D1395548

Clinics in Developmental Medicine No. 101/102

LANGUAGE DEVELOPMENT AND DISORDERS

Edited by:
William Yule
Michael Rutter

1987
Mac Keith Press
OXFORD: Blackwell Scientific Publications Ltd.
PHILADELPHIA: J. B. Lippincott Co.

First published 1987

British Library Cataloguing in Publication Data

Language development and disorders. ——
  (Clinics in developmental medicine, ISSN
  0069-4835; 101/102)
  1. Speech, Disorders of
  I. Yule, William   II. Rutter, M.
  III Series
  612'.78   QP306

ISBN (UK) 0-632-01522-5
    (USA) 0-397-48003-2

Printed in Great Britain at The Lavenham Press Ltd., Lavenham, Suffolk
Mac Keith Press is supported by **The Spastics Society, London, England**

CONTENTS

CONTRIBUTORS

MARTIN BAX — Research Fellow in Paediatrics, Charing Cross and Westminster Medical School.

DOROTHY BISHOP — MRC Senior Research Fellow, Department of Psychology, University of Manchester.

SUSAN BLOCKBERGER — Speech and Language Pathologist, Sunny Hill Hospital for Children, Vancouver, B.C.

DENZIL BROOKS — Principal Physicist, Regional Audiology Unit, Withington Hospital, Manchester.

A. G. M. CANAVAN — Lecturer, Department of Clinical Psychology, Institute of Psychiatry, De Crespigny Park, London S.E.5.

KAY COOMBES — Senior Lecturer in Speech Pathology, Central School of Speech and Drama, London N.W.3.

RICHARD CROMER — Senior Research Psychologist, MRC Cognitive Development Unit, Gordon Street, London W.C.1.

DAVID CRYSTAL — Honorary Professor of Linguistics, University College of North Wales, Bangor.

PAUL FLETCHER — Lecturer in Linguistic Science, University of Reading.

ROGER FREEMAN — Clinical Professor of Psychiatry, University of British Columbia; Consultant Psychiatrist, Children's Hospital, Deaf Children's Society of B.C., and Western Institute for the Deaf, Vancouver, B.C.

PRUE FULLER — Director of ACE (Aids to Communication in Education), Ormerod School, Waynflete Road, Oxford.

ANN GATH — Consultant Child Psychiatrist, Department of Psychiatry, West Suffolk Hospital, Bury St. Edmunds.

ROBERT GOODMAN — Senior Research Fellow, Department of Child Psychiatry, The Hospital for Sick Children, Great Ormond Street, London W.C.1.

NEIL GORDON — Consultant Paediatric Neurologist, Booth Hall Children's Hospital, Charlestown Road, Blackley, Manchester.

MARY GUTFREUND   Research Unit, School of Education, University of Bristol.

C. A. HEYWOOD   Research Psychologist, Department of Experimental Psychology, South Parks Road, Oxford.

SHEILA HOLLINS   Senior Lecturer and Honorary Consultant in the Psychiatry of Mental Handicap, St. George's Hospital Medical School, London.

PATRICIA HOWLIN   Senior Lecturer in Psychology, Institute of Psychiatry, De Crespigny Park, London S.E.5.

CHRIS KIERNAN   Director, Hester Adrian Research Centre, University of Manchester.

CATHERINE LORD   Associate Professor, Department of Pediatrics, University of Alberta; Department of Psychology, Glenrose Rehabilitation Hospital, Edmonton, Alberta, Canada.

MARGARET MARTLEW   Lecturer, Department of Psychology, University of Sheffield.

CHRISTINE PUCKERING   Research Psychologist, Institute of Psychiatry, De Crespigny Park, London S.E.5.

HARRY PURSER   Lecturer, School of Speech Pathology, Leicester Polytechnic.

JEAN RONDAL   Professor of Psychology, Laboratoire de Psychologie du Langage et de Logopédie, Université de Liège.

LEWIS ROSENBLOOM   Consultant Paediatric Neurologist, Child Development Centre, Alder Hey Children's Hospital, Liverpool.

MICHAEL RUTTER   Honorary Director, MRC Child Psychiatry Unit, Institute of Psychiatry, De Crespigny Park, London SE5 8OF.

HOWARD SHANE   Director, Communication Enhancement Clinic, Children's Hospital, 300 Longwood Avenue, Boston, Massachusetts.

PHIL SILVA   Director, Dunedin Multidisciplinary Health & Development Research Unit, Department of Paediatrics and Child Health, University of Otago Medical School, Dunedin, New Zealand.

TIM SOUTHGATE   Head Teacher, Ormerod School, Waynflete Road, Oxford.

C. G. WELLS   Department of Curriculum, Ontario Institute for Studies in Education, Toronto, Ontario.

WILLIAM YULE   Professor of Applied Child Psychology, Department of Psychology, Institute of Psychiatry, De Crespigny Park, London S.E.5.

FOREWORD

As science and medicine progress, so generally does the care and treatment of the sick and the disabled. But this is not the automatic consequence one might suppose. New discoveries, inventions and procedures do not flow directly into new treatments and new educational practices. Even when a discovery or invention is linked in a direct way to a specified condition, such as the development of a vaccine for a particular viral agent, the vaccine must be tested, produced, distributed and the conditions appropriate to its use specified. Between the initial research and the eventual clinical utilisation a great deal has to be done.

Bridging the gap between basic research and its practical utilisation is no easy business. In cases that involve the manufacture of a product, commercial motives will probably see the process through along well-worked 'trade routes'. Where there is no apparent commercial involvement, the transfer of new knowledge and new methods is more difficult. Scientific and professional societies, through their meetings and journals, play a rôle: but unless there are already established lines of communication this can be rather a hit-and-miss affair, especially where ideas and information have to be transmitted across several subject boundaries and where the number of people involved is fairly large. The making of this book is a reflection of this problem and illustrates the invaluable work of organisations such as the Spastics Society which provides a nexus for several professional groups.

This book had its origins in the problems and anxieties of the teaching staff within the Spastics Society's schools and colleges. Communication difficulties are common, though the precise nature and degree of the disability varies greatly between individuals. They are among the most handicapping of disabilities because they isolate a person and in so doing restrict social, educational and occupational opportunities; and of course they are of the greatest importance to the disabled and their families. The staff were aware that basic and applied research on language and communication was being done in many countries. They were familiar with some of the alternative communication systems that had been devised for the disabled, and aware that rapid progress was being made with augmented systems as micro-electronic technology advanced. In this welter of material, what to do for any particular child and when to do it is often the teacher's responsibility.

Faced with these pressing issues the Society's Educational Advisory Committee set itself a number of tasks. One of these was to bring together theoretical, practical and clinical knowledge from several disciplines that bear on language and communication into some reasonably accessible form. Given the large area which had to be covered it seemed sensible to bring together a group of experts and have them review and discuss the state of the art and the state of the science. With the help of the Society's Medical Education and Information Unit, a three day study group was arranged in 1984. The group included research workers, clinicians and teachers and drew on people from several countries. The papers and discussions from this meeting were used as a basis on which to plan a book. Some of the papers presented to the study group are included in the book, others were commissioned as a result of the discussions.

What the editors and the Mac Keith Press have sought to do in designing and publishing this book is to provide a broad and multi-faceted view of language development and language disorders. Thus contributions from education, linguistics, psychology, paediatrics, psychiatry, neurology, neuropsychology and speech therapy are included. They describe our current knowledge of language development, suggest classifications for language pathology, outline what is known of the epidemiology of language difficulties, consider assessment and therapy, alternative communication systems and the impact of the new technology on communication aids. The book is larger than originally envisaged but we believe that the variety of perspectives that it provides will make it particularly useful to the range of specialists who are concerned with the development of communication skills and language disorders.

KEVIN CONNOLLY

1
EPIDEMIOLOGY, LONGITUDINAL COURSE AND SOME ASSOCIATED FACTORS: AN UPDATE

Phil A. Silva

Introduction

In 1972 Mac Keith and Rutter reviewed the literature to that point, and concluded that

> '1 per cent of children come to school with a marked language handicap and a further 4 to 5 per cent may show the sequelae of earlier language difficulties. The commonest condition associated with language delay is intellectual retardation, but deafness, cerebral palsy and developmental disorders are also common, the last two particularly as a cause of mild to moderate language delay. Infantile autism is a less common cause of mild to moderate language retardation but is more important as a cause of severe and persistent language retardation.'

This chapter provides a brief update of some of the published research that has appeared since 1972.

To a large extent, many of the earlier epidemiological studies reviewed by Mac Keith and Rutter were handicapped by a lack of standardised tests of language development. They generally used criterion-referenced approaches and assessed such aspects as 'intelligibility' of expressive language. Another problem was that the earlier estimates tended to be based on expressive language only; verbal comprehension is more difficult to assess clinically. Although language understanding and usage develop in parallel there can be deficits in one but not both skills. In recent years, standardised tests of language have become available (Cantwell and Baker 1985); of these the Reynell Developmental Language Scales (Reynell 1969, 1977) are particularly useful because they evaluate both verbal comprehension and verbal expression in preschool children. Despite the norms being based on relatively small samples of English children, they have been found to be applicable to children in New Zealand (McKerracher *et al.* 1977). The Reynell Scales show satisfactory split-half reliability, but the test-retest reliabilities are likely to be lower because of the day-to-day variability in performance of young children. The Reynell Scales manuals describe high content validity, and the manual supplement (Silva *et al.* 1978) gives details of their concurrent and predictive validity.

Despite increased recognition of the importance of language development, there has been a notable lack of progress in understanding factors that may be associated with it, and much remains to be learned about language acquisition and language handicap (Howlin 1981). Silva and Fergusson (1980) found the maternal general mental ability, education and training in child development, socio-economic status, birthweight, and child experiences were the six factors most strongly associated with the language development of three-year-olds. However, these variables explained only 11 per cent of the variance of verbal comprehension and 7 per cent of the variance of verbal expression.

There is an important distinction between a developmental delay in expressive language and poorly developed speech articulation. Clarity of speech is only one aspect of expressive language development. Children with unclear speech articulation are more likely to have slow language development and behavioural problems than children with clear speech, regardless of whether they are of normal or low intelligence (Morley 1965, Silva *et al.* 1984). However, there is some evidence (*e.g.* Baker and Cantwell 1982*a*) that a 'pure articulation disorder' is less likely than a 'language disorder' to be associated with psychiatric problems.

There is also a close relationship between language and intelligence (Silva *et al.* 1978) and between language delay and low intelligence (Silva 1981). Indeed, the items in tests of language and intelligence are often the same. While language tests such as the Reynell Scales contain items that appear to assess language, they also require the child's sustained attention and involve a certain amount of reasoning. Likewise, many intelligence test items involve language comprehension and expression. This is especially the case with the Stanford-Binet Intelligence Scale (Terman and Merrill 1960). The correlation between this test and the Reynell Developmental Language Scales is high—about 0.6 to 0.7 in one study of five-year-olds (Silva *et al.* 1978). Also, both show a similar correlation with WISC IQ (Wechsler 1974) and reading tests given several years later (Silva *et al.* 1978).

Prevalence studies since 1972

Most studies of delayed language development have focused on preschool rather than school-age children because it is at that age that language develops dramatically. Most studies have focused on three-year-old children.

Randall *et al.* (1974) found nine out of 160 three-year-old London children (5.6 per cent) to be 'severely language delayed', using a definition of having a score on either Reynell Verbal Comprehension or Verbal Expression or on a test of speech articulation of two or more standard deviations below the mean.

Stevenson and Richman (1976) carried out an epidemiological study of developmental language delay involving a sample of 705 London three-year-old children. They used a variety of standardised measures and from their definitions estimated that 3.1 per cent had delayed language development, 0.6 per cent had specific language delay, and 0.4 per cent had severe retardation.

Fundudis *et al.* (1979), in a study of 3300 Newcastle upon Tyne children, found 4 per cent to be 'speech retarded' in that they were not using 'three or more words strung together to make some sort of sense by the age of 36 months' (p.3). They considered their 4 per cent estimate as 'conservative'. They then followed up 102 of the speech-retarded group and classified 18 of them as 'pathologically deviant', that is having an intellectual handicap alone (N = 7); cerebral palsy (N = 5); autism (N = 2); elective mutism (N = 2); severe dysphasia (N = 1); or cleft palate dysarthria (N = 1). The remaining 84 children were classified as having a 'residual speech handicap' and their estimated prevalence was about 2 to 3 per cent of children of school age. While some associated factors were uncovered in this research, the assumed causes of these problems were largely unexplained for the larger 'residual speech handicapped' group.

Chazan *et al.* (1980) surveyed 7320 children aged 3¾ years to 4¼ years, who were 99.5 per cent of all children born in a six-month period in two local authority areas, one in Wales and one in England. A simple first-stage screening schedule was filled in by health visitors, teachers, or playgroup leaders. The results showed that 3.2 per cent were judged as having a 'definite speech and language development problem'. When 'possible' problems were added, the percentage increased to 12.4 per cent. A second-stage, more detailed screening schedule was then filled in for children who had been screened out as having 'definite' or 'possible' problems. This resulted in 4.4 per cent of the total sample being identified as having 'severe problems' of speech and language and 11.4 per cent as having 'some problems' of speech and language.

Jenkins *et al.* (1980) found 15 per cent of a sample of 323 three-year-old children who were 'not talking adequately'. 8 per cent were assessed by paediatricians as having either 'normal', 'possibly abnormal' or 'abnormal' speech or language. Their ratings of abnormality correlated very closely with independent assessments by a speech therapist using the Reynell Scales (Bax *et al.* 1980).

There appears to have been less research into the prevalence of language delay on the other side of the Atlantic. Tuomi and Ivanoff (1977) from a study of a sample of 900 kindergarten and grade one children in Canada considered that 6 to 7 per cent had 'language problems'. A similar prevalence rate for language 'disabilities' was estimated in the USA by Marge (1972), who said that 6.2 per cent of four- to 17-year-olds have 'delayed language acquisition'.

The most recent description of developmental language delays from the Dunedin Multidisciplinary Health and Development Study (Silva *et al.* 1983) defined a language delay as a score at or below the fifth percentile in verbal comprehension, verbal expression, or both from 1027 three-year-old children examined. The sample was assessed with the Reynell Developmental Language Scales (Reynell 1969). This definition identified 7.6 per cent as 'language delayed'. They were further grouped as to whether they had a delay in comprehension only (2.6 per cent), a delay in expression only (2.3 per cent), or a general language delay (*i.e.* delayed in both) (2.6 per cent).

While the recent studies of the prevalence of language delay have resulted in prevalence rates from 3 to 15 per cent (with a median of about 6 to 8 per cent), there has been no general agreement as to where the cut-off point in the normal distribution should be drawn. In a discussion of this issue, Richman and Stevenson (1976) emphasised that 'a decision about what constitutes abnormality would be strengthened if prognostic validation data were available but such information has not yet been provided for language delay' (p. 431). Since then, there have been three major longitudinal studies of developmental language delay which have highlighted the longer-term course and significance of these disorders. They, in turn, have thrown further light on criteria that should be used to define preschool children as language delayed.

Longitudinal significance of preschool language delays
Of the prevalence studies cited above, three followed up their samples after several years. These were the Waltham Forest Study (Stevenson and Richman 1976, Richman *et al.* 1983), the Newcastle study (Fundudis *et al.* 1979), and the Dunedin study (Silva *et al.* 1983). As pointed out by Stevenson (1984), there were remarkable similarities between the three studies. All assessed the children near their third birthdays, and followed them up at either age seven (Newcastle and Dunedin) or eight years (Waltham Forest). All three studies reported results from the Wechsler Intelligence Scale for Children (Wechsler 1974) and from reading tests. Results for one or both of the Rutter Behaviour Scales (Rutter *et al.* 1970) were reported for the Waltham Forest and Newcastle studies and are available from the Dunedin study. Data from the Dunedin seven-year follow-up have been reanalysed, and new analyses carried out to allow a more complete comparison of the three studies than was given by Stevenson (1984). Results for one language-delay group only was reported from the Waltham Forest and Newcastle studies, while results from three groups (comprehension delay only, expressive delay only and general language delay) were reported from Dunedin.

Intelligence
Table I sets out the percentage of children defined as having a low IQ on follow-up from the language-delay groups and comparison groups. From 29.2 per cent to 72.7 per cent of the language-delay groups had a low Full Scale IQ compared with from 4 to 12 per cent in the comparison groups. The percentage with low Verbal IQs in the language-delay groups ranged from 54.0 to 68.2 per cent (comparison-group range from 9.5 to 23.0 per cent). As would be expected, the percentages with low Performance IQs were lower, ranging from 21.0 to 50.0 per cent for the language-delayed groups compared with 4.0 to 7.8 per cent for the comparison groups. These data show that the definitions of language delay used identified a group of children who later had a high prevalence of low IQs. Thus, to some extent, the data provide some degree of support for the validity of the definitions of language delay used.

Reading
Similar results were found regarding the later reading ability of the language-delayed children. The Waltham Forest study found 41.0 per cent to be 16 months or more backward in reading (comparison group 14.0 per cent) and the Newcastle study had mean reading quotient of 80 (comparison group mean reading quotient 94). From the Dunedin study, all three language-delay groups had lower mean Burt Word Reading scores (Scottish Council for Research in Education 1976) which were 17.2, 17.1, and 12.8 (for comprehension delay, expression delay and general

4

language delay respectively) compared with a mean of 30.7 for the remainder of the sample. In terms of reading delay (*i.e.* a delay of a year or more at age seven), 37.5, 31.8, and 63.6 per cent respectively had a reading delay compared with 7.9 per cent for the remainder of the sample. When all three Dunedin language-delay groups were combined, 44.1 per cent were delayed in reading at age seven. All reading score differences between the Dunedin language-delay groups and the remainder of the sample were significant (p<0.05). Again, these data provide support for the usefulness of the definitions.

Behaviour problems
Because of the differences in the way the study samples were drawn, it is not possible directly to compare the rate of later behaviour problems as measured by the Rutter Behaviour Scales (Rutter *et al.* 1970) and to test the differences for significance. However, as noted by Stevenson (1984), both English studies showed a discernible tendency for the language-delayed children to have a higher degree of later behavioural deviance than those without an early language delay. When the three Dunedin language delay groups were combined, 28 per cent had high Rutter Parent Scale scores (*i.e.* 13 or more) at age seven, compared with 21 per cent for the remainder of the sample—a non-significant difference. However, 27 per cent of the combined language-delayed group had high Rutter Teacher Behaviour scores (*i.e.* 9 or more) compared with 13 per cent for the sample remainder, a significant difference (p<0.05).

Conclusions from the three longitudinal studies
Despite their different locations, definitions of language delay and the different measures of reading ability used, the three longitudinal studies resulted in remarkably similar findings relating to later intelligence and reading. It was clear that early language delay was a strong predictor of low IQ and reading problems four to five years later. Also, there was an association between early language delay and later behaviour problems.

The Dunedin study identified three different subgroups of language-delayed children who, in total, comprised 7.6 per cent of the total sample: in contrast to about 3 per cent of children identified by the two English studies. As shown in Table I, each of the three Dunedin language-delay groups had a higher rate of later low intelligence than the comparison group. This was similar to the rate of later low intelligence found in the English studies. Also, each Dunedin delayed-language subgroup had a relatively high rate of later reading problems. Of the three Dunedin subgroups, the general language-delay group had the highest later prevalence of low IQ or reading problems. There were no significant differences in the prevalence of later low IQ or reading problems when the comprehesion-delayed and expressive language-delayed groups were compared, suggesting that comprehension delay as well as expressive delay should be included when screening out children with language delay. The results suggest that the definitions of language delay used in the Dunedin study were useful when judged according to their ability to define a group of language-delayed children who would be expected to have a high rate of

5

TABLE I

Percentages of language-delayed children with later low IQs[1] from three longitudinal studies

Studies and Groups	Full Scale IQ		Low Verbal IQ		Low Performance IQ	
	Language-delay group	Comparison[2] group	Language-delay group	Comparison[2] group	Language-delay group	Comparison[2] group
Waltham Forest	36.0	4.0	59.0	23.0	27.0	4.0
Newcastle	39.0	12.0	54.0	21.0	21.0	7.0
Dunedin comprehension delay only	29.2	8.0	54.2	9.5	33.3	7.8
Dunedin expressive delay only	45.5	8.0	54.5	9.5	27.3	7.8
Dunedin general language delay	72.7	8.0	68.2	9.5	50.0	7.8
All Dunedin delay groups combined	48.5	8.0	58.8	9.5	36.8	7.8

[1]Low IQs for the English studies were <86 and for the Dunedin study <91 (the mean IQ for each scale of the WISC in Dunedin was 106 to 107)
[2]Comparison groups for the English studies were specially selected. The comparison group for the Dunedin study comprised the remainder of the sample (i.e. N = 800 + those without language delay at age three)

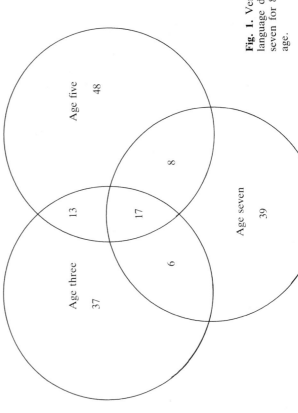

Fig. 1. Venn diagram shows overlap of language delay at ages three, five and seven for 857 children assessed at each age.

later low IQ or reading problems.

Perhaps the most important conclusion to be drawn from the three longitudinal studies was that emphasised by Stevenson (1984). He suggested that the estimate of the prevalence rate for language delay originally suggested by Mac Keith and Rutter (1972) should be increased. According to the Dunedin study results, this estimate could be as high as 7 to 8 per cent of preschool children and should include children at or below the fifth percentile on the Reynell Scales in language comprehension, expression or both.

Stability of language delay

The Dunedin research group (Silva *et al.* 1983) investigated the stability of language delay in 851 children in their sample who had language assessments at age three and five based on the Reynell Scales, and at age seven based on the Illinois Test of Psycholinguistic Abilities (Kirk *et al.* 1968). The definition of language delay was the same at each age, and included children scoring at or below the score nearest to the fifth percentile on either the verbal comprehension, verbal expression or both scales. About one in five children (19.6 per cent) scored at or below the cut-off point on at least one occasion over the three assessments. The overlap of any type of language delay at each age is depicted in Figure 1.

The Venn diagram shows that 37 children scored below the cut-off point at age three only, 48 at age five only, and 39 at age seven only (a total of 14.6 per cent of the sample) on one or both scales. Low scores at two ages were found for 13 children at three and five, eight at five and seven, and six at ages three and seven (3 per cent of the sample). Only 17 children (2 per cent of the sample) gained a low score at all three ages. Of the three subtypes of language delay, general language delay was the most stable over time.

Of those children with a low score at one age only, 42.5 per cent had a low Full Scale WISC IQ (<91) and/or reading problems (one year or more below average) at age seven. This increased to 65.2 per cent for those with low scores on two occasions, and to 82.6 per cent for those with low scores at all three assessments. All prevalence rates of low IQ and/or reading problems significantly exceeded the sample prevalence rate, which was 17.5 per cent. These data show that even those with a low score on only one assessment had a significantly increased rate of later problems, although those with low scores on more than one assessment had an even higher prevalence of later low IQ and/or reading problems.

Associated factors

It has long been known that developmental language delay is often associated with intellectual handicap, deafness, cerebral palsy, or is a reflection of infantile autism or elective mutism (Mac Keith and Rutter 1972, Fundudis *et al.* 1979), so these associations are not discussed here. This section summarises the evidence on sex and social-class differences, and discusses some further findings of the association between language delay and behavioural problems.

Sex differences

Sex differences in language development and developmental language delay favouring girls have been found in a number of studies. For example, the Dunedin studies (Silva 1980; Silva *et al.* 1982*a*, 1983) found that the girls began to talk, on average, a month earlier than the boys and they gained significantly higher scores on all the language tests. Also, about twice as many boys as girls are usually found to have a language delay (Morley 1965, Stevenson and Richman 1976, Fundudis *et al.* 1979, Silva 1980). While it is well known that more boys than girls have developmental language delays, it is not known why this should be so. It should be noted, however, that not every type of language delay has a male preponderance. For example, Bartak and Rutter (1973) found no significant sex difference in children with severe receptive language disabilities.

Social-class differences

There is a large literature showing an association between low socio-economic status and low intelligence, and because of the high correlation between intelligence and language test scores it is not surprising to find a similar association between low socio-economic status and slow language development. Because of the high degree of overlap between language and intelligence it is not possible to separate out 'pure language' or to control for differences in intelligence in looking at relationships between socio-economic status and language delay.

In the Dunedin study, the average language score of the lowest SES group at age five was about a year below that of the children in the highest SES group (Silva *et al.* 1982*b*). A similar social-class gradient relating to the level of language ability has also been found by others (Lawton 1968). For example, Wooster (1970) found social-class differences in the ability to understand and produce language. He went on to express the view that in England, 'children from lower class homes often speak a distinctive dialect and show retarded development on measures of language skills and cognitive functioning' (p. 118). More recent studies have confirmed the association between lower socio-economic status and language delay (Fundudis *et al.* 1979).

While the association between socio-economic status and cognitive ability (including language ability) is well recognised, less progress has been made in determining why the association exists. Socio-economic status or social class are useful measures, but as pointed out by Bloom (1974) they are too general and too static to serve as the environmental measure for such specific human characteristics as verbal ability. Bloom went on to argue that it is what parents and others in the environment *do* in their interaction with the individual that are likely to influence the development of a specific characteristic rather than the more static or status attributes of the parents. Apart from some notable exceptions (*e.g.* White and Watts 1973) little real progress has been made in advancing understanding about the assessment and significance of the environmental and experiential processes that influence the cognitive development of the young child, let alone how these vary with socio-economic status to influence the child's language development.

Behavioural problems in children with developmental language delay
As pointed out by Friedlander and Wetstone (1974), it is a common clinical observation that there is an association between language delay and behavioural problems. Some have argued that language disorder is secondary to a primary emotional disability (Kessler 1966) while others have expressed the view that language delay is the primary problem. For example, Rutter (1972) argued that there are

> 'at least five different ways in which language retardation indirectly leads to emotional and behavioural difficulties: through educational failure, through the effects of communication difficulties in social relationships, through lack of social integration, through the effects of teasing and rejection by other children, and through associated brain dysfunction' (p. 185).

Cantwell and Baker (1977) critically reviewed the literature on psychiatric disorder in children with speech and language retardation. They noted that most studies referred to more severe rather than mild or moderate language disorders. They expressed the belief that, although serious methodological problems made interpretation of many studies difficult, the evidence confirmed the probability of the association. However, they warned that 'little can be stated with great certainty' (p. 586). They concluded that, except in rare instances, psychiatric disorder does not cause speech and language retardation, and that in most cases psychiatric disorder is indirectly caused by speech and language retardation. They also pointed out that both problems may have a common cause, such as mental retardation, deafness, brain damage, family factors, or low socio-economic status.

In the 14 years since Rutter (1972) reported the state of knowledge regarding children with delayed language, several epidemiological studies on the association between language delay and behavioural problems have been reported, two from London, one from Newcastle, one from Dunedin and a series of studies from Los Angeles. These are briefly described.

The Waltham Forest study
The prevalence of language delay found in this study has already been briefly described (Stevenson and Richman 1976). Further results on language development and behaviour problems are described in two further papers (Richman *et al.* 1975, Stevenson and Richman 1978), a chapter (Richman *et al.* 1983), and a book bringing together the longitudinal results (Richman *et al.* 1982). The sample was selected from 705 children of non-immigrant families by a variety of screening methods which identified 101 children with behavioural problems. A matched comparison group of similar size without behavioural problems was also selected. A final group included 20 language-delayed children, eight from the behaviour problem group, two from the matched comparison group, and 10 from the larger sample from which the above samples were drawn.

The results of studies of the relationship between language delay and behaviour problems in the three-year-olds were described by Stevenson and Richman (1978). They found behaviour problems to be present in 59 per cent of the language-delayed three-year-old children, compared with 14 per cent in the full sample of 705 children (p<0.001). They also found that 12.9 per cent of the children with behaviour problems had a language delay, compared with 3.1 per cent of the full sample (p<0.001). The types of behaviour problems found to be significantly associated with language delay were social relationship problems (dependency, relationships with siblings and peers), parental control of behaviour, unhappy moods, poor appetite, overactivity, and problems of attention. The behaviour problem group also performed significantly more poorly than the matched comparison group on a range of psychometric measures, many of which assessed aspects of language development. These results held regardless of whether children with language delay were included or excluded from the comparison.

As already described, Richman *et al.* (1983) reported follow-up results, and found that those with language delay at age three still had significantly more behavioural problems at age eight compared with those without a language delay at age three. Discussing the association between early language disorders and behavioural problems, they suggested that both problems may possibly be influenced by some other factor, rather than one causing the other.

The North London study
Jenkins *et al.* (1980) reported a study of behavioural problems in a sample of 418 children under the age of five years. In addition to collecting information on behaviour problems, each child's speech was assessed clinically and rated as 'normal', 'possibly abnormal', or 'definitely abnormal'. For those children over two years of age (N = 168), 18 per cent with no behaviour problems and 36 per cent with behaviour problems were judged to have speech or language abnormalities. This difference was statistically significant (p<0.05). When the group was further subdivided according to age, the association was found to be significant only at age two.

The Newcastle study
The prevelance of developmental language delay and its association with cognitive development at age seven (Fundudis *et al.* 1979) has been described above. The Newcastle group also followed up their sample at age seven; they compared their two language-delayed groups ('residual speech retarded' and 'pathological speech retarded') with a matched comparison group and studied their behaviour, personality, temperament and psychiatric status. On the Rutter Teacher Scale (Rutter *et al.* 1970) both language-delay groups were found to have significantly more behaviour problems than the comparison group. The residual speech-retarded group was found to be significantly more introverted than the comparison group on the Junior Eysenck Personality Inventory (Eysenck 1965). The residual speech-retarded group was clinically judged by a psychologist to be less confident and to have a poorer level of attention span than the comparison group. Finally, both language-delay groups were rated as more psychiatrically disturbed than the comparison group, and the pathologically speech-retarded group were judged to be even more psychiatrically disturbed than the residual speech-retarded group.

They summarised their detailed findings by concluding that:

'The weight of evidence that we have set out above provides incontrovertible proof of long-term behavioural sequelae of speech disorders in the early years of life. Those speech disorders which are more clearly pathological have by far the severest consequences. The most clear-cut pattern identified is that of speech delay and later introversion and withdrawal. Finally, there is evidence that severity of disturbance correlates inversely with performance on tests of intelligence and language irrespective of whether the child belongs to a study group or the control group.' (p. 77).

Fundudis *et al.* (1979) concluded by suggesting that behaviour problems were, in part at least, secondary to cognitive, speech, and language problems.

The Dunedin study
The association between behavioural problems and language development was investigated by the Dunedin Multidisciplinary Health and Development Research Unit (McGee *et al.* 1983). A group of 52 boys and 32 girls with stable behaviour problems (*i.e.* behaviour problems identified at both age five and seven) were compared with the remainder of the sample ($N = 410$ boys, 392 girls). The stable behaviour problem group was not significantly delayed in the early acquisition of language (*i.e.* talking in single words or sentences). However, they had significantly poorer verbal comprehension at age seven in comparison with the remainder of the sample. These findings remained significant when maternal mental ability was controlled.

The Los Angeles studies
The Los Angeles studies involved taking consecutive cases referred to a clinic for speech and language problems and carrying out a full psychometric and psychiatric evaluation based on information obtained from the child, his or her parents and teachers. Various types of language and speech delay were defined and psychiatric diagnoses were made using DSM-III criteria (American Psychiatric Association 1980). Several studies based on different numbers of the referred children have been reported. All covered a wide age range (age two to about 16 years—mean about six years) and no comparison groups were used.

Cantwell *et al.* (1979) reported results from the first 100 of the referred children and 53 received at least one DSM-III diagnosis. Attention deficit disorder was diagnosed in 19 children, oppositional disorder in 13 and various anxiety disorders in 12. Cantwell *et al.* (1980) identified factors that discriminated between various language-disorder groups and the psychiatrically ill and well group.

Baker and Cantwell (1982*a*) described the developmental, social and behavioural characteristics of 180 of the referred children. The results confirmed those of the earlier study, and further indicated that adverse environmental conditions did not appear to be responsible for the psychiatric disorders identified. They gave a DSM-III psychiatric diagnosis to 53 per cent of the sample. However, when the sample was divided into those with 'pure speech disorders' (*i.e.*

11

articulation problems N = 76) and those who were 'language-disordered' (N = 104), only 23 per cent of the former group were given a psychiatric diagnosis compared with 63 per cent of the 'language disordered' group. They concluded that psychiatric screening and intervention programmes should concentrate on language-disordered children rather than those with speech articulation problems only.

In yet another report (Baker and Cantwell 1982*b*), 291 of the referred children were divided into three major groups according to type of communication disorder: 'pure speech disorder' (*i.e.* speech articulation problems, N = 108), 'pure language disorder' (N = 19), and 'disorder of both speech and language' (N = 164). It was found that psychiatric diagnoses were the highest in the 'pure language-disordered' group (95 per cent), followed by the 'speech- and language-disordered' group (45 per cent), then the 'pure speech-disordered' group (29 per cent).

The final Los Angeles study to be described (Cantwell and Baker 1983) reported on the prevalence of affective disorders among 600 children referred to the speech and hearing clinic. 4 per cent were diagnosed as having some type of affective disorder. Major depression was the most common diagnosis (N = 10) followed by cyclothymic disorder (N = 7), dysthymic disorder (N = 5), and bipolar disorder (N = 1). The children with affective disorder tended to have language rather than speech problems and were older, and there appeared to be a strong correlation between academic failure and psychiatric disorder.

Conclusions
There is general agreement that about 1 per cent of children have a 'severe' developmental language delay. Various definitions of less severe forms of developmental language delay have resulted in between 3 and 15 per cent being defined as language delayed. The median from the various studies, and the results from the longitudinal study from Dunedin, suggest that 6 to 8 per cent of preschool children could usefully be defined as 'language delayed': far higher than the rate suggested by Mac Keith and Rutter (1972). While the more severe forms of language delay, general language delay, and those associated with other problems such as mental retardation or deafness, are likely to be the most stable, many who have language delays in the preschool years do not have them later. This suggests the need for some caution in classifying children as language delayed on the basis of one assessment only. Any diagnosis of less severe forms of language delay should remain tentative until confirmed by later assessments. While children with early language delay may not necessarily have these particular problems later, longitudinal studies have shown that they are at increased risk of having a later low IQ and/or reading difficulties in the early school years. This risk appears to be greatest with general language delay and delays that persist over time. These findings give strong support to the view that early language delays are an important problem, and suggest that efforts to arrange identification and intervention programmes may be worthwhile. However, further research is necessary to show the effectiveness of such strategies. An important caveat should be added. Not all children with early language delays turn out to have later problems. To some

extent, the degree of risk of later problems is determined by the type and severity of language delay.

Language delays are about twice as common in boys, and more common in children from low socio-economic levels. However, the differences are not strong enough to justify targeting early identification or intervention programmes on these groups alone as all children are at risk.

Children with developmental language delays appear to have a high rate of immediate and longer-lasting behaviour problems and psychiatric disorders. While the nature of the relationship is not yet clear, current opinion is equally divided between the view that language delay may cause behavioural problems directly or that both problems reflect some other cause. It is probable that both explanations may be true for some children, but further research is necessary to clarify the nature of the relationship. The association between language delay and behavioural problems provides further evidence for the importance of early language delay.

Some progress has been made since Mac Keith and Rutter (1972) reviewed the literature on the epidemiology of language delay. However, two important gaps remain. Firstly, there is a need for further information on the long-term developmental and educational implications of language delay. There is still no reliable information on the significance of language delay for academic progress beyond the first few years of schooling. Secondly, further longitudinal research is needed on the long-term significance of language delay for behaviour problems and mental health. The available research has clarified the situation up to the age of eight, and the Los Angeles studies have shown that older children with language delay are at risk of mental health problems. Further longitudinal study should investigate the implications of different types of early language delay and associated factors for long-term development, education, employment, and mental health.

ACKNOWLEDGEMENT

The author acknowledges the support of the Medical Research Council of New Zealand, the main funding body for the Dunedin Multidisciplinary Health and Development Research Unit.

REFERENCES

American Psychiatric Association (1980) *Diagnostic and Statistical Manual of Mental Disorders.* Washington: American Psychiatric Association.

Baker, L., Cantwell, D. P. (1982a) 'Developmental, social and behavioural characteristics of speech and language disordered children.' *Child Psychiatry and Human Development,* **12,** 195–206.

—— —— (1982b) 'Psychiatric disorder in children with different types of communication disorders.' *Journal of Communication Disorders,* **15,** 113–126.

Bartak, L., Rutter, M. (1973) 'Special educational treatment for autistic children: a comparative study. I: Design of study and characteristics of units.' *Journal of Child Psychology and Psychiatry,* **14,** 161–179.

Bax, M., Hart, H., Jenkins, S. (1980) 'Assessments of speech and language development in the young child.' *Pediatrics,* **63,** 350–354.

Bloom, B. S. (1974) 'Preface.' *In:* Marjoribanks, K. (Ed) *Environments for Learning.* Windsor: NFER Company.

Cantwell, D. P., Baker, L. (1977) 'Psychiatric disorder in children with speech and language retardation: a critical review.' *Archives of General Psychiatry,* **34,** 583–591.

—— —— Mattison, R. E. (1979) 'The prevalence of psychiatric disorder in children with speech and language disorder. An epidemiologic study.' *Journal of the American Academy of Child Psychiatry,* **18,** 450–461.

—— —— —— (1980) 'Psychiatric disorders in children with speech and language retardation: factors associated with development.' *Archives of General Psychiatry,* **37,** 423–426.

—— —— (1983) 'Depression in children with speech, language and learning disorders.' *Journal of Contemporary Psychotherapy,* **15,** 51–59.

—— —— (1985) Reference suggested by M. Rutter?

Chazan, M., Laing, A. F., Bailey, M. S., Jones, G. (1980) *Some of Our Children: The Early Education of Children With Special Educational Needs.* London: Open Books.

Eysenck, S. B. G. (1965) *Junior Eysenck Personality Inventory (Manual).* London: University of London Press.

Friedlander, B. Z., Wetstone, H. S. (1974) 'Systematic assessment of selective language listening deficit in emotionally disturbed preschool children.' *Journal of Child Psychology and Psychiatry,* **15,** 1–12.

Fundudis, T., Kolvin, I., Garside, R. F. (1979) (Eds) *Speech Retarded and Deaf Children: Their Psychological Development.* London: Academic Press.

Howlin, P. (1981) 'Language'. *In:* Rutter, M. (Ed) *Scientific Foundations of Developmental Psychiatry.* London: Heinemann Medical; Baltimore: University Park Press. pp 198–220.

Jenkins, S., Bax, M., Hart. H. (1980) 'Behaviour problems in preschool children.' *Journal of Child Psychology and Psychiatry,* **21,** 5–17.

Kessler, J. W. (1966) 'Personality theory and psychopathology.' *In:* Kessler, J. W. (Ed) *Psychopathology of Childhood.* New Jersey: Prentice Hall.

Kirk, S. A., McCarthy, J. J., Kirk, W. D. (1968) *The Illinois Test of Psycholinguistic Abilities (Revised Edn)* Urbana, Ill.: University of Illinois Press.

Lawton, D. (1968) *Social Class, Language, and Education.* London: Routledge & Kegan Paul.

McGee, R. O., Silva, P. A., Williams, S. M. (1984) 'Perinatal, neurological, environmental, and developmental characteristics of seven year old children with stable behaviour problems.' *Journal of Child Psychology and Psychiatry,* **25,** 573–586.

Mac Keith, R. C., Rutter, M. (1972) 'A note on the prevalence of speech and language disorders.' *In:* Rutter, M., Martin, M. A. (Eds) *The Child With Delayed Speech. Clinics in Developmental Medicine No. 43.* London: S.I.M.P. with Heinemann; Philadelphia: Lippincott.

McKerracher, D. W., Saklofske, D. H., Silva, P. A. (1977) 'An evaluation and cross cultural comparison of the Reynell Developmental Language Scales.' *Australian Reading Education Journal,* (Spring); 14–17.

Marge, M. (1972) 'The general problems of language disabilities in children.' *In:* Irwin, J. W., Marge, M. (Eds.) *Principles of Childhood Language Disabilities.* New York: Appleton Century Crofts. pp 75–98.

Morley, E. M. (1965) *The Development and Disorders of Speech in Childhood.* Edinburgh: E. & S. Livingstone.

Randall, D., Reynell, J., Curwen, M. (1974) 'A study of language development in a sample of three-year-old children.' *British Journal of Disorders of Communication,* **9,** 3–16.

Reynell, J. (1969) *Reynell Developmental Language Scales.* Windsor: N.F.E.R.

—— (1977) *Reynell Developmental Language Scales (Revised).* Windsor: N.F.E.R.

Richman, N., Stevenson, J. E. and Graham, P. J. (1975) 'Prevalence of behaviour problems in 3-year-old children: an epidemiological study in a London borough.' *Journal of Child Psychology and Psychiatry,* **16,** 277–287.

—— —— —— (1982) *Preschool to School: A Behavioural Study.* London: Academic Press.

—— —— —— (1983) 'The relationship between language, development, and behaviour.' *In:* Schmidt, M. H., Remschmidt, H. (Eds) *Epidemiological Approaches in Child Psychiatry: II.* New York: Thieme-Stratton.

Rutter, M. (1972) 'The effects of language delay on development.' *In:* Rutter, M., Martin, J. A. (Eds) *The Child with Delayed Speech,* London: S.I.M.P. with Heinemann; Philadelphia: Lippincott.

—— Tizard, J., Whitmore, K. (1970) *Education, Health and Behaviour.* London: Longman.

Scottish Council for Research in Education (1976) *The Burt Word Reading Test, 1974 Revision.* London; Hodder & Stoughton.

Silva, P. A. (1980) 'The prevalence, stability, and significance of developmental language delays in preschool children.' *Developmental Medicine and Child Neurology,* **22,** 768–777.

—— (1981) 'The predictive validity of a simple two item developmental screening test for three year olds.' *New Zealand Medical Journal,* **93,** 39–41.

—— Bradshaw, J., Spears, G. F. (1978) 'A study of the concurrent and predictive validity of the Reynell Developmental Language Scales: report from The Dunedin Multidisciplinary Child Development

14

Study.' Windsor: N.F.E.R.

—— Fergusson, D. (1980) 'Some factors contributing to language development in three year old children.' *British Journal of Disorders of Communication*, **15**, 205–214.

—— Justin, C., McGee, R., Williams, S. M. (1984) 'Some developmental and behavioural characteristics of seven year old children with delayed speech development.' *British Journal of Disorders of Communication*, **19**, 147–151.

—— McGee, R. O., Williams, S. M. (1982a) 'The predictive significance of slow walking and talking.' *British Journal of Disorders of Communication*, **17**, 133–139.

—— —— Thomas, J., Williams, S. M. (1982b) 'A descriptive study of socio-economic status and child development in Dunedin five year olds: a report from the Dunedin Multidisciplinary Child Development Study.' *New Zealand Journal of Educational Studies* **17**, 21–32.

—— —— Williams, S. M. (1983) 'Developmental language delay from three to seven years and its significance for low intelligence and reading difficulties at age seven.' *Developmental Medicine and Child Neurology*, **25**, 783–793.

Stevenson, J. (1984) 'Predictive value of speech and language screening.' *Developmental Medicine and Child Neurology*, **26**, 528–538.

—— Richman, N. (1976) 'The prevalence of language delay in a population of three year old children and its association with general retardation.' *Developmental Medicine and Child Neurology*, **18**, 431–441.

—— —— (1978) 'Behaviour, language and development in three-year-old children.' *Journal of Autism and Childhood Schizophrenia*, **8**, 299–313.

Terman, L. M., Merrill, M. R. (1960) *Stanford Binet Intelligence Scale*. Boston: Houghton Mifflin.

Tuomi, S., Ivanoff, P. (1977) 'Incidence of speech and hearing disorders among kindergarten and Grade 1 children.' *Special Education in Canada*, **51**, (4), 5–8.

Wechsler, D. (1974) *The Wechsler Intelligence Scale for Children—Revised*, New York: Psychological Corporation.

White, B. J., Watts, J. C. (1973) *Experience and Environment: Major Influences on the Development of the Young Child*. New Jersey: Prentice-Hall.

Wooster, A. D. (1970) 'Social and ethnic differences in understanding the spoken word.' *British Journal of Disorders of Communication*, **5**, 118–125.

15

2

CHILDHOOD LANGUAGE DISORDERS: CLASSIFICATION AND OVERVIEW

Dorothy Bishop and Lewis Rosenbloom

The medical approach to classification

The traditional classification of childhood language disorders has adopted a medical framework which uses a variety of aetiological and functional criteria for defining groups. A broad distinction is usually made between:

(1) Pure speech disorders, *i.e.* dysphonia, dysfluency, and dysarthria

(2) Language disorder secondary to hearing loss

(3) Language disorder associated with more general intellectual impairment, and secondary to brain disorder or damage

(4) Dysphasia arising from brain lesions acquired after language has developed

(5) Language disorder associated with behavioural or psychiatric disorder

(6) Language disorder as a consequence of environmental deprivation

(7) Language disorder not attributable to any of the above: 'developmental dysphasia' or 'specific developmental language disorder'.

In recent years, however, there has been growing dissatisfaction with this medical approach to classification of language disorders.

Principally, such classifications attempt to list or separate diagnoses in a variety of different ways that often overlap. Thus diagnostic labels may be used, for example, (i) to describe observed clinical features, such as dysfluency; (ii) to indicate the underlying mechanism, *e.g.* hearing loss; or (iii) to indicate aetiology, *e.g.* 'rubella syndrome'. Often ignorance as to the underlying pathological or aetiological processes, rather than adherence to a system of classification, determines which label is used in a specific medical condition. As a result of these deficiencies, the use of multi-axial medical classification has been advocated: but this has not been widely adopted, except in the field of psychiatry.

The traditional medical classification works well within category (1), where one can identify a number of diseases affecting the speech apparatus (*e.g.* cleft palate, upper motor neuron lesions, malocclusion of the jaw), each of which produces distinctive patterns of speech abnormality, depending on the location and the nature of the physical disorder. For categories (2) to (6), however, the classification is less satisfactory on both medical and linguistic grounds. Suppose one considers children with language disorder secondary to general intellectual impairment. From the medical viewpoint this is an unsatisfactory category because it says nothing about the cause, nature, management or prognosis of the brain lesions causing intellectual impairment, and clearly therefore can cover a multitude of disorders. The medical diagnosis fails to provide any perspective on the natural (or unnatural) history of individual disorders, how they might evolve, or their potential for resolution. From the linguistic viewpoint the label is even less helpful. Quite apart from the thorny problem of deciding how severe intellectual impairment must be to 'explain' a language disorder, there is considerable variation in the language problems found in children of low intelligence (Karlin and Strazzulla 1952, Chapman and Nation 1981). The label 'language disorder associated with general intellectual impairment' tells us nothing about the nature of the child's language deficits, and may indeed hinder treatment by implying that the language disorder cannot improve.

It is with the final category, 'developmental dysphasia' or 'specific developmental language disorder', that there is most dissatisfaction. The terminology is confusing on several counts. First, it suggests we are dealing with a single condition, whereas the label is in fact applied on the basis of largely negative criteria (*i.e.* the child is *not* deaf, intellectually impaired, physically handicapped, or psychiatrically disturbed), and, not surprisingly, there is considerable variety in the pattern and severity of language disorders included in this group. Second, aetiology is likely to be heterogeneous. The term 'developmental' indicates that the disorder emerges during development, but does not specify whether it is secondary to congenital structural or functional anomalies of the brain, or whether it is an acquired disorder attributable to covert disease processes. We might expect to find a spectrum of disorders included under this heading, and indeed this is seen in practice. The use of a single term to cover such a variety of disorders has not only made speech therapists cynical about the relevance of a medical approach to language disorders, but has also caused confusion in the research literature, where different studies may obtain contradictory results simply because they are using different populations of children. The term 'developmental dysphasia' is particularly unhelpful, since it implies that we are dealing with a condition analogous to that found in adults with lesions of the left cerebral hemisphere, whereas in fact the only clear point of similarity between these disorders is that language is impaired in both.

The linguistic approach to classification
One reaction has been to turn away from a medically oriented classification, and to describe children in terms of linguistic criteria instead (Bloom and Lahey 1978, Wood 1982). In the past, descriptions of the language of language-disordered children seldom went beyond distinguishing between receptive and expressive language. This distinction has been retained, but is now applied separately to the different components of language, *i.e.* phonology (the sound system), grammar (syntax and morphology), semantics (representation of meaning in language), and pragmatics (how language is used). Furthermore, the focus of interest is shifting from quantitative descriptions of language in terms of 'age-equivalent' or standardised scores, to consideration of qualitative aspects of language. A child with poor language may resemble a younger normal child ('immature language'), or may have linguistic features not found in the course of normal development ('deviant language'). Table I uses this framework to illustrate the wide variety of linguistic deficiencies encompassed by the term 'language disorder'.

The medical and linguistic approaches to classification have been regarded as

TABLE I
A linguistic classification of disordered language

Type of language disorder			Examples
Phonology	Expressive	Immature	Cluster reduction; final consonant deletion; 'k' and 'g' produced as 't' and 'd' *e.g.* string → 'ti'; cake → 'tate'
		Deviant	Initial consonant deletion: *e.g.* van → 'an': sheep → 'eep'
	Receptive	Immature	? Conflicting research: see Barton (1980)
		Deviant	?
Grammar	Expressive	Immature	Simple 'telegrammatic' sentence structure 'I would like an apple and a banana' → 'Me want apple . . . me want banana' Over-generalisation of grammatical rule 'I goed shopping'
		Deviant	Restricted use of a single sentence frame such as subject-verb-object Bizarre syntax: 'Me buy go sweets'
	Receptive	Immature	Tends to ignore inflectional endings
		Deviant	Systematic misunderstanding of some structures (Bishop 1982)
Semantics	Expressive	Immature	Overextension of word meaning, *e.g.* all animals called 'dog'
		Deviant	Anomia: frequently fails to produce word despite knowing it
	Receptive	Immature	Weak vocabulary
		Deviant	Confused if one word has different meanings
Pragmatics	Expressive	Immature	Failure to use polite forms 'Get me an ice-cream', rather than 'May I have an ice-cream, please'
		Deviant	Use of inappropriately stilted language
	Receptive	Immature	Failure to recognise sarcasm
		Deviant	Tendency to respond to utterances literally without regard to situation, *e.g.* adult with arms full asks 'Can you open the door?' child says 'Yes I can, I am very strong' without opening door (Wood 1982)

alternatives (Aram and Nation 1975). This is unfortunate, as it implies they are independent and unrelated ways of describing language disorders, with the linguistic approach concentrating upon the observed clinical features and the medical one concentrating upon aetiology and pathology. While, however, there is no one-to-one correspondence between medical and linguistic levels of description, the relationship between the two is far from random. We aim to demonstrate that the medical and linguistic approaches are complementary, and that both are necessary in classification.

A two-way classification of language disorders
Table II outlines a two-way classification of childhood language disorders, in which identifiable medical factors are represented by the columns, and broad groupings of language disorder by rows. Entries in the body of the Table indicate disorders where a particular medical category is associated with a particular type of language disorder. We shall consider these disorders, taking each column in turn.

Structural or sensorimotor defect of the speech apparatus
This category includes congenital structural abnormalities (*e.g.* cleft palate), neuromotor impairment (*e.g.* suprabulbar palsy), and diseases that temporarily affect the speech apparatus (*e.g.* laryngitis). 'Dysarthria' refers to speech problems associated with weakness, spasticity or inco-ordination of the speech musculature,

TABLE II

A two-way classification of childhood language disorders

MEDICAL FACTORS

	Structural or sensorimotor defect of speech apparatus	Hearing loss	Brain damage or dysfunction acquired in prenatal or perinatal period	Brain damage or dysfunction acquired in childhood	Emotional/behavioural disorders	Environmental deprivation	Aetiology unclear
Speech limited in quality and/or quantity but other language skills normal	Dysphonia; dysarthria	Deafness acquired after language developed			Elective mutism		Stuttering; 'developmental apraxia of speech'
Generalised delay of language development		? With chronic conductive hearing loss	Common with most types intellectual retardation			Result of neglect	? Delayed language
Specific problems with syntax and phonology		? Particularly with selective high-frequency loss		With left-hemisphere lesions in older children			Phonologic-syntactic syndrome
Specific problems with semantics and pragmatics			Cocktail-party syndrome; infantile autism (mild)				Semantic-pragmatic disorder
Poor understanding and limited verbal expression		With severe or profound prelingual deafness	Severe mental handicap	With bilateral lesions of language areas; Landau-Kleffner syndrome			Congenital auditory imperception
Severe impairment of non-verbal as well as verbal communication			Severe mental handicap; infantile autism	Ultimate outcome of degenerative disorders			

and 'dysphonia' to abnormalities of voice control. Unless there are additional handicaps, these disorders impair only the articulation of speech, without affecting other aspects of language (Worster-Drought 1968, Ingram 1972, Darley *et al.* 1975, Peterson-Falzone 1982).

The distinction between speech and language disorders
When a child is unable to speak or difficult to understand, this may be the manifestation of an underlying disorder of language formulation, or it may reflect a relatively peripheral disturbance in the function of the speech apparatus. Traditionally a distinction has been made between 'speech disorders', where damage to or dysfunction of the speech apparatus impairs the ability to transmit language through the medium of sound, and 'language disorders', where the ability to formulate meaning is disturbed. As with other terminology in this area, confusion has arisen (i) because different authors use terms such as 'speech disorder' in highly specific but disparate ways, and (ii) because some disorders are difficult to classify according to this dichotomy. Crystal (1980) preferred to adopt a more linguistic approach, in which the traditional 'speech disorders' are regarded as varieties of language disorder in which there are disturbances at the phonetic or phonological levels. Nevertheless, the traditional distinction does highlight the fact that the spoken language produced by a person is not necessarily an accurate reflection of underlying linguistic competence. Although this is easy to accept in principle, in practice it can be difficult to determine whether a child's problems are restricted to speech or whether there is more widespread linguistic impairment, particularly in the case of cerebral-palsied children with severe motor impairment. The important questions are (i) does the child have normal understanding of language? (ii) if the child is intelligible, is the grammatical structure of language normal? and (iii) in older children, is written language appropriate for a child of that age? Individuals who are quite unable to speak may develop normal or above-average linguistic skills which are only apparent when comprehension tests are used (Lenneberg 1962) or when a communication aid is provided (Fourcin 1975). These cases not only demonstrate the importance of providing communication aids for the physically handicapped, but also pose problems for theories that maintain that the child must practise speaking in order to learn to understand language (Liberman *et al.* 1967).

However, although normal language comprehension can develop in individuals with disorders of spoken language, in many cases it does not, and it is then important to assess the child further to see whether the language problem is attributable to hearing loss or associated with more general intellectual impairment. Hearing loss is particularly common in children with cleft palate and other cranio-facial abnormalities, and in children with athetoid cerebral palsy.

Many children with clear oromotor deficits do have language disorders that cannot be explained either in terms of the motor handicap, or as a secondary consequence of hearing loss or intellectual impairment. Rapin and Allen (1983), for example, describe children who have clear oromotor deficits (such as dribbling or difficulty in swallowing and chewing), but who also have comprehension deficits

20

and abnormal expressive language structure.

Assessing the child with an unexplained disorder of speech-sound production
We have so far considered the issue of language skills in children whose articulatory disorders have a clear physical basis. Another diagnostic problem arises when a child presents with defective speech-sound production in the absence of obvious physical handicap.

In some children, more detailed investigation may give evidence of minor physical problems of oromotor control, either in the history (feeding problems or dribbling), or on direct examination. Martin (1981) emphasised that one should examine sensory as well as motor skills. Discussions of dysarthria have focused almost exclusively on the relationship between speech and motor status, ignoring the rôle of sensation. It may be that in an adult who has already learned to speak, oral sensation is relatively unimportant for fluent speech, but it seems plausible that sensory feedback plays an important rôle in developing articulatory skills. If this is so, then a congenital oral sensory loss might have much more severe consequences for speech than a similar loss acquired in adulthood. A similar situation is seen in children with hemiplegic cerebral palsy. Here the presence and extent of sensory loss in the affected limbs is the major factor determining both their growth and functional status.

It would, however, be wrong to assume that minimal motor or orosensory deficits are responsible for all unexplained problems with speech-sound production. One has only to consider the speech of a normal two-year-old, that of a profoundly deaf child, or that of a Japanese adult speaking English, to realise that such problems can arise for reasons other than neurological impairment. The speech a person produces reflects not only sensorimotor integrity, but also the internal representation of the sound system of the language. If mastery of the language is incomplete or deviant, then difficulty in producing correct speech sounds may occur as a consequence of *linguistic* rather than *sensorimotor* handicap. In other cases, it has been suggested that problems with speech sound sequencing arise because of a specific disorder of motor programming. Such disorders cannot be attributed to structural or sensorimotor defects of the speech apparatus, and are discussed more fully below (p. 29).

Hearing loss
Sensorineural deafness
A hearing loss acquired after language has fully developed has little effect on verbal skills, other than interfering with understanding of spoken language, and causing a deterioration in precision of articulation and voice quality. Deafness acquired prenatally or in early childhood, however, has profound consequences for language development, even with early diagnosis and amplification. There is a strong relationship between degree of deafness and language skills in the prelingually deaf (Bench 1979). The most striking characteristic of these children is their limited, inflexible use of vocabulary and sentence structures (Moores 1972, Swisher 1976): the example of deviant expressive syntax in Table I is typical of a profoundly deaf

child. These problems are not restricted to speech, but extend to written language and signed analogues of English (Simmons 1962, Bishop 1983). It has often been remarked that the spoken language of profoundly prelingually deaf children is delayed, but more detailed analyses suggest that it is also deviant in many respects, including phonology (Oller and Eilers 1981), vocabulary, and syntax (Bishop 1983). For many deaf people, sign language is the main means of communication. There is no research support for the idea that mastery of sign language interferes with spoken language development, but nor is there any evidence of positive transfer from signed analogues of English to spoken or written language (Bishop 1983).

It is known that a selective high-frequency hearing loss can seriously affect language development (Roach and Rosecrans 1972), but there has been little work on the nature of the linguistic difficulties of such children. Before pure-tone audiometry was routinely used, children with a high-frequency hearing loss tended to be diagnosed as cases of 'developmental dysphasia' (Ewing 1930), and some children continue to be misdiagnosed (Merklein and Briskey 1962, Rosenberg 1966, Matkin 1968).

It is often assumed that 'deaf language' is easily recognised, but while this may be true for children with a severe hearing loss, it is not the case for milder losses or those affecting only the high frequencies (Matkin 1968). It is worth noting Rapin and Wilson's caution (1978) that 'the single most common error in investigating a child who fails to develop language is to overlook a peripheral hearing loss'.

Conductive hearing loss
Middle ear disease is often regarded as a relatively minor complaint, since associated hearing loss is mild and does not significantly impair communication in adults. However, although there is no conclusive proof of a causal relationship (Paradise 1981), it has been argued that children who sustain several episodes of otitis media in the preschool years are at risk for language disorder, with poor listening skills, phonological problems, and persisting educational handicaps being remarked upon (Holm and Kunze 1969, Kaplan *et al.* 1973, Lewis 1976, Needleman 1977, Brandes and Ehinger 1981). However, not all studies find this association (Allen and Robinson 1984).

Brain damage or dysfunction acquired prenatally or perinatally
There is a wide range of genetic abnormalities and perinatal insults causing brain damage or dysfunction and resulting in a slow rate of cognitive development, so that the child's pattern of intellectual abilities is normal but the level of development is appropriate for a younger child. Sparks (1984) has recently reviewed the patterns of speech and language disorders resulting from a variety of birth defects. Retarded language development may be the first indication that anything is wrong, but assessment of abilities in other areas will then indicate that motor skills, non-verbal ability and social development are all at a similar low level.

Medical investigation of children with known or assumed chronic brain dysfunction is often unrewarding. Nevertheless it is crucial to search for an underlying cause, to attempt to demonstrate the site and nature of the lesion, and to suggest treatment and indicate prognosis. A disciplined approach to the use of modern investigative methods will be determined both by good clinical practice and the availability of such techniques as cytogenetic investigations, metabolic screening, cerebral-evoked response measurement and computerised tomography. All these methods can provide important information about the nature of the brain disorder in individual children.

Morley (1972) noted that mentally retarded children tend to show poverty or absence of language rather than frank abnormality, and several studies have shown close similarities between the language of retarded children and that of younger normal children (Lackner 1968). Mutism, or speech limited to occasional single words, is not normally found except in cases of severe subnormality (Karlin and Kennedy 1936).

Although intellectual retardation usually takes the form of a generalised slowing of cognitive development, the pattern of impairment is less even in some children in whom language may be disproportionately delayed. It is uncertain whether environmental factors, including the educational programmes offered to these children, contribute to this state of affairs. In the past there was a tendency to use intellectual retardation as an 'explanation' for language disorder, but as research progresses there is increasing interest in investigating the patterns of verbal and non-verbal deficit found in different syndromes.

Chromosomal disorders
One of the commonest chromosomal disorders is Down's syndrome, in which there is an excess of normal genetic material on chromosome 21. Virtually all children with Down's syndrome are moderately or severely intellectually retarded, but language does seem disproportionately impaired in many cases, so that verbal attainments are poor even when compared with other children of similar non-verbal ability. Dodd (1976) showed that children with Down's syndrome made significantly more phonological errors than either normal or severely subnormal children matched on mental age. Although the Down's group did better when imitating than when spontaneously naming, under no condition did their performance approach that of the two comparison groups, and they made a large number of inconsistent substitutions and omissions of sounds that could not be regarded as phonological simplifications. It remains unclear how far these speech problems can be accounted for in terms of structural abnormalities of the articulators. Dodd favoured an alternative explanation in terms of specific difficulty in programming the motor movements of speech. In addition, children with Down's syndrome also have a greatly raised incidence of conductive hearing problems (Brooks *et al.* 1972, Balkany 1980), which may play a part in causing their language problems.

The fact that typical abnormalities are found in Down's syndrome supports the general hypothesis that identifiable genetic factors may underlie certain patterns of language disability. An increased incidence of chromosomal defects of various types has been found in children with language disorders (Mutton and Lea 1980, iedrich *et al.* 1982). More recently it has been found that one or more fragile sites n the x chromosome appear to be markers for a pattern of sex-linked moderate mental retardation occuring in males that is associated with disproportionate disabilities of expressive language and articulation (Howard-Peebles *et al.* 1979. Paul *et al.* 1984). This condition may be identical to the Renpenning syndrome (McLaughlin and Kriegsmann 1980). As chromosome mapping proceeds, it is possible that further relationships between gene loci and clinical features will be found.

Hydrocephalus and the 'cocktail-party' syndrome

A specific kind of linguistic impairment has been described in hydrocephalic children of low intelligence, some of whom have language which, at least on superficial observation, seems disproportionately *good* compared to their other skills. These children use long, complicated sentences incorporating sophisticated vocabulary, but the content of their language is empty or irrelevant, and formal testing reveals poor comprehension (Tew 1979, Tew and Lawrence 1979). This phenomenon, known as the cocktail-party syndrome (Hadenius *et al.* 1962), is of particular interest since it suggests that mastery of the form of language (syntax and phonology) can occur despite fairly limited cognitive ability. The pattern of deficit of children with the cocktail-party syndrome seems to be the mirror-image of the phonologic-syntactic disorder, where the child attempts to convey relevant and sensible messages, but is constrained by inability to cope with language form (see below). It is intriguing to note that while the latter disorder occurs mainly in boys, the 'cocktail-party' syndrome is more common in girls (Tew 1979). It must be stressed, however, that many hydrocephalic children do not show any features of the cocktail-party syndrome.

Infantile autism

Language disorder is a major component of the syndrome of infantile autism, where it is associated with a profound disturbance of social relationships, and obsessional patterns of behaviour. It is now generally accepted that the constellation of behavioural and linguistic abnormalities in autism reflects a cognitive disturbance with an organic basis (Rutter 1983). Autistic children have a severe disorder in understanding the meaning and use of language, which extends to non-verbal forms of communication.

The most severe form of language impairment is mutism, which occurs in around 50 per cent of autistic five-year-olds (Rutter 1966). Other children show a range of abnormalities, many of which appear deviant rather than immature. Articulation may be immature, and prosody is often abnormal (Pronovost *et al.* 1966), but the most striking deficits are in language content and use. Echolalia (repeating another person's utterance), and pronoun reversal (referring to the self as 'you' and others as 'I') are two features associated with autism that have been interpreted as signs of psychiatric disturbance, but which seem better explained as behaviours that result when the child does not understand (Fay and Schuler 1980). The apparently complex utterances made by some autistic children are usually stereotyped or echolalic. Comprehension is usually very poor. There may be an inconsistent response to non-verbal sounds with loud noises sometimes eliciting no response, and soft sounds producing a strong reaction or even distress (Rutter 1966). Some autistic children use language in a ritualistic way, and may repeat advertising jingles or catch-phrases over and over again. In such cases there seems to be some similarity with the cocktail-party syndrome, in that the child has a superficial mastery of language, but little or no understanding of the ideas that the language expresses. A similar dissociation between performance and understanding may occur with written language, where the child shows good mechanical reading ability but poor comprehension of what is read. The term 'hyperlexia' has been used for such cases, some of whom have an obsessional tendency to read out loud any written material they encounter.

The developmental outlook for autistic children, and their ultimate ability to live independently, is constrained primarily by their over-all cognitive functioning. When this is severely impaired, continued dependence is very likely. For those who are less severely mentally handicapped, a greater or lesser degree of language is likely to be acquired, although there are usually overt limitations to its competent social usage. Indeed, even when the autistic person's language becomes superficially appropriate, the individual is likely to remain socially isolated and it is exceptional for normal interpersonal relationships to be established or maintained.

Brain damage or dysfunction acquired in childhood
Localised cerebral lesions
The effects of localised brain lesions on language are very different for children and adults. In the adult, damage to circumscribed areas of the left hemisphere is associated with dysphasia, and there is a close relationship between locus of injury and type of dysphasia. Such language disturbances often persist for many years. In children, the effects of similar lesions depend on age. In infants, left-hemisphere lesions typically depress general intelligence without causing characteristic dysphasic symptoms. This reflects the plasticity of functional organisation in the immature brain, which enables language to develop in the right hemisphere if the left is damaged early in life (Basser 1962, Lenneberg 1967, Rasmussen and Milner 1977, Bishop 1981). Persistent dysphasia is seldom found in young children except where there are bilateral lesions, when the compensatory development of right-hemisphere language is not possible. Unilateral left-hemisphere lesions acquired after the child has learned to speak may result in language impairment, but the type of linguistic deficit is unlike that found in adults. Jargon, paraphasias, persistent comprehension problems or frank agrammatism are all uncommon. Most children are reticent, and have expressive problems especially in the area of phonology (Alajouanine and Lhermitte 1965; Hecaen 1976, 1983). If the lesion is acquired under the age of eight years, the child's dysphasia typically recovers, although careful testing reveals persisting verbal deficiencies (Woods and Carey 1979), and many children have intellectual deficits and do not succeed at school (Byers and McLean 1962, Alajouanine and Lhermitte 1965). The older the child, the greater the probability that the dysphasia will not recover fully (Woods and

Carey 1979).

Acquired aphasia with convulsive disorder: Landau-Kleffner syndrome
In 1957 Landau and Kleffner described a rare language disorder in which severe comprehension problems developed in children with previously normal language. This disorder has also been referred to as 'acquired auditory-verbal agnosia'. Cooper and Ferry (1978) recently reviewed all published cases. Children with this syndrome start to develop normal language but then regress, either suddenly or over a period of weeks or months. All cases in the original series had seizures around the time of onset, but other cases have been reported where the EEG was abnormal but no seizures were observed. Most children have few or no seizures after the initial onset, although cases have been reported where seizures recur after several years, often preceded or accompanied by language deterioration. Gascon *et al.* (1973) noted that anticonvulsant medication might normalise the EEG without improving the language disorder. An auditory basis for the disorder is suggested on several counts. First, these children seem to respond best to language in a visual modality, and most special schools make heavy use of written and signed language. Second, the comprehension problems of these children closely resemble those of profoundly deaf children. Understanding is deviant rather than immature in both groups (Bishop 1982). Third, although the usual forms of behavioural and evoked-response audiometry typically show no deficit in these children, Costello and McGee (1965) found abnormal auditory adaptation in two cases, and a recent study by Stefanatos (unpublished) found abnormal cortical auditory evoked responses to frequency modulated stimuli. Finally, as with deafness, outcome is strongly related to age at onset (Toso *et al.* 1981, Bishop 1985), with the best prognosis for children who had good language prior to onset.

It is usually fairly straightforward to differentiate between Landau-Kleffner syndrome and deafness on the basis of audiometry. Differentiation between Landau-Kleffner syndrome and infantile autism is occasionally problematic. The majority of children with Landau-Kleffner syndrome have normal social behaviour, but some children do react very badly to the frightening experience of finding that they can no longer understand what people are saying, and may become very timid or have frequent temper tantrums. However, these emotional disturbances are typically quite unlike the aloofness and avoidance of eye-contact found in autistic children.

Degenerative disorders
Speech and language can be lost progressively as part of the more generalised loss of psychosocial skills that is seen in a variety of degenerative brain disorders. The causes, clinical features and differential diagnosis of these uncommon conditions are described by Rosenbloom (1981). Deterioration is often slow. As with other disorders in which cognitive functions are globally impaired, retardation of linguistic progress may be the first indication that anything is wrong. More comprehensive assessment then indicates the widespread range of disabilities.

Very occasionally the presenting feature of degenerative brain disorders in childhood can be a severe form of acquired autistic behaviour, with loss of language, social isolation and obsessional characteristics. Corbett *et al.* (1977) have termed this progressive disintegrative psychosis. Evans-Jones and Rosenbloom (1978) have defined a further group of such psychotic children who develop normal language and other skills, then rapidly lose these abilities between three and five years of age, often at a time of severe psychological stress, and become severely autistic and retarded. No specific aetiology has been demonstrated in these children who, on prolonged follow-up, remain profoundly handicapped but do not show further deterioration.

Emotional and behavioural disorders
Emotional disorders may make children reluctant to communicate. However, emotional and behavioural disturbances are an implausible explanation for delayed language acquisition in children, especially in those who show no other sign of psychiatric disturbance, and we would suggest scrupulous care in assuming this aetiology.

Elective mutism
This term is used to describe children who refuse to speak in all but a few situations, and appear to be excessively shy. It may be necessary to observe the child with a parent through a one-way screen in order to obtain a language sample. A significant proportion of electively mute children do have articulatory or language deficits (Wright 1968, Kolvin and Fundudis 1981). In such cases reticence may be an understandable reaction to the experience of being teased, criticised, or not understood. Others can speak normally but fail to do so. Such individuals do not have a language disorder but they may have other features of childhood psychiatric disorder.

Environmental deprivation
When considering the rôle of environmental factors in the genesis of language disorders, we may make a broad distinction between two components of environmental deprivation: physical deprivation (poverty, malnutrition, poor housing, *etc.*) and social deprivation (*i.e.* lack of caring relationship between child and caretaker and/or inadequate linguistic stimulation).

Both forms of deprivation tend to co-occur, making it difficult to disentangle specific effects. However, the importance of social factors is demonstrated by studies of institutionalised children, whose physical needs are looked after but who lack the opportunity to develop individual relationships with adults.

Such children are usually retarded in all aspects of development, but verbal impairments are particularly striking (Provence and Lipton 1962, Lefevre 1972). Abused children living with their families, in contrast, do not seem to be delayed in language development unless they are also subjected to neglect, *i.e.* inadequate physical environment (Allen and Oliver 1982). Thus a poor relationship between child and caretaker seems less detrimental to language development than no relationship at all. It is encouraging to find that some children with gross verbal impairments arising from appallingly severe physical, social and linguistic deprivation have shown impressive levels of language development once they are put in a normal home, with some showing complete recovery (Skuse 1984). However, some forms of severe deprivation early in life affect the way in which the brain develops, producing irreversible handicaps. For example, malnutrition *in utero* can result in microcephaly and intellectual retardation (Lefevre 1972).

Turning to less extreme situations, we know that there are cultural differences between social classes in the ways in which language is used, and one might wonder whether the 'restricted code' used by working-class parents puts their children at a disadvantage when learning language. However, Tizard *et al.* (1983) concluded that it was seriously misleading to suppose that working-class children suffered from a 'verbal deficit'. They found that working-class four-year-olds did use language for complex purposes less frequently than middle-class children, but both groups displayed all the essential verbal skills. Irrespective of social class, children had far more complex language directed to them at home than at nursery. If one matches groups as closely as possible in terms of physical environment, then social-class differences in language attainments are detectable but not large. Cultural differences between social classes cannot be regarded as an important determinant of developmental language disorders.

This conclusion is strengthened by the finding that children can develop normal language in the face of fairly severe 'verbal deprivation'. Hearing children growing up with profoundly deaf parents seldom have long-term language problems, even though they may be exposed to grossly abnormal spoken language in the preschool years (Critchley 1967, Mayberry 1976, Schiff 1979).

Specific developmental speech and language disorders of unknown origin
Many children present with a language disorder for which there is no obvious explanation. Peripheral hearing is normal, nor-verbal intelligence is good, the family home is perfectly adequate and there is no sign of physical or psychiatric abnormality. Little is known about the aetiology of these disorders. The vast majority of children have no detectable genetic or physical abnormality, even after detailed investigation. Research on the classification of these 'specific developmental disorders' is still in its infancy. The classification described should not be regarded as either comprehensive or definitive, and is certain to be refined or altered in the light of future investigations.

Stuttering
Stuttering is the term applied to forms of dysfluent speech in which production of individual words is disrupted by syllable or sound repetition or sound prolongation. Despite considerable research into the aetiology of stuttering, no single organic or environmental factor has been shown to be a necessary and sufficient cause of this disorder. There is, however, broad agreement that stuttering is considerably more common in boys than in girls and that it runs in families. It seems increasingly likely that stuttering results from the interaction of organic and environmental factors, rather than being caused by one or the other. Thus a child may have a genetic

predisposition to stutter which is only manifested under particular environmental conditions (Kidd 1983). Furthermore, it may be that we are dealing with a variety of disorders with different aetiologies under the umbrella term 'stuttering'.

Johnson (1959) has argued that it is normal for young children to go through a period of dysfluency as they learn language, and that parental reaction to this dysfluency plays a rôle in the development of stuttering in many children. The parent who becomes anxious about dysfluency and seeks to correct it exacerbates the problem by making the child aware that something is wrong. Most speech therapists welcome referrals of preschool children whose parents are anxious about apparently trivial dysfluencies, since by counselling the parents they can prevent more serious difficulties developing. Usually they would only work directly with a child if he or she was aware of stuttering and showed marked tension and signs of struggle.

More detailed reviews of the aetiology and treatment of stuttering may be found in Dalton and Hardcastle (1977) and Freeman (1982).

'Developmental apraxia of speech'
It would be convenient if we could easily divide all disorders of speech-sound production into those attributable to linguistic or to sensorimotor deficits. However, some children seem to fit neither category. Language skills are good, and the child is not dysarthric. However, speech production is faulty, and there is a discrepancy between what the child seems physically capable of articulating and what he or she does articulate. In mild cases, the only sign of the disorder may be a tendency to become muddled on long words (so that 'buttercup' is produced as 'bukkertup' for example), or to make inconsistent pronunciation errors, so that 'van' is pronounced variably as 'van', 'fan' or 'ban' on different occasions). Such a child is clearly capable of producing the individual speech sounds, but appears to have difficulty in organising the correct sequence of sounds. In severe cases, the child may be able to imitate words or phrases, but be extremely limited in spontaneous speech. Rapin and Allen (1983) have described a pattern of disorder which they term 'severe expressive syndrome with good comprehension' where the child is mute, or produces only single-word utterances, despite having adequate oromotor skills and normal understanding of language. Given the linguistic competence of these children, it seems reasonable to conceptualise this disorder as a motor programming deficit. A similar deficit has been described in brain-damaged adults, and is referred to as 'apraxia of speech' or 'verbal dyspraxia'. These terms have also been applied to children: but, as with 'dysphasia', they have generated confusion. Some authors use these terms in the classical neurological sense, to refer only to those rare cases where language comprehension appears normal, and where there is a clear discrepancy between the child's physical capacity for speech-sound production and the erratic articulatory performance in spon-taneous connected speech. Some would insist that there be independent evidence of brain damage before using the term 'apraxia', while others adopt the circular argument that the speech disorder itself is evidence of brain damage. To add to the confusion, many authors use the terms 'developmental apraxia of speech' or

'developmental verbal dyspraxia' in a much looser sense, with some regarding any difficulty in sequential production of speech sounds as 'dyspraxia', irrespective of the child's language skills and the nature of the speech errors. Such a definition would include, for example, a child with immature language who regularly omitted final consonants from words. This is a misleading usage of 'apraxia', since it would imply that the child had a primary motor-programming deficit, when in fact the observed speech-production errors are easily accounted for in terms of an immature phonological system, which is part of a more general language deficit (see p. 31). Others have altered the meaning of the 'apraxia' to include speech problems with a sensory basis (cf. the original definition of this term by Rosenbek *et al.* 1984). Guyette and Diedrich (1981) have drawn attention to the wide variety of definitions of 'developmental apraxia of speech', concluding that:

> First, there is little reported agreement on which symptoms/behaviors are important in the diagnosis of this disorder. Second, there is a paucity of data to support claims even when agreement is found. (p. 8)

Guyette and Diedrich conclude that the diagnosis 'developmental apraxia of speech' is neither appropriate nor useful. However, we do need terms to describe those rare children whose speech difficulties cannot be accounted for in terms of dysarthria or sensory loss, nor in terms of a restricted phonological system. We would recommend that labels such as 'developmental apraxia of speech' be limited to such children, and that research studies use precise objective criteria to define what they mean when they use these terms.

Developmental language delay
This term is often used loosely to talk about any type of language difficulty in a child, but should really be reserved for those children whose over-all development is normal except in the area of language, where development progresses at a slow rate, with essentially normal language appearing by the age of six years or less.

A distinction between language delay and language disorder seems justified both logically and empirically. Logically we know that for any developmental milestone there will be variation in the age at which it is passed, and that children will exist who are statistically abnormal, in that the age at which they pass the milestone will be unusually late. It does not necessarily follow, however, that these children are suffering from any biological abnormality. For example, a small proportion of girls will not have reached puberty by the age of 17, despite being perfectly healthy. In other cases there may be underlying disease (*e.g.* a pituitary disorder) which is responsible for failure to reach puberty. It is important to distinguish between the two types of girl, since the prognosis and treatment will be different. In language development, similarly, we can make a conceptual distinction between children who are delayed (*i.e.* immature but not abnormal) and those who are disordered. Empirical data lend support to such a distinction. Epidemiological studies (Morley 1972, Silva 1980) typically find that the prevalence of specific language problems in childhood falls off fairly steeply between the ages of three and five years, so it is clear that many children 'recover' after a history of slow language development in the preschool years. Other children identified as having language disorders in the preschool years have persistent linguistic, educational, social and behavioural difficulties (Aram *et al.* 1984).

The problem for the paediatrician and speech therapist is how to distinguish delay and disorder in practice. When confronted by a three-year-old who is only producing single words, how can we tell if the child's language is simply delayed, or if there is a language disorder such as the phonologic-syntactic syndrome? One obvious cue to outcome is the severity of the disorder. Currently we have no hard data to say how severe a problem must be before we decide that the child needs special help in the form of a language group or speech therapy. It is advisable to monitor the progress of young children at six-monthly intervals. As a rule of thumb one can say that if an otherwise normal child has only a handful of words at three years, speaks in single words at 3½, or in two-word utterances at four years, then the problem is certainly severe enough to cause concern.

It may be that the *pattern* as well as severity of the language disorder can give a guide to its prognosis: for instance, children whose phonological systems resemble those of younger normal children may prove to have better outcome than those with deviant characteristics.

One might imagine that the child with a genuine delay of language development should give little cause for concern, since the language problem will resolve itself without intervention. However, there is mounting evidence that such children are at risk for educational problems even though their language appears superficially normal. Fundudis *et al.* (1979) followed up a group of 24 children who had poor language at three years of age, but who were developing normally in other respects. When followed up at seven years of age, the group as a whole did significantly more poorly than a control group on a variety of cognitive and educational tasks, especially those involving language.

Specific problems with language form: phonologic-syntactic syndrome
This is the most common variety of developmental language disorder in which an apparently normal child has a selective difficulty with language form, but normal language content. The child has a normal urge to communicate, and says sensible and appropriate things. A wide range of severity of disorder is encompassed by this category. At one extreme we have the child who would traditionally be referred to as a 'developmental expressive aphasic' (Morley 1972), where speech may be highly unintelligible, with syntactic structure several years behind age-level. At the other extreme is the child whose main problems are with phonology, who would in the past be regarded as a case of 'functional articulation disorder'. Research studies have found receptive as well as expressive problems with phonology and syntax in both sorts of child (Shriner *et al.* 1969; Whitacre *et al.* 1970; Marquardt and Saxman 1972; Bishop 1979, 1982).

Parents typically report that language development was slow from birth. A positive family history of language or reading difficulties is common in such children, suggesting a genetic aetiology. Any child with problems of this kind persisting beyond the age of six years will need a great deal of special help.

Language does improve slowly, but the child usually has difficulty learning to read, and will be far behind in basic school attainments and social development by the time reasonable expressive speech is acquired. The incidence of this disorder is hard to ascertain, since criteria for diagnosis vary. All authors agree that boys are about two or three times more likely to be affected than girls.

The term phonologic-syntactic syndrome has been taken from Rapin and Allen (1983), whose description of this type of disorder corresponds very closely with this account. However, they differ on some points of detail. They regard oromotor dysfunction as common in such children, and mention that many have a history of difficulty in swallowing, sucking, or chewing. In Bishop's (1979) sample, only a few children presented with such problems. The difference may arise because Rapin and Allen's sample were referred for paediatric neurological assessment, so may be more likely to have evident neurological problems.

Rapin and Allen noted the similarities between the symptoms of Broca's aphasia and phonologic-syntactic syndrome, and speculate that prefrontal pathology may be involved. But one must then explain why these children typically have no hard neurological signs, while children with unequivocal lesions of Broca's area do not have the phonologic-syntactic syndrome.

There may be difficulty in deciding whether a child with a speech-sound production problem is a case of 'developmental apraxia of speech', minimal dysarthria, or phonological-syntactic syndrome. While some authorities would regard symptoms such as gross motor clumsiness as indicative of 'developmental apraxia of speech, we would argue that the criterion of diagnosing 'apraxia' should be the nature of the speech errors. Analysis of the child's sound system should enable one to distinguish between apraxia (where errors are inconsistent and increase in likelihood with complexity of utterance) and phonological disability (where errors are systematic, and can be described in terms of a delayed or deviant phonological system) (Compton 1970, Oller 1973, Leonard 1982). Differentiation from dysarthria is only problematic when the child has signs of neuromotor handicap. The question then is whether the sensorimotor deficit is adequate to account for the speech difficulty. Where the child has expressive and receptive problems with syntax as well as phonology, a diagnosis of phonologic-syntactic syndrome is indicated.

Specific problems with language use and content: semantic-pragmatic disorder
The term semantic-pragmatic syndrome was used by Rapin and Allen (1983) to describe a group of children who use superficially complex language with clear articulation, but whose use and understanding of language is defective. We prefer to talk of a 'disorder' rather than a 'syndrome', reflecting our view that we are describing a set of behaviours that are loosely associated, which shade into autism at one extreme and normality at the other. These children have relatively little problem with language form, but are characterised by abnormal language content and use. They may produce apparently irrelevant utterances, and tangential answers to questions. A nice example is given by Wood (1982), who describes the following exchange:

Child: My mother took me and my sister
Adult: Took you where?
Child: Yeah
Adult: Your mother took you and your sister *where?*
Child: Yes, she did. That will be the last one I'd ever seen.

At present the literature on this disorder is limited to clinical description, and research studies using objective criteria to categorise children are urgently needed. The following comments are based on our experience with this type of child, and may be regarded as working hypotheses in need of formal tests.

This type of language tends to occur in association with other behavioural and cognitive abnormalities, many of which resemble mild forms of the deficits found in infantile autism.

(1) The history is typically one of delayed language development, with some children producing very little language until five or six years of age. The child may give inconsistent responses to sound, making it difficult to exclude deafness. Early language may be characterised by echolalia or jargon.

(2) Young children with this sort of disorder sometimes produce paradoxical results when expressive and receptive language skills are compared, in that their comprehension seems worse than expression. For example, a child may spontaneously name a set of pictures correctly, but then make errors when asked to pick out the same pictures named by another person.

(3) There may be fascination with the sound of language without regard to the meaning, so that nursery rhymes or advertising jingles may be repeated playfully over and over again.

(4) If the child is asked to name objects or pictures, three features may be observed: (i) the child may misperceive the object or situation. Typically the child thinks the picture is of something that strongly resembles the pictured item, but which would be very unlikely in that context. Examples observed by the authors are a five-year-old who described a crescent moon with stars as 'banana with stars', and a four-year-old who thought that a girl putting a red flower in a boy's lapel was a girl setting fire to a boy; (ii) the child may produce a word that is quite different in meaning, but similar in sound: *e.g.* catapult for caterpillar; (iii) there may be a word-finding problem, with the child hesitating and groping for a word that he or she knows.

(5) Some children continually ask questions, but do not seem to take notice of replies. For example, a boy with this sort of language disorder responded to pictures of animals by immediately saying, 'Where does the horsie live? Where does the doggie live?' He was quite capable of responding to these questions, and seemed to be simply re-enacting an earlier session with his teacher.

(6) The child may fail to understand or produce such cues to meaning as facial expression or tone of voice.

(7) Although fluent and grammatically complex sentences are produced, minor problems with syntax and phonology may persist in the school-age child. Pronoun and tense distinctions give particular difficulty.

(8) There may be a marked difference between the child's ability to understand in a structured, concrete situation, such as a multiple choice test, and ability to comprehend normal conversation, where the speaker refers to events that are not immediately deducible from the physical context.

(9) Understanding is highly literal, so that sarcasm or metaphorical use of language are misunderstood.

(10) Inattention is often a serious problem in young children with this disorder.

(11) Children may be thought of as naughty by their teachers because they tend not to obey instructions, and they are often insensitive to social etiquette. For example, a child may suddenly walk out of morning assembly at school, or may sing a favourite song when everyone is quiet for prayers. Normal fear of strangers may be absent, and the child may kiss or stroke unfamiliar adults.

(12) Imaginative play is usually poorly developed, and there may be fascination with mechanical objects.

(13) Unlike other language-disordered children, a few of these children learn to read at the normal age, or even earlier. However, their comprehension for what they read tends to be poor.

(14) Many, but not all, such children are significantly clumsy in gross motor skills.

Most children of this kind would never be called autistic: they do not have the avoidance of eye-contact and aloofness typical of infantile autism, and only mild tendencies to ritualistic and obsessional behaviour. Ability to cope in normal school depends heavily on the extent of social abnormality associated with the disorder.

Similar clusters of linguistic, behavioural, and cognitive abnormalities have been described by de Ajuriaguerra *et al.* (1976) in what they describe as 'verbally unrestrained' language disorder. More recently, Wing (1981) has described a rather similar pattern of disorder in her account of Asperger's syndrome. However, while Wing's cases tended to be of normal verbal intelligence, children with semantic-pragmatic disorder typically have a large discrepancy between Verbal and Performance IQ, reflecting their difficulty in understanding abstract questions. Furthermore, many children with semantic-pragmatic disorder relate to other people reasonably well, whereas all of Wing's cases had severe difficulties in this area. The existence of these different types of disorder indicates that, while these social and linguistic deficits tend to co-occur, they can be dissociated. Individuals with predominantly social difficulties tend to be referred to a psychiatrist as cases of Asperger's syndrome, whereas individuals with predominantly linguistic difficulties will be seen by speech therapists. Where both social and linguistic difficulties are pronounced, the individual will be diagnosed as a case of infantile autism. But the boundaries between these conditions are not precise, and it would be inappropriate to agonise over a differential diagnosis between semantic-pragmatic disorder, Asperger's syndrome and infantile autism if a child appeared to have some features of each condition.

It is important, however, to differentiate semantic-pragmatic disorder from hearing loss, elective mutism, Landau-Kleffner syndrome and intellectual retardation. Techniques such as electrocochleography and evoked-response audiometry will be necessary if the child cannot be tested by normal audiometric techniques, or if results are inconsistent. Elective mutism may be suspected if the child is usually mute but then produces a long and complex utterance. However, it is only an appropriate diagnosis if it can be shown that the child regularly uses complex and appropriate language in a familar setting. Differentiation from Landau-Kleffner syndrome may be difficult in preschool children who appear unresponsive to sound. Points to consider are developmental history (regression in Landau-Kleffner syndrome), electro-encephalography (EEG abnormalities or seizures in Landau-Kleffner syndrome) and play and social behaviour (normal in Landau-Kleffner syndrome). Young children with semantic-pragmatic disorder often give the impression that they are intellectually retarded, because their poor language is associated with limited imaginative play, inattention and clumsiness. However, testing with a non-verbal scale (*e.g.* the Leiter International Performance Scale) in a non-distracting environment will show the child to have normal non-verbal abilities.

Finally, semantic-pragmatic disorder is one of the few language disorders where there may be a difficulty in distinguishing the disorder from normality. The types of linguistic difficulty manifested by school-age children are often not immediately obvious, and are typically not picked up by standardised language tests. Where a parent or teacher persists in worrying about the language development of an apparently normal child, one should investigate comprehension skills carefully, using open-ended rather than multiple choice tests, before concluding that there is nothing to worry about.

Auditory imperception and central auditory disorders
When a child appears to be unresponsive to sound, the usual course followed is referral to an audiologist who will look for evidence of sensorineural or conductive hearing loss. If the child responds at normal thresholds to pure-tone stimuli, it is usually concluded that auditory impairment is not an adequate explanation for the language disorder. However, this overlooks the possibility that there may be disruption or dysfunction of the auditory pathways at a more central level. As Taylor (1964) pointed out:

> Interest in the conducting mechanism of the middle ear and in the mechanism of cochlear function and dysfunction is not sufficient; the central and cortical areas together with the whole of cerebral mechanisms have to be taken into account.

The effects of lesions of the auditory pathways at different levels have been studied in adults using electrophysiological and behavioural measures, and distinctive patterns of impairment are found. Ability to detect pure tones is typically unimpaired with central auditory lesions, but patients have difficulty in discriminating speech when this is presented in noise or against a competing message (Jerger 1964, Keith 1982).

In principle, these techniques would seem promising for application to children, but there are difficulties. Cortical auditory-evoked response audiometry has been used relatively seldom with language-disordered children, presumably because of methodological and interpretative difficulties (Parving *et al.* 1981), although brainstem-evoked response techniques seem more satisfactory (Jerger *et al.* 1980). Behavioural tests analogous to those used with adults have been devised, but these pose problems of interpretation. Virtually all these tests require the child to respond to linguistic stimuli. We might therefore expect a language-disordered child to perform poorly regardless of the status of the central auditory pathways. Indeed, in normal children, performance on these tests is highly dependent on age (Willeford 1977).

Because we do not yet have reliable and validated behavioural indices of central auditory disorder, we recommend that terms such as 'central auditory disorder' be reserved for cases where there is electrophysiological or neurological confirmation of involvement of the central auditory pathways (Lenhardt 1981). Where such evidence is lacking, it is preferable to use descriptive terms such as 'auditory imperception', and to regard central auditory disorder as a hypothesis rather than a diagnosis.

Auditory imperception may be defined as lack of responsiveness to sound in a child with normal peripheral hearing. Severe forms of this disorder are rare, usually occurring in the context of the syndrome of acquired aphasia with convulsive disorder (Landau and Kleffner 1957). However, occasional cases have been described where the severe auditory comprehension problems appear to be present from birth, and there is no evidence of electroencephalographic abnormalities. The first clear description of such a case was by Worster-Drought and Allen in 1929, who used the term 'congenital auditory imperception'. Their case had a persistent and severe language disorder.

Ward and Kellett (1982) described a group of eight preschool children who showed highly variable responses to sound in conjunction with severe expressive and receptive language problems. These children made good progress on a home treatment programme. In our experience, many audiologists interpret variable or anomalous results on audiometry as indicative of either fluctuating conductive hearing loss or incompetent audiology. Taylor (1964), however, has pointed out that variability of response to auditory stimuli may be a characteristic of central auditory disorder, and that responsiveness may vary according to whether the child is attending to visual stimuli. Clearly further research is needed to develop reliable and valid techniques for detecting central auditory disorders in children.

Conclusion
Our attempts to impose an order on the chaotic variety of language disorders in children are bound to be imperfect. No sooner does one identify a set of categories than one encounters children who seem to belong to no category, or whose characteristics fall between two categories. Does this mean that we should abandon attempts at classification altogether, and concentrate on describing each individual child in as much detail as possible? We would counteract this sort of argument by adopting the same position as Kendell (1975) in his defence of diagnosis in psychiatry. Quite simply, without some sort of classificatory framework, scientific communication is impossible. 'If every patient is different from every other then we

can learn nothing from our colleagues, our textbooks, or the accumulated experience of our predecessors' (pp. 5–6). The response to the shortcomings of our current classificatory scheme should be not to abandon classification, but to seek ways of refining and improving the classification so that it leads to greater understanding of the conditions we are dealing with. To do so we need to expand our knowledge in three areas.

First, we need to investigate the possibility of multifactorial causation of childhood language disorders. Our experience is that many language-disordered children have a history of multiple adverse factors: thus a child may be living in poor social circumstances, have suffered a difficult birth, and then had several prolonged episodes of conductive hearing loss in early childhood. While it is possible that these factors are simply coincidental with the language disorder, it seems worth investigating the possibility that 'the sum is greater than the parts', and that a language disorder may result from a combination of adverse factors, none of which alone would be sufficient to impair language development seriously.

Second, further research is needed into the organic basis of childhood language disorders. We would stress the inadequacy of models based on research with adult neurological patients for explaining childhood language disorders. Adult anatomical, physiological and clinical studies correlate poorly with what is seen in paediatric practice, as we might expect from what we know of the plasticity of the immature nervous system. Techniques relevant to infants and young children need to be developed. We have indicated the relevance of cytogenetic studies. Other promising techniques include newer radiological investigative methods, including nuclear magnetic resonance and regional bloodflow measurement, as well as neurophysiological and neurochemical evaluations.

Finally, we need more information about the time course, patterns of evolution and the natural and modified histories of childhood language disorders. Classifications such as we have described are largely based on observations of children over short periods of time and on cross-sectional data, and hence are of limited value in remediation. Such descriptions need to be supplemented by prospective longitudinal studies of language-disordered children.

A 45-minute videotape entitled 'Varieties of Developmental Language Disorder' has been produced by the first author and is available for purchase. Further details from the TV Unit, Department of Mental Health, Whitla Medical Building, Belfast City Hospital, Belfast BT9 7BL.

REFERENCES

Alajouaine, T., Lhermitte, F. (1965) 'Acquired aphasia in children.' *Brain*, **88**, 653–662.
Allen, D. V., Robinson, D. O. (1984) 'Middle ear status and language development in preschool children.' *ASHA*, **26**, 33–37.
Allen, R. E., Oliver, J. M. (1982) 'The effects of child maltreatment on language development.' *Child Abuse and Neglect*, **6**, 299–305.
Aram, D., Nation, J. (1975) 'Patterns of language behavior in children with developmental language disorders.' *Journal of Speech and Hearing Research*, **18**, 229–241.
—— Ekelman, B. L., Nation, J. E. (1984) 'Preschoolers with language disorders: 10 years later.' *Journal of Speech and Hearing Research*, **27**, 232–244.
Balkany, T. J. (1980) 'Otologic aspects of Down's syndrome.' *Seminars in Speech, Language and*

Hearing, **1,** 39–47.

Barton, D. (1980) 'Phonemic perception in children.' *In:* Yeni-Komshian, G. H., Kavanagh, J. F., Ferguson, C. A. (Eds.) *Child Phonology: Vol. 2: Perception.* New York: Academic Press.

Basser, L. S. (1962) 'Hemiplegia of early onset and the faculty of speech with special reference to the effects of hemispherectomy.' *Brain,* **85,** 427–460.

Bench, J. (1979) 'Introductory review.' *In:* Bench, J., Bamford, J. (Eds.) *Speech–Hearing Tests and the Spoken Language of Hearing-Impaired Children.* London: Academic Press.

Bishop, D. V. M. (1979) 'Comprehension in developmental language disorders.' *Developmental Medicine and Child Neurology,* **21,** 225–238.

—— (1981) 'Plasticity and specificity of language localization in the developing brain.' *Developmental Medicine and Child Neurology,* **23,** 251–255.

—— (1982) 'Comprehension of spoken, written and signed sentences in childhood language disorders.' *Journal of Child Psychology and Psychiatry,* **23,** 1–20.

—— (1983) 'Comprehension of English syntax by profoundly deaf children.' *Journal of Child Psychology and Psychiatry,* **24,** 415–434.

—— (1985) 'Age of onset and outcome in "acquired aphasia with convulsive disorder" (Landau-Kleffner syndrome).' *Developmental Medicine and Child Neurology,* **27,** 705–712.

Bloom, L., Lahey, M. (1978) *Language Development and Language Disorders.* New York: John Wiley.

Brandes, P. J., Ehinger, D. M. (1981) 'The effects of early middle ear pathology on auditory perception and academic achievement.' *Journal of Speech and Hearing Disorders,* **46,** 301–307.

Brooks, D. N., Wooley, H., Kanjilal, G. C. (1972) 'Hearing loss and middle ear disorders in patients with Down's syndrome.' *Journal of Mental Deficiency Research,* **16,** 21–29.

Byers, R. K., McLean, W. T. (1962) 'Etiology and course of certain hemiplegias with aphasia in childhood.' *Pediatrics,* **29,** 376–383.

Chapman, D. L., Nation, J. E. (1981) 'Patterns of language performance in educable mentally retarded children.' *Journal of Communication Disorders,* **14,** 245–254.

Compton, A. J. (1970) 'Generative studies of children's phonological disorders.' *Journal of Speech and Hearing Disorders,* **35,** 315–339.

Cooper, J. A., Ferry, P. C. (1978) 'Acquired auditory verbal agnosia and seizures in childhood.' *Journal of Speech and Hearing Disorders,* **43,** 176–184.

Corbett, J., Harris, R., Taylor, E., Trimble, M. (1977) 'Progressive disintegrative psychosis in childhood.' *Journal of Child Psychology and Psychiatry,* **18,** 211–219.

Costello, M. R., McGee, T. M. (1965) 'Language impairment associated with abnormal auditory adaptation.' *In:* Graham, A. (Ed.) *Sensorineural Hearing Processes and Disorders.* Boston: Little, Brown.

Critchley, M. (1967) 'Language development of hearing children in a deaf environment.' *Developmental Medicine and Child Neurology,* **9,** 274–280.

Crystal, D. (1980) *Introduction to Language Pathology.* London: Edward Arnold.

Dalton, P., Hardcastle, W. J. (1977) *Disorders of Fluency.* London: Edward Arnold.

Darley, F. L., Aronson, A. E., Brown, J. R. (1975) *Motor Speech Disorders.* Philadelphia: W. B. Saunders.

De Ajuriaguerra, J., Jaeggi, A., Guignard, F., Kocher, F., Maquard, M., Roth, S., Schmid, E. (1976) 'The development and prognosis of dysphasia in children.' *In:* Morehead, D. M., Morehead, A. E. (Eds.) *Normal and Deficient Child Language.* Baltimore: University Park Press.

Dodd, B. (1976) 'A comparison of the phonological systems of mental age–matched normal, subnormal and Down's syndrome children.' *British Journal of Disorders of Communication,* **11,** 27–42.

Evans-Jones, L. G., Rosenbloom., L. (1978) 'Disintegrative psychosis in childhood.' *Developmental Medicine and Child Neurology,* **20,** 462–470.

Ewing, A. W. G. (1930) *Aphasia in Children.* Oxford: Oxford Medical Publications.

Fay, W. H., Schuler, A. L. (1980) *Emerging Language in Autistic Children.* Baltimore: University Park Press.

Fourcin, A. J. (1976) 'Language development in the absence of expressive speech.' *In:* Lenneberg, E. H., Lenneberg, E. (Eds.) *Foundations of Language Development: Vol. 2.* New York: Academic Press.

Freeman, F. J. (1982) 'Stuttering.' *In:* Lass, N. J., McReynolds, L. V., Northern, J. L., Yoder, D. E. (Eds.) *Speech, Language and Hearing: Vol. 2.* Philedelphia: W. B. Saunders Co.

Friedrich, U., Dalby, M., Staehelin-Jensen, T., Bruun-Petersen, G. (1982) 'Chromosomal studies of children with developmental language retardation.' *Developmental Medicine and Child Neurology,* **24,** 645–652.

Fundudis, T., Kolvin, I., Garside, R. (1979) *Speech Retarded and Deaf Children: Their Psychological*

Development. London: Academic Press.

Gascon, G., Victor, D., Lombroso, C., Goodglass, H. (1973) 'Language disorder, convulsive disorders, and electroencephalographic abnormalities.' *Archives of Neurology*, **28**, 156–162.

Guyette, T. W., Diedrich, W. M. (1981) 'A critical review of developmental apraxia of speech.' *In:* Lass, N. J. (Ed.) *Speech and Language: Advances in Basic Research and Practice: Vol. 5.* New York: Academic Press.

Hadenius, A. M., Hagberg, B., Hyttnas-Bensch, K., Sjogren, I. (1962) 'The natural prognosis of infantile hydrocephalus.' *Acta Paediatrica*, **51**, 117–118.

Hecaen, H. (1976) 'Acquired aphasia in children and the ontogenesis of hemispheric functional specialization.' *Brain and Language*, **3**, 114–134.

—— (1983) 'Acquired aphasia in children: revisited.' *Neuropsychologia*, **21**, 581–587.

Holm, V. A., Kunze, L. H. (1969) 'Effects of chronic otitis media on language and speech development.' *Pediatrics*, **43**, 833–839.

Howard-Peebles, P. N., Stoddard, G. R., Mims, M. G. (1979) 'Familial X-linked mental retardation, verbal disability, and marker X chromosomes.' *American Journal of Human Genetics*, **31**, 214–222.

Ingram, T. T. S. (1972) 'The classification of speech and language disorders in young children.' *In:* Rutter, M., Martin, J. A. M. (Eds.) *The Child with Delayed Speech. Clinics in Developmental Medicine, No. 43.* London: Spastics International Medical Publications.

Jerger, J. (1964) 'Auditory tests for disorders of the central auditory mechanism.' *In:* Fields, W. S., Alford, B. R. (Eds.) *Neurological Aspects of Auditory and Vestibular Disorders.* Springfield, Illinois: C. C. Thomas.

—— Hayes, D., Jordan, C. (1980) 'Clinical experience with auditory brainstem response audiometry in pediatric assessment.' *Ear and Hearing*, **1**, 19–25.

Johnson, W. (1959) *The Onset of Stuttering: Research Findings and Implications.* Minneapolis: University of Minnesota Press.

Kaplan, G. J., Bender, T. R., Baum, C., Clark, P. S. (1973) 'Long term effects of otitis media: a ten-year cohort study of Alaskan Eskimo children.' *Pediatrics*, **52**, 577–585.

Karlin, I. W., Kennedy, L. (1936) 'Delay in the development of speech.' *American Journal of Diseases of Childhood*, **51**, 1138–1149.

—— Strazzulla, M. (1952) 'Speech and language problems of mentally deficient children.' *Journal of Speech and Hearing Disorders*, **17**, 286–294.

Keith, R. W. (1982) 'Central auditory tests.' *In:* Lass, N. J., McReynolds, L. V., Northern, J. L., Yoder, D. E. (Eds.) *Speech, Language and Hearing, Vol. 3: Hearing Disorders.* Philadelphia: W. B. Saunders.

Kendell, R. E. (1975) *The Role of Diagnosis in Psychiatry.* Oxford: Blackwell Scientific Publications.

Kidd, K. K. (1983) 'Recent progress on the genetics of stuttering.' *In:* Ludlow, C. L., Cooper, J. A. (Eds.) *Genetic Aspects of Speech and Language Disorders.* New York: Academic Press.

Kolvin, I., Fundudis, T. (1981) 'Elective mute children: psychological development and background factors.' *Journal of Child Psychology and Psychiatry*, **22**, 219–232.

Lackner, J. R. (1968) 'A developmental study of language behaviour in retarded children.' *Neuropsychologia*, **6**, 301–320.

Landau, W. M., Kleffner, F. R. (1957) 'Syndrome of acquired aphasia with convulsive disorder in children.' *Neurology*, **7**, 523–530.

Lefèvre, A. B. (1975) 'Language development in malnourished children.' *In:* Lenneberg, E. H., Lenneberg, E. (Eds.) *Foundations of Language Development, Vol. 2.* New York: Academic Press.

Lenhardt, M. L. (1981) 'Childhood central auditory processing disorder with brainstem evoked response verification.' *Archives of Otolaryngology*, **107**, 623–625.

Lenneberg, E. H. (1962) 'Understanding language without ability to speak: case report.' *Journal of Abnormal and Social Psychology*, **65**, 419–425.

—— (1967) *Biological Foundations of Language.* New York: John Wiley.

Leonard, L. B. (1982) 'Phonological deficits in children with developmental language impairment.' *Brain and Language*, **16**, 73–86.

Lewis, N. (1976) 'Otitis media and linguistic incompetence.' *Archives of Otolaryngology*, **102**, 387–390.

Liberman, A. M., Cooper, F. S., Shankweiler, D. P., Studdert-Kennedy, M. (1967) 'Perception of the speech code.' *Psychological Review*, **74**, 431–461.

Marquardt, T. P., Saxman, J. H. (1972) 'language comprehension and auditory discrimination in articulation deficient kindergarten children.' *Journal of Speech and Hearing Research*, **15**, 382–389.

Martin, J. A. M. (1981) *Voice, Speech, and Language in the Child: Development and Disorder.* Vienna: Springer.

Matkin, N. D. (1968) 'The child with a marked high-frequency hearing impairment.' *Pediatric Clinics of*

39

North America, **15,** 677–690.

Mayberry, R. (1976) 'An assessment of some oral and manual language skills of hearing children of deaf parents.' *American Annals of the Deaf,* **121,** 507–512.

McLaughlin, J. F., Kriegsmann, E. (1980) 'Developmental dyspraxia in a family with X-linked mental retardation (Renpenning syndrome).' *Developmental Medicine and Child Neurology,* **22,** 84–92.

Merklein, R. A., Briskey, R. J. (1962) 'Audiometric findings in children referred to a program for language disorders.' *Volta Review,* **64,** 294–298.

Moores, D. (1972) 'Language disabilities of hearing-impaired children.' *In:* Irwin, J. V. Marge, M. (Eds.) *Principles of Childhood Language Disabilities.* New York: Appleton-Century Crofts.

Morley, M. (1972) *The Development and Disorders of Speech in Childhood (3rd edn.)* Edinburgh: Churchill Livingstone.

Mutton, D. E., Lea, J. (1980) 'Chromosome studies of children with specific speech and language delay.' *Developmental Medicine and Child Neurology,* **22,** 588–594.

Needleman, H. (1977) 'Effects of hearing loss from early recurrent otitis media on speech and language development.' *In:* Jaffe, B. H. (Ed.) *Hearing Loss in Children.* Baltimore: University Park Press.

Oller, D. K. (1973) 'Regularities in abnormal child phonology.' *Journal of Speech and Hearing Disorders,* **38,** 36–47.

—— Eilers, R. E. (1981) 'A pragmatic approach to the phonological systems of deaf speakers.' *In:* Lass, N. J. (Ed.) *Speech and Language: Advances in Basic Research and Practice. Vol. 6.* New York: Academic Press.

Paradise, J. L. (1981) 'Otitis media during early life: how hazardous to development? A critical review of the evidence.' *Pediatrics,* **68,** 869–873.

Parving, A., Elberling, C., Salomon, G. (1981) 'Slow cortical responses and the diagnosis of central hearing loss in infants and young children.' *Audiology,* **20,** 465–479.

Paul, R., Cohen, D. J., Greg, W. R., Watson, M., Herman, S. (1984) 'Fragile X syndrome: its relations to speech and language disorders.' *Journal of Speech and Hearing Disorders,* **49,** 328–332.

Peterson-Falzone, S. T. (1982) 'Articulation disorders in orofacial anomalies.' *In:* Lass, N. J., McReynolds, L. V., Northern, J. L., Yoder, D. E. (Eds.) *Speech, Language, and Hearing. Vol. 2: Pathologies of Speech and Language.* Philadelphia: W. B. Saunders.

Pronovost, W., Wakstein, M. P., Wakstein, D. J. (1966) 'A longitudinal study of speech behaviour and language comprehension of fourteen children diagnosed as atypical or autistic.' *Exceptional Children,* **33,** 19–26.

Provence, S., Lipton, R. C. (1967) *Infants in Institutions: A Comparison of their Development with Family-Reared Infants during the First Year of Life.* New York: International University Press.

Rapin, I., Wilson, B. C. (1978) 'Children with developmental language disability: neurologic aspects and assessment.' *In:* Wyke, M. (Ed.) *Developmental Dysphasia.* London: Academic Press.

—— Allen, D. (1983) 'Developmental language disorders: nosologic considerations. *In:* U. Kirk (Ed.) *Neuropsychology of Language, Reading, and Spelling.* New York: Academic Press.

Rasmussen, T., Milner, B. (1977) 'The role of early left-brain injury in determining lateralization of cerebral speech functions.' *Annals of the New York Academy of Sciences,* **299,** 355–369.

Roach, R. E., Rosecrans, C. J. (1972) 'Verbal deficit in children with hearing loss.' *Exceptional Children,* **38,** 395–399.

Rosenbek, J. C., Kent, R. D., LaPointe, L. L. (1984) 'Apraxia of speech: an overview and some perspectives.' *In:* Rosenbek, J. C., McNeil, M. R., Aronson, A. E. (Eds.) *Apraxia of Speech.* San Diego, California: College-Hill Press.

Rosenberg, P. E. (1966) 'Misdiagnosis of children with auditory problems.' *Journal of Speech and Hearing Disorders,* **31,** 279–283.

Rosenbloom, L. (1981) 'Chronic central nervous system disease in childhood.' *In:* Hull, D. (Ed.) *Recent Advances in Paediatrics,* **6.** Edinburgh: Churchill Livingstone.

Rutter, M. (1966) 'Behavioural and cognitive characteristics of a series of psychotic children.' *In:* Wing, J. K. (Ed.) *Early Childhood Autism.* Oxford: Pergamon.

—— (1983) 'Cognitive deficits in the pathogenesis of autism.' *Journal of Child Psychology and Psychiatry,* **24,** 513–531.

Schiff, N. B. (1979) 'The influence of deviant maternal input on the development of language during the preschool years.' *Journal of Speech and Hearing Research,* **22,** 581–603.

Shriner, T. H., Holloway, M. S., Daniloff, R. G. (1969) 'The relationship between articulatory deficits and syntax in speech defective children.' *Journal of Speech and Hearing Research,* **12,** 319–325.

Silva, P. (1980) 'The prevalence, stability and significance of developmental language delay in preschool children.' *Developmental Medicine and Child Neurology,* **22,** 768–777.

Simmons, A. A. (1962) 'A comparison of the type token ratio of spoken and written language of deaf and hearing children.' *Volta Review,* **64**, 417–421.

Skuse, D. (1984) 'Extreme deprivation in early childhood—II. Theoretical issues and a comparative review.' *Journal of Child Psychology and Psychiatry,* **25**, 543–572.

Sparks, S. N. (1984) *Birth Defects and Speech-Language Disorders.* San Diego: College-Hill Press.

Stefanatos, G. A. (1984). Nonverbal abilities in communication disorders.' D. Phil. thesis, University of Oxford *(unpublished).*

Swisher, L. (1976) 'The language performance of the oral deaf.' *In:* Whitaker, H., Whitaker, H. A. (Eds.) *Studies in Neurolinguistics, vol. 2.* New York: Academic Press.

Taylor, I. (1964) 'Differential diagnosis of hearing disorders.' *In:* Renfrew, C., Murphy, K. (Eds.) *The Child who does not Talk. Clinics in Developmental Medicine, No. 13,* London: S.I.M.P. with Heinemann, pp. 65–68.

Tew, B. (1979) 'The Cocktail Party Syndrome in children with hydrocephalus and spina bifida.' *British Journal of Disorders of Communication,* **14**, 89–101.

—— Laurence, K. M. (1979) 'The clinical and psychological characteristics of children with the "Cocktail Party Syndrome".' *Zeitschrift für Kinderchirurgie,* **28**, 360–367.

Tizard, B., Hughes, M., Carmichael, H., Pinkerton, G. (1983) 'Language and social class: is verbal deprivation a myth?' *Journal of Child Psychology and Psychiatry,* **24**, 533–542.

Toso, V., Moschini, M., Gagnin, G., Antoni, D. (1981) 'Aphasie acquise de l'enfant avec épilepsie. Trois observations et revue de la littérature.' *Revue Neurologique,* **137**, 425–434.

Ward, S., Kellett, B. (1982) 'Language disorder resolved?' *British Journal of Disorders of Communication,* **17**, 33–52.

Whitacre, J. D., Luper, H. L., Pollio, H. R. (1970) 'General language deficits in children with articulation problems.' *Language and Speech,* **13**, 231–239.

Willeford, J. A. (1977) 'Assessing central auditory behaviour in children: a test battery approach.' *In:* Keith, R. W. (Ed.) *Central Auditory Dysfunction.* New York: Grune & Stratton.

Wing, L. (1981) 'Asperger's syndrome: a clinical account.' *Psychological Medicine,* **11**, 115–129.

Wood, M. L. (1982) *Language Disorders in School-age Children.* Englewood Cliffs, New Jersey: Prentice-Hall.

Woods, B. T., Carey, S. (1979) 'Language deficits after apparent clinical recovery from childhood aphasia.' *Annals of Neurology,* **6**, 405–409.

Worster-Drought, C., Allen, I. M. (1929) 'Congenital auditory imperception (congenital word-deafness): with report of a case.' *Journal of Neurology and Psychopathology,* **9**, 193–208.

—— (1968) 'Speech disorders in children.' *Developmental Medicine and Child Neurology,* **10**, 427–440.

Wright, H. L. (1968) 'A clinical study of children who refuse to talk at school.' *Journal of the American Academy of Child Psychiatry,* **7**, 603–617.

3
CONCEPTS OF LANGUAGE DEVELOPMENT
A REALISTIC PERSPECTIVE

David Crystal

Problems for the clinician

There are five main problems for clinicians and researchers who approach the field of language development and disorders. First, there is the enormous number of variables that have to be taken into account when dealing with such tasks as screening, assessment, diagnosis and treatment. In English pronunciation (phonology) there are over 40 sound-units (or phonemes) in most accents, and several hundred ways in which these units combine to produce words. There are over a thousand features of grammatical construction. The vocabulary is conservatively estimated to contain over a million words; and English has a range of dialects and styles of use which, because of its worldwide status, has produced more usage variation than any other language.

Secondly there is the problem of description. Some aspects of language have received a fairly thorough surface description, but their underlying organisational principles have been little investigated. A good example is vocabulary; there are many good, large dictionaries, but there is very little explanation available of how networks of words define each other and come to be learned. The alphabetic organisation of a dictionary is useless as a guide to learning, since children do not learn words in alphabetical order. Another example is pronunciation: such features as intonation and tone of voice have been given a very limited surface description. Thirdly, even for those areas that have been studied in detail, there is the problem of describing and labelling the symptoms. Obtaining accurate information about language, in the form of recordings and transcriptions, describing and analysing the patterns in the data, and (from a clinical viewpoint) reducing the number of variables, have been major preoccupations of clinical linguistic researchers in recent years (Crystal 1981). But the descriptions are inevitably somewhat abstract (in the interests of making generalisations) or technical (in the interests of precision), and this raises the question of how to promote the use of a satisfactory clinical 'language for talking about language'. The everyday terminology of linguistic description (terms such as 'sentence', 'word', 'vowel', 'syllable') is inadequate because people's definitions are often very different. Those who wish to specialise in language development and disorders need to develop an awareness of terminology for describing linguistic symptoms which goes beyond the popular.

Fourthly, all the remarks so far have been made with the description of normal adult language in mind. Hardly any of the major categories of *child* language handicap have been described in a linguistically comprehensive manner—comparable to the kind of meticulous and all-embracing symptomatology which is routine in medical science. Whether the handicap is identified aetiologically (*e.g.* deafness, mental retardation, cleft palate) or impressionistically (*e.g.* delayed, functional, deviant), a thorough behavioural description is usually lacking. One therefore lacks a clear sense of the range of symptoms involved, of their consistency of distribution in samples, and of their frequency.

Finally, while a great deal of clinical linguistic research is now being devoted to the task of describing the linguistic properties of samples taken from language-disordered children, with the aim of providing better assessments and individual remediation programmes, hardly any of this research is longitudinal in orientation. For instance, there are now several published studies of the range of grammatical variability one would expect to find in the grammatical skills of language-delayed four-year-olds. But I know of no published study that plots the 'natural history' of the delay, and monitors its subsequent development during treatment. At present, predicting the course of a language disorder's development can only be guesswork (Crystal 1984).

Such reasons presumably explain why accounts of language abilities and disabilities in local government record forms, and suchlike, are generally so vague as to be meaningless, or opt for variables which (though irrelevant) are at least easier to identify. Examples of the former include the heading 'language', without further gloss, on one record chart; another had the same heading, but also a subheading which read, optimistically, 'scores'. Examples of the latter include the mania for counting things, which at times is seen almost as a panacea: one counts the number of words children have been observed to use, or the number of words in their sentences, or the number of distinct sounds they have articulated. But simple quantitative measures of this kind do not lead very far. For example, to say that two children both have a vocabulary of 50 words (not an easy matter to decide about in the first place, incidentally) does not say anything about their relative level of language learning. One child might have learned the words by heart, whereas the other might be using them productively and creatively; one might have basic, concrete vocabulary, whereas the other might have more advanced, abstract vocabulary; and so on. Similarly, to say that two children are both producing four-word sentences tells us very little: the crucial question is 'which kind of words?', 'what sort of sentence structure?'. It is easy to count the length of a sentence; but, having counted, you are no nearer understanding the basis of a child's language disorder, without further linguistic study. To stay with quantitive measures, without supplementing them by qualitative criteria, is to be looking in the wrong place for an explanation of language disorder.

Basic concepts

Language and communication are not synonymous. There are many functions of language other than for interpersonal communication—for example, to release emotion when one is on one's own, or to build up a rhythm for work or play. Likewise, there are many ways of communicating other than by language. All such behaviours are included in the descriptive framework of *semiotics*. Semiotics has received many definitions, but the one that seems most relevant for clinical

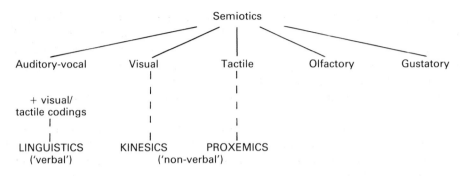

Fig. 1. The semiotic frame.

purposes is 'patterned communication in all modalities' (Sebeok *et al.* 1964). The approach stresses 'the interactional and communicative context of the human use of signs, and the way in which these are organised in transactional systems involving sight, hearing, touch, smell, taste'. This broad perspective is to be welcomed, to remind us of the potential communicative rôle of all sensory modalities, including those (such as touch) whose relevance has been underestimated, and those (such as smell and taste) whose relevance is generally ignored—though one can hardly doubt the importance to children of the 'passive' signals they receive through these modalities. However, only the first three of the five modalities have been studied extensively and become institutionalised in the academic literature (see Fig. 1), which recognises the domains of linguistics, kinesics and proxemics.

The use of the auditory-vocal channel as a means of human communication (*i.e.* 'speech', or, more precisely, 'spoken language') is pre-eminently the concern of *linguistics*. But other visual or tactile 'codings' based on speech would also be subsumed under the heading of linguistic study—first-order codes, such as writing ('written language'), or second-order codes, such as finger-spelling. More complex signing systems, too, have to be allowed for: those that have a direct relationship with the patterns of spoken or written language (such as the Paget-Gorman Signing System) and those that do not (such as British Sign Language); see Crystal and Craig's 1978 review of various systems. *Kinesics* includes the study of facial expression and bodily gesture—purely visual systems of communication, lacking any derivational connection with spoken or written language, and lacking the scope and productivity that one associates with deaf signing systems. *Proxemics* studies the tactile medium of communication (*e.g.* hand-shaking), or the way that variations in physical distance between human beings can be used as a communicative signal. Again, a distinction must be drawn between the everyday use of proxemic behaviour, which is quite limited in scope, and the contrived use of such behaviour in specially designed signalling systems, such as are used with the deaf-blind.

The distinction between linguistic behaviour on the one hand, and kinesic/proxemic behaviour on the other, is similar to that often encountered in psychology between 'verbal' and 'non-verbal' communication. But the verbal/non-verbal terminology obscures the importance of non-segmental features of intonation, rhythm, tone of voice and the like, which are clearly vocal but not verbal. No binary division does them justice, for at one extreme such features interact closely with the structures of spoken language (in such contexts as stating/questioning, or focusing attention on particular words in a sentence), and at the other extreme they are used for the communication of emotion, in a similar way to kinesic or proxemic behaviour.

There is little to be gained by extending the use of the word 'language' to cover all the domains of semiotic enquiry, as is often done through the use of such expressions as 'body language'. In these expressions, the term has become synonymous with 'communication', and a valuable distinction is in danger of being lost. However, clear differences exist between the kind of behaviour demonstrated by the use of spoken/written language and that encountered in the kinesic/proxemic domain. The remarkable *productivity* (or creativity) of the grammar and lexicon of language is one criterion of difference; another is the *dual structure* of language (a level of meaningless units—such as sounds or letters—combining to form a level of meaningful units, such as words and sentences). Some writers have argued that there are major qualitative differences between spoken/written language, and the various kinds of non-verbal communication (Hockett 1958, Hockett and Altmann 1968). Concept-based deaf signing systems sit somewhat uneasily between the two, but current social attitudes forcefully support their characterisation as 'language'. Focusing on the dissimiliarities between spoken/written language and signing systems is generally felt to be counter-productive.

The structure of language
All linguistic theories draw a distinction between the structural properties of language and the range of functions to which language can be put, and this distinction is highly relevant to the investigation of language handicap. On the one hand, there are people whose handicap limits their ability to use the structures of spoken/written language; on the other hand, there are those whose control of structure is relatively advanced, but who lack the ability to put these structures to good use in real communicative situations. Within these two broadly defined areas of *language structure* and *language use,* several important dimensions have come to be routinely identified.

Most accounts recognise three main branches of language structure: *semantics, grammar,* and the properties of the *transmission system* chosen (*i.e.* whether spoken, written or signed). Semantics is the study of how meaning is structured in language. At the most general level, it involves the study of the way we organise the meaning of what we want to say or write into stretches of language (often called discourses or texts). Discourse breakdowns are common in handicapped language, such as when questions are not answered appropriately, or when irrelevant or disjointed remarks are introduced into a conversation. At a more detailed level, semantics involves the study of vocabulary – not just by making lists of words (more precisely, 'lexical items'), but a study of how these items relate to and define each other (Crystal 1981, 1982). It is the learning of these relationships that constitutes the main task in the acquisition of vocabulary. One cannot assess lexical ability simply by counting the number of words someone uses, for as we have seen two people may have similar sizes of vocabulary, but be very different in their awareness of how the lexical items relate to each other.

The distinction between semantics and grammar can be made in the following way. If we want to make a request for a locked door to be opened, there are innumerable ways in which we might express this, using the same vocabulary, and also many ways in which the language does not permit us to express this request. Among the permitted ways are such sentences as 'I need a key to open the door', 'This door needs a key', and 'If we had a key we could open this door'. Among the disallowed sentences are 'Need I a key this door to open', 'Open could the door a locked', and so on. Grammar is the study of sentence structures and sequences, from the viewpoint of which strings of words are acceptable in a language, and how they relate to each other. It is often subdivided into *morphology* (the study of the way individual words can be changed by adding different prefixes or suffixes, and by joining units together in various ways, *e.g. go/going/gone, nation/nationalisation)* and syntax (the study of the way in which words are strung together to make up the phrases and sentences of a language, and the relationships between these patterns, *e.g.* questions/statements, positive/negative, active/passive). Not surprisingly, in view of the complexity involved, grammatical disability is a major feature of most kinds of language handicap. And, as with semantic analysis, simple measures of grammar in terms of sentence length (for instance) do not capture this complexity: two people may use similar sentence lengths, but be vastly different in the kind of grammatical structures they are able to handle (Crystal *et al.* 1976).

The third branch of language structure refers to the way we transmit the message—whether in speech, or in writing, or using some other medium. Restricting the case to speech, we immediately have to distinguish between those properties of the transmission system which are independent of a particular language, and those which are dependent. The problems which arise from the first of these headings are very different from those which arise from the second. Unfortunately the everyday term 'pronunciation' does not make this distinction clear, and so new terminology has to be introduced to deal with it. It is now conventional to distinguish between *phonetics* (the vast range of sounds that the human vocal tract can produce and the human ear perceive) and *phonology*—the much more restricted range of sounds which actually appear in a language.

In the absence of any pathology, all human beings are born with the same capacities for sound in their ears, vocal tracts and brains. Similarly, pathologies of hearing, articulation or nervous system affect speakers all over the world in the same way, regardless of the language community in which they live—for example, the nasal resonance of a cleft-palate child will be apparent whether the child learns German or Chinese. But when speakers have an intact auditory, articulatory and nervous system, it does not therefore follow that they will be able to learn the sound system of their language efficiently—and when there is a disability here (a 'specific' learning disability for some of the sounds of this system), each language has to be studied in its own terms. A child with an immature or deviant

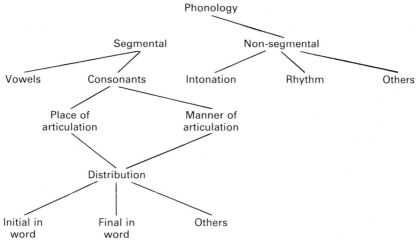

Fig. 2. Levels of detail in phonological analysis.

pronunciation of English will seem very different from one with an immature or deviant pronunciation of French or Chinese. The assessment procedures must be different, and remedial work proceeds along quite different lines.

So it is unhelpful to say that a child has 'poor pronunciation', unless it is clear whether the problem is seen primarily as biological (as conventionally defined in terms of anatomical, physiological or neurological abnormality) or as a psycho—linguistic one (as conventionally defined in terms of the learning of psychological processes or linguistic rules). Many children suffer from both kinds of handicap. The cleft-palate child, for instance, will have poor pronunciation which is partly explained by the anatomical deficiency and the associated neurophysiological abnormalities. But other aspects of the problem may not be so easily explained, suggesting that there may be elements of a learning difficulty as part of the history of that handicap too. Part of the difficulty of making a good diagnosis and planning appropriate remedial help is due to the complex way in which phonetic and phonological aspects of a disorder interact and overlap. It is especially easy to assume, in cases of severe physical handicap, that the problems are solely phonetic in character; but the existence of phonological learning problems in these children is widespread, and may be universal.

These problems can be illustrated by looking at the way in which a phonological investigation can probe a child's pronunciation problems, at increasingly detailed levels (Fig. 2). An initial division is made between those features of sound which can be identified as segments, and those which cannot. Under the first heading, we have all the consonants and vowels, and the ways in which they combine to form syllables. Under the second heading there is intonation and rhythm, which stretch over whole words and sentences. Children may develop a phonological problem in their vowel/consonant segments, or in their intonation/rhythm patterns, or in both. Next we have to ask whether all segments are likely to

47

be affected, or only vowels, or only consonants; and then what kinds of vowels or consonants might be affected. One needs to classify consonants according to their place of articulation (lips, teeth-ridge *etc.*) or their manner of articulation (whether they are nasal, voiced, plosive, etc.). Lastly one has to describe their distribution—whether the errors appear whenever a phoneme is used, or only sometimes (*e.g.* only at the ends of words).

The use of language
The range of linguistic variables discussed so far concerns the relatively 'tangible' dimension of language structure—the strings of sounds, words and structures that come 'out of the mouth and into the ear'. The study of written language or of signing would have led to a similar structural account, though terminology would have differed to some extent (for instance, the notion of phonology being replaced by graphology, in the study of writing). Under the heading of language in use, a quite different range of variables is involved, as here we are dealing with the analysis of the situations in which language is found, and of the people who are involved in the act of communication. To impose some order on the enormous scope of this dimension, it is common to identify three broad parameters of variability, relating to temporal, social and psychological factors. *Temporal* variation in language use refers to the way in which language changes over time, both in the long term (as when Anglo-Saxon develops into modern English) and in the short term (as in current debates about English usage). *Social* variation in language use refers to the way in which language varies in terms of the regional or social background of the users – a domain which includes such notions as dialects, occupation, social status and social rôle, and which is generally studied under the heading of sociolinguistics. The sociolinguistic consequences of biological differ- ence (such as sex, age or handicap—'Does he take sugar?') can also be included in this category. Thirdly, *psychological* variation in language use refers to the way in which language varies in terms of the capacities of the individual user—a domain which includes memory, attention, intelligence and personality, and which is generally studied) under the heading of psycholinguistics. The analysis of individual differences, and of task effects on language, is also a major concern for the psycholinguist, and one which is of particular relevance to clinical studies. So too is the field of language learning, which is usually placed under this heading because of its dependence on cognitive abilities; the more restricted field of child language acquisition therefore often being referred to as 'developmental' psycholinguistics (see below).

The distinction between language structure and language use is a simple and attractive one, but it is misleading in one important respect. There are several features of language that cannot be identified without the equal participation of both dimensions. Terminology varies, but these days reference is generally made to them under the heading of *pragmatics*, and recently the pragmatic aspects of language development and language handicap have attracted particular attention (Ochs and Schieffelin 1979, Gallagher and Prutting 1983). Pragmatics has received many definitions, but essentially it refers to the study of the factors that govern users' choice of utterance, arising out of their social setting. It includes the assumptions people make when they communicate, the intentions underlying what they say, the way context influences the amount they say or the way they say it, the turn-taking which makes a conversation run smoothly, and the appropriateness of the subject matter to a situation. Problems of a pragmatic kind are widespread in the study of language handicap, due to the limited awareness children have of the nature of linguistic interaction, and the uncertainty many adults feel about how they should act when they meet a handicapped child. Nor are professionals free of pragmatic uncertainty: witness the current debates over what level of language to use to a child, whether one should speak or sign or both, and whether one should adopt a structured or a free conversational therapeutic style. Language is primarily an interactive phenomenon. The description, assessment and remediation of a handicap depend totally on taking into account the implications of this axiom.

Recent textbooks on pragmatics (*e.g.* Leech 1983, Levinson 1983) illustrate the great breadth of this subject, and show how difficult it is to present a single classification of pragmatic variables which would satisfy everyone. At one extreme, pragmatics is closely related to semantics and to other structural levels of language—so much so that some scholars would be prepared to call it a 'level' of language structure. At the other extreme, pragmatics is closely related to sociolinguistics and psycholinguistics, focusing upon matters of usage and extralinguistic context which have no direct relationship to language structure. In relation to the first extreme, there are clear cases where it is possible to make a pragmatic error by wrongly using aspects of language structure—using *tu* instead of *vous* in certain circumstances in French, for example. On the other hand, it is also a pragmatic 'error' to tell a joke at a funeral, but here there is nothing in the structure of the language to explain why this is wrong. Because of this range of subject matter, I think it is premature to talk of 'pragmatic disorders', as it is not possible to provide an unequivocal theoretical definition of what is involved. But the importance of pragmatic factors in the investigation of language handicap is undeniable.

These observations about language structure and use are summarised in Figure 3 (with reference to the spoken medium only).

Psycholinguistics
If psycholinguistics had remained a theoretical field, it would doubtless have developed a clear identity, as a bridge between theoretical linguistics and cognitive psychology—as is suggested by several definitions of the subject. Slobin (1971) defined it as 'the mental processes underlying the acquisition and the use of language'. Clark and Clark (1977) described psycholinguistics as 'the study of three mental processes—the study of listening, speaking, and of the acquisition of these two skills by children'. But very early on, people wanted to use psycholinguistics to solve problems in language acquisition and use, especially in relation to speech pathology, the teaching of reading, and learning a second language. There has also been a recent trend to investigate problems from fields as diverse as medicine and literary criticism. The result has been a considerable diversification of subject

matter, and a range of overlapping interpretations about what psycholinguistics is. It is therefore important to distinguish clearly between theoretical psycholinguistics, as defined above, and applied psycholinguistics, where the aim is (as the editorial policy of *Applied Psycholinguistics* states) to report work 'in which applied *problems* are approached from the standpoint of basic research and theory' (my italics).

Clinical psycholinguistics may be defined as the study of breakdown in linguistic behaviour, and of the principles governing this breakdown, as people interact, socially and biologically, with their environment—and especially with their clinicians, clinical materials and clinical settings (Crystal 1984). Similarly, with reference to the analogous situation in schools, one might define a *remedial* psycholinguistics, where the same definition would apply, except that the last part would read 'teachers, teaching materials and educational settings'. Clinical/remedial psycholinguistics tries to explain language breakdown by exploring the relationship between linguistic behaviour and such psychological factors as memory, attention and perception. The clinical linguist can describe the patterns of linguistic disability which emerge, and can sometimes explain the nature of a patient's handicap purely with reference to his procedures. But more often the explanation of a patient's difficulty lies elsewhere—in a limited auditory short-term memory, for example, or in emotional disturbance. In such circumstances the linguist's account is inadequate, and a more general perspective must be achieved. It is this perspective which a psycholinguist aims to provide.

The investigation of all these factors is routine in speech pathology/therapy, as part of assessment and remediation, but the aim there is to intervene and obtain progress. The aim of psycholinguists is not so vocational: they wish to study these factors in order to understand the reasons for the linguistic handicap. Their aim is to model and predict patients' language behaviour, in the light of other behavioural abilities. Clinical/remedial psycholinguists, *qua* psycholinguists, will stop their investigation once they can model a patient's performance this way. They will not attempt to do anything about it. That is the business of others, such as speech therapists and remedial language teachers.

In practice, however, this distinction is sometimes obscured by individual personalities and clinical settings. Many clinicians and teachers have now been trained in psycholinguistic techniques, and use them routinely in their work. This is beneficial, for the more that therapy or teaching can be informed by principles deriving from psycholinguistics, the more systematic, economical and effective the intervention is likely to be. Likewise, many psycholinguists these days work routinely in clinics and classrooms, which they see as a testing ground for their hypotheses about breakdown. But there is no identity between the two rôles.

Nor, lastly, is there identity between the rôles of speech pathologist/therapist and the profession of remedial language teacher—even though some individuals exercise both rôles by virtue of a dual training. The rôle of the speech pathologist/therapist is to establish a patient's control over all the linguistic skills necessary to ensure a happy and successful life in the world at large—which means primarily the 'core' of skills involved in everyday conversation. The remedial

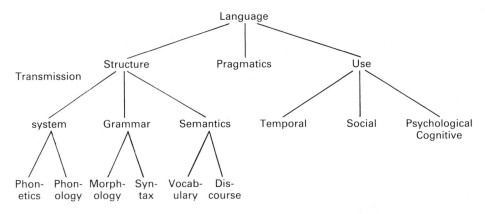

Fig. 3. The main areas of spoken language structure and use.

language teacher, by contrast, has to lead a child through the educational curriculum, and must bridge the gap between the child's core language abilities and the demands placed upon those abilities by the curriculum. Maths, science projects, reading, religious education and other subjects all have their own linguistic identity, and have to be approached differently.

Conclusions

A normal development of language requires balanced progress under each of the headings in the above figures (Figs. 1–3). It is of little value to be able to articulate sounds beautifully if one has few words or structures to use them in; and conversely, an excellent control of grammar and a deviant phonology is of limited use. Any valid procedure to be used in screening, assessment, diagnosis or treatment must, at the very least, have a slot available for each of these headings.

How far it is possible to reduce the many details encountered under each of these headings to a very small set, capable of being reduced routinely in clinical situations, is less clear. For example, in the grammatical assessment procedure known as LARSP (Crystal 1982), there are over 100 grammatical variables (in itself a massive simplification of the range available in English). As a result of current research, it is gradually beginning to emerge which of these variables are the most diagnostic. The central rôle of verbs, pronouns, question-words, certain types of clause structure and clause sequence, and several other features, are factors whose significance repeatedly emerges, in working with children in the second and third year (see Chapter 5). And similar selections are beginning to be made for other areas of language. What is essential is that all such findings are integrated within a general framework, to avoid ending up with an incoherent inventory of facts. It is this framework which familiarity with the terminology and conceptual apparatus of scientific language thinking can help to provide.

REFERENCES

Clark, H. H., Clark, E. V. (1977) *Psychology and Language: An Introduction to Psycholinguistics*. New York: Harcourt, Brace, Jovanovich.

Crystal, D. (1981) *Clinical Linguistics*. Vienna: Springer.

—— (1982) *Profiling Linguistic Disability*. London: Edward Arnold.

—— (1984) *Linguistic Encounters with Language Handicap*. Oxford: Blackwell.

—— Craig, E. (1978). 'Contrived sign language.' *In:* Schlesinger, I., Namir, L. (Eds.) *Sign Languages of the Deaf: Psychological, Linguistic and Sociological Perspective*. New York: Academic Press, 141–68.

—— Fletcher, P., Garman, M. (1976) *The Grammatical Analysis of Language Disability*. London: Edward Arnold.

Gallagher, T. M., Prutting, C. A. (1983) *Pragmatic Disorders of Spoken Language*. San Diego: College Hill Press.

Hockett, C. F. (1958) *A Course in Modern Linguistics*. New York: Macmillan.

—— Altmann, S. (1968) 'A note on design features.' *In:* Sebeok, T. A. (Ed.) *Animal Communication* Bloomington: Indiana University Press, pp. 61–72.

Leech, G. N. (1983) *Principles of Pragmatics*. London: Longman.

Levinson, S. C. (1983) *Pragmatics*. Cambridge: C.U.P.

Ochs, E., Schieffelin, B. B. (Eds.) (1979) *Developmental Pragmatics*. New York: Academic Press.

Slobin, D. I. (1971) *Psycholinguistics*. Glenview: Scott, Foresman.

Sebeok, T. A., Hayes, A. S., Bateson, M. C. (Eds.) (1964) *Approaches to Semiotics*. The Hague: Mouton.

4
PRELINGUISTIC COMMUNICATION

Margaret Martlew

Prelinguistic communication has justifiably attracted a great deal of research interest over the past 10 years, in two major areas. How do infants make themselves understood with the means they have available? And what implications do these non-verbal communicative skills have for the acquisition of language? Communication requires at least two participants, one to signal meaning and the other to interpret it. The mother, therefore, as the person most likely to be interacting with the infant, plays a significant rôle. Initially there is an obvious imbalance in any infant/adult interaction. Neurological immaturity constrains both what and how the very young infant can communicate. Despite this, communication does take place because mothers impute meanings that the young infant could not possibly intend (Macfarlane 1977). Infants cannot fend for themselves so they have to rely on having their needs interpreted. Initially innate signals, such as distress cries, support these needs. Whatever preadaptive mechanisms the child may have, however, the mother encourages the child's communicative progress by providing predictable routines and appropriate opportunities for diversification and elaboration. Over the first year, mothers' interactions with their children reflect increasing elaboration, complexity and co-ordination. Early forms of infant behaviour grow in complexity, and develop into conventional patterns of non-verbal exhanges.

Bruner (1981) suggests that intention is evident when an individual shows persistence in reaching a goal, chooses among alternatives in order to reach a goal, and ceases activity when the goal has been achieved. It is not necessary for the actor to be able to account for, or be conscious of, the nature of his intentions. Generally, intentional communication is assumed to be established towards the latter part of the first year. Bruner's definition allows for some intentionality in the infant's responses to the environment before this. Such intentional activity is used in tracing how infants achieve communicative goals.

Communicative activity can be subdivided into elementary units. These constituents reflect individual change and development as well as being co-ordinated into higher-level structures. Eye gaze, orientation, gesture and early vocalisations are essential components of the infant's communicative repertoire before the emergence of language. Initially used singly, these come to be co-ordinated into one action sequence by the end of the first year in reciprocal exchanges with parents. The processes by which the infant figures out the rules governing the composition and co-ordination of these systems are related to affective, social and cognitive development. This chapter traces the development of these communicative components, their eventual co-ordination within a communicative framework and their possible significance for language acquisition.

Affect

The infant appears to be born with a repertoire of affective behaviours that allows for the expression of basic needs. These complex behaviours equip the infant to elicit appropriate nurturance responses (Brazelton 1979). Before the advent of language or the intentional use of other symbolic forms of communication, affective expressive behaviours are the only reliable indications of the infant's reactions. They are the primary means by which the infant can communicate wishes, dislikes and so on.

Initially the infant's response to the environment is in terms of the physical properties of stimuli, such as size or brightness (Fogel *et al.* 1982). By six weeks, infants are responding to the content of events (Sroufe 1979). By two months familiar people and objects will evoke a smile, which shows not only that the infant is capable of retrieving events to make comparisons, but also that recognition carries with it the expectation of the event being enjoyable (Sroufe 1979). Similar effects can be observed where failure to assimilate can lead to withdrawal and crying. Fogel *et al.* (1982) suggest that, in this respect, the two-month-old can behave in much the same way as the older child. Mothers gain great pleasure from eliciting these positive responses. They seem sensitive to encouraging what are the most highly developed skills in the infant's repertoire, and to providing situations in which their infant can use them.

Possibly infant affect is not merely a reaction to an experience but is intrinsically involved in shaping the experience (Demos 1982). Exchanges are regulated by the mother disposing her infant to act in ways which reflect the saliency of an event and to act also as a communicative partner. While interacting, both partners are showing recognition of the rules of exchanges. If displays are emitted that are not appropriate to the anticipated communicative procedures, then the partner has to take appropriate action. If reorganisation is unsuccessful, the rule violation leads to changes in the partner's display. This has been observed in infants' behaviour in naturalistic studies and demonstrated experimentally. Tronick (1981), for example, reported a study where mothers interacted normally or maintained a still, immobile face. Infants of three months responded to the still face by staring, looking away, giving wary glances and eventually engaging in self-comforting behaviours. Cohn and Tronick (1982) suggested it can be damaging if the mother gives wrong or distorted cues in early infancy, but by about nine months the infant is more able to cope. For example, when encountering mothers in the still-faced situation, nine-month-old infants could redirect their activities: for instance by playing with objects. By this time the infant has a greater repertoire of behaviours and can switch goals, thus demonstrating ways of coping more easily with failure of reciprocity.

Timing and turn-taking

Closely bound up with affect is the rhythmic compatibility which normally exists between mothers and their infants. This, as Bullowa (1979) points out, is a communicative system which is intrinsically functional in its own right. The mother uses it even when she expects no response from the infant. Sharing meaning may initially, according to Bullowa, be sharing rhythm.

Wolff's (1968) work on sucking rhythms and state show how organised the infant is. The development of these complexly organised behaviours depends on endogenous timing mechanisms that also make the initial rhythmicities possible. Sucking and crying are organised into high-frequency temporal sequences which are relatively unaffected by external events. Brazelton (1979) claims that the infant's regulation of his/her states of consciousness becomes the behavioural basis from which the mother knows how to adapt her timing. The mother has an idea of what she wants her infant to achieve, and shows an awareness of state. She keeps the infant at a moderate level of arousal, which Kaye (1982) suggests is the optimal level for performance and learning. The asymmetry of the relationship between the mother and her infant has important results (Kaye 1979). The mother's superior flexibility in anticipating the infant's fairly regular cycling encourages progress. She adopts a kind of intuitive curriculum, monitors and controls changes of expression, and is creative in introducing new variations.

Condon and Sander (1974) attempted to demonstrate a subtle synchrony of neonatal movements and adult speech. They observed changes in the direction of infants' movements, which they claimed were co-ordinated with phoneme boundaries. This has not been replicated, and the more likely co-ordination is in relation to stress, rhythm or tempo. Rhythmic cycles of attention and non-attention during face-to-face interactions were observed by Brazelton *et al.* (1974). They observed that the interactions took the form of a regulated homeostatic system. Tronick *et al.* (1980) found that with infants of 100 days, both mother and infant changed to similar behavioural and affective states at the same time. One did not tend to lead while the other followed.

These rhythms become entrained to environmental events as the infant becomes capable of goal-directed action (Sander 1977). These goal-directed actions, such as the rooting reflex, emerge from well-established contexts when the infant is in an appropriate temporal and physical environment.

The infant's capacity to modify and organise his/her communicative acts becomes more elaborated and diversified over the prelinguistic period. At about two months, interactions show the beginnings of regulated, reciprocal exchanges. There is affective vocal and motor play around caretaking activities. This is a form of skilled performance on a complex task which requires the sharing of time, content and intent (Tronick 1981). Successful communicative acts need the understanding of both participants who can modify their responses to accord.with the other's expressed intent while still satisfying their own intent.

Patterned sequences in turn-taking have been seen as the precursors of conversational turns. Bateson (1975) uses the term 'protoconversations' to refer to these interactive, non-random sequences. She found that there was a greater likelihood of mother's vocalisations being followed by infant vocalisation, and vice versa, than would be expected by chance. Mutual organisation of turn-taking in mother/infant interaction has been seen to operate in ways similar to adult exchanges (Collis 1979). Schaffer *et al.* (1977) found that there were few instances of overlap in vocalisation in one- and two-year-olds. Stern *et al.* (1975) however did find that co-actional vocalisation occurred more often than turn-taking in the two-to three-month-old twins they studied. They suggest that this could be seen as an adaptation to some kind of constraint on processing auditory material during production. Vocal exchanges are simple at this time and little useful information is lost. As the child becomes older, the turn-taking pattern becomes more important.

Attention, eye gaze, orientation
Newborns are able to see and aim their gaze. This is the first sign, together with orienting movements, that can be used to detect infant attention. Attention signals a receptive state. Mutual attention is the basis for communication based on conscious intention.

By four months, infants have essentially mature voluntary control of gaze behaviours. They show a preference for visual stimuli which are co-ordinated with sound. This suggests they have the ability to co-ordinate auditory and visual information (Cohen 1982). Neck muscles controlling head orientation, and striated muscles involved in sucking and oculomotor control, are the first to come under voluntary control: therefore instrumental head-turning is observable in the neonatal period. These behaviours are important for communication. Gaze and face orientation are major signals of readiness in the three- to-six-month period when the infant is seeking and enjoying social interaction involving auditory and vocal channels (Stern 1981). By this time, the infant is in command of quite a range of communicative behaviours. Gaze and head aversion, with the head lowered, is interpreted by mothers as a termination signal. A raised head is taken as a 'holding' signal. Loss of all visual contact is perceived as withdrawal, while a full enface with a glazed look is interpreted as a different form of unreadiness (Stern 1981). By six months, as Stern points out, the infant is operating with a surprisingly mature system.

Gaze initiation and gaze termination are a function of both the internal state of the infant (on-off visual behaviour) and stimulation provided by the mother who is constantly altering her behaviour in response to changes in the infant's visual attention and state (Stern 1974). Infants' gaze aversion is attributed to their need to modulate arousal or to process information from a prior stimulus (Field 1981). There is considerable variability in attention, arousal and affective behaviours when infants are observed in interactive sequences: though all too often this is not taken into account. Individual differences and organismic variables such as state and developmental change might contribute to this.

Memory
The establishment and development of intentional communication depends upon memory for external events. Infant memory appears to be robust but selective. Characteristics that are most salient are retained for longer periods of time. Cohen (1982) reports a study where five-month-old infants were familiarised with a

three-dimensional figure. They were then tested for recall with the same figure and one differing in shape, colour, size or orientation, either immediately afterwards, 10 minutes later or 24 hours later. All features were recognised in the immediate condition, colour and form after 10 minutes, but only form was recognised after 24 hours.

Infants as young as 10 weeks were found to show differential responding to a specific mobile after 72 hours, even though they had seen other mobiles in the meantime (Rovee-Collier and Fagan 1981). It seemed that two successive encounters with a different exemplar were sufficient for the infants to extract general features. Rovee-Collier and Fagan propose that there may be an automatic frequency-processing mechanism. Efficient and adaptive, such a mechanism would allow infants to respond appropriately to multiple variations of recurring stimuli. At the same time, it would permit appropriate differential responses to stimuli remaining invariant over successive encounters.

They also demonstrated that brief reminders can facilitate access to stored information for periods extending over several days and that the reminder was as effective as the original training. Cuing procedures produced significant differences between two groups of 12-week-old infants after 14 days. Failure to find retention in young infants, therefore, should be considered in terms of retrieval failures rather than memory deficits. This is supported by Kagan *et al.* (1978), who proposed that the only difference between two- and eight-month-olds is that the older infants can establish and retrieve schemas more quickly and hold them for longer.

Person/object interaction
The infant's responses to objects and people also show increasing elaboration and differentiation over the first year. Changes in the infant's ability to respond to objects and people separately, before being able to co-ordinate these responses into a single action sequence, mean that communicative intentions are achieved in different ways according to the level of development. Person-to-person interaction develops first. The infant can achieve this because, according to Tronick (1981) he possesses programmes that permit the decoding and generation of affective signals.

There is, however, some disagreement about the point at which infants can clearly differentiate between people and objects. Trevarthan (1979) claimed that this distinction is observable by two months of age. Infants react to people using expressive movements, while they treat objects as sources of perceptual information or interest. Infants of this age have a wide repertoire for indicating mood, and possess the intent to transmit specific contents of experience and purpose. Differences in the responses of two-month-olds to moving objects and people were also observed by Brazelton *et al.* (1974). With objects, infants would focus attention for up to two minutes without shifting their gaze, then they would pounce and strike out, registering an intense facial expression and using jerky movements.

Their responses to their mothers showed a cyclic pattern of attention: their movements were smooth and gestural, their facial expressions varied. If mothers simulated objects by using jerky movements that were non-contingent on their infant's approaches, the infant would stare at them as though they were objects (Cohn and Tronick 1982). Bullowa (1979) described differences in the behaviour of four-month-olds when their mother was present and absent. She found they displayed a much smaller repertoire of behaviours when alone than in the presence of their mothers, when they engaged in complicated interaction sequences. Similarly, Contole and Over (1981) found observers could detect whether three-month-olds were alone or with a person and whether that person was interacting or not.

Frye *et al.* (1983) queried this unambiguous differentiation of people and objects. They claimed it is linked to social behaviour, and dependent on infants detecting intention in a way that may not be possible until the second half of the first year. They found no differences in infants' responses at three months to an object or to their mother. These were only discernable at 10 months. Also at three months, greeting and withdrawal were judged to be present for both objects and mothers.

Sugarman-Bell (1978) defined three steps in the preverbal period which reflect the infant's differentiated behaviour towards objects and people. Initially there is a simple, single orientation where unitary activities are directed towards either an adult or a toy. From about four to seven months, the infant begins to show differentiated actions towards persons or objects and by eight to 10 months the child has integrated adult and object activities. These are now co-ordinated into one action sequence and the infant can, for example, solicit the mother's attention by touching her arm, looking at her face and grasping a desired object. These constituent patterns are developed separately before being combined into a hierarchy of communication skills.

Gesture and vocalisation
The relationship between language and gesture has been the subject of much discussion (Gardner and Gardner 1969, Hewes 1976, Kimura 1976, Klima and Bellugi 1979). The significance of gesture and its association with emergent linguistic skills has led to the suggestion of continuity in intentional signalling between verbal and non-verbal modes (Bates *et al.* 1975, 1977, 1979; Bruner 1975).

Intentional gestures probably derive from earlier forms of behaviour, which had different functions initially (Trevarthen 1979, Fogel 1981, Thelen 1981, Lockman and Ashmead 1983). Some movement forms, such as primary walking in neonates or index-finger pointing in the first month, appear before the age when they seem necessary or functionally significant. It is possible that these early acts are transformed into gestures and the development of complex systems has origins in simpler, earlier forms.

It is difficult to assess the rôle played by preadaptive mechanisms and/or eliciting conditions in the environment. Newborns can move their arms towards perceived objects (Bower 1974, Trevarthen 1979, Lockman and Ashmead 1983) and the precision of these movements increases at three to five weeks. By four to five months, infants are using accurate directional reaching even for moving objects. Directional accuracy is achieved initially by hand/arm adjustments which precede fine distal adjustments of the fingers. Initially infants will use whatever movements are available, responding to different situations with the same limited and stereotyped movements before developing the appropriate differentiated responses which are goal-corrected for the specific context.

Gestures indicate a communicative intention, and in this respect they are distinct from acts. Acts reflect an awareness of the world and responses to it, subjectivity in Trevarthen's (1979) terms, but not an awareness of the subjectivity of others. Acts are an end in themselves, rather than being movements whose primary function is to convey a message. It is likely that adults facilitate the emergence of intentional gestures by recognising and reinforcing those acts which show fairly close approximations to conventional gestures. Clark (1978) suggested that mothers interpret and fulfil the child's actions and so construct the acts as they perceive them. He illustrates this by tracing the reaching gesture emerging from the act of reaching. Eventually the act is not used simply to get an object but to produce a change in the mother's behaviour.

Pointing is one of the most important pre-verbal gestures. Pointing is a manual gesture involving index finger extension in which the finger may or may not touch the referent. Fogel (1981) observed pointing in the first few months, directed towards the mother, which he inferred showed a primitive signification of attraction. So pointing may take on an exploratory function (Bates *et al.* 1975). When object and person become integrated into one action schema at about nine months, pointing serves to isolate a referent and eye-gaze is used to draw the mother into the communicative framework. Children demonstrate deictic ability by gestural pointing before they use verbal labels to refer to objects. Bates *et al.* (1979) consider pointing to be a sensorimotor form of naming. They found it to be the strongest predictor of language development of all the gestures they studied in nine- to 18-month-old infants. (Other gestures they examined but which did not correlate with language development were those signifying requests, refusals and showing off.)

Masur (1982) looked at three object-related gestures: pointing, extending objects and open-handed reaching in infants aged nine to 18 months. Pointing was the last of these gestures to emerge, at around 12 to 14 months. The ability to co-ordinate gaze with gestures for signalling in more than one direction at a time (for example, child extending object to mother while gazing at the camera) occurred concurrently across all three types of gestures. Only after there was dual directional signalling were words used in conjunction with gestures. Murphy (1978) also found that pointing emerged at nine months but was not integrated with vocalisations until 14 months. In the early stages, pointing seemed to be an act rather than a gesture. Pointing was well established by 20 months. It could be used in successive strings and was well synchronised with labelling. Mothers help to establish the communicative function of pointing by giving verbal acknowledgements, by looking at what is indicated (Leung and Rheingold 1981) and by using pointing gestures themselves. Infants are able to understand the significance of pointing at a nearby object, before they can interpret pointing directed at more distant ones (Lempers 1979). Infants' ability to comprehend distal points increases between nine to 14 months. Initially, infants can usually only interpret pointing gestures when the pointing hand is in the same visual field as the indicated object. By about 14 months, infants can follow a variety of points which cross their midline (Lempers 1979, Murphy and Messer 1977).

Barten (1977) has suggested a functional taxonomy of gestures covering four major areas of children's expressive movements. These functions cover gestures that gain services and regulate or change the behaviour of others (instrumental); express feelings, either positive or negative (expressive); point out objects and events (deictic); represent actions on objects or performed with objects (enactive). In Sheffield, we have used a modified version of these categories to study changes in children's use of gesture over the period when they were 10 to 21 months (Zinober and Martlew 1985). We found that instrumental gestures were used more frequently than the others but tended to decline around 21 months. Expressive and enactive gestures were idiosyncratic: one child, whose mother engaged in a lot of fantasy play, used them frequently, the other hardly at all. Deictic gestures showed a steady increase over time, particularly in the book context, though points were not well established till 14 months. Depictive gestures did not occur.

When comparing acts, gestures and vocalisations, we found that acts predominated in the 10- to 14-month-period and then declined, particularly in the picture-book context; gestures increased from 10 to 18 months before declining; vocalisations increased, and by 21 months 70 per cent of the turns in the play situation and 90 per cent in the picture-book situation had vocalisations. Initially gestures were used on their own but were then co-ordinated with vocalisations. At about 14 months, gestures were accompanied by protowords [aet] [dis], pointing being well established at this time. Protowords were used till about 19 months, when they were superseded by single-word utterances with gestures.

Protowords are a transitional phenomenon that have been observed to occur between babbling and conventional words. They have definable characteristics but are limited in their expressive functions (Halliday 1975, Dore *et al.* 1976, Carter 1978). They tend to refer to general aspects: approval, disapproval, wanting and rejecting. The first use of conventional words is also limited. There may be a period of several months when, for instance, object words are only to label and not to make requests. Until words become plurifunctional in usage, gestures continue to be used with them to add another function. Initially the gesture and the vocalisation will carry the same message, the gesture often being the easier to interpret. From the middle of the second year, once the two modes are integrated and elaborated, the gesture and the vocalisation can begin to convey different (though complementary) messages.

The transition from non-verbal to verbal communication
The extent to which prelinguistic communication is a facilitative precursor, a prerequisite or largely irrelevant to language acquisition depends on the emphasis given to the internal organising capacities of the child. Language acquisition strategies can be seen to be linked to general cognitive abilities or specific linguistic mechanisms. A characteristic of these different approaches is that different

grammars are used to describe the child's developing language; and whereas linguists try to describe language, psychologists attempt to explain the processes underlying its development and use.

In the sixties, little attention was paid to communicative precursors as the child was assumed to possess an innate linguistic processing device. This device permitted relevant linguistic data to be extracted from a degraded input with minimal environmental assistance (Chomsky 1965, McNeill 1970). The alternative of semantic universals (Fillmore 1968) and pragmatic implications (Searle 1969) focused interest on cognitive-based strategies, formulated in the prelinguistic period, which could facilitate language acquisition. Bloom (1973), for example, suggested that linguistic categories are coded onto previously established conceptual categories and Bruner (1975) maintained that linguistic concepts are first coded in action. The importance of knowing about the context in which language is used is stressed by Bates *et al.* (1979) as most of the semantics of early child speech was pragmatic. Such socio-cognitive approaches emphasise the illocutionary force of communicative exchanges, tracing the emergence of primitive speech acts back to early vocalisations and gestures (Dore 1975, 1978; Bates *et al.* 1979). Alternatively, Halliday (1975) proposed that the functions for which language are used, and which are emerging in the preverbal period, are implicated in the conventionalised structure of language.

The significant transitional period from prelinguistic communication begins in the last quarter of the first year. The infant's intention to communicate and the nature of his intentions are observable in his behaviour in interactive situations. The infant begins to combine gaze, orientation, gesture and vocalisations within a patterned framework where reciprocity in exchanges shows increasing conventionalisation and flexibility. Initially each combination is limited in scope, serving single functions, but these are extended and elaborated throughout the one-word period.

A co-ordinated control of sensorimotor systems, however, has to be viewed in relation to the child's socio-cognitive development. This co-ordination of abilities seems to occur after the infant has reached Piaget's stage V when there are observable increases in symbolic capacity.

There have been various speculations about what cognitive developments must occur for language acquisition to proceed and what predictions can be made (Bloom 1973, Sinclair 1970). Ingram (1978) found that linguistic milestones occurred with particular sensorimotor stages, and concluded that two—means-ends and imitative achievements—may be important for the emergence of pragmatic and syntactic forms of language. On another measure, that of object permanence, Corrigan (1978) found no correlation with language development, and advised against accepting any one-to-one relationship in cognitive and language development.

A notion of means-ends relationships reflects the infant's understanding of using objects or people as tools for obtaining other objects. But reaching this cognitive level is not a sufficient condition for establishing communication skills. Harding and Golinkoff (1979), for instance, found that patterns of mother/infant conversations and games exchanges were related to different levels of communicative skills in observations they made on two groups of infants, all operating at stage V on Piagetian tasks of causality. The group they defined as non-intentionally communicating had mothers who tended to direct the conversation, filling in for their infants and missing the infants' cues for responses. Nelson (1973) also indicated that this kind of directive speech may delay language growth. However, she also pointed out that children bring different strategies to language learning and it is important that there is a match between the child's cognitive organisation and the mother's use of language in interactions.

Two of the most detailed descriptions of how language stems from the elaboration and co-ordination of abilities developed in the prelingustic period stem from the different approaches adopted by Bruner and Bates. Bruner (1975) related language with action. Grammatical rules are learned by analogy with the rules of action and attention. 'What may be innate about language acquisition is not linguistic innateness but some special features of human action and human attention that permit language to be decoded by the uses to which it is put' (1975, p.2). How action sequences aid children to acquire standard communicative forms is explored by tracing the growth of joint action and joint activity in exchanges between mothers and children aged from three to 15 months. The mother plays an important rôle in the acquisition of these concepts by providing, elaborating and creatively exploiting appropriate situations. She interprets the child's intentions before intentional signalling has developed, and then helps to conventionalise the forms used. For instance, referential abilities are seen to emerge from an understanding of the social rules for engaging in dialogue, together with the realisation of the rules existing between sign and significate. The mother provides a scaffolding framework whereby earlier communicative forms, such as smiling, reaching, pointing and vocalisation are interpreted as requests for labels. These gradually become more ritualised until eventually verbal labelling is accomplished (Bruner 1981). Scaife and Bruner (1975) found that infants of four months could follow their mother's direction of gaze and therefore establish joint attention. This, they claim, marks the beginning of joint reference which is a prerequisite for all later forms of communication. Games and social exchanges (Ratner and Bruner 1978) assist the child to master language by limiting the domain in which utterances are used. Games provide an easily predicted task structure, in which it is also possible to introduce variants and promote the development of rôle-reversible relationships. All this is achieved within a playful context where an optimum level for learning can be sustained. The concepts of agent, action, object, and recipient are established in games, and these facilitate the grasping of linguistic concepts. Initially the child understands the requirements of joint action, differentiates these into components, realises they are sequentially ordered and then substitutes standard elements of the lexicon. Bruner, therefore, assumed isomorphism between certain linguistic and cognitive processes. Predication and attention processing are linked, as are case structure and the organisation of action. Predication corresponds to regrouping and reorganisation in perceptual attention and memory. Case grammatical forms correspond to action concepts.

Bates *et al.* (1975, 1979) also emphasised continuity between concepts formed in the prelinguistic period and the onset of language. 'Context does not just cause language, but is an integral part of the structure of language. Meanings are conveyed through a creative combination of utterances and social settings' (1979, p. 412).

Bates and colleagues adopted a Speech Act framework for delineating the child's transition from non-verbal to verbal communication. They studied three infants, aged two, six and 12 months, over a period of eight months. They identified three stages in their development, corresponding to perlocutionary, illocutionary and locutionary functions.

The perlocutionary stage stretched from birth to ten months. During this time the child was not aware of the communicative value of his signals. Furthermore, these signals were not recognised as conventional communications. From 10 to 15 months, in the illocutionary stage, the infant shows an intentional use of adults to obtain objects and also uses objects to obtain adult attention. Bates *et al.* have related the intentional use of people to achieve goals to the emergence of conventional exchanges. They term this behaviour 'protoimperative'. The infant begins showing or giving objects to the mother, and then alternates eye-contact between the mother and object. Once the infant realises that his actions can influence the adult in satisfying his goal-directed efforts, his signals become more ritualised and economic. For example, the infant progresses from reaching and grasping, to ritualised open and shut hand movements and then to pointing. Also, if one strategy fails, the infant is capable of trying alternatives.

As well as this type of communication, which serves to regulate the behaviour of others, Bates *et al.* also looked at 'protodeclaratives', actions involving infants' use of objects to elicit or maintain social interactions. Initially infants will just show or give objects, then they will continue with these behaviours, or variants of them, until a response has been elicited from the adult. The use of these functions emerged about the same time as a third function whereby the infant could use an object to obtain another object. This is viewed as co-ordinating two aspects into a single concept of tool use and expressing a means-end relationship which corresponds to sensorimotor stage V.

Finally, in the locutionary stage (whose onset varied between 12 and 16 months in the three children studied) the children began attaching words to their previously developed schemas, for example, naming a wanted object or labelling while pointing.

Because two events can be described with the same terminology does not mean the processes are related. Because two events occur at the same time does not necessarily mean that they are connected. In language development there are many temptations to form firm conclusions on the basis of circumstantial links. Action schemas may be emerging concurrently with linguistic strategies for extracting relevant data, or grammatical rules may be an extension of action rules. What is certain is that the prelinguistic child knows a lot about communication before he acquires language. Without knowing about shared meanings, reciprocal rôles and expressive intent, grammatical rules could remain a contextless abstraction.

Language gains its significance in communication, and intentional communication is established before speech.

Prelinguistic communication: implications for handicapped children

In the early months, communicative links depend largely on mothers interpreting their infants' needs, which are inferred from the context and the limited signals the child can use. As behaviour becomes more integrated and the realisation of expressive intent more conventionalised, communicative exchanges develop within a more economic and flexible framework.

Throughout the first year the infant shows increasing control and elaboration of sensory and motor functions. The rôle of component behaviours, initially used singly and then in co-ordination in communicative acts, raises questions in relation to handicap. If children have sensory or motor impairments, this might affect their ability to acquire communication and linguistic skills. Tronick (1981) proposed that no particular modalities are of unique importance to the infant in his capacity to generate communicative signals. However, even if language is not modality specific, each modality facilitates communication and increases the young infant's potential for experiential learning. Limitations on the infant's capacity to produce or interpret certain signals may impair the ability to generate change.

With handicapped infants, the question arises as to how much variation the system can withstand. How, and to what extent, is the development of communication affected when constrained by a child's neurological or physical impairment?

Depending on the severity and nature of the impairment, the child's ability to experience the world and effect change through his own actions will be curtailed. This limited experience can have deleterious effects on the infant's ability to organise and co-ordinate information. Such children therefore need a very supportive and sensitive environment. But infants suffering from impairments are likely to be further handicapped by their disabilities, disrupting the environmental support they need. If infants can only give minimal, distorted or inconsistent signals, mothers will have difficulty both in interpreting their child's needs and in establishing predictable routines.

The handicapping condition therefore disrupts normal patterns and puts mothers in a difficult and paradoxical position. Mothers are known to be sensitive to their children's level of development. They also encourage their children to perform increasingly complex actions. If a child remains at a low developmental level, but grows physically larger, these characteristics of the mother's rôle are in conflict. What adjustments can a mother make when the child is too old chronologically but not developmentally to be playing the supportive games of infancy?

Any impairment can have deleterious effects on interactions. Observations of blind children (Fraiberg 1974) and children with Down's syndrome (Berger and Cunningham 1981) show that mothers can be negatively affected by not receiving expected signals from their infants. Not surprisingly, mothers of multiply handicapped children show the greatest difficulties in developing and maintaining interactions (Kogan 1980, Brooks-Gunn and Lewis 1984).

Some mothers seem to be more fluent and flexible in working with their children to reach communicative goals than others are. If we are to help mothers who find difficulty in adapting to their infant's needs, we need to be able to work from an informed base of both specific and general patterns of disability. Blind children, for instance, cannot develop joint attention in the way Bruner proposes, nor do they use gestural signalling for communicating (Fraiberg 1974). These and other associated problems can have enormously deleterious effects on the child and the child's environment, but they can be overcome (Adelson 1983). Als *et al.* (1980) observed a blind child who developed normally by having compensatory emphasis given to auditory and tactile stimulation.

There is now a growing amount of information available on the likely disruptive effects of sensory deficits on presymbolic communication. Little, however, is known about the consequences of multiple handicap or motor deficits. What are the likely outcomes for the development of communication and cognition when infants cannot, for instance, give consistent signals, cannot use their hands to gesture or manipulate objects and establish control over their environment? Currently we are observing the ways mothers of cerebral-palsied infants try to establish shared meaning. We are attempting to assess the extent to which this is influenced by the severity of the impairment and the mothers' strategies for encouraging interaction (Martlew 1984).

Another important factor in the impaired infant's acquisition of communicative skills is the further handicapping condition that can affect the transition from presymbolic to symbolic communication. Normally, presymbolic communication facilitates the smooth transition to language acquisition. Children's early utterances emerge and develop in the same highly motivating and socially supportive environment provided by mothers who continue to interpret intended meaning. However, even children with only mild impairments may not be able to acquire spoken language and may have to be taught an alternative communication system. Often these are taught, not by the mother as a natural progression in a social context, but by other adults often less aware of the child's communicative intentions. There may be parallels here with the difficulties many normal children find in acquiring written language. For most children, written language is an abstract cognitive exercise with no immediate rewards. Children from supportive homes, where literacy is encouraged from an early age as part of social interaction with parents, do not seem to encounter these problems (Bissex 1980, Martlew 1985).

We need to give more consideration to the timing and methods of teaching of alternative systems, taking particular cognisance of the communicative links that have been established between mothers and their infants. This should go some way to ensuring that handicapped infants benefit from the continuity of communication which normal children experience and help to decrease rather than increase their problems.

Certain kinds of learning may be optimally accomplished in infancy, not necessarily because the infant learns more efficiently but because the experience is constructed in a specific way. It is possible that some features of language and communication are more difficult to acquire or require more external help than others. Genie (Curtiss *et al.* 1975) is a classic example of the effects of degraded input. Five years after being rescued from the appalling and isolated conditions she had experienced for her first 14 years of life, her language use was still bizarre in some ways but not in others. For example, she had still not acquired pro-forms or auxiliaries. Similarly there may be some components of the non-verbal system involved in the infant's developing communication skills which may be more important or need greater environmental support. At present we have only a sketchy knowledge of how adaptive the child can be or what specific features of language development are affected by the kind of environmental support infants experience in communicative exchanges with their mothers.

However it seems particularly important to concentrate on the whole spectrum of communicative behaviour when considering language acquisition in both normal and impaired children, because the major function of language lies in communication.

REFERENCES

Adelson, E. (1983) 'Precursors of early language development in children blind from birth.' *In:* Mills, A. E. (Ed.) *Language Acquisition in the Blind Child.* Sevenoaks, Kent: Croom Helm.
Als, H., Tronick, E., Brazelton, B. (1980) 'Affective reciprocity and the development of autonomy: the study of a blind child.' *Journal of the American Academy of Child Psychiatry,* **19,** 22–40.
Barten, S. (1977) 'The development of gesture.' *In:* Smith, N. R., Franklin, M. B. (Eds.) *Symbolic Functioning in Childhood.* Hillsdale, New Jersey: Lawrence Erlbaum.
Bates, E., Camaioni, I., Volterra, V. (1975) 'The acquisition of performatives prior to speech.' *Merrill Palmer Quarterly,* **21,** 206–226.
—— Benigni, L., Bretherton, I., Camaioni, L., Volterra, V. (1977) 'From gesture to first word: on cognitive and social prerequisites.' *In:* Lewis, M., Rosenblum, L. (Eds.) *Interaction, Conversation and the Development of Language.* New York: Wiley.
———————— (1979) *The Emergence of Symbols: Communication and Cognition in Infancy.* New York: Academic Press.
Bateson, M. C. (1975) 'Mother-infant exchanges: the epigenesis of conversational interaction.' *Annals of the New York Academy of Sciences.* **263,** 101–113.
Berger, J., Cunningham, C. C. (1981) 'The development of eye contact between mothers and normal versus Down's Syndrome infants.' *Developmental Psychology,* **17,** 678–689.
Bissex, G. (1980) *GNYS AT WRK: A Child Learns to Read and Write.* Harvard: Harvard University Press.
Bloom, L. (1973) *One Word at a Time: The Use of Single Word Utterances before Syntax.* The Hague: Mouton.
Bower, T. F. R. (1974) *Development in Infancy.* San Francisco: W. H. Freeman.
Brazelton, T. B. (1979) 'Evidence of communication in neonatal behavioral assessment.' *In:* Bullowa, M. (Ed.) *Before Speech: The Beginning of Interpersonal Communication.* Cambridge: Cambridge University Press.
—— Koslowski, B., Main, M. (1974) 'The origins of reciprocity.' *In:* Lewis, M., Rosenblum, L. (Eds.) *The Effect of the Infant on its Caregiver.* New York: Wiley.
Brooks-Gunn, T., Lewis, M. (1984) 'Maternal responsivity in interactions with handicapped infants.' *Child Development,* **55,** 782–793.
✗ Bruner, J. (1975) 'From communication to language: a psychological perspective.' *Cognition,* **3,** 255–287.
—— (1981) 'Intention and the structure of action and interaction.' *In:* Lipsitt, L., Rovee-Collier, C. (Eds.) *Advances in Infancy Research, Vol.1.* New Jersey: Ablex.
Bullowa, M. (1979) 'Introduction: Prelinguistic communication: a field for scientific research.' *In:*

Bullowa, M. (Ed.) *Before Speech: The Beginning of Interpersonal Communication*. Cambridge: Cambridge University Press.

Carter, A. L. (1978) 'From sensori-motor morphemes to words.' *In:* Lock, A. (Ed.) *Action, Gesture and Symbol: the Emergence of Language*. New York: Academic Press.

Chomsky, N. (1965) *Aspects of the Theory of Syntax*. Cambridge, Mass.: M.I.T. Press.

Clark, R. A. (1978) 'The transition from action to gesture.' *In:* Lock, A. (Ed.) *Action, Gesture and Symbol: The Emergence of Language*. New York: Academic Press.

Cohen, L. B. (1982) 'Developing knowledge of infant perception.' *In:* Belsky, J. (Ed.) *In the Beginning: Readings in Infancy*. New York: Columbia University Press.

Cohn, J. F., Tronick, E. Z. (1982) 'Communicative rules and the sequential structure of infant behaviour during normal and depressed interaction.' *In:* Tronick, E. (Ed.) *Social Interchange in Infancy: Affect, Cognition and Communication*. Baltimore: University Park Press.

Collis, G. M. (1979) 'Describing the structure of social interaction in infancy.' *In:* Bullowa, M. (Ed.) *Before Speech: The Beginning of Interpersonal Communication*. Cambridge: Cambridge University Press.

Condon, W. S., Sander, L. (1974) 'Synchrony demonstrated between movements of the infant and adult speech.' *Child Development*, **45**, 456–462.

Contole, J., Over, R. (1981) 'Change in the selectivity of infant social behavior between 15 and 30 weeks.' *Journal of Experimental Child Psychology*, **32**, 21–35.

Corrigan, R. (1978) 'Language development as related to Stage 6 object permanence development.' *Journal of Child Language*, **5**, 173–189.

Curtiss, S., Fromkin, V., Rigler, D., Rigler, M., Kraschen, S. (1975) 'An update on the linguistic development of Genie.' *In:* Dato, D. P. (Ed.) *Georgetown University Round Table on Languages and Linguistics*. Washington, D.C.: Georgetown University Press.

Demos, E. V. (1982) 'Facial expressions of infants and toddlers: a descriptive analysis.' *In:* Field, T., Fogel, A. (Eds.) *Emotion and Early Interactions*. New Jersey: Lawrence Erlbaum.

Dore, J. (1975) 'Holophrases, speech acts and language universals.' *Journal of Child Language*, **2**, 21–40.

—— (1978) 'Conditions on the acquisition of speech acts.' *In:* Markova, I. (Ed.) *The Social Context of Language*. New York: Wiley.

—— Franklin, M., Miller, R., Ramer, A. L. M. (1976) 'Transitional phenomena in early language acquisition.' *Journal of Child Language*, **3**, 13–28.

Field, T. (1981) 'Infant arousal, attention and affect during early interactions.' *In:* Lipsitt, L. P., Rovee-Collier, C. (Eds.) *Advances in Infancy Research, Vol.1*. New Jersey: Ablex. pp.58–99.

Fillmore, C. (1968) 'The case for case.' *In:* Bach, E., Harms, R. T. (Eds.) *Universals in Linguistic Theory*. New York: Holt, Rinehart & Winston.

Fogel, A. (1981) 'The ontogeny of gestural communication: the first six months.' *In:* Stark, R. (Ed.) *Language Behavior in Infancy and Early Childhood*. New York: Elsevier.

—— Diamond, G., Langhorst, B., Demos, V. (1982) 'Affective and cognitive aspects of the 2 month old's participation in face to face interaction with the mother.' *In:* Tronick, E. Z. (Ed.) *Social Interchange in Infancy: Affect, Cognition and Communication*. Baltimore: University Park Press.

Fraiberg, S. (1974) 'Blind infants and their mothers: an examination of the sign system.' *In:* Lewis, M., Rosenblum, A. (Eds.) *The Effects of the Infant on its Caregiver*. New York: Wiley.

Frye, D., Rawling, P., Moore, C., Myers, I. (1983) 'Object-person discrimination and communication at 3 and 10 months.' *Developmental Psychology*, **19**, 303–309.

Gardner, R. A., Gardner, B. T. (1969) 'Teaching sign language to a chimpanzee.' *Science*, **165**, 664–672.

Halliday, M. (1975) *Learning How to Mean: Explorations in the Development of Language*. London: Arnold.

Harding, C. G., Golinkoff, R. M. (1979) 'The origins of vocalisations in prelinguistic infants.' *Child Development*, **50**, 28–32.

Hewes, G. W. (1976) 'The current status of gestural theory of language origin.' *Academy of Science*, **280**, 482.

Ingram, D. (1978) 'Sensori-motor intelligence and language development.' *In:* Lock, A. (Ed.) *Action, Gesture and Symbol: the Emergence of Language*. New York: Academic Press.

Kagan, J., Kearsley, R., Zelazzo, P. (1978) *Infancy: its Place in Human Development*. Cambridge: Harvard University Press.

Kaye, K. (1979) 'Thickening thin data: the maternal role in developing communication and language.' *In:* Bullowa, M. (Ed.) *Before Speech: the Beginning of Interpersonal Communication*. Cambridge: Cambridge University Press.

—— (1982) 'Organism, apprentice and person.' *In:* Tronick, E. Z. (Ed.) *Social Interchange in Infancy: Affect, Cognition and Communication.* Baltimore: University Park Press.

Kimura, D. (1976) 'The neural basis of language qua gesture.' *In:* Whitaker, H., Whitaker, H. (Eds.) *Studies in Neurolinguistics, Vol.2.* New York: Academic Press.

Klima, E. S., Bellugi, U. (1979) *The Signs of Language.* Cambridge, Mass.: Harvard University Press.

Kogan, K. L. (1980) 'Interaction systems between preschool handicapped or developmentally delayed children and their parents.' *In:* Field, T. M., Goldberg, S., Stern, D., Sostek, A. (Eds.) *High Risk Infants and Children.* New York: Academic Press.

Lempers, J. D. (1979) 'Young children's production and comprehension of non-verbal (deictic) behaviors. *Journal of Genetic Psychology, 135,* 92–102.

Leung, E. H., Rheingold, H. L. (1981) 'The development of pointing as a social gesture.' *Developmental Psychology, 17,* 215–220.

Lockman, J. L., Ashmead, D. H. (1983) 'Asynchronies in the development of manual behavior.' *In:* Lipsitt, L., Rovee-Collier, C. K. (Eds.) *Advances in Infancy Research, Vol.2.* New Jersey: Ablex.

Macfarlane, A. (1977) *The Psychology of Childbirth.* London: Fontana.

McNeill, D. (1970) *The Acquisition of Language.* New York: Harper & Row.

Martlew, M. (1984) 'Communication between mothers and infants with cerebral palsy.' *Paper given at British Association meeting, University of East Anglia, Norwich.*

X —— (1985) 'The development of written language.' *In:* Durkin, K. (Ed.) *Language Development through the School Years.* Sevenoaks, Kent: Croom Helm.

Masur, E. F. (1982) 'Mothers' responses to infants' object-related gestures: influences on lexical development.' *Journal of Child Language, 9,* 23–30.

Murphy, C. (1978) 'Pointing in the context of a shared activity.' *Child Development, 49,* 371–380.

—— Messer, D. J. (1977) 'Mothers, infants and pointing: a study of gesture.' *In:* Schaffer, H. R. (Ed.) *Studies in Mother-Infant Interaction.* London: Academic Press.

Nelson, K. (1973) 'Structure and strategy in learning to talk.' *Monograph of the Society for Research in Child Development, 38.*

Ratner, N. K., Bruner, J. (1978) 'Games, social exchange and the acquisition of language.' *Journal of Child Langue. 5,* 391–401.

Rovee-Collier, C., Fagan, J. W. (1981) 'The retrieval of memory in early infancy.' *In:* Lipsitt, L., Rovee-Collier, C. (Eds.) *Advances in Infant Research, Vol.1.* New Jersey: Ablex.

Sander, L. W. (1977) 'The regulation of exchange in the infant-caretaker system and some aspects of the context-content relationship.' *In:* Lewis, M., Rosenblum, L. (Eds.) *Interaction, Conversation and the Development of Language.* New York: Wiley.

Scaife, M., Bruner, J. (1975) 'The capacity for joint visual attention in the infant.' *Nature, 253,* 265–266.

Schaffer, H. R., Collis, G. M., Parsons, G. (1977) 'Vocal interchange and visual regard in verbal and preverbal children.' *In:* Schaffer, H. R. (Ed.) *Studies in Mother-Infant Interaction.* London: Academic Press.

Searle, J. (1969) *Speech Acts.* Cambridge: Cambridge University Press.

Sinclair, H. (1970) 'The transition from sensory-motor behaviour to symbolic activity.' *Interchange, 1,* 119–126.

Sroufe, A. (1979) 'The ontogenesis of emotion in infancy.' *In:* Osofsky, J. (Ed.) *Handbook of Infant Development.* New York: Wiley.

Stern, D. (1974) 'Mother and infant at play: the dyadic interaction involving facial, vocal and gaze behaviors.' *In:* Lewis, M., Rosenblum, L. (Eds.) *The Effect of the Infant on its Caregiver.* New York: John Wiley. pp. 187–214.

—— (1981) 'The development of biologically determined signals of readiness to communicate, which are language "resistant".' *In:* Stark, R. (Ed.) *Language Behavior in Infancy and Early Childhood.* New York: Elsevier. pp. 45–63.

—— Jaffe, J., Beebe, B., Bennett, S. L. (1975) 'Vocalizing in unison and in alternation: two modes of communication within the mother-infant dyad.' *In:* Aaronson, D., Rieber, R. W. (Eds.) *Developmental Psycholinguistics and Communication Disorders.* New York: New York Academy of Sciences.

Sugarman-Bell, S. (1978) 'Some organisational aspects of pre-verbal communication.' *In:* Markova, I. (Ed.) *The Social Context of Language.* New York: Wiley.

Thelen, E. (1981) 'Rhythmical behaviour in infancy: an ethological perspective.' *Developmental Psychology, 17,* 237–257.

Trevarthen, C. (1979) 'Communication and cooperation in early infancy: a description of primary intersubjectivity.' *In:* Bullowa, M. (Ed.) *Before Speech: the Beginning of Interpersonal Communication.* Cambridge: Cambridge University Press.

Tronick, E. Z. (1981) 'Infant communicative intent: the infant's reference to social interaction.' *In:* Stark, R. (Ed.) *Language Behaviour in Infancy and Early Childhood.* New York: Elsevier North Holland.

—— Als, H., Brazelton, B. (1980) 'Monadic phases: a structural descriptive analysis of infant-mother face-to-face interaction.' *Merrill Palmer Quarterly,* **26,** 3–24.

Wolff, P. H. (1968) 'The serial organisation of sucking in the young infant.' *Pediatrics,* **42,** 943–956.

Zinober, B., Martlew, M. (1985) 'Developmental changes in gesture and vocalisation from ten to twenty-one months.' *British Journal of Developmental Psychology.*

5
ASPECTS OF LANGUAGE DEVELOPMENT IN THE PRESCHOOL YEARS

Paul Fletcher

Theoretical background

A child's learning of language is an impressive feat. By the first birthday, there is limited understanding and no productive language, but four years later a child can argue, ask questions, tell stories, lie, talk about events in the past and consider events in the future. Admittedly there is still a lot to learn before the child matches the adult in these skills; and he still has to learn to read and write. But the development in spoken language over these four years has been dramatic. How does language develop in these early years, and what can go wrong? What counts as 'normal' in the child's spoken language development? I will address these questions by looking first at spoken language development between birth and the beginnings of words. I will then consider phonology and grammar, as relatively independent systems that the child has to learn and organise between the ages of one and five. To begin with, however, it is appropriate to step back a little from the details of development and consider theoretical issues in language acquisition. For assessing if a child is language-impaired, it is crucial to be able to compare his linguistic abilities with those of normal children. To determine why language impairment occurs, however, it will be important to identify the variables that are relevant to successful language acquisition, and to itemise the processes that underlie the normal child's convergence on adult abilities. We may then be able to examine the significance of certain variables, and the breakdown of certain processes, in language impairment. It has to be said at the outset that intensive research into normal child language development of the last 20 years has not furnished a monolithic explanatory theory. Theoretical discussion has nevertheless been extensive. Here we outline two influential strands of research which may have relevance for understanding language impairment.

The modern history of language development research began in earnest with Chomsky, whose initial statement of an 'idealised language acquisition device' envisaged a considerable innate language-learning mechanism for the child (Chomsky 1965). In an ingenious application of Occam's razor, this mechanism was specified in the same terms as the principles of the theory of transformational generative grammar, which Chomsky had developed for characterising languages like English. In brief, the argument is that if it is possible to discover a set of linguistic universals in the languages of the world, despite their diverse surface forms, the simplest way to account for the presence of these features is in terms of an innate endowment. Language is (impaired individuals apart) a feature common to—indeed the most important distinguishing characteristic of—the human species.

If instead of marvelling at the diversity of the languages of the world we concentrate on what it is that languages, as a biological phenomenon, have in common we discover a consistent set of organisational principles, the most plausible explanation for which (so Chomsky argues) is that the human infant is endowed with them.

It is important to note that this view of language acquisition does not totally discount the linguistic environment in which the child grows up, though it does minimise its importance. In more recent statements of the Chomskyan view, the language that the child hears is said to be a 'trigger' for the generation of the innate principles:

> The environmental stimulus is thus viewed only as a trigger; much of the ability eventually attained is determined by genetically encoded principles, which are triggered or activated by environmental stimulus rather than formed by it more or less directly (Lightfoot 1982)

Since the most famous 'principle of grammar' in the early development of Chomsky's work was the transformational rule, research efforts in the study of language development in the 1960s examined longitudinal records of children's conversations, for evidence of rule-learning that might provide indirect support for the nativist principles. Of course the 'innateness hypothesis' could not be tested directly. This would require human infants to be raised in an environment which used a communication system artificially constructed to contravene the principles of universal grammar. Even if this were possible, it would be profoundly unethical.

The early research seemed to indicate that children learning English did proceed at least in part by formulating rules about the language they were learning. The best evidence for the child's active, constructive approach to the problems of acquisition came from the errors he made. The most frequently cited example is that of past-tense over-generalisations such as 'comed' or 'goed' (see below). The child could not simply repeat such forms from the language he hears around him. Rather, on the basis of the restricted examples of '-ed' coding for past on regular verbs that he has heard, the child has formulated a rule for past-tense formation which, for a time, is extended to all verbs in the language, including the irregular ones.

However at the beginning of the 1970s there was a shift in the research focus, away from an exclusive concentration on the child's language, to include the nature of the linguistic input to the child. There were two reasons for this. First, if the language of parents to the child is modified in ways that might make it easier to assimilate and learn, then the explanatory load on innate capacities is correspondingly reduced. The second reason reflected an increasing interest in language as communication, and language acquisition as learning how to communicate— *Learning How to Mean* was the title of an influential book of the time—(Halliday 1975). Since meaning is transacted in conversation, the details of interactions between children and their parents became of interest. Details of the characteristics of parental speech to young children appeared in Snow (1986). She made it clear that parental (or child-directed) speech has structural characteristics that set it apart from that used to other adults. It tends to be short and syntactically simple, to use a restricted vocabulary and to have 'identifying' features (such as a higher fundamental frequency) that set it apart from other varieties. Child-directed speech is well formed—parents use grammatical sentences to children, and the range of topics is limited: the semantics of these utterances are also simple, which may in part account for the lack of syntactic complexity. In early stages of language learning, then, the linguistic environment is adapted by parents in ways that may facilitate the language-learning task. The potential importance of these findings is, as Snow says, 'to constrain hypotheses concerning the nature and variety of language learning mechanisms'. Such work as there has been is limited and programmatic (Gleitman et al. 1984). It is possible, however, to conclude that successful language acquisition requires both an intact learning mechanism (whatever the specifics might be) and an appropriately facilitative linguistic environment. We may assume further that deficiencies in either will lead to language impairment. While in the future we may expect to learn more about deficiencies in the acquisition mechanism in some language-impaired individuals, and about the effects of an inappropriate linguistic environment on others, in the current state of knowledge we will find it most fruitful to concentrate on the *identification* of a language-impaired individual in terms of his non-correspondence to the normal developmental course.

The first year
It is very unusual for children to use recognisable words before their first birthday; but the first year, particularly the second half of it, is of profound importance for later language development. It is at this time that the child is initiated into conversation-like interaction, and begins to take part in other relevant social rituals—playing games like peek-a-boo or ring-a-roses, with their repetitive action-linked language, or looking at pictures in books. The child also starts practising sounds. It is true that the sounds are not used meaningfully: if a nine-month-old says 'tata', it is unlikely to be an intentional reference to 'daddy', but he is at least working on the articulatory movements that will need to be refined increasingly as he learns to use meaningful words in his second year. As well as 'practising' individual sounds, from six months onwards the infant will reproduce these sound sequences in tonal patterns resembling speech. The parent may hear a short sound-sequence that does not have any determinable meaning, but the intonation of the sequence may be very like that used by adults when they are asking a question, for example. In the second half of the first year, the child seems able to reproduce the intonational tunes of the language around him; often a parent, hearing sequences of sounds intoned like a question, an exclamation or a declaration, will think that the baby is 'saying' something. In fact he is just giving a firm indication that he can hear, extract and produce salient tonal features of the language he hears around him. It follows from this that anything which prevents him hearing the patterns in the language around him, such as intermittent or permanent hearing loss, will affect his language development.

The first six months

The first sound the baby makes is crying, soon after the moment of birth. For the first two months the infant makes only reflexive sounds, predominantly crying, but also what have been referred to as 'vegetative' sounds, connected with burping, swallowing and spitting up. Cries can occur in long series; each portion of the cry (the actual sound we hear) lasts for about a second, and can be likened to a long vowel sound, produced on an outward stream of air from the lungs. Each cry is followed by a very brief period of inhaling as the child prepares himself for the next burst. During the period of inhaling for crying the baby breathes through his mouth—otherwise he is a compulsive nasal breather. It is interesting to note that the basic mechanism of speech—the modification of an outgoing airstream—is used by infants from birth in their cry sounds.

Cries are associated with discomfort on the part of the infant—hunger and pain particularly. At six to eight weeks of age the first comfort sounds are produced, often in response to the mother smiling or talking. The sounds are usually called 'cooing' sounds because of a characteristic vowel quality, which tends to be like the 'oo' in 'boot' when the child first produces the sounds. Quite soon the range of vowels heard is diversified, however, and the cooing sounds also contain consonants, particularly 'g' or 'k' sounds. The first cooing sounds begin as single segments, about half a second in length, but soon they are linked into groups of three to 10 segments. The child still expresses discomfort by crying, but from the age of about three months the frequency of crying episodes tends to fall off. And at about four months of age, laughter-like sounds emerge.

Normal infants are naturally noisy. We must not think of them as making this noise in a vacuum, but in the context of an extremely close relationship with their mothers, whose response to vocalising by the child is immediate. If an infant vocalises, the mother will generally respond with some words of her own. Even if she does not say anything, she will smile at the infant or touch him. This prototype conversation can begin very early, as a typical exchange between a mother and her three-month-old daughter shows. Notice that while the mother is herself prepared to speak sentences, she is content to accept almost anything from the baby's (naturally) rather limited repertoire as her contribution to the 'conversation'.

Mother	*Ann*
	(smiles)
Oh what a nice little smile	
Yes isn't that nice	
There	
There's a nice little smile	(burps)
What a nice wind as well	
Yes that's better, isn't it?	
Yes	
Yes	(vocalises)
Yes!	
There's a nice noise.	

73

This particular mother in fact reacted to *all* Ann's burps, yawns, sneezes, coughs, cooing, vocalisations and smiles with utterances like those illustrated above (see Snow 1977).

So far in discussing the baby's development we have concentrated on production, for obvious reasons—it is much easier to describe what we hear than what the baby can hear. But the baby's perception of the language around him, and his understanding of it, is an equally significant part of learning how to talk. It is however much more difficult for us to describe. The first step in his perceptual development involves the perception of speech versus non-speech. A baby may stop crying when spoken to, or may give some differential behavioural response to speech (opening his eyes when his father talks to him) versus non-speech (keeping them closed when his father coughs). He may react to the sound of his own name by turning his head to the speaker. He does not actually recognise his name, but he can recognise the tone in which it is said. This can be checked by substituting someone else's name, in the same tone of voice. If the child makes a reliable response to his own name, it is likely that he will make the same response to someone else's name enunciated in the same way.

Six months to one year
The next (and major) step for the child is to recognise the connection between a particular word and an object or a situation. What the word might be will depend very much on the family situation. One family might, for example, encourage the child's realisation of the association between 'tick-tock' and a clock by holding him up to look at and hear a loudly ticking clock. By six months, he may respond to the word 'tick-tock' by looking at the clock. It is important to remember that some children may not give evidence of this association between sound and meaning till much later, and also that the association, when it comes, may be linked to social rituals, not objects: so the mother saying 'bye-bye' will, after long weeks of practice which may have begun with the mother shaking the baby's hand at his departing father in the morning, eventually elicit a spontaneous waving by the child. 'Clap hands', after similar intensive parental intervention, will bring about the infant's appropriate reaction. Different families have different games and rituals. What they all have in common is that they impress on the child the all-important relationship between sounds and meanings, without which no development can take place. Between six and nine months, a child may show signs of recognising one or two words for objects or situations, but he will not produce these words yet. His vocalising will be developing however, and he will make a wider range of noises and sounds. This more extensive repertoire of sounds is referred to as babbling—a term which has implications, quite accurately, both of quantity and meaninglessness in the vocalising it refers to. The baby produces a much wider range of sounds, apparently as a kind of oral play. As well as clicks, trills, and grunts the baby will, particularly as he approaches his first birthday, produce a variety of consonant-like and vowel-like sounds, either on their own or in sequences. So you may hear towards the end of the first year, strings of syllables like 'mamamama', or 'papap', or 'dededede'. Occasionally some of the sounds in the sequences may appear

unusual—one hears consonants that do not exist in English. The available studies on this issue (summarised in Locke 1986) concur that infant vocalisation in the second half of the first year shows patterned behaviour, both in terms of its syllabic structure (which is predominantly open syllables as in the 'mamama' example above) and the segments used. By far the majority of consonants used are stops (like *p, d*), nasals (like *m, n*) and glides (like *w*). The other major consonant classes—fricatives (like *s* or *f*), affricates (like *ch*) and liquids (like *l*) appear less than 20 per cent of the time. The same consonantal preferences are reported in studies of babbling by the deaf (Locke 1983) and in studies of Down's syndrome infants. Both Dodd (1972) and Smith and Oller (1981) found that these infants did not differ from normals in their babbling repertoire. The studies of non-normals suggest that children do not need to hear themselves in order to babble (though they may very well babble more if they do hear themselves—the studies reported here do not address that issue) and that infant vocalisation in the first year is not a learned behaviour. This in turn suggests that it will be difficult to use babbling patterns diagnostically.

Between six and 12 months the child's production repertoire is increasing in terms of the sounds he can make and (as we mentioned at the beginning) the tunes he can reproduce. But it is rare for the sounds to have any meaning. As the child listens, he begins to link one or two words consistently with meanings—objects or situations. However, he may appear to understand a great deal more. Parents have been heard to say of their nine-month-old: 'He understands everything we say'. He may understand a good deal more than he did six months earlier, both about the fact that speech sounds are significant and about the situations he finds himself in. But there are limits to what he knows. If for example a mother says to her child 'wave to daddy', and points at the departing father and then waves at him—it is not at all necessary for the child to understand the words 'wave' and 'to' to comply with the mother's instruction. It is possible to check this by saying in the same circumstances (gesture, wave and daddy location) 'sing to daddy': almost inevitably waving will result. To take another example, reported of a nine-month-old girl: there was a photograph of her on the wall which she liked, possibly because of the reflections from the glass covering the photograph, as much as the picture itself. Her mother repeatedly said 'baby' and pointed at the picture. When the child heard one of her parents say 'where is the baby?' she would turn right round in her high chair to look at the picture. But she reacted in the same way to the question 'where is daddy?' The two words sounded too similar for her to distinguish at this stage. These examples show that the child's interpretation of constantly repeated words will be greatly assisted by gestures, actions and consistent situations. It is consistency and regularity which mark the child's early experience. For instance, we can account fairly comprehensively for what the infant experiences in terms of a quite restricted range of situations; from most to least frequent, they are: mother's lap, crib or bed, infant seat, bath, sofa, playpen, floor and jumper-swing. In these situations there are routine interactions, with often highly specific and repeated utterances from the mother. These will be some extension of the range of situations for the older infant, more to do with his own increased mobility than any radical change in the household routine. But there will still be a good deal of repetitive association between sounds and objects or events in familiar situations. (For further details on language behaviour in the first years see Crystal 1986, Stark 1986.)

First words and the transition to linguistic structure

The event every parent is on the lookout for is the occurrence of the child's first recognisable word. This is perhaps the right place to emphasise that this is a distinctly moveable feast. Those who have watched the development of two or more children will know that even in the same family two children only a couple of years apart will differ dramatically in the time at which they speak their first word, and in the subsequent rate of language development, particularly up to the age of about three. The appearance of the first word (that is, the first recognisable English word) may come around the first birthday—or it may be as late as two. Notice that we are discussing the *production* of the first word, and, as already indicated, producing words is only one side of the story. If a child is understanding words, this temporary absence in production should not be a cause for too much concern. Furthermore, the ages referred to are averages, and a child can delay the appearance of this behaviour considerably and still be within normal limits.

Before the first recognisable word appears, many children have been observed to use 'words' which, while consistent in sound and meaning, are not recognisable English words (Ferguson 1976). For instance a baby may say 'ah' when hugging his teddy, or mother, or in relation to similar displays of affection to anyone else. The child will then pick up this sound and use it in similar circumstances. Exclamations of this kind can eventually take on word-like status. One three-year-old girl, it is reported, used to refer to her comforter blanket as 'my ah'. This presumably dates back to this early, repetitive kind of association between the parent's exclamation and a specific situation. It is very difficult to predict what these pre-words will be, or indeed if they will be used at all. They are highly idiosyncratic, and difficult to recognise because they are not standard words. The kind of pre-words reported range from the 'ah' we have already mentioned, to a 'dadada' sequence, said in a loud voice and taken to understand that the child was telling someone off, to an 'oo' sound used of birds and animals to signify something like 'look it's moving'. Recognising the relationship between babbling, pre-words and first words is particularly important: that they are not successive stages of development, and all three types of sound-making may coexist. Some children around their first birthday will chatter continually, and give the impression of real speech. Most of this will be babble; there will be a few pre-words, and possibly a few attempts at standard English words. Other children will babble less, and have a more extensive vocabulary. The *range* of behaviour is extensive—from children with a productive vocabulary of nil, to one of about 40 words (including pre-words, and expressive words like 'ah', 'bye', 'hi'). Most children are at the lower end of this scale (Garman 1981).

Comprehension

Unfortunately this is quite difficult to assess. The first problem is the apparent difference between naturalistic observation of children's understanding, and their performance in experimental settings (Chapman 1978). Parents of one-year-old children who are starting to talk, typically report that their children understand everything they say. Children who are at the level of putting two words together in production respond appropriately to parental commands (Shipley *et al.* 1969). Longitudinal studies of children's production show that by the age of 3½ they are engaged in quite complex conversations and give every sign of understanding what their interlocutors are saying (Fletcher 1985). In experimental studies, however, there is a wide range of evidence that contrasts with the naturalistic picture. Here we will just give two examples.

Chapman (1978) report that many children are unable to use constituent order in active sentences as a cue to agent-of-action and object-of-action, when the task is appropriate picture selection. With certain tasks, lack of success in the experimental situation may continue up to four years of age. In production, however, children will be using appropriate word-order in the sentences they produce by the middle of their third year. Bridges (1980) reported in detail on individual responses to the comprehension of active and passive sentences. Children were given toy cars and asked to act out a sentence like 'the red car is pushed by the green car'. Up to 2½, a child in Bridges' study would tend to ignore one car and push the other himself. Between 2½ and four years, individual children differed. One child might assume that the car nearest his hand is the agent of the action the verb refers to; another child of similar age would move the first-mentioned car. After about four years of age, children tended to respond appropriately. What is of most interest here are the individual responses of the children younger than four. If the child is using a consistent strategy to respond, he will sometimes be correct, but at other times wrong. If he is presented with 'the red car is pushed by the green car', the green car is nearer to his hand, and he is using the 'near car as agent' strategy, then he will appear to respond appropriately. The strategy he is using to cope will become apparent only when he responds incorrectly to the same stimulus when the red car is closest to him. The example emphasises that for the young language-learner the comprehension process may be based on partial linguistic knowledge, and success may be based on one of a number of *comprehension strategies*. It is by invoking the existence of such strategies that we can resolve the paradox we began with. In normal interactions, the linguistic stimulus to the child is often heavily supported by the situation in which it is uttered. Suppose, for example, a child between 18 and 24 months is given a ball and a lorry and asked 'why don't you put the ball in the lorry?' The chances are that the child will put the ball in the lorry, but we cannot assume that the child comprehends the syntax of negative questions, or even the verb 'put'. Rather, he understands 'ball', 'lorry' and typical ways of acting with respect to the objects (Shatz 1978). Experimental contexts such as those constructed by Bridges (1980), or the typical comprehension tests (*e.g.* Miller and Yoder 1985, Bishop 1983) deliberately exclude or limit situational clues so that the experimenter or examiner can unequivocally interpret the child's response. This goes some way towards resolving the apparent discrepancies between naturalistic and experimental understanding in the child.

If partial linguistic understanding (and occasional failures to understand) are normal aspects of language behaviour for the child under four, we have to expect similar performance for an extended period in the language-impaired child. Most of our information about the comprehension of such children comes from standardised tests, which would appear in the context of this discussion to be inappropriate for informing us about the comprehension strategies used, unless response patterns are carefully analysed.

Early production

We would normally expect the first word to have appeared by the age of two: but some children start talking much later than this, and manage perfectly well (and we hear anecdotes of famous people, like Macaulay and Einstein, who reputedly failed to talk until the age of four.) Nevertheless such children are unusual, and if a child does not use any recognisable words by 18 months, it is worth considering assessment by the appropriate professional.

The actual words used or understood by a child will vary from family to family: but there are usually some common features. In the first 50 words in comprehension, a majority will be either names (Mummy, Daddy, Paddington, Spot) or common nouns. These will be names for objects like toys, clothes, parts of the body, food or household items, people or animals. The child will also understand a smaller number of action words: games like 'clap hands', 'peek-a-boo', 'ring-of-roses'; verbal games like 'what does a doggie say'; words which are linked at a regular activity like 'bath', 'dance', 'give'; place words, that require the child to locate something, or put it in a particular place—'where's' (the dog), 'look at' (the flowers). Apart from nominals and action words, one or more words like 'hot', 'no' or 'don't touch', which inhibit action by the child, will also be understood (Benedict 1979).

In the first 50 production words, the discrepancy between nominals and action words is more marked. We can expect 60 per cent of these words to be nominals (names for family members, pets or toys), but only about two out of 10 to be action words. Other categories found are demonstratives like 'there', and possessives (particularly 'mine'). Even though the child uses a high proportion of nominals, these will very often be action-related. So the mother might say 'give me the ball' and the child will pass it over to her, saying 'ball' at the same time. A list of the words used in production by one 14-month-old child appears in Figure 1.

Over-extension in production

A common feature of early production vocabularies is the use of words by the child to name objects to which adults would not apply the same word. The child's limited vocabulary, applied to an expanding world, in his second year, causes him to extend words inappropriately, often on the most tenuous of associations. For example, one child is reported to have use the word 'door' when she wanted her mother to open the door, and then to have extended the application of the word to

Nominals		Action words		Other		
Mummy	Babar	run	down	no	we	thanks
Daddy	Aba	all gone	eat	bye bye	please	doo doo
baby	bear	more		pee pee		
dog	milk					
dolly	juice					
kitty	cheese					
girl	raisin					
bottle	cracker					
egg	book					
shoe	sock					
eye	car					
choo choo	bus					
lorry	noon					
star						

Fig. 1. The vocabulary of one 14-month-old girl (total = 39)

asking her mother to take the top off a tube of smarties. The connection here is the 'opening' involved in both cases. Another child used the term 'bow-wow' to refer to a dog, then extended it to a piece of fur with glass eyes, then to his father's cuff links, then to the pearly buttons on a dress of his mother's, then to a thermometer. If there is a link throughout this set of items, it comes perhaps from the iridescence of the dog's eyes. The example emphasises that while most children do over-extend the words in their vocabulary, they have highly individual ways of doing it. In general we can expect about one in three of the child's early production words to be over-extended (Rescorla 1980). Frequently cited words in lists of children's over-extended words include 'car', 'shoe', 'hat', 'apple', 'ball', 'cat', 'dog', 'hot', and 'Dada.'

Pronunciation
It is appropriate to consider the child's pronunciation development independently from grammar and semantics in this chapter because, while normal children progress through the components of language in succession (despite individual variations), it seems to be possible for an impaired child's pronunciation system to be affected independently of his grammatico-semantic system. The perspective within which phonological development is currently considered (like language development generally) is that of the child as active problem-solver, both as hearer and speaker. These two aspects of his rôle as a language-user present rather different problems. Recent work on perception (*e.g.* Menyuk *et al.* 1986) emphasises the likely reliance, by the young child beginning to develop a vocabulary, on the recognition and storage of larger units (syllables and words) rather than analysing what he hears into individual segments or distinctive features.

In the course of the evening they came into the drawing-room, and, as an especial treat, were to sing some of their hymns to me, instead of saying them, so that I might hear how nicely they sang. Ernest was to choose the first hymn, and he chose one about some people who were to come to the sunset tree. I am no botanist, and do not know what kind of tree a sunset tree is, but the words began, 'Come, come, come; come to the sunset tree for the day is past and gone.' The tune was rather pretty and had taken Ernest's fancy, for he was unusually fond of music and had a sweet little child's voice which he liked using.

He was, however, very late in being able to sound a hard 'c' or 'k', and, instead of saying 'Come,' he said 'Tum, tum, tum.'

'Ernest,' said Theobald, from the arm-chair in front of the fire, where he was sitting with his hands folded before him, 'don't you think it would be very nice if you were to say "come" like other people, instead of "tum"?'

'I do say tum,' replied Ernest, meaning that he has said 'come'.

Theobald was always in a bad temper on Sunday evening. Whether it is that they are as much bored with the day as their neighbours, or whether they are tired, or whatever the cause may be, clergymen are seldom at their best on Sunday evening; I had already seen signs that evening that my host was cross, and was a little nervous at hearing Ernest say so promptly 'I do say tum', when his papa had said he did not say it as he should.

Theobald noticed the fact that he was being contradicted in a moment. He got up from his arm-chair and went to the piano.

'No, Ernest, you don't,' he said, 'you say nothing of the kind, you say "tum", not "come". Now say "come" after me, as I do.'

'Tum,' said Ernest, at once; 'is that better?' I have no doubt he thought it was, but it was not.

'Now, Ernest, you are not taking pains: you are not trying as you ought to do. It is high time you learned to say "come", why Joey can say "come", can't you, Joey?'

'Yeth, I can,' replied Joey, and he said something which was not far off 'come'.

'There, Ernest, do you hear that? There's no difficulty about it, nor shadow of difficulty. Now, take your own time, think about it, and say "come" after me.'

The boy remained silent a few seconds and then said 'tum' again.

I laughed, but Theobald turned to me impatiently and said, 'Please do not laugh, Overton; it will make the boy think it does not matter, and it matters a great deal', then turning to Ernest he said, 'Now Ernest, I will give you one more chance, and if you don't say "come", I shall know that you are self-willed and naughty.'

He looked very angry, and a shade came over Ernest's face, like that which comes upon the face of a puppy when it is being scolded without understanding why. The child saw well what was coming now, was frightened, and, of course, said 'tum' once more.

'Very well, Ernest,' said his father, catching him angrily by the shoulder. 'I have done my best to save you, but if you will have it so, you will,' and he lugged the little wretch, crying by anticipation, out of the room. A few minutes more and we could hear screams coming from the dining-room, across the hall which separated the drawing-room from the dining-room, and knew that poor Ernest was being beaten.

'I have sent him up to bed,' said Theobald, as he returned to the drawing-room, 'and now, Christina, I think we will have the servants in to prayers', and he rang the bell for them red-handed as he was.

Fig. 2. (Reprinted from Butler 1980.)

80

When the vocabulary is limited the child does not have to make the precise distinctions (*e.g.* between t/d, s/sh) which will be eventually necessary to distinguish between say, 'tuck' and 'duck', 'sip' and 'ship'. The reflection in production of the child's global perception strategies, as he builds up a vocabulary of about 50 words in the six months or so after his first word, is variability and imprecision in pronunciation. The word 'fish', for example, may be pronounced at separate times as 'kish' or 'ish'; 'milk' may sometimes be pronounced with an initial consonant (with perhaps a 'b' in place of an 'm') but no final 'k', and sometimes with the 'k' but no initial consonant. The child may say 'dog' without the final 'g', or it may come out as 'gogi', with an initial 'g' as well as the final one, and an extra 'i' vowel at the end. This last example is instructive in showing us how the child, at a particular point in his development (around the age of two), will simplify the production task. By 'harmonising' the initial consonant with the second consonant, the child avoids the problem of having different consonants either side of the vowel. And by effectively constructing an extra syllable by adding the 'i' vowel, he avoids the problem that many children have in pronouncing final consonants, in the CVC syllables which are so common in English.

Studies of the pronunciations of words in early vocabularies, then, indicate considerable inter-word variation in the pronunciation of individual segments. This suggests that a purely segment-based characterisation of early pronunciations, which assumes that the child can distinguish individual sounds, would be inappropriate. In the early stages of establishing a vocabulary, the child can get by with relatively accurate pronunciations, using a very limited set of sounds. As his vocabulary increases during the end of the second and the beginning of the third year, the child's strategies must provide an increasingly differentiated set of sounds, which need to be organised within the phonological structure of the language he is learning.

The next stage of the child's development is referred to by Ingram (1986) as the 'phonology of the simple morpheme', and lasts up to about four years of age. Ingram described the phonological patterns that can be found in this period in terms of processes that the child's pronunciations undergo by comparison with the adult forms they are trying to pronounce. Two of these, *consonant harmony* and *final consonant deletion*, we have already referred to. Other common processes are:

(1) *Stopping:* replacing fricative consonants with plosives: so 'sea' is pronounced the same as 'tea', and 'sing' as 'ting'.

(2) *Fronting:* back consonants are replaced by those further forward in the mouth (Butler 1980). This is a general tendency of learners of English, as shown in Figure 2.

The reaction here of the Victorian father, as depicted by Butler, to his son's mistake is rather different from that to be expected from the modern parent. It is of course exaggerated for the novelist's purposes. But certain features of the anecdote ring true. We do know that substituting a 't' for a 'c' or 'k' at the beginning of words ('fronting') is a very common feature of young children's speech (though most four-year-olds—Ernest's age at this point in the novel—will have learned to pronounce 'come' or 'kick' correctly). Modern studies also show that children can *perceive* in the speech of others a difference which they may not be able to produce. In the extract Ernest shows no sign of puzzlement when his father pronounces 'come' and 'tum' one after the other; but he is still unable to reproduce the required sound even in immediate imitation. The third point of contact with recent research is that the child may appear not to be aware that he *has* made a mistake. Ernest maintains that he pronounces 'come' correctly, though to the adult ear his pronunciation sounds like 'tum'. He cannot get it right: '"Tum" said Ernest, at once; "is that better?" I have no doubt he thought it was, but it was not.' It is not immediately clear why the child is unable to perceive his own mistakes. One explanation is that the child is in fact making sub-phonemic adjustments in his pronunciation which adults, habituated to categorising speech sounds in quite specific ways, are not able to attend to. This 'pseudo-homonymy' is discussed by Priestley (1980) and documented by Macken and Barton (1980).

A further common process apparent in speech of young learners is that of cluster reduction. A number of words in English begin (phonetically) with a 'cluster' of two consonants: 'pray', 'bray', 'dray', 'speak', 'play', 'blind', and so on. It is common for children learning these in their third year to reduce these to a single consonant. For the stop-initial clusters—those beginning 'p', 'b', *etc.*, the 'l' or 'r' will be omitted. So 'pram' becomes 'pam', and 'tram' is pronounced 'tam'. The clusters that for the adult begin with 's' have the 's' omitted by the child at first—'speak' becomes 'peak' or 'beak'.

Clinical concerns

By 3½, apart from such features as lisps and the occasional immature pronunciation, the child will have mastered most of the sounds of his language in relatively simple words. New words that are polysyllabic may combine to present difficulties into primary school. Before returning to grammatical development, it may be worth reviewing the clinical relevance of the picture of development which is emerging. By comparison with aspects of the normal course of development, what will alert us to possible difficulties?

If we are using the normal course of development as our reference base, then clearly any deviation from this will be a cause for concern. The non-appearance, or the very late appearance, in the first couple of years of life, of any of the behaviours we have discussed will alert us to possible problems. In this regard it is perhaps worth making some points that have so far remained implicit. First, there is a good deal of prelinguistic behaviour, before the start of language proper, which appears crucial to successful language development. This involves vocalising on the child's part, and the development of perception and comprehension skills, in the context of constant linguistic interaction with an adult. Second, there is considerable variability in the age at which children do begin to use language, and this variability bedevils early assessment. As a rough guide, however, most children have produced their first word by about two. Third, there is variability in the kind of behaviour that is evidenced. One child's first words may be largely nominal (Fig. 1); another child may use mostly expressive words, to greet or show affection. One child may always aim for precision in pronunciation (and thus not use many of the phonological processes), whereas another may not worry so much about precision so long as he is understood. From an early stage, what characterises children's language at all levels is the individual's selection of strategies to cope with particular problems, in comprehension and production, which may result in apparent errors—for example, the pronunciation of 'speak' as 'peak' or 'beak', or the past tense of 'come' as 'comed'. One of the unexplained mysteries of language development is how children move on from these adaptive strategies to a convergence on the adult standard. It is an index of abnormality when a child either (i) does not utilise the kind of strategies illustrated, particularly the grammatical strategies discussed below, or (ii) is unable to develop on from immature strategies, particularly in the area of phonology.

Grammatical development

The first obvious development after the child's use of single-word utterances culled from his early vocabulary is the juxtaposition of two elements in the first syntactic sequences ('doggie tail', 'in there', 'more juice'). The next development involves the incorporation of verbs into these sequences—the first clauses in the child's output ('drink juice', 'kiss mummy') and eventually three-element sequences ('Mary see me'). A little more than a year after her first words at 14 months, an English child called Sophie could take part in this kind of conversation:

Extract A   2;5

    M: What's what lovey
     S: Me want that
    M: What is it
     S: [si:n]   (= plasticine)
5 *M:* Plasticine
     S: Mm
    M: What are you going to make
     S: See Jack
          Amy see me
10   See me
         Not Jack
         Only me
    M: Only you
     S: You take a bissy   (= biscuit)
15 *M:* Cos I was hungry
     S: Me want a bissy
    M: There you are
(S = Sophie, M = her mother)

While it is difficult to generalise from a single child (most particularly with respect to the age at which a structure is used), Sophie turns out to follow a course of development very similar to that of other children in the literature (Fletcher 1985). We will therefore use the extract above, and extracts from later conversations, as a framework for the discussion of salient features of language development between two and four years.

Already the child can take part in a conversation—she can understand simple questions (e.g. 1.3/4) and respond, and she can use simple declarative clauses to express wants and requests. She can differentiate between speaker and addressee by using 'me' and 'you' appropriately. She appears to have the idea of negation (see 1.11). Some progress has evidently been made in the preceding 12 months, but there is a good deal yet to be learned. If we simply take one area that is crucial for both development and impairment (Fletcher and Peters 1984), that of verb inflection and premodification, we see some of the limitations. In Extract A, the verbs are uninflected and do not have premodification: Sophie says 'Amy see me', not 'Amy will see me'. She says 'you take a bissy', not 'why did you take a bissy'. Her mother is able to interpret what she says as a question, but Sophie has yet to learn the formal structure for asking questions. It is true that in the development of a vocabulary differentiated by word-class, and the construction of simple, telegraphic clauses which are well formed for English, a framework for syntactic structure has been built. But much about grammatical systems has yet to be learned.

The second brief extract comes a little over six months later, just after the child's third birthday.

Extract B   *3;0*
    S: Why did—Hester be fast asleep mummy
    M: She was tired
    S: And why did her have—two sweets mummy
    M: Because you each had two
5   That's why
       She had the same as you
       Ooh dear
       Now what
    S: Daddy didn't give me two in the end
10 M: Yes he did
    S: He didn't
    M: He did
    S: Look
       He given one to—two to Hester and two to us

Even with such a brief extract, differences are apparent which demonstrate quite dramatic strides over a relatively short period:
(1) Her utterances are generally longer. A common way of measuring this difference is in mean length of utterance (MLU), where the number of items (words or morphemes—more commonly the latter) is averaged over 100 utterances. MLU is often used, because of the variation in rate of development across children, as a 'language-age' measure for spontaneous speech data. So instead of looking at the language ability of a group of three-year-olds, an investigator will look instead at a group of children who all lie within a specific MLU range. Despite its problems (Crystal 1974), MLU remains a widely used measure, and one which may well be

related to age (Miller and Chapman 1981). The MLU of the sample from which Extract A is taken is 2.58, while the sample from which Extract B comes has an MLU of 3.82.

(2) Measures of length, while potentially helpful in grouping children of similar language ability, do not give us any qualitative information about the nature of the language they are using. There are widely used clinical procedures such as LARSP (Language Assessment, Remediation and Screening Procedure—see Crystal *et al.* 1981) which provide a systematic approach to qualitative assessment. Such a procedure would highlight the grammatical differences between the two samples. We note in Extract B: (i) longer and more structured clause sequences—1.9 and 1.14. These contain adverbials ('in the end') and co-ordinated phrases ('two to Hester and two to us'); (ii) interrogative structures which while not quite adult-like are nevertheless reasonably successful; (iii) auxiliaries 'did' and 'didn't', and a verb inflection—the '-en' on given; (iv) a wider range of pronouns—we find 'her', 'he' and 'us' in this extract.

The expansion of simple clause structure, the emergence of interrogatives and the start of the development of grammatical systems, are the major features of this next stage of development. Again the indices of normal progress can be used as a set of criteria to which problem cases can be referred. But there is another feature of this stage of development, not apparent in the extract, which bears on our discussion of strategies in phonology and our earlier discussion of acquisition mechanisms. Within two months Sophie was using over-regularised past tenses such as 'comed' and 'doed'. Two decades of language-acquistion research, mostly in English, have made us familiar with the appearance of these kinds of 'errors' in young children's speech. One of the mechanisms the child brings to language-learning might be termed a 'morpheme-recognition' device, that extends regularities present in the language (like 'ed' for past tense) to irregular verbs, for a period. The function of such a strategy is to simplify the task of on-line language production for the child. By treating all verbs in the language as regular, he can avoid the problem of retrieval of the idiosyncratic past tenses of irregular verbs when formulating sentences.

As well as using forms like 'comed', Sophie also had a more unusual over-regularisation, exemplified in forms like 'putten', 'hurten', 'touchen'. Generally speaking, the '-en' suffix was limited to verbs which ended in certain sounds; but she used it quite often, for nearly a year.

The significance of Sophie's adoption and elimination of the '-en' form is not that we expect every child, or even many children learning English, to use similar forms. Rather, this child's uptake of a particular form available to her in the input data is further evidence of a powerful mechansim which is available to most children as they learn a language. Children can construct certain kinds of generalisations about their language on the basis of rather limited data. Similarly, as indicated in this case by the disappearance of the '-en' form (and by the rather more gradual elimination of the over-regularised '-ed' form from most children's speech), children can modify their output to eliminate these non-adult forms. If these facilities are generally available to normal children, it would seem important to consider their development (or lack of them) in the language-handicapped child. This would seem to call for detailed longitudinal studies, to supplement the widely available cross-sectional studies on language-impaired children, which have been the norm to date. We would like to know if language-impaired children take the kind of approach to language-learning which over-regularisation errors indicate that normal children do. If so, we also need to determine whether the language-impaired children can drop such strategies when they have outlived their usefulness.

Our final extract from Sophie's conversations with her mother comes from just before her fourth birthday.

Extract c

    S: You see
        He had a precious thing
        And it was a round thing that had pockets in
        Like that
5   All the way round
        And you see there was this button
        And a thing
    M: Start again Sophie
        Start again
10   *S:* And you see
        You know the new person
    M: The new person
    S: Not at playgroup
    M: No
15   *S:* On television

The crucial feature of this extract comes at 1.3, where Sophie demonstrates what has been a major advance over the last year, the construction of complex sentences. The language provides various devices for linking together simple clauses. These include co-ordinations (clauses linked with 'and' or 'but') and subordinations (clauses linked with such words as 'after', 'before', 'while', 'since', 'if' and 'because') and also the linkage exemplified here, with 'that' introducing a relative clause. The potential available to the child for narrative sequencing, for indicating temporal relation between events, for expressing causal, purpose and resultative relations, is just beginning to be tapped. This development, the beginnings of which can be identified in the fourth year, goes on well into primary school.

Apart from this major index of change, other developments in the fourth year are more subtle. As we have already indicated, verb suffix overgeneralisations die out. More auxiliary verbs are learned, and the past tense (which was previously only marked on main verbs) is marked on auxiliaries also. Passives, like 'he got hurt', begin to appear. Children demonstrate that they can understand that word-order differences can reflect differences in function (*i.e.* 'the red car pushes the green car' is different from 'the red car is pushed by the green car').

The appearance of auxiliary verbs, of interrogative structures and of complex sentences, are obvious and tangible indices of development. Using such indices for the assessment of specific language impairment is a beginning. But it is important to bear in mind that there is more to normal language acquisition, and to the characteristics of language impairment, than grammar. Grammar may provide the most convenient and direct point of entry into the linguistic system. But it is unlikely that we will achieve a complete account of language development, or a typology of specific language impairment, if we restrict our attention to purely syntactic characteristics. Two examples should serve to clarify this. In normal development, children learning English use tenses from the second half of their third year. But the use of temporal adverbials, to specify duration or the time at which an event takes place (*e.g.* 'last week', 'for several hours', 'after mum comes home'), is a much more protracted process which continues well into the primary-school years. Temporal specification is an important part of language-learning, about which we currently know very little (Weist 1986). The structures through which time is expressed do not present a problem for normal children. What is at issue is the semantics of time, and its conceptual underpinnings. Since temporal language may also cause problems for language-impaired children, it is clear that we will have to consider in detail the semantics of this, and other conceptual areas (such as conditionability, causality, and modality), to compare the performance of normal children and those thought to have problems.

A second instance of the limitations of a purely grammatical approach comes when we consider that many children with complex, high-level language impairment ('semantic-pragmatic disorder') evidence word-finding problems of various kinds. The child may not be able to access a particular noun when presented with a picture of an object, and may paraphrase it ('it's a thing where you get water', instead of 'well'). Accessing the appropriate verb may also cause difficulty, as in these extracts:

> *Adult:* What do you think those things are for? (pointing to windmill sails)
> *Child:* For the wind to go round

> *Child:* You know what he's doing
> *Adult:* No
> *Child:* He's doing like this (demonstrates crawling)

If lexical accessing problems are characteristic of a particular group of language-impaired children, it is obvious that to identify and explain them we will need to go outside the confines of grammar, strictly interpreted, and consider initially how normal children develop the skills of appropriate lexical choice. Examples such as the use of 'go' in the first extract have been reported for some normal children by Bowerman (1982). But currently we have very little information on the scope and frequency of these and other lexical errors in the later stages of normal development.

Extensions of our interest outside the confines of grammar will require careful and intensive descriptions of the performance of normal and impaired language-learners in the areas indicated. This will inevitably refine our view of indices of development, and of the characteristics of impairment. It may also lead us towards the building and testing of models to address the issue of the processes underlying normal and abnormal learning and use.

REFERENCES

Benedict, H. (1979) 'Early lexical development: comprehension and production.' *Journal of Child Language,* **6,** 183–200.
Bishop, D. (1983) *Test for Reception of Grammar.* University of Newcastle: Department of Speech.
Bowerman, M. (1982) 'Reorganisational processes in lexical and syntactic development'. *In:* Wanner, E., Gleitman, L. (Eds.) *Language Acquisition: The State of The Art.* Cambridge: Cambridge University Press.
Bridges, A. (1980) 'SVO comprehension strategies reconsidered: the evidence of individual patterns of response.' *Journal of Child Language,* **7,** 89–104.
Butler, S. (1980) 'The tum phenomenon.' *Journal of Child Language,* **7,** 428–9
Chapman, R. (1978) 'Comprehension strategies in children.' *In:* Kavanaugh, J., Strange, W. (Eds.) *Speech and Language in the Laboratory, School and Clinic.* Cambridge, Mass.: MIT Press.
Chomsky, N. (1965) *Aspects of the Theory of Syntax.* Cambridge, Mass.: MIT Press.
Crystal, D. (1974) 'Review of R. Brown: *A First Language. Journal of Child Language,* **1,** 289–307.
—— (1986) 'Prosodic development.' *In:* Fletcher, P., Garman, M. (Eds.) *Language Acquisition: Studies in First Language Development* Cambridge. Cambridge University Press.
—— Fletcher, P., Garman, M. (1981) *The Grammatical Analysis of Language Disability.* London: Edward Arnold.
Dodd, B. (1972) 'Comparison of babbling patterns in normal and Down-Syndrome infants.' *Journal of Mental Deficiency Research,* **16,** 35–40.
Ferguson, C. (1976) 'Learning to pronounce: the earliest stages of phonological development in the child.' *Papers and Reports on Child Language Development,* **11,** 1–27. Stanford University: Department of Linguistics.
Fletcher, P. (1985) *A Child's Learning of English.* Oxford: Basil Blackwell.
—— (1986) 'Grammar and "semantic-pragmatic" disorders.' *Paper presented at the ICAA Conference on Semantic-pragmatic Disorders, Dawn House, Mach.*
—— Peters, J. (1984) 'Characterising language-impairment in children: an exploratory study.' *Language Testing,* **1,** 33–49.
Garman, M. (1981) 'Microprofile of Stage I.' *In:* Crystal, D. (Ed.) *Working with LARSP.* London: Edward Arnold.
Gleitman, L., Newport, E., Gleitman, H. (1984) 'The current status of the motherese hypothesis.' *Journal of Child Language,* **11,** 43–79.
Halliday, M. A. K. (1975) *Learning How to Mean: Exploration in the Development of Language.* London: Edward Arnold.
Ingram, D. (1986) 'Phonological development: production.' *In:* Fletcher, P., Garman, M. (Eds.) *Language Acquisition: Studies in First Language Development.* Cambridge: Cambridge University Press.
Lightfoot, D. (1982) *The Language Lottery: Towards a Biology of Grammars.* Cambridge, Mass.: MIT Press.
Locke, J. (1983) *Phonological Acquisition and Change.* New York: Academic Press.
—— (1986) 'Speech perception and the emergent lexicon.' *In:* Fletcher, P., Garman, M. (Eds.) *Language Acquisition: Studies in First Language Development. 2nd edn.* Cambridge: Cambridge University Press.
Macken, M., Barton, D. (1980) 'The acquisition of the voicing contrast in English: a study of voice onset time in word-initial stop consonants.' *Journal of Child Language,* **7,** 41–74.
Menyuk, P., Menn, L., Silber, R. (1986) 'Early strategies for the perception and production of words and sounds.' *In:* Fletcher, P., Garman, M. (Eds.) *Language Acquisition: Studies in First Language Development. 2nd edn.* Cambridge: Cambridge University Press.
Miller, J., Chapman, R. (1981) 'The relation between age and mean length of utterance.' *Journal of Speech & Hearing Research,* **24,** 154–161.
—— Yoder, D. E. (1985) *Miller-Yoder Test of Grammatical Comprehension.* Baltimore: University

Park Press.

Priestley, T. (1980) 'Homonymy in child phonology.' *Journal of Child Language, 7*, 413–427.

Rescorla, L. (1980) 'Overextension in early language development.' *Journal of Child Language, 7*, 321–336.

Shatz, M. (1978) 'Children's comprehension of their mothers' question directives.' *Journal of Child Language, 5*, 39–46.

Shipley, E. F., Smith, C. S., Gleitman, L. R. (1969) 'A study in the acquisition of language: free responses to commands.' *Language, 45*, 322–343.

Smith, B. L., Oller, D. K. (1981) 'A comparative study of pre-meaningful vocalisations produced by normally developing and Down's Syndrome infants.' *Journal of Speech and Hearing Disorders, 46*, 46–51.

Snow, C. (1977) 'The development of conversation between mothers and babies.' *Journal of Child Language, 4*, 1–22.

—— (1986) 'Conversations with children.' *In:* Fletcher, P., Garman, M. (Eds.) *Language Acquisition: Studies in First Language Development (2nd Edn.)* Cambridge: Cambridge University Press.

Stark, R. E. (1978) 'Prespeech segmental feature development comprehension strategies in children.' *In:* Kavanaugh, J., Strange, W. (Eds.) *Speech and Language in the Laboratory, School and Clinic.* Cambridge, Mass.: MIT Press.

Weist, R. (1986) 'Tense and aspect.' *In:* Fletcher, P., Garman, M. (Eds.) *Language Acquisition: Studies in First Language Development.* Cambridge: Cambridge University Press.

6
THE CONVERSATIONAL REQUIREMENTS FOR LANGUAGE LEARNING

Gordon Wells and Mary Gutfreund

It is no longer controversial to assert that language is learned through participation in conversations with more mature members of the language community. There is now a general consensus that the primary function of language is communicative: to enable members of a social group to collaborate in the construction of shared meanings as a means of achieving various purposes which transcend the purely linguistic. Control of the language code, in other words, provides one of the major resources that adults draw upon in interacting with each other. And it is by being included in such conversations that the young child gradually comes to master the way in which the code is organised, and learns to use it to participate in interaction more fully and effectively.

However, although the establishment of the essential nature of conversational experience for language learning is certainly helpful in defining the framework within which to pose questions about how that learning takes place, it does not in itself provide any answers. For example, it does not tell us how far children are autonomous in constructing their linguistic repertoire, and how far they are influenced by the specific characteristics of their linguistic experience. For this reason, it also says little about what kinds of conversational interventions are most likely to benefit those whose progress is impeded by various handicaps.

To address this issue, we have used data drawn from the British Language Development Study, a longitudinal research programme in which a representative sample of 128 normal children were regularly observed at home over the age-range 15 to 60 months. Samples of entirely naturalistic conversation were obtained at each observation by means of a radio-microphone, controlled by a preset timing device; no observer was present during the recording, but contextual information was obtained the same evening by replaying the tape to the parents and asking them to recall in detail the setting, activity and participants in each recorded conversational sample (Wells 1981, 1985).

Following transcription, all the child's utterances in each recording were coded according to a comprehensive scheme of linguistic analysis (Wells 1975), on the basis of which it has been possible to establish developmental trends in the emergence of options within the various pragmatic, semantic and syntactic subsystems. These constitute a speaker's linguistic repertoire (together with the phonological subsystems, which were not investigated). Certain aspects of the speech addressed to the children were also investigated; and for a subsample of the children, a study was made of the relationship between characteristics of the children's conversational experience at one specific stage of development and their progress in language learning over the subsequent nine months. From these (admittedly somewhat slender) sources of evidence, we shall try to give a more specific account of how children learn from their experience of conversational interaction.

The child's construction of language

One of the most significant findings of the study is the extent to which the sequence of development is constant, irrespective of the child's sex, position in family and social background. Despite quite wide variation in the amount and quality of their conversational experience, our sample of British-born children seemed to follow a common path in acquiring the basic resources of English. Even within individual subsystems, such as the auxiliary verbs or the structural options in the noun phrase, items regularly emerged in the same order. This was equally true when items from different subsystems were compared (Wells 1985). The similarity is so great, that it may be able to form the basis of an instrument for the assessment of language development (Satterly *et al.* 1984).

There was not perfect unanimity in every point of detail, of course. When relatively small samples of naturally occurring speech are recorded at three-monthly intervals, the data are inevitably subject to error. It is also possible that the over-all similarity may hide consistent individual differences; but such differences can only be relatively small and are unlikely to lead to any substantial modification to the claim for a common sequence of development.

A common sequence calls for a common explanation: and immediately two apparently contradictory candidates suggest themselves. On the one hand, it could be explained by very substantial similarity in the input that the children receive, where this similarity is conceived in terms of the relative frequency of items. On the other hand, the common sequence could be due largely to intrinsic characteristics of the language to be learned, irrespective of frequency. Note that both these possible explanations assume an essential similarity between children in what they bring to the learning task; both also assume that all children are exposed to a sufficiently representative sample of conversational input to provide the evidence necessary for learning. Where they differ is in putting the emphasis for the determination of the order in which learning takes place, either on the relative frequency of items in the input (which is potentially under the control of people with whom the learner interacts), or on intrinsic characteristics of what has to be learned (for example, the differential complexity of particular items, which is independent of their frequency).

These two candidate explanations were evaluated with respect to the order in which items emerged in four linguistic systems: pronouns, auxiliary verbs, sentence-meaning relations and pragmatic functions (Wells 1985). For each subsystem, rank orders were derived for (i) the relative frequency with which the items occurred in the speech addressed to the children, and (ii) the relative complexity of items in terms of the semantic and syntactic features required for their description. These rank orders were then correlated with the rank orders of emergence of the items within each system.

Correlations between order of emergence and relative complexity were highly significant for all the linguistic systems investigated (r_s = 0.79 to 0.95). Equally high correlations were recorded between order of emergence and relative frequency in the input, but only for three of the systems investigated (r_s = 0.78 to 0.89). The exception was the system of pragmatic functions, where the correlation was only r_s = 0.31 (n.s.). These results were interpreted as providing stronger support for the explanation that the order of emergence is determined by the relative complexity of the items to be learned. However, since complexity and input frequency were themselves significantly correlated for all systems except pragmatic functions, there is a qualification to the above explanation. The relative complexity of items determines the order in which they can be learned; however, where there are two or more items of equal complexity, the order in which they are actually learned is influenced by the relative frequency with which they occur in the input.

If we now return to the question posed earlier, concerning the relative contribution of the child and his environment to the language-learning task, it seems that the most parsimonious explanation is that the 'what' and 'how' of language-learning is the responsibility of the learner. In broad outline, the sequence of learning is determined by an interaction between the relative complexity of items to be learned and what the child brings to the task by way of prior information and strategies for forming and testing hypotheses about the linguistic evidence to which he is exposed. Except in minor details, it appears, the frequency characteristics of the input do not substantially affect the sequence in which learning takes place.

The rôle of the input

This does not mean that the input is of no importance. Indeed, without the evidence provided by the utterances addressed to the child, it is difficult to see how learning could take place at all. What is more, there is a strong tendency (at least in Western cultures) for adults and older children to adjust their speech when talking with language-learners so that it is simpler, better formed, more repetitive and redundant in context than when talking with more mature language-users (Sachs and Devin 1976, Snow 1977). It seems, therefore, that in these cultures the evidence is presented to children in a particularly clear form. Furthermore, in certain respects, it is progressively adjusted to the level of development that the child has reached (Cross 1977). This does not seem to be the case in all cultures, however (Schieffelin 1979), nor even in all subcultural groups within the United States (Heath 1983).

In the present study this is strikingly demonstrated by the frequency data just considered. The rank orders of relative frequency that were used in the correlations with order of emergence were based on total frequencies of items over all observations. However, when frequencies are plotted by increasing age of the children, very clear trends emerge, which show that for those systems that are optional (*i.e.* systems from which a choice need not be made in every utterance, such as auxiliaries) all items start with a very low frequency and then rise fairly sharply to a peak before levelling off or even declining slightly in frequency. What is particularly interesting about these results is that the increases in input-frequency occur a few months before the same items emerge in the children's speech. Group data no doubt hide individual differences, the magnitude of which we are only just beginning to investigate, but in general there seems to be substantial evidence of the kind of 'fine-tuning' in frequency of at least some items, similar to that found by Cross in her study of accelerated developers (1977).

Not all items, however, can initially be used with very low frequency. Every utterance requires that some options be chosen, and in the early stages some occur with very high frequency indeed. Nor are these necessarily the least complex linguistically: for example, the very high incidence of questions to very young children reported by Newport *et al.* (1977). They argue that it is not possible to substantiate the claim that adults deliberately control the frequency of different items in their speech, in an attempt to teach them in the most efficient manner. Anyway this claim is rendered implausible by the implied requirement for constant and careful monitoring of speech, even assuming that adults in general have the necessary knowledge. Nevertheless, despite the force of the arguments against the occurrence of widespread systematic teaching by means of deliberate 'tuning' of frequency, it is still true that, for many items, adult speech does seem to provide an input that is well suited to the language learner's needs.

So what guides adult behaviour if not a deliberate, well-planned teaching strategy? The answer probably lies largely in cues provided by the child himself. As the child begins to show some understanding of a particular item, the adult begins to use it more frequently. After a period during which the child works on the evidence provided by the input to integrate the item into his repertoire, he begins to use it in his own speech. In other words the frequency characteristics of the adult input seem to be accounted for largely by the child's linguistic development, which, in turn, is largely determined by the relative complexity of the items to be learned. Other cues are also provided by the child's physical, social and intellectual development, all of which follow a largely inbuilt sequence.

The one linguistic system examined where this relationship between input frequency, complexity and order of emergence did not hold was that of pragmatic functions; but this result is not incompatible with the above explanation. For many linguistic systems, the adult can match his or her selection of options to the range available to the child. For the system of functions, however, the relationship between the options selected in adjacent moves is one of reciprocity: questions are followed by answers, statements by acknowledgements, requests by compliances or refusals. The frequency with which functional options are selected by adults is thus in part reciprocally determined by the options chosen by the child when he initiates the exchange, and partly constrained by the speech rôles that the adult has to adopt as the child's caretaker. It is not surprising, therefore, that the frequency in the input does not match the order of emergence in this case.

Responsiveness to the child's own behaviour, particularly communicative behaviour, thus seems to be the major determinant of the progressive modification of the input that renders it a well-adjusted source of evidence for the learner. This adds a new significance to the notion of 'learning through interaction'. It is not simply that the child learns by observing and participating in linguistic interaction—though this is certainly important. He also has his task facilitated by the adjustments that adults make in their manner of speaking, in response to the cues provided by the child's own contributions to the interaction. These adjustments which parents make to normal children appear to be largely unconscious.

However, with language-impaired children, adults (therapists, teachers and parents) consciously modify their language input according to the demands of structured programmes designed specifically to teach language (Gillman 1979, 1983; Leeming *et al.* 1979). Many of these programmes are formal and didactic and do not use language for communicating social, control, information, affective or expressive functions as it is with normal children. In some, however (Cooper *et al.* 1978), the adult language is changed in degree, but not in kind: the normal settings and functions of language are maintained, but the pace is deliberately slowed so that the parents can focus on small steps successively.

Variation in rate of learning

So far we have considered only the question of responsibility for the course that learning takes, and found that this is very largely determined by the learner himself. On the evidence from our own and other studies of the sequence of development (Brown 1973), it is difficult to dispute Chomsky's claim that 'our systems of belief are those that the mind, as a biological structure, is designed to construct. We interpret experience as we do because of our special mental design' (1976). However, many writers have taken this claim to imply that the environment plays an insignificant part in learning—including Chomsky himself, although earlier in the paragraph just quoted he adds 'though the data of sense were necessary to evoke and elicit this knowledge'.

By contrast, we see no contradiction in emphasising the very considerable importance of the environment, whilst still accepting the relative autonomy of the learner in constructing his knowledge. First, as already pointed out, without the evidence provided by the environment, in the form of language in use in interaction, there would be no learning. Secondly, we have just considered ways in which the learning task may be facilitated by linguistic input which is responsive to the child's developing ability to process increasingly complex evidence. Next we shall consider additional support for this view which comes from a closer examination of possible reasons for the differences between children in the rate at which their learning progresses.

These differences are very substantial. When the children in our sample of 'normal' children were compared at the age of 3½ years with respect to the level attained on our scale of language development, the range represented by the difference between children scoring 2 SD above and below the mean was equivalent to an age difference of approximately three years. So we tried to find systematic differences in the children's experience which might account for this difference in rate of progress.

Adults have been shown to have a general tendency to adjust their speech when talking to young children. But it would be surprising to find that they all did this equally effectively. Several studies have examined the differential frequency with which certain features occur in the speech addressed to individual children and sought to relate observed differences to differences in the children's rate of progress. Although the results are somewhat equivocal in matters of detail, there is now substantial evidence of a significant relationship, with the greatest consensus being found with respect to pragmatic features, such as the differential frequencies with which particular speech acts occur and in the extent to which adult utterances incorporate previous child contributions (Wells and Robinson 1982).

McDonald and Pien (1982) have suggested that mothers can be broadly distinguished in terms of the relative emphasis they give, in interacting with their children, to the two intentions of controlling their non-verbal behaviour or encouraging their participation in conversation. Olsen-Fulero (1982) has suggested a somewhat similar three-way distinction between conversational, controlling and didactic intentions. Both authors suggest that it is conversations in which the adult seeks to encourage the child's participation in conversation that facilitate his linguistic development.

Our own investigation (Barnes *et al.* 1983) supports the suggestion that adults differ in their relative emphases on different intentions in interaction, but these, we believe, are likely to vary according to context and also according to the children's stage of development. When the children were about two years old, we examined the features of adult speech that were found to be significantly associated with rapid progress in language learning. They were: over-all amount of speech and, in particular, a higher frequency of direct requests to control the child's behaviour, of polar interrogatives and of utterances which extended the topic of the child's preceding contribution. In interpreting these results, we suggest that all these features can encourage the child's active participation in interaction and hence facilitate his linguistic development. Direct requests frequently refer to an action to be performed in the course of a familiar routine: in our own study, a substantial proportion of the direct requests occurred in contexts of joint activity such as baking or doing the housework together.

Thus such requests provide particularly clear evidence of the relationship between utterance and situation. They also provide opportunities for the child with minimal expressive resources to take his turn appropriately in the interaction. Polar interrogatives, requiring only a 'yes' or 'no' in reply, also provide easy slots for the child to fill. However, it was the proportion of extending utterances that was found to be most strongly related to subsequent rate of progress (Wells 1986).

What is interesting about the results of these investigations, and of those reported by Cross (1977, 1978), is that the features of the input that emerge as differentially facilitating are not so much those that concern the formal properties of utterances—their structure and complexity—but rather those which relate to their properties as contributions to interaction. With respect to the former features, it appears, almost all adults modify their speech to suit the developmental level of their child interlocutor.

Learning through interaction
In an attempt to clarify the picture which is beginning to take shape concerning the significance of collaborative interaction, Wells (1985) proposed that there are certain intentions which guide most participants in framing their contributions to conversational exchanges, and that some of these may have particular value in facilitating interaction when one of the participants is still relatively immature.

1. SECURING AND MAINTAINING INTERSUBJECTIVITY OF ATTENTION
The gaining of attention was found to be the major reason given by the mothers reported by Garnica (1977) for a variety of modifications to the prosodic and paralinguistic features of the speech they addressed to their two-year-old child (Trevarthen and Hubley 1978).

2. ENSURING MUTUAL COMPREHENSION
It is always necessary to ensure that conversational partners understand one another. Where there is gross disparity between participants in communicative ability, it is of particular importance. Many studies have reported that adults modify their own speech to make it comprehensible (see above), but fewer have drawn attention to the need for the adult to check that she or he understands the child's meaning intentions. However it seems highly likely that this intention accounts to a large extent for the high frequency of utterances by some adults which expand or reformulate the child's utterance, often with a questioning intonation (Brown *et al.* 1969; Cross 1977, 1978; Wells 1980). Such utterances have the function of restating what the child is believed to have meant and of offering him the opportunity to confirm or reject the proffered interpretation.

3. INCORPORATING SOME ASPECT OF THE CHILD'S PREVIOUS CONVERSATION IN THE ADULT RESPONSE
Extending the topic or some other aspect of the child's utterances—or inviting the child to do so—is one very effective way of ensuring topical continuity across turns, and thus of achieving some degree of conversational coherence. This conversational strategy also helps the child to map the speech signal onto his representation of the situation referred to, since such extending adult utterances are likely to refer to aspects of the situation which are already being attended to by the child and are likely therefore to be of interest to him. High frequencies of extending utterances in the speech of some parents are reported by Cross (1977, 1978), Wells (1980) and Barnes *et al.* (1983).

4. SUSTAINING THE DESIRE TO CONVERSE
This strategy of ensuring that the child wishes to continue the conversation takes many forms, from the provision of the attention, goods and services that the child requests, to the extending of the child's conversational topics that has just been discussed. Several authors have referred to the importance of this aspect of adult speech: Nelson (1973) found an 'accepting' style to be predictive of later progress; Gleason (1977) discussed several types of positive 'feedback'; Kaye and Charney

(1980) described the prevalence of 'turnabouts', utterances that both respond to the child's previous utterance and solicit a further one; and Howe (1981) emphasised the general importance of maintaining the child's motivation to communicate.

5. DIRECT TEACHING

An important distinction has to be made between teaching language and the provision of opportunities for language learning. Several writers have argued that the characteristic speech style that almost all adults adopt when talking to young children is ideally designed to teach language (Snow 1977), although Newport *et al.* (1977) questioned this claim. It might be more appropriate to describe this spontaneously adopted speech style as providing particularly clear evidence from which to learn. On the other hand, where adults deliberately set out to teach (except in the case of vocabulary teaching), their efforts do not usually meet with much success. A particularly striking example of the ineffectiveness of this strategy is cited by McNeill (1970).

The preceding intentions have been suggested as ones that might underlie adult contributions to conversations with young children, independently of the purposes of those conversations and of the contexts in which they occur. It has further been suggested that some of the conversational strategies through which these intentions are realised might be important in facilitating the child's mastery of the skills and resources needed to participate effectively in conversation.

The available evidence certainly supports this claim, although it must be admitted that it is almost entirely correlational in nature. Cross (1978) found that, compared with normally developing children, a sample of accelerated developers received a higher proportion of utterances that corresponded to intentions 2 and 3 above. She hypothesised that 'synergistic sequences', which combined expansions and extensions with repetitions of the children's utterances, were the most powerful facilitating feature in the speech addressed to the accelerated developers. Barnes *et al.* (1983) also found that children who received speech with similar characteristics at the stage when their mean length of utterances was 1.5 morphemes made greater than average progress over the ensuing nine months. Evidence for the facilitating effect of motivation-enhancing feedback is reported by Nelson (1973) and by Howe (1981). Indeed, the findings of Cross and Barnes *et al.* could equally be said to support the importance of this characteristic of adults' conversational style. Direct teaching, on the other hand, has not been shown to be facilitative—at least where it takes the form of correction and modelling of linguistic form. However, if the arguments advanced above for the relative autonomy of the child's mastery of the language system are correct, this is only to be expected.

Two short extracts from the recordings of one child aged about two years illustrate the sort of conversation that we believe is likely to provide the most helpful environmental support for the child's language learning (Wells 1981, 1986). The relevant hypothesised adult intentions are glossed in brackets in the right-hand column.

97

Example 1. Mark (aged 27 months) is standing by the radiator.

Mark	Mother	Gloss
Ot mummy (v)?		
	Hot?	(Checks interpretation)
	Yes that's the radiator	(Confirms; extends; offers specific vocabulary item)
Been? (= burn?)		
Burn?		
	Burn?	(Checks interpretation)
Yeh		
	Yes you know it'll burn don't you?	(Extends; invites confirmation)
Oh!		
Ooh!		
	Take your hand off it	
A man (he can see a man out of the window)		
A man er dig . . down there		
	A man walked down there?	(Checks interpretation)
Yeh		
	Oh yes	(Acknowledges. Note, however, misunderstanding has occurred)
Oh yes		
A man's fire Mummy (v)		
	Mm?	(Requests repetition)
A man's fire		
	Mummy's flower?	(Checks interpretation)
No		
	What?	(Requests repetition)
Mummy (v)		
The man, fire (emphasising individual words)		
	Man's fire?	(Checks interpretation)
Yeh		
	Oh yes the bonfire	(Confirms; offers specific vocabulary item)

Bonfire (imitating)

                   Mm.   (Confirms)

Bonfire
Oh bonfire . .
Bonfire

Example 2. Mark (aged 23 months) is looking at birds in the garden.

Mark	*Mother*	*Gloss*
/ɛð/(= look at that)		
Birds Mummy (v)		
	Mm	(Acknowledges; signals joint attention)
Jubs (= birds)		
	What are they doing?	(Invites Mark to extend)
Jubs breads		
	Oh look	
	They're eating the berries aren't they?	(Extends; invites confirmation)
Yeh		
	That's their food	
	They have berries for dinner	(Extends)
Oh		

It will come as no surprise to learn that Mark progressed more rapidly than average in his language-learning. However, we should be wary of attributing his accelerated development exclusively to his mother's intuitive skill in providing a particularly rich and responsive learning environment. From the evidence of recent research it is becoming clear that there are differences between children in personality, and perhaps also in language-learning style, that lead them to make different uses of their linguistic resources and therefore to provide differential opportunities to their parents to respond in ways that might further facilitate their learning (Wells 1986). If, as Lock (1980) put it, the child is engaged in 'the guided reinvention of language', there is little doubt that some children are also better able than others to guide their parents in the best ways to guide them.

Language-learning by handicapped children
It would be presumptuous of us to offer prescriptions to those who are concerned

with the problems in language-learning experienced by handicapped children. In the first place, the evidence from normal children is still somewhat sketchy and inconclusive; and in the second place, there are many forms of handicap, both single and multiple, each presenting specific problems of which we have no experience. At most, therefore, we can raise a number of issues for consideration.

Perhaps the most fundamental question is how, and to what extent, a handicap affects the strong predisposition of the normal child to construct a lingusitic repertoire on the basis of the evidence obtained through interaction. The difficulties could be of one or more of the following kinds:

(1) A reduction or distortion of the ability to obtain the relevant evidence from the environment.

(2) A limitation, partial or total, on the ability to use whatever resources are available in speech production.

(3) A reduced ability to form and test hypotheses about the organisation of the language system and its use as a resource for communication.

Only in the last case, it seems to us, would there be grounds for believing that the relationship between the learner and his environment differed in kind rather than merely in degree from that of the normal child. If that is the case, it may well be that a totally different style of interaction is called for.

On the other hand, unless there is such a radical difference in the mode of learning, the general arguments developed in this paper concerning the rôle of the environment would still seem to apply. That is to say, the aim of those interacting with the child should still be to facilitate his engagement in interaction, leaving it to him to select from the evidence thus made available that which he is able to assimilate at each stage.

Unfortunately it is our impression that, because of his restricted ability to participate in conversational interaction, the cues that the handicapped child gives to his adult interlocutors often lead them, in turn, to modify their behaviour in ways that are inhibitive rather than facilitative of their further development. Studies of partially hearing children, for example, (Gregory 1983, Wood 1983), have found that the parents' difficulties in communicating with their children lead them to adopt a strongly didactic style, concentrating on eliciting words and phrases that they select, rather than attempting to support and extend their children's attempts to converse with them as best they are able. But this, they argue, is just as counterproductive for these children as it is for those with normal hearing. Indeed it seems that the difficulties in learning to communicate that handicapped children experience may often be further compounded by the distortions in the input that they themselves elicit.

It would seem to us, however, that it is precisely the child who has difficulty in learning to communicate who is most in need of interactional experience in which the adult's contributions are characterised by the intentions described in the previous section: establishing and maintaining intersubjectivity of attention; ensuring mutual comprehension; and creating shared structures of meaning by, whenever possible, incorporating some aspect of the child's contribution in the following adult contribution. These intentions may better be realised if speech alone is supported by gesture and/or sign. If either or both child and adult use such supplemented speech where necessary the interaction becomes more like that experienced by normal children. These strategies seem to be the ones most likely to enhance the child's motivation to communicate: and this, with a tailoring of the form of adult utterances to the child's level of development, is probably the most effective assistance that the child's caretakers can give.

ACKNOWLEDGEMENT

The research reported here has been supported by grants from the SSRC, the Nuffield Foundation, the Boots Charitable Trust, the Spencer Foundation and the DES.

REFERENCES

Barnes, S. B., Gutfreund, M., Satterly, D. J., Wells, C. T. (1983) 'Characteristics of adult speech which predict children's language development.' *Journal of Child Language,* **10,** 65–84.
Brown, R. (1973) *A First Language: The Early Stages.* London: Allen & Unwin.
—— Cazden, C., Bellugi, U. (1969) 'The child's grammar from 1 to 3.' *In:* Hill, J. P. (Ed.) *Minnesota Symposium on Child Psychology, Vol. 2.* Minneapolis: University of Minnesota Press.
Chomsky, N. A. (1976) *Reflections on Language.* London: Temple Smith.
Cooper, J., Moodley, M., Reynell, J. (1978) *Helping Language Development.* London: Edward Arnold.
Cross, T. G. (1977) 'Mother's speech adjustments: the contribution of selected child listener variables.' *In:* Snow, C. E., Ferguson, C. A. (Eds.) *Talking to Children: Language Input and Acquisition* Cambridge: Cambridge University Press.
—— (1978) 'Mother's speech and its association with rate of linguistic development in young children.' *In:* Waterson, N., Snow, C. (Eds.) *The Development of Communication.* Chichester: John Wiley.
Garnica, O. K. (1977) 'Some prosodic and paralinguistic features of speech in young children.' *In:* Snow, C. E., Ferguson, C. A. (Eds.) *Talking to Children: Language Input and Acquisition.* Cambridge: Cambridge University Press.
Gillham, B. (1979) *The First Words Language Programme.'* London: Allen & Unwin.
—— B. (1983) *Two Words Together.* London: Allen & Unwin.
Gleason, J. B. (1977) 'Talking to children: some notes on feedback.' *In:* Snow, C. E., Ferguson, C. A. (Eds.) *Talking to Children: Language Input and Acquisition.* Cambridge: Cambridge University Press.
Gregory, S. (1983) 'Language development in deaf children: delayed or different?' *Paper presented at Child Language Seminar, University of Strathclyde, March 1983.*
Heath, S. B. (1983) *Ways with Words.* Cambridge: Cambridge University Press.
Howe, C. (1981) *Acquiring Language in a Conversational Context.* London: Academic Press.
Kaye, K., Charney, R. (1980) 'How mothers maintain dialogue with two-year olds.' *In:* Olson, D. (Ed.) *The Social Foundations of Language and Thought.* New York: Norton.
Leeming, K., Swann, W., Coupe, J., Mittler, P. (1979) *Teaching Language & Communication to the Mentally Handicapped.* London: Evans/Methuen Educational.
Lock, A. (1980) *The Guided Reinvention of Language.* London: Academic Press.
McDonald, L., Pien, D. (1982) 'Mother conversational behaviour as a function of interactional intent.' *Journal of Child Language,* **9,** 337–358.
McNeill, D. (1970) *The Acquisition of Language: The Study of Developmental Psycholinguistics.* New York: Harper & Row.
Nelson, K. (1973) 'Structure and strategy in learning to talk.' *Monographs of the Society for Research in Child Development,* **38,** nos. 1–2. (Series No. 149.)
Newport, E. L., Gleitman, H., Gleitman, L. R. (1977) 'Mother I'd rather do it myself: some effects and non-effects of maternal speech style.' *In:* Snow, C. E., Ferguson, C. A. (Eds.) *Talking to Children Language: Input and Acquisition.* Cambridge: Cambridge University Press.
Olsen-Fulero, L. (1982) 'Style and stability in mother conversational behaviour: a study of individual differences.' *Journal of Child Language,* **9,** 543–564.
Sachs, J., Devin, J. (1976) 'Young children's use of age-appropriate speech styles in social interaction and role-playing.' *Journal of Child Language,* **3,** 81–98.

Satterly, D. J., Wells, C. G., Gutfreund, M., Barnes, S. B. (1984) *Manual to Accompany the Bristol Scale of Language Development.* University of Bristol School of Education.

Schieffelin, B. B. (1979) 'Getting it together: an ethnographic approach to the study of the development of communicative competence.' *In:* Ochs, E., Schieffelin, B. B. (Eds.) *Developmental Pragmatics.* New York: Academic Press.

Snow, C. E. (1977) 'Mother's speech research: from input to acquisition.' *In:* Snow, C. E., Ferguson, C. A. (Eds.) *Talking to Children: Language Input and Acquisition.* Cambridge: Cambridge University Press.

Trevarthen, C., Hubley, P. (1978) 'Secondary intersubjectivity: confidence, confiding and acts of meaning in the first year.' *In:* Lock, A. (Ed.) *Action Gesture and Symbol: The Emergence of Language.* London: Academic Press.

Wells, C. G. (1975) *Coding Manual for the Description of Child Speech in its Conversational Context. (Revised edition)* University of Bristol School of Education.

Wells, C. G. (1980) 'Adjustments in adult-child conversation: some effects of interaction.' *In:* Giles, H., Robinson, W. P., Smith, P. M. (Eds.) *Language: Social-Psychological Perspectives.* Oxford: Pergamon.

—— (1981) *Learning Through Interaction: The Study of Language Development.* Cambridge: Cambridge University Press.

—— (1985a) *Language Development in the Pre-School Years.* Cambridge: Cambridge University Press *(in press).*

—— (1986) 'Variation in child language' *In:* Fletcher, P. and Garman, M. (Eds.) *Language Acquisition (2nd Edn.).* Cambridge: Cambridge University Press.

—— Robinson, W. P. (1982) 'The role of adult speech in language development.' *In:* Freser, C., Scherer, K. (Eds.) *The Social Psychology of Language.* Cambridge: Cambridge University Press.

Wood, D. (1983) 'Teaching: natural and contrived.' *Child Development Society Newsletter,* **31,** 2–7.

7
ENVIRONMENTAL INFLUENCES ON LANGUAGE DEVELOPMENT

Christine Puckering and Michael Rutter

The influence of environmental factors on children's language development is obvious in two rather different respects. Firstly, the *particular* language that children learn is that of the environment in which they grow up. Thus, no one doubts that it is because of environmental influences that children learn English rather than French if they are brought up in an English speaking home. Secondly, children who are reared in very extreme circumstances of privation such as in isolation in dark cupboards or attics do not learn to speak until they are removed from their isolation (Skuse 1984b). Thus, exposure to some sort of language is necessary for language to develop. However, there has been considerable controversy on most other matters regarding environmental influences on language development. For example, it would seem reasonable to extrapolate from the studies of total isolation to lesser degrees of deprivation so that one might expect that children brought up in homes providing a markedly limited amount of conversational interchange would be impaired in their language development. But in apparent contradiction of this supposition is the finding that children reared by deaf parents are not usually delayed in their language development (Vernon 1974). So just what is necessary for the promotion of language development? In so far as conversational interchange of some kind promotes language growth, what aspects of the language environment are helpful? Do children have to be taught the specifics of grammar, or of vocabulary, or is it enough that they simply hear language about them? These are some of the issues that we consider in this chapter. In doing so it will be necessary to make several distinctions. Firstly, a differentiation is required between influences that lead to a clinically significant language delay and those that are concerned with variations within the normal range. Secondly, (a point that is perhaps related to the first) we need to distinguish between definitely abnormal circumstances and reasonably normal environments that for one reason or another are not optimal for language growth.

Thirdly, we need to ask whether the environments that promote language in a normal child are the same ones that are required to facilitate language development in children with language handicaps of one kind or another. Fourthly, there is the difficult methodological issue of distinguishing between environmental influences that aid intellectual development generally and those that have a specific effect on language *per se*.

Family structure
Birth order and family size
In spite of methodological difficulties, there are many studies demonstrating that
first-born and only children have a slight advantage in intellectual ability and school
achievement (Rutter and Madge 1976). This advantage is most apparent in males
(Douglas *et al.* 1968, Belmont and Marolla 1973), and with respect to verbal
intelligence (Douglas *et al.* 1968); but reading attainment is also affected (Record *et
al.* 1969, Davie *et al.* 1972). The differences are small however (about 3½ IQ points
between first and fifth born children within the same sibship—Record *et al.* 1969).
While the explanation for this ordinal position effect is not known with any
certainty it is likely to reflect the differences in interaction of parents with their first
and later born children. In Davie *et al.*'s (1984) observational study of preschool
children family position had a greater effect than social class on interactions. Only
and eldest children received more adult attention, while youngest children played
and talked with other children and tagged along with older children's games. The
youngest children were about 5 IQ points below first and only children on the
Stanford Binet test, a language rich IQ test, though no formal tests of language were
given. Bradley and Caldwell (1984) similarly reported the highest 'HOME' (Home
Observation for the Measurement of the Environment) scores for only children,
with birth order and overcrowding between them accounting for a large proportion
of the total variance in the child's environment.

Overall family size has also been related to intelligence in a number of studies;
most strongly to verbal intelligence and later reading abilities (Rutter and Madge
1976). This difference is evident in the early school years and holds true even when
social class is held constant. It is influenced by the number of both older and
younger siblings (Douglas 1964, Nisbet and Entwistle 1967, Davie *et al.* 1972) and
by family spacing (Douglas *et al.* 1968).

The growth of language seems to be facilitated by the extent of the child's early
contact with the relatively rich language environment that can be provided by
adults, rather than by interactions with other small children or by the undifferentiated noisiness of a large family (Wachs and Gruen 1982).

Multiple births
The limiting case of close spacing between children is the birth of twins, or larger
sets of children. There is a long history of interest in twins from a social and
psychological point of view and agreement that such children are likely to be
slightly slower than singletons in general (and especially in language) development
(Scottish Council for Research in Education 1953, Zazzo 1960, Koch 1966, Mittler
1969). This disadvantage of about six months in language test scores up to the age
of 11 is not accounted for by family size or structure, environmental factors such as
overcrowding, or socio-economic factors – even though these are related to
intelligence test scores of both twins and singletons (Scottish Council for Research
in Education 1953, Zazzo 1960, Koch 1966, Mittler 1969).

One possible explanation for the slight language deficit of twins might be that
generally they are of lower birth weight than singletons, and suffer more prenatal

and perinatal difficulties. Record *et al.* (1970), however, found that if one twin died at or shortly after birth, the survivor had an IQ at 11 years only marginally below the singletons in the study. Mittler (1971) put the difference between twins and singletons down to undefined postnatal factors, which he calls 'the twin situation'.

Lytton *et al.* (1977) illuminated this twin-situation by naturalistic home observation of twins and singletons with their parents. Their data showed that twins experienced fewer verbal interactions with their parents and less affection from their parents. However, the twins tended to approach parents more and stay in close proximity, perhaps seeking affection, or simply as one aspect of general immaturity. These results held even when mothers' education and perinatal factors are taken into account.

A fascinating, but little researched area of twin language is the occurrence of 'secret language', 'cryptophasia', or 'autonomous speech' (Luria and Yudovitch 1959, Zazzo 1960, Lubbe 1974, Savic 1980). Zazzo (1969) estimated the frequency of cryptophasia at about 40 per cent, and Mittler (1969) suggested a similar figure of 47 per cent, although with an inexplicably high rate in dizygotic twin boys. Luria and Yudovitch (1959) gave a detailed account of speech between a pair of twins in which what was said was understood only by the twins or other children in the family, and not by adults.

Savic (1980) denied the secret nature of the speech and claimed that it was no more than baby talk compounded by articulation difficulties. Baby talk is now recognized as a special 'register' which exists alongside many adult languages and which has common features across cultures. These include particular phonological, grammatical and lexical features (Ferguson 1977). An example in English would be: M: Rebecca go bye-bye now = Go to sleep now, Rebecca.

Savic (1980) argued that reports of autonomous speech were erroneous in describing it as a secret language, because in her detailed study of a very small sample of families with twins the characteristics of the twins' speech took the form of baby talk and was used with other family members as well as with the co-twin. She suggested that this was no more than the idiosyncratic family baby talk that evolves as a transitional form of speech in many families because of the immaturity of the child. Under normal conditions baby talk is gradually supplanted by the mature form, but when twins are thrown together, and when they have a reduced amount of interaction with adults, such talk may be maintained longer than usual. This view was endorsed by Lebrun (1982) who described it as a 'degenerate rendition of the language representing a delay in language acquisition'. However, Mittler (1969) found no difference in test scores on the Illinois Test of Psycholinguistic Abilities between twins with and without cryptophasia, which would seem to run counter to the immature speech hypothesis. It has to be said that there is a lack of data to decide whether or not cryptophasia constitutes more than baby talk. Doubtless that is part of the story but clinical experience suggests that it is only part. There are undoubted cases of twin pairs who, despite adequate language skills, persist in a style of talk between themselves that excludes others. Such talk may share some features with baby talk, but what is remarkable about it is not so much the linguistic features as its exclusiveness to the twin pair and its

105

persistence well beyond the normal phase of baby talk. However, almost certainly this form of cryptophasia is considerably less common than the 40 per cent or so of occurrence reported in some studies of twins. The factors leading to this supposedly private language are not known but possibly they may include unusual shared personality features in the twins, a particularly close twin relationship, the presence of language difficulties, and the relative isolation of the twin pair within a family that is limited in communication and interaction.

Social class

The analysis of the meaning of associations between social class and language development is much complicated by the need to separate genetic and environmental effects, and the parallel need to differentiate effects on language *per se* from effects on cognition more generally. Furthermore, the identification of a social class effect in itself says nothing about mechanisms. Are the effects a consequence of parental intelligence and education, of differing styles of parent-child interaction and communication, of differences in the uses to which language is put, of family size, or of psychosocial stresses and adversity?—to mention but some of the alternatives. Clearly, language development is strongly related to social class (Douglas, 1964, Davie *et al.* 1972), but that observation does not identify the specific aspects of social class that are relevant.

Bernstein (1975) described the differences between working class and middle class children's use of language in terms of what he called 'restricted' and 'elaborated' codes. An elaborated code is one in which the meaning of the communication can be understood without specific foreknowledge of the surroundings and circumstances of the conversation. For example, 'The vase was in the British Museum' is elaborated, while 'We saw it there' is restricted.

Both types of code are useful in different contexts. Thus, restricted codes are used in all social groups to avoid unnecessarily lengthy communications and to emphasize social group cohesion, by 'in'-jokes and by private references that are meaningless to outsiders. Moreover, it is clear that these codes refer to *styles* of language usage and not to language capacities. Working class children can and do use elaborated codes when it is made explicit to them that a formal explanation is needed (Robinson 1965), but they use them less readily than middle class children in the school setting where they are thought to be advantageous. Bernstein's work has stimulated heated controversy, but experimental studies have tended to confirm that there are social differences in language *use*, and these have implications for development (Hawkins 1969). Robinson (1980) criticized Bernstein's theory on the grounds that it was inconsistent and untestable and argued that, while there are socioeconomic class differences in language use, these are not a function of confinement to a restricted code; rather they reflect different interpretations of set tasks. Middle class children are more likely to observe the conventions of 'good' academic performance, and elaborate more fully even when 'telling teachers things they already know', a task often met in the school setting. He ascribed the later lack of success of the working class children in school to the lower expectations of their teachers based on the pupils' use of language. This, he suggested, is perceived by the children and becomes self-fulfilling via reduced self-esteem and disillusioned antagonism to the school and academic values.

Robinson's hypothesized mechanisms are plausible but they are even less tested than Bernstein's theory. However, it should be emphasized that there are at least four separate issues involved here. First, there is the basic question of whether or not there are social class-related differences in patterns of language usage. The evidence is consistent in showing that such differences do indeed exist, although the extent to which they are manifest varies markedly according to language context and task demands. Second, there is the concern regarding the meaning of such differences. While Bernstein specifically rejected the notion that the social class differences in *use* of language reflected an underlying deficit in language competence (Gahagan and Gahagan 1970) his work has too often been taken to imply just that. In confirmation of Bernstein's view, Tizard *et al.* (1983) demonstrated vividly that working class nursery school girls use little complex language in conversation with teachers in spite of such use at home. 'Complex language' was defined in terms of categories such as comparisons, explanations, reminiscences and future plans. Their very limited use of complex language in school however was not a reflection of inability, as all the girls talked more and with more complexity with their mothers at home. It is noteworthy that this home-school difference in language usage was less evident in children from more privileged backgrounds. Middle class girls were somewhat more reticent in their communication at school, but the discrepancy between home and school was not so great as for working class girls. We may conclude that the main social class effect seen in children's language is a matter of patterns of usage, rather than basic language skills. Nevertheless, the same data do show some differences between social classes in language competence.

The third issue concerns the origins of the class-related differences in language. Until relatively recently there was a general assumption that working class homes provided a less 'stimulating' linguistic environment than that in middle class families (Bullock Report 1975, Tough 1976). The recent study by Tizard and her colleagues (Tizard *et al.* 1983, Tizard and Hughes 1984) have forced some modification in that assumption. Their observational study showed there was more, and more varied, conversational interchange between parents and their children in working class homes than the same children experienced at nursery schools – although compared with middle class mothers those in the working class used fewer examples of complex language. The findings have been used to infer that, contrary to prior assumptions, working class homes *do* provide a 'stimulating' language environment; furthermore the 'stimulation' that working class children receive at home is superior to what they get at school so that it would be an error to suppose that nursery schools can compensate for language deficiencies at home.

This issue has sufficiently great policy implications to warrant some detailed discussion. Paediatricians often advise that language retarded children from socially disadvantaged homes would benefit from nursery school attendance. Are they wrong to do so? Before that question can be answered, certain further factual matters must be mentioned. First, it is important that the Tizard sample did *not* include the socially disadvantaged families that have given rise to most concern. Single parent and ethnic minority families were excluded and there were very few children from large or indigent families. Communication patterns might be rather different in those groups.

Second, the parent-child conversations at home were deliberately recorded in circumstances when the mothers were relatively unpressured by competing demands on their time. Hence, the findings indicate what happens in optimal circumstances, but not necessarily what happens in the more usual conditions of multiple stresses and pressures. Thus, the results indicate that the mothers are capable of producing complex language and, consequently, that when limitations are found they may derive from psychosocial constraints on the mothers rather than from any maternal incapacity.

Third, it is a general finding from numerous studies in the USA that socially disadvantaged children show cognitive *gains* (albeit not necessarily persisting) when they go to nursery schools (Clarke-Stewart and Fein 1983). Whether or not the same applies to ordinary British nursery schools is uncertain; certainly many of the observed benefits derive from schools of special quality. Nevertheless, if the Tizard findings apply to those children, we are forced to conclude that we must revise our ideas on what constitutes a 'stimulating' environment. If the home environment is linguistically richer, but the children nevertheless make better progress after starting nursery school, then presumably we have focussed on the 'wrong' aspect of the environment. In that connection, it may be important that teachers use more didactic talk for teaching than parents although there is less open-ended exploratory conversation at school. Perhaps children need *both* types of communicative interchange, so that home and school provide complementary environments that meet rather different needs.

With those considerations in mind we need to return to the question of whether nursery schools are beneficial for language impaired children from socially disadvantaged homes. Clearly, the Tizard findings indicate that it would be wrong to expect schools to provide the same language environment as that found in 'good' homes. Equally, they emphasize that we should be wary of assuming that the language that children use outside the home is representative of what they can produce in optimal conditions. Even so, the results of studies of nursery schools suggest that they *may* be beneficial, perhaps especially for children from seriously disadvantaged homes (Clarke-Stewart and Fein 1983). However, such studies also indicate that nursery schools vary greatly in the quality of the environment that they provide. The best are likely to be beneficial, the worst may be deleterious. The implication is that we should know something about the nursery schools that we recommend *and* that we should monitor the progress of individual children in order to determine as best we can whether or not they actually benefit from the experience.

The last issue with respect to the social class differences in language usage is whether or not they *matter* in terms of the children's later development and, if they do, by what mechanism the effects are mediated. Insofar as children learn through talking with others, any communication limitation is likely to impede later learning whether or not the limitation stems from a deficit in language capacity or from a difference in style of usage. Moreover, it is clear that there are substantial social class differences in scholastic attainment. What is not known is whether or not these are a consequence of environmentally induced differences in patterns of language usage.

Bilingualism

Gros-Jean (1982) defined bilingualism as 'the regular use of two or more languages' and proceeded to the conclusion that bilingualism as such has no effect, positive or negative, on the cognitive development of children. Some writers have claimed accelerated development in abstract and analytic capacities (e.g. Peal and Lambert 1962, Ben-Zeev 1977) and even more studies claim to have demonstrated delayed development (e.g. Jones and Stewart 1951). However, it seems likely that the effects of bilingualism may be either positive or negative depending on circumstances (McLaughlin 1984, Paradis and Lebrun 1984).

Inevitably conclusions are constrained by inadequacies in the evidence and by a lack of comparability between studies. Most research is based on small specialized samples, often with cross-sectional rather than longitudinal data. Many of the studies failed to use tests that were fair and well standardized in both languages and/or failed to make allowance for social class differences. A test requiring the use of either language may be unfair to one group, and many general intelligence tests are influenced by language abilities. A series of studies in Wales have shown that the apparent inferiority of bilingual children depends on the type of testing used. Verbal tests, or tests mediated by language do show a deficit, particuarly where there is a premium on speed (Jones 1966). A longitudinal study, the St. Lambert Project, which had the advantage that the children were matched on IQ and other relevant variables before their bilingual experience, showed no intellectual disadvantage on yearly retesting thereafter (Lamber and Tucker 1972). Apparent dissimilarities in these studies may reflect the age and situation when the second language is introduced.

Bilingual or multilingual children may have poorer vocabulary scores in each language, because they have had their experience spread across two or more vocabularies, but as a result they may have greater cognitive flexibility and an ability to conceptualize language in a different way, where the structure of language and the arbitrary assignation of symbol to referent becomes opaque (Feldman and Shen 1971, Ianco-Worral 1972, Ben-Zeev 1977). Although there are a few published references to trilingualism and multilingualism (Murrel 1966, Oksaar 1977, Chamot 1978, Oskaar 1981) none of these address directly the interesting question of whether this metalinguistic awareness of language is of any assistance in learning a third language. Studies of the types of errors made by extra language learners however show that they are often very similar regardless of the first language of the speaker (Romantic, Japanese, Chinese, or Iranian) and are also similar to those of naive first language learners (Hatch 1978, McLaughlin 1984). This suggests that the task to be mastered is similar for first and subsequent language learners, and that previous language learning is of lesser importance either as a help or interference.

The evidence on the effects of age on the acquisition of second language skills is surprisingly sparse and inconclusive (McLaughlin 1984, Paradis and Lebrun 1984). Nevertheless, it is clear that preschoolers do not make more rapid progress than older children during the first year of exposure to a foreign language (Snow and Hoefnagel-Hohle 1978). The greater cognitive skills of adolescents puts them at an initial advantage. On the other hand, it may be that ultimately the linguistic habits acquired after adolescence do not achieve the same degree of automaticity and 'naturalness' as those formed earlier in life.

Some fascinating studies of the language development of individual children have been made by linguists looking at their own children. Burling (1959) described the immersion of his 16-month-old son of English speaking parents into a Garo-speaking community in India where he was cared for by a Garo-speaking nurse, and where he mixed with local children. Very rapidly he began to produce some Garo consonant and vowel sounds not normally heard in English. At 18 months he began to use both Garo and English words separately for the same objects. The hospitalization of his mother was followed by word combinations and inflexions in Garo by two years. Two months later he was away from the Garo Hills though still with a Garo-speaking nurse, and for the first time he seemed to recognize that there were two separate languages, refusing to speak Garo in the presence of non-Garo speakers, and becoming shy when asked questions in Garo in their company. By two years nine months he had completely differentiated the two languages.

Imedadze (1967) described similar progress for her child with Georgian speaking parents but a nurse and grandmother who spoke Russian. At 14 months she had a mixed vocabulary and no grammatical structures, later developing pairs of equivalent words in the two languages. By 21 months she spoke less and less in mixed phrases, and by 27 months she refused to answer a stranger in Russian when with mother and father.

The general picture is that a child of normal or good abilities learning two languages simultaneously may be a little slow to develop each language because of reduced exposure to each, but does so perfectly well, and indeed learns the language structures independently in an order consistent with that of monolingual children, based on the relative complexity of the structures in each particular language. For example Mikes and Vlahovic (1966) described a Serbo–Croatian–Hungarian speaking child who could use locatives (onto, in, under *etc.*) in Hungarian but not in Serbo-Croatian where the noun has to change case to agree with the locative, and undergo a complex transformation expected only of older children.

Children learning a second language after consolidation of the first may be undertaking a somewhat different task (Felix 1978). The naive learner begins by developing a large vocabulary and then juxtaposing words to express a conceptual relationship, thereby 'inventing' his own grammatical relation *e.g.* 'allgone shoe'. The second language learner however brings to the task more cognitive strategies, and an experience of syntax and begins to produce a restricted range of grammatically correct sentences. Nevertheless, it does appear that first and second language acquisition involve essentially similar cognitive strategies in most respects (McLaughlin 1984).

It is clear, however, that the development and maintenance of a second language depends on more than exposure alone. Lambert *et al.* (1958) showed that classes of English speaking kindergarten children spoke French as well as monolinguals after a short 'immersion' programme in school where all teaching was in French. In contrast Ervin-Tripp (1973 *a, b*) showed that Chicano (Spanish-speaking) children did not succeed in the English speaking schools. She put their relative failure down to competition from native English speakers, in which they were sure to be beaten in the early stages, and the social expectations and blame for failure from the dominant culture. Similarly she demonstrated (Ervin-Tripp 1967) that the fluency of Japanese war-brides in America was dependent on their attitudes to and desire to merge with the American culture. Social support and approval is required for the maintenance of two languages, though even when one is apparently lost it can be relearned more easily. Speech markers may also carry information about social identity and therefore be espoused or rejected (Ervin-Tripp 1973 *a, b*).

While the evidence is incomplete on the factors that influence the outcome of early bilingualism, certain tentative conclusions may be drawn (Paradis and Lebrun 1984). Firstly, a positive attitude towards each of the languages to be mastered appears to be important for bilingual proficiency; difficulties are more likely when one of the languages is subject to discriminatory attitudes (either personal or cultural). Secondly, active parental support for bilingualism is highly influential. Thirdly, probably it is crucial for the children to have the opportunity to use both languages actively in conversation to express ideas and intentions. On the other hand, it appears advisable to keep the two languages as distinct as possible. Given these favourable circumstances, a bilingual upbringing is most unlikely to be disadvantageous and may well carry advantages with respect to cognitive and linguistic flexibility. Probably, such positive effects (when they occur) derive from the initial cognitive tasks required to understand and produce a second language, rather than from proficiency in two languages as such (Diaz 1985). On the whole, when there are ill-effects they stem, *not* from the fact of having to learn two languages simultaneously (which normal children manage perfectly well), but rather from the negative social set associated with the particular bilingual combination or from the lack of adequate language learning opportunities.

It seems that children from a wide range of backgrounds and with all levels of intelligence within the normal range can cope well with the learning of two languages simultaneously. However, does the same apply to children with language disabilities? The findings are limited but it appears that children showing a marked first language delay are likely to have particular difficulty managing the acquisition of two languages simultaneously (see chapters by Rondal and Triley in Paradis and Lebrun 1984). If the culture as a whole requires bilingualism, persistence with both languages may be justified (given appropriate remedial help); if, however, mastery of two languages is not essential it may be advisable for the family to use only one language with children who experience serious problems in language acquisition. Painstaking assessment in both languages is essential for the language disabled child in a bilingual environment (Langdon 1983); nevertheless the types of language errors in the one language tend to be paralleled by those in the second. The relative strengths and weaknesses of the two languages should lead to a remedial programme which may involve general remedial education, special speech and language therapy, and in some cases teaching of English as a second language.

Extreme isolation and deprivation

Mythical and historical accounts of children raised in isolation from normal human contact, sometimes even by wild animals, probably begin with the twin founders of the city of Rome, Romulus and Remus. According to legend, they were raised by a she-wolf. Thereafter the literature is peppered with accounts of such children. Accounts often appear in waves, suggesting the possibility that some of the more fantastic versions owe more to imagination than science (Malson 1972). The first well documented case is the Wild Boy of Aveyron (Itard 1801) who was found living entirely wild on acorns and roots in 1798 at the age of about 11 years. Itard undertook to educate the boy to prove that human intelligence is constructed on the basis of experience and education. Victor did indeed slowly learn to understand simple language and to recognize written words, but his vocal speech and understanding remained very limited.

Skuse (1984 *a*, *b*) provided a well documented summary of nine children raised in conditions of extreme social deprivation for periods from 2½ to 12 years. Their horrific experience included grossly impoverished environments and sometimes malnourishment, neglect, physical restraint, and physical abuse. To this series Clarke (1984) has added another recent example. At discovery the children ranged in age from 2½ to 13½ years and all showed little comprehension or expressive language, and gross retardation in other cognitive areas.

In chronological order, the first modern case of such severe deprivation is that of Anna (Davis 1940, 1947) who was found at the age of five wedged into a tilted chair in a storeroom with her hands tied above her head. She had been there since babyhood, malnourished and unable to talk or move. At first she was believed to be deaf and possibly blind but on removal to a children's home she began to develop visual attention, and colour preferences, and to emerge from her severe withdrawal. In spite of moving to a foster home Anna remained grossly deficient in language and cognitive skills up to her death at 10 years.

At about the same time, a 6½-year-old girl was found living shut away with her deaf-mute mother (Mason 1942, Davis 1947). She was withdrawn and fearful of strangers. Isabelle and her mother were removed from their enforced seclusion and by the age of eight Isabelle was reported to have age appropriate skills and language. It is interesting to note that although she lived in an impoverished environment she had the company of her deaf-mute mother, and indeed had some understanding and use of signs, though not of spoken language, when discovered.

In 1972 Koluchova reported the discovery at the age of seven of twin boys whose mother had died shortly after their birth. They had been raised by their stepmother who kept them isolated in a small unheated cupboard. They slept on the floor and were often beaten. When discovered they were malnourished, and suffering from rickets. After removal from this inhuman environment and some time in a foster home, the boys developed good relationships with other people and progressed to a level of language and non-verbal competence consistent with their age (Koluchova 1976). It is again noteworthy that the twins had always had the advantage of each other's company although deprived of mature human verbal communication.

The most prolonged period of deprivation was experienced by Genie (Curtiss 1977) who was not discovered until she was nearly 14. She had spent 12 years confined either to an infant's potty chair or a strait-jacket-like sleeping bag, and had been beaten for making any noise. Her social contacts were with her father and brother who only made dog-like noises in her earshot. She neither spoke nor understood language, and was unable to walk. She was incontinent of urine and faeces, and spat copiously. Although she was alert and eager for human contact and was given intensive individual attention Genie remained retarded in non-verbal skills and grossly handicapped in both understanding and using language. Curtiss produces evidence that she had failed to demonstrate the left cerebral hemsiphere specialization in language usual in right handed individuals, but did not exclude the possibility of cortical anomalies as a cause.

Alice and Beth (Douglas and Sutton 1978) were discovered at five years of age; they were lacking in intelligible speech although they understood some simple language. They had been brought up by a depressed and isolated mother in conditions of extreme environmental impoverishment although they were not malnourished. They appeared to be able to communicate with each other but were unintelligible to other people in spite of a keen social interaction and friendly interest. With placement in a nursery group and intervention they were both within normal limits on language and intellectual achievement by 6½.

Mary and Louise (Skuse 1984a) were found at 2½ and 3½ years respectively living with their mentally handicapped and functionally mute psychiatrically disturbed mother who kept them tied to the bed with leashes. The two girls behaved like little animals, sniffing and grunting at strangers. After placement in a nursery group and children's home Louise began to develop socially, emotionally and intellectually – eventually achieving age appropriate language. Mary was initially more withdrawn, and made poorer progress socially and in language though her non-verbal skills were age appropriate. She had congenital anomalies (including microcephaly); probably these were responsible for her poor development.

Of the nine cases with sufficiently full information, three (Anna, Genie and Mary) remained severely handicapped in language skills. Of these only Mary had non-verbal abilities in the normal range. Mary is known to have had organic abnormalities in addition to her depriving experiences and Genie, too, may well have had biological impairment.

The remaining six children gained language skills at or approaching their chronological age. Isabelle, the Koluchova twins, and the Douglas and Sutton twins

(Alice and Beth), had all had the benefit of some social interaction with a deaf mute mother (Isabelle) or their co-twin which might have mitigated the direst of their deprivations. Both sets of twins also had fairly normal experiences of language and social experience in their first year before experiencing more profound deprivation. However Isabelle attained reasonable language without this early experience, and Genie failed to make normal language gains although she too had about 20 months in a relatively normal environment, so that the stimulation in the first year does not seem to be the only critical variable to be considered.

Two findings stand out from those detailed case reports. Firstly, it is clear that severe environmental privation can lead to devastating cognitive and language impairment; many of these grossly isolated children were without useful language and functioned in the severely retarded range at the time they were rescued. Secondly, in most cases there was almost complete (or at least very substantial) recovery when the children were placed in a normal environment. It is a point of great clinical importance that in all cases major language and cognitive gains were already obvious within a few months after restoration to a normal environment. Often it was much longer (up to several years) before the children had 'caught up' to age appropriate levels. Nevertheless, substantial improvements were evident very early. It seems probable that if such gains do not occur within a matter of months after rescue there must be doubt as to whether the language delay was solely due to social isolation.

Three further issues, however, lack adequate resolution. The first question is what is different about the few children who do not recover after rescue. It appears that at least part of the explanation is that some suffered from an additional biological handicap. Whether or not unusually severe social isolation can on its own lead to a permanent irreversible language handicap is not known. The possibility cannot be ruled out but it seems unlikely that this is other than a rare occurrence. Perhaps one important consideration in that connection is that, with the partial exception of Genie, the children either started to improve rapidly or they did not recover language at all. There is no indication of a *gradient* of severity with respect to recovery.

The second question is whether the degree of recovery is influenced by either protective features during the period of isolation or by special remedial measures after removal from the isolation. It seems possible that both features may be operative but we lack data on their importance. The third question is whether or not there is a critical period beyond which language cannot develop for the first time. If there is such a period it must extend over many years in early and middle childhood. Nevertheless there is some suggestion that language acquisition must occur in the first 12 years if it is to proceed normally (Lenneberg 1967, Curtiss 1981, Rutter 1981).

Hearing children of deaf parents

It might be thought that hearing children of deaf parents would be particularly prone to speech delay because of the lack of language input in the early years. Parents with hearing loss may have poor articulation particularly of consonants and

114

high frequency sounds, and undeveloped grammatical structures (for example plurals or past and future tenses). Where sign language is used there is no means of expressing tense of the verb. These factors mean that children of deaf parents experience a distorted and limited language environment. Nevertheless, both Lenneberg (1967) and Vernon (1974) reported that language development is not delayed in this group, but that the child becomes 'bilingual' in speech and sign language.

Some case reports of language and communication studies do exist showing syntactic deficits (Todd 1972, Sachs *et al.* 1981). Two unpublished doctoral dissertations (Brelje 1971, Todd 1972) appear to come down one on each side of the argument and Sachs et al (1981) claimed to show syntactic deficits. Perhaps, more importantly, these case reports suggest that some aspects of language (such as recursions—that is, units that by the logic of the system are derived from themselves) develop with very little in the way of environmental input, whereas others (such as the use of auxiliaries) are quite environmentally sensitive (Sachs *et al.* 1981). Ervin-Tripp (1971) mentioned anecdotally her contact with two hearing children of deaf parents, who at three years were unable to understand or produce speech in spite of prolonged exposure to television. This suggests the critical importance of meaningful and contingent language experience, as opposed to general bombarding with noise. Jones and Quigley (1979), however, showed that two chidlren of profoundly deaf parents learned to use standard English questions in the same order and at the same rate as children raised in a normal speech environment. Both children simultaneously learnt American Sign Language and used the two languages in conjunction when talking to their parents although their parents could hear little of what they said. This study is all the more remarkable considering the poor intelligibility and non-standard forms of grammar used by the parents.

Critchley's study (1967) is equivocal. Of the four children he studied, one child had deviant articulation and poor grammar together with initial reading difficulties; a second child had a lower verbal IQ compared with her performance IQ. The remaining two children were reported to have few problems; one of these was a very lively and ambitious boy who entered nursery school at three years.

Schiff and Ventry (1976) studied 34 physically healthy hearing children being reared by deaf parents. Two-thirds (23) showed normal speech and language development, but a third (11) exhibited problems. In one case this consisted of an articulation problem only, but 10 had both expressive and receptive language deficits. Unfortunately, the report did not provide details of the degree of language impairment that was present. Nevertheless, the findings suggest that although most hearing children reared by deaf parents develop normally some do not. Curiously, the language problems were not associated with any difference in the length of time spent with hearing adults; however, they were somewhat more frequent when there was an older sibling with speech problems and when the mother's speech was unintelligible.

The Schiff and Ventry study brings out another point of clinical relevance. In addition to the 34 healthy hearing children mentioned above, there were six children with presumably unsuspected hearing loss and six with other disorders (psychomotor retardation, emotional disturbance and brain damage). The authors noted the difficulty experienced in convincing deaf parents of audiological or speech problems in children who clearly respond to sounds their parents do not hear, and who may have been declared free of problems at birth. Schlesinger and Meadow (1972) enlarged on the psychological as well as practical reasons for this. Deaf parents may look to their hearing child to be a helper and guide to them, and be reluctant to admit the possibility of the child too having problems. Fant and Schuchman (1974) stressed the pressure on hearing children to be interpreters in a variety of situations that are beyond the usual experience of a child; this may constitute a problem or be a spur to maturity.

Although some writers have concluded that hearing children of deaf parents have few or no speech and language problems (Lenneberg 1967, Vernon 1974) this seems to be an over-optimistic estimation. These children appear more likely to have hearing loss themselves, and also to be at a somewhat greater risk for articulation and grammar problems than a normal group, although there are unknown protective factors that allow many children to escape unscathed. One of these may be average or better IQ, but it is unclear how others may contribute.

Institutional upbringing

Early studies of institutionalized children found high rates of cognitive and language delay (*e.g.* Burlingham and Freud 1944, Goldfarb 1945) and it came to be thought that rearing away from parents necessarily damaged intellectual development. However, three separate findings clearly indicated that this was an erroneous inference. Firstly, several studies showed that transfer from a poor institution to a better one was followed by important cognitive gains (*e.g.* Garvin and Sachs 1963). Secondly, following improvements in the quality of residential nurseries, cognitive and language delays were no longer characteristic of institution-reared children (Tizard *et al.* 1972, Tizard and Rees 1974). Thirdly, the same studies demonstrated that variations in children's language progress were systematically associated with differences in the qualities of the institutional environment. Thus, it became apparent that it was not separation from parents, or group rearing as such that interfered with language growth; rather it was the particular features of the patterns of care provided that mattered.

Tizard *et al.* (1972) made a careful observational study of 13 well equipped and well staffed long stay residential nurseries. In all the nurseries the children's mean language comprehension scores were at or above that expected for their ages. The finding suggested that the children, most of whom were of lower working class parentage, had actually benefited from the language environment of the institution since their arrival there before the age of 12 months. Tizard stressed that the children were healthy and well cared for, and that the nurseries had very favourable adult-child ratios. Probably, the children received more adult talk than in the average home, where the mother's time is divided among a variety of duties of which child care is only one.

The difference between the average and best nurseries was in the quality of the staff talk. Children's language comprehension was significantly better in nurseries when there was ample informative staff talk and answering of children's questions. Where nurseries allowed staff more autonomy and more responsibility it seemed that the caregivers were more able to engage in play and conversation with the infants (rather than having their duties restricted to caretaking and management); these nurseries tended to promote better language comprehension. No comparable effect was seen in expressive language, and the children were described as rather uncommunicative, even in the best nurseries.

Tizard and Rees (1974) found that these nursery reared children further improved their cognitive development between two and four as they were spoken and read to with increasing frequency, and had more varied experiences like trips to the zoo. Children who returned to their own mothers, and consequently lost the nursery's rich environment of books and toys were actually doing worse than the children who remained in the nursery, although children adopted into good families were doing best of all.

It may be concluded that rearing in a residential nursery need not impede language development provided that there is ample play and conversation with the infants and plenty of activities shared by staff and children.

Parental mental disorder
Numerous studies have demonstrated that the children of parents with mental disorder have an increased risk of psychiatric problems; moreover the evidence suggests that, to an important extent, this risk reflects an environmental effect associated with the family discord and disruption associated with adult mental illness (Rutter and Quinton 1984, Rutter 1987). However, on the whole, the risks to the children seem to be greater with respect to socio-emotional-behavioural functioning than to cognition (Rutter 1985a, b). Nevertheless, there have been various clinical reports of language delay in young children exposed to maternal depression (Richman et al. 1982, Mills et al. 1984) or subjected to abuse or serious neglect (Allen and Oliver 1982). One recent study (Coghill et al. 1986) suggested that maternal depression may be particularly likely to be associated with cognitive impairment if it occurs during the first year of the infant's life—a provocative finding that needs replication. Richman et al. (1982) found that maternal depression when children were aged three years was associated with somewhat lower language and reading scores at seven years, even when mother's intelligence, social class and current depression was taken into account statistically. Mills et al. (1984) showed that depressed mothers tended to make fewer informative comments on their children's current activities; moreover depressed mothers were less likely to elicit a response or acknowledgement from the children. However, this tendency applied only to a subgroup of depressed mothers whose children also showed marked expressive language deficits and behaviour problems. The measures of communication used in these studies of depressed mothers parallel Tizard's 'complex uses' of language (Tizard et al. 1983) and the Dunn and Kendrick's (1980) 'highlighting' measures. All reflect the extent to which mothers 'tune' their conversation to the child's level and interests. The data are too few for

firm conclusions on causal processes. However, it seems that the occurrence of depression may sometimes impair parents' abilities to interact responsively with their children and that this impairment may have adverse consequences for their children's language development. But it is important that this is evident in only some families. We do not know whether the main effect stems from the depression *per se* or rather from the family discord and social disadvantage with which it is so often associated. It would be wrong to assume that parental depression necessarily predisposes to language problems, but when parents are depressed, clinicians should be alert to the need to assess possible effects on family interactions.

Home environment

Controversy has raged over the rôle of the family environment in language development. On the one hand, Skinner (1957) claimed that language is learnt by reinforcement of the child's production of imitated words and phrases; on the other hand Chomsky (1971) postulated an innate inbuilt capacity that enabled children to construct language for themselves given only an exposure to people speaking. Of course neither view is entirely tenable. Clearly, reinforcement constitutes a wholly inadequate explanation for several rather different reasons. To begin with, children acquire language far too rapidly for this process to account for its development (Miller 1964); but also children construct their own meaningful rules of grammar with the result that initially they misconstrue irregular verbs (fighted, comed) – *i.e.* using constructions that they have not heard. In addition, recordings of family conversations show that parents tend to respond to the factual content (ie truth or otherwise) of what their children say, rather than to its grammatical correctness (Brown and Hanlon 1970)[1]. On the other hand, the Chomskian view underplays the extent to which children's language usage is influenced by their experiences. The difficulty concerns the determination of just which aspects of the environment matter for different aspects of language development. Chomsky focused on grammar as the essence of what is special about language. That may well be correct, and certainly there is no evidence that children acquire syntactical capacities as a result of particular teaching techniques. But the practical usage to which such syntactical capacities are put will depend on children's semantic and pragmatic skills and on their ability to use spoken language to express ideas and concepts. These various other aspects of language may be more open to environmental influences.

Numerous studies have shown how adults and older children adjust their style of speaking when talking to a young child – using certain kinds of simplifications, repetitions, special tone qualities and systematic emphases on key words to facilitate the child's understanding (Garnica 1977). It is tempting to suppose that this highly adapted 'motherese' talk actually aids children's language development. However, although indeed it may be useful in fostering children's communication there is no evidence that the variations in the extent to which it is used account for any of the variations between children in the speed with which they learn to talk. It

[1]However, later studies have shown differences in parental responses to grammatical and ungrammatical utterances (Penner, S. G., 1987, *Child Development,* **58,** 376–384).

118

seems most unlikely that this particular form of speaking to children is of crucial importance in language learning.

There are several studies that have shown links between qualitative aspects of children's home environment and their language development; a few investigations have demonstrated that these remain even after controlling for parental social class and for educational level. For example, Bradley and Caldwell (1984) found a correlation of 0.41 between the HOME Inventory (Home Observation for the Measurement of the Environment) and scores on the Illinois Test of Psycho-linguistic Abilities. The key features included variety in daily interactions with the children, appropriate play materials, and maternal responsivity. Wulbert *et al.* (1975) differentiated between language delayed and matched normal preschool children on the basis of their HOME Inventory scores. The findings were spread right across the socio-economic strata suggesting that the mother-child relationship was a more powerful factor than social class in relation to language delay. Similarly Jones (1972) showed that in a sample of older boys (10 to 12 years), matched on non-verbal IQ but discrepant on language ability, the highly verbal boys came from homes that gave more encouragement to talk, had higher academic and vocational aspirations, more materials such as books and games to encourage language, and an investment in verbal facility as important for the child's future.

Wachs and Gruen (1982) and Gottfried and Gottfried (1984) illustrated the heterogeneity of possible environments even within a given social class. Gottfried (1984) showed that for preschool children a variety of parent-child interactions, maternal involvement, and the promotion of exploration and academic behaviour were the most potent positive influences on cognitive and language development in middle class homes. Overcrowding and a dirty, dangerous, or restricted environ-ment were the most potent negative factors when mother's IQ and nursery attend-ance were held constant. Gottfried noted that a noisy and distracting environment with too many sources of stimulation was deleterious to children's cognitive de-velopment. It seems that it is not the sheer quantity of stimulation, but its coherence and relevance that is pertinent for cognitive/language development. Wachs (1984), too, attacked the myth that global early stimulation is what is needed.

Three separate issues arise in the interpretation of these findings. Firstly, there is the question of whether the cross-sectional correlations between how parents talk to their children and the rate of their children's language development (*e.g.* Gross 1977) represent causal effects, and insofar as there are causal influences, who is influencing whom? Or are the communications of both parents and children due to some third factor (such as genetic endowment or broader social circumstances)? There are a variety of statistical techniques that help in deciding which alternative is more likely. For example, longitudinal data, using so-called 'cross-lagged' designs, can determine whether early child language predicts later maternal language better than the converse (*e.g.* Clarke-Stewart 1973, Bradley *et al.* 1979). Unfortunately, there are several statistical hazards in these approaches (Rogosa 1980) and they do not provide an entirely satisfactory solution. An alternative approach to the causal issue lies in the use of experimental manipulations. Thus, it has been found that modelling can enhance language development (Brown et al 1969) and that recasting

e into a new grammatical form can facilitate the development of
and Nelson 1984). These findings show that such manipulations
what they cannot indicate is whether these influences *actually*
nal course of language development. However, the combination
strategy with a naturalistic longitudinal study goes far to resolve
…ions (Bryant 1985). Unfortunately, we lack data from such a
…ategy applied to language development.

Nevertheless, deaf children's learning of gestural communication constitutes a naturalistic approximation to this strategy, as the recent study by Goldin-Meadow and Mylander (1984) shows. They found that deaf children reared by hearing parents developed a gestural communication system that bore some resemblance to early conventional spoken language. The findings that in some respects the parents' use of gesture was impoverished compared with that of their children, and that the children's gestures did not mirror those of their parents, were used to argue that some, but not all, aspects of language are relatively environment-insensitive or resilient. However, the same data indicated that some language features are sensitive to environmental input. Clearly children are active and creative language learners and, equally clearly, language is not primarily learned either by direct imitation or by differential reinforcement. On the other hand, environmental influences do have effects; not mainly in terms of specific teaching or shaping of language elements, but rather on the basis of a broad language or communication model from which the child intuitively draws generalizations (Maratsos, 1983).

The second issue is whether the identifiable environmental influences operate more generally with respect to cognitive development as a whole or, rather, whether they have a specific impact on language development as such. Insofar as the home and parental correlates of children's intelligence are so similar to the correlates of children's language it is evident that many (probably most) of the environmental effects are general rather than specific. Because researchers have not sought to partial out effects on language from those on intelligence, however, we lack knowledge on which is which.

The third query is whether the family features that account for variations within the *normal* range of language development are the same as those that lead to *abnormal* language delay. While it is not possible to give an unambiguous answer to that question, it is apparent that when clinically significant language delay is due to environmental factors it is usually associated with fairly gross environmental deficits or distortions. Of course, it may be that rather lesser degrees of experiential limitations may have important effects in children who already suffer from some intrinsic language problem that renders them more vulnerable.

With these very considerable reservations in mind regarding the uncertainty of our knowledge, some cautious inferences may be drawn. Firstly, probably parents do not consciously set out to teach language to their children; rather they seek to communicate with a 'limited and inattentive listener' (Newport *et al.* 1977). To achieve this end, parents change several aspects of their usual speech; speaking in a higher pitched voice, exaggerating tonal variation, and stressing key words in a sentence (Garnica 1977). This both attracts the child's attention and highlights the main message in the utterance. Speech to young children tends to be repetitive (Gross 1975), restricted in content to the present tense (Snow 1977) and centred on objects already of interest to the child (Collis 1975). The use of well formed short sentences, and an increase in questions and imperatives (Newport *et al.* 1977) may be aimed at increased intelligibility and compliance, but incidentally it presents children with frequent examples of certain grammatical forms. In yes-no questions, the verb auxiliary (as in *'Can* you put the brick in') is in the highly salient initial position, and mothers who use large numbers of yes-no questions tend to have children who learn to use verb auxiliaries earlier. Similarly deixis (pointing out a referent *e.g.* 'There is a ball', 'Here are your giraffes') relates to the development of plural inflexions in nouns.

Self repetition by mothers is very frequent, but it does not directly relate to language growth, though it may increase intelligibility. Repetition of the *child's* utterance, and expansion of the child's utterance correlate with the use by the child of the verb auxiliary. The device of repeating what the child has said in a corrected and expanded form may teach complex grammar (Nelson *et al.* 1973, Gross 1977), or may work more indirectly, by providing reinforcement in the form of expressing an interest in what the child is saying, and a means of checking meaning with the child (Brown 1977). Baker and Nelson (1984) showed experimentally that 'recasting' what the child has just said in a new grammatical form highlights the grammar in an understandable context and can be used to promote the learning of passives, relative clauses, and auxiliaries at an unusually early age.

Evidence suggests, however, that active social interaction, as opposed to any particular aspect of partial speech, promotes language development. Experimental studies demonstrate that early babbling is encouraged and formed by contingent reinforcement, particularly social and vocal stimulation together (Irwin 1960, Routh 1969, Dodd 1972). Nelson (1973) and Clarke-Stewart (1973) confirmed that language development is correlated with maternal interaction and responsiveness; and with the children's outings and contact with additional adults rather than with the grammatical form of speech. Television watching was not an effective facilitator of language, presumably because the stimulation it provides is non-interactive.

Forced imitation or reinforced practice has little effect. For example McNeil (1968) quoted 10 repetitions of a child being prompted to say 'Nobody likes me' after saying 'Nobody don't like me'. Eventually the light dawned and he said 'Nobody don't likes me'. In addition, as previously noted, parents appear to reinforce those sentences that are true rather than those which are grammatically correct but untrue (Brown and Hanlon 1970).

Most aspects of child language, however, are impervious to parental speech style. Children seem to be biased to attend selectively to initial items in utterances and to those items where the referent is immediately obvious to them, and in this way filter input and extract linguistic information in an orderly and patterned way (Slobin 1973, Newport *et al.* 1977). While general attitudinal and environmental factors provide a suitable springboard and reinforcement for language learning, there is little evidence for the usefulness, or even existence, of specific language tuition in the home.

Parental influences on the language of handicapped children

Clinically, there tends to be an assumption that what is beneficial for the language development of normal children will also be beneficial for handicapped children. There has been remarkably little study of whether or not this is in fact the case. Of course, at one level there are almost certain to be parallels. If language normally derives from responsive, reciprocal social interaction between children and other people it would seem probable that the same applies when language development is impaired for some reason. Nevertheless, two considerations raise questions as to whether the parallels are complete. Firstly, if language has failed to develop normally in spite of good environmental conditions, should one assume that the children merely require more of the same? Or does the language delay mean that a more directive teaching approach might be beneficial? Secondly, do the same environmental influences apply when the children's handicaps reflect limitations in their ability to perceive or process normal language input? This issue arises most obviously in the case of deaf children who cannot hear the conversational interchanges that seem to benefit the language development of normal children. Probably it is no accident that some deaf children make better progress reared by deaf than by hearing parents. The inference is that the crucial experience is the communicative interaction and that, if children cannot hear spoken words, gesture and signs may serve as a substitute.

However, broader issues are also involved. Thus, several studies have shown that the parents of deaf children tend to differ in their styles of interaction from the parents of hearing children (Meadow 1980). In particular, they are inclined to be more intrusive and directive with their children. Somewhat comparable findings apply with the parents of autistic children. It is noteworthy that these differences in style apply not only to the parents' but also to other adults' interactions (Gardner 1977). Moreover, the differences also apply within the same family as shown by McDonald-Wikler *et al*.'s (1984) study of mother-child interaction in a family with non-identical triplets of the same sex, two of whom were autistic. The mother was more directive and less responsive, the greater the extent of the child's verbal and social handicap. It appears that the combination of the child's lack of language and his severely limited social responsiveness cause people to be much more directive, controlling and structured in their approaches than they might be otherwise. Similarly, deaf children's limitations induce particular parental styles. Of course, the fact that parents *do* communicate with deaf or with autistic children in particular ways does not necessarily mean that these styles *benefit* the children's language progress. Howlin and Rutter's (1987) analysis of the changes over time in patterns of mother-child interaction in an intervention study with families containing an autistic child casts some light on the matter. With the most severely handicapped autistic children, the gravity of the children's lack of communicative skills meant both that there was little scope for mothers to do other than adopt a directive style, and also that interventions made little difference to the children's progress. However, interventions made some difference with the children who had already made some start with language. The findings suggested (but did not prove) that it was the change in maternal interactions that facilitated the children's language. However, it was not possible to determine just which aspects of maternal communication and interactions were most beneficial. A deliberate focus on and attention to their children's communications (spoken or otherwise) seemed important, and most often a combination of directiveness and responsiveness was needed. The emphasis on structure and intrusiveness (to overcome the children's lack of social responsiveness) certainly meant that the changes could not be described in terms of making interactions more 'normal'. Perhaps unusual handicaps that interfere with normal communicative responsiveness mean that unusual conditions may be most beneficial; however, the data needed to substitute that rather general suggestion are lacking.

Patterns of parent-child interaction with other groups of language delayed children have tended to differ less from those found with normal children, but three tentative conclusions may be drawn (Cunningham *et al.* 1985). First, children with developmental language disorders tend to initiate fewer social interactions with both peers (Siegel *et al.* 1985) and parents (Cunningham *et al.* 1985). This tendency may increase the risk of psychiatric problems (see chapter by Howlin and Rutter) but also it may mean that parents need to be more socially directive than usually necessary. Second, parents tend to modify their interactions more according to their children's behaviour and level of understanding of language, than according to the children's speech production. Third, there is some suggestion that children's language progress may be less when the complexity of parental language is greatly in excess of their children's linguistic comprehension.

Conclusions

It is clear that we have not found all the answers to the questions we posed initially. In spite of enormous progress in psycholinguistics it is still not at all clear how children develop language in such a regular and ordered way. Certain very adverse conditions can retard the development of language, but it is so strongly self-righting, at least in early childhood, that even after gross deprivation it will recover in a more enhancing environment. Within the normal range of environments, rearing in a socially disadvantaged home, being one of a pair of twins, being brought up in a very large family, and having parents who play and talk little with the children may retard language development. Rearing in a family that provides unusually rich and varied interactions and responsive, reciprocal conversation may accelerate it similarly. However, such differences may be of little practical importance if they reflect only variations in *rates* of language acquisition and not the extent to which children achieve eventual *mastery* of language concepts (Robinson 1980). Probably that is the case to a considerable extent but the modest linkages between early language skills and later scholastic achievements provide a warning that the effects may not be wholly free of later significance.

As to the particular environmental features that influence language development, it is clear that we should abandon certain discredited notions. 'Stimulation' is not an appropriate term to describe what is needed; undifferentiated noise is more likely to retard than to accelerate language development. Also talking 'at' children is not what is required. The need is for a responsive, reciprocal interaction and communication with the child rather than any one-way sensory input or bombardment with auditory (or any other kind of) stimuli. It seems that the traditional teaching models also miss the mark. Undoubtedly children learn language from their language environment. However, for the most part, they do not acquire particular linguistic skills as a result of anyone specifically teaching them those skills. Rather language develops in ways that we do not fully understand, as a result of children engaging in varied two-way communicative interchanges with others. That same process probably applies to children with language handicaps but, in some cases, the nature of the handicaps may mean that more directive, intrusive approaches are needed in addition to the general language-enhancing qualities of social interaction.

REFERENCES

Allen, R. E., Oliver J. M. (1982) 'The effects of maltreatment on language development.' *Child Abuse and Neglect,* **6,** 299–305.
Baker, N. D., Nelson, K. E. (1984) 'Recasting and related conversational techniques for triggering syntactic advances by young children.' *First Language,* **5,** 3–22.
Belmont, L., Marolla, F. A. (1973) 'Birth order, family size and intelligence.' *Science,* **182,** 1096–1101.
Ben-Zeev, S. (1977) 'The influence of bilingualism on cognitive strategy and cognitive development.' *Child Development,* **48,** 1009–1018.
Bernstein, B. (1975) *'Class, Codes and Control.' Vol. 3.* London: Routledge.
Bradley, R. H., Caldwell, B. M., Elardo, R. (1979) 'Home environment and cognitive development in the first two years—a cross lagged panel analysis.' *Developmental Psychology,* **15,** 246–250.
—— —— (1984) '174 children: a study of the relationship between home environment and cognitive development during the first 5 years.' *In:* Gottfried, A. W. (Ed.) *Home Environment and Early Cognitive Development.* Orlando: Academic Press.
Brelje, H. W. (1971) 'A study of the relationship between articulation and vocabulary of hearing impaired parents and their normally hearing children.' *Doctoral dissertation.* University of Portland: Oregon.
Brown, R. (1977) 'Introduction.' *In:* Snow, C. E., Ferguson, C. A. (Eds.) *Talking to Children: Language Input and Acquisition.* Cambridge: Cambridge University Press.
—— Cazden, C., Bellugi-Klima, H. (1969) 'The child's grammar from I–III.' *In:* Hill, J. P. (Ed.) *Minnesota Symposium on Child Psychology, Vol. 2.* Minneapolis: University of Minnesota Press.
—— Hanlon, C. (1970) 'Derivational complexity and the order of acquisition in child speech.' *In:* Hayes, J. R. (Ed.) *Cognition and the Development of Language.* New York: John Wiley.
Bryant, P. (1985) 'Parents, children and cognitive development'. *In:* Hinde, R. A., Perret-Clermont, A. N., Stevenson-Hinde, J. (Eds.) *Social Relationships and Cognitive Development.* Oxford: Oxford University Press.
Bullock, A. (Chairman) (1975) *A Language for Life. Report of the Committee of Inquiry of the Department of Education and Science.* London: HMSO.
Burling, R. (1959) 'Language development of a Garo and English speaking child.' *Word,* **15,** 45–68.
Burlingham, D., Freud, A. (1944) *'Infants Without Families.'* New York: International Universities Press.
Chamot, A. U. (1978) 'Grammatical problems in learning English as a third language.' *In:* Hatch, E. M. (Ed.) *Second Language Acquisition: A Book of Readings.* Rowley, Ma. Newbury House.
Chomsky, N. (1971) 'Recent contributions to the theory of innate ideas.' *In:* Searle, J. R. (Ed.) *The Philosophy of Language.* Oxford: Oxford University Press.
Clarke, A. M. (1984) 'Early experience and cognitive development.' *Review of Research in Education,* **II,** 125–160.
Clarke-Stewart, K. A. (1973) 'Interactions between mothers and their young children: characteristics and consequences.' *Monographs of the Society for Research in Child Development,* **38,** nos. 6–7 (Serial no. 153).
—— Fein, G. G. (1983) 'Early childhood programs.' *In:* Haith, M. M., Campos, J. C. (Eds.) *Infancy and Developmental Psychobiology. Vol. 2. Mussen's Handbook of Child Psychology, 4th edn,* New York: John Wiley. pp. 917–999.

Coghill, S. R., Caplan, H. L., Alexander, H., Robson, K. M., Kumar, R. (1986) 'Impact of maternal postnatal depression on the cognitive development of young children.' *British Medical Journal,* **292,** 1165–1167.

Collis, G. (1975) 'The integration of gaze and vocal behaviour in the mother-infant dyad.' *Cited by Newport et al. 1977.*

Critchley, E. (1967) 'Language development of hearing children in a deaf environment.' *Developmental Medicine and Child Neurology.* **9,** 274–280.

Cunningham, C. E., Siegel, L. S., van der Spuy, H. I. J., Clark, M. C. and Bow, S. J. (1985) 'The behavioural and linguistic interactions of specifically language-delayed and normal boys with their mothers.' *Child Development,* **56,** 1389–

Curtiss, S. (1977) *Genie: a Psycholinguistic Study of a Modern Day 'Wild Child'.* London: Academic Press.

—— (1981) 'Dissociations between language and cognition: cases and implications. *Journal of Autism and Developmental Disorders,* **11,** 15–30.

Davie, C. E., Hutt, S. J., Vincent, E., Mason, M. (1984) *The Young Child at Home.* Windsor: NFER-Nelson.

Davie, R., Butler, N., Goldstein, H. (1972) *From Birth to Seven: A Report of the National Child Development Study.* London: Longman.

Davis, K. (1940) 'Extreme social isolation of a child.' *American Journal of Sociology,* **45,** 554–565.

—— (1947) 'Final note on a case of extreme isolation.' *American Journal of Sociology,* **52,** 432–437.

Diaz, R. M. (1985) 'Bilingual cognitive development: addressing three gaps in current research.' *Child Development,* **56,** 1376–1388.

Dodd, B. J. (1972) 'Effects of social and vocal stimulation on infant babbling.' *Developmental Psychology,* **7,** 80–83.

Douglas, J. E., Sutton, A. (1978) 'The development of speech and mental processes in a pair of twins: a case study.' *Journal of Child Psychology and Psychiatry,* **19,** 49–56.

Douglas, J. W. B. (1964) *The Home and the School.* London: MacGibbon & Kee.

—— Ross, J. M., Simpson, H. R. (1968) *'All Our Future: a Longitudinal Study of Secondary Education.'* London: Peter Davies.

Dunn, J., Kendrick, C. (1980) 'Studying temperament and parent child interaction: comparison of interview and direct observation.' *Developmental Medicine and Child Neurology,* **22,** 484–496.

Ervin-Tripp, S. (1967) 'An Issei learns English.' *Journal of Sociological Issues,* **23,** 78–90.

—— (1971) 'An overview of theories of grammatical development.' *In:* Slobin, D. I. (Ed.) *The Ontogenesis of Grammar: A Theoretical Symposium.* New York: Academic Press.

—— (1973a) 'Structure and process in language acquisition.' *In:* Dil, A. S. (Ed.) *Language Acquisition and Communicative Choice.* Stanford: Stanford University Press.

—— (1973b) 'On becoming a bilingual.' *In:* Dil, A. S. (Ed.) *Language Acquisition and Communicative Choice.* Stanford: Stanford University Press.

Fant, L. J., Schuchman, J. S. (1974) 'Experiences of two hearing children of deaf parents.' *In:* Fine, P. J. (Ed.) *Deafness in Infancy and Early Childhood.* Baltimore: Williams & Wilkins.

Feldman, C., Shen, M. (1971) 'Some language related cognitive advantages of bilingual 5 year olds.' *Journal of General Psychology,* **118,** 235–244.

Felix, S. W. (1978) 'Some differences between 1st and 2nd Language Acquisition. *In:* Waterson, N., Snow, C. A. (Eds.) *The Development of Communication.* Chichester: John Wiley.

Ferguson, C. A. (1977) 'Baby talk as a simplified register.' *In:* Snow, C. E., Ferguson, C. A. (Eds.) *Talking to Children: Language Input and Acquisition.* Cambridge: Cambridge University Press.

Gahagan, D. M. and Gahagan, G. A. (1970) *Talk Reform: explanations in language for infant school children.* London: Routledge and Kegan Paul.

Gardner, J. (1977) *Three Aspects of Childhood Autism: Mother-child Interactions, Autonomic Responsivity, and Cognitive Functioning.* Ph.D. Thesis, University of Leicester.

Garnica, O. (1977) 'Some prosodic and paralinguistic features of speech to young children.' *In:* Snow, C., Ferguson, C. A. (Eds.) *Talking to Children: Language Input and Acquisition.* Cambridge: Cambridge University Press.

Garvin, J. B., Sachs, L. S. (1963) 'Growth potential of preschool aged children in care: a positive approach to a negative condition.' *American Journal of Orthopsychiatry,* **33,** 399–408.

Goldfarb, W. (1945) 'Effects of psychological deprivation in infancy and subsequent stimulation.' *American Journal of Psychiatry,* **102,** 18–33.

Goldin-Meadow, S., Mylander, C. (1984) 'Gestural communications in deaf children: the effects and effects of parental input on early language development.' *Monographs of the Society for Research in Child Development,* **49,** Nos. 3–4 (Serial No. 207).

125

Gottfried, A. W. (Ed.) (1984) *Home Environment and Early Cognitive Development.* Orlando: Academic Press.

—— Gottfried, A. E. (1984) 'Home environment and cognitive development in young children of middle socioeconomic status families.' *In:* Gottfried, A. W. (Ed.) *Home Environment and Early Cognitive Development.* Orlando: Academic Press.

Gros Jean, F. (1982) *Life with Two Languages.* Cambridge Mass: Harvard University Press.

Gross, T. G. (1975) 'Some relationships between motherese and linguistic level in accelerated children.' *Papers and Reports on Child Language Development No. 10.* Stanford, California, Stanford University Press.

—— (1977) 'Mothers' speech adjustments: the contributions of selected child listener variables.' *In:* Snow, C. E., Ferguson, C. A. (Eds.) *Talking to Children: Language Input and Acquisition.* Cambridge: Cambridge University Press.

Hatch, E. M. (Ed.) (1978) *Second Language Acquisition: A Book of Readings.* Rowley. Ma. Newbury House.

Hawkins, P. R. (1969) 'Social class, the nominal group and references.' *Language and Speech,* **12,** 125–135.

Howlin, P., Rutter, M. (1987) 'Mothers' speech to autistic children: a preliminary causal analysis.' *Journal of Child Psychology and Psychiatry (in press).*

Ianco-Worral, A. D. (1972) 'Bilingualism and cognitive development.' *Child Development,* **43,** 1390–1400.

Imedadze, N. V. (1967) 'On the psychological nature of child speech formation under condition of exposure to two languages.' *International Journal of Psychology,* **2,** 129–132.

Irwin, O. C. (1960) 'Infant speech: effect of systematic reading of stories.' *Journal of Speech and Hearing Research,* **3,** 187–190.

Itard, J. (1801) 'The Wild Boy of Aveyron.' *In:* Malson, L. (Ed.) *Wolf Children. Translated by* Fawcett, E., White, J. (1972) London: New Left Books.

Jones, M. L., Quigley, S. P. (1979) 'The acquisition of question formation in spoken English and American Sign Language by two hearing children of deaf parents.' *Journal of Speech and Hearing Disabilities,* **44,** 196–208.

Jones, P. A. (1972) 'Home environment and the development of verbal ability.' *Child Development,* **43,** 1081–1086.

Jones, W. R. (1966) *Bilingualism in Welsh Education.* Cardiff: University of Wales Press.

—— Stewart, W. A. (1951) 'Bilingualism and verbal intelligence.' *British Journal of Psychology,* **4,** 3–8.

Koch, H. L. (1966) *Twins and Twin Relations.* Chicago: Chicago University Press.

Koluchova, J. (1972) 'Severe deprivation in twins: a case study.' *Journal of Child Psychology and Psychiatry,* **13,** 107–114.

—— (1976) 'The further development of twins after severe and prolonged deprivation: a second report.' *Journal of Child Psychology and Psychiatry,* **17,** 181–188.

Lambert, W. E., Havelka, J., Crosby, C. (1958) 'The influence of language acquisition contexts on bilingualism.' *Journal of Abnormal and Social Psychology,* **56,** 239–244.

—— Tucker, G. R. (1972) *Bilingual Education of Children: The St. Lambert Experiment.* Rowley, Mass. Newbury House.

Langdon, H. W. (1983) 'Assessment and intervention strategies for the bi-lingual language disordered student.' *Exceptional Children,* **50,** 37–46.

Lebrun, Y. (1982) 'Cryptophasie et retard de langage chez les jumeaux.' *Enfance,* **3,** 101–108.

Lenneberg, E. (1967) *Biological Foundations of Language.* New York: John Wiley.

Lubbe, H. (1974) 'Preliminary report on a study of language acquisition process of a pair of twins.' *VIIIth International Congress of Sociology.* Montreal, August 1974.

Luria, A. R., Yudovitch, E. I. (1959) *Speech and the Development of Mental Processes in the Child.* London: Staples.

Lytton, H., Conway, D., Sauve, R. (1977) 'The impact of twinship on parent-child interaction.' *Journal of Personality and Social Psychology,* **35,** 97–107.

McDonald-Wikler, L., Maynard, D. W., Frankel, R. C., Hammarlund, T. (1984) 'A mother with triplets, two of whom are autistic: a study of mother-child interaction.' *Unpublished paper delivered at the Annual Convention, American Association for Mental Deficiency; Minneapolis, Minnesota, May, 1984.*

McLaughlin, B. (1984) *Second Language Acquisition in Childhood: Vol. 1. Preschool Children.* 2nd edn. Hillsdale, New Jersey. Lawrence Erlbaum.

McNeil, D. (1968) 'Developmental psycho-linguistics.' *In:* Smith, F., Miller, G. A. (Eds.) *The Genesis of Language.* Cambridge Mass.: MIT Press.

126

Malson, L. (1972) *Wolf Children. Translated by:* White, J. London: New Left Books.

Maratsos, M. (1983) 'Some current issues in the study of the acquisition of grammar.' *In:* Flavell, J. H., Markman, E. M. (Eds.) *Mussen's Handbook of Child Psychology, 4th edn. Vol III: Cognitive Development.* New York: John Wiley, 707–786.

Mason, M. K. (1942) 'Learning to speak after six and one half years of silence.' *Journal of Speech and Hearing Disorders,* **7**, 295–304.

Meadow, K. P. (1980) *Deafness and Child Development.* Berkeley: University of California Press.

Mikes, Vlahovic (1966) 'Studies of child language development.' *Quoted in* Ferguson, C. A., Slobin, D. A. (Eds.) (1973) *Studies of Child Language Development.* New York: Holt, Rinehart & Winston.

Miller, G. A. (1964) 'The psycho-linguists.' *Encounter, 5,* **23**, 29–37.

Mills, M., Puckering, C., Pound, A., Cox, A. D. (1984) 'What is it about depressed mothers that influences their children's functioning?' *In:* Stevenson, J. E. (Ed.) *Recent Research in Developmental Psychopathology. Journal of Child Psychology and Psychiatry. (Book Supplement 4).* Oxford: Pergamon Press.

Mittler, P. (1969) *Psycho-linguistic Skills in Four-year-old Twins and Singletons.* Ph.D. thesis. University of London.

—— (1971) *The Study of Twins.* Harmondsworth: Penguin Books.

Murrel, M. (1966) 'Language acquisition in a trilingual environment: notes from a case study.' *Studia Linguistica, 20,* 9–35.

Nelson, K. (1973) 'Structure and strategy in learning to talk.' *Monographs of the Society for Research in Child Development,* **38**. nos. 1–2. (Serial number 149).

—— Carskaddon, G., Bonvillian, J. D. (1973) 'Syntax acquisition: impact of experimental variation in adult verbal interation with the child.' *Child Development,* **44**, 497–504.

Newport, E. L., Glectman, H., Glectman, L. R. (1977) 'Mother, I'd rather do it myself: some effects and non-effects of maternal speech style.' *In:* Snow, C., Ferguson, C. A. (Eds.) *Talking to Children: Language Input and Acquisition.* Cambridge: Cambridge University Press.

Nisbet, J. D., Entwistle, N. J. (1967) 'Intelligence and family size, 1949–1965.' *British Journal of Educational Psychology,* **37**, 188–193.

Oksaar, E. (1977) 'On becoming trilingual: a case study.' *In:* Molony, C., Zobl, H., Stotling, W. (Eds.) *Deutsch in Kontackt mit anderen Sprachen.* Kronberg, Scriptor.

—— (1981) 'Linguistic and pragmatic awareness of monolingual and multilingual children.' *In:* Dale, P. S., Ingram, D. (Eds.) *Child Language: An International Perspective.* Baltimore: University Park Press.

Paradis, M., Lebrun, Y. (Eds.) (1984) *Early Bilingualism and Child Development.* Lisse: Swets & Zeitlinger.

Peal, E., Lambert, W. E. (1962) 'The relation of bilingualism to intelligence.' *Psychological Monographs,* No. 546.

Record, R. G., McKeown, T., Edwards, J. H. (1969) 'The relation of measured intelligence to birth order and maternal age.' *Annals of Human Genetics,* **33**, 61–69.

—— —— (1970) 'An investigation of the differences in measured intelligence between twins and single births.' *Annals of Human Genetics,* **34**, 11–20.

Richman, N., Stevenson, J., Graham, P. J. (1982) *Preschool to School—a Behavioural study.* London: Academic Press.

Robinson, W. P. (1965) 'The elaborated code in working class language.' *Language and Speech,* **8**, 243–252.

—— (1980) 'Language Management.' *In:* Hersov, L. A., Berger, M., Nicol, A. R. (Eds.) *Language and Language Disorders in Childhood.* Oxford: Pergamon.

Rogosa, D. (1980) 'A critique of cross-lagged correlation.' *Psychological Bulletin,* **88**, 245–258.

Routh, D. K. (1969) 'Conditioning of vocal response differentiation in infants.' *Developmental Psychology.* **1**, 219–226.

Rutter, M. (1981) *Maternal Deprivation Reassessed. 2nd edn.* Harmondsworth: Penguin Books.

—— (1985a) 'Family and school influences on behavioural development.' *Journal of Child Psychology and Psychiatry,* **26**, 349–368.

—— (1985b) 'Family and school influences on cognitive development.' *Journal of Child Psychology and Psychiatry,* **26**, 683–704.

—— (1987) 'Parental mental disorder as a psychiatric risk factor'. *In:* Hales, R. E., Frances, A. J. (eds). *American Psychiatric Association's Annual Review, Vol. 6.* Washington, D.C.: American Psychiatric Association.

—— Madge, N. (1976) *Cycles of Disadvantage.* London: Heineman.

127

——— Quinton, D. (1984) 'Parental psychiatric disorder: effects on the children.' *Psychological Medicine,* **14,** 853–880.

Sachs, J., Bard, B. and Johnson, M. L. (1981) 'Language learning with restricted input: case studies of two hearing children of deaf parents.' *Applied Psycholinguistics,* **2** (1), 33–54.

Savic, S. (1980) *How Twins Learn to Talk.* London: Academic Press.

Schiff, N. B., Ventry, I. M. (1976) 'Communication Problems in Hearing Children of Deaf Parents.' *Journal of Speech and Hearing Disorders,* **41,** 348–358.

Schlesinger, H. S., Meadow, K. P. (1972) *Sound and Sign.* Berkeley: University of California Press.

Scottish Council for Research in Education (1953) *Social Implications of the 1947 Scottish Mental Survey.* London: University of London Press.

Siegel, L. S., Cunningham, C. E. van der Spuy, H. I. J. (1985) 'Interactions of language delayed and normal preschool boys with their peers.' *Journal of Child Psychology and Psychiatry,* **26,** 77–83.

Skinner, B. F. (1957) *Verbal Behaviour.* New York, Appleton-Century-Crofts.

Skuse, D. H. (1984*a*) 'Extreme deprivation in early childhood – **I.** Diverse outcome for three siblings from an extraordinary family.' *J. Child Psychol. Psychiat.,* **25,** 523–541.

——— (1984*b*) 'Extreme deprivation in early childhood—**II.** Theoretical issues and a comparative review.' *Journal of Child Psychology and Psychiatry,* **25,** 543–572.

Slobin, D. I. (1973) 'Cognitive prerequisites for the development of grammar.' *In:* Ferguson, C. A., Slobin, D. I. (Eds.) *Studies in Child Language Development.* New York. Holt, Rinehart & Winston.

Snow, C. (1977) 'The development of conversation between mothers and babies.' *Journal of Child Language,* **4,** 1–22.

——— Hoefnagel-Höhle, M. (1978) 'The critical period for language acquisition: evidence for second language learning.' *Child Development,* **49,** 1114–1128.

Tizard, B., Cooperman, O., Joseph, A., Tizard, J. (1972) 'Environmental effects on language development: a study of young children in long stay nurseries.' *Child Development,* **43,** 337–358.

——— Rees, J. (1974) 'A comparison of the effects of adoption, restoration to the natural mother, and continued institutionalization on the cognitive development of 4-year-old children.' *Child Development,* **45,** 92–99.

——— Hughes, M., Carmichael, H., Pinkerton, G. (1983) 'Language deprivation and social class: is verbal deprivation a myth?' *J. Child Psychol. Psychiat.,* **24,** 533–542.

——— ——— (1984) *Young Children Learning: Talking and Thinking at Home and School.* London: Fontana.

Todd, P. H. III (1972) 'From sign language to speech: delayed acquisition of English by a hearing child of deaf parents.' Unpublished Doctoral dissertation. Berkeley: University of California.

Tough, J. (1976) *The Development of Meaning: A Study of Children's Use of Language.* London, Allen & Unwin.

Vernon, M. (1974) 'Effects of parents' deafness on hearing children.' *In:* Fine, P. J. (Ed.) *Deafness in Infancy and Early Childhood.* Baltimore: Williams & Wilkins.

Wachs, T. D., Gruen, G. E. (1982) *Early Experience and Human Development.* New York: Plenum.

——— (1984) 'Proximal experience and early cognitive-intellectual development: the social environment.' *In:* Gottfried, A. W. (Ed.) *Home Environment and Early Cognitive Development.* Orlando: Academic Press.

Wulbert, M., Inglis, S., Kriegsman, E., Mills, B. (1975) 'Language delay and associated mother child interactions.' *Developmental Psychology,* **11,** 61–70.

Zazzo, R. (1960) *Les Jumeaux: Le Couple et la Personne.* **II.** *L'Individuation Psychologique.* Paris: Presses Universitaires de France.

8
THE DEVELOPMENTAL NEUROBIOLOGY OF LANGUAGE

Robert Goodman

This chapter considers some of the connections between brain development and language development. In order to set the scene, the first section provides a brief outline of the main stages of normal brain development. The following section on cerebral lateralisation is about the normal division of labour between the left and right cerebral hemispheres, starting with the situation in a typical adult, then turning to cerebral lateralisation during development, and finally considering the situation in left-handers.

The emphasis of the chapter subsequently shifts from normal development to abnormal development, examining first the possibility that inadequate exposure to language adversely affects the development of language-related parts of the brain. This section asks: is there a sensitive period for language acquisition? Following on from the possible effects of language deprivation on brain development, the following two sections look at possible effects of abnormal brain development on language functions. The first of these two sections addresses three related questions: are developmental language disorders due to delays in brain maturation? Or are they due to atypical patterns of cerebral lateralisation? Or are they due to focal brain abnormalities? Moving on from postulated to definite brain abnormalities, the penultimate section considers recovery from brain damage, starting with some of the relevant general principles, and then examining the widely held notion that brain damage is less disabling when it occurs early in life.

It is easier to pose questions about the connections between brain development and language development than to provide adequate answers. Nevertheless, developmental neurobiology is an expanding research field, and provisional answers are beginning to emerge. Since advances in this area may depend on new technology, the final section of this chapter assesses the potential promise of some of the new brain-imaging modalities.

Normal brain development
When considering embryological development, it is sometimes useful to distinguish between additive and subtractive processes. Additive (or progressive) development can be likened to the production of a motor car or a computer, with a series of parts being added, each in the right place, until the final version is completed. Subtractive (or regressive) development can be likened to the process of sculpting a statue from a block of stone, with bits of stone being chipped away until the finished statue remains. Although embryology has traditionally stressed the rôle of additive development in organogenesis and histogenesis, subtractive processes are

also important. As Glücksman (1951) pointed out, selective cell loss plays a part in the development of practically all biological systems, including the vertebrate CNS. As a first approximation, additive processes largely determine the broad outline of brain organization, while subtractive processes contribute to subsequent fine-tuning (see Cowan *et al.* 1984).

For the sake of simplicity, brain development can be divided into a number of overlapping stages (Ebels 1980, Geschwind and Galaburda 1985).
The principal stages are:

(1) Formation of the neural tube and its derivatives. In the human embryo this process is largely completed by the fifth postconceptual week (O'Rahilly and Gardner 1977). Failure at this stage leads to gross anatomical disorders such as anencephaly or holoprosencephaly.

(2) Cellular proliferation within germinal zones generates neuronal and glial precursors. The cells of the cerebral cortex arise from the subependymal germinal layer surrounding the lateral ventricles. After the completion of the proliferative phase, neuronal losses cannot be made good by additional proliferation. In the case of the human cerebral cortex, the proliferative phase ends before birth.

(3) Cellular migration. In humans, migration from the subependymal germinal layer into the cerebral cortex occurs mainly between the third and eighth foetal month (Geschwind and Galaburda 1985). Generalised failure of migration is rare, leading to severe mental retardation and gross brain malformation, *eg.* lissencephaly (Lemire and Workany 1982). Patchy failure of migration is commoner (Geschwind and Galaburda 1985), producing ectopic collections of neurons, or localised areas of abnormally formed (dysplastic) brain.

(4) Cellular differentiation of post-proliferative cells into specific types of neurons is largely completed by the time of birth.

(5) Further elaboration of axons and dendrites leads to a progressive growth in the number of synapses. In humans, this process occurs after birth as well as before. In the prefrontal cortex, for example, the pyramidal cells may increase their dendritic length tenfold or more in the first six postnatal months (Schadé and van Groenigen 1961). Dendritic development in a particular brain region seems to parallel the development of function (Parmelee and Sigman 1983). (Regional myelinisation is a cruder index of functional maturation but it has the compensatory advantage of being relatively easy to measure.)

(6) Selective elimination of neurons, neuronal processes, and synapses plays an important part in brain development. In most neuronal systems, roughly half of the original neurons die off during a well-defined period that is characteristic of each neuronal population (Cowan *et al.* 1984). This selective cell death may eliminate neurons that have formed erroneous connections, as well as helping to match the size of each neuronal population to the size of its target field. Selective elimination of some of the axon collaterals of an individual neuron can increase the specificity of that neuron's connections (Cowan *et al.* 1984). Fine-tuning by selective loss probably continues throughout childhood. In the human frontal cortex, for example, synaptic density reaches a peak in the second year of life and then progressively declines until late adolescence, presumably as a result of selective loss

(Huttenlocher 1979). In addition to the synapses that physically disappear, other synapses remain in place but become functionally inactive—the so-called *latent synapses* (see Wall 1977).

Stages (1) to (4) occur before birth and appear to be relatively impervious to external environmental influences (Goldman-Rakic *et al.* 1984). By contrast, stages (5) and (6) continue after birth and can potentially be affected by the individual's experiences of the world (van Hof 1981).

Different parts of the brain develop at different rates. For example, dendritic maturation occurs much earlier in the primary visual cortex than in the prefrontal cortex (Schadé and van Groenigen 1961, Takashima *et al.* 1980). Consequently, different neural systems may vary not only in the extent to which they can be fine-tuned by the individual's experiences, but also in the timing of the fine-tuning.

Although the developmental processes described in this section may seem remote from the study of normal and abnormal language acquisition, an understanding of normal brain development is relevant to two of the topics discussed later in this chapter: the possible effect of language deprivation on brain development, and the effects of brain damage on language development.

Cerebral lateralisation

Some general principles

Asymmetries at various levels of the nervous system have been documented in all vertebrate groups (Geschwind and Galaburda 1985). The human cerebral hemispheres provide a particularly striking instance of asymmetrical specialisation, with the left hemisphere specialising in some functions, and the right hemisphere in others (Bradshaw and Nettleton 1983, Springer and Deutsch 1985). Since more is known about hemispheric specialisation in adults than in children, this section begins with some generalisations derived mainly from studies of lateralisation in adults. The section continues with current ideas about cerebral lateralisation in infancy and childhood, and finally turns to left-handedness and atypical patterns of cerebral lateralisation.

The evidence for asymmetrical cerebral lateralisation in humans comes from a variety of studies involving normal and brain-damaged individuals (Bradshaw and Nettleton 1983, Springer and Deutsch 1985). Hemispheric asymmetries in normal individuals have been demonstrated by neuro-anatomical and neuroradiological studies, by EEG and evoked-response studies, and by studies of perceptual asymmetries, mainly involving dichotic listening or tachistoscopic viewing. Patients with unilateral brain lesions are an important source of clinical information about cerebral lateralisation. Additional clinical information has come from studies on two groups of neurosurgical patients: split-brain patients who have undergone surgical division of their major interhemispheric commissures (Bogen 1979); and patients undergoing the intracarotid sodium amytal (Wada) test, which involves the temporary inactivation of first one hemisphere and then the other (Wada and Rasmussen 1960).

Studies of normal and brain-damaged individuals allow a number of generalisations to be made about hemispheric asymmetry. Some of these

131

generalisations are presented below.

The so-called *dominant* hemisphere is the hemisphere that can speak up for itself. Although the term 'dominance' is still commonly used, it places an excessive emphasis on language lateralisation (Kinsbourne and Hiscock 1983). It is now outdated to think of one hemisphere dominating the other; each hemisphere is predominant in some domains. In a typical right-handed adult, for example, the left hemisphere is predominant in language functions, and the right hemisphere is predominant in visuospatial functions (Corballis 1983).

A major skill may involve component subskills that are lateralised in opposite directions. In the case of musical appreciation, for example, the left hemisphere may contribute more to the appreciation of rhythm, while the right hemisphere may contribute more to the appreciation of melody (Gordon 1983). Language skills may also be divided between the two hemispheres, with the left hemisphere specialising in the grammatical and semantic aspects of language, and with the right hemisphere specialising in the production and comprehension of prosody and emotional gesturing (Ross and Mesulam 1979). 'Prosody' refers to the distribution of stress and melodic contour in speech—the way something is said rather than what is said. The same sentence spoken with a different emphasis or with a different tone of voice can convey a subtly or markedly different message. Right hemisphere lesions can selectively impair the production and comprehension of prosody and emotional gesturing (Ross 1981, Weintraub *et al.* 1981). When subskills are lateralised to different hemispheres, co-operation between the hemispheres is clearly of great importance.

Lateral specialisation may be a matter of degree rather than an all-or-nothing phenomenon. Thus, although the left hemisphere is more specialised in the grammatical and semantic aspects of language, the right hemisphere does have some linguistic capabilities even in these domains (Bradshaw and Nettleton 1983, Searleman 1983). These capabilities are vividly demonstrated during a Wada test: although most individuals are unable to speak after their left hemisphere has been anaesthetised, they are usually able to follow verbal instructions, indicating that the unanaesthetised right hemisphere does have some capacity to understand language, even if it cannot express itself in speech.

The degree of lateralisation varies between skills and between people (Bradshaw and Nettleton 1983). In general, receptive language skills are less lateralised than expressive language skills. Language skills also appear to be less strongly lateralised in left-handers than in right-handers.

The hemisphere that is most skilled in some particular function may actively suppress the opposite hemisphere's ability to carry out the same function. Some of the recovery that occurs after a unilateral brain injury may result from the remaining hemisphere escaping from the results of long-term suppression. For example, the eventual return of some speech after a left-hemisphere stroke may be mediated by the intact right hemisphere (Kinsbourne 1971)—an expressive capability that had previously been suppressed, perhaps because the left hemisphere had monopolised the brainstem centres controlling vocalisation.

Cerebral lateralisation during development

Contrary to the traditional view that the two hemispheres are functionally equivalent at birth and only become asymmetrically specialised as childhood progresses, there are now many studies suggesting that the two hemispheres are already asymmetrically specialised by the time of birth. Indeed, Kinsbourne and Hiscock (1983) argued that the degree of hemispheric asymmetry neither increases nor decreases during development, but remains constant across the lifespan. The evidence for early hemispheric asymmetry derives from three main areas: anatomical studies; psychological and neurophysiological studies of normal children; and clinical studies of brain-damaged children.

Anatomically, hemispheric asymmetry has been demonstrated from infancy onwards (Geschwind and Galaburda 1985). Indeed, hemispheric asymmetry is already evident during fetal life. For example, the planum temporale, which is a language-related region of cerebral cortex, is already generally larger on the left at the 29th week of gestation (Wada *et al.* 1975).

Studies of normal infants and children have revealed functional asymmetries from birth onwards (Kinsbourne and Hiscock 1983). Even in premature babies, cortical-evoked responses suggest that the left hemisphere is differentially sensitive to speech sounds (Molfese and Molfese 1980). Dichotic-listening tests produce similar results: from three weeks of age, there are indications of a left-hemisphere advantage for speech sounds (consonant-vowel nonsense syllables), and a right-hemisphere advantage for musical sounds (Entus 1977). Similarly, an EEG study (Gardiner and Walter 1977) of six-month-old infants suggested that the left hemisphere is preferentially activated by speech, and the right hemisphere by music. While this evidence indicates that prelinguistic functions are already lateralised during infancy, other evidence indicates that language itself is clearly lateralised from (or soon after) the time it is first acquired (Kinsbourne and Hiscock 1983). This early lateralisation of language was elegantly demonstrated by the dual-task study of Piazza (1977), in which three- to five-year-old children were asked to tap either their left or right index finger as fast as possible while either humming or reciting a rhyme. In all age groups, concurrent humming disproportionally impaired left-sided tapping, while concurrent speech disproportionally impaired right-sided tapping. The inference was that language was lateralised to the left hemisphere, and that two left-hemisphere tasks (speech and right-sided tapping) were interfering with one another.

Early lateralisation is also demonstrated by clinical studies with brain-damaged children. Recent studies of acquired childhood aphasia suggest that from the time language is first acquired, right-hemisphere lesions are much less likely to produce aphasia than left-hemisphere lesions (Woods and Teuber 1978). Indeed, the incidence of crossed aphasia (*i.e.* aphasia after a right-hemisphere lesion) may be no higher in children than in adults (Woods and Teuber 1978). Kinsbourne and Hiscock (1983) discuss possible reasons why early hemispheric lateralisation was not detected by the older studies of acquired aphasia in childhood. Although the capacity for language recovery is greater after left-sided brain damage sustained during childhood than after comparable damage sustained in later life (see below), this childhood advantage can most plausibly be attributed to the developing brain being better at respecialisation after injury—and not to the developing brain being unspecialised prior to injury, as used to be taught (Kinsbourne and Hiscock 1983).

While damage to the developing left hemisphere is more likely to impair most linguistic functions, there are some hints that damage to the developing right hemisphere may selectively impair prosody. Thus Weintraub and Mesulam (1983) found a possible link between early damage or dysfunction affecting the right hemisphere and a long-term impairment in prosody and emotional gesturing.

Left-handedness and atypical cerebral lateralisation

In most individuals, the left hemisphere typically predominates in language functions and hand-control, while the right hemisphere typically predominates in visuospatial functions. A substantial minority of the general population do not show this typical pattern of cerebral lateralisation. In left-handed individuals, for example, language and hand-control commonly lateralise to opposite hemispheres, while language and visuospatial functions may lateralise to the same hemisphere (see Geschwind and Galaburda 1985). Furthermore, in some individuals, different language skills are lateralised to opposite hemispheres (Rasmussen and Milner 1975).

Left-handedness is common, accounting for roughly 10 per cent of the general population in a variety of cultures (Oldfield 1971, Teng *et al.* 1977, Silverberg *et al.* 1979). As the most visible mark of atypical lateralisation, left-handedness has attracted considerable attention from neurologists and neuropsychologists. Although most left-handers resemble right-handers in having their speech lateralised to the left hemisphere, a substantial minority of left-handers either have their speech lateralised to the right hemsiphere, or have bilateral speech representation (Bradshaw and Nettleton 1983). Whatever the direction of lateralization, left-handers generally show a lesser degree of lateralisation than typical right-handers (Bradshaw and Nettleton 1983).

In order to make sense of some of the theories connecting left-handedness with learning disabilities, it is useful to distinguish between ordinary left-handedness (which is common) and pathological left-handedness (which is rare).

Pathological left-handedness arises when damage to the left hemisphere converts someone who would otherwise have developed into a right-hander into a left-hander instead (Satz 1972). For example, in the extreme case of individuals whose left hemispheres have been extensively and severely damaged before birth, all the individuals become left-handed although about 90 per cent would have become right-handed had they not been brain-damaged.

Ordinary left-handedness is commonly familial. Thus roughly half of the offspring of two left-handed parents are themselves left-handed (Annett 1983). The simplest genetic model of left-handedness is that of McManus (1985), modified from Annett (1978). This model postulates a single gene locus with two alleles, that can be represented R and r. In the general population, R is commoner than r. In the common homozygote (RR), language and handedness always lateralise to the left hemisphere (unless that hemisphere is severely injured). In the rarer homozygote (rr), handedness and language functions are assumed to lateralise independently of one another, with each being equally likely to lateralise to the left or right hemisphere. In the heterozygote (Rr), handedness and language are usually, but not invariably, lateralised to the left hemisphere. If this genetic model is correct, the presence of a balanced polymorphism for right- and left-handedness in a variety of populations suggests a heterozygote advantage (as in the case of the sickle-cell polymorphism).

Is there a sensitive period for language acquisition?

This section considers the possibility that language exposure may affect brain development. It is widely accepted that the development of the brain is influenced not just by the organism's genes, but also by the developing organism's experiences of the world (Gottleib 1983). This sensitivity to experience represents one of the major differences between the brain and a computer: the wiring diagram of the brain can be permanently changed by the information it processes (particularly in the developmental period), while the wiring diagram of a contemporary computer cannot be altered in this way.

The reciprocal relationship between brain development and environmental experience has been most extensively investigated in the case of visual perception. In experimental animals, restricted visual input in early life can affect the development of vision-related parts of the brain, thereby inducing permanent changes in visual acuity, binocular vision, and orientation-sensitivity (Stein and Dawson 1980, van Hof 1981, Parmelee and Sigman 1983). In these instances, the effects of experience on brain development appear to be mediated by the selective loss or inactivation of underused pathways, and possibly by the selective amplification of well-used pathways (van Hof 1981). In human infants too, there seems to be a sensitive period in early postnatal life during which adequate visual input is needed if later visual processing is to be normal (Vaegan and Taylor 1979). Thus, a congenital cataract in one eye can lead to that eye becoming amblyopic and remaining so even if the cataract is eventually removed (Rice and Taylor 1982).

The term *sensitive period* (or *critical period*) refers to the developmental stage when brain organisation is most easily affected by the quality of an individual's experiences. The deleterious effects of environmental deprivation during the sensitive period are either irreversible or relatively difficult to reverse, even when the individual is later exposed to a normal environment. There is no reason to suppose that the sensitive periods for two different sorts of experience (*e.g.* vision and hearing) will necessarily occur at the same developmental stage.

Since early visual deprivation affects the development of vision-related parts of the brain, with long-term effects on visual functioning, it is at least plausible that early linguistic deprivation affects the development of language-related parts of the brain, with long-term effects on linguistic functioning (as suggested by Lenneberg 1967). Although there is no direct evidence, two lines of indirect evidence do suggest that there may indeed be one or more sensitive periods during which temporary language deprivation can lead to persistent verbal deficits.

The first line of evidence comes from follow-up studies of children who had suffered from middle-ear disease in their preschool years. These studies suggest that mild or fluctuating conductive deafness in early childhood may be followed by persistent verbal deficits, including speech impairments, comprehension difficulties, reading problems, and selective impairments in verbal reasoning (Reichman and Healey 1983, Silva *et al.* 1985).

A second line of evidence for a sensitive period for language acquisition comes from a detailed case study (Curtiss 1977) of a severely deprived girl, referred to as Genie. Between the ages of 20 months and 13½ years, Genie was practically continuously confined to a small dark room, where she spent her days tied to a potty chair, and her nights tied into a sleeping bag. She was not spoken to, and she had practically no opportunity to overhear any conversation. She was severely beaten if she made any sound. After being discovered at the age of 13½, Genie went on to acquire some language, though her language development was not normal: her comprehension developed better than her speech; and her vocabulary developed better than her grammar. Although Genie was right-handed, dichotic-listening tests suggested that her language was strongly lateralised to her right hemisphere. Furthermore, Genie's profile of language abilities and deficits resembled that of the right hemisphere of a commissurotomised or hemispherectomised adult (Searleman 1983). Taken together, these results do provide some support for the existence of a prepubertal sensitive period for language acquisition, at least for the left hemisphere. It is not possible, though, to be certain that Genie had not sustained left-hemisphere damage as a result of chronic malnutrition, illness, or beatings (Skuse 1984).

Can developmental language disorders be attributed to brain abnormalities?

The preceding section has considered the possibility that language exposure may affect brain development. This section examines the opposite sort of connection, considering the possibility that brain abnormalities are the cause of developmental language disorders. Although it is true that brain-damaged children are particularly prone to language disorders (see Chapter 9), it does not necessarily follow that all children with developmental language disorders have minimal brain damage. (Consider the logic of: people who have strokes are prone to limp, so anyone who limps must be suffering from a minimal stroke.) At present, the hypothesis that all developmental language disorders have a neurological basis is attractive but unproven.

Neurological explanations of developmental language disorders tend to fall into one of three groups. First, *maturational lag* hypotheses assume that developmental disorders arise from maturational delays in specific brain systems. Second, *atypical lateralisation* hypotheses attribute developmental language disorders to atypical patterns of cerebral lateralisation, including those associated with left-handedness. Third, *focal abnormality* hypotheses attribute developmental language disorders to localised brain abnormalities. These three groups of theories will be considered in turn, though it should be noted that some theories combine elements from two or three groups.

Maturational lag?

Everyday experience teaches us that different children mature at different rates, and that the same child may mature quickly in one area and slowly in another. It is not difficult to imagine that developmental language disorders are just extreme forms of this abnormal variability, resulting from maturational lags in the relevant neural systems. Thus dyslexia has been attributed to delayed maturation of the left hemisphere (Satz and Sparrow 1970). Although this sort of hypothesis is intuitively appealing, the supporting evidence is weak (Kinsbourne and Hiscock 1983). Furthermore, maturational-delay hypotheses have some difficulty explaining why children with developmental language disorders do not necessarily catch up in the end, and why these children often show deviant (and not just delayed) patterns of development (Rutter 1983). Nevertheless, it remains possible that maturational delays do account for at least some developmental language disorders.

Atypical lateralisation?

For half a century, developmental language disorders have been attributed to incomplete or atypical patterns of cerebral lateralisation (Orton 1937, Zangwill 1960, Critchley 1970). The evidence for an association between left-handedness and developmental language disorders is controversial (Kinsbourne and Hiscock 1983). For example, Geschwind and Behan (1984) found stuttering to be almost five times commoner in strongly left-handed individuals than in strongly right-handed individuals, whereas a large epidemiological survey (Andrews and Harris 1964) found no overrepresentation of left-handers among stutterers. Similarly, some studies have found a striking association between left-handedness and developmental reading problems (Geschwind and Behan 1984), while other large studies have shown no significant association (Rutter and Yule 1981). Furthermore, an association between left-handedness and a developmental language disorder would not prove that the atypical pattern of cerebral lateralisation caused the developmental disorder: it would be just as plausible that an underlying brain abnormality caused both the developmental disorder and a high rate of pathological left-handedness.

Stuttering is one instance in which neurological investigations have been used to investigate the rôle of atypical cerebral lateralisation in a developmental language disorder. Jones (1966) described four individuals who had stuttered from early childhood onwards, and who subsequently needed neurosurgery—following a subarachnoid haemorrhage in three adults, and for a cerebral tumour in one 13-year-old. In each case, a preoperative Wada test showed speech to be represented bilaterally (*i.e.* in both hemispheres). In all four cases, the stutter disappeared after neurosurgery, and a repeat Wada test showed that speech control was now lateralised just to the unoperated side. Although these striking findings suggest that stuttering is related to bilateral speech representation, other studies provide little support for this conclusion. Thus in two small series (Andrews *et al.* 1972, Luessenhop *et al.* 1973), Wada tests on six developmental stutterers demonstrated normal lateralisation of speech in each case. For stuttering, as for other developmental language disorders, the rôle of atypical cerebral lateralisation remains uncertain.

Focal abnormalities?

Since the adult pattern of hemispheric specialisation antedates birth (see above), it is plausible that focal congenital abnormalities of the brain could lead to specific problems in acquiring particular skills, in much the same way that focal brain injury in adult life leads to specific losses of particular skills. Some experimental studies have looked for links between developmental language disorders and localised abnormalities of brain structure or function. Two recent reports illustrate the potential relevance of this sort of study.

Galaburda *et al.* (1985) describe four consecutive cases of dyslexia that came to autopsy. In each case, detailed neuropathological examination revealed patchy areas of cortical dysplasia, particularly affecting language-related areas of the left hemisphere.

Lou *et al.* (1984) used emission CT scanning to examine regional cerebral bloodflow in eight children with various sorts of developmental dysphasia. By comparison with controls, the dysphasics were more likely to show hypoperfusion of the regions around the Sylvian fissure, and were less likely to respond to word-naming tasks with the normal pattern of increased bloodflow.

Recovery from brain damage

Severe brain damage can be followed by a striking degree of functional recovery, both in humans and experimental animals (Finger and Stein 1982). Brain-damaged adults can regain lost abilities, and brain-damaged children can acquire abilities that would normally have been localised to the damaged parts of their brains. Although early brain damage is accompanied by an increased rate of language problems (see Chapter 9), language development after early brain damage is often surprisingly normal.

Recovery from brain damage is generally studied by one of two complementary approaches. Outcome studies look at an individual's abilities and deficits at various times after brain injury. Neuronal studies look at the ways in which neurons can form new connections after brain injury. Outcome studies represent a 'black box' approach, while neuronal studies represent a 'wiring diagram' approach. Studies combining these two approaches have been particularly informative.

Functional recovery: some general principles

Functional recovery after brain injury depends on a variety of factors, including the location and extent of the brain damage, and the developmental stage at which the damage occurs. Several general principles can be abstracted from the results of outcome studies (reviewed in Finger and Stein 1982). These principles are relevant to language acquisition (or reacquisition) after brain damage in humans.

Lost abilities can be regained by *restitution*, in which the original strategy for achieving a particular end is fully or partly recovered, or by *substitution*, in which an alternative strategy is used to achieve the same end. For example, if a right-handed individual has a stroke affecting the right side of the body, the ability to write may be regained by recovering right-hand skill (restitution) or by learning to use the left hand instead (substitution). Both restitution and substitution can vary in their degree of adequacy, and restitution is not necessarily better than substitution.

After a focal brain injury, the functions of a damaged region may be taken over by other regions of the brain. It is useful to distinguish between *contralateral* and *ipsilateral* transfer of function. Contralateral (or interhemispheric) transfer is characteristically from a damaged area of one hemisphere to the corresponding area on the other side, *e.g.* from damaged left temporal cortex to intact right temporal cortex. Ipsilateral (or intrahemispheric) transfer is characteristically from a damaged area of brain to an adjoining undamaged area of the same hemisphere, *e.g.* from damaged left precentral cortex to intact left postcentral cortex.

In the case of asymmetrically lateralised abilities, including linguistic abilities, contralateral transfer can lead to substantial functional recovery after unilateral brain damage. In general, the earlier the brain damage occurs, the more complete the restitution. Thus when the left hemsiphere has been extensively damaged *in utero* or during infancy, the individual with an intact right hemisphere can still acquire normal or nearly normal language (Smith and Sugar 1975, Dennis and Whittaker 1977, Woods and Carey 1979). A child whose left hemisphere is injured after infancy is more likely to develop persistent linguistic deficits, though these deficits can be relatively subtle (Woods and Carey 1979). After puberty, the capacity for contralateral transfer is still present in some individuals (see Chapter 9 and Kinsbourne 1971), but is generally less dramatic than after early brain damage. It would seem, then, that as brain development progresses, the right hemisphere generally becomes less able to take over the skills that are normally lateralised to the left hemisphere. Conversely, the left hemisphere becomes progressively less able to take over right-hemisphere functions (Woods 1980). This progressive restriction in the capacity for contralateral transfer used to be attributed to an age-related increase in hemispheric asymmetry. As described above, however, hemispheric asymmetry is prominent in the normal infant as well as in the normal adult. Consequently, the developing brain's greater potential for contralateral transfer seems to be related to a greater capacity for respecialisation after injury, and not to the absence of specialisation prior to injury.

Particularly when brain damage occurs very early in development, the functions of a damaged region may be taken over by an intact region of the same hemisphere. In cats, for example, recovery of pattern sensitivity after damage to the visual cortex depends primarily on the surviving lateral suprasylvian cortex, with much more visual recovery occurring after neonatal brain damage than after comparable adult damage (Spear 1979). In monkeys too, there are some suggestions that very early lesions may lead to successful ipsilateral relocation. For example, bilateral damage to prefrontal cortex causes little or no long-term impairment on delayed-response tasks if the damage occurs *in utero*, whereas comparable damage sustained in infancy or adulthood does result in long-term impairment (Goldman-Rakic *et al.* 1983). Ipsilateral transfer has not yet been shown to play a significant rôle in the preservation of language functions after brain damage.

The degree of recovery after brain injury depends not just on the location, extent and timing of the injury, but also on whether the damage was inflicted over an extended period or all at once. In general, brain damage inflicted in two or more stages is followed by a greater degree of functional restitution than comparable brain damage inflicted in a single stage (Finger and Stein 1978). Although it is not known why sequential lesions are more conducive to a transfer of function, the phenomenon clearly has important implications for elective neurosurgery.

Neuronal responses to brain injury
Although dead neurons cannot be replaced after the prenatal proliferative phase, there is now abundant evidence that surviving neurons can form new synaptic connections in response to brain injury, particularly when the injury occurs early in life. The neuronal responses to brain injury are well reviewed by Finger and Stein (1982). These processes may be involved in language recovery after brain injury.

When an axon is transected, the distal portion dies, but the proximal portion may form growth cones and regenerate new terminals. This *regenerative sprouting* can result in the formation of appropriate new connections close to the site of injury (*e.g.* Kromer *et al.* 1981*a,b*). Successful axonal regeneration over longer distances is probably hampered because brain injury disrupts tissue alignment and vascularisation, and also leads to the production of glial and connective-tissue barriers (Finger and Stein 1982). In some circumstances, regenerative sprouting can be promoted by *neurotrophic* factors, such as nerve growth factor (NGF) (Björklund and Stenevi 1972).

When brain injury eliminates some of the axons innervating an area, the remaining axons may produce collateral sprouts that reoccupy the vacated synaptic sites. This *collateral sprouting* may be involved in functional restitution (Finger and Stein 1982).

Recovery from brain injury may involve the reactivation of latent synapses (Wall 1977) as well as the creation of new synapses. This reactivation can probably be facilitated by pharmacological manoeuvres, such as local perfusion of the cortex with noradrenaline (van Hof 1981).

The neuronal responses to early and late brain damage differ both quantitatively and qualitatively (van Hof 1981, Finger and Stein 1982). First, both regenerative and collateral sprouting occur more readily in younger animals. Second, when the brain is injured before the developing axons have reached their normal destination, some of the growing axons eventually reach alternative destinations instead. Finally, if the brain is damaged before the stage of selective axonal loss, the accidental losses of some axonal collaterals could potentially be counterbalanced by a reduction in the normal losses of other axonal collaterals. As a result of these various differences, early brain damage is more likely to elicit the production of *anomalous* connections, *i.e.* neuronal connections that are either absent or inconspicuous in a normal brain. Because early brain damage elicits more regeneration and remodelling, the young brain is said to show greater *neuro-*

plasticity.

In some studies, the degree of functional recovery after a brain injury has been correlated with the neuronal responses to that injury (Schneider 1979, Spear 1979). These correlational studies demonstrate that the immature organism's greater neuroplasticity may be adaptive, but is not invariably so. The anomalous connections formed after brain injury can restore normal functions, but they can also lead to maladaptive responses if the anomalous connections are between the 'wrong' sites.

Brain damage: the earlier the better?
Early brain damage has widely been held to be less disabling in the long term than comparable brain damage sustained later in life. Thus Hans-Lukas Teuber, a well-known neuropsychologist, once stated: 'If I'm going to have brain damage, I'd best have it early rather than late' (quoted in Finger and Stein 1982). Although there is clearly some truth in this view, it is an oversimplification.

The developing brain's greater capacity for recovery is most evident when the focus is on the preservation of specific neurological or psychological functions. Kennard (1942) reached the influential conclusion that early damage to the motor cortex caused less long-term motor impairment than comparable later damage. Although Kennard seems to have been mistaken as far as motor recovery is concerned (see Chapter 9 and Passingham *et al.* 1983), greater recovery after early brain damage has been found for other functions: visual functions in cats (Spear 1979); performance on delayed-response tasks in monkeys (Goldman-Rakic *et al.* 1983): and language functions in humans (see above). Despite this association with greater recovery of specific functions, early brain damage does have disadvantages, as described below.

Brain injury in early life is more likely to be followed by the production of anomalous neural connections, and some of these connections may impair rather than improve function. In brain-damaged children, for example, anomalous connections may mediate hyperaesthesia and abnormally persistent mirror movements (Schneider 1979).

Although focal brain damage is less likely to result in specific psychological deficits when it occurs early in life, it is more likely to result in general intellectual and scholastic impairment (Rutter 1983, Rutter *et al.* 1983). Intuitively, it is tempting to suppose that this general impairment is the result of crowding too many functions into too little remaining brain. The inadequacy of this simple view is highlighted by a case report (Smith and Sugar 1975) of a congenital right hemiplegic who had his left hemisphere completely excised at the age of five and who not only acquired normal language but also had above-average intelligence in adult life. This sort of outcome reopens the issue of why early brain injury so often results in general cognitive impairment. Perhaps early focal lesions are commonly accompanied by diffuse generalised brain damage as well. Alternatively, or in addition, the anomalous connections formed after early damage could potentially impair general cognitive processing by channelling random information ('noise') between unrelated neural systems.

Brain injury may disrupt the capacity for new learning more than it disrupts the capacity to retain skills learned prior to the injury (Hebb 1942). If true, this effect would inevitably be more handicapping to the individual whose brain damage occurred early in life, before learned skills had yet been acquired.

In summary, although early brain damage is less likely to result in long-term deficits in specific skills, including language skills, this advantage is often purchased at a heavy price.

The potential promise of new brain-imaging techniques

Until recently, the available brain-imaging techniques were relatively crude, and were often unpleasant and potentially harmful for children. The new generation of brain-imaging techniques are beginning to provide ways to visualise brain structure and function without exposing children to invasive procedures or high doses of radiation. Consequently, it is becoming increasingly possible to correlate brain and language development, both in normal children and in children with developmental disorders. The next decade may well see major advances in our understanding of the neurological components of children's language disorders. Gross brain damage is already readily detected by CT scanning, and the latest generation of CT scanners are able to detect relatively subtle structural deficits.

Imaging by nuclear magnetic resonance (NMRi) produces an image of brain structure that is at least as good as that produced by the best CT scans, while exposing the child to much less radiation (Brownell *et al.* 1982, Dubowitz *et al.* 1986). NMRi can show the pattern of myelinisation particularly well. Even better, NMRi may eventually be able to provide 3D maps of brain function, *e.g.* by phosphorus imaging to obtain 3D maps of ATP turnover. Unfortunately, the practicalities of NMRi make it a difficult technique to use with children. In order to obtain an NMRi scan, the child has to lie still in an enclosed coffin-like space. If this is too frightening for the conscious child, maintaining and monitoring anaesthesia within an NMRi scanner also presents difficulties.

Emission CT scanning, using inhaled xenon 133, is a newly established method for obtaining 3D images of brain function. Computerised analysis of the emission pattern from the blood-borne isotope permits the reconstruction of 3D regional cerebral bloodflow. Radiation exposure is low. As described above, emission CT scanning has been used to investigate developmental dysphasia (Lou *et al.* 1984). Although PET scanning can also produce 3D maps of brain function (Brownell *et al.* 1982), the radiation exposure is higher, making the technique less suitable for children.

Very premature babies are a high-risk population for perinatal brain damage (Stewart 1983). Ultrasound scanning in the neonatal period can delineate at least some of the brain damage that occurs, particularly now that high-frequency transducers can detect periventricular leucomalacia (Levene *et al.* 1985). Follow-up studies may reveal significant associations between particular patterns of initial brain damage and later developmental disorders.

REFERENCES

Andrews, G., Harris, M. (1964) *The Syndrome of Stuttering. Clinics in Developmental Medicine, No. 17.* London: S.I.M.P. with Heinemann; Philadelphia: Lippincott.

—— Quinn, P. T., Sorky, W. A. (1972) 'Stuttering: an investigation into cerebral dominance for speech.' *Journal of Neurology, Neurosurgery, and Psychiatry*, **35**, 414–418.

Annett, M. (1978) *A Single Gene Explanation of Right and Left Handedness and Brainedness.* Coventry: Lanchester Polytechnic.

—— (1983) 'Hand preference and skill in 115 children of two left-handed parents.' *British Journal of Psychology*, **74**, 17–32.

Björklund, A., Stenevi, U. (1972) 'Nerve growth factor: stimulation of regenerative growth of central noradrenergic neurons.' *Science*, **175**, 1251–1253.

Bogen, J. E. (1979) 'The Callosal Syndrome.' *In:* Heilman, K. M., Valenstein, E. (Eds.) *Clinical Neuropsychology.* New York: Oxford University Press. pp. 308–359.

Bradshaw, J. L., Nettleton, N. C. (1983) *Human Cerebral Asymmetry.* Englewood Cliffs, N. J.: Prentice-Hall.

Brownell, G. L., Budinger, T. F., Lauterbur, P. C., McGeer, P. L. (1982) 'Positron tomography and nuclear magnetic resonance imaging.' *Science*, **215**, 619–626.

Corballis, M. C. (1983) *Human Laterality.* New York: Academic Press.

Cowan, W. M., Fawcett, J. W., O'Leary, D. D. M., Stanfield, B. B. (1984) 'Regressive events in neurogenesis.' *Science*, **225**, 1258–1265.

Critchley, M. (1970) *The Dyslexic Child.* London: Heinemann.

Curtiss, S. (1977) *Genie: A Psycholinguistic Study of a Modern-Day "Wild Child".* New York: Academic Press.

Dennis, M., Whitaker, H. A. (1977) 'Hemispheric equipotentiality and language acquisition.' *In:* Segalowitz, S. J., Gruber, F. A. (Eds.) *Language Development and Neurological Theory.* New York: Academic Press. pp. 93–106.

Dubowitz, L. M. S., Pennock, J. M., Johnson, M. A., Bydder, G. M. (1986) 'High-resolution Magnetic resonance imaging of the brain in children.' *Clinical Radiology*, **37**, 113–117.

Ebels, E. J. (1980) 'Maturation of the Central Nervous System.' *In:* Rutter, M. (Ed.) *Scientific Foundations of Developmental Psychiatry.* London: Heinemann. pp. 25–39.

Entus, A. K. (1977) 'Hemispheric asymmetry in processing of dichotically presented speech and nonspeech stimuli by infants.' *In:* Segalowitz, S. J., Gruber, F. A. (Eds.) *Language Development and Neurological Theory.* New York: Academic Press. pp. 63–73.

Finger, S., Stein, D. G. (1982) *Brain Damage and Recovery: Research and Clinical Perspectives.* New York: Academic Press.

Galaburda, A. M., Sherman, G. F., Rosen, G. D., Aboitiz, F., Geschwind, N. (1985) 'Developmental dyslexia: four consecutive patients with cortical anomalies.' *Annals of Neurology*, **18**, 222–233.

Gardiner, M. F., Walter, D. O. (1977) 'Evidence of hemispheric specialization from infant EEG.' *In:* Harnad, S., Doty, R. W., Goldstein, L., Jaynes, J., Krauthamer, G. (Eds.) *Lateralization in the Nervous System.* New York: Academic Press. pp. 481–500.

Geschwind, N., Behan, P. O. (1984) 'Laterality, hormones, and immunity.' *In:* Geschwind, N., Galaburda, A. M. (Eds.) *Cerebral Dominance: The Biological Foundations.* Cambridge, Mass.: Harvard University Press. pp. 211–224.

—— Galaburda, A. M. (1985) 'Cerebral lateralization: biological mechanisms, associations, and pathology: I. A hypothesis and a program for research.' *Archives of Neurology*, **42**, 428–459.

Glücksman, A. (1951) 'Cell death in normal vertebrate ontogeny.' *Biological Reviews*, **26**, 59–86.

Goldman-Rakic, P. S., Isseroff, A., Schwartz, M. L., Bugbee, N. M. (1983) 'The Neurobiology of Cognitive Development.' *In:* Haith, M. M., Campos, J. J. (Eds.) *Mussen's Handbook of Child Psychology, 4th ed., vol. II, Infancy and Developmental Psychobiology.* New York: Wiley. pp. 281–344.

Gordon, H. W. (1983) 'Music and the right hemisphere.' *In:* Young, A. W. (Ed.) *Functions of the Right Cerebral Hemisphere.* London: Academic Press. pp. 65–86.

Gottlieb, G. (1983) 'The psychobiological approach to developmental issues' *In:* Haith, M. M., Campos, J. J. (Eds.) *Mussen's Handbook of Child Psychology, 4th ed., vol. II, Infancy and Developmental Psychobiology.* New York: Wiley. pp. 1–26.

Hebb, D. O. (1942) 'The effect of early and late brain injury upon test scores, and the nature of normal adult intelligence.' *Proceedings of the American Philosophical Society*, **85**, 275–292.

Huttenlocher, P. R. (1979) 'Synaptic density in human frontal cortex—developmental changes and effects of aging.' *Brain Research*, **163**, 195–205.

143

Jones, R. K. (1966) 'Observations on stammering after localized cerebral injury.' *Journal of Neurology, Neurosurgery, and Psychiatry,* **29,** 192–195.

Kennard, M. A. (1942) 'Cortical reorganization of motor function: studies on series of monkeys of various ages from infancy to maturity.' *Archives of Neurology and Psychiatry,* **48,** 227–240.

Kinsbourne, M. (1971) 'The minor cerebral hemisphere as a source of aphasic speech.' *Archives of Neurology,* **25,** 302–306.

Kinsbourne, M., Hiscock, M. (1983) 'The normal and deviant development of functional lateralization of the brain.' *In:* Haith, M. M., Campos, J. J. (Eds.) *Mussen's Handbook of Child Psychology, 4th ed., vol. II, Infancy and Developmental Psychobiology.* New York: Wiley. pp. 157–280.

Kromer, L. F., Björklund, A., Stenevi, U. (1981*a*) 'Innervation of embryonic implants by regenerating axons of cholinergic septal neurones in the adult rat.' *Brain Research,* **210,** 153–171.

—— —— —— (1981*b*) 'Regeneration of the septohippocampal pathways in adult rats is promoted by utilizing embryonic hippocampal implants as bridges.' *Brain Research,* **210,** 173–200.

Lemire, R. J., Warkany, J. (1982) 'Normal development of the central nervous system: correlation with selected malformations.' *In:* American Association of Neurological Surgeons, *Pediatric Neurosurgery: Surgery of the Developing Nervous System.* New York: Grune & Stratton. pp. 1–22.

Lenneberg, E. H. (1967) *Biological Foundations of Language.* New York: Wiley.

Levene, M. I., Williams, J. L., Fawer, C. (1985) *Ultrasound of the Infant Brain. Clinics in Developmental Medicine, No. 92.* London: S.I.M.P. with Blackwell; Philadelphia: Lippincott.

Lou, H. C., Henriksen, L., Bruhn, P. (1984) 'Focal cerebral hypoperfusion in children with dysphasia and/or attention deficit disorder.' *Archives of Neurology,* **41,** 825–829.

Luessenhop, A. J., Boggs, J. S., La Borwit, L. J., Walle, E. L. (1973) 'Cerebral dominance in stutterers determined by Wada testing.' *Neurology,* **23,** 1190–1192.

McManus, I. C. (1985) 'Handedness, language dominance and aphasia: a genetic model.' *Psychological Medicine, Monograph Supplement* 8.

Molfese, D. L., Molfese, V. J. (1980) 'Cortical responses of preterm infants to phonetic and nonphonetic speech stimuli.' *Developmental Psychology,* **16,** 574–581.

Oldfield, R. C. (1971) 'The assessment and analysis of handedness: the Edinburgh Inventory.' *Neuropsychologia,* **9,** 97–113.

O'Rahilly, R., Gardner, E. (1977) 'The developmental anatomy and histology of the human central nervous system.' *In:* Vinken, P. J., Bruyn, G. W. (Eds.) *Handbook of Clinical Neurology, vol. 30, Congenital Malformations of the Brain and Skull, Part I.* Amsterdam: North-Holland Publishing. pp. 15–40.

Orton, S. T. (1937) *Reading, Writing and Speech Problems in Children: A Presentation of Certain Types of Disorders in the Development of the Language Faculty.* New York: Norton.

Parmelee, J. R., Sigman, M. D. (1983) 'Perinatal brain development and behaviour.' *In:* Haith, M. M., Campos, J. J. (Eds.) *Mussen's Handbook of Child Psychology, 4th ed., vol. II, Infancy and Developmental Psychobiology.* New York: Wiley. pp. 95–155.

Passingham, R. E., Perry, V. H., Wilkinson, F. (1983) 'The long-term effects of removal of sensorimotor cortex in infant and adult rhesus monkeys.' *Brain,* **106,** 675–705.

Piazza, D. M. (1977) 'Cerebral lateralization in young children as measured by dichotic listening and finger-tapping tasks.' *Neuropsychologia,* **15,** 417–425.

Rasmussen, T., Milner, B. (1975) 'Clinical and surgical studies of the cerebral speech areas in man.' *In:* Zulch, K. J., Creutzfeldt, O., Galbraith, G. (Eds.) *Cerebral Localization: An Otfrid Foerster Symposium.* Berlin: Springer-Verlag. pp. 238–257.

Reichman, J., Healey, W. C. (1983) 'Learning disabilities and conductive hearing loss involving otitis media.' *Journal of Learning Disabilities,* **16,** 272–278.

Rice, N. S. C., Taylor, D. (1982) 'Congenital cataract: a cause of preventable blindness in children.' *British Medical Journal,* **285,** 581–582.

Ross, E. D. (1981) 'The aprosodias: functional-anatomical organization of the affective components of language in the right hemisphere.' *Archives of Neurology,* **38,** 561–569.

—— Mesulam, M-M. (1979) 'Dominant language functions of the right hemisphere? Prosody and emotional gesturing.' *Archives of Neurology,* **36,** 144–148.

Rutter, M. (1983) 'Issues and prospects in developmental neuropsychiatry.' *In:* Rutter, M. (Ed.) *Developmental Neuropsychiatry.* Edinburgh: Churchill Livingstone. pp. 577–598.

—— Chadwick, O., Schaffer, D. (1983) 'Head injury.' *In:* Rutter, M. (Ed.) *Developmental Neuropsychiatry.* Edinburgh: Churchill Livingstone. pp. 577–598.

—— Yule, W. (1981) 'Neurological aspects of intellectual retardation and specific reading retardation.' *In:* Rutter, M., Tizard, J., Whitmore, K. (Eds.) *Education, Health and Behaviour.* Huntington, N.Y.: Krieger. (Originally published in London, 1970.) pp. 54–74.

144

Satz, P. (1972) 'Pathological left-handedness: an explanatory model.' *Cortex,* **8,** 121–135.

—— Sparrow, S. S. (1970) 'Specific developmental dyslexia: a theoretical formulation.' *In:* Bakker, D. J., Satz, P. (Eds.) *Specific Reading Disability: Advances in theory and method.* The Netherlands: Rotterdam University Press. pp. 17–40.

Schadé, J. P., van Groenigen, W. B. (1961) 'Structural organization of the human cerebral cortex. I. Maturation of the middle frontal gyrus.' *Acta Anatomica,* **47,** 74–111.

Schneider, G. E. (1979) 'Is it really better to have your brain lesion early? A revision of the "Kennard principle".' *Neuropsychologia,* **17,** 557–583.

Searleman, A. (1983) 'Language capabilities of the right hemisphere.' *In:* Young, A. W. (Ed.) *Functions of the Right Cerebral Hemisphere.* London: Academic Press. pp. 87–111.

Silva, P. A., Stewart, I., Kirkland, C., Simpson, A. (1985) 'How impaired are children who experience persistent bilateral otitis media with effusion?' *In:* Duane, D. D., Leong, C. K. (Eds.) *Understanding Learning Disabilities: International and Multidisciplinary Views.* New York: Plenum. pp. 27–37.

Silverberg, R., Obler, L. K., Gordon, H. W. (1979) 'Handedness in Israel.' *Neuropsychologia,* **17,** 83–87.

Skuse, D. (1984) 'Extreme deprivation in early childhood – II. Theoretical issues and a comparative review.' *Journal of Child Psychology and Psychiatry,* **25,** 543–572.

Smith, A., Sugar, O. (1975) 'Development of above normal language and intelligence 21 years after left hemispherectomy.' *Neurology,* **25,** 813–818.

Spear, P. D. (1979) 'Behavioural and neurophysiological consequences of visual cortex damage: mechanisms of recovery.' *In:* Sprague, J. M., Epstein, A. N. (Eds.) *Progress in Psychobiology and Physiological Psychology, vol. 8.* New York: Academic Press. pp. 45–90.

Springer, S. P., Deutsch, G. (1985) *Left Brain, Right Brain. Revised edition.* San Francisco: Freeman.

Stein, D. G., Dawson, R. G. (1980) 'The dynamics of growth, organization and adaptability in the central nervous system.' *In:* Brim, O. G., Kagan, J. (Eds.) *Constancy and Change in Human Development.* Cambridge, Mass.: Harvard University Press. pp. 163–228.

Stewart, A. (1983) 'Severe perinatal hazards.' *In:* Rutter, M. (Ed.) *Developmental Neuropsychiatry.* Edinburgh: Churchill Livingstone. pp. 15–31.

Takashima, S., Chan, F., Becker, L. E., Armstrong, D. L. (1980) 'Morphology of the developing visual cortex of the human infant: a quantitative and qualitative Golgi study.' *Journal of Neuropathology and Experimental Neurology,* **39,** 487–501.

Teng, E. L., Lee, P., Yang, K., Chang, P. C. (1977) 'Handedness in a Chinese population: biological, social, and pathological factors.' *Science,* **193,** 1148–1150.

Vaegan, Taylor, D. (1979) 'Critical period for deprivation amblyopia in children.' *Transactions of the Ophthalmological Society of the United Kingdom,* **99,** 432–439.

Van Hof, M. W. (1981) 'Development and recovery from brain damage.' *In:* Connolly, K. J., Prechtl, H. F. R. (Eds.) *Maturation and Development: Biological and Psychological Perspectives. Clinics in Developmental Medicine, No. 77/78.* London: S.I.M.P. with Heinemann; Philadelphia: Lippincott. pp. 186–197.

Wada, J. A., Clarke, R., Hamm, A. (1975) 'Cerebral hemispheric asymmetry in humans: cortical speech zones in 100 adult and 100 infant brains.' *Archives of Neurology,* **32,** 239–246.

—— Rasmussen, T. (1960) 'Intracarotid injection of sodium amytal for the lateralization of cerebral speech dominance.' *Journal of Neurosurgery,* **17,** 266–282.

Wall, P. D. (1977) 'The presence of ineffective synapses and the circumstances which unmask them.' *Philosophical Transactions of the Royal Society of London* (Series B), **278,** 361–372.

Weintraub, S., Mesulam, M-M., Kramer, L. (1981) 'Disturbances in prosody: a right-hemisphere contribution to language.' *Archives of Neurology,* **38,** 742–744.

—— —— (1983) 'Developmental learning disabilities of the right hemisphere: emotional, interpersonal and cognitive components.' *Archives of Neurology,* **40,** 463–468.

Woods, B. T. (1980) 'The restricted effects of right-hemisphere lesions after age one: Weschler test data.' *Neuropsychologia,* **18,** 65–70.

—— Teuber, H-L. (1978) 'Changing patterns of childhood aphasia.' *Annals of Neurology,* **3,** 273–280.

—— Carey, S. (1979) 'Language deficits after apparent clinical recovery from childhood aphasia.' *Annals of Neurology,* **6,** 405–409.

Zangwill, O. L. (1960) *Cerebral Dominance and its Relation to Psychological Function.* London: Oliver & Boyd.

9
DEVELOPMENTAL NEUROPSYCHOLOGICAL CORRELATES OF LANGUAGE

C. A. Heywood and A. G. M. Canavan

Introduction

Language development in the normal child has been considered elsewhere in this volume, and so the intention in this chapter is to provide a consideration of the neuropsychological underpinnings of such development. Inevitably, the myriad neuropsychological functions contributing to the complex system of language comprehension and production are best described by their absence—a perfectly functioning system gives little clue as to its component parts; only when a part is missing or damaged does its contribution to the over-all system become obvious. Consequently much of this chapter will be devoted to failures in the normal development of language, to developmental dysphasias. Within this volume the present chapter is most closely related to Chapter 8, and the two should be read in conjunction. An issue raised there and also to be considered here is that of whether early childhood dysphasias are comparable in their symptomatology and course to their adult counterparts, or rather reflect differing neuropsychological dysfunctions. Finally, two other aspects of language development, reading and writing, will be discussed once again in the context of abnormality, known as dyslexia and dysgraphia respectively.

Developmental dysphasia

There is consensus agreement that language development in the normal child follows a steady and predictable route from birth to the age of four years, regardless of the nationality into which the child is born, and with environmental factors affecting only the rate of this progress and not its sequence. This sequence has been described in detail elsewhere in this volume. Thus, as noted by Rutter (1982), the usual consequence of early brain damage (with regard to language) is to produce a developmental delay rather than to produce the kind of dysphasic abnormalities associated with later injury.

Developmental dysphasia has been defined as 'slow, limited or otherwise faulty development of language in children who do not otherwise give evidence of gross neurological or psychiatric disability' (Zangwill 1978). Hence difficulties in language accompanying hemiplegia or mental handicap, or secondary to deafness are not regarded as instances of developmental dysphasia. Nevertheless, according to Zangwill dysphasic children often grow up dyslexic, with reduced verbal intelligence, although verbal comprehension is generally normal. Semantic memory may be spared, as are visual and manipulative skills, and mathematical ability is rarely affected.

Ingram (1976) has argued that on the whole the general pattern of developmental dysphasia reflects that of normal speech development, hence verbal abilities usually acquired later are those most prone to error or omission. Thus for instance defective articulation of consonants is common, these usually being acquired later than vowels. Again speech is usually characterised by poverty of content, limited syntactical structure and poor use of rhythm.

Despite the assertion that developmental dysphasics display no gross neurological disabilities, a growing number of specific neurological and neuropsychological disorders have come to light, as demonstrated, for instance, by Rapin and Wilson (1978). First and foremost partial hearing loss (in the high-frequency range) which does not present as deafness, and which for most purposes can be compensated for by the sufferer, may result in a profound inability to discriminate between consonants, leaving the ability to distinguish between vowel sounds (the low-pitched components of language) intact. Hence the dysphasic child might substitute one consonant for another, or fail to develop certain consonants at all. Second, deficits in the rate of processing of auditory information have been described in a number of developmental dysphasics (Tallal and Piercy 1978), and since language comprehension involves the processing of rapidly changing acoustic information the consequences of such deficits are obvious.

Rapin and Wilson (1978) have also described a small number of developmental dysphasics, mostly with nonspecific EEG abnormalities, who appear to be suffering from verbal auditory agnosia, a syndrome previously thought to be confined to adulthood. In this rare condition all aspects of language appear to be intact except for comprehension of the spoken word—such patients may be able to speak themselves, read, write and display no auditory defects apart from the inability to decode the phonological aspects of speech.

On a more general level Rapin and Wilson also investigated 60 preschool and school-age children suffering from language disorders with regard to neurological and neuropsychological function, and while it is not clear whether these represented mostly developmental or acquired dysphasic syndromes the results are nevertheless of interest. In short, most of the children displayed oromotor deficits, and were delayed in reaching milestones such as walking. Deficits of fine motor abilities tended to persist into school age. The rest of their results revealed a heterogeneous assortment of impairments, with some children deficient on auditory tasks while others were deficient in the visual modality, and it is also apparent that the children differed markedly in their linguistic abilities. As yet, no clear system of categorising developmental dysphasias has emerged, and therefore no one-to-one relationship between different dysphasias and different neuropsychological syndromes has been constructed.

As a final example, Benton (1978) has pointed out that in a number of developmental dysphasics the underlying disorder may be one of sequential perception. Such children have been shown to be defective in learning or discriminating between both visual and auditory sequences, abilities clearly central to language development. The same author reviews the evidence for impairments in intermodal associative learning and habituation in a limited number of

147

developmental dysphasics, and appeals for large-scale studies involving the co-operation of many centres in order to determine the relative contributions of all these neuropsychological impairments to childhood disorders of language. Such studies are still awaited, but it is already quite clear that developmental dysphasia represents not a single syndrome, with a single set of neuropsychological correlates, but rather a conglomerate of syndromes, each likely to be related to its own neuropsychological factors. It is also clear that the normal course of language development can be halted at any one of its stages, by a variety of factors, preventing the child from progressing to the next stage.

In this context, we need now to consider acquired dysphasias of childhood, rather than developmental dysphasias, since these represent a retardation of language (usually as the result of organic insult) in children in whom language has already begun to develop normally. In particular it has been widely claimed that brain damage at this age does not result in such dire consequences as brain damage sustained in adulthood, the implication being that the younger brain is more flexible than the adult's and can go on to develop language in a way that the adult brain cannot. If this were true it would mean that the developmental neuropsychological correlates of language differed from their adult counterparts, or at the very least that the young brain could accommodate a redistribution of myriad neuropsychological functions in the way that the adult brain could not. The following sections examine these possibilities.

Acquired dysphasia in childhood

It is commonly stated that the effects of brain damage sustained in infancy are less deleterious than those sustained in adulthood. While it is true that children injured before the age of 12 years tend not to display lesion-laterality effects (Rutter 1982), it is certainly not true that they display no impairment at all. Rutter points to three areas in which even mild brain damage may be of serious consequence to the young child. First, in studies of children with only slight local trauma and no generalised damage there may be long-term scholastic difficulties even if there is no effect on IQ. Second, there is an increased risk of psychiatric disorder in children with neurological 'soft signs'. Finally, even low-level lead exposure may be associated with increased cognitive and attentional difficulties. Furthermore, with regard to age-effects within childhood, there is at least one study (Chadwick *et al.* 1981) in which there was a tendency for cognitive test scores, and especially for measures of scholastic attainment, to show greater impairment in children under the age of five years at the time of injury.

The view, then, that the younger brain is more resilient has grown from observations on the restitution of speech in patients suffering early damage to the classical speech areas (Lenneberg 1967, Newcombe 1969). The better prognosis for infant dysphasics has generated a great deal of animal research aimed at establishing whether or not the immature nervous system shows a greater plasticity than its adult counterpart. With a growing body of animal literature that attempts to elucidate the possible mechanisms underlying behavioural sparing or recovery from neural damage (Stein *et al.* 1974, Finger 1978), it is possible to take a retrospective look at the clinical investigations. In this way pitfalls can be highlighted that illustrate the difficulties in characterising the neuropsychological status of the developing child.

The first reference to an optimistic prognosis for the infant dysphasic can be attributed to Bernhardt (1897) who, while challenging the then prevalent view that childhood dysphasia did not exist, stated that: 'True aphasia is not rare in childhood; it is a frequent symptom of infantile cerebral hemiplegia, mostly transient, rarely permanent. It is mostly motor in type.'

It was not until 1942, however, that the first thorough review of the symptomatology and evolution of childhood dysphasia was presented (Guttman 1942). Guttman reviewed 10 cases. The observation that six patients recovered completely and the remaining four showed only slight dysphasic residue led Guttman to conclude: 'If after four weeks aphasic signs are still noticeable, prognosis as to the final outcome has to be more guarded, or in other words that aphasia in children recovers within four weeks in benign cases.'

More recent evidence does not contradict the broad conclusion that acquired dysphasia in infancy is invariably followed by a remarkable degree of recovery. There is for example, the oft-cited study of Byers and McLean (1962) who reported on a group of children, nearly all of whom recovered language ability in the presence of permanent right hemiplegia. Nevertheless two points remain at issue. First, there is considerable disagreement regarding the time course of recovery, which inevitably has serious implications when an infant-adult comparison is attempted. Second, it is not clear at what age the infant loses the plasticity which is deemed responsible for enhanced recovery. Before embarking on a discussion of these issues, some mention should be made of animal studies that exemplify problems inherent in the study of age/brain-damage relationships.

Some lessons from animal studies
Experiments on recovery of function can be dated from the paradigmatic works of Kennard (1936, 1938, 1940, 1942) who examined the effects of lesions of the precentral motor cortex in infant and adult rhesus monkeys. Kennard claimed, although less strenuously than many who have quoted her and with some provisions, that precentral lesions sustained in adulthood were more deleterious than when sustained in infancy. Her conclusions are questionable for four reasons: (i) the juvenile monkeys sustained more extensive lesions than the infant monkeys (Isaacson 1975); (ii) in none of her studies were juvenile-operated animals allowed as long to recover as the infant-operated animals; (iii) Kennard herself noted that the differences between the groups lessened with time; and (iv) the most conspicuous impairment was of fine finger movements, which are not fully developed in infants who may therefore appear to be less impaired compared with controls of the same age.

The problems in evaluating Kennard's work demonstrate two precautions that must be taken in studies of age/brain damage relationship. The first concerns the importance of equal recovery time for both infant and adult operated groups. The second concerns delayed onset of certain deficits following damage sustained in infancy. Behavioural effects of 'early' versus 'late' lesions might reflect differences in maturity of the neural area at the time of trauma rather than the function of the area itself. An infant cannot lose abilities it has yet to develop and therefore cannot recover functions that have not been lost. When the first of these precautions was carefully observed, that of allowing for equal recovery times, the differences reported by Kennard were not confirmed (Passingham *et al.* 1983).

A second example serves to make the same point. The ability of the normal infant monkey to perform delayed response tasks depends on the integrity of the caudate nucleus (Goldman 1974). During development the maturing prefrontal cortex begins to subserve an important rôle in such tasks. If dorsolateral prefrontal cortex is removed in monkeys after birth, the ability to perform delayed response tasks is unimpaired in infancy (Goldman 1971). However, as the operated monkey matures, a deficit on delayed-response tasks appears (Goldman 1974, 1976).

A comparison of infants with adults

Russell and Espir (1961) made observations on 255 patients who had sustained penetrating head wounds. These authors argued that dysphasias acquired during adult life, that is after the age of 18, may show a limited degree of recovery but only in the first three to six months post trauma. This is in agreement with Kertesz and McCabe (1977) who suggested that no significant recovery occurs beyond six months. In contrast Teuber (1960) proposes that children can show steady improvement for up to several years post trauma and eventually suffer no dysphasic residue. However, a comparison between infant and adult dysphasics presents a problem akin to that confronting Kennard. Children have not traversed all the stages of language acquisition and thus display characteristically impoverished speech. They have, in effect, much less to lose and consequently are required to make fewer gains to achieve recovery from acquired dysphasia. This is clearly not the case in the adult dysphasic who has far to go in the retrieval of sophisticated competence.

There are a number of clinical exceptions that argue against the view that acquired dysphasia in adulthood leads to a poor prognosis. Broida (1977) noted improvement in adult cases under therapy for many years after a stroke. Marks *et al.* (1957) studied 205 patients most of whom suffered from dysphasia secondary to disease. Ages ranged from three to 80 years and the majority of participants underwent between one month and one year of therapy considered efficacious by some authors (Butfield and Zangwill 1956). Since only 7 per cent of this population was under the age of 30, it was not possible to draw conclusions regarding the relationship between age and prognosis. The authors reported that 50 per cent made poor recovery, 21 per cent good recovery and 22 per cent and 7 per cent made fair or excellent recovery, respectively.

This compares favourably with recovery rates quoted in other investigations. However, Marks *et al.* (1957) cited two cases exhibiting acute symptoms. One was a 37-year-old man, the other a 46-year-old woman, both of whom recovered completely. It is just the existence of these and other similar cases that suggest that age alone does not entirely determine prognosis. These include a patient of Geschwind (1974) who showed little recovery in the first year after the onset of dysphasia, but showed complete recovery in the subsequent year. However, such cases are often presented with little more data than can be gleaned from cursory clinical examination.

The greater part of the literature concerned with dysphasia has concentrated on classification of symptoms and its relation to site of pathology. For example, voluminous reviews of Broca's dysphasia have relied on cases presented in the latter years of last or the early years of the present century. But these reports often establish only the initial occurrence of the deficit. Whether this be transient or permanent is not settled by the classical literature. Thus Mohr (1976) has shown from long-term follow-up that there were indeed considerable improvements in the 20 cases of Broca's dysphasia that have been adequately documented in the published reports.

A further two notable exceptions have provided a wealth of data clearly demonstrating the possibility of full recovery of the adult dysphasic. Luria (1970), in his examination of penetrating head wounds, presented evidence that 32 per cent of those patients with gross invasion of the classical speech areas either recover fully or show only a mild dysphasic residue. Similarly, an examination of the 19 cases of Penfield and Roberts (1959) suggests the same trend. These authors argued that the removal of speech cortex leads to no permanent disability. It is therefore significant to note that 12 of these cases, all showing near complete recovery, have underlying pathology originating in adulthood.

There are recurrent problems in the assessment of clinical studies that concern recovery and sparing. First, in the composition of case reports, the emphasis may be on any one of the many variables that can be used in classifying the patient and this varies considerably between reports. Furthermore, by reshuffling patients under different classifications of age, aetiology, pathology and symptoms (as sometimes occurs when the same patients are studied in different investigations), any connections between the many variables are disguised. Second, there is commonly a lack of homogeneity in patient populations. Recovery has been shown to be dependent on aetiology, type of dysphasia, and indeed the method of evaluation of the disorder (Kertesz 1979). Some investigators have restricted their studies to severe dysphasics (Sarno and Levita 1971) while others (Basso *et al.* 1975) have categorised their patients only as Broca's or Wernicke's dysphasias, resulting in populations that cannot be compared.

In an effort to resolve this problem Kertesz and McCabe (1977) studied 83 patients matched for initial severity, aetiology and type of dysphasia. Complete recovery was observed in over half of the post-traumatic cases. Moreover, in agreement with some other authors (Sarno and Levita 1971, Smith 1972), a negative correlation was observed between age and initial recovery rates (0 to three months) which did not however reach statistical significance.

In summary, patients can show recovery or sparing whether the damage is incurred early or late in life. There are, however, several problems when a comparison of the rate or degree of recovery between patient populations is attempted. Amongst these is the failure to elucidate additional factors that determine prognoses. This results in a lack of homogeneity in patient populations that are compared. Second, the problem is exacerbated by the discrepancy in initial language ability of infant and adult patients which makes comparisons of final outcomes difficult.

Mechanisms of recovery

Having indicated that the relationship between age and brain damage is at best controversial, it is of interest to turn to an evaluation of one possible mechanism underlying recovery. It is possible that the hemispheres are equipotential early in development, enabling language to develop in the remaining, uncommitted hemisphere following unilateral damage to speech areas. It is at this point that some mention should be made of a large literature on the consequences of hemispherectomy in which the second area of disagreement may be found; namely, the age at which the infant brain loses the plasticity that possibly confers on it superior recovery following damage.

Data from infant hemiplegics, who have undergone dominant hemi-spherectomy to alleviate intractable epilepsy, have added weight to the argument for greater anatomo-functional plasticity in the infant brain (Basser 1962). Krynauw (1950) studied 10 such patients aged between seven months and 21 years. Left hemispherectomy resulted in no impairments of speech as a consequence of operation and in some cases striking improvements. In all but one patient the injury was sustained in the first 21 months, the other had a history of a difficult birth and febrile illness at four and a half years.

Similarly, McFie (1961), reporting observations on 34 patients and reviewing over 300 cases of infantile hemiplegia, concludes that the most striking difference in mean change of IQ following hemispherectomy is that associated with the age at which the injury to the hemisphere is incurred.

Finally, Gardner *et al.* (1955) and Hillier (1954) reported the effects of left dominant hemispherectomy for glioma on patients 10 and 14 years old, respectively. In these instances, although hemispherectomy was followed by speech loss, there was subsequent alleviation of dysphasic symptoms. In contrast, left dominant hemispherectomy in the adult results in a persistent dysphasia with limited recovery as exemplified by the patients of Smith (1966), Zollinger (1935) and Crockett and Estridge (1951). In agreement with the foregoing reports McKissock (1953) stated that the criteria for recommending dominant hemi-spherectomy are infantile hemiplegia accompanied by epilepsy and behaviour disorder. The mechanism of functional recovery to which most authors subscribe is summarised by Penfield (1965):

> When the major speech area is severely injured in later life, the adult cannot do what he might have done as a child. He may improve but he is apt to be using the remaining uninjured cortex on the side of the injury. He can never establish a completely new centre on the non-dominant side, as far as our experience goes . . . because he has, by that time, taken over the initially uncommitted convolution of the non-dominant side of his brain for other uses.

It should be noted, however, that no solid evidence exists in support of the proposed mechanism. Indirect evidence is suggested by Basser (1962) and Krashen (1973) who report a high incidence of dysphasias resulting from right-hemisphere damage in children. This diffuse representation of language functions in the infant implies that early in development the hemispheres are equipotential for language learning. This in turn leads to the conclusion that early damage to one hemisphere may result in normal language acquisition by the other. However, this phenomenon has been accepted without any proper consideration of the possibility of left hemisphere pathology accompanying right hemisphere damage in the cases cited above.

More recently several authors (see Woods 1983) have subscribed to the view that language is lateralised within the first few months after birth (a theory of developmental invariance) and have questioned the notion that the right hemisphere plays an active rôle in speech production early in development with a gradual lateralisation of language over time (the developmental maturation hypothesis). However, this is not to deny the ability of the right hemisphere to take over language functions in the event of early left-hemisphere damage.

The upper age limit for the proposed hemispheric transfer of language function is unclear. Lenneberg (1967) claims that language invariably returns to a child if he is less than nine years old at the time of neural damage. This conclusion was based on an evaluation of 25 case reports. Alajouanine and Lhermitte (1965), on the other hand, based their conclusions on a study of 32 patients aged between six and 15 years. A comparison of children less than 10 years old with children of 10 years or more failed to find a significant difference in speed or level of recovery. Furthermore eight patients showed an incomplete recovery and suffered a pronounced dysphasic residue. Moreover, Geschwind (1974) suggested that a similar mechanism must be involved in instances of recovery of adult dysphasics following massive dominant hemisphere lesions.

Without speculating on the conditions responsible for functional transfer, suffice it to say that evidence suggests that the potential for recovery is related to handedness and degree of cerebral laterality of language functions (Gloning *et al.* 1969). Thus, left-handedness is frequently accompanied by decreased lateralisation of language ability, compared with right-handedness, and therefore greater potential for recovery following unilateral damage to the dominant hemisphere.

In conclusion, then, the neuropsychological correlates of acquired dysphasias in childhood are much the same as those of adulthood. This is not to deny that the prognosis for infant dysphasics is somewhat better than that for adults: younger tissue heals more quickly than old, and the young may enjoy a longer recovery time. It is important, however, to emphasise this distinction between 'good outcome' and 'recovery' processes: the better outcome for infants does not necessarily imply greater recovery ability.

It was mentioned earlier that infant dysphasia is often accompanied by dyslexia, and no account of the development of language would be complete without some discussion of reading and writing skills. It is also clear that the neuropsychological correlates of reading and writing must share much in common with those of the spoken word. The final section, then, is devoted to dyslexia and dysgraphia.

Dyslexia and dysgraphia

Disorders of reading or writing may be either 'acquired' or 'developmental', the former term referring to the loss of either or both of these linguistic skills following brain damage, the latter referring to a failure to acquire the abilities during the course of development. Although much of the following discussion will be devoted to developmental dyslexia, it should be pointed out that the features characterising this syndrome are essentially the same as those known as 'specific reading retardation', (Rutter and Yule 1973). As these authors point out, in both cases full-scale IQ remains intact, there is a ratio of about 3.5 : 1 of boys to girls, overt neurological signs are more frequent than in the general population and there is no tendency for the children to arise from any particular social class.

It should also be pointed out that neither developmental dyslexia nor specific reading retardation is quite so selective as it sounds. With regard to the latter, for instance, Rutter and Yule (1973) found that the reading impairment was commonly associated with other speech and language difficulties. The same studies revealed a host of aetiological factors at work in this syndrome. Among these were genetic factors, a relative failure in cerebral maturation, brain damage and a lack of suitable environmental stimulation. Rutter and Yule also noted that this developmental impairment was often associated with adverse temperamental features, and that all these factors interacted with family, school and social circumstances to give rise to reading difficulties. Nevertheless, apart from these more general considerations, many investigations have uncovered specific neuropsychological correlates of dyslexia and dysgraphia, as will be seen below.

The most extensive study of developmental dyslexia to date is probably that of Petrauskas and Rourke (1979). They located 133 retarded readers of seven and eight years of age, and compared them with 27 normal children on 44 dependent measures. A factor-analysis of the results suggested that the retarded readers comprised at least three subtypes. The first group displayed deficiencies in verbal IQ and auditory-verbal tasks as well as poor reading, but were not impaired on tests of tactile-perceptual, motor, visuospatial or abstract-conceptual functions. A second group showed deficiencies only in motor functions and immediate memory for visual sequences, while the third group displayed relatively normal performance on all tests except for an apparent crossed-dominance on motor tasks.

Mattis *et al.* (1975) had previously come to a similar conclusion regarding the number of subtypes of dyslexia to be found in children and young adults. Their study had taken into account the possibility of brain damage as a concomitant of one or all of these subtypes, employing extensive history-taking, EEG recording and the taking of skull x-rays as well as other measures to determine this. In short they were unable to find any consistent neurological correlate of dyslexia in their sample.

The heterogeneity of dyslexic disorders is probably responsible for the conflicting reports to be found in the literature and discussed recently by Corballis *et al.* (1985). As they point out, Orton's theory of developmental dyslexia (or 'word blindness' as it was originally termed, Orton 1925) held that the condition be characterised by weak lateralisation and left-right confusions. However, there have been as many failures to find these differences as there have been positive findings—but in the light of the work described above it is likely that such deficits occur in only a particular subgroup of dyslexics.

The experimental results reported by Corballis *et al.* (1985) conform to these expectations. They tested normal and reading-disabled children aged from 11 to 13 years on the ability to discriminate 'b' from 'd'. When these letters were presented in their normal orientations, the good readers displayed the usual right visual hemifield advantage, but the disabled readers did not. The difference between the two groups however did not reach statistical significance. On the other hand a close inspection of the data reveals considerable variability within the disabled group, such that some children were clearly abnormally lateralised with respect to the task.

The second part of Corballis *et al.'s* task required the children to discriminate the same letters in varying angular rotations. In this case neither the normal readers nor the dyslexic children displayed any hemifield advantage, and there were no significant differences between the groups. Once again though the disabled readers displayed greater variability, and so the failure to find a significant correlate of dyslexia may rest in treating all dyslexics as a single group.

One source of variability has been described by Rutter and Yule (1973). They point out that although verbal language processes are generally the more strongly related to reading ability in older children, in very young children visuospatial defects are an important cause of reading impairment. Bryant and Bradley (1983) have studied backward readers from a similar perspective. They have shown that as children begin to read and write they tend to treat words as patterns, and depend largely upon visual codes when reading, but phonological codes when spelling. This initial separation was seen to be stronger and to last longer in backward readers than in other children.

Not all specific neuropsychological defects attributed to dyslexics have stood the test of time. Thus for instance Bakker (1972) showed that poor readers experienced particular difficulty in sequencing letters. However, Nelson (1980) has demonstrated since then that such sequencing errors are a consequence of poor reading ability rather than a cause. Many of the findings regarding dyslexia are correlational in nature, and so this demonstration represents an important lesson to be applied when considering other studies.

Dyslexia and dysgraphia only rarely occur in isolation, the rule being to find them in varying combinations. Nelson and Warrington (1974) assessed two groups of children in the eight to 14 years age range, one of which displayed severe reading and spelling retardation of more than three years, while the other displayed only spelling retardation of equivalent severity. They found the dyslexic and dysgraphic group to be much poorer in terms of verbal IQ than the group with dysgraphia alone. Frith (1980) compared primarily dysgraphic children with primarily dyslexic children on a spelling test, and found them to be equally impaired. Interestingly, the dysgraphic children produced twice as many phonetic as non-phonetic spelling

155

errors compared with the dyslexics, who produced equal amounts of each, leading to the conclusion that phonological difficulties in spelling are associated with reading problems. These two studies point to the possibility that dyslexia is the more serious of the written-language disorders, being associated with more widespread verbal impairment and usually encompassing some degree of dysgraphia as well, while the latter is more likely to occur in isolation, though still rarely so.

Finally, it should be noted that early dyslexia does not usually lead to a favourable outcome. Schonhaut and Satz (1983) recently reviewed 18 studies in which children with primary reading disability were followed up for two to 25 years. Reading and writing deficits were seen to persist well into later life in the better studies, while favourable outcomes were reported only in anecdotal form. In this respect childhood dyslexia is no less severe than acquired dyslexia of adulthood.

Summary

Comprehension and expression of the spoken word develops inexorably over the first four years of life in the normal child, passing through fixed stages regardless of the language into which the child is born, comprehension always leading the way. However, developmental dysphasia may strike at any of these stages, and various neuropsychological dysfunctions have been described to account for such failures.

Acquired dysphasia of childhood has also been described. The classical literature has it that such childhood dysphasia is mild and transient, unlike its adult counterpart. It has also been suggested that there is a critical period for language development in childhood, during which time the right hemisphere may adopt the left hemisphere's functions should the need arise. While there is little doubt that the prognosis for childhood dysphasics is better than that for adults, more recent work undermines each of these classical assumptions, which have been dealt with in detail here.

Finally a discussion of other developmental linguistic problems—dyslexia and dysgraphia—led to the conclusion that disorders of reading and writing may be just as variable, and reflect just as many neuropsychological dysfunctions, as dysphasia itself. The prognosis for dyslexia is unfavourable, once again underlining the severity of developmental neuropsychological disorders.

REFERENCES

Alajouanine, T., Lhermitte, F. (1965) 'Acquired aphasia in children.' *Brain*, **88**, 653–662.
Bakker, D. J. (1972) *Temporal Order in Disturbed Reading*. Rotterdam: University Press.
Basser, L. S. (1962) 'Hemiplegia of early onset and the faculty of speech.' *Brain*, **85**, 427–460.
Basso, A., Faglioni, P., Vignola, L. A. (1975) 'Etude controllée de la rééducation du langage dans l'aphasie: comparison entre aphasiques traités et nontraités.' *Revue of Neurology*, **131**, 607–614.
Benton, A. (1978) 'The cognitive functioning of children with developmental dysphasia.' *In:* M. A. Wyke (Ed.) *Developmental Dysphasia*. London: Academic Press.
Bernhardt, M. (1897) *In:* Nothnagel, *Spezielle Pathologie und Therapie*, 9, Part 2, Vienna.
Broida, H. (1977) 'Language therapy effects in long term aphasia.' *Archives of Physical Medicine and Rehabilitation*, **58**, 248–253.
Bryant, P. E., Bradley, L. (1983) 'Auditory organisation and backwardness in reading.' *In:* Rutter, M.

(Ed.) *Developmental Neuropsychiatry.* New York: Guilford Press.

Butfield, E., Zangwill, O. L. (1956) 'Reeducation in aphasia: a review of 70 cases.' *Journal of Neurology, Neurosurgery and Psychiatry,* **9,** 75–79.

Byers, R. K., McLean, W. T. (1962) 'Etiology and course of certain hemiplegias with aphasia in childhood.' *Pediatrics,* **29,** 376–383.

Chadwick, O., Rutter, M., Thompson, J., Shaffer, D. (1981) 'Intellectual performance and reading skills after localised head injury in childhood.' *Journal of Child Psychology and Psychiatry,* **22,** 117–139.

Corballis, M. C., Macadie, L., Beale, I. L. (1985) 'Mental rotation and visual laterality in normal and reading disabled children.' *Cortex,* **21,** 225–236.

Crockett, H. G., Estridge, N. M. (1951) 'Cerebral hemispherectomy.' *Bulletin of the Los Angeles Neurology Society,* **16,** 71–87.

Finger, S. (Ed.) (1978) *Recovery from Brain Damage.* New York: Plenum.

Frith, U. (1980) 'Unexpected spelling problems.' *In:* Frith, U. (Ed.) *Cognitive Processes in Spelling.* London: Academic Press.

Gardner, W. J., Karnosh, L. J., McClure, C. C., Gardner, A. K. (1955) 'Residual function following hemispherectomy for tumour and for infantile hemiplegia.' *Brain,* **78,** 487–502.

Geschwind, N. (1974) 'Late changes in the nervous system: an overview.' *In:* Stein, D. G., Rosen, J. J., Butters, N. (Eds.) *Plasticity and Recovery of Function in the Central Nervous System.* New York: Academic Press. pp. 467–508.

Gloning, I., Gloning, K., Haub, G., Quatember, R. (1969) 'Comparison of verbal behavior in right-handed and non right-handed patients with anatomically verified lesions of one hemisphere.' *Cortex,* **5,** 43–52.

Goldman, P. S. (1971) 'Functional development of the prefrontal cortex in early life and the problem of neuronal plasticity.' *Experimental Neurology,* **32,** 366–387.

—— (1974) 'An alternative to developmental plasticity: heterology of CNS structures in infants and adults.' *In:* Stein, D. G., Rosen, J. J., Butters, N. (Eds.) *Plasticity and Recovery of Function in the Central Nervous System.* New York: Academic Press. pp. 149–174.

—— (1976) 'Maturation of the mammalian nervous system and the ontogeny of behavior.' *In:* Rosenblatt, J. S., Hinde, R. A., Shaw, E., Beer, C. (Eds.) *Advances in the Study of Behavior. Vol. 7.* New York: Academic Press. pp. 1–90.

Guttman, E. (1942) 'Aphasia in children.' *Brain,* **65,** 205–219.

Hillier, W. F. (1954) 'Total left cerebral hemispherectomy for malignant glioma.' *Neurology,* **4,** 718–721.

Ingram, T. T. S. (1976) 'Speech disorders in childhood.' *In:* Lenneberg, E. H., Lenneberg, E. (Eds.) *Foundations of Language Development, Vol. 2.* New York: Academic Press.

Isaacson, R. L. (1975) 'The myth of recovery from early brain damage.' *In:* Ellis, N. R. (Ed.) *Aberrant Development in Infancy.* Potomac, MD. Lawrence Erlbaum.

Kennard, M. A. (1936) 'Age and other factors in motor recovery from precentral lesions in monkeys.' *American Journal of Physiology,* **115,** 138–146.

—— (1938) 'Reorganization of motor functions in the cerebral cortex of monkeys deprived of motor and premotor zones in infancy.' *Journal of Neurophysiology,* **1,** 477–496.

—— (1940) 'Relation of age to motor impairment in man and in subhuman primates.' *Archives of Neurology and Psychiatry,* **44,** 377–397.

—— (1942) 'Cortical reorganization of motor function, studies on a series of monkeys of various ages from infant to maturity.' *Archives of Neurology and Psychiatry,* **48,** 227–240.

Kertesz, A. (1979) 'Recovery and treatment.' *In:* Heilman, K. M., Valenstein, E. (Ed.) *Clinical Neuropsychology.* Oxford: Oxford University Press. pp. 503–534.

—— McCabe, P. (1977) 'Recovery patterns and prognosis in aphasia.' *Brain,* **100,** 1–18.

Krashen, S. (1973) 'Lateralization, language learning and the critical period: some new evidence.' *Language Learning,* **23,** 63–74.

Krynauw, R. A. (1950) 'Infantile hemiplegia treated by removing one cerebral hemisphere.' *Journal of Neurology, Neurosurgery and Psychiatry,* **13,** 243–267.

Lenneberg, E. H. (1967) *Biological Foundations of Language.* New York: John Wiley.

Luria, A. R. (1970) *Traumatic Aphasia.* The Hague: Mouton. pp. 27–76.

Marks, M., Taylor, M., Rusk, L. A. (1957) 'Rehabilitation of the aphasic patient: a survey of three years experience in a rehabilitation setting.' *Neurology,* **7,** 837–843.

Mattis, S., French, J. H., Rappin, I. (1975) 'Dyslexia in children and young adults: three independent neuropsychological syndromes.' *Developmental Medicine and Child Neurology,* **17,** 150–163.

McFie, J. (1961) 'The effects of hemispherectomy on intellectual functioning in cases of infantile hemiplegia.' *Journal of Neurology, Neurosurgery and Psychiatry,* **24,** 240–249.

McKissock, W. (1953) 'Infantile hemiplegia.' *Proceedings of the Royal Society of Medicine,* **46,** 431–434.

Mohr, J. P. (1976) 'Rapid amelioration of motor aphasia.' *Archives of Neurology,* **28,** 77–82.

Nelson, H. (1980) 'Analysis of spelling errors in normal and dyslexic children.' *In:* Frith, U. (Ed.) *Cognitive Processes in Spelling.* London: Academic Press.

—— Warrington, E. K. (1974) 'Developmental spelling retardation and its relation to other cognitive abilities.' *British Journal of Psychology,* **65,** 265–274.

Newcombe, F. (1969) *Missile Wounds of the Brain. A Study of Psychological Deficits.* Oxford Neurological Monographs.

Orton, S. T. (1925) 'Word blindness in school children.' *Archives of Neurology and Psychiatry,* **14,** 581–615.

Passingham, R. E., Perry, V. H., Wilkinson, F. (1983) 'The long-term effects of removal of sensorimotor cortex in infant and adult rhesus monkeys.' *Brain,* **106,** 675–705.

Penfield, W. (1965) 'Conditioning the uncommitted cortex for language learning.' *Brain,* **88,** 787–798.

—— Roberts, L. (1959) *Speech and Brain-Mechanisms.* Princeton, NJ.: Princeton University Press.

Petrauskas, R. J., Rourke, B. P. (1979) 'Identification of subtypes of retarded readers: a neuropsychological, multivariate approach.' *Journal of Clinical Neuropsychology,* **1,** 17–37.

Rapin, I., Wilson, B. C. (1978) 'Children with developmental language disability: neurological aspects and assessment.' *In:* M. A. Wyke (Ed.) *Developmental Dysphasia.* London: Academic Press.

Russell, W. R., Espir, M. L. E. (1961) *Traumatic Aphasia.* Oxford: Oxford University Press.

Rutter, M. (1982) 'Developmental neuropsychiatry: concepts, issues and prospects.' *Journal of Clinical Neuropsychology,* **4,** 91–115.

—— Yule, W. (1973) 'Specific reading retardation.' *In:* Mann, L., Sabatino, D. (Eds.) *The First Review of Special Education.* Philadelphia: Buttonwood Farms.

Sarno, M. T., Levita, E. (1971) 'Natural course of recovery in severe aphasia.' *Archives of Physical Medicine and Rehabilitation,* **52,** 175–179.

Schonhaut, S., Satz, P. (1983) 'Prognosis for children with learning disabilities: a review of follow-up studies.' *In:* Rutter, M. (Ed.) *Developmental Neuropsychiatry.* New York: Guildford Press.

Smith, A. (1966) 'Speech and other functions after left dominant hemispherectomy.' *Journal of Neurology, Neurosurgery and Psychiatry,* **29,** 467–471.

—— (1972) 'Dominant and non-dominant hemispherectomy.' *In:* Smith, W. S. (Ed.) *Drugs, Development and Cerebral Function.* Springfield, Ill.: C. C. Thomas.

Stein, D. G., Rosen, J. J., Butters, N. (Eds.) (1974) *Plasticity and Recovery of Function in the Central Nervous System.* New York: Academic Press.

Tallal, P., Piercy, M. (1978) 'Defects of auditory perception in children with developmental dysphasia.' *In:* Wyke, M. A. (Ed.) *Developmental Dysphasia.* London: Academic Press.

Teuber, H. L. (1960) 'Perception.' *In: Handbook of Physiology, Section 1: Neurophysiology 3.* American Physiology Society.

Woods, B. T. (1983) 'Is the left hemisphere specialized for language at birth?' *Trends in Neurosciences,* **6,** 115–117.

Zangwill, O. L. (1978) 'The concept of developmental dysphasia.' *In:* Wyke, M. A. (Ed.) *Developmental Dysphasia.* London: Academic Press.

Zollinger, R. (1935) 'Removal of left cerebral hemisphere. Report of a case.' *Archives of Neurology and Psychiatry,* **34,** 1055–1064.

10

THE 'WHAT' AND 'HOW' OF LANGUAGE DEVELOPMENT: A NOTE ON SOME OUTSTANDING ISSUES AND QUESTIONS

Michael Rutter

The preceding chapters have summarized some of the key features of what is known on the course of language development and of its environmental correlates. It is clear that a good deal is known about both, but much less about just what constitutes the essential nature of language and less still about *how* these skills are acquired. Yet these are crucial issues in the understanding of language problems and in the planning of language remediation programmes. In this brief chapter, some of the more important issues and questions on this topic are noted.

What is language

As Crystal points out in Chapter 3, language involves several subsystems. These include: (i) *syntax* or grammar, namely the ways in which words are combined to form phrases, sentences and subclauses; (ii) *phonology,* the organization of sounds and the rules regulating that usage; (iii) *semantics,* that is the meaning of words both in isolation and in subsets and combinations; and (iv) *pragmatics,* those aspects of meaning controlled by the ways in which language is used in relation to the perspectives of a speaker and listener.

The controversies over the nature of language came to the fore in the late 1950s with the clash between Skinner (1957) and Chomsky (1959). Skinner's behaviourist hypothesis specified that each word and word combination was learned separately by means of associations, imitation, practice and reinforcement. In contrast, Chomsky proposed that linguistic structure was innate; the specifics of a particular language were learned but the essential elements that constituted the basis of language were not.

There are reasons why the Skinnerian position is no longer accepted (see Cromer 1980, 1974; Howlin 1980; Maratsos 1983). However, most stem from the observation that language structures cannot be accounted for in terms of their 'surface' features in the sentences used. Thus, a single word order can convey quite different grammatical relations (*e.g.* 'John is eager to please' and 'John is easy to please' where John is the actor in the former and is acted upon in the latter). Conversely the same grammatical relation can be indicated by quite different surface categories (*e.g.* 'John gave Mary the gift', 'Mary was given the gift by John' and 'The gift was given to Mary by John'). Moreover, a language is a system that exceeds the data; a speaker exposed to one use of a wholly novel term will be able to predict a new grammatical usage for it (Berko 1958). Thus, if a person is told:

'Today John glizzes. Yesterday he did the same thing. Yesterday he _____';
'glizzed' will be readily inserted for the missing word. Chomsky's solution was to hypothesize the existence of a deep structure that was purely grammatical. There is no longer any doubt that children are indeed actively engaged in the acquisition of a system of rules that allows for the generation of novel word combinations (Brown 1973). Moreover, the utterances that they produce derive from their own rule system, rather than from any direct imitation of what they have heard. One essential feature of language is its extremely rich creativity. Some kind of abstract representations of linguistic knowledge must be involved. What is much less clear is just what that representation entails.

Chomsky claimed that the essence was purely grammatical, that the grammatical rules were transformational in character (*i.e.* the patterns that allow one grammatical construction to be seen as equivalent to another, *e.g* the interrogative 'are you coming' can be derived from the declarative 'you are coming'), and that the rule system was innate and not taught. The notion of transformational grammar was intuitively appealing and at first it seemed to account for many of the most important features of language. However, firstly the number of transformations in an utterance is not consistently related to the speed with which the utterance is processed (as would be predicted on a transformational view of language); secondly although, on the whole, transformational complexity predicts the order with which grammatical structures are acquired, there are exceptions and developmental order of acquisition is also predicted by semantic complexity; and thirdly transformational grammar does not provide an entirely adequate account of the patterns of children's language errors (Maratsos 1983).

Parental shaping of children's language
Chomsky also argued that parents not only failed to shape children's language usage but also that their own lingusitic input to the child was so degenerate and error-filled that it failed even to provide an adequate model for the child to imitate. It was inferred that the child must already innately possess highly developed abstract ideas about the forms of grammar. The first part of this proposition has received broad support, but the second has not. Brown and Hanlon's (1970) detailed study of three mother-child pairs showed that parental responses rarely served to correct grammatical errors or to reward grammatical accuracy; rather they tended to focus on the truth value of what their children said. Moreover, there was only a very modest positive correlation between the frequency with which mothers used particular linguistic forms and the order of acquisition of these forms by the children (Brown 1973). It cannot be said that there has been much further naturalistic study of this matter but such evidence as there is shows only weak associations between the specific features of the speech children hear and that which they produce (Baker and Nelson 1984; Scherer and Olswang 1984; Schwartz *et al.* 1985; Hoff Ginsberg 1985, 1986). Children *can* be taught grammar by experimental procedures (see review by Rutter 1980) but ordinarily that is not how grammar is acquired.

On the other hand, it appears that adult speech to children is much more grammatical than Chomsky supposed (see review by Maratsos 1983). Furthermore, the characteristics of speech as used to young children ('motherese') has several features likely to facilitate understanding. There tends to be exaggerated intonation, clear enuciation, slower tempo, and distinct pauses between utterances and between clause boundaries. Also, the topics tend to be confined to the here and now, the vocabulary is restricted, and the major content words are more likely to denote concrete objects, activities and properties. As children's understanding (rather than production) of language increases so parents tend to adjust their complexity of language usage (Cunningham *et al.* 1985), adults tend to speak to language retarded children as if they were younger than their chronological age (Cross *et al.* 1985, Howlin and Rutter 1987); and even children tend to adapt their style of language when speaking to younger children (Shatz and Gelman 1973, Sachs and Devlin 1976).

The question is whether this style of speaking facilitates the development of language. It seems unlikely that people deliberately talk in this way to aid grammar. As Brown (1977) pointed out, many of the speech characteristics are common to utterances made to foreigners and even to talk between lovers! Instead it is likely that parents are attempting to keep their children interested and to ensure that they understand, rather than tutor them in grammar. Even so, it is probable that the speech characteristics may be helpful. Children seem less likely to respond to sentences that are too complex or that they do not understand (Shipley *et al.* 1969). However, that observation raises the further issue of which aspects of parental language most matter in this connection. As Wells and Gutfreund argue (Chapter 6), the evidence suggests that the structure and complexity of utterances probably matter far less than the social communicative features that both prolong conversations and make them interesting to the children.

Of course, the nature of the language input to children in no way explains language acquisition. Most of all, it fails to account for the special qualities of the structure of language. Also it is clear that children acquire complex language despite rearing in environments that seem to lack the qualities necessary to facilitate language development (Lieven 1978). Furthermore, a comparison of adoptees and biologically reared children indicates that at least some of the associations represent genetic rather than environmental effects (Hardy-Brown and Plomin 1985). At most, the findings provide only a general guide to the conversational features likely to encourage children's language. It is not probable that the fine grained features of parental language make much difference to the process of language acquisition. Moreover, it is not self-evident that the features most beneficial for normal children will be the same ones that are most helpful for those with language handicaps (see below).

Does the pace of early language development matter?
Most of the evidence on early language development has been concerned with variations in the speed with which young normal children acquire particular linguistic skills during the preschool years. The clinician has to pose the further query as to whether it matters whether children acquire language early or late.

Entirely normal children may be using single words as early as eight months whereas others do not do so until after their second birthday. As Fletcher points out (Chapter 5), the range of normality is very wide. Are variations within this normal range of any clinical significance? Clearly, *abnormal* delays are a matter of concern in view of the frequency with which there are persisting sequelae (see Chapters 1 and 17) but it is much more dubious whether early or late speech acquisition as such is of any great moment in the absence of pathology.

It is necessary to ask, for example, whether variations in the pace of early language development correlate with later verbal prowess, IQ, educational attainments, or socio-emotional functioning? Surprisingly little is known on this score. Probably there is a low positive correlation but the associations appear rather inconsistent apart from an unexplained stronger correlation in boys than in girls (Plomin and DeFries 1985).

The meaning of even these very modest associations remains uncertain. Does the early mastery of language provide the child with skills that give an advantage in later psychological functioning? Or is the early acquisition of language a *result* of superior cognitive endowment? Alternatively, are the associations between early language and later cognition (or socio-emotional functioning) a function of continuities in environmental influences? It is probable that all these explanations have some validity. Studies of the continuities and discontinuities in psychological development from infancy to later childhood reveal a complex set of two-way reciprocal interactions in which skills in one area facilitate progress in another; with children influencing their parents as well as vice versa; and with later experience (beneficial and adverse) both partially determined by earlier happenings and also sometimes over-riding the effects of what has gone before (Rutter in press).

Grammar, semantics, cognition and pragmatics

The growing appreciation during the late 1960s and early 1970s of the limitations of Chomsky's transformational theory led to a research focus on both cognitive and semantic facets of language acquisition. Various theorists proposed that language grew out of some mix of general cognitive analytic abilities (Cromer 1981, Maratsos 1983). These theorists differed from Chomsky in their postulate that language was an outgrowth of general cognition rather than an entirely separate skill that was a function of an inbuilt system of grammatical rules. Also most attributed a greater (albeit still minor) rôle to environmental influences than that suggested by Chomsky. However, they agreed with Chomsky in their emphasis on children as active agents in language learning. But, in contrast to transformational theory, the motivation was thought to come from an active desire to express meanings made available through conceptual development. Two somewhat different types of cognitive theory have been proposed. First, there are those that concentrate on the cognitive mechanisms and operations that make a structured language system possible. Thus, attention has been paid to the rôle of auditory short term memory in verbal comprehension (Menyuk 1969, Conrad 1972): and to the need for hierarchical planning in the production and comprehension of linguistic structure. The second type of theory emphasizes the importance of meaning in language acquisition. The hypothesis is that the major aspects of grammar can be accounted for by the child's active application of major semantic categories. In other words, it is suggested that children pay attention to and acquire only those aspects of language that encode the ideas and concepts that they already understand or wish to express; those outside their understanding are ignored. Moreover, children's word combinations are thought to reflect semantic connections more than grammatical structures, with semantic factors central to the definition of grammatical rules. As conceptual understanding grows, so does linguistic competence.

There is an extensive body of evidence that seeks to test out these ideas (Maratsos 1983) but some of the key findings may be summarized succinctly. To begin with, there is general agreement that there is truly some kind of systematic patterning in children's earliest utterances. It follows that young children have *categories* for describing the regularities of word combinations. The question is whether these reflect grammatical units or semantic features (Lyons 1968). It is clear that there is both great individual variation and great specificity in many children's early grammars (Braine 1976). Probably these variations do not reflect differences in linguistic capacities, it is more likely that they reflect differences in what children like to talk about or differences in cognitive style in how language capacities are applied (Maratsos 1983). On the whole, it seems that early grammars tend not to employ formal grammatical categories and relations such as noun and verb or noun and subject. Early speech does not involve the complex grammatical coordinations that were once supposed to occur. Rather, semantic properties such as action or location, or pragmatic factors such as focus, appear to serve to group words, at least in part. In the English language there seems to be a cognitively 'natural' order (subject—verb—object) but this is not so in many other languages. It is evident from comparative language study that there is no truly 'natural' order for grammatical elements and children readily learn the order(s) of the language to which they are exposed.

The subsequent phases of grammatical acquisitions in English involve the appearance of numerous small morphemes and inflections (-ing; plural 's'; -ed etc); the use of auxiliary verbs (such as do, can etc); the emergence of sentence embedding (*e.g.* 'I think he will come', in which the last three words denote what is thought); and then the use of conjunctions together with verb and noun phrases. Brown's (1973) classical study of morpheme appearance showed that often these were acquired gradually, and not suddenly as the result of a rule-guided insight. On the other hand, the overall sequence of acquisition of the 14 morphemes examined was remarkably stable in the three children studied. The order was not a function of frequency of parental use; to some extent it related to transformational complexity, and to a rather greater extent to semantic complexity. Other work, too, has shown the importance of concepts for linguistic usage. Slobin (1966) noted that the hypothetical is grammatically easily expressed in Russian but still it appeared late, as it does in English where its expression is more complex. It seems that children do not use speech forms until they develop the concepts to which the forms refer (Cromer 1974).

It may be accepted that the semantic properties of words and of word combinations play a rôle in language development. But equally it is clear that the growth of grammar can *not* be seen as merely a function of meaning. Concepts are, of course, important in language acquisition because they provide a motivation for children to find words to express their ideas, because they provide ways of constructing sentences, and because the lack of a concept may make it more difficult for the child to develop the relevant word or morpheme association. However, there is no one-to-one relation between non-linguistic concepts and corresponding grammatical expressions. If there were, it would be expected that grammatical constructions encoding similar meanings should all appear at the same time. Both within-language and cross-language comparisons show that this is not so (Maratsos 1983). Cognitive development does not constitute a sufficient explanation of grammar. This is shown, too, by the observation that even when children have the concepts, they do not acquire the relevant adult linguistic forms straight away; the process of acquisition may even take several years (Bellugi 1971). Furthermore, in children with pathological conditions, syntax and semantics may be substantially disconnected. Some aphasic children understand concepts that they cannot encode in language (Cromer 1978); conversely, some mentally retarded children have syntactical skills above their general cognitive level (Curtiss 1981).

In summary, it appears that semantic properties *per se* cannot be the sole source of lexical categories. The earliest general categories tend to be of a semantically defined kind but by the age of three or four shared grammatical combinations are providing the bases for category organization (Maratsos 1983). However, it is not that syntactical structures come to predominate over semantic ones. Rather most rules and categories involve complex mixtures of formal, semantic and pragmatic features.

Concepts and meaning
Language is used to convey meaning and hence it is necessary to consider some aspects of the growth of children's understanding of meaning and use of concepts (Clark 1983). It is clear that the ability to categorize and group objects appears early—from nine months or so onwards. However, children's meanings are not the same as those of adults. At first there may be underextensions so that, for example, the word 'dog' may be used to refer only to one particular dog. A bit later, usually between 12 and 30 months, overextensions become quite common. Thus 'dog' may be used to refer to all manner of animals (Rescorla 1980). Overextensions tend to be based on the *appearance* of relevant objects (in terms of size, shape *etc.*) rather than function (Clark 1973, Bowerman 1978). The proportion of words overextended generally decreases as children's vocabulary increases.

This process of overextending words is strikingly similar in all languages, suggesting that the overextensions themselves may offer clues to the concepts that children use (Clark 1983). The ability to make similarity judgements seems crucial for word usage as well as cognitive representations. It appears that children acquire meanings by working out what category each word picks out (the reference) and how adjacent word meanings contrast with each other (the sense). The complexity of children's initial word uses suggests that the overextensions derive from their desire to communicate (Braunwald 1978). Children are producing words to try to make themselves understood while talking about a much wider range of objects, situations and states than they have the vocabulary for.

Over-and under-extensions are not the only ways in which child meanings depart from adult meanings. Overlaps and mismatches also occur. Overlaps involve simultaneous over-and under-extensions so that, for example, a child might use 'dog' for large dogs and calves but not for small dogs or cows (Clark 1983). Alternatively, words may be acquired first as part of particular routines or formular expressions without the child realizing that the word has a more general usage. Mismatches are those instances when the child starts out with a wrong hypothesis about the adult convention governing the meaning of a word, a hypothesis so wrong that the child's meaning is quite different. Clark and Clark (1977) cited the example of a child who frequently forgot to wipe his boots when he came in. On one occasion his mother remonstrated 'You did that on purpose!'. When asked later what 'on purpose' meant the child's reply was 'It means you're looking at me!'. The guess was reasonable but wrong. Sometimes the wrong usage may be so peculiarly wrong from an adult perspective that it seems that a wholly new word has been invented. Ordinarily if children's misuse of words is met with incomprehension on the adult's part, the word is dropped from the repertoire.

It is unclear how these normal misuses of words and phrases relate to the abnormal language of autistic individuals—described in terms of 'metaphorical' usages and neologisms (see Chapter 13). However there are obvious parallels and it may be that what is abnormal is not so much the occurrence of these language features but their persistence and stereotyped application. Perhaps the lack of social reciprocity and the impaired understanding of language mean that the autistic child fails to make use of the feedback he needs to regulate his language in accord with adult conventions.

It is a general observation that children seem to understand words long before they produce them. Of course, adults, too, have a much larger passive than active vocabulary—recognizing words that they hear but that they never use themselves. However, the relationship between comprehension and production is more complex than simply a lag of the latter behind the former. Clark (1983) argued that the processes involved are rather different. In production, the child knows the concept he wants to use and then searches his memory store for the word that provides the best match to communicate what he means to the other person. In comprehension, the reverse applies. The child seeks to recognize the word he hears and so to identify the conceptual category to which it refers. Both processes are necessary for language mastery.

The later phases of language development involve a tremendous increase in vocabulary; Templin (1957) suggested that it rose to about 14,000 by six years of age. The order in which new words are acquired seems to depend on several different factors. Firstly there is the relative complexity of meaning of words; simpler ones tend to be acquired earlier. Secondly, there is the child's reliance on non-linguistic strategies based on a prior organization of object and situation categories. Thus, across a wide range of language (including even American Sign Language) 'in' is learned before 'on', with both of these being acquired before 'under' (Clark 1983). This order reflected the children's ease in using locative terms when required simply to copy adult's actions. The semantic feature hypothesis was proposed to account for children's acquisition of meaning (Clark 1973). It assumed that meanings break down into combinations of units; the proposal being that children start with partial meanings to which they add elements until gradually the meaning matches that of adults—moving from the most general to most specific characteristics. This suggestion seemed in keeping with the data on overextensions. However, it is noteworthy that overextensions in comprehension are much rarer than those in production. That observation, together with the evidence on the use of nonlinguistic strategies, suggests that the acquisition of meaning must rely on conceptual as well as semantic features, on non-linguistic constructs, and also on patterns of usage and experience with the objects/situations concerned (Clark 1983).

Clark (1983) argued that in acquiring meanings children use two basic principles of lexical organization—*contrast* and *conventionality*. In other words, the meaning of words depends on contrasts with other paired words (*e.g.* children learn the meaning of 'dog' through contrasts with 'cat', 'lamb' *etc.*); and for certain meanings there is a conventional word or meaning that should be used in the language community. The implication is that children's knowledge of meaning builds up through their testing of hypotheses about what words can be used for. Such hypotheses are likely to be based on non-linguistic knowledge initially but linguistic information later. The process, however, is essentially social. Children look for new words to fill gaps in their communication systems and, also, when they hear new words they assume that they must contrast with ones with which they are already familiar. This filling of lexical gaps leads to overextensions, to the use of general purpose words like 'that', and also to the coinage of new words.

It may be envisaged that this process of filling lexical gaps will be more prominent in children with impairments in language comprehension and more prolonged in those who lack the social interchange skills needed to move on to conventional adult usages. Although not exploited up to now, the approach suggests a way of tackling some of the language abnormalities associated with autism. It also emphasizes that conceptual categories and word meanings, although linked, are by no means synonymous. But, perhaps most of all, lexical contrast theory is important in making communication (rather than any aspect of speech) primary. The implication is that the acquisition of figurative language ('spill the beans', 'hit the sack' *etc.*) and of colloquial language is likely to depend on social communicative skills as much as linguistic competence *per se*.

Communication

Much communication does not involve language (*e.g.* smiles of welcome or frowns of disapproval) and some language lacks communicative intent (as with talking to one's self to express feelings of irritation, or daydreaming or in organizing thoughts). Nevertheless, the main purpose of language is social communication and it is necessary to consider both its roots during the prelinguistic phase and also the later integration with language (see Chapter 4).

Homo sapiens is a social animal and it is reasonable to suppose that there is some kind of innate predisposition for the seeking of social interaction (Bowlby 1969/82). However, although babies are indeed socially responsive in ways that make them rewarding to parents, at first the social dialogues are mainly regulated by adults rather than infants. Nevertheless within the period of about nine to 18 months it seems that infants develop the ability to have intentional states and to base interactive behaviour upon such states (Shatz 1983). Piaget supposed that infants were initially egocentric in their thinking and that it was this characteristic that limited their communicative skills. However this does not provide an adequate explanation both because infants are already intensely social in orientation and because young children produce communications that are inadequate even for themselves (Asher and Oden 1976).

Instead it seems that social communication arises on the basis of a mixture of skills. Thus, it depends on people's ability to judge the social needs of any particular situation. Not only do children as young as 4 years of age adapt their speech when talking to a younger child, but also they do so differently when they see themselves in a teaching rôle than when they are trying to engage the younger child in informal play (Shatz and Gelman 1977). In addition, it is neccessary that they learn to alternate turn taking and to build a discourse in a way that is dependent upon and related to preceding adult utterances—a skill that is evident by the age of two years or so (Shatz 1983). Referential skills, too, are important; that is the ability to appreciate the other speaker's perspective. Charney's (1979) data suggest that this skill is already present in the third year of life although children's ability to apply the skill adequately varies considerably by situation and takes some four to five years more before it is well established. Furthermore, even preschool children have some appreciation of age and status relationships and adjust their speech accordingly (Corsaro 1979). However, conversational skills also rely on the ability to make inferences about the other person's intentions, feelings and needs. Preschoolers have some skills of this kind but the quality and complexity of their inferences increases substantially during the primary school years (Shantz 1983).

The precise links between these social cognitive skills and language are far from well understood. Nevertheless, it is clear that children's ability to *use* language for communicative purposes will be affected by their competencies in social cognition as well as in linguistics. Moreover, it is not difficult to see that the informality of colloquial language relies to a considerable extent on the person's appreciation of what can be understood in context. It is probable that the pedantic formality of the spoken language used by many autistic individuals stems from deficits in this area. There is substantial potential for using knowledge on normal language and communicative development to delineate more accurately the specific deficits associated with language disorders; however most of their potential has yet to be realized (but see Chapter 11).

Clinical implications

During the 1960s most research on language development was concerned with syntax but the last decade or so has been characterized by a burgeoning of investigations into the several other systems that make up language—semantics, phonology, pragmatics and the cognitive processes and concepts thought to underlie them. It is no longer clinically acceptable to use vague descriptions such as 'immature or inappropriate language' or 'language is impaired'. Rather, it is imperative to specify the nature of the language disorder more precisely in order both to devise adequate remedial or therapeutic programmes and to advise families on prognosis. Some of the ways in which this may be tackled are outlined in Chapters 2, 13 and 18.

It is clear that, although the different facets of language tend to develop roughly in parallel in normal children, frequently this is not the case when there is a serious language delay. The identification of the particular aspects of language that are delayed or deviant in their development is not just an academic exercise, because the processes and influences involved in different language systems are not identical. Moreover, the balance between the factors implicated in language development alter somewhat as language development progresses. However, at all ages, language cannot be considered as an isolated skill. There are indeed features that are unique to language but so also language is a code for the communication to other people of ideas. As such, social processes are important in its development. Concepts and cognitive skills both help shape the course of language acquisition and the uses to which language is put. Many questions on the 'what' and 'how' of language development still await answers but already the findings from research have implications for clinicians in terms of how they assess language, how aetiological processes are conceptualized, and how prognosis is evaluated.

ACKNOWLEDGEMENTS

I am much indebted to the excellent accounts of different facets of language development in Mussen's Handbook of Child Psychiatry by Eve Clark, Michael Maratsos, Carolyn Shantz and Marilyn Shatz, on which the chapter leans heavily.

REFERENCES

Asher, S. R., Oden, S. (1976) 'Children's failure to communicate: an assessment of comparison and egocentrism explanations.' *Developmental Psychology,* **12,** 132–139.

Baker, N., Nelson, K. (1984) 'Recasting and related conversational techniques for triggering syntactic advances by young children.' *First Language,* **5,** 3–22.

Bellugi, U. (1971) 'Simplification in children's language.' *In:* Huxley, R., Ingram, E. (Eds.) *Language Acquisition: Models and Methods.* New York and London: Academic Press. pp. 95–119.

Berko, J. (1958) 'The child's learning of English morphology.' *Word,* **14,** 150–177.

Bowerman, M. (1978) 'Semantic and syntactic development: a review of what, when and how in language acquisition.' *In:* Schiefelbusch, R. L. (Ed.) *Bases of Language Intervention.* University Park Press: Baltimore. pp. 98–189.

Bowlby, J. (1969/82) *Attachment and Loss I: Attachment.* London: Hogarth.

Braunwald, S. R. (1978) 'Context, word and meaning: towards a communicational analyses of lexical acquisition.' *In:* Lock, A. (Ed.) *Action, Gesture and Symbol.* Academic Press: New York.

Braine, M. D. (1976) 'Children's first word combinations.' *Monographs of the Society for Research in*

Children, Vol. 41., Serial No. 164.

Brown, R. (1973) *A First Language.* Cambridge, Mass.: Harvard University Press.

—— (1977) 'Introduction.' *In:* Snow, C., Ferguson, C. A. (Eds.) *Talking to Children.* Cambridge: Cambridge University Press.

—— Hanlon, C. (1970) 'Derivational complexity and the order of acquisition in child speech.' *In:* Hayes, J. R. (Ed.) *Cognition and the Development of Language.* New York: John Wiley. pp. 11–53.

Charney, R. (1979) 'The comprehension of "here" and "there". *Journal of Child Language,* **6,** 69–80.

Chomsky, N. (1959) 'A review of B. F. Skinner's verbal behaviour.' *Language,* **35,** 26–58.

Clark, E. V. (1973) 'What's in a word? On the child's acquisition of semantics in his first language.' *In:* Moore, C. T. E. (Ed.) *Cognitive Development and the Acquisition of Language.* New York and London: Academic Press. pp. 65–110.

—— (1983) 'Meanings and concepts'. *In:* Flavell, J. H., Markman, E. M. (Eds.) *Cognitive Development. Vol III. Mussens Handbook of Child Psychology, (4th Edn.)* New York: John Wiley.

Clark, H., Clark, E. V. (1977) *Psychology and Language: An Introduction to Linguistics.* New York: Harcourt Brace.

Conrad, R. (1972) 'The developmental role of vocalising in short-term memory.' *Journal of Verbal Learning and Verbal Behaviour,* **11,** 521–533.

Corsaro, W. A. (1979) 'Young children's conception of status and role.' *Sociology of Education,* **52,** 46–59.

Cromer, R. F. (1974) 'The development of language and cognition: the cognition hypothesis.' *In:* Foss, B. M. (Ed.) *New Perspectives in Child Development.* Harmondsworth: Penguin. pp. 184–252.

—— (1978) 'The basis of childhood dysphasia: a linguistic approach.' *In:* Wyke, C. M. A. (Ed.) *Developmental Dysphasia.* New York and London: Academic Press. pp. 85–134.

—— (1980) 'Normal language development: recent progress.' *In:* Hersov, L. A., Berger, M., Nicol, A. R. (Eds.) *Language and Language Disorder in Childhood.* Oxford: Pergamon.

—— (1981) 'Reconceptualizing language acquisition and cognitive development.' *In:* Schiefelbusch, R., Bricker, D. (Eds.) *Early Language: Acquisition and Intervention.* Baltimore: University Park Press.

Cross, T. G., Nienhuys, R. G., Kirkman, M. (1985) 'Parent-child interaction with receptively disabled children: some determinants of maternal speech style.' *In:* Nelson, K. E. (Ed.) *Children's Language, Volume 5.* Hillsdale, N. J.: Erlbaum.

Cunningham, C. E., Siegel, L. S., van der Spry, H. I. J., Clark, M. L., Bow, S. J. (1985) 'The behavioral and linguistic of specifically language-delayed and normal boys with their mothers.' *Child Development,* **56,** 1389–1403.

Curtiss, S. (1981) 'Dissociations between language and cognition: cases and implications.' *Journal of Autism and Developmental Disorders,* **11,** 15–30.

Hardy-Brown, K., Plomin, R. (1985) 'Infant communicative development: evidence from adoptive and biological families for genetic and environmental influences on rate differences.' *Developmental Psychiatry,* **21,** 378–385.

Hoff Ginsberg, E. (1985) 'Relations between discourse properties of mothers' speech and their children's syntactic growth.' *Journal of Child Language,* **12,** 367–385.

—— (1986) 'Function and structure in maternal speech: their relation to the child's development of syntax.' *Developmental Psychology,* **22,** 155–163.

Howlin, P. (1980) 'Language' *In:* Rutter, M. (Ed.) *Scientific Foundations of Developmental Psychiatry.* London: Heinemann. pp. 198–220.

—— Rutter, M. (1987) 'The verbal interaction between autistic children and their mothers.' *Journal of Child Psychology and Psychiatry (in press).*

Lieven, E. V. M. (1978) 'Turn-taking and pragmatics. Two issues in early child language.' *In:* Campbell, R. N., Smith, P. T. (Eds.) *Recent Advances in the Psychology of Language.* New York: Plenum.

Lyons, J. (1968) *Introduction to Theoretical Linguistics.* Cambridge: Cambridge University Press.

Maratsos, M. (1983) 'Some current issues in the study of the acquisition of grammar.' *In:* Flavell, J. H., Markman, E. M. (Eds.) *Cognitive Development, Vol III, Mussens Handbook of Child Psychology. (4th Edn.)* New York: Wiley.

Menyuk, P. (1969) *Sentences Children Use.* Cambridge, Mass: MIT.

Plomin, R. DeFries, J. C. (1985) *Origins of Individual Differences in Infancy: The Colorado Adoption Project.* Orlando, Florida: Academic Press.

Rescorla, L. (1980) 'Overextensions in early language development.' *Journal of Child Language,* **7,** 321–335.

Rutter, M. (1980) 'Language training with autistic children: how does it work and what does it achieve?'

In Hersov, L. A., Berger, M. (Eds.) *Language and Language Disorders in Childhood*. Oxford: Pergamon. pp. 147–172.

—— (1987) 'Continuities and discontinuities from infancy.' In Osofsky, J. (Ed.) *Handbook of Infant Development (2nd Edn.)*. New York: Wiley (in press).

Sachs, J., Devlin, J. (1976) 'Young children's knowledge of age appropriate speech styles.' *Journal of Child Language, 3,* 81–98.

Scherer, M., Olswang, L. (1984) 'Role of mothers' expansions in stimulating children's language production.' *Journal of Speech and Hearing Research, 27,* 387–396.

Schwartz, R., Chapman, K., Prelock, P., Terrell, B., Rowan, L. (1985) 'Facilitation of early syntax through discourse structure.' *Journal of Child Language, 12,* 13–25.

Shantz, C. U. (1983) 'Social cognition.' *In:* Flavell, J. H., Markman, E. M. (Eds.) *Cognitive Development Vol. III, Mussens Handbook of Child Psychology. (4th Edn),* New York: Wiley.

Shatz, M. (1983) 'Communication.' *In:* Flavell, J. H., Markman, E. M. (Eds.) *Cognitive Development Vol. III, Mussens Handbook of Child Psychology. (4th Edn)*. New York: Wiley.

Shatz, M., Gelman, R. (1973) 'The development of communication skills: modifications in the speech of young children as a function of listener.' *Monographs of the Society for Research in Child Development, 38,* No. 5, Series No. 152.

—— —— (1977) 'Beyond syntax: The influences of conversational constraints on speech modifications.' *In:* Snow, C., Ferguson, C. (Eds.) *Talking to Children: Language Input and Acquisition*. Cambridge: Cambridge University Press.

Shipley, E. F., Smith, C. S., Gleitman, L. R. (1969) 'A study in the acquisition of language: free responses to command.' *Language, 45,* 322–342.

Skinner, B. F. (1957) *Verbal Behavior*. New York: Appleton Century Crofts.

Slobin, D. I. (1966) 'Comments on developmental psycholinguistics by D. McNeil.' *In:* Miller, G. A., Smith, F. (Eds.) *The Genesis of Language*. Cambridge, Mass: MIT.

Templin, M. C. (1957) 'Certain language skills in children: their development and interrelationships.' *University of Minnesota Institute of Child Welfare Monographs, 26.*

170

11
LANGUAGE ACQUISITION, LANGUAGE DISORDER AND COGNITIVE DEVELOPMENT

Richard F. Cromer

Introduction

Over the past two decades, research on language acquisition has shifted its focus from one to another of what can be called the various *subsystems* that comprise language. In Chapter 3, David Crystal has given descriptions of these subsystems. One of the major problems facing clinicians who have attempted to keep abreast of the research literature has been the competing claims for the primacy of one or another of these subsystems as providing the only useful explanation for language development or language disorder. Such claims are often accompanied by the downgrading of explanations offered by researchers who have focused their attention on the currently less favoured subsystems. I will argue that an understanding is needed of all of the subsystems of language.

In the first part of this chapter some of the recent research findings on language in the handicapped will be reviewed in terms of the four subsystems of language. The aim is to illustrate how considering language in this way may aid in clarification of the language problems faced by particular handicapped groups or individuals. In a final section, I will claim that this subsystem approach is by itself inadequate. Its purpose is merely to aid in descriptive adequacy. Real advances for therapy and intervention will only be achieved with an understanding of the underlying impairments that result in the observed language characteristics that are described in terms of the subsystems. As part of that claim, some possible cognitive and other impairments and their effects will be described.

Subsystem deficits

Syntax

It might be thought that with so much research on the syntactic component of grammar, a good deal would now be known about syntactic impairments in children with various language disorders. But in fact very few individuals can adequately be described as having language disorders primarily due to problems with syntax. For example, a good deal of research effort has been expended on examining the language of mentally retarded children. One of the most commonly found characteristics of mental retardation is that many non-language developmental processes, while the same as in normal children, proceed at a slower rate and thus evidence delay in appearance. Much the same conclusion has been reached for syntactic development. In the well-known early study by Lenneberg *et al.* (1964), 61 Down's syndrome children living at home were found to perform like younger normal children on imitation tests. Language development was best predicted by the passing of particular motor milestones.

Lackner (1968) wrote transformational grammars of the utterances of five retarded children suffering congenital or early acquired encephalopathy. He found that sentence length increased with mental age and was the same as in normal children at that age. Their syntactic rules developed regularly and became more differentiated with increasing mental age, as did the number and types of transformations that were understood on imitation and comprehension tests. Lackner concluded that the language of normal and retarded children is not qualitatively different. Both groups follow similar developmental trends. This basic conclusion has been repeatedly supported by various recent studies, although some tasks reveal a delay in acquisition beyond what would be predicted on the basis of mental age (Cromer 1987). Retarded children, if they acquire language, do not seem to have basic syntactic impairments: but they do evidence problems with the other subsystems of language.

Autistic children might also be thought to show specifically syntactic language impairments. Many of these children, of course, have no language or evidence only non-productive echolalia. Nothing can be said about a specifically syntactic impairment in such cases, since the entire language faculty is affected. But in those autistic children who acquire some language, can any of the oddness of that language be attributed to syntactic deficits?

The evidence for a syntactic disability in autistic children is somewhat conflicting. Earlier experiments appeared to indicate some syntactic deficit. Hermelin and O'Connor (1967) compared subnormal autistic children with severely subnormal non-autistic children. They made use of the common finding that most subnormal children have extremely short memory spans, but can increase the amount of information they can process by using sentence structure. In Hermelin and O'Connor's experiment, the 12 children in each group were prematched on the basis of their immediate memory span for digits, as well as on their scores from the Peabody Picture Vocabulary Test. The experimental task was to repeat words that were arranged either randomly or in sentences. While the severely subnormal non-autistic children performed significantly better with sentences than with random sequences, no such difference was found for the autistic children. It appeared that the autistic children were not able to use sentence structure to improve their memory span.

Aurnhammer-Frith (1969) obtained similar results. In her experiment, the autistic children were prematched for digit span performance with normal children of comparable mental age. Subjects had to recall word lists of four, six, eight, 10, 12, or 14 words that were arranged either as grammatically correct and meaningful sentences, or as meaningless strings of words without syntactical connection. The results showed that both groups benefited from grammatical structure and performed better on sentences than on randomly arranged words. However, the normal children benefited significantly more than the autistic group did. That is, as compared to normal children, the autistic group was somewhat impaired in the ability to make use of sentence structure. Fyffe and Prior (1978) have recently replicated this finding. But it is important to note that the autistic children did in fact benefit to some extent from syntactic structure. Similarly, Fay and Mermelstein (1982) report a study by Voeltz (1976) that obtained confirmatory evidence on imitation by autistic children of grammatical sentences and their scrambled equivalents. In Aurnhammer-Frith's study, it was merely that normal children benefited significantly more.

Pierce and Bartolucci (1977) assessed the syntactic abilities of 10 autistic, 10 retarded, and 10 normal children who had been matched for a non-language mental age of about six years on the Leiter scale. Free-speech samples were obtained, and each child's level of syntactic development was assessed by Lee's Developmental Sentence Scoring (DSS) carried out on 50 utterances from each child. The normals obtained a DSS score in keeping with Lee's (1974) norms for six-year-olds. The mentally retarded group attained a mean score comparable to that of normal 4½-year-olds. The mean score of the autistic group was at the level of syntactic ability achieved by 3½-year-olds. Pierce and Bartolucci concluded that the syntax used by autistic children lags behind that of both normal and mentally retarded children who are at the same level of mental functioning.

In a transformational grammatical analysis of the data, Pierce and Bartolucci (1977) found that the grammars of children with mental ages below their group mean tended to have simpler base grammars in which relative clauses, verb phrase complements, some modals, the perfect and the passive voice were missing. This was true regardless of the group to which the child belonged. They argued that since the variability in mental-age scores was greater for the autistic and retarded groups, with each containing several children of a lower mental age than any in the normal group, it was not surprising that only those two groups had simpler base grammars. So while the grammars of some autistic and mentally retarded children were simpler than those found in any of the normal children, they were not deviant. Pierce and Bartolucci argue that if younger children of normal intelligence had been studied, they too would be using the same sorts of simplified base grammars found in the less advanced mentally retarded and autistic children in their study. They concluded that the syntax of autistic children is rule-governed but less complex than that of normal children.

A series of experiments on high-level autistic children with reading ability was conducted by Frith and Snowling (1983). The eight autistic children who were examined were between nine and 17 years old chronologically, and their reading ages ranged from 8:1 to 10:2 on the British Ability Scale Reading Test, a test of single-word naming. In one of the experiments, intact syntactic processing was demonstrated in an ingenious way. The autistic children read sentences that contained a nonsense word marked either for singular or plural. The pronunciation of words with a final 's' depends on this distinction in English. Note the pronunciation in words marked for singularity: 'One yellow *bippis* is enough for me'; 'I like to fly in a *gakis*'. Compare the pronunciation when these identical nonsense items are marked for plurality: 'All these *bippis* are fresh today'; 'Twenty *gakis* lived in a box.' These sentences originally came from Ruth Campbell (unpublished material) who studied normal children. Frith and Snowling compared their results to Campbell's, as both groups were in the same reading age-range. The pronunciations by the normal and the autistic children were remarkably similar, and for both groups the difference between singular and plural pronunciation was highly significant. The autistic children were clearly able to use phonology to mark the distinction between singular and plural forms. This would serve as further evidence that syntactic development in autistic children is not deviant; the autistic children were sensitive to syntactic constraints.

Probably the best candidate group for a syntactic impairment would be developmentally aphasic children. Adults with Broca's aphasia, who have damage in the anterior portion of the left hemisphere (specifically in Broca's area—though this is often not true for many of the reported cases) are claimed to be agrammatic in that they leave out the little 'function words' in production, and fail adequately to process them in comprehension. These 'agrammatic aphasics' are said to have a specifically syntactic deficit. It is useful to ask what could be meant by a syntactic deficit, and to examine evidence for its occurrence.

One problem concerns the notion of 'function words' which Broca's aphasics handle so poorly. Black (1979, 1980) has seriously questioned the validity of analyses based on problems with 'function words'. She has argued that the notion of 'function words' is poorly defined. Although most researchers treat 'function words' as if they were a syntactic category, in fact they give this class a semantic definition, not a syntactic one. That is, 'function words' are viewed—indeed they are usually *defined* by most researchers—as words with little semantic content, and it is claimed that only information-carrying elements in the sentence are preserved by Broca's aphasics. This *semantic* definition, however, does not yield a homogeneous *syntactic* class; 'function words' include prepositions, particles, auxiliaries and relatives. Black interprets her own experimental data, obtained from six Broca's aphasics, as being more adequately accounted for primarily in terms of a phonological impairment (see also Kean 1977, 1978).

Other researchers, however, give additional evidence for considering Broca's aphasics as syntactically impaired. Saffran *et al.* (1980) and Schwartz *et al.* (1980) have carried out tests of both comprehension and production on five agrammatic patients who had language profiles on the Boston Diagnostic Aphasia Test that were characteristic of Broca's aphasia. Among the tasks, one assessed performance on active and passive sentences; another employed reversible locative statements (*e.g.* 'The square is on top of the circle'). Another studied transitive verbs (*e.g.* 'The square is shooting the circle' where stick figures of a square shooting a circle and of a circle shooting a square were the pictured comprehension choices). The over-all general conclusion from their results was that agrammatic patients lack sensitivity to the rules that assign semantic rôles (agents, objects to be located) to sentence positions. In their paper on comprehension, Schwartz *et al.* (1980) concluded that agrammatic patients have a syntactic mapping defect that renders them unable to use a fixed set of procedures to recover the relational structure of sentences. In their paper on production, Saffran *et al.* (1980) went further and claimed that agrammatic patients have a basic syntactic deficit such that their speech is generated without underlying structures that represent logical relations. They claim that in production, agrammatic patients take the salient elements of a cognitive representation and map them directly into language on a one-to-one basis.

Does this constitute a basic syntactic deficit? Schwartz *et al.* (1980) appear to believe that it does, and that agrammatic patients lack underlying syntactic structures. However, if Broca's aphasics have a basic syntactic impairment, it would be difficult to explain the observed performance by such patients on those tasks not requiring rôle differentiation, or on which word-order is used consistently but incorrectly. It may be that agrammatic patients have trouble mapping word-order onto semantic interpretations. But that is a very different claim from one that posits a specifically syntactic impairment.

So what would a syntactic deficit look like? The clearest case would be the inability to assign words to constituent categories. Comprehension would be seriously impaired, and perhaps limited to the understanding of content words. Production would show little evidence of any constituent structure. A few years ago, I collected and analysed language samples from a number of severly aphasic children (Cromer 1978*a*, *b*). These children appear to be suffering from a rare aphasic syndrome, referred to in the literature as 'acquired aphasia with convulsive disorder in children' (Landau and Kleffner 1957). Children who are described by this syndrome neither comprehend nor produce oral language. In the group studied, children were specially chosen so that deafness, mental deficiency, motor disability, and severe personality disorder could be excluded as the causes of their language difficulties. These children have been taught in their special residential school to read and write, and it was their written productions in controlled situations that were analysed. Some of the results will be described in the section where underlying impairments are examined. One child in the group, however, produced written language that was qualitatively different from the others, and which could possibly be taken as an example of what productions without constituent knowledge might look like.

Children were shown actions with toys that formed short, non-verbal 'stories'. Their task was merely to observe the story, and after its completion to write a description of what they had seen. No language was used; the words the children wrote were generated from their internal lexicons. One of the stories involved a camel pulling a cart up an incline. At various points other animals jumped into the cart as it passed—a lion, then a tiger, then a horse. When next a cow climbed in, the horse got out to push. At the top of the incline, the animals jumped into a larger cart. The empty cart rolled back down the hill dragging the camel with it, and the camel and cart landed in a heap at the bottom. Here is the description of that story written by an aphasic boy, aged 14:4, and with an IQ in the normal range (94 on the Collins-Drever Test). His story is reproduced, retaining his spelling, punctuation and alignment:

a camel hill a cart stop a lion and a tiger up.
a cart hill stop camel up horse stop cow good up. 169
tirid happy backwards up a camel down rolling camel.
dangerous cart camel down hurt hospital broken arm

This might be an example of what language output with a severe syntactic deficit would look like. Even here, however, there are some indications of constituent structure. Where determiners occur, they always appear before a noun: a camel, a cart, a lion, a tiger. And two inflections are correctly attached to verb constituents: rolling, broken. One might have expected errors in these. For the most part, then, it is difficult to observe cases in which there is primarily a syntactic deficit. The syntax in various language-disordered children may be delayed, but short of lacking language altogether, it is rare to find basic syntactic defects.

Semantics

Tager-Flusberg (1981) compared the semantic and syntactic abilities of autistic children in two experiments. In one, she compared the comprehension scores as well as the strategies used by normal and autistic children to interpret active and passive sentences which varied in terms of their real-world probability. Sentences like 'the car hits the truck' are called unbiased, since its reverse, 'the truck hits the car' is an equally possible sentence given in isolation. By contrast, a sentence like 'the dog wears the hat' has high positive bias since its reverse results in a sentence which is very low in real-world probability. Sentences of varying degrees of probability were used. For example, the sentence 'the truck hits the boy' is still biased, but not as strongly as the previous example, since its reverse, 'The boy hits the truck' is also possible, but with a lower degree of probability than the former, as rated in isolated sentences by adults. Children heard the sentences and had to carry out their interpretations with toys that were provided. 18 autistic children of an average chronological age of 8:1 (range 3:11 to 11:10) were compared to a group of 30 normal children (mean chronological age 3:10, range 2:9 to 4:8) who were matched as a group on the Peabody Picture Vocabulary Test and on the Raven's Progressive Matrices. The results showed that the autistic and the normal children both used word-order strategies in sentence comprehension. However, although the comprehension scores of both groups showed an *over-all* effect of probability, a close analysis of individual sentences revealed that the autistic children were not sensitive to the individual probability levels of the words. Furthermore, while only two of the 18 autistic children (11 per cent) used a probable-event strategy for performing on the sentences, 13 of the 30 normal children (43 per cent) used such a strategy.

To test this result further, a second experiment on these children employed only content words rather than full sentences. Children had to give interpretations to strings such as 'girl touch boy', 'boy touch girl' and 'girl boy touch'. The results revealed that while there was no significant difference between the normals and the autistic children in the use of word-order to perform the task, significantly more normal children used a probable-event strategy (54 per cent) than did the children in the autistic group (12 per cent—only two subjects using such a strategy). The use of word-order indicates the extraction of a language-related rule—a mapping property whereby the order of words signals relations such as agent-action-object. Since autistic children used such a strategy as often as normal children, Tager-Flusberg concluded that autism does not involve a basic inability to use linguistic rules—at least in those children who used such a strategy, it should be added. By contrast, most of the autistic children did not use a probable-event strategy; they appeared not to use semantic knowledge for their interpretations to the same extent as normal children. In the experiment with sentences, they were not as sensitive to the individual probability levels, and in both experiments very few autistic children used a probable-event strategy. Tager-Flusberg argued that when normal children use a probable-event strategy, it shows that they are responding to linguistic input on the basis of some minimal understanding of the content words. This input is then mapped directly onto conceptual knowledge.

In another of the experiments on autistic children with reading ability conducted by Frith and Snowling (1983), passages from the Gap Test (McLeod 1970) were presented to autistic, dyslexic and normal children who had been matched on reading age. The task on that test is to write in the missing words that are indicated by spaces in the passage that do not give clues to the length of the words. An example would be 'There was a chest of —— and a cupboard to put things ——.' Completions were scored not only in terms of correct and incorrect, but also whether the incorrect responses belonged to the same syntactic class as the target word. Frith and Snowling found that although autistic children made significantly more errors than the control groups, the errors that they made belonged to the same syntactic class as the targets approximately twice as often as to incorrect classes, and this was the same ratio as that found for normal and dyslexic readers. So while their syntactic competence (at least as gauged by answers on this test) was similar to that of the control groups, they were less able to provide the correct target word within each syntactic class. To check this possible semantic disability still further, another experiment employed short stories in which, at intervals, the subject was faced with various word choices. Some of these required the subject to choose the correct verb, as in:

(swim)
'Tom could (hear) something else nearby'.
(heat)

Others forced a choice on nouns, as in:

(holes)
'He looked in the (drawers) in the riverbank. . . '.
(books)

Still others required a choice of 'function words' as in:

(of)
'The duck flew (for) the air'.
(into)

The results revealed that the autistic children, while scoring above chance, nevertheless performed significantly more poorly on this task than the reading-matched normal and dyslexic children, who scored near ceiling. The autistic children were less able than the controls to use context in order to choose the correct word semantically within a given syntactic class.

However, it does not seem that autistic children have a basic semantic impairment; for in another of the experiments by Frith and Snowling (1983), some intact semantic functioning by autistic children was demonstrated. This experiment employed the Stroop interference task. In this task, each colour name is written in ink of a conflicting colour and placed in a circle of that same colour. For example, the word 'blue' might be written in red ink and placed within a red circle. The task for the child was merely to name aloud the colour of the circles. They were told to ignore the words inside the circles, and practice ensured that the task was understood. The classic Stroop effect is that when the meaning of the word conflicts with the ink colour, performance is significantly slowed down. In Frith and Snowling's experiment, all three groups—the autistic and the reading-age-matched normals and dyslexics—showed the Stroop effect to the same degree. Frith and Snowling concluded that the autistic children are accessing the printed words and are doing so automatically. It should also be recalled that in their results on choices of the correct word in a story, the autistic children—while scoring significantly poorer than the control children—nevertheless scored significantly above chance, thus indicating some semantic processing.

It would appear that autistic children do not suffer a primary semantic defect. They perform adequately on some semantic tasks, especially those requiring the reading of single words. But they sometimes fail to use contextual semantic cues when reading.

Nevertheless, some degree of semantic deficit has been noted. Hermelin and O'Connor (1967) have observed the use of less semantic clustering in recall than did mental-age-matched controls. Tager-Flusberg (1981) found a tendency towards less use of semantic strategies (the probable-event strategy) for interpreting sentences and other linguistic strings. In the experiments cited here, and in those of Frith and Snowling (1983), basic semantic abilities were found to be largely unimpaired, but autistic children were less able to make use of meaningful context. What is made manifest as a semantic deficit in language itself, may really be reflective of underlying conceptual deficits.

Curtiss (1981) has been studying the dissociations between language and cognitive abilities in individual cases of various language-disordered children. Two of her cases are of especial interest here. One of these, Antony, was studied from the age of 6:5 to 7:2. His IQ was estimated to be between 50 and 56. The syntax of his language, however, despite his low IQ, was described as having an impressive range of features—third-person pronouns, demonstratives, infinitive markers, object sentential complements, 'wh' pronouns, and nearly the full range of auxiliary forms. His sentences were grammatically well formed, but his speech was described as being semantically inappropriate. Some of his modal auxiliaries were inappropriate, tenses were used inconsistently, and he occasionally employed the wrong 'wh' word in questions (*e.g.* 'where I took' in a context where 'what' appeared to be more appropriate to the meaning). Curtiss further reported that he was unable to respond to 'how' or 'why' questions, frequently misinterpreted questions as assertions, and often misunderstood the inferential content of utterances. She reports the following exchanges as examples (where A is Antony):

s: You sew with that (explaining spool)
A: No, I don't sew with that
s: Other people do
A: No, my mom do

J: Draw a picture of Vivian
A: No. It's not Vivian's, it's mine
s: Draw a picture of Mrs w
A: No. It's not Mrs w's

In a second case, Marta, cognitive deficit in an adolescent was explored in relation to language. Marta was 16 years old and had an IQ of 44. She was described by Curtiss as being 'barely testable, has severely limited attentional capacity, and often cannot understand or perform tasks that normal two-year-olds perform successfully.' Nevertheless, her syntactic and morphological abilities were said to be richly developed. She produced sentences that Curtiss described as involving relativisation, complementation, pronominalisation, passivisation, word-order reversals, and full-blown noun-phrase and verb-phrase morphology. She produced such complex sentences as 'He's my third principal I've had since I've been here' and 'She does paintings, this really good friend of the kids who I went to school with last year, and really loved.' However, in spite of the richness of her syntactic and morphological system, Marta's speech was described as often being confusing or even meaningless. Her sentences were frequently ill formed semantically even when taken in context, and incorrect tense, aspect, pronoun, and adverb usage often occurred. More complete reports of these cases and others can be found in Curtiss *et al.* (1978), Curtiss and Yamada (1981) and Yamada (1981). Some other children with language disorders also appear to have primary semantic impairments. Rapin and Allen (1983) used the label 'semantic pragmatic syndrome without autism' for children who have very fluent expressive language. They described the utterances produced by such children as being 'syntactically well formed, phonologically intact, and, on the surface, "good language". On closer examination, however, one discovers that the language is often not really communicative' (p. 174). Children with this type of language show an impairment in the ability to encode meaning relevant to the conversational situation. Questions may be answered, for example, with seemingly irrelevant responses. Rapin and Allen reported that one child with this syndrome answered the question 'Where do you go to school?' with 'Tommy goes to my school because I see him in the hall everyday, but we have different teachers, and I like arithmetic but Tommy likes reading'. It would be difficult to pinpoint the problem here as affecting the semantic component, in the sense that Curtiss reported for Antony. The syndrome described by Rapin and Allen has usually been observed in children with hydrocephaly.

Some children with internal hydrocephaly talk excessively, but if they are mentally retarded their language has been described as lacking in content. Taylor

(1959) described such children as having an impressive vocabulary. Hadenius *et al.* (1962) reported on six hydrocephalic children in whom mental retardation was observed along with 'a peculiar contrast between a good ability to learn words and talk, and not knowing what they are talking about' (p. 118). They described these children as loving to chatter but thinking illogically, and they coined the term 'cocktail-party syndrome' for the condition. Ingram and Naughton (1962) described 16 cerebral-palsied patients with arrested hydrocephalus, nine of whom fit this description. There was a marked disparity between what they could say and what they could do. Ingram and Naughton described these children as 'chatterboxes', 'excessively talkative' or 'bletherers', and the term 'chatterbox syndrome' has now also come to be used to describe this condition.

Anderson and Spain (1977) reported a study of spina-bifida children, 40 per cent of whom showed the hyperverbal syndrome—although only about half of that number exhibited it to any significant degree. The hyperverbal children were typically female, and were poor intellectually, with considerably higher verbal than performance skills. Analysis of the children's spontaneous speech showed that they used quite complex syntax, but often inaccurately. Their utterances were described as bizarre, and the children rarely seemed to understand the meaning of some adult-type phrases that they used. Hyperverbal children, then, may evidence some degree of semantic impairment. A more complete review of children with this type of language can be found in Cromer (1987).

Pragmatics
The work so far reviewed on language in speaking autistic children appeared to show no basic impairment in either the syntactic or the semantic components. However, there is some evidence that autistic children suffer from basic impairment or impairments that affect the pragmatic use of language. Christiane Baltaxe (1977) made an in-depth study of the language of five high verbal-level adolescents who had been diagnosed as autistic in childhood. At the time of her study they were between 14 and 21 years of age. Their IQ range, as assessed on the Wechsler Intelligence Scale, was 86 to 118. They were all from a middle-class background. None was institutionalised and all lived at home with their parents. Baltaxe analysed the utterances that she collected from a recorded interview that was structured to elicit various types of verbal responses. Based on this analysis, Baltaxe found impairment in three pragmatic areas. One of these had to do with the relationship between the shifting rôles of a speaker and a listener in a conversational dialogue. For example, subjects would encode information as if they were still in the listener rôle when reporting a former dialogue, rather than taking the rôle of a speaker in the present. Baltaxe quoted one child as saying, 'I told my parents I'd be good at home but I feel you're too old to be at home, we feel you should be away.'

A second pragmatic impairment centred on problems with rules governing a dialogue. The autistic children appeared to be ignorant of the rules of acceptability and politeness. For example, the social rules that govern linguistic interchanges between older and younger speakers had not been acquired, and the autistic child's speech often appeared inappropriate, rude or tactless. A good example of the way this pragmatic deficit can affect other aspects of the linguistic system comes from work on the difference between polite and familiar forms of address in languages where these are morphologically marked. In a study of German-speaking adolescent autistics, Baltaxe and Simmons (1977) observed the inability to differentiate between the polite and familiar forms, 'Sie' and 'Du', and the use of these forms interchangeably in the same utterance referring to the same referent.

A third pragmatic impairment was found in the foregrounding and back-grounding of information. Baltaxe (1977) found that the autistic children were unable to differentiate old and new information, and this was observed in their misuses of anaphoric pronouns, definite articles, and relative clauses. For example, in discourse where one would expect the use of anaphoric pronouns to refer to old information, these autistic children would use nouns and fully specified noun phrases, giving their speech a sense of pedantic literalness and redundancy that has often been reported for autistic children.

It would appear that autistic individuals suffer primarily from a pragmatic deficit when their language is considered. This pragmatic deficit, of course, affects all the other subsystems of language—syntax, semantics, and phonology—in ways that can be specified increasingly carefully.

Phonology

It may be that particular handicapped groups of children show specifiable differences from normal children in some aspects of their phonology. One such disorder that has recently received considerable attention is developmental dyslexia (Frith 1981).

Snowling (1980) studied a group of dyslexic children who were substantially behind their peers in reading ability, but whose low reading scores could not be attributed to low intelligence. 18 such children, of mean chronological age 12:1 and a mean IQ of 106, were matched on reading age with 36 normal readers. These were of course younger, with a mean chronological age of 9:5; their mean IQ was 105. Pronounceable nonsense-words were presented either auditorially or visually. The task was merely to make a same/different judgement. The stimuli were presented in various combinations in which the first word was presented either auditorially or visually in combination with the second word, also being presented either auditorially or visually, resulting in four possible presentation types. Both groups did well on the auditory-auditory condition, thus showing that the dyslexic children had no problems with auditory discrimination. But on the visual-auditory task (the task most like real reading) the groups showed a significant difference in performance, with the dyslexic group performing poorly. Snowling concluded that the dyslexic readers performed in a qualitatively different way from normal readers, for it should be recalled that they were matched to the normal readers in terms of reading age. These children appear to have difficulties in visual-sound decoding; they are not merely the low end of a normal distribution of readers. Jorm (1979) has also reviewed evidence that developmental dyslexics have difficulty with a phonological route to meaning, although he attempts to explain this in terms of a short-term memory deficit. Phonological impairments of other types may also be implicated in the problems of other handicapped groups.

Underlying impairments

So far it has been argued that it is useful to consider the description of language deficits in a modular way. It is true that all of the subcomponents of language interact in important ways, and there are many language researchers who would view a modular approach as inaccurate and misleading; the child acquires all the aspects of language simultaneously, and these acquistitions are closely interrelated. So why should language be broken up into arbitrary subsystems? One reason should already be obvious: through careful description, one observes that in many cases a single subcomponent of the language is primarily impaired, *i.e.* a modular approach is descriptively valid. But there is a second and more important reason. Mere description of language impairment is useless on its own. Adequate description is only the first step towards more important aims. Two major purposes that are better served by more specific descriptions of language disorder are the design of appropriate intervention procedures and the uncovering of underlying impairments that result in the observed language behaviour. Intervention procedures will not be discussed here. This section will briefly mention some of the hypotheses that have been put forward to account for observed language deficits.

Cognitive impairments

There are several theories that directly implicate underlying cognitive impairments to account for the observed language behaviour of language-disordered individuals.

MEMORY

One process that might be impaired in some individuals is memory. The rôle that short-term auditory memory plays in verbal comprehension has been demonstrated in a variety of experiments (Conrad 1972, Rapin and Wilson 1978). Menyuk (1964, 1969) found that a memory deficit could account for some language deficits in children. She argued that the language-disordered children in her study produced deviant language. Furthermore, in an imitation task, these children performed differently from normal children in that they omitted the first part of the sentence (which could indicate a short-term memory deficit), and could not retain strings greater than three to five morphemes in length. This contrasted with normal children whose imitation errors consisted of modifications of sentence structure. Menyuk speculated that if the language-disordered children could not remember more than two or three morphemes, they would be unable to carry out a deepening linguistic analysis of language input.

Graham (1968, 1974; Graham and Gulliford 1968) also hypothesised that memory deficits limited the language of educationally subnormal children. Repetition and comprehension scores on a number of different sentence types increased regularly with short-term memory, as assessed by a task of repeating random words and digits. Graham concluded that the children were unable to process sentence types that made excessive demands on their short-term memory capacity.

Some researchers have speculated that the cause of language difficulty in some aphasic children might be attributable to auditory storage deficits. For example, Rosenthal and Eisenson (1970) presented both speech and non-speech sounds to aphasic and to normal children. The child's task was to identify sounds presented singly, and to put in temporal order those presented in pairs. Both groups of children could identify the single sounds. The aphasic children, however, performed poorly when they had to report the order of two sounds that were presented in close temporal proximity. Rosenthal and Eisenson interpreted this in terms of an auditory storage deficit. Auditory traces that could be identified when presented on their own could not be retained long enough for a perceptual analysis of temporal order to be made.

RATE OF AUDITORY PROCESSING

Other researchers of childhood aphasia have implicated a different underlying cognitive deficit. Tallal and Piercy (1973*a,b*, 1974, 1975, 1978) have found that when the rate of presentation of auditory signals is too great, the aphasic child is unable to analyse their order. Furthermore, they demonstrated that these children could not discriminate particular speech sounds unless the formant transitions were synthetically increased (Tallal and Piercy 1974, 1975). From these experiments, Tallal and Piercy concluded that the language deficit in aphasic children is due to an inability to process rapidly occurring acoustic information.

SEQUENCING

It has long been known that some adult aphasics appear to suffer from temporal order deficit (Hughlings-Jackson 1888, Critchley 1953). Hirsh (1959) emphasised the importance of a central temporal sequencing ability for making sense of auditory input and language. Monsees (1961) speculated that the basic disability in aphasic children is a central disorder involving the perception of auditory sequences. Efron (1963), who worked with adult aphasics, and Lowe and Campbell (1965) who studied children described as 'aphasoid', found that the ability to judge which of two sounds came first was impaired. Their language-disordered groups required large auditory, interstimulus gaps in order to make sequence judgements. Additional support for a sequencing impairment comes from a study by Sheehan *et al.* (1973) who found that adult aphasics could be aided by the insertion of silent intervals between phonemes. These same patients were not aided by silent intervals between words.

In some research, the sequencing impairment is not limited to the auditory modality. For example, Poppen *et al.* (1969) studied the ability of six aphasic children, aged 5:8 to 9:3, to press frosted panels in the same order they had seen them lighted. Although they performed better on this task than on a purely auditory sequencing task, they still performed poorly.

There are problems with theories of sequencing impairments for explaining language disorder. First, the sequencing deficits observed may not be primary but merely the result of other cognitive deficits. Earlier it was noted that Rosenthal and

Eisenson (1970) interpreted temporal-order identification problems as being due to storage deficits. Tallal and Piercy, in their experiments, claim the basic deficit to be one of rate of auditory processing. A second problem is that the observed sequencing deficits, whatever is said to be their ultimate cause, cannot adequately account for the observed language disorders. Leonard (1979) has pointed out, for example, that the nature of the speech used by language-impaired children suggests that both auditory processing problems and sequencing deficits are a corollary to and not the cause of the observed language difficulties. He noted that if sequencing deficits of the type proposed in most theories were truly causal, they should result in utterances with word reversals (actually, one might expect phoneme reversals); instead the observed language usually takes the same form as that of younger normal children, (*e.g.* deletion of elements that are obligatory in adult syntax).

HIERARCHICAL PLANNING IMPAIRMENT
An analysis of the language of some severely aphasic children, and the fact that they are almost totally arhythmic, has suggested the possibility that at least some rare groups of aphasic children have a more basic cognitive deficit that involves a central hierarchical planning ability. Cromer (1983) has shown that severely aphasic children of normal intelligence perform significantly more poorly than chronological-age-matched normals and profoundly deaf children on non-verbal tasks requiring the drawing and the construction of hierarchically structured figures. The aphasic children could perform the tasks as long as they were allowed to make their drawings or constructions in a serial manner. When they were required to interrupt their procedures and perform the task in terms of subunits, their ability deteriorated and often they could not complete the task at all.

IMPAIRMENT OF A 'SYMBOLIC' CAPACITY
Ricks and Wing (1976) have suggested that one of the basic cognitive impairments in autistic children involves the ability to form symbols. They define symbols in the sense of one thing standing for something else. They claim that among the most severely impaired autistic children, there are some who have no ability to use or understand symbols. These children do not respond to their own names, nor to any words or gestures. Some limited conditioning to simple stimuli is sometimes possible, but nothing higher can be achieved. Other autistic children produce only meaningless echolalia. Ricks and Wing suggest that while this shows an ability to store the sounds of words and to reproduce them under appropriate stimulation, there is no real understanding. They claim that the echolalic process in these children is automatic and does not constitute true symbolic activity.

Using words as symbols is clearly necessary for language. The exact cognitive processes that allow symbol use have never been adequately delineated. Presumably some hints about the implications of such an impairment will come from a few brain-damaged cases described as suffering from asymbolia. (See also Duffy and Liles 1979, who provide a translation of Finkelnberg's 1870 paper viewing all aphasia as 'asymbolia'.)

Conceptual impairments

It has been suggested that some deficiencies of language are due to conceptual limitations. The cases mentioned earlier (Curtiss *et al.* 1978, Curtiss 1981, Curtiss and Yamada 1981, Yamada 1981) showed that the semantic component of language can be severely affected by the low conceptual level in retarded children. The cases of Antony and Marta demonstrated adequate acquisition of syntax, but with accompanying semantic deficiencies in tense, aspect, and pronoun and adverb usage, attributable to conceptual limitations.

It has been observed that some aspects of language acquisition in normal children are determined by the growth of the particular concepts to be encoded. Brown (1973) noted several linguistic constructions that children began to produce only after having reached a developmental level which allowed for conceptual understanding of what was being encoded. If some handicapped children fail to acquire particular concepts, then their observed language may be deficient not only in the ideas expressed (as Curtiss has found) but also in the acquisition of particular grammatical devices that are specifically used to express those concepts.

Social/affective impairments

In the review of language subsystem impairments, it was observed that pragmatic deficiencies most adequately described the language of speaking autistic children. It is not yet clear what cognitive impairments might be responsible for problems of language use. It is possible that such impairments may be more adequately conceptualised as social/affective, rather than purely cognitive in nature. Menyuk (1978) has pointed out that during the first year of life the normally developing child uses vocalisations communicatively, to indicate needs and feelings and to socialise. By one or two months of age, the normal infant is sensitive to turn-taking in vocalisation. In addition, the infant is sensitive to acoustic features that communicate intent, mark speech-sound boundaries, and identify the speaker. Though incapacities in these areas observed in autistic children may be traceable to particular cognitive impairments, it is also possible to hypothesise a basic impairment in the social/affective processes that usually characterise members of the human species.

Conclusion

This review has attempted to point out the importance of adequate clinical descriptions of the observed language behaviour of handicapped individuals. It was suggested that a modular approach to language can be useful in that it may clarify more precisely the nature of the observed deficits. In some cases, it may be that one particular component of language is primarily affected. In other cases, the deficit may manifest itself across all of the subsystems. In either case, clear descriptions of the observed language are only the first step in identifying underlying impairments.

Language intervention programmes with the handicapped can be more skilfully designed only when one has a better understanding of the particular underlying impairment in each language-disordered individual.

REFERENCES

Anderson, E. M., Spain, B. (1977) *The Child with Spina Bifida.* London: Methuen.

Aurnhammer-Frith, U. (1969) 'Emphasis and meaning in recall in normal and autistic children.' *Language and Speech,* **12,** 29–38.

Baltaxe, C. A. M. (1977) 'Pragmatic deficits in the language of autistic adolescents.' *Journal of Pediatric Psychology,* **2,** 176–180.

—— Simmons, J. Q. (1977) 'Language patterns of adolescent autistics: a comparison between English and German.' *In:* Mittler, P. (Ed.), *Research to Practice in Mental Retardation, Volume II: Education and Training.* Baltimore: University Park Press. pp. 267–278.

Bates, E. (1976) *Language and Context: The Acquistion of Pragmatics.* New York: Academic Press.

Black, M. (1979) 'Broca's aphasia: a review of current approaches.' *Paper presented at the 2nd European meeting of the International Neuropsychological Society, The Netherlands.*

—— (1980) 'Differential processing of "function words" in expressive aphasia.' *Paper presented at the 3rd European meeting of the International Neuropsychological Society, Chianciano, Italy.*

Bloom, L. (1970) *Language Development: Form and Function in Emerging Grammars.* Cambridge, Mass: MIT Press.

Brown, R. (1970) *Psycholinguistics: Selected Papers by Roger Brown.* New York: The Free Press.

—— (1973) *A First Language: The Early Stages.* Cambridge, Mass: Harvard University Press.

Chomsky, N. (1959) 'A review of B. F. Skinner's *Verbal behaviour.*' *Language,* **35,** 26–58.

Conrad, R. (1972) 'The developmental role of vocalizing in short-term memory.' *Journal of Verbal Learning and Verbal Behaviour,* **11** , 521–533.

Critchley, M. (1953) *The Parietal Lobes.* London: Edward Arnold.

Cromer, R. F. (1978a) 'The basis of childhood dysphasia: a linguistic approach. *In:* Wyke, M. A. (Ed.) *Developmental Dysphasia.* London & New York: Academic Press. pp. 85–134.

—— (1978b) 'Hierarchical disability in the syntax of aphasic children.' *International Journal of Behavioral Development,* **1,** 391–402.

—— (1983) 'Hierarchical planning disability in the drawings and constructions of a special group of severely aphasic children.' *Brain and Cognition,* **2,** 144–164.

—— (1987) 'Differentiating language and cognition.' *In:* Lloyd, L., Schiefelbusch, R. L. (Eds.) *Language Perspectives II.* Austin: Pro-Ed.

Curtiss, S. (1981) 'Dissociations between language and cognition: cases and implications.' *Journal of Autism and Developmental Disorders,* **11,** 15–30.

—— Fromkin, V., Yamada, J. E. (1978) 'The independence of language as a cognitive system.' *Paper presented at the First International Congress for the Study of Child Language, Tokyo, August 7–12.*

—— Yamada, J. (1981) 'Selectively intact grammatical development in a retarded child.' *U.C.L.A. Working Papers in Cognitive Linguistics,* **3,** 61–91.

Duffy, R. J., Liles, B. Z. (1979) 'A translation of Finkelnburg's (1870) lecture on aphasia as "asymbolia" with commentary.' *Journal of Speech and Hearing Disorders,* **44,** 156–168.

Efron, R. (1963) 'Temporal perception, aphasia, and déjà vu.' *Brain,* **86,** 403–424.

Fay, D., Mermelstein, R. (1982) 'Language in infantile autism.' *In:* Rosenberg, S. (Ed.) *Handbook of Applied Psycholinguistics.* Hillsdale, New Jersey: Lawrence Erlbaum, pp. 393–428.

Frith, U. (1981) 'Experimental approaches to developmental dyslexia: an introduction.' *Psychological Research,* **43,** 97–109.

—— Snowling, M. (1983) 'Reading for meaning and reading for sound in autistic and dyslexic children.' *British Journal of Developmental Psychology,* **1,** 329–342.

Fyffe, C., Prior, M. (1978) 'Evidence for language recoding in autistic, retarded and normal children: a re-examination.' *British Journal of Psychology,* **69,** 393–402.

Graham, N. C. (1968) 'Short term memory and syntactic structure in educationally subnormal children.' *Language and Speech,* **11,** 209–219.

—— (1974) 'Response strategies in the partial comprehension of sentences.' *Language and Speech,* **17,** 205–221.

—— Gulliford, R. A. (1968) 'A psychological approach to the language deficiencies of educationally subnormal children.' *Education Review,* **20,** 136–145.

Hadenius, A-M., Hagberg, B., Hyttnäs-Bensch, K., Sjögren, I. (1962) 'The natural prognosis of infantile hydrocephalus.' *Acta Paediatrica,* **51,** 117–118.

Hermelin, B., O'Connor, N. (1967) 'Remembering of words by psychotic and subnormal children.' *British Journal of Psychology,* **58,** 213–218.

Hirsh, I. J. (1959) 'Auditory perception of temporal order.' *Journal of Acoustic Society of America,* **31,** 759–767.

186

Hughlings-Jackson, J. (1888) 'On a particular variety of epilepsy ("intellectual aura"), one case with symptoms of organic brain disease.' *Brain,* **11,** 179–207.

Ingram, T. T. S., Naughton, J. A. (1962) 'Paediatric and psychological aspects of cerebral palsy associated with hydrocephalus.' *Developmental Medicine and Child Neurology,* **4,** 287–292.

Jakobson, R. (1960) 'Closing statement: linguistic and poetics.' *In:* Sebeok, T. A. (Ed.) *Style in Language.* Cambridge, Mass: MIT Press. pp. 350–377.

Jorm, A. F. (1979) 'The cognitive and neurological basis of developmental dyslexia: a theoretical framework and review.' *Cognition,* **7,** 19–33.

Kean, M-L. (1977) 'The linguistic interpretation of aphasic syndromes: agrammatism in Broca's aphasia, an example.' *Cognition,* **5,** 9–46.

—— (1978) 'The linguistic interpretation of aphasic syndromes.' *In:* Walker, E. (Ed.) *Explorations in the Biology of Language.* Hassocks, Sussex: Harvester Press. p . 67–138.

Lackner, J. R. (1968) 'A developmental study of language behavior in retarded children.' *Neuropsychologia,* **6,** 301–320.

Landau, W. M., Kleffner, F. R. (1957) 'Syndrome of acquired aphasia with convulsive disorder in children.' *Neurology,* **7,** 523–530.

Lee, L. (1974) *Developmental Sentence Analysis.* Evanston, Illinois: Northwestern University Press.

Lenneberg, E. H., Nichols, I. A., Rosenberger, E. F. (1964) 'Primitive stages of language development in mongolism.' *In:* Rioch, D. McK, Weinstein, E. A. (Eds.) *Disorders of Communication. Research Publications of the Association for Research in Nervous and Mental Diseases, Vol. 42.* Baltimore: Williams & Wilkins, pp. 119–137.

Leonard, L. B. (1979) 'Language impairment in children.' *Merrill-Palmer Quarterly,* **25,** 205–232.

Lowe, A. D., Campbell, R. A. (1965) 'Temporal discrimination in aphasoid and normal children.' *Journal of Speech and Hearing Research,* **8,** 313–314.

Macnamara, J. (1972) 'Cognitive basis of language learning in infants.' *Psychological Review,* **79,** 1–13.

McLeod, J. (1970) *GAP Reading Comprehension Test.* London: Heinemann Educational.

Menyuk, P. (1964) 'Comparison of grammar of children with functionally deviant and normal speech.' *Journal of Speech and Hearing Research,* **7,** 109–121.

—— (1972) *Sentences. Children Use.* Cambridge, Mass: MIT Press.

—— (1978) 'Language: what's wrong and why.' *In:* Rutter, M., Schopler, E. (Eds.) *Autism: A Reappraisal of Concepts and Treatment.* New York: Plenum Press, pp. 105–116.

Miller, G. A., Chomsky, N. (1963) 'Finitary models of language users.' *In:* Luce, R. D., Bush, R. R., Galanter, E. (Eds.) *Handbook of Mathematical Psychology Vol. II.* New York: John Wiley. pp. 419–491.

Monsees, E. K. (1961) 'Aphasia in children.' *Journal of Speech and Hearing Disorders,* **26,** 83–86.

Pierce, S. Bartolucci, G. (1977) 'A syntactic investigation of verbal autistic, mentally retarded, and normal children.' *Journal of Autism and Childhood Schizophrenia,* **7,** 121–134.

Poppen, R., Stark, J., Eisenson, J., Forrest, T., Wertheim, G. (1969) 'Visual sequencing performance of aphasic children.' *Journal of Speech and Hearing Research,* **12,** 288–300.

Rapin, I. Allen, D. A. (1983) 'Developmental language disorders: nosologic considerations.' *In:* Kirk, U. (Ed.) *Neuropsychology of Language, Reading, and Spelling.* New York: Academic Press. pp. 155–184.

—— Wilson, B. C. (1978) 'Children with developmental language disability: neurological aspects and assessment.' *In:* Wyke, M. A. (Ed.) *Developmental Dysphasia.* London: Academic Press. pp. 13–41.

Ricks, D. M., Wing, L. (1976) 'Language, communication, and the use of symbols.' *In:* Wing, L. (Ed.) *Early Childhood Autism 2nd edn.* Oxford: Pergamon. pp. 93–134.

Rosenthal, W. S., Eisenson, J. (1970) 'Auditory temporal order in aphasic children as a function of selected stimulus features.' *Paper presented at the 46th annual convention of the American Speech and Hearing Association, New York.*

Saffran, E. M., Schwartz, M. F., Marin, O. S. M. (1980) 'The word order problem in agrammatism. II: Production.' *Brain and Language,* **10,** 263–280.

Schwartz, M. F., Saffran, E. M., Marin, O. S. M. (1980) 'The word order problem in agrammatism. I: comprehension.' *Brain and Language,* **10,** 249–262.

Sheehan, J. G., Aseltine, S., Edwards, A. E. (1973) 'Aphasic comprehension of time spacing.' *Journal of Speech and Hearing Research,* **16,** 650–657.

Snowling, M. J. (1980) 'The development of grapheme-phoneme correspondence in normal and dyslexic readers.' *Journal of Experimental Child Psychology,* **29,** 294–305.

Tager-Flusberg, H. (1981) 'Sentence comprehension in autistic children.' *Applied Psycholinguistics,* **2,** 5–24.

Tallal, P., Piercy, M. (1973a) 'Defects of non-verbal auditory perception in children with developmental aphasia.' *Nature,* **241,** 468–469.

—— —— (1973b) 'Developmental aphasia: impaired rate of non-verbal processing as a function of sensory modality.' *Neuropsychologia,* **11,** 389–398.

—— —— (1974) 'Developmental aphasia: rate of auditory processing and selective impairment of consonant perception.' *Neuropsychologia,* **12,** 83–93.

—— —— (1975) 'Developmental aphasia: the perception of brief vowels and extended stop consonants.' *Neuropsychologia,* **13,** 69–74.

—— —— (1978) 'Defects of auditory perception in children with developmental dysphasia.' *In:* Wyke, M. A. (Ed.) *Developmental Dysphasia.* London: Academic Press, pp. 63–84.

Taylor, E. M. (1959) *Psychological Appraisal of Children with Cerebral Defects.* Cambridge, Mass: Harvard University Press.

Voeltz, L. (1976) *An Analysis of the Linguistic Behaviors of Severely Developmentally Handicapped Children Diagnosed as Autistic.* Doctoral dissertation, Indiana University. (*Dissertation Abstracts International, 1977,* **37,** 5045.)

Yamada, J. (1981) 'Evidence for the independence of language and cognition: case study of a "hyperlinguistic" adolescent.' *U.C.L.A. Working Papers in Cognitive Linguistics,* **3,** 121–160.

12

DEVELOPMENTAL DISORDERS OF SPEECH AND LANGUAGE

Neil Gordon

A child's first words are awaited with great anticipation by most parents and their pleasure is likely to be a very positive reinforcement to the child in efforts to communicate verbally. The first meaningful words are usually around a year, but the normal variation extends from about eight to at least 18 months. Although the first words used by a child are a fairly late stage in language development, it is one of the few events that may be able to be identified retrospectively when assessing language development. This is well illustrated by the histories of Laura Bridgman (Gordon 1969) and Helen Keller who had begun to use words before the onset of their illnesses, and if inner language and comprehension of verbal symbols had not been established they would have been much less likely to have accomplished what they did. If the months pass and the child does not talk, concern is likely to arise, especially on the part of the parents. Exactly when these worries start will depend on factors such as comparisons with siblings, or what the neighbour's child of the same age is doing, or the parents' involvement with an only child. If it is decided that a period of observation is desirable in order to assess progress over a longer period it may be a comfort to parents to realise that the first word an infant uses is a fairly late stage, and the development of inner language and the understanding of verbal symbols must come first. This may persuade parents that it is vital to talk to the child so that words can be heard in a meaningful situation, asking little in return for a long time.

In some instances it can be the health visitor who raises the question of delayed speech and suggests a referral to the clinic for this to be checked, or such a delay may be noted by the clinical medical officer during a routine medical examination at 24 or 36 months of age (says single words with meaning at 24 months; simple sentences of at least three words with a verb at 36 months).

Reasons for delayed development of speech and language
The classification of speech and language disorders is considered in detail in Chapter 2, but a useful and brief scheme proposed by Ingram has stood the test of time (Ingram 1969, Purvis 1977). He defined six categories:
(1) Disorders of voicing (dysphonia)
(2) Disorders of respiratory co-ordination (dysrhythmia)
(3) Disorders of speech sound production (dysarthria), *e.g.* neurological abnormalities such as cerebral palsy, and structural abnormalities such as palatal disproportion and cleft palate
(4) Disorders of speech sound production *secondary* to other diseases or adverse

environmental factors, *e.g.* mental defect, deafness, psychiatric disorders and acquired dysphasias.

(5) Developmental speech disorders – developmental expressive and receptive dysphasias

(6) Mixed speech disorders involving two or more of the above categories.

Concern about a child's development of speech and language, whoever may express this, but especially the parents, must be considered a matter of paramount importance, and one that warrants an urgent assessment. Many of the above disorders are discussed in other chapters, but it can be emphasised that it will be rare for affected children to have only a single handicap. Some of these may be remedial and some may not, but learning disorders of this kind are often more severe than the sum of any individual cause; and if even one can be rectified, the result may be a surprisingly disproportionate improvement.

The effects of social factors, mental handicap, certain neurological disabilities and psychiatric disorders will be considered elsewhere, and only defective sensory input and some types of acquired dysphasia will be discussed before describing the problems of developmental speech disorders.

Defective sensory input

When faced with the need to assess and investigate a child with developmental delay there are certain priorities. In the case of language it is first of all imperative to ensure an adequate sensory input. Permanent deafness whatever the cause, and even if it is only of moderate degree and only involves certain frequencies, is likely to affect language development. Minor degrees of high-tone deafness can be particularly difficult to diagnose, especially if it is associated with other handicaps such as cerebral palsy (athetosis). In the case of sensorineural deafness particular care must be taken in screening low-birthweight babies and those suffering from jaundice or those who have been given drugs (aminoglycosides).

Although there may be no well-controlled trials to prove the importance of early diagnosis, it is certainly an entirely logical approach. Many parents will suspect if their baby has impaired hearing by the age of six or seven months, and if they do not raise the subject they should be questioned about it. Nine months of age is a reasonable time for an initial screening for deafness and action should be taken if the child fails the tests. However such screening tests at this and later ages have their limitations. They may fail to identify children with intermittent deafness, usually due to recurrent otitis media.

It is probably more important to follow up children with upper respiratory tract infections, whether at the time of examination they are deaf or not; as they are certainly at risk of intermittent conductive deafness due to infection of the middle ear, effusions into the middle ear, or blockage of the Eustachian tube. It is suggested that there may be a connection between intermittent deafness and learning disorders. Zinkus *et al.* (1978) examined 40 children with academic underachievement. One group of 18 had severe and frequent episodes of ear infections during this time and the remaining 22 only relatively mild attacks. All the first group had had myringotomies and all the children had an IQ of 85 or above. At the time of the study there were seven children in the first group with bilateral hearing loss of 10 to 20 dB, six had unilateral hearing loss of 10 to 20 dB and five had normal hearing. In the second group only two children had a bilateral hearing loss of 10 to 20 dB. On examination there were no significant differences between the groups in the age of developing walking skills, but there were in the acquisition of a four to 10-word vocabulary and in the ability to formulate and utilise sentences of three or more words. Those in the first group showed a poorer performance on tests that depended on auditory processing skills such as mental arithmetic and auditory sequential memory. There were also deficits in word decoding and spelling skills. The authors concluded that severe otitis media before the age of three may not be the only cause of subsequent disabilities, but it does seem to be a factor.

Sak and Reuben (1982) assessed the association of recurrent middle ear effusions in the preschool period with subsequent cognitive, linguistic and academic performance. In each case a sibling without a history of ear infection was used as a control, and the children were aged between eight and 11 years. None of them had been diagnosed as learning disabled. Children with an IQ below 85 were excluded, and all of them had a pure-tone audiometric average $15 \leq$ dB in the better ear. There were 18 pairs, 13 boys and five girls in the group with a history of ear infections, and 8 boys and 10 girls in the control group. All in the former group had had one or more myringotomies.

The first group had significantly depressed verbal quotients (WISC-R) and a lower spelling achievement, and on the ITPA given to 13 pairs they were deficient in auditory recognition; deficits which may have been related to the early history of middle-ear infections. They did have particular strengths in visual sequential memory which suggests the availablity of compensatory strategies for auditory deficits. These were obviously minimally affected children as those with previous learning difficulties had been excluded, and they also had no particular social problems. Holm and Kunze (1969) have speculated that children from a lower socio-economic background might be disadvantaged in attempting to compensate for depressed language functioning associated with conductive hearing loss. They examined 16 children who had suffered from chronic otitis media with fluctuating hearing loss confirmed by audiometry, and a similar number of unaffected controls matched for age, sex and socio-economic background. A series of language and articulatory tests were used and the children with a history of ear infections showed that there was a delay of language skills which required the receiving or processing of auditory stimuli or the production of verbal responses, but there was no difference from the controls in primarily visual and motor skills. Fluctuating hearing loss seemed likely to be the cause of the delay, perhaps due to a lack of appropriate stimulation during a critical period of development. However it is uncertain how long this may persist when normal hearing has been established.

In the study of Bennett et al. (1980) there were 37 boys and 16 girls who were attending language and learning disability classes, and as controls there were 41 boys and 15 girls who had no learning problems. They were all aged between seven and 12 years. By the history, 12 of the learning-disabled children and five of the control children had recurrent ear infections. 20 of the first group had abnormal audiograms, seven on both sides, and only nine, four on both sides, of the controls. Acoustic impedance measurements showed that 26 learning-disabled children, compared with 12 controls, had abnormal tympanograms in one or both ears, and 12 of the 26, and five of the 12, also had a hearing loss. Of the 12 learning-disabled children with positive histories only one had normal middle-ear function at the end of the study. None of the five control children with such a history were deaf and only two had abnormal tympanograms. There was therefore among these middle-class schoolchildren an increased incidence of ear infections and of ongoing middle-ear dysfunction in those with language and learning disabilities. Also many of the young learning-disabled children had evidence of active unrecognised middle-ear problems. The findings suggest that children with ear infections and transient deafness are at increased risk of learning disorders.

It is suggested that not only spoken language but the acquisition of reading skills may be affected by recurrent middle-ear disease. Eaton and Nowell (1983) selected a control group of 59 children from a normal school and 55 children from remedial centres. All were from comparable backgrounds and aged between seven and 11 years. The children in both groups were examined with an impedance bridge test. Abnormal results were found in four of the control group but were seen in 14 of those with reading problems. This raises a possible correlation between middle-ear pathology and reading difficulties.

Paradise (1981) has reviewed these and other studies on the effects of repeated attacks of otitis media in the first few years of life on language and learning development. Animal experiments support the importance of critical or sensitive periods during which artificially imposed sensory deprivation can apparently result in permanently impaired cortical function or abnormal brain cell morphogenesis. He divided the human studies into those in which the experimental subjects had been selected on the basis of their having impaired hearing at the time of testing, and those which were all retrospective with the experimental subjects having at the time normal or only slightly depressed hearing. Only the second group are relevant to the hypothesis that otitis media in early life leads to delayed development. There are a number of criticisms such as uncertainties about the diagnosis of otitis media in early life, the exact hearing levels in infancy, and the matching of subjects and controls. The association between the early deafness and developmental impairment could be due to other factors such as socio-economic status, impaired parenting, subtle unrecognised CNS disorders, poor over-all health, especially chest infections and allergies, pregnancy and perinatal risk factors and large numbers of siblings.

If there is an association between early deafness and later development it may not be a permanent effect. Dalzell and Owrid (1976) reassessed a group of children who five years previously had shown a conductive hearing loss and poor performance on language tests, and found a satisfactory improvement in hearing and in language function in the majority. However for individual children problems may still be present in secondary school. Persistent learning difficulties may well depend on persistence of impaired hearing (Bennett *et al.* 1980).

In the opinion of Paradise (1981), impairment in children's speech, language and cognition does seem to relate to chronic and continuous middle-ear disease and conductive hearing loss, but once hearing recovers developmental impairment tends to disappear, and at present there is no convincing evidence that lasting developmental disorders can result from episodes of otitis media during the first few years of life as long as there is no persistent deafness. However there is no evidence that they do not.

In practice there are certainly some children who do seem to have literacy problems and have a history of recurrent ear troubles, and others with an equally long catalogue of such illnesses who do not. Personal experience suggests that one reason for this discrepancy may be multiple handicaps, for example a history of significant difficulties at birth, or impaired intelligence or adverse social factors. Hall and Hill (1986) support this possibility. They suggest that the impact of secretory otitis media on language development depends on at least five factors; the age of onset, the duration of the episodes, the severity of the hearing loss, the intrinsic qualities of the child such as intelligence and temperament, and the linguistic environment which is certainly not always related to social class. They suggest that in certain research studies the effect of middle-ear disease is diluted by the inclusion of many children in whom the disorder is of brief duration and trivial importance.

Also care has to be taken not to draw too many conclusions from limited studies. For example in a paper from Denmark (Lous and Fiellau-Nikalajsen 1984) a prospective study on more than 500 children, followed from their third to ninth year of life, revealed no difference in school class-level between the 9 per cent of the children who constantly had abnormal tympanometry during a six-month period at the age of three and the other pupils in the same community. Also on a silent reading test there was no difference between case pupils and controls; although the authors are careful to point out that this analysis was only based on the pupils' ability to understand a silent reading test which is only a special part of reading ability, which is only a special part of language, and that on a specific day. They also stress that a factor which is often not considered is the classroom situation.

A particularly important result of intermittent deafness in early childhood may be a poor listening ability, leading to poor understanding and a poor sequential auditory memory. This may be a reason for language improving after deafness is no longer a problem, but not spelling, because there is no well-developed sound/symbol coding system to rely on (Quinn and Macauslan 1986). There is still controversy on the best treatment for recurrent ear troubles in early life which is beyond the scope of this chapter to consider, but the subject is well reviewed by Paradise (1980).

Acquired dysphasias
Although in a separate category to developmental disorders, lost language skills should be considered as in children there is often an overlap. If brain damage due to injury or disease occurs before the age of about seven there is always a resulting mixture of loss of function on the one hand and interference with development on

the other, the relative proportions depending on the age of the child. Causes may vary from trauma to cerebral tumours and their treatment, and from meningitis to degenerative cerebral disease.

Epilepsy can be taken as an example as it is often associated with impaired language function, whether this is the result of brain damage from status epilepticus, or the fact that focal epilepsy affecting in particular the left temporal lobe may be one symptom of dysfunction of this part of the brain, while dysphasia and learning difficulties may be others (Stores 1977). Also schoolchildren with epilepsy have a number of other problems to cope with which may well impair their learning abilities. In particular the incidence of the fits themselves, even of minor type, has to be considered; the side-effects of drugs can be highly relevant and emotional problems are frequent (Corbett *et al.* 1985).

The Landau-Kleffner syndrome of acquired aphasia
There are a number of progressive cerebral diseases resulting in dementia and epilepsy, with loss of language skills among other disabilities, but in the acquired aphasia syndrome there is a special relationship between epilepsy and language development. No definite cause has been found for this condition although some form of 'encephalopathy' has been suspected, which is often the case with syndromes of unknown origin. It has been well described by Landau and Kleffner (1957). Typically a previously normal child loses language skills between the ages of three and nine, without other neurological abnormalities or known brain pathology. The disorder of language function includes both reception and expression, and the former may be so severe that the child does not respond to verbal commands and may be thought to be deaf; and the sudden onset of the loss of ability to communicate can lead to severe behaviour disorders (Miller *et al.* 1984). At about the same time most, but not all, of these children develop generalised or partial seizures. Part of the definition of the syndrome however is the occurrence of an abnormal EEG with asymmetrical paroxysmal activity, mainly over the post central areas. The onset of the condition may be sudden or gradual and its course is very variable. One important factor must be the age range of the syndrome which is also a critical one for language development. Also the prognosis varies enormously. Some of the affected children have a severe language disorder persisting into adulthood but others make a reasonable recovery (Cooper and Ferry 1978, Mantovani and Landau 1980), and as pointed out by the latter authors, this is one of the most puzzling features of the disorder. This does not seem to be due to the frequency of the seizures but could be due to different aetiologies (Deonna *et al.* 1977). These authors identified three different clinical varieties. The first are those children in which aphasia develops suddenly, progresses rapidly, and fluctuates usually in association with seizures in a similar way to epileptic aphasia in adults; and the aphasia probably represents a functional disconnection of language mechanisms without a newly acquired lesion. The second group comprises those in whom there is no recovery for a long time and this may be due to the other hemisphere taking over speech function. In the third group a deficit in auditory comprehension gradually develops, recovery is usually minimal and the cause may

be an encephalopathy affecting both sides of the brain. It is strange that no definite aetiologies have been established in such a striking syndrome. One can only speculate, but can a possible explanation, in some instances anyhow, be that it is more a disorder of function than structure? Obviously it can be argued that the abnormal EEG findings, a definite feature of the syndrome, and the language disorder are both due to the underlying pathology, but can another explanation for the typical features of the syndrome be a disconnection or disruption of cerebral function by epileptic activity, whether associated with overt fits or not, at a critical period of development. As first suggested by Landau and Kleffner (1957), Gascon *et al.* (1973) proposed that, in the absence of any evidence of an 'encephalitis', the condition involving both temporal lobes may be related, in some unknown way, to the convulsive disorder, and Sato and Dreifuss (1972) maintained that language regression can result from continuous bilateral synchronous temporal-spike activity causing dysfunction of both hemispheres, which surely may have lasting effects. Such epileptic activity can certainly disrupt cerebral function in the part of the brain involved which cannot be used for normal function; and localisation must be a vital factor. This is well shown by post-ictal phenomenon, and in a more prolonged way by the states of bewilderment described by Goldie and Green (1961). If you talk to older children with epilepsy they will tell you that on some days it is not much use going to school as they know they will not be able to learn satisfactorily, although they do not necessarily have a fit on such a day. Perhaps in the case of this syndrome such activity prevents the complex associations underlying language function being established, and it is known that if such connections are not formed during certain periods of life they may never develop (Dobbing 1970). Holmes *et al.* (1981) studied two children with this syndrome, and reviewed the literature on 43 other children with epilepsy and aphasia. Speech abnormalities in acquired or congenital aphasia were not closely related to epileptiform activity on the EEG and speech did not necessarily improve when the EEG did. It was therefore suggested that the EEG abnormalities were an epiphenomenon of the underlying pathology, rather than the cause of the speech abnormality. This may be so, but the findings do not seem to exclude the possibility that the development of speech function may be disrupted over a period of time, apart from the fact, pointed out by Goldie and Green (1961), that the routine EEG only reveals cortical activity to a limited extent, and unless depth electrodes are used, such activity in the diencephalon is missed.

Bishop (1985) in a review of the literature examined the outcome of the syndrome related to the age of onset and found that in the Landau-Kleffner syndrome the older the child the better the prognosis, which is the opposite to that for childhood aphasia after structural lesions of the left hemisphere. Anti-epileptic drugs are worth trying but there is no evidence that they benefit the disorder of language (O'Donohoe 1979).

Developmental disorders of speech and language
TYPES OF DEVELOPMENTAL DYSPHASIA
When the child is late in talking and conditions such as deafness, mental handicap and other significant factors have been assessed with negative results, the

possibility of a specific disorder of language development must be considered. As has been stated, the start of spoken speech varies considerably so that there is no exact point dividing the normal from the abnormal. This is to be expected as it is intrinsic to the whole of biology and applies not only to individuals but to differences between systems within individuals. For example there is similar variation in the onset of puberty, the development of athletic abilities and many of the ageing processes. A family history of difficulties of language development is suggestive, and the extremes of delay are more likely to be abnormal. There are no exact parallels between the severity of the delay and clinical findings which must be regarded as abnormal, but a specific disorder of language development is likely when subsequently there are difficulties in acquiring reading skills, and there are defects in other aspects of development such as impaired emotional stability and social relationships. Also there is an increased male preponderance with most of the more severe delays. The sex difference in the timing of language acquisition in the normal range is quite small, so that this factor must not be made an excuse for doing nothing when a boy is thought to be slow to speak. The fact that girls do mature earlier in certain aspects of language development may well be due to genetic reasons, as phytogenetically survival may have depended on the early development of certain skills, sometimes related to visuo-motor and sometimes to language function. The pattern of language skills may be seen to be deviant (Chapters 2, 9 and 14), and in the case of some children there are known relationships to medical disorders such as chromosome abnormalities.

There is no doubt that, in particular, sex chromosome aberrations can affect language development, although the exact cause is not known (Garvey and Mutton 1973); but in the opinion of Ludlow and Cooper (1983), this is not a common cause of primary disorders of speech and language. The evidence suggests that supernumerary x chromosomes depress verbal abilities, and certainly delayed language development is common in such disorders, while in Turner's syndrome (45x) the deficits are in spatial and non-verbal functions. Children with extra x chromosome material can present with auditory rate processing and auditory memory deficits, and manifest expressive language, reading and spelling difficulties (Walzer 1985). The growth rates of x chromosome aneuploids differ from normal and this may apply also to brain development. A possible hypothesis is that disturbances in the maturational processes of the brain, beginning early in life, affect the functional organisation of neurons and therefore the development of abilities (Nettley 1983).

Delayed speech development of mild degree, on the borderland of normal variation, will usually be overcome through advice to the parents and a sympathetic understanding of the child's difficulties without the need for special treatment. Those children who have developed a good comprehension of speech by the age of three almost always acquire adequate expressive speech without undue delay.

Developmental dysphasias can be almost entirely of an expressive type and are then often accompanied by abnormalities of word-sound production. As these dysphasias become more severe, and more deviant from normal development, there will be an increasing element of receptive dysphasia. Often the parent will say that their child seems to understand all that is said to them, but this statement must be checked as young children can be remarkably good at picking up visual clues and responding to requests in a reasonable manner.

Often with increasing degrees of severity there begins to be evidence of a spread of the disability to other functions. There are indications that sounds, other than those of speech, are incorrectly interpreted. Worster-Drought (1943) coined the term 'congenital auditory imperception' to cover this type of disability, although severe developmental dysphasia can occur without any other evidence of auditory agnosia. Very occasionally the auditory agnosia can be the dominant feature with the child showing little or no response to sounds of any kind, so that the term central deafness has been used. In some of these children assessment over a long period may show evidence of both peripheral and central deafness, which is perhaps not surprising when the cause is, for example, anoxia which can affect both the cerebral cortex and the auditory nuclei in the brainstem. Gradually as these children grow older they do begin to respond to sounds, presumably as alternative pathways for auditory stimuli to reach the cortex are established (Gordon 1966).

The more that disorders of language development are analysed the more subgroups are likely to be found, such as semantic pragmatic disorders discussed in Chapter 3. This must be in part due to the complexity of language function, and it is surely not surprising that there may be overlap between different syndromes resulting from an interaction between the disturbance of cerebral function whatever the cause, the personality of the child, and environment influences.

Accepting that language development goes through various stages from the foundations of inner language, as shown in make-believe play which the infant must first of all develop without the use of verbal symbols, then the understanding of the sounds used by those in close contact, endowing them with meaning mainly by association, and finally by learning to use these sounds as a means of communication, it must be realised that this is not the only function of language. Language is also used to control behaviour and in problem solving. This may well be one of the reasons for children with delayed language development also presenting with behaviour problems. It is not just that one cannot reason with them, but they have no means of resolving the situation. As language function gradually improves, it is common for the behaviour disorders to do likewise. The use of language in other ways may be influenced significantly by the children's family encouragement, for example to use language in imaginative creation, commenting on what is going on around them, and defending their rights (Tough 1973).

Assessment of delayed speech. When a child with delayed speech development is considered to be suffering from a specific disorder the first step will be to analyse the disability with the help of the speech therapist and psychologist. Tests such as the Reynell Developmental Language Scales (Reynell 1977) will help to show to what extent comprehension and/or expression of language are involved, and on this will depend both prognosis and treatment. The more that comprehension is involved the more guarded the prognosis has to be, especially when the use of symbols of any kind is severely affected. Assessment will be considered in other chapters.

Possible pathogenesis. Among adults it is widely accepted that so many of the syndromes of acquired dysphasia can be explained by the disconnection of one part of the brain from another (Geschwind 1965), and the more specific the developmental disorders of language are the more possible is the theory of non-connection syndromes. Such a theory can explain why this particular aspect of learning is defective, while other aspects of intelligence are developing normally. A child who cannot communicate with spoken speech may not be able to integrate information from the auditory cortex with patterns of movement subserving articulation, with the memory of past experiences, and with emotional factors.

There are a number of reasons why such connections are not established. They may never be formed due to an interference with the growth of the brain, as when malnutrition occurs during the main spurt of brain growth. In humans this occurs from about mid-pregnancy to about the end of the second year of life; and is not related to the increase of neurons which occurs much earlier in pregnancy, but to the proliferation of glial tissue and myelination. A significant factor may be dysmaturity, as obviously the fetus must have suffered from malnutrition, whatever the cause, if the birthweight at term is well below average. This correlates well with studies such as Drillien's (1972). She showed that infants who had suffered from hypoxia and malnutrition in the third trimester are less likely to have major handicaps but may show an increase in mild degrees of mental retardation and minor neurological abnormalities. Also Dobbing (1970) has shown in his experimental evidence that if malnutrition does occur during the main spurt of brain growth complete recovery may be impossible due to a failure of dendritic connections to form. Admittedly there may be other reasons than malnutrition for infants showing learning difficulties later in life, and studies on acute starvation, chronic malnutrition and nutritional supplementation on the child's development are not in favour of this hypothesis (Stein and Susser 1985). However there is no doubt that this is a complex subject and it is difficult to believe that malnutrition at certain critical periods never has an effect.

It is easier to understand the destruction of connections from such factors as anoxia during pregnancy and birth. Brown (1967) followed up a group of infants with symptomatic neonatal asphyxia and found, on comparison with normal controls, evidence of an association between the asphyxia and various handicaps, including motor inco-ordination, epilepsy, speech retardation and school problems.

In the case of cerebral lesions after birth, for example from trauma, vascular lesions or tumours, the evidence is compatible with the findings among adults, allowing for the fact that sometimes the younger the child the better the prognosis as the brain is more adaptable in infancy before functions have become firmly established.

This may only apply to unilateral lesions with inter-hemisphere transfer, and the effects may be different rather than lesser or greater. For example general intellectual impairment with poor performance at school may be commoner than specific defects, and newly learned tasks may be more vulnerable than well-established ones. There is also the fact that the more immature the brain the more at risk it seems to be from insults of all kinds, and its further development may result in malfunction rather than true recovery (Rutter 1982). Landau *et al.* (1960) reported a child who had congenital aphasia, and cyanotic congenital heart disease. The latter caused the child's death at the age of 10 and autopsy showed bilateral old infarctions in the Sylvian regions and retrograde degeneration in the medial geniculate nuclei. Language function had developed to a degree and this must have been subserved by phytogenetically older auditory pathways in the brainstem and medial thalamus. The aphasia was a form of word deafness due to bilateral disconnection of the auditory input from Wernicke's area. However there must be caution in attributing a particular function to a particular part of the brain because it is lost when that part is destroyed. What you are seeing is the brain working as a whole without the help of the affected part. F.M.R. Walshe used to illustrate this in his teaching by saying that if there was something wrong with the gearbox in your car one of the results would be a nasty noise but it was not the purpose of the gearbox to prevent this noise. It had other jobs to do.

In some individuals the findings may well be due to disconnection of one part of the brain from another rather than the destruction of a primary speech area. Such syndromes as alexia without agraphia splenium with a right visual-field defect can be explained by a lesion in the splenium of the corpus callosum so that due to disconnections, the patient is unable to comprehend written language but can copy words that cannot be read. Also letters cannot be read aloud but can be read when traced on the back of the hand due to the use of other sensory input channels. In the case of alexia with agraphia the lesion is found in the angular gyrus of the left hemisphere, a primary area of speech function. There may be no hemianopia but, apart from the failure to read, including letters traced on the back of the hand, writing is incorrect, either spontaneously or on dictation, and there is difficulty in copying (Geschwind 1985).

Galaburda *et al.* (1985) reported the findings on the brains of four men, aged 14 to 32 years, diagnosed as having dyslexia and dying from trauma, myocarditis or subarachnoid haemorrhage. All the brains showed developmental anomalies of the cerebral cortex, consisting of neuronal ectopias and achitectonic dysplasias, mainly in the perisylvian regions and predominantly affecting the left hemisphere. There was also a deviation from the standard pattern of cerebral asymmetry, with symmetry of the planum temporale. The evidence suggests that the lesions in these brains are developmental anomalies acquired before birth, at a time when most of the neuronal migration from the germinal zone to the cerebral cortex is taking place. The lesions were fairly scattered, although predominating on the left side, and to explain this the authors suggest that the disturbed neuronal migration may result in an anomalous pattern of growth and development of connections in the cortex. Lesions inhibiting the development of language related structures may be accompanied by greater development of other structures which would explain the better visual motor functions among many of those with dyslexia.

Among young children whose brains are still developing it may be better to concentrate on the organisation of the brain as a whole and how this may be disturbed by noxious agents rather than thinking in terms of isolated lesions in particular parts of the brain. It is suggested that damage to the fetal brain on one side may have particularly great effects on future function because the corresponding region on the opposite side develops more intraneural connections than normal to the permanent detriment of the originally damaged area (Geschwind 1985).

Finally there is evidence that if connections are not used this may have a profound influence on cerebral function, and possibly on structure. Experimental work on animals has been mainly on visual function by such procedures as occluding one eye or producing a squint which interferes with the interaction of stimuli from the two eyes. Certainly if excellence in a particular skill is to be acquired, the earlier in life this is first studied the better. In humans there may not be critical periods of learning as in lower animals but there are optimum periods. In the case of language, Lenneberg (1966) suggests that such a period may extend up to 12 years. For example those who became deaf after the age of two are much more easily trained in language than the congenitally deaf child, but the optimum age may be lower than that (Helen Keller lost her hearing and sight at the age of one year seven months). Then there is evidence of an upper limit of around 13, based on such evidence as the age of injury to the left hemisphere after which it is more difficult to relearn language, and studies on 'wolf children'; but some would favour a much younger upper age limit (Krashen 1975).

Multiply handicapped children

Children with learning disorders are obviously at risk from more than one type of disability. Clumsiness due to visuo-motor dysfunction may also delay language development. This is not surprising when the cause is one that can result in generalised brain damage such as anoxia, even if certain parts of the brain may be more at risk than others due to their relative immaturity (Ounsted and Taylor 1972). Certain aspects of communication such as eye-contact, absence of gesture and lack of speech prosody, in addition to emotional and interpersonal difficulties, shyness, visuo-spatial disturbances and problems with mathematics can occur with right cerebral hemisphere lesions (Weintraub and Mesulam 1983). There are also speech problems among so-called clumsy children because articulation involves a complex degree of co-ordination and because these children so often find it difficult to put their thoughts into words, and to organise words into coherent sentences (Garvey 1980).

Another good example of the child with multiple handicaps is one with severe cerebral palsy. Because of the physical disability the child will be deprived of opportunities to gain experience from the environment, but in addition there may be features of dysphasia due to cortical brain damage, and almost inevitably of dysarthria. Words the child can say may be unintelligible because of a spastic, ataxic, dystonic or mixed type of dysarthria depending on the form of the cerebral palsy. Such dysarthria may be very difficult to treat, but it is vital to confirm if there are other contributing factors such as palatal disproportion or malocclusion about which a great deal can be done.

It must also be remembered that occasionally delayed language development may be the presenting symptom of a totally unrelated disorder, a classical example being Duchenne muscular dystrophy. Kaplan and Elias (1986) suggested that any child showing expressive verbal impairment should be evaluated for motor function.

Left-handers

One particular group at risk arises from studies on left-handers which are undoubtedly a heterogeneous group. The evidence is that a number of left-handers are 'pathological' left-handers, 5 per cent according to Bishop (1983), and not natural left-handers. This results from impairment of left hemisphere function, insufficient to produce a right hemiplegia but enough to cause clumsiness of the right hand, making it easier to use the left hand. Bishop (1984) has shown that not only is there clumsiness of the right hand which can be shown by, for example, a square tracing task, but there is also a high incidence of language disorders, presumably due to left cerebral hemisphere lesions causing disruption of both language areas and of motor areas on that side.

There are two particular theories on the dominance of the left cerebral hemisphere for language. Annett's (1985) right-shift theory proposed a dominant gene which shifts language function to the left hemisphere as it is more efficient to have a speech output-input loop system on one side of the brain. Then the close proximity of the mouth and hand areas in the sensory-motor cortical strip suggests that any advantage to the left hemisphere mouth area would be likely to give an incidental advantage to the right hand. Geschwind and Galaburda (1985) maintained that there is a genetically determined dominance of the left cerebral hemsiphere for language function, but that there are various environmental influences, including the interuterine environment, which shift dominance towards symmetry between the two hemsipheres, and occasionally to the right hemsiphere.

The management of children with specific disorders of language development

Management is discussed in other chapters but as soon as a child is suspected of having delayed speech development professional help must be provided. Initially with the very young child it may be a matter of advice to the parents rather than any formal therapy. The importance of talking with such children must be stressed, and doing this at close hand as children who are late in talking will almost certainly be walking and less likely to be content with sitting on mother's knee. If the older child with a specific disorder has failed to learn language structure in the home, even under optimum conditions, it seems very unlikly that duplicating this process in an educational setting is going to be any more successful (Griffiths 1979). This is especially true if the pattern of the child's language is not only delayed but deviant. McNeil (1974) suggests that just as linguists and phoneticians have to become conscious of the language processes of syntax and phonology, so with children who have specific difficulties with language development. The mother tongue then has to be consciously taught, starting with the learning of individual sounds and words.

The exact method of teaching will be the choice of the experts involved; the psychologist, the teacher, the therapist, preferably working together and with the parents. It should be as flexible an approach as possible to the individual child, and most methods rightly depend on some form of association, making links between sounds, objects and symbols.

Among children with delayed development of speech and language the majority will be able to be helped within the normal school, although sometimes in a special class, if possible with the teacher and speech therapist working together. It will only be a few severely affected children who need expert help with assessment and treatment which can only be provided in a special school.

The latest Education Act in the United Kingdom strongly encourages integration of handicapped children into normal school, a laudable objective in many ways; however only if the resources of the school are adequate and a careful check is kept on the child's progress. Children with language disorders very easily become isolated because of their inability to communicate, and particularly if they are well behaved, may sit at the back of the class, bothering no one but falling further and further behind in their education.

There will be occasional children who for various reasons, (physical handicap, mental retardation and severity of the language disorder), fail to develop useful spoken speech after adequate teaching given over a long time. Then the use of non-speech communication systems have to be considered (Kiernan *et al.* 1982). There are many such systems so that choices can be made for the individual child.

Reading disabilities

There is no doubt that children who have difficulty in acquiring spoken speech are at considerable risk later on in childhood of being unable to learn to read and spell in spite of an adequate level of intelligence, so it should be the responsibility of anyone involved with such children to notify schools of this possibility. This subject is discussed in Chapter 17.

Conclusions

Among all the disabilities that can affect children, difficulties with communication are among the most severe and distressing. Normal learning depends almost entirely on an ability to understand spoken speech and to use it adequately. In the severely multiply handicapped child it must be the one function that makes life tolerable. Therefore any suspicion that a child's speech is delayed, expressed by anyone, must be a signal for urgent assessment and necessary treatment.

For the clinician there should be a systematic approach, first of all checking contributory factors such as adequate auditory input, mental development, physical and emotional disabilities, and social disorders. Then if the disability appears to be a specific disorder of language development its severity must be established and decisions taken on the type of help required. Among children with abnormal speech, especially when sounds other than those of speech seem to be involved, a 'let's wait and see what happens' attitude may be quite unjustified. It may be vital to keep alive an awareness of sounds, using for example auditory stimuli converted into visual ones on a television screen. The brain seems well equipped to suppress unmeaningful stimuli, a suppression which may become permanent. This may be one of the reasons why children who do not speak by a certain age may never do so.

Most children with delayed language development will acquire adequate speech. The fact that they may do so over the years without extra help is no argument for not providing it; as this will only be done with an inevitable loss of the child's potential, quite apart from the frustrations and distress experienced by the child and the family. Also there will be some who will never be able to communicate adequately if not given expert help. The visible effects of the disability may be few but its consequences are profound and although more studies are needed, it is likely to be a false economy to restrict the necessary services.

Investigations employing newer techniques, such as nuclear magnetic resonance and emission computed tomography, may well throw more light on the subtle changes which may underlie learning disabilities. Lou *et al.* (1984) used the latter technique to study regional bloodflow. Children with language and attention disorders were investigated and abnormalities were found in both hemispheres. Areas of hypoperfusion, and by inference low metabolic activity, were predominantly seen in the periventricular white matter and in border zones between major arterial territories. Among the children with dysphasia parts of both perisylvian regions showed impaired perfusion, while in those with attention deficit disorders there was hypoperfusion in the white matter of the mesial frontal lobes, and in some of them in the region of the caudate nuclei as well. Such findings are consistent with a rôle for early hypoxic-ischaemic events in the etiology of learning disorders in childhood, and the more that can be learned about their underlying mechanisms the more can be done to prevent them.

REFERENCES

Annett, M. (1985) *Left, Right Hand and Brain: The Right Shift Theory.* London: Lawrence Erlbaum Associates.
Bennett, F. C., Runska, S. H., Sherman, R. (1980) 'Middle ear function in learning-disabled children.' *Pediatrics,* **660,** 254–260.
Bishop, D. V. M. (1983) 'How sinister is sinistrality?' *Journal of the Royal College of Physicians of London,* **17,** 161–172.
—— (1984) 'Using non-preferred hand skill to investigate pathological left-handedness in an unselected population.' *Developmental Medicine and Child Neurology,* **26,** 214–226.
—— (1985) 'Age of onset and outcome in "Acquired Aphasia with Convulsive Disorder" (Landau-Kleffner Syndrome).' *Developmental Medicine and Child Neurology,* **27,** 705–712.
Brown, J. K. (1976) 'Infants damaged during birth. Perinatal asphyxia.' *In:* Hull, D. (Ed.) *Recent Advances in Pediatrics.* Edinburgh: Churchill Livingstone.
Cooper, J. A., Ferry, P. C. (1978) 'Acquired auditory verbal agnosia and seizures in childhood.' *Journal of Speech and Hearing Disorders,* **43,** 176–184.
Corbett, J. A., Trimble, M. R., Nichol, T. C. (1985) 'Behavioural and cognitive impairments in children with epilepsy: the long term effects of anticonvulsant therapy.' *Journal of the American Academy of Child Psychiatry,* **24,** 17–23.
Dalzell, J., Owrid, H. L. (1976) 'Children with conductive deafness: a follow up study.' *British Journal of Audiology,* **10,** 87.
Deonna, T., Beaumanoir, A., Gaillard, F., Assali, G. (1977) 'Acquired aphasia in childhood with seizure disorder: a heterogeneous syndrome.' *Neuropadiatrie,* **8,** 263–273.
Dobbing, J. (1970) 'Undernutrition and the developing brain.' *American Journal of Disease in Childhood,* **126,** 411–415.
Drillien, C. M. (1972) 'Aetiology and outcome in low birth weight infants.' *Developmental Medicine and*

Child Neurology, **14,** 563–574.

Eaton, D. M., Nowell, H. (1983) 'Reading disability and defects of the middle ear.' *Archives of Disease in Childhood,* **58,** 1010–1012.

Galaburda, A. M., Sherman, G. F., Rosen, G. D., Aboritiz, F., Geschwind, N. (1985) 'Developmental dyslexia: four consecutive patients with cortical anomalies.' *Annals of Neurology,* **18,** 222–233.

Garvey, M. (1980) 'Speech therapy.' *In:* Gordon, N., McKinlay, I. (Eds.) *Helping Clumsy Children.* London: Churchill Livingstone.

—— Mutton, D. E. (1973) 'Sex chromosome aberrations and speech development.' *Archives of Disease in Childhood,* **48,** 937–941.

Gascon, G., Victor, D., Lambroso, C. T., Goodglass, H. (1973) 'Language disorder, convulsive disorder, and electroencephalographic abnormalities.' *Archives of Neurology,* **28,** 156–162.

Geschwind, N. (1965) 'Disconnection syndromes in animals and man.' *Brain,* **88,** 237–294, 585–652.

—— (1985) 'Biological foundations of reading.' *In:* Duffy, F. H., Geschwind, N. (Eds.) *Dyslexia: A Neuroscientific Approach to Clinical Evaluation.* Boston: Little Brown & Co.

—— Galaburda, A. M. (1985) 'Cerebral lateralisation. Biological mechanisms, associations, and pathology. A hypothesis and a program for research.' *Archives of Neurology,* **42,** 428–459.

Goldie, L., Green, J. M. (1961) 'Observations on episodes of bewilderment seen during a study of petit mal.' *Epilepsia,* **2,** 306–312.

Gordon, N. (1966) 'The child who does not talk. Problems of diagnosis with special reference to children with severe auditory agnosia.' *British Journal of Disorders of Communication,* **1,** 78–84.

—— (1969) 'A history of Laura Bridgman—from American Notes by Charles Dickens.' *British Journal of Disorders of Communication,* **4,** 107–116.

Griffiths, P. (1979) 'An approach to language therapy for children with specific language disabilty.' *New Zealand Speech Therapist Journal,* **34,** 14–30.

Hall, D. M. B., Hill, P. (1986) 'When does secretory otitis media affect language development.' *Archives of Disease in Childhood,* **61,** 42–47.

Holm, V. A., Kunze, L. H. (1969) 'Effects of chronic otitis media on language and speech development.' *Pediatrics,* **43,** 833–839.

Holmes, G. L., McKeever, M., Saunders, Z. (1981) 'Epileptiform activity in aphasia of childhood: an epiphenomenon?' *Epilepsia,* **22,** 631–639.

Ingram, T. T. S. (1969) 'Disorders of speech development in childhood.' *British Journal of Hospital Medicine,* **4,** 1608–1625.

Kaplan, L. C., Elias, E. R. (1986) 'Diagnosis of muscular dystrophy in patients referred for evaluation of language delay.' *Developmental Medicine and Child Neurology,* **28,** 110.

Kiernan, C., Reid, B., Jones, L. (1982) *Signs and Symbols.* London: Heinemann Medical.

Krashan, S. (1975) 'The development of cerebral dominance and langauge learning: more new evidence.' *In:* Dato, D. P. (Ed.) *'Developmental Psycholinguistics: Theory and Applications.* Washington, D. C.: Georgetown University Round Table on Language and Linguistics.

Landau, W. M., Kleffner, F. R. (1957) 'Syndrome of acquired aphasia with convulsive disorder in children.' *Neurology,* **7,** 523–530.

—— Goldstein, R., Kleffner, F. (1960) 'Cogenital aphasia. A cliniciopathologic study.' *Neurology,* **10,** 915–921.

Lenneberg, E. G. (1966) 'The natural history of language.' *In:* Smith, F., Miller, G. R. (Eds.) *The Genesis of Language: a Psycholinguistic Approach.* Cambridge, Mass: MIT Press.

Lou, H. C., Henriksen, L., Bruhn, P. (1984) 'Focal cerebral hypoperfusion in children with dysphasia and/or attention deficit disorder.' *Archives of Neurology,* **41,** 825–829.

Lous, J., Fiellau-Nikalajsen, M. (1984) 'A 5-year prospective case-control study of the influence of early otitis media with effusion on reading achievement.' *International Journal of Pediatric Otorhinolaryngology,* **8,** 19–30.

Ludlow, C. L., Cooper, J. A. (1983) 'Genetic aspects of speech and language disorders: current status and future directions.' *In:* Ludlow, C. L., Cooper, J. A. (Eds.) *Genetic Aspects of Speech and Language Disorders.* New York: Academic Press.

Mantovani, J. F., Landau, W. M. (1980) 'Acquired aphasia with convulsive disorder: cause and prognosis.' *Neurology,* **30,** 524–529.

McNeil, D. (1974) 'How to resolve two paradoxes and escape a dilemma.' *In:* Connolly, K., Bruner, J. (Eds.) *The Growth of Competence.* London: Academic Press.

Miller, J. F., Campbell, T. F., Chapman, R. S., Weismer, S. E. (1984) 'Language behaviour in acquired childhood aphasia.' *In:* Holland, A. (Ed.) *Language Disorders in Children.* San Diego: College Hill Press.

Nettley, C. (1983) 'Sex chromosome abnormalities and the development of verbal and nonverbal abilities.' *In:* Ludlow, C. L., Cooper, J. A. (Eds.) *Genetic Aspects of Speech and Language Disorders.* New York: Academic Press.

O'Donohoe, N. V. (1979) *Epilepsies of Childhood.* London: Butterworths.

Ounsted, C., Taylor, D. C. (1972) *Gender Differences: Their Ontogeny and Significance.* London: Churchill Livingstone.

Paradise, J. L. (1980) 'Otitis media in infants and children.' *Paediatrics,* **65,** 917–943.

—— (1981) 'Otitis media during early life: how hazardous to development? A critical review of the evidence.' *Pediatrics,* **68,** 869–873.

Purvis, R. J. (1977) 'Speech disorders.' *In:* Drillien, C. M., Drummond, M. B. (Eds.) *Neurodevelopmental Problems in Early Childhood.* Oxford: Blackwell Scientific Publications.

Quinn, V., Macauslan, A. (1986) *Dyslexia. What Parents Ought to Know.* London: Penguin.

Reynell, J. (1977) *Manual for the Reynell Developmental Language Scales (Revised).* Windsor: NFER.

Rutter, M. (1982) 'Developmental neuropsychiatry: concepts, issues and prospects.' *Journal of Clinical Neuropsychology,* **4,** 91–115.

Sak, R. J., Reuben, R. J. (1982) 'Effects of recurrent middle ear effusion in pre-school years on language and learning.' *Developmental and Behavioural Pediatrics,* **3,** 7–11.

Sato, S., Dreifuss, F. E. (1972) 'Electroencephalographic findings in a patient with developmental expressive aphasia.' *Neurology,* **23,** 181–185.

Stein, Z., Susser, M. (1985) 'Effects of early nutrition on neurological and mental competence in human beings.' *Psychological Medicine,* **15,** 717–726.

Stores, G. (1977) 'Sex-related differences in "attentiveness" in children with epilepsy attending ordinary school.' *In:* Meinardi, H., Rowan, A. J. (Eds.) *Advances in Epilepsy.* Amsterdam: Sinets and Zeitilinger.

Tough, J. (1973) *Focus on Meaning: Talking to Some Purpose with Young Children.* London: Allen and Unwin.

Walzer, S. (1985) 'X chromosome abnormalities and cognitive development: implications for understanding normal human development.' *Journal of Child Psychology and Psychiatry,* **26,** 177–184.

Weintraub, S., Mesulam, M. M. (1983) 'Development or learning disabilities of the right hemisphere.' *Archives of Neurology,* **40,** 463–468.

Worster-Drought, C. (1943) 'Congenital auditory imperception (congenital word deafness) and its relation with idioglossia and allied speech defects.' *Medical Press and Circular,* **210,** 410–420.

Zinkus, P. W., Gottlieb, M. I., Shapiro, M. (1978) 'Developmental and psychoeducational sequelae of chronic otitis media.' *American Journal of Diseases of Childhood,* **137,** 1100–1104.

13
LANGUAGE DISORDERS ASSOCIATED WITH PSYCHIATRIC DISTURBANCE

Michael Rutter and Catherine Lord

The strong association between language impairment and psychiatric disorder in young children (see Chapter 17) is both theoretically and clinically important. The finding raises questions on the nature of the processes and mechanisms involved in the connections between the two. It is crucial to appreciate that the association arises in several different ways. In this chapter we focus on the heterogeneity of psychiatric disorders that involve language problems, in order to discuss issues of differential diagnosis and of treatment decisions as they face clinicians dealing with language disorders in young children.

There is a need to differentiate between a distorted *use* of language in individuals with a normal language capacity and a delay or impairment in language skills – *i.e.* an *incapacity* in language development. Of course, distorted language use and language delay frequently coexist, and one of the key issues to be considered is the extent to which patterns of language impairment are of diagnostic importance. However, the scope of the chapter is confined to language problems that present in early childhood. We will not consider the loss of language skills in adult life, nor will we discuss abnormalities of language usage associated with psychiatric disorders arising after the preschool years. Such abnormalities (*e.g.* thought disorder in schizophrenia or mutism in severe depression) are of great psychiatric significance but are of very limited relevance in the clinical practice of those dealing with disorders of the development of language.

Nature of relationship between language impairment and psychiatric disorder
For children six years or younger, delays in language constitute a major precipitant of psychiatric referral (Chess and Rosenberg 1974). Yet identification of disordered speech and/or language is as often an entry point for the recognition of other problems as an endpoint for itself. Since speech and language difficulties are usually quite easy to observe, parents and teachers can often identify them earlier and professionals can quantify them sooner than delays in other areas of behaviour, such as socio-emotional development (Lichtenstein 1984, Rutter 1984).

Historically, there has been an assumption that when language impairment is associated with psychiatric disturbance this means that somehow the psychological disorder caused a problem in the child's use and/or development of language. However, the relationship may take different forms, few of which are straightforward or unidirectional.

Figure 1 summarizes some of the main patterns that this association may take. First there is the case of a psychiatric disorder causing a secondary language

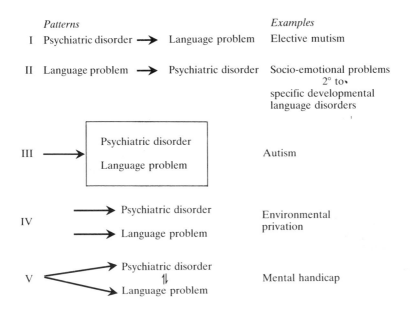

Fig. 1. *Psychiatric disorder and language problems*
(Varied patterns of association)

problem. Elective mutism constitutes the only common example of this kind in early childhood. The electively mute child *has* language capabilities, but for socio-emotional reasons does not use them normally.

Second, there is the reverse unidirectional causal process; namely the situation in which there is a primary language disability that causes a secondary psychiatric disturbance. The example, here, is provided by the socio-emotional problems that may arise as a secondary consequence of a specific developmental language disorder (see Chapter 17). The mechanisms involved are ill-understood and probably are multiple. However, at least in some cases, it seems that the social stresses and difficulties caused by the language handicap (or by the intellectual or educational deficits with which it may be associated) predispose to psychiatric disturbance.

Third, the association between the language delay and the psychiatric disorder may not represent a causal process at all; rather both may constitute different facets of some other underlying problem. Autism provides the best example of this pattern. The precise nature of the underlying problem is not known, but it involves some kind of cognitive-developmental deficit (Rutter 1983). That is to say, the language delay does not constitute a specific or 'pure' language disorder; instead it forms part of a broader cognitive impairment that includes thought processes as well as linguistic features. Similarly, the disturbed social relationships involve an impairment in the appreciation and processing of socio-emotional cues or stimuli.

Fourth, there is the rather different pattern in which the language delay and

207

psychiatric disorder arise from *different* causal processes that happen both to stem from some broader risk situation. This is the case with the language delay and psychiatric disorder that can arise in children who experience severe environmental privation, as in poor quality institutional care or parental neglect (see Chapter 7). It is evident that the language delay and the psychiatric disorder do *not* reflect the same underlying problem because the specific risk mechanisms have been shown to be different. Thus, in modern residential nurseries and Children's Homes it is quite unusual to find children who are substantially delayed in their language development but socio-emotional disturbance is common. The language impairment in old-style poor quality institutions stemmed from a lack of the necessary learning experiences involved in adult-child communication and interaction (Rutter 1985a); the socio-emotional difficulties, on the other hand, probably derive from the severe discontinuities in parenting involved in multiple changing caregivers (Rutter 1981).

Fifth, there is the pattern of multiple interconnected causal processes. Mental retardation provides the best example of this circumstance. Children with mental handicap (particularly when it is severe) frequently exhibit psychiatric problems (Corbett 1985) and usually, they are delayed in their language development (see chapter by Rondal). In addition, to the interrelationships between the language and psychiatric disturbances exemplified in patterns I to IV, the two disorders may arise from different causal processes. For example, in some cases of mental handicap, the speech difficulty may derive from a motor problem (as in the dysarthrias associated with cerebral palsy) or from deafness (as in congenital rubella) – neither of which play a central rôle in the causation of the psychiatric problem. On the other hand, basically all these problems derive from the organic brain condition that caused the mental handicap.

The consequence of these varied patterns of association is that the co-occurrence of language delay and psychiatric disorder does not, in itself, identify the causal processes involved. Rather, the clinician is required to make a careful differential diagnosis of both the language problem and the psychiatric disturbance in order to draw conclusions about the relevant mechanisms.

Implications for assessment
The need for a systematic appraisal of the child's level and pattern of functioning in cognition, language and socio-emotional development is outlined in Rutter's chapter on assessment (Chapter 18). The findings from such an evaluation may be used to differentiate between the various psychiatric disorder-language disability patterns outlined above.

Figure 2 summarizes some of the main ways in which the five disorders considered above show contrasting pictures with regard to language and cognition. Thus, very marked situational variations in children's use of spoken language are most likely to be found with elective mutism. A lack of social communication is characteristic of both elective mutism and autism. However, autism is distinctive in that there is a major deficit in language comprehension, whereas in elective mutism there is not. Deviant features in the form of spoken language are common only with

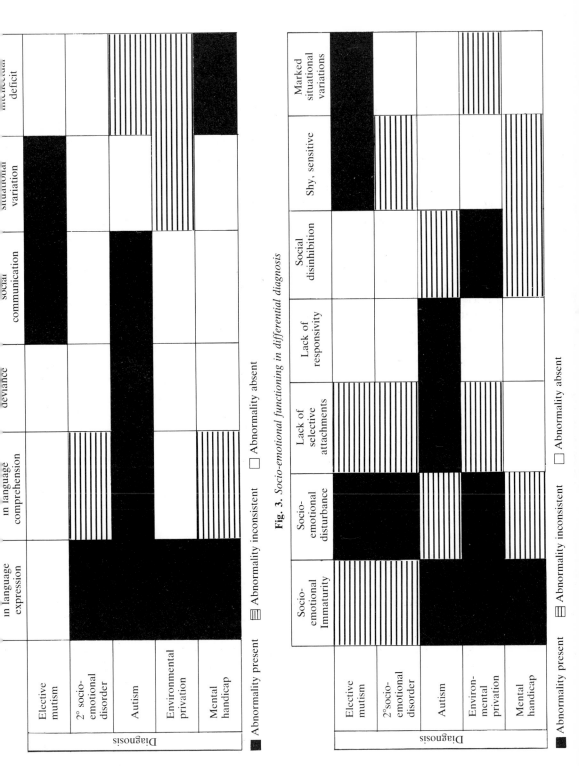

Fig. 3. *Socio-emotional functioning in differential diagnosis*

209

autism. By definition, mental handicap is characterized by the presence of a general intellectual deficit. Such a deficit is commonly found in autism, too, but the language deviance and the lack of social communication serve as differentiating features from mental handicap.

The two patterns most difficult to distinguish from one another on the basis of language and cognition alone are (i) the secondary emotional disturbances associated with a specific developmental language disorder and (ii) the pattern of language delay and psychiatric disorder associated with severe environmental privation. In both cases, the usual picture is that of a major deficit in language expression, with little in the way of other abnormalities. If there is also a major deficit in language comprehension, however, this makes it less likely that the problem is solely a result of environmental privation.

Figure 3 shows how the findings on socio-emotional functioning may provide a guide to differential diagnosis. As one might expect, the mere presence of socio-emotional abnormalities is of little significance in itself (as it is that which defines the presence of psychiatric disorder); although conditions differ in the extent to which they reflect immaturity (i.e. behaviour appropriate to a younger child) or disturbance (meaning fears, anxiety, aggression and the like). The pattern associated with environmental privation stands out, however, in terms of the presence of social disinhibition and indiscriminate 'over'-friendly behaviour. Thus, children reared by multiple changing caretakers in an institutional setting tend to be clinging as toddlers; during early and middle childhood they appear attention-seeking and demanding of attention; and during the school years they tend to be overactive, inattentive and intrusively personal in their approaches to strangers. If the environmental privation occurred in a family context rather than an institution (as with parental neglect or abuse), probably this pattern would not be found. Rather it is likely that there would be an insecure attachment. The children might be clinging or rebuffing of their parents, but the parent's presence would not create the reassurance and confidence that would be expected ordinarily.

The socio-emotional disturbances that arise as a secondary consequence of a specific developmental language disorder are distinctive in terms of a *lack* of distortion of the normal development of social attachments. Thus, the children may be fearful or aggressive, and may have difficulties in peer relationships, but on the whole, their attachments to their parents are normal in form.

In sharp contrast, it is the severe distortion of that developmental process that most characterizes the syndrome of autism. Young children with autism tend to lack strongly selective attachments to their parents. However, most of all, they lack the normal reciprocity and to-and-fro responsiveness that is typical of ordinary social interchanges. This lack is evident in all social encounters although it is most strikingly shown in encounters with other children.

In elective mutism, a defining feature is the marked situational variation so that the children appear friendly and reactive with some individuals but unresponsive with others. Typically, however, there may be some more pervasive social difficulty in terms of shyness, sensitivity or social awkwardness.

There is no one type of psychiatric disorder associated with mental handicap and there is no distinctive socio-emotional pattern of diagnostic importance. However, in keeping with the general developmental delay the pattern is likely to be markedly immature in relation to the child's chronological age (but roughly appropriate in relation to mental age).

Psychiatric disorders secondary to language delay
With these general considerations in mind, we turn now to a more detailed consideration of some of the main varieties of language disorder associated with psychiatric disturbance. Probably the most common pattern is that of the psychiatric disorders that arise as a secondary consequence of a developmental language delay. The clinical features of specific developmental speech and language disorders are described in Chapter 12 and will not be discussed further here.

Secondary psychiatric disturbances are least likely to occur when there is a disorder of articulation alone (although the psychiatric risk is still increased), and most likely to arise when the disorder involved language comprehension as well as expression (Griffiths 1969, Mattison *et al.* 1980; see chapter by Howlin and Rutter for a more detailed account of findings). Probably, too, psychiatric disturbances are more common when the speech or language problem is accompanied by, or part of, a more general intellectual impairment (Fundudis *et al.* 1979, Richman *et al.* 1982). Language delay in the preschool years is more likely to be associated with persistent psychiatric problems in boys than in girls (Richman *et al.* 1982).

The psychiatric disorders associated with language delay do not follow any distinctive pattern. Rates of anxiety disorders, conduct disturbance, and attention deficit syndromes are all increased (Baker and Cantwell 1982).

Because the association between psychiatric disorder and language delay is nonspecific in type, no one form of treatment can be recommended. Obviously there is a need to foster normal speech and language development in so far as that is possible. But that is not sufficient in itself for two rather different reasons. Firstly, there is no *necessary* connection between language delay and psychiatric disturbance. Some children with quite marked language difficulties show a normal socio-emotional development. The language handicap provides a social challenge but the strategies used in meeting that challenge may be protective or the reverse. Treatment needs to be planned to aid adaptive social problem-solving strategies. Secondly, although secondary, the psychiatric problems may be far from trivial; some are both persistent and handicapping. As a result, they need attention in their own right according to whatever style or intervention is most appropriate in the individual circumstances.

Language disorders associated with serious psychosocial adversity
It has long been thought that language development is particularly sensitive to adverse environmental influences like psychosocial deprivation. Yet children growing up in a wide range of environments develop adequate speech and language, implying that few *positive* factors are critical to language development (Houston, 1970). In this connection, it is interesting that the delays associated with

psychosocial adversity seem to be about equally common in boys and girls, which is not the case for most other language difficulties (Sandgrund *et al.* 1974). The general topic of environmental influences on language development is considered in the chapter by Puckering and Rutter; here we will confine discussion to clinically significant language delays associated with lacks or distortions in the child's life experiences.

Children raised from infancy in poor quality institutions or in multiple foster placements exhibit a raised incidence of delays in expressive language, of articulation disorders and of reading problems (Tizard and Tizard 1974, Singer and Fagan 1984). Comprehension of language is usually not impaired to the same extent (Klaus and Gray 1968). The sheer amount of adult-infant interaction and communication in institutions may be lower than that in most families, although this need not be the case. However, qualitative factors may be as influential for language development. Such factors include the extent to which language is used to inform rather than to direct behaviour, the amount of spontaneous conversation and the degree to which staff communications are modified to the developmental levels of the children (Tizard and Tizard 1974).

Factors similar to those studied in institutions have also been linked to relations between maternal behaviours and language development. Children who have been severely neglected show more limited vocabulary, more problems in articulation and less complex sentence structure than control groups matched for social class and race, including non-neglected, but physically abused children (Blager and Martin 1976, Allen and Oliver 1982). Neglected children and their mothers typically interact verbally *and* non-verbally at very low rates (Bousha and Twentyman 1984, Hoffman-Plotkin and Twentyman 1984). This is the one group of children who are most likely to experience true privation of interactive language (Yarrow 1961).

Children who have been physically abused (Blager 1979; Bousha and Twentyman, 1984), children from very large families (Gaines *et al.* 1978; Richman *et al.* 1982) and children of mothers with psychiatric disorder (Baldwin *et al.* 1982, Sameroff *et al.* 1982) may also show language difficulties, particularly in the grammatical complexity of their spontaneous sentences and in their responses during structured tests.

As in studies of institutions, the effects on language development may well be mediated by the quality of mother-child interaction including mothers' responsiveness, restrictiveness or use of explanation (Wulbert *et al.* 1975, Schachter 1979). Of course, the same issues apply to father-child interaction; however in most families mothers talk more with young children (see Greenbaum and Landau 1979, Tizard *et al.* 1983). Moreover, maternal features tend to be stronger predictors of language difficulties (Baldwin *et al.* 1982).

Diagnosis of communication disorders due to environmental circumstances cannot be made solely on the basis of a child's speech and language characteristics, although they can be suggestive (see above). Identification of psychosocial adversities of a type and of a severity likely to lead to language delay is the most critical factor in diagnosis. It should be added, however, that the presence of such adversities is not sufficient in itself for the inference that environmental privation is the cause of all the difficulties. Deprived children can and do suffer from all sorts of language disorders and the diagnosis requires *both* the relevant type of language/socio-emotional pattern *and* the presence of a relevant environmental risk factor.

Prognosis for psychosocially deprived children depends on factors such as whether or not there are other handicaps (physical or intellectual) as well as severity of language delay and possibly the age of the child at the start of treatment (Blager 1979, Singer and Fagan 1984).

Children who lack adequate linguistic experiences may also be deprived of food, freedom of movement or access to environments in which conversation is possible (Fromkin *et al.* 1974, Skuse 1984*a*). In fact, delayed *onset* of speech (as opposed to immaturities in complexity and vocabulary) has been reported primarily in severely malnourished children whose physical growth is also retarded and who have suffered extremes of deprivation in many areas (Powell *et al.* 1967, Skuse 1984*a*). For infants, gross deprivation may be required to affect the development of basic language skills; while in later years, more subtle but persistent aspects of the environment may influence a child's *use* of language (Rutter 1981). However, longterm effects depend most heavily on whether or not the deprivation continued (Rutter 1981). Hospitalization or foster-home placement of children suffering from extreme deprivation typically results in improvements within weeks, at least in the use of language for communication and in vocabulary (Koluchova 1972, Fromkin *et al.* 1974, Skuse 1984*b*). However, the long-term prognosis in these rare cases is difficult to determine, and may be related to such diverse factors as malnutrition, congenital abnormalities, organic dysfunction, presence of language at discovery and rate of progress during initial stages of treatment (Powell *et al.* 1967, Skuse 1984*a*). Clearly the prime objective of treatment is the provision of an environment more conducive to normal development. Where possible, this should be achieved through improvements in the child's existing family setting but in some cases the need to protect the child may require removal of the child from a severely neglectful or damaging home.

Mental handicap

Mental handicap constitutes the most common condition associated with significant speech and language delay. However, probably it is also the most common *mis*diagnosis—at least among primary care professionals who lack an adequate training in developmental disorders. This error occurs because, in the absence of a systematic assessment, it may be assumed that a child who is severely delayed in speaking must also be retarded in other areas of development. Of course, statistically speaking, that is likely, but still there are many children whose delays are specific to language. Whether or not that is so in an individual child can be determined only by means of a thorough clinical appraisal combined with an appropriate psychological assessment. The qualifying adjective 'appropriate' is necessary because many tests of intelligence are heavily weighted with verbal tasks. In children with impaired language, cognitive testing must include separate assessment on non-verbal tests (see Chapter 19).

Chapter 15 provides a fuller account of the language disorders associated with mental handicap. It is necessary, here, only to make a few points that are particularly pertinent with respect to language disorders associated with psychiatric disturbance. Because mental handicap is a term that describes a *general* intellectual impairment that is associated with a handicap in adaptive functioning, it may be expected that a delay in language will form part of the global developmental delay. However, it is common for such delay to be uneven in pattern with some functions more affected than others. With severe degrees of mental handicap it is common for language to be *more* retarded than other areas of development but the reverse can occur. Development of speech and language skills in intellectually retarded people follows a generally normal course (Lackner 1968), but onset of language occurs later, articulation is often poor, acquisition of speech and language skills takes longer, and most intellectually retarded people remain limited in use of language throughout their lives (Ryan 1977). The relationship among the various aspects of speech and language may also be different for intellectually retarded individuals than for normally developing children. Thus, receptive vocabulary in children with intellectual retardation often exceeds grammatical complexity (Ryan 1977). Assessment of *spontaneous* language in retarded children often indicates greater knowledge than one would expect on the basis of formal test results (Prutting *et al.* 1975).

In general, the greater a child's deficit on adaptive and non-verbal cognitive tasks, the more likely that spoken language will be substantively impaired. However, for any given level of intellectual retardation there is considerable individual variation in language skills. Whether or not an individual child acquires language (either spoken or sign) depends on factors such as social skills, motor abilities and the opportunities provided by the environment as well as on mental age level (Bonvillian and Nelson 1982). This finding underscores the need for a multidimensional assessment of the child's abilities and deficits. It also emphasizes that the presence of mental handicap does not in itself explain the language problem. In some intellectually retarded children the language delay may be no more than another facet of a general cognitive immaturity. However, mentally handicapped children (particularly those with severe handicap) commonly have other problems besides low IQ. These include hearing deficits and neurological disorders—both of which may lead to language problems independently of the intellectual impairment (Ryan 1977). For example, children with Down's syndrome often have particular difficulties with articulation (Evans and Hampson 1968). In addition, it is important to assess the possible rôle of psychosocial influences. Children with mild mental retardation are disproportionately likely to come from socially disadvantaged families; a lack of adequate linguistic experiences may have played a part in the genesis of the language delay. Also, psychosocial factors may influence children's use of language, whatever the degree of delay. While cognitive deficits may limit the complexity of concepts expressed by a child with intellectual retardation (Cromer 1976), it may be that social factors such as the responsiveness of the listener (Ryan 1977) and the confidence the child has in his or her own knowledge (Zigler and Butterfield 1968) determine the extent to which an

214

intellectually retarded child successfully uses his linguistic skills in communication and cognition.

Because children with mental handicap are delayed in their general development, their behaviour is likely to be roughly commensurate with their mental age. It is important not to mistake appropriately immature behaviour with psychiatric disorder. Thus, the emotional difficulties of an intellectually retarded six-year-old with tantrums who has difficulty separating from her mother may well be no more than behaviour that is within normal limits for a mental age of, say, two to three years. On the other hand, intellectual retardation is associated with a substantially increased risk of the same wide range of emotional and conduct problems seen in normally developing children (Corbett 1985). These problems, even when seemingly due to the general immaturity of the retarded child, deserve the same consideration as equivalent problems in other children, although treatment may vary according to developmental needs.

In addition to a raised frequency of common types of psychiatric problems, the most severely retarded children also have a greater likelihood of autistic-like social impairment associated with stereotyped repetitive behaviour (Wing and Gould 1979). Often, however, the clinical picture does not fulfil the usual criteria for autism. At present, it remains uncertain whether these disorders represent atypical varieties of autism or some phenocopy of different medical aetiology. Either way, three clinical considerations remain. First, it is apparent that the autistic-like problems have their basis in cognitive deficits; they are most likely to be found in those with severe mental handicap and a comprehension age below 20 months. Second, the presence of autistic features does not indicate that radically different methods of treatment are indicated or that the prognosis is better than that for other severely mentally handicapped children. The children's development is likely to be more a function of the very low IQ than of the autistic features, but, if anything, the presence of the latter suggest a worse outlook. Thirdly, although necessarily modified by the degree of mental handicap, the social impairment raises much the same treatment issues as those that apply with autism (see Rutter 1985c; also below). The language deficit is usually severe, and in most cases, it does not respond well to speech training (see chapter 23).

Infantile autism

Autism constitutes not only the most severe psychiatric disorder arising in early childhood but also the condition associated with the most pervasive abnormality in language development. Abnormal or delayed communication is the most common reason for initial referral (DeMyer 1979) and also one of the four main diagnostic criteria for autism. The remaining criteria are: specific deficits in basic aspects of social development, some form of ritualistic or repetitive behaviour, and developmental impairment or distortion that is manifest before three years (usually before 30 months) (American Psychiatric Association, 1980; Rutter 1985b).

Autism is a relatively rare condition that occurs in a 'pure' form in about four per 10,000 persons. However, when partial forms are included, up to 21 per 10,000 persons may be affected (Wing and Gould 1979). The syndrome is much more common in males than females, with a ratio of about three males to every female (Lotter 1966). About 70 to 80 per cent of autistic persons have significant intellectual retardation as well as autism (Lockyer and Rutter 1970, Lotter 1974). Autism is a lifelong condition. However, the prognosis in terms of eventual independence and academic status varies greatly across individuals, being worst in those with a non-verbal IQ below 50. Because of its importance in prognosis and in understanding other aspects of behaviour and development, a comprehensive appraisal of intelligence is a crucial first step in assessment.

Language and speech characteristics
Most children with autism show *delays* in the development of language, with a deficit in comprehension being especially marked (Tager-Flusberg 1981, Lord 1984a). About a fifth of autistic children are reported to learn a few words and then to show regression in language development sometime between 15 and 30 months of age (Rutter 1985b). Such a regression appears to have no particular clinical significance but, if anything, it carries a worse (rather than a better) prognosis.

About half of autistic individuals never develop functional speech; most of these persons also show severe mental handicap (Lotter 1978). At the other extreme, a small proportion of autistic children develop sufficient language to score in the average range on verbal tests by early adolescence (Lockyer and Rutter 1970). This is most likely to occur when the non-verbal IQ is within the normal range and when there is useful communicative language already manifest by the age of five years.

Immediate echolalia, or repeating back what someone has just said, is very common (Rutter 1966) but it is not specific to autism. Some repetition is a normal part of language development up to about 30 months; persistent echoing seems to be particularly associated with comprehension deficits. It can serve a variety of communicative functions such as allowing a child to take a turn in a conversation even though he or she has not understood what was said (Curcio and Paccia 1982, Prizant 1983).

Unlike immediate echoing, delayed echolalia, in which a child repeats something someone said minutes to months before (including television commercials or other stereotyped phrases), occurs almost exclusively in children with autism or other severe social deficits (Bartak *et al.* 1975). It is most common in young autistic children, though it continues to occur into adulthood in some persons. At two and three years of age, echolalia (as opposed to no speech at all) is associated with a relatively good prognosis for the eventual development of language (Howlin 1981).

Echolalia can be particularly confusing to parents. Children with delayed echolalia sometimes produce quite complicated but inappropriate sentences that they have memorized. These utterances may misrepresent both their comprehension and their ability to use language flexibly (*i.e.* the child may not be able to use the words in other contexts or other sentence forms).

A tendency to say 'you' instead of 'I' is also particularly associated with autism. To a substantial extent, this appears to be a function of an echoing tendency

216

(Bartak and Rutter 1974). Rote auditory memory and articulation are often less delayed in autistic children than are other aspects of language (Tubbs 1966, Bartolucci 1976).

The second deficit in communication associated with autism is a failure to compensate for limited oral language skills by using alternative methods of communication. Thus, unlike children with other types of severe language impairment, young autistic children do not use gesture, facial expression or normal intonation patterns to express a variety of intentions, nor are they able to use these 'paralinguistic features' to aid their understanding of what others say. A deaf child might indicate that he wants to go outside by vocalizing, catching his mother's eye across a room and gesturing toward the door using pantomime and facial expression. An autistic child typically would take his mother's wrist and soundlessly without ever looking at her, pull her across the room until he can place her hand on the door-knob.

Third, even when delays in the form (*e.g.* vocabulary, grammar) of language are overcome, abnormalities in *use* of language remain associated with autism throughout childhood. The introduction and continuation of appropriate conversational topics are matters of extreme difficulty. Of those autistic adults who are capable of speaking fluently, few are able to use language flexibly in a reciprocal to-and-fro conversational manner that both includes a response to and a development of what the other person has said. Autistic persons with fluent language may talk to themselves or 'at' others without really understanding the social nature of most conversations.

Aetiology and medical implications
Autism constitutes a descriptive rather than aetiological diagnosis. It is associated with a diverse array of diseases, including congenital rubella, infantile spasms, tuberous sclerosis, congenital cytomegalovirus and the fragile x syndrome, as well as with a raised rate of perinatal problems and of minor congenital abnormalities (see Rutter 1985*b*). Most of these features are as much associated with mental handicap as with autism. However, autism differs from non-autistic mental handicap in its pattern of association with medical conditions, in that it is relatively rare in individuals with Down's syndrome, or cerebral palsy (Wing and Gould 1979). It also differs sharply in the age of onset of epileptic seizures (Rutter 1970, Deykin and MacMahon 1979). About a quarter of autistic individuals develop seizures. This rate is not markedly different from that in mental handicap, but whereas the usual onset in autistic individuals is during adolescence, in mentally retarded persons typically it is in early childhood.

Three sets of findings suggest a heritable component to autism (Folstein and Rutter in press). First, the concordance rate for autism and for cognitive/language disorders is higher in monozygotic than dizygotic pairs (Folstein and Rutter 1977). Second, the estimated 2 per cent rate of autism in siblings (the figure is approximate because it is based on small numbers and unstandardized diagnoses—Gottesman *et al.* 1982) is considerably greater than the 1 per 2,500 rate in the general population (Lotter 1966). Third, the rates of language disorder, learning disability and mental retardation are raised in the siblings of autistic children; in one study the rate was about 15 per cent (August *et al.* 1981). The evidence suggests that there is some kind of genetic association between autism and some other cognitive and language deficits; nevertheless it is unclear just what is inherited and it is not known whether the genetic risk applies to most cases of autism or only to a subgroup.

Recent studies have shown that some cases of autism are associated with the fragile x phenomenon. However, the reported rates have varied from 0 per cent to 17 per cent (see Rutter and Schopler in press) and it is not known whether there is any specific connection with autism (as distinct from mental handicap). It may be that the fragile x accounts for some of the familial loading for cognitive deficits but at present, we lack evidence on the extent to which it does so. As a result of these various uncertainties on genetic mechanisms, parents can be given general guidance on the possible risks of having a further child with autism or some other cognitive disorder, but precise quantification is not possible.

Because of these various medical findings, it is now generally accepted that autism is due to some organic condition (Rutter 1985*b*). However, it still remains the case that most autistic children do not have recognizable CNS disease; unlike the situation with severe mental handicap neuropathological studies have been disappointingly inconclusive. No marked differences have been found between autistic children who have clear-cut brain dysfunction and those who do not (Rutter and Lockyer 1967). Moreover, no clear pattern of structural or chemical brain abnormalities has emerged (see Rutter and Schopler in press). That there is an organic basis for autism is not in doubt, but its nature remains obscure.

Altogether, the chances that a particular autistic child will have a treatable medical condition, or even one that is relevant for specific genetic counselling, are relatively low. Highly intrusive medical investigations should therefore be kept to a minimum. On the other hand, it is important to take a systematic medical history (for perinatal complications, postnatal brain disorders *etc.*); to obtain a family history for cognitive and language disorders; to undertake a neurodevelopmental assessment (including tests for hearing and vision); to carry out urine and blood screening for metabolic disorders; and to perform chromosome examinations (including assessment for the fragile x in males).

Cognitive and intellectual aspects of autism

About three quarters of persons with autism are also intellectually retarded, meaning that they show at most only very isolated skills close to their chronological age level. However, autistic children and adolescents show a pattern of cognitive abilities and disabilities that is distinct from that of children with non-autistic intellectual retardation, behaviour problems or specific language disorders (Lockyer and Rutter 1970, DeMyer *et al.* 1974, Bartak *et al.* 1975. For autistic children, strongest performance is generally in visuo-spatial, concrete object-oriented tasks such as puzzles and matching tasks. Performance tends to be weakest on tasks that require greater abstraction or sequencing of separate ideas, as well as on language tests (Lockyer and Rutter 1970, De Meyer *et al.* 1974).

218

To date, the strongest factor in predicting outcome in autism has been non-verbal IQ, though language and social skills also have some predictive value (Lotter 1978). Autistic children who are severely retarded almost inevitably remain severely handicapped. Autistic children who are mildly retarded generally remain handicapped, but may be able to participate in some community functions. Autistic children without clear mental retardation have about a 50 per cent chance of living independently, albeit usually with continuing marked social problems. However, within the non-retarded range, we lack good prognostic indications of the level of adaptation in adult life. The outlook is worst for those with severe communication problems that persist beyond the preschool years, but, apart from that, the outcome may depend almost as much on the available educational, vocational and social resources as on the specific particular behavioural problems or cognitive skills (Schopler *et al.* 1981).

Emotional and behavioural characteristics
Most autistic children are socially abnormal from infancy, although sometimes abnormalities in social behaviour do not become apparent until language fails to develop (or regresses) towards the end of the second year. As infants and toddlers, autistic children may look at people's faces, but they do not use the catching of another's gaze as a means of directing attention. They cannot coordinate 'social looking' with other behaviours such as facial expressions, vocalizations or gestures (Mirenda *et al.* 1983, Lord 1984*b*).

Some autistic children are remarkably unexpressive emotionally. Others smile, frown and show some 'normal' emotions; however, these emotions tend not to be related to the emotions of others. A toddler with autism might smile at the light reflecting off a toy but would not accompany this smile with a glance at his mother. The same child would be unlikely to join in the laughter of his family at the antics of a sibling. Many *young* autistic children ignore people or look through them as if they were not there. A few actively withdraw from affection. However, other children may cling without particular interest in communicating or indiscriminately may enjoy physical approaches even from strangers (particularly tickling or roughhousing). The early failure to develop attachments, and often even to discriminate parents and siblings from others, is particularly important in differentiating autism from other severe communication disorders. The effect of this lack of early attachment on parents is also often very marked.

As autistic children reach school age, most show some attachment to their parents and familiar adults (Sigman and Ungerer 1984), but social abnormalities continue to be particularly obvious with peers and in unstructured situations (Clark and Rutter 1981). Most of all, autistic children do not discriminate or make use of socio-emotional cues (Hobson 1986), social reciprocity is missing from their relationships with other people, and they fail to develop intense emotional ties that involve a concern for the other person. They especially lack inferential behaviour in their social interactions (van Engeland *et al.* 1985); a lack that may stem from a more general inability to draw inferences about other people's intentions or beliefs or expectations (Baron-Cohen *et al.* 1985, 1986). Among those with associated mental handicap, a lack of imaginary play beyond very simple levels, meaningless use of objects (*e.g.* spinning, lining up) and an inordinate amount of time spent doing nothing are also characteristic (Wing and Gould 1979, Lord 1984*b*).

By adolescence, many autistic youngsters are interested in the company of others, but still do not show either sufficient knowledge of social conventions (*e.g.* how to begin a conversation), or an adequate sense of what potential friends might be feeling to establish truly reciprocal friendships (Rutter 1983). Autistic adolescents and adults may have normal sexual feelings but their lack of social skills make the development of a normal sexual relationship unlikely; few persons with autism marry or have children (Rutter 1985*b*).

Flicking the fingers, gazing at the hands, tiptoeing and hand-flapping also occur in many young austistic children (Ornitz *et al.* 1977). Other self-stimulatory behaviours associated with mental retardation and/or sensory deficits, such as eye-poking, rocking or head-banging may also be seen. Rituals and compulsive behaviours range from simple actions such as touching puzzle pieces to the upper lip to obsessive routines such as asking the same series of questions every evening before bed. An abnormal seeking for sameness and unusual preoccupations such as those seen in the repetitive drawing of geological formations or in attachments to unusual objects (such as a pepper shaker) may also occur.

Differential diagnosis
As indicated earlier in this chapter, the differential diagnosis between autism and other severe language disorders depends both on the pattern of language deficits and on the presence of particular socio-emotional abnormalities. Because of inconsistent responses to sound and delayed language, a common initial concern of parents is that their autistic child is deaf. Audiological tests usually rule out hearing impairment, but children with severe hearing impairments are also clearly different from autistic children in their intention to communicate and in their gestures, facial expressions and play. Children with severe developmental receptive language, who are even rarer than autistic children, may show somewhat more restricted use of non-verbal communication than deaf children, but can be discriminated from children with autism by their normal attachments and social behaviour with familiar adults and children (Bartak *et al.* 1975). These language-delayed children also show more articulation errors and a greater incidence of hearing impairment than do children with autism.

The lack of play and social skills in young autistic children often results in aimless wandering or behaviours such as running up and down the hall screaming or seeking out small objects and repetitively dumping them. A diagnosis of attention deficit with hyperactivity can usually be ruled out by assessment of the child's social, cognitive and language skills. Non-autistic children with hyperactivity should show relatively normal social interactions and imaginative play when contexts are created that minimize their attention deficits, in contrast to autistic children who have real *incapacities* in these areas. Whereas the behaviour of all children, including those with autism, varies across situation, autistic children's social behaviour is qualitatively different from others' even in the best of circumstances. In addition, *severe* delays in communication are not typical of hyperactive children of normal intelligence (Ross and Ross 1982).

Autism also shows substantial overlap with a pattern of persistent social deficits and circumscribed interests that occurs in non-retarded children with relatively intact language skills, the so-called 'schizoid disorder of childhood' (Wolff and Barlow 1979) or 'Asperger's syndrome' (Wing 1981). It is not clear if this clinical picture represents the mild end of the range of autism, a discrete group within autism or a quite separate group that overlaps with autism in some symptoms. Typically these children are diagnosed later and fare somewhat better in school than children with classic autism.

Differential diagnosis between schizophrenia and autism is usually straightforward, except in rare cases of highly verbal autistic adolescents (Noll and Benedict 1981; Petty *et al.* 1984). Schizophrenia is a disorder or group of disorders characterized by *deterioration* of social and cognitive functioning. It typically involves delusions, hallucinations and/or markedly illogical thinking accompanied by disturbances in motivation, affect, and/or movement that usually are first manifest only in late childhood or adolescence (Rutter and Garmezy 1983).

Schizophrenia is not usually associated with the severe difficulties in the acquisition of basic aspects of language, particularly comprehension, that are seen even in autistic persons of normal intelligence (Kolvin 1971, Bartak *et al.* 1975, Rutter 1985*b*). While schizophrenics may use language in unusual ways that reflect abnormal thoughts and perceptions, *major* immaturities in speech and actual errors in grammar such as pronoun reversals do not usually occur. Systematic studies have indicated no consistent tendency for autistic children to resemble schizophrenic children at similar chronological ages (Green *et al.* 1984).

Finally, there may be occasional diagnostic confusion between autism and Rett's syndrome. The latter is a progressive dementing disorder that is associated with a loss of facial expression and of interpersonal contact, stereotyped 'handwashing' movements, a broad-based stance, ataxia and loss of purposeful hand use (Hagberg *et al.* 1983). The condition is confined to girls. In the early stages of the disease, the hand movements show some similarities with the mannerisms characteristic of autism. However, the clinician should be alerted to the difference from autism by the increasing ataxia, progressive generalized dementia, lack of chewing, lack of complex obsessive-like behaviours, and inability to use the hands for purposeful activities (Olsson and Rett 1985).

There are also rare children with deviant language, unusual interests and severe social difficulties, who do not seem to fit into *any* reliable diagnostic category. Diagnostically, the extent to which a child's social, cognitive and language deficits represent true incapacities rather than variations in performance is the most important issue in differentiating autism from other disorders (Rutter 1985*d*). However, from a clinical point of view, precise categorization is less important than careful assessment of a child's strengths and weaknesses and the identification of factors most likely to enhance learning and development.

Treatment

The treatment of autism should comprise adequate medical care, appropriate educational programming and family-oriented services (see Rutter 1985*b*). Although the effects of treatment are often modest, when interventions are carefully directed toward practical goals related to the needs of a particular child and his or her family, the results can be real and worthwhile. Because the diverse sources of help required vary from year to year, someone needs to coordinate the different services. It is important to have someone who knows the child and family and who maintains regular contact with them over time. Periodic reassessments, not only of the child's skills, but also of his or her needs, the concerns of the family and the availablity of community resources are essential.

With families of autistic children, the goal of treatment is to help the family, including the autistic child, lead as normal a life as possible and to help the family keep the child at home as long as it is sensible. Providing parents with an understanding of the condition and with realistic expectations is often the start of treatment. Providing information and access to community resources is also important.

Treatment programmes typically combine two strategies. First, parents are taught behavioural methods for dealing with their child's maladaptive actions and for teaching behaviours that lead to more independence (*e.g.* toilet training, riding a bus). Second, parents are helped to discover activities and situations that may provide positive experiences for them and their child.

There are no specific pharmacological treatments for autism (see Rutter 1985*b*). However, occasionally drugs may be of value for symptomatic relief in the reduction of tension, aggression or overactivity or in the management of sleep disturbance.

Educational placements must be considered on an individual basis for each child, as must extra services such as speech therapy. Special classes for autistic children are appropriate in many cases. However, provided adequate support services are available, some of the most handicapped are better placed in schools for severely retarded children; others do well in classes for the language disabled; and a few of the most highly functioning may cope in ordinary schools. There are definite *social* advantages for autistic children to be integrated into programmes with children who are not autistic, but only *if* there are the skills and resources required to take advantage of the opportunities.

While there is no known cure for autism, treatment geared to the individual needs of children and families can make real differences in daily living.

Disintegrative 'psychosis'

The rather unsatisfactory term 'disintegrative psychosis' is applied to a heterogeneous group of disorders in which, following apparently normal development up to the age of three or four years (or occasionally later), there is a profound disintegration of behaviour involving loss of receptive and productive language, serious cognitive impairment and the emergence of various behavioural abnormalities such as overactivity and motor stereotypies.

Clinical characteristics
Typically, the onset is between three and six years of age. It is characterized by a vague period of premonitory illness or mood changes (*e.g.* sudden increase in fearfulness or irritability), followed by a deterioration in articulation and in complexity of grammar and sometimes by motor changes such as difficulty in walking or unusual movements (Heller 1930, Hulse 1954, Hudolin 1957). Usually, there is social withdrawal, loss of bowel and bladder control, and decreasing use and understanding of language until the child stops speaking entirely. In addition, there may be general intellectual deterioration, manifested in preschool children by the sudden onset of extreme passivity, loss of adaptive skills such as dressing, and the replacement of previous patterns of imaginative play by repetitive, meaningless use of objects (Corbett *et al.* 1977).

For schoolage children, deterioration in academic performance often represents the first source of concern followed by the appearance of articulation difficulties, problems in language use and comprehension, poor attention, and emotional instability (Malamud 1959, Corbett *et al.* 1977). Rather than becoming mute, older children may show more obvious signs of adult-like aphasia such as word-finding problems and autistic-like changes in the social appropriateness of their language.

In some children, behaviour may stabilize after six to nine months (Evans-Jones and Rosenbloom 1978), but others experience continued deterioration with bizarre behaviours such as auditory and visual hallucinations, and the development of rituals or sensory anomalies such as smelling things (Malamud 1959, Corbett *et al.* 1977). Because of such behaviours, the term 'psychosis' has been used to describe these children.

Differential diagnosis
These disintegrative disorders tend to follow one or other of two contrasting courses. First, after a period of regression lasting a few months up to a year or so, there is a plateau followed by a slow improvement, but usually within the context of continuing severe handicap (Evans-Jones and Rosenbloom 1978). Thereafter, the clinical picture closely resembles that of autism and it remains quite uncertain whether such disorders represent atypical varieties of autism or some rather different condition. The later onset after a definite period of normal development lasting several years, together with the clear loss of skills, might seem to constitute a crucial difference from autism, but, so far, the difference has not been shown to have any aetiological or prognostic significance. As with autism, an organic cause is probable but no specific aetiology has been identified as yet. The main differential diagnosis (apart from autism) in this non-progressive variety is from emotionally determined changes in speech usage (as in elective mutism), on the one hand and from acquired aphasia with epilepsy—the Landau-Kleffner syndrome—on the other (see chapters by Cromer and by Gordon). The latter is a rare condition in which, following normal development, there is a loss of receptive and productive language over the course of a few months (Miller *et al.* 1984). Usually, this is associated with the onset of seizures (which typically do not continue for more than

a few years) and/or transient gross abnormalities on the EEG (Worster-Drought 1971, Mantovani and Landau 1980). However, sometimes, the seizures may develop later (Cooper and Ferry 1978) and occasionally a mild delay in speech development may have preceded the dramatic language loss (Rapin *et al.* 1977, Miller *et al.* 1984) but this is unusual.

Because of the severity of the loss of receptive language the children may appear to be deaf (Worster-Drought 1971). Not infrequently, the children exhibit severe distress in response to their communication failure but usually warm responsive social relationships are maintained. The initial picture of loss of receptive language may be very similar in acquired aphasia and disintegrative psychosis but the former syndrome differs markedly in the retention of normal intellect and normal social responsiveness. Also, a grossly abnormal EEG is *not* usual in the latter.

The second course is of a progressive deterioration (Rivinus *et al.* 1975, Corbett *et al.* 1977). At first there may be no detectable signs of a neurological disorder and no indications of the underlying pathology. However, later on there may be increasing obvious motor dysfunction, sometimes with seizures or localized neurological signs. The medical conditions that occasionally present in this way include Wilson's disease, the cerebral lipoidoses, leukodystrophies and encephalitides. Clearly, the course and outcome after the initial phase is dependent on the particular disease in each case. It is important to appreciate that the diagnosis can be very difficult in the early stages and it is not uncommon for diagnostic tests misleadingly to be negative at first only to become positive later. When this happens the disorder may wrongly be labelled 'hysterical' (Caplan 1970, Rivinus *et al.* 1975). This misdiagnosis is made more likely by the fact that the clinical picture of disintegrative psychosis is an atypical presentation for many of the neurological conditions that may cause it. It is important, therefore, to be aware that a slowly *progressive* loss of previously well established language and cognitive skills is rarely due to hysteria and usually heralds some serious neurological disorder. It may be added that the same diseases when they occur in infancy are more often first shown by retardation in growth or by alterations in motor function than by loss of language (Wilson 1972, Noronha 1974).

As with the non-progressive variety, it is necessary to differentiate the clinical picture of disintegrative psychosis from the more benign functional loss of speech usage (but not speech capacity), as in elective mutism. The most important diagnostic feature is the presence or absence of impaired language comprehension, as shown by systematic testing. If there is such impairment, and, especially if this is accompanied by general intellectual impairment, some form of disintegrative psychosis is likely. In addition, the associated socio-emotional features are very different in the two groups of disorders (see above).

Assessment and treatment
Because diagnosis may be difficult in the early stages it is not uncommon for there to be a period of 18 months to two years between the onset of symptoms to appropriate clinic referral (Rivinus *et al.* 1975, Evans-Jones and Rosenbloom

224

1978). This delay can produce stress in families of affected children, especially since many parents firmly believe that their child's condition is associated with specific environmental events (*e.g.* a holiday or hospitalization of the mother) for which they feel responsible and guilty, but yet which makes them unwarrantedly hopeful for eventual complete recovery. Thorough neurological assessment is necessary to provide parents with appropriate information on diagnosis and prognosis and to alleviate family stress and uncertainty (Corbett *et al.* 1977). Unfortunately, however, it rarely reveals a treatable medical condition. As noted above, repeated medical investigations may be required before the cause of progressive deterioration is identified.

Periodic psychological reassessments are needed in order to measure changes over time (in terms of either deterioration or improvement). In the long run, improvements in behaviour and learning in children with non-progressive conditions are most often realized through appropriate education and behaviour management. The goals for treatment and the strategies required to carry them out entail the same multi-dimensional approach used for autism. It is critical to have an understanding of the child's skills and deficits in all areas and of the situations at home and at school (Evans-Jones and Rosenbloom 1978). As with autism, the role of the health professional is often to provide a stable contact across time and to coordinate services that shift as the child grows older and his or her and the family's needs change.

Elective mutism

Elective mutism is a descriptive term that refers to children who can speak but who do so only with very few people and/or in a small number of environments (Kratochwill 1981). The most common situation consists of a child who speaks to parents and siblings at home, but who refuses to talk to teachers or other children at school (except perhaps to a few peers) or to speak above a whisper to strangers in any setting (Kolvin and Fundudis 1981).

Clinical characteristics

The most common age of onset is three to five years, although often children are not referred for treatment until they have begun formal schooling (Kratochwill *et al.* 1979, Kolvin and Fundudis 1981). Shyness and refusal to speak are quite common in five- or six-year-olds during the first few months after starting school (Brown and Lloyd 1975), perhaps, especially among children of immigrants (Bradley and Sloman 1975). However, these cases usually resolve themselves without intervention (Parker *et al.* 1960). Elective mutism lasting a year or more appears to be even more rare than autism (Kolvin and Fundudis 1981, Rutter and Garmezy 1983).

Since elective mutism beginning in adolescence follows a different pattern from that in earlier childhood (Kaplan and Escoll 1973, Kratochwill 1981), this chapter will focus on the latter group. In contrast to most other speech and language disorders, elective mutism occurs with equal frequency in the two sexes, or perhaps even slightly more often in girls than boys (Hayden 1980, Kolvin and

225

Fundudis 1981). No clear association with social class, birth order or family size has been found (Halpern *et al.* 1971, Koch 1976); though twins and siblings have made up a disproportionate number of case reports (Wright 1968).

Elective mutism was previously considered to be a situation-specific emotional disorder that occurred in otherwise well-functioning children. However, more recent studies indicate that the majority of electively mute children are excessively shy and manifest very poor peer relationships across a variety of situations (Kolvin and Fundudis 1981). In addition, many electively mute children are somewhat delayed in the onset of language and, at 6 to 10 years of age, still show significant immaturities in communication, particularly articulation (Lerea and Ward 1965, Kolvin and Fundudis 1981).

More general (although usually mild) cognitive delays are also quite common in children initially diagnosed as electively mute (Parker *et al.* 1960, Reed 1963). Of the population of elective mutes studied by Kolvin and Fundudis (1981), 20 per cent scored in the range of intellectual retardation and a further 20 per cent were significantly below average on a *non-verbal* test of intelligence.

Besides extreme shyness and limited peer relations, elective mutism has also been related to behavioural immaturities, difficulties in bowel and bladder training and tics (Reed 1963, Kolvin and Fundudis 1981). Two groups of electively mute children have been proposed: frightened, timid, sensitive children who experience 'combat anxiety' in school (Reed 1963) and apathetic, slow, negative children who seem to seek attention through their refusal to speak (Friedman and Karagan 1973, Kolvin and Fundudis 1981). However, mixed clinical pictures are common.

Family disturbances including marital difficulties, distorted mother-child relationships and psychiatric disorder in one or more parents (Browne *et al.* 1963, Bradley and Sloman 1975) are frequently present; less commonly, family patterns of slow language development (Parker *et al.* 1960) or of not speaking to each other (Kaplan and Escoll 1973) have been reported. Finally, although children may stop speaking for a short while after injuries or traumatic events, it is rare for this to develop into a persistent elective mutism (Reed 1963, Wright 1968).

Differential diagnosis
For a diagnosis of elective mutism, it must be clear that the child *can* speak in some situations and does comprehend language, *i.e.* that the lack of speech cannot be accounted for by specific *incapacities* in language (such as those seen in dysphasic or autistic children). Having parents take language samples or tape record their child's speech at home is often sufficient to eliminate these concerns. In addition, if there is evidence of delayed language, the possiblity of general intellectual retardation must also be addressed through cognitive assessment. Once it has been determined that a child *can* speak and is *electively* mute, attention must be paid to the various factors that may have played a part in causation. It is usual to find an admixture of extreme personality features, social anxiety, problems in peer relationships, and some type of family difficulty (perhaps most commonly an unduly intense and restrictive mother-child relationship). However, in addition, mild speech or language problems or cognitive limitations may have been contributory factors.

In contrast to elective mutism, hysterical reactions involving speech are generally characterized by loss of ability to speak in *all* situations, occurring suddenly over a very short period of time (*e.g.* several hours) usually in children over 5 years of age (Rock 1971, Goodyer 1981). Other somatic complaints such as headaches and stomach aches are common, as is the existence of psychiatric disorder in the parents of these children (Kaplan and Escoll 1973, Goodyer 1981). Rate of improvement is good and often quite rapid. However, given the high frequency of misdiagnosis associated with hysteria, careful medical examination is warranted (Caplan 1970, Rivinus *et al.* 1975).

Elective mutism shows some overlap with school refusal or school phobia (Parker *et al.* 1960, Halpern *et al.* 1971), with maternal overprotectiveness said to play a role in both disorders (Browne *et al.* 1963). Also, occasionally, elective mutism may be confused with depression (Kaplan and Escoll 1973), although this difficulty is more typical of varieties occurring in adolescence.

Prognosis and treatment
The outlook is best when the children are in well functioning families and, probably also, if the mutism is not accompanied by markedly abnormal temperamental features or lasting severe difficulties in peer relationships (Koch 1976, Kolvin and Fundudis 1981). Prognosis is worse if mutism continues after 10 years of age and if it is associated with significant cognitive impairment (Wright 1968, Koch 1976). Even when the mutism is resolved, a substantial minority of the children continue to have academic and social difficulties during early and late adolescence (Koch 1976, Kolvin and Fundudis 1981), though these may improve once school is completed (Reed 1963).

The finding that a child speaks in one situation and not in another (and thus shows elective mutism) is indicative of an emotional disorder, but it does not necessarily indicate the psychological mechanism involved. These require separate diagnostic appraisal. However, the refusal to speak in particular situations (commonly school) produces practical problems of its own. Thus, treatment must be directed towards modifying the child's refusal to speak in specific situations, as well as addressing concerns about the child's emotional disturbance.

Most treatments have focused directly on the elimination of the maladaptive behaviour of refusing to speak, based on the assumption that if this goal is accomplished, other general treatment goals (i.e. fostering normal development, alleviation of family distress) will fall into place. Behavioural methods of treatment have included the use of systematic positive reinforcement for speaking (*e.g.* tokens, social rewards—see Kratochwill 1981), prompting of speech so that the child knows exactly when he or she is expected to speak (Conrad *et al.* 1974) and desensitization procedures such as gradually moving from a one-to-one interaction with a therapist to speaking in a classroom with other students. There is a necessity for coordination of treatment across teachers, parents and therapists (Parker *et al.* 1960, Wright 1968); for interventions to occur in the everyday situations in which the child must participate (*e.g.* school); and for eliminating secondary gains such as extra help and attention that the child receives for not speaking. The value of very frequent, brief treatment sessions has also been stressed (Friedman and Karagan 1973, Kratochwill *et al.* 1979).

While both speech therapy and behavioural approaches have generally proved successful in getting children to use *some* speech in the classroom, the resulting language is often at a low level and not particularly communicative. In addition, only some children show significant gains in their spontaneous initiation of conversation (Conrad *et al.* 1974, Sanok and Striefel 1979). These difficulties illustrate the need for somewhat more systematic consideration of treatment goals beyond decreasing the maladaptive behaviour of not speaking in specific situations. In contrast to behavioural methods, psychotherapeutic approaches have emphasized the need for treatment of broader concerns but have generally not provided systematic documentation of their effectiveness. Since developmental (*e.g.* speech problems, academic difficulties, and social deficits) and family factors clearly play a rôle in many cases of elective mutism, these issues need to be addressed as part of its treatment just as they are in other psychiatric and language disorders of childhood.

Conclusions

The relationship between language impairment and psychiatric disorder in childhood is strong, but not simple. Interactions between language, cognitive and social deficits, and specific behaviour problems vary greatly across disorder, development and situation. One direct implication of this complexity is that each of these current and past aspects of development (language, social, cognitive and behaviour) must be carefully assessed. Diagnostic formulations must be made on multiple axes including factors both internal (*e.g.* non-verbal cognitive skills) and external (*e.g.* psychosocial circumstances) to the child (Rutter and Garmezy 1983, Rutter 1985*d*).

Furthermore, judgements about a child's skills or deficits in one domain cannot be reached without direct observation of behaviour in *that* area. For example, one cannot reach conclusions about the language skills of an electively mute child without hearing him or her speak. The non-verbal cognitive level of an autistic child cannot be evaluated on the basis of his or her social behaviour during a physical examination, but requires direct assessment. Language provides a window through which to observe other domains and also serves as a communication skill necessary in its own right. Evaluation must address both of these aspects of development and potential deviance.

Information on areas other than language may also be critical in reaching conclusions about a specific aspect of a child's development or diagnosis. Thus, you cannot be sure that an electively mute child does not have an articulation disorder or an expressive language delay without hearing him speak (for example, by listening to a tape recording made at home). Nevertheless, you *can* differentiate the electively mute child from an autistic child by watching his facial expressions, use of gesture, social responsiveness and play.

The fact that there are few cures for the disorders described in this chapter means that treatment must focus on clear, functional goals. These goals can range from immediate and specific (*e.g.* getting an autistic child to respond to his or her name) to long-term and general (*e.g.* helping an electively mute child to develop better peer relations). Both types of goals must be monitored to determine the extent to which they are achieved. We are not at a stage in our understanding of these disorders or their treatment where we can safely assume without reevaluation, that any treatment will succeed.

There is little evidence, except in the case of psychosocial deprivation, that parental shortcomings or difficulties are the source of deviant or delayed language development. On the other hand, there is reason to believe that parents can bring about real improvements in communication and help avoid the development of secondary problems (Schopler 1976, Howlin 1981). Besides families, education remains the primary source of change for many children with language and psychiatric difficulties. Direct treatment by specialists may provide some help in amelioration of specific problems and acquisition of specific skills. However, in many cases, the input of professionals (whether physicians, speech therapists, psychologists or other health care workers) is best judged in terms of the extent to which it facilitates the work of parents and teachers in fostering children's normal development. Of course, the specifics of the ways in which this is done will vary according to the type of language disorder and of psychiatric problem. The recognition that there is an association between the two provides a starting point but the diagnostic process must go on to delineate the particular mechanisms involved in that association in each case; treatment must then be planned accordingly.

REFERENCES

Allen, R. E., Oliver, J. M. (1982) 'The effects of child maltreatment on language development.' *Child Abuse and Neglect,* **6,** 299–305.

American Psychiatric Association. (1980) *Diagnostic and Statistical Manual of Mental Disorders (3rd edn).* Washington: American Psychiatric Association.

August, G. J., Stewart, M. A., Tsai, L. (1981) 'The incidence of cognitive disabilities in the siblings of autistic children.' *British Journal of Psychiatry,* **138,** 416–422.

Baker, L., Cantwell, D. P. (1982) 'Language acquisition, cognitive development, and emotional disorder in childhood.' *In:* Nelson, K. E. (Ed.) *Children's Language, Volume 3.* Hillsdale, NJ: Lawrence Erlbaum. pp. 286–331.

Baldwin, A. L., Cole, R. E., Baldwin, C. P. (Eds.) (1982) 'Parental pathology, family interaction, and the competence of the child in school.' *Monographs of the Society for Research in Child Development,* **47,** (5).

Baron-Cohen, S., Leslie, A. M., Frith, U. (1985) 'Does the autistic child have a "theory of mind"?' *Cognition,* **21,** 39–46.

Baron-Cohen, S., Leslie, A. M., Frith, U. (1986) 'Mechanical behavioural and intentional understanding of picture stories in autistic children.' *British Journal of Developmental Psychology,* **4,** 113–125.

Bartak, L., Rutter, M. (1974) 'Use of personal pronouns by autistic children.' *Journal of Autism and Childhood Schizophrenia,* **4,** 217–222.

—— Rutter, M., Cox, A. (1975) 'A comparative study of infantile autism and specific developmental receptive language disorder. I—The Children.' *British Journal of Psychiatry,* **126,** 127–145.

Bartolucci, G. (1976) 'Formal aspects of language in childhood autism.' *In:* Steffen, J. J., Karoly, P. (Eds.) *Autism and Severe Psychopathology: Advances in Child Behavioral Analysis and Therapy, Volume two.* Toronto: Lexington Books. pp. 159–185.

Blager, F. B. (1979) 'The effect of intervention on the speech and language of abused children.' *Child Abuse and Neglect,* **5,** 991–996.

Blager, F., Martin, H. P. (1976) 'Speech and language of abused children.' *In:* Martin, H., Kempe, C. H. (Eds.) *The Abused Child: A Multidisciplinary Approach to Developmental Issues and*

Treatment (pp. 83–92). Cambridge, Mass.: Ballinger.

Bonvillian, J. D., Nelson, K. E. (1982) 'Exceptional cases of language acquisition.' *In:* Nelson, K. E. (Ed.) *Children's Language, Volume 3* Hillsdale, NJ: Lawrence Erlbaum. pp. 322–391.

Bousha, D. M., Twentyman, C. T. (1984) 'Mother-child interactional style in abuse, neglect, and control groups: naturalistic observations in the home.' *Journal of Abnormal Child Psychology,* **93,** 106–114.

Bradley, S., Sloman, L. (1975) 'Elective mutism in immigrant families.' *Journal of the American Academy of Child Psychiatry,* **14,** 510–514.

Brown, J. B., Lloyd, H. (1975) 'A controlled study of children not speaking in school.' *Journal of Ass. Workers Maladjusted Child,* 49–63.

Browne, E., Wilson, V., Laybourne, P. C. (1963) 'Diagnosis and treatment of elective mutism in children.' *Journal of the American Academy of Child Psychiatry,* **2,** 605–617.

Caplan, H. L. (1970) *Hysterical 'conversion' symptoms in childhood.* Unpublished M. Phil. dissertation, University of London.

Chess, S., Rosenberg, M. (1974) 'Clinical differentiation among children with initial language complaints.' *Journal of Autism and Childhood Schizophrenia,* **4,** 99–109.

Clark, P., Rutter, M. (1981) 'Autistic children's response to structure and to interpersonal demands.' *Journal of Autism and Developmental Disorders,* **11,** 201–217.

Conrad, R. D., Delk, J. L., Williams, C. (1974) 'Use of stimulus fading procedures in the treatment of situation specific mutism.' *Journal of Behavior Therapy & Experimental Psychology,* **5,** 99–100.

Cooper, J. A., Ferry, P. C. (1978) 'Acquired auditory verbal agnosia and seizures in childhood.' *Journal of Speech and Hearing Disorders,* **43,** 176–184.

Corbett, J. A. (1985) 'Mental retardation: psychiatric aspects.' *In:* Rutter, M., Hersov, L. (Eds.) *Child and Adolescent Psychiatry: Modern Approaches* (2nd edn). Oxford: Blackwell Scientific. pp. 661–678.

Corbett, J., Harris, R., Taylor, M. (1973) 'Progressive disintegrative psychosis of childhood.' *Journal of Child Psychology and Psychiatry,* **18,** 211–219.

Cromer, R. F. (1976) 'The cognitive hypothesis of language acquisition and its implications for child language deficiency.' *In:* Morehead, D. M., Morehead, A. E. (Eds.) *Normal and Deficient Child Language* Baltimore: University Park Press. pp. 283–334.

Curcio, F., Paccia, J. M. (1982) 'Strategies in evaluating autistic children's communication.' *Topics in Language Disorders,* **3,** 43–49.

DeMyer, M. K. (1979) *Parents and Children in Autism.* New York: Wiley.

—— Burton, S., Alpern, G. D., Kimberlin, C., Allen, J., Yung, E., Steele, R. (1974) 'The measured intelligence of autistic children.' *Journal of Autism and Childhood Schizophrenia,* **4,** 42–60.

Deykin, E., MacMahon, B. (1979) 'The incidence of seizures among children with autistic symptoms.' *American Journal of Psychiatry,* **136,** 1310–1312.

Evans, D., Hampson, M. (1968) 'The language of mongols.' *British Journal of Disorders of Communication,* **3,** 171–181.

Evans-Jones, L. G., Rosenbloom, L. (1978) 'Disintegrative psychosis in childhood.' *Developmental Medicine and Child Neurology,* **20,** 462–470.

Folstein, S., Rutter, M. (1977) 'Infantile autism: a genetic study of 21 twin pairs.' *Journal of Child Psychology and Psychiatry,* **18,** 297–321.

Folstein, S., Rutter, M. (in press) 'Autism: familial aggregation and genetic implications.' *Journal of Autism and Developmental Disorders.*

Friedman, R., Karagan, N. (1973) 'Characteristics and management of elective mutism in children.' *Psychology in the Schools,* **10,** 249–252.

Fromkin, V., Krashen, S., Curtiss, S., Rigler, D., Rigler, M. (1974) 'The development of language in Genie: a case of language acquisition beyond the critical period.' *Brain and Language,* **1,** 81–107.

Fundudis, T., Kolvin, I., Garside, R. F. (Eds.) (1979) *Speech Retarded and Deaf Children: Their Psychological Development.* London: Academic Press.

Gaines, R., Sandgrund, A., Green, A. H., & Power, E. (1978) 'Etiological factors in child maltreatment: a multivariate study of abusing, neglecting, and normal mothers.' *Journal of Abnormal Child Psychology,* **87,** 531–540.

Goodyer, I. (1981) 'Hysterical conversion reactions in childhood.' *Journal of Child Psychology and Psychiatry,* **22,** 179–188.

Gottesman, I. I., Shields, J., Hanson, D. R. (1982) *Schizophrenia: The Epigenetic Puzzle.* New York: Cambridge University Press.

Green, W. H., Campbell, M., Hardesty, A. S., Grega, D. M., Padron-Gayol, M., Shell, J., Erlenmeyer-Kimling, L. (1984) 'A comparison of schizophrenic and autistic children.' *Journal of*

230

American Academy of Child Psychiatry, **23,** 399–409.

Greenbaum, C. A., Landau, R. (1979) 'The infant's exposure to talk by familiar people: mothers, fathers, and siblings in different environments.' *In:* Lewis, M., Rosenblum, L. A. (Eds.) *The Child and its Family.* New York: Plenum. pp. 67–89.

Griffiths, C. P. S. (1969) 'A follow-up study of children with disorders of speech.' *British Journal of Disorders of Communication,* **4,** 46–56.

Hagberg, B., Aicardi, J., Dias, K., Ramos, O. (1983) 'A progressive syndrome of autism, dementia, ataxia, and loss of purposeful hand use in girls: Rett's syndrome: report of 35 cases.' *Annals of Neurology,* **14,** 471–479.

Halpern, W. I., Hammond, J., Cohen, R. (1971) 'A therapeutic approach to speech phobia: elective mutism reexamined.' *Journal of American Academy of Child Psychiatry,* **10,** 94–107.

Hayden, T. L. (1980) 'Classification of elective mutism.' *Journal of the American Academy of Child Psychiatry,* **19,** 118–133.

Heller, T. (1930) 'About dementia infantilis.' *Reprinted in:* Howells, J. G. (Ed.) (1969) *Modern Perspectives in International Child Psychiatry.* Edinburgh: Oliver & Boyd. pp. 610–616.

Hobson, R. P. (1986) 'The autistic child's appraisal of expressions of emotion.' *Journal of Child Psychology and Psychiatry,* **27,** 321–342.

Hoffman-Plotkin, D., Twentyman, C. T. (1984) 'A multimodal assessment of behavioral and cognitive deficits in abused and neglected preschoolers.' *Child Development,* **55,** 794–802.

Houston, S. H. (1970) 'A re-examination of some assumptions about the language of the disadvantaged child.' *Child Development,* **41,** 947–963.

Howlin, P. (1981) 'Effectiveness of operant language training with autistic children.' *Journal of Autism and Developmental Disorders,* **11,** 89–106.

Hudolin, V. (1957) 'Dementia infantilis Heller: diagnostic problems with a case report.' *Journal of Mental Deficiency Research,* **1,** 79–90.

Hulse, W. C. (1954) 'Dementia infantilis.' *Journal of Nervous and Mental Disease,* **119,** 471–477.

Kaplan, S. L., Escoll, P. (1973) 'Treatment of two silent adolescent girls.' *Journal of the American Academy of Child Psychiatry,* **12,** 59–71.

Klaus, R. A., Gray, S. W. (1968) 'The early training project for disadvantaged children: a report after five years.' *Monographs of the Society for Research in Child Development,* **33,** 1–66.

Koch, M. (1976) 'Elective mutism in children: a follow-up study.' *In:* Sankar, D. S. (Ed.) *Mental Health in Children.* Westbury, NY: PJD Publications. pp. 405–415.

Koluchova, J. (1972) 'Severe deprivation in twins: a case study. *Journal of Child Psychology and Psychiatry,* **13,** 107–114.

Kolvin, I. (1971) Psychosis in childhood—a comparative study. *In:* Rutter, M. (Ed.), *Infantile Autism: Concepts, Characteristics, and Treatment.* Edinburgh: Churchill Livingstone. pp. 7–26.

—— Fundudis, T. (1981) 'Elective mute children: psychological development and background factors.' *Journal of Child Psychology and Psychiatry,* **22,** 219–232.

Kratochwill, T. R. (1981) *Selective Mutism: Implications for Research and Treatment.* Hillsdale, NJ: L. Erlbaum Associates.

Kratochwill, T. R., Brody, G. H., Piersel, W. C. (1979) 'Elective mutism in children.' *In:* Lahey, B., Kazdin, A. E. (Eds.) *Advances in Clinical Child Psychology, Vol. 2.,* New York: Plenum. pp. 193–240.

Lackner, J. R. (1968) 'A developmental study of language behavior in retarded children.' *Neuropsychologia,* **6,** 301–320.

Lerea, L., Ward, B. (1965) 'Speech avoidance among children with oral-communication defects.' *Journal of Psychology,* **60,** 265–270.

Lichtenstein, R. (1984) 'Predicting school performance of preschool children from parent reports.' *Journal of Abnormal Child Psychology,* **12,** 79–94.

Lockyer, L., Rutter, M. (1970) 'A five to fifteen-year follow-up study of infantile psychosis: IV. Patterns of cognitive ability.' *British Journal of Social and Clinical Psychology,* **9,** 152–163.

Lord, C. (1984*a*) 'Language comprehension and cognitive disorder in autism.' *In:* Siegel, L., Morrison, F. J. (Eds.) *Cognitive Development in Atypical Children.* New York: Springer-Verlag. pp. 67–82.

—— (1984*b*) 'The development of peer relations in children with autism.' *In:* Morrison, F. J., Lord, C., Keating, D. P. (Eds.) *Advances in Applied Developmental Psychology.* New York: Academic Press. pp. 165–229.

Lotter, V. (1966) 'Epidemiology of autistic conditions in young children. I. Prevalence.' *Social Psychiatry,* 124–137.

—— (1974) 'Social adjustment and placement of autistic children in Middlesex: a follow-up study. *Journal of Autism and Childhood Schizophrenia,* **4,** 11–32.

231

—— (1978) 'Follow-up studies.' *In:* Rutter, M., Schopler, E. *Autism: A Reappraisal of Concepts and Treatment.* New York: Plenum Press. pp. 475–496.

Malamud, N. (1959) 'Heller's disease and childhood schizophrenia.' *American Journal of Psychiatry,* **16,** 215–218.

Mantovani, J. F., Landau, W. M. (1980) 'Acquired aphasia with convulsive disorder: course and prognosis.' *Neurology,* **30,** 524–529.

Mattison, R. E., Cantwell, D. P., Baker, L. (1980) 'Dimensions of behavior in children with speech and language disorders.' *Journal of Abnormal Child Psychology,* **8,** 323–338.

Miller, J. F., Campbell, T. F., Chapman, R. S., Weismer, S. E. (1984) 'Language behavior in acquired childhood aphasia.' *In:* Holland, A. (Ed.) *Language Disorders in Children.* San Diego: College-Hill Press. pp. 57–99.

Mirenda, P. L., Donellan, A. M., Yoder, D. E. (1983) 'Gaze behavior: a new look at an old problem.' *Journal of Autism and Developmental Disorders,* **13,** 397–410.

Noll, R. B., Benedict, H. (1981) 'Differentiations within the classification of childhood psychoses: a continuing dilemma.' *Merrill-Palmer Quarterly,* **27,** 175–195.

Noronha, M. J. (1974) 'Cerebral degenerative disorders in infancy and childhood.' *Developmental Medicine and Child Neurology,* **16,** 228–241.

Olsson, B., Rett, A. (1983) 'Behavioral observations concerning differential diagnosis between the Rett syndrome and autism. *Brain Development,* **7,** 281–289.

Ornitz, E. M., Guthrie, D., Farley, A. H. (1977) 'The early development of autistic children.' *Journal of Autism and Childhood Schizophrenia,* **7,** 207–229.

Parker, E. B., Olsen, T. F., & Throckmorton, M. C. (1960) 'Social casework with elementary school children who do not talk in school.' *Social Work,* **5,** 64–70.

Petty, L. K., Ornitz, E. M., Michelman, J. D., Zimmerman, E. G. (1984) 'Autistic children who become schizophrenic.' *Archives of General Psychiatry,* **41,** 129–135.

Powell, G., Brasel, J., Blizzard, R. (1967) 'Emotional deprivation and growth retardation simulating idiopathic hypopituitarism. I. Clinical evaluation.' *New England Journal of Medicine,* **276,** 1271–1278.

Prizant, B. M. (1983) 'Echolalia in autism: assessment and intervention.' *Seminars in Speech and Language,* **4,** 63–77.

Prutting, C., Gallagher, T., Mulac, A. (1975) 'The expressive portion of the N.S.S.T. compared to a spontaneous language sample.' *Journal of Speech and Hearing Disorders,* **40,** 40–49.

Rapin, I., Mattis, S., Rowan, A. J., Golden, G. G. (1977) 'Verbal auditory agnosia in children.' *Developmental Medicine and Child Neurology,* **19,** 192–207.

Reed, G. F. (1963) 'Elective mutism in children: a re-appraisal.' *Journal of Child Psychology and Psychiatry,* **4,** 99–107.

Richman, N., Stevenson, J., Graham, P. J. (1982) *Pre-school to School: A Behavioral Study.* New York: Academic Press.

Rivinus, T. M., Jamison, D. L., Graham, P. J. (1975) 'Childhood organic neurological disease presenting as psychiatric disorder.' *Archives of Disease in Childhood,* **50,** 115–119.

Rock, N. L. (1971) 'Conversion reactions in childhood: a clinical study on childhood neuroses.' *Journal of the American Academy of Child Psychiatry,* **10,** 65–93.

Ross, D. M., Ross, S. A. (1982) *Hyperactivity: Current Issues, Research, and Theory. 2nd edn.* New York: John Wiley.

Rutter, M. (1966) 'Behavioral and cognitive characteristics of a series of psychotic children.' *In:* Wing, J. K. (Ed.) *Early Childhood Autism.* London: Pergamon.

—— (1970) 'Autistic children: infancy to adulthood.' *Seminars in Psychiatry,* **2,** 435–450.

—— (1981) *Maternal Deprivation Reassessed (2nd edn).* Harmondsworth, Middlesex: Penguin.

—— (1983) 'Cognitive deficits in the pathogenesis of autism.' *Journal of Child Psychology and Psychiatry,* **24,** 513–532.

—— (1985a) 'Family and school influences on cognitive development.' *Journal of Child Psychology and Psychiatry,* **26,** 683–704.

—— (1985b) 'Infantile autism and other pervasive developmental disorders.' *In:* Rutter, M., Hersov, L. (Eds.) *Child and Adolescent Psychiatry: Modern Approaches* (2nd edn.). London: Blackwell Scientific. pp. 545–566.

—— (1985c) 'The treatment of autistic children.' *Journal of Child Psychology and Psychiatry,* **26,** 193–214.

—— (1985d) 'Infantile autism: Assessment, differential diagnosis and treatment.' *In:* Shaffer, D., Erhardt, A., Greenhill, L. (Eds.) *A Clinician's Guide to Child Psychiatry* (pp. 48–78). New York: Free Press.

—— Garmezy, N. (1983) 'Developmental psychopathology.' *In:* Mussen, P. H. (Ed.) E. M. Hetherington (volume editor), *Mussen's Handbook of Child Psychology. IV. Socialization, Personality and Social Development* (4th edn.). New York/Chichester: John Wiley & Sons. pp. 775–912.

—— Lockyer, L. (1967) 'A five to fifteen year follow-up study of infantile psychosis. I: Description of sample.' *British Journal of Psychiatry,* **113,** 1169–1182.

—— Schopler, E. 'Autism and pervasive developmental disorders: concepts and diagnostic issue.' *Journal of Autism and Developmental Disorders (in press).*

Ryan, J. (1977) 'The silence of stupidity.' *In:* Morton, J., Marshall, J. M. (Eds.) *Psycholinguistics: Developmental and Pathological.* Ithaca. NY: Cornell University Press. pp. 99–124.

Sameroff, A. J., Seifer, R., Zax, M. (1982) 'Early development of children at risk for emotional disorder.' *Monographs of the Society for Research in Child Development,* **47,** (7).

Sandgrund, A., Gaines, R. W., Green, A. H. (1974) 'Child abuse and mental retardation: a problem of cause and effect.' *American Journal of Mental Deficiency,* **79,** 327–330.

Sanok, R. L., Striefel, S. (1979) 'Elective mutism: generalization of verbal responding across people and settings.' *Behavior Therapy,* **10,** 357–371.

Schachter, F. F. (1979) *Everyday Mother Talk to Toddlers: Early Intervention.* New York: Academic Press.

Schopler, E. (1976) 'Towards reducing behavior problems in autistic children.' *In:* Wing, L. (Ed.) *Early Childhood Autism 2nd edn.* London: Pergamon Press. pp. 221–246.

—— Mesibov, G. B., DeVellis, R., & Short, A. (1981) 'Treatment outcome for autistic children and their families.' *In:* Mittler, P. (Ed.) *Frontiers of Knowledge in Mental Retardation Vol. 1.* Baltimore: University Park Press. pp. 293–301.

Sigman, M., Ungerer, J. (1984) 'Attachment behaviors in autistic children.' *Journal of Autism and Developmental Disorders,* **14,** 231–244.

Singer, L. T., Fagan, J. F. (1984) 'Cognitive development in the failure-to-thrive infant: a three-year longitudinal study.' *Journal of Pediatric Psychology,* **9,** 363–383.

Skuse, D. (1984*a*) 'Extreme deprivation in early childhood. I: Diverse outcomes from an extraordinary family.' *Journal of Child Psychology and Psychiatry,* **25,** 523–542.

—— (1984*b*) 'Extreme deprivation in early childhood. II: Theoretical issues and a comparative review.' *Journal of Child Psychology and Psychiatry,* **25,** 543–572.

Tager-Flusberg, H. (1981) 'On the nature of linguistic functioning in early infantile autism.' *Journal of Autism and Developmental Disorders,* **11,** 45–56.

Tizard, B., Hughes, M., Carmichael, H., Pinkerton, G. (1983) 'Language and social class: is verbal deprivation a myth?' *Journal of Child Psychology and Psychiatry,* **24,** 533–542.

Tizard, J., Tizard, B. (1974) 'The institution as an environment for development.' *In:* Richards, M. P. M. (Ed.) *The Integration of a Child into a Social World.* London: Cambridge University Press. (pp. 137–152).

Tubbs, V. K. (1966) 'Types of linguistic disability in psychotic children.' *Journal of Mental Deficiency Research,* **10,** 230–240.

van Engeland, R., Bodnar, F. A., Bolhuis, G. (1985) 'Some qualitative aspects of the social behaviour of autistic children: an etiological approach.' *Journal of Child Psychology and Psychiatry,* **26,** 879–893.

Wilson, J. (1972) 'Investigation of degenerative disease of the central nervous system.' *Archives of Disease in Childhood,* **47,** 163–170.

Wing, L. (1981) 'Asperger's syndrome: a clinical account.' *Psychological Medicine,* **11,** 115–129.

—— Gould, J. (1979) 'Severe impairments of social interaction and associated abnormalities in children: epidemiology and classification.' *Journal of Autism and Developmental Disorders,* **9,** 11–29.

Wolff, S., Barlow, A. (1979) 'Schizoid personality in childhood: a comparitive study of schizoid, autistic and normal children.' *Journal of Child Psychology and Psychiatry,* **20,** 29–46.

Worster-Drought, C. (1971) 'An unusual form of acquired aphasia in children.' *Developmental Medicine and Child Neurology,* **13,** 563–571.

Wright, H. L. (1968) 'A clinical study of children who refuse to talk in school.' *Journal of the American Academy of Child Psychiatry,* **7,** 603–617.

Wulbert, M., Inglis, S., Kriegsmann, E., Mills, B. (1975) 'Language delay and associated mother-child interactions.' *Developmental Psychology,* **11,** 61–70.

Yarrow, L. Y. (1961) 'Maternal deprivation—toward an empirical and conceptual reevaluation.' *Psychological Bulletin,* **58,** 459–490.

Zigler, E., Butterfield, E. C. (1968) 'Motivational aspects of changes in IQ test performance of culturally deprived nursery school children'. *Child Development,* **39,** 2–14.

LANGUAGE DEVELOPMENT AND SENSORY DISORDER: VISUAL AND HEARING IMPAIRMENTS

Roger Freeman and Susan Blockberger

Hearing and visual impairment are both intriguing as experiments of nature. The former raises a host of issues about language, how people without spoken and heard language function socially, culturally, emotionally and academically. The latter involves the rôle of vision as the child relates language to knowledge of the environment and the relationship between non-verbal, visually perceived communicative behaviours and the acquisition of language. In the situation of double handicap, even more fundamental questions arise about how such an individual experiences self and the world in the absence of both well-developed distance senses.

Visual impairment
Definitions and important variables
Under ordinary conditions, only the most severe degrees of visual impairment with onset at birth or shortly thereafter are likely to lead to deviations or delays in language development. (Lesser degrees of severity may be influential when combined with other impairments produced by intellectual retardation or brain damage.) This discussion will therefore be limited to those children who have no useful pattern recognition (though they may have light perception). It is important, however, to be aware that a partially sighted child's delayed or deviant language may sometimes be wrongly attributed to the visual impairment.

Language development
Although acquisition of first words may be slightly delayed, blind children achieve major language milestones at or near the ages expected for sighted children. Differences exist, however, in the use and the nature of the language acquired. Traditionally, researchers and educators working with blind children expressed concern about 'verbalisms', or words used without tangible sense experience, which was wrongly thought to lead to loose thinking (Dokecki 1966). In recent years the concept of verbalism has been abandoned in favour of a more detailed analysis of the blind child's language comprehension and linguistic competence. This approach has been given its impetus from recent theories of language acquisition in sighted children, which have emphasised the importance of visually perceived information. While some researchers (*e.g.* Landau 1984) have stressed the similarities in language acquisition between sighted and blind children, others (*e.g.* Andersen *et*

al. 1984) have noted subtle differences. These include difficulties in acquisition of word-meaning, differences in use of first words, a strong reliance on standardised or formulaic exchanges, and problems in the understanding of deictic words (where word-meaning shifts according to the perspective of the speaker: I/you, here/there, this/that).

A pioneering study of normal blind babies was reported by Fraiberg (1977). She studied 10 blind babies intensively and longitudinally from the age of less than 12 months, and made some comparisons with scales of normal development in sighted children. Fraiberg noted that blind children acquire the milestones of using two words and two-word sentences later than sighted children, although most blind children were credited with these items within the range of normal development as defined in the Bayley Scales of Infant Development. Other milestones, such as 'responds to verbal requests' and 'uses words to make wants known' were achieved at a similar or even younger median age by the blind group. Fraiberg also observed delays in locomotion, mother-infant signalling, and adaptive hand use in the blind children. She concluded that objects in the babies' environment were therefore delayed in acquiring 'representational substantiality'. Object concepts, which the sighted child acquires through vision, must be discovered by the blind child through a comparatively laborious manual-tactile-acoustic exercise.

Fraiberg's observations suggest that blind children have difficulty in acquiring the meaning of certain words because of their restricted experience which results in conceptual difficulties. Landau (1984) compared the meanings expressed by three blind children in their early vocabulary with those expressed by sighted children. She concluded that 'blind children do talk about objects and their locations in space, actions, and events, and do so in just the same way as sighted children at the same linguistic level' (p. 66). Andersen *et al.* (1984) disputed this claim in their study of six blind children aged nine months to 40 months. They noted three differences in the early lexicons of blind children, which seem to suggest that they use language in a more restricted, less creative fashion: (i) blind children did not use idiosyncratic forms and did not abandon use of any of their early words; (ii) words for actions were restricted to actions that they themselves were performing, rather than actions involving other people or objects; and (iii) blind children did not use functional or relational terms such as 'no', 'more' or 'again' to encode information about dynamic states (such as 'more' to comment on the additional instance of something), but only to satisfy their own needs. Andersen *et al.* suggested that these differences indicate that blind children have less understanding of words as 'symbolic vehicles', and are less likely than sighted children to form active hypotheses about the meaning of words.

Andersen *et al.* (1984) supported this claim with an analysis of the over-extensions of words exhibited by the blind children they were studying. A commonly noted phenomenon in the early word usage of sighted children is their tendency to over-extend the use of some words to include referents which are not included in the adult meaning of that word. They may, for example, go through a stage of calling all four-legged animals 'doggie'. These over-extensions often are made on the basis of visual-perceptual characteristics (such as four-leggedness), but are also sometimes made on the basis of other properties such as function or texture. In contrast to sighted children, the blind children that Andersen *et al.* studied rarely over-extended early-acquired words.

A more obvious difference that is frequently observed in the language acquisition of the blind child is a delay in mastery of I/you pronouns. Fraiberg (1977) noted a significant delay in the acquisition of a stable 'I' in the third and fourth years. This was tied to delays in development of representational play and both were felt to represent an inability to use another object as a symbolic representation of the self.

Urwin (1984) noted a restricted use of pronouns in her blind subject Suzanne. She suggested that because of Suzanne's restricted access to surrounding context she had little opportunity to comment on others. Urwin implied that she therefore had little opportunity to master the pronoun system. Episodes were recorded where Suzanne reproduced entire conversations using two different voices, and Urwin compared these exchanges to rôle-playing sequences enacted by sighted children. Similar exchanges have been noted by Fraiberg (1977) and Andersen *et al.* (1984), and are related to delayed echolalia, discussed below. Although these exchanges involve pronoun forms which shift with the 'speakers', Urwin noted that this does not guarantee that these distinctions will be correctly deployed in conversation.

But many blind children do become competent language users, demonstrating a knowledge and understanding of language equal to their sighted peers. Landau (1984) examined one blind child's understanding and use of 'sighted terminology' such as 'look' and 'see'. This child responded to instructions such as 'look up,' 'look behind you', or 'look at the table' by exploring the area or object in question with her hands. She distinguished between 'look at —' (to which she responded with perceptual exploration) and 'touch —' (which led her to simply make manual contact). Surprisingly, she demonstrated an understanding of these words in relation to activities of sighted people. Her responses to instructions such as 'Let mommy look at —' revealed an appreciation that sighted people need to have objects correctly oriented in space to be able to see them, and cannot see through barriers. Furthermore, it is misleading to assume that apparently similar functions of language represent comparable developmental achievements in blind and sighted children (Urwin 1984). For example, early restrictions in the blind child's object-naming may indicate that s/he has not yet learned to refer to objects that are, from the child's perspective, absent or concealed. On the other hand, the sighted child's naming is largely elicited and supported by visual cues; the ability to refer to absent things develops later.

Echolalia, imitation, and social routines: alternative routes?
Blind children are often noted to make extensive use of vocal imitation, apparently unanalysed 'chunks' of language reproduced in highly predictable social routines, and immediate and delayed echolalia. However, these phenomena have been under-reported in the normal population (Peters 1983). Urwin (1984) discussed the rôle these patterns seemed to serve for the blind children she studied: keeping the

listener's attention, topic maintenance in the absence of visual cues, social rehearsal analogous to the sighted child's pretend-play re-enactments of previously observed social interactions, and (at least for one child) efforts to elicit the parent's voice to use it as a reference point for mobility.

A subgroup of blind children has been described as autistic-like (Elonen and Cain 1964, Fay and Schuler 1980) based partly upon similarities in language symptomatology: excessive echolalia and I/you pronoun difficulties. An autistic-like profile has been associated with retrolental fibroplasia (now known as retinopathy of prematurity) (Keeler 1958, Chase 1972) but is not limited to this group (Wills 1979). Echolalia in autistic children has been shown to serve a variety of communicative and cognitive functions (Prizant and Duchan 1981, Prizant and Rydell 1984, Prizant 1985). Prizant suggested that echolalia may represent an alternative path in the development of language.

There are several possible explanations for the blind child's alternative type of language acquisition (Prizant 1985). Characteristics of parental input, described below, may be involved. Delayed language comprehension, coupled with a relatively more sophisticated rote memory for speech, has been associated with echolalia. Finally, blind children may have more difficulty in segmenting a continuous flow of speech into words, due to the unavailability of visually perceived cues such as gesture and gaze.

Difference in parent-child interaction

Discussion thus far has focused primarily on the impact of visual impairment on the acquisition of word-meaning. But language almost always involves social inter-action, and here the effect is immediate and obvious.

In the early months of life, sighted babies interact with their caretakers through a rich array of visually perceived acts, including gaze, facial expression and gestures. Adults respond to these behaviours in infants as if they had communicat-ive intent, even when they are still reflexive. In turn, the infant quickly learns to use these behaviours to regulate social interaction, signal wants and communicative feelings, while learning also to attend to the messages of parental actions (such as following the direction of gaze to determine the topic or focus).

Deprived of this rich source of information, feedback, and socialisation, the parents' interactions with their blind baby are affected in both obvious and subtle ways. Mothers of sighted babies tend to talk about what their child is already attending to, as signified by gaze. Blind babies often signify that they are attending to something through much less transparent means, such as momentary stilling or characteristic hand movements. But parents vary in their discernment and response to these subtle signals, and parental counselling is frequently recommended (Fraiberg 1977, Als et al. 1980, Kekelis and Andersen 1984, Urwin 1984). Even when these signals are perceived, it is still difficult to determine the focus of the child's attention, due to the vagueness and nonspecificity of the signal (Urwin 1984). In addition, the blind baby is denied one powerful way of initiating an interaction, that of making eye-contact. Often the blind child must wait until the parent decides to initiate an interaction or is close enough to touch. Given these problems, it is not surprising that mothers of blind children are more likely than those of sighted children to be the initiators of topics in exchanges with their children (Kekelis and Andersen 1984). These writers noted that most of the topics focused on child-centred activities rather than other people or events in the environment. Faced with uncertain cues as to their child's interest and attention, mothers tended to opt for the 'safe' topics of what the child was actually doing or holding. Furthermore, their comments on these topics tended to take the form of labelling rather than providing additional information of which the blind child might be unaware.

Fraiberg (1977) and others have remarked upon the characteristic flat facial expression of many blind children, often wrongly interpreted as reflecting retardation, aloofness, depression or boredom. Faced with this lack of feedback from facial expression, and in apparent unconscious effort to determine if the blind child is in fact attending to and understanding them, mothers tend to use many more directives and questions which require either a verbal or motoric response. Input high in directives has been associated with language delays in other populations, but a causal link has not been proved.

Als *et al.* (1980) systematically videotaped interaction from just after birth between an otherwise normal blind baby and its parents. It was their conclusion that the blind baby, like other babies, strives to accomplish biologically preset goals, but must accomplish this in a different way. If these differences can be interpreted by the caregiver as useful and necessary (perhaps with some skilled advice) then a parent's patience and sensitivity can foster flexibility rather than the stereotyped patterns often described in blind children. This perspective on the plasticity of human development is in agreement with that of Warren (1977), Chess (1978), and Thomas and Chess (1980).

Non-verbal communication
Important information in a communicative exchange is carried through non-verbal channels. Often the perception or use of these behaviours is dependent upon vision. Along with their difficulty in learning normal gestures, some blind children develop idiosyncratic gestures that sighted people find hard to interpret (Fraiberg 1977). Changes in body posture can be misleading, as in the case described by Urwin (1984) where the blind child dropped his head while listening. Parke *et al.* (1980) compared blind to sighted school children in the use of three non-verbal communicative behaviours: smiling, nodding and raising the eyebrows. Differences were found between the groups on all three. Blind children nodded their heads less frequently, although at appropriate moments. They spent much more time smiling, and indeed some were described as 'chronic smilers'. Although the amount of eyebrow-raising did not differ between groups, blind children tended to raise their eyebrows inappropriately compared with sighted children who raise theirs to indicate interest or emphasise a word. Blind children have often been noted to have difficulty in appropriate modulation of vocal loudness. Usually they stray toward being too loud, termed the 'broadcasting voice' of the blind (Jan *et al.* 1977). The broadcasting voice has been attributed to a lack of awareness of the exact location

and distance of the listener(s) or the presence of strangers within earshot. The strident quality of the broadcasting voice may also represent an effort by the blind speaker to maintain the listener's attention. Sighted speakers continually monitor listeners' attention by observing visual cues such as facial expression, intermittent eye contact and nodding. The blind speaker may learn to compensate for the absence of these cues by relying on sheer volume to attract and maintain the listener's attention to his message.

Possibilities for intervention
In trying to help blind children who have language problems there are several considerations, despite the preliminary state of our knowledge. First, are the observed differences actually a problem in the sense that they require intervention? Or do they reflect an adaptive alternative path? Second, are they part of another disability or impairment combined with blindness?

Clearly a speech and language pathologist should be involved in the assessment of language problems and in the development of intervention strategies. For the blind child, strategies are focused on: (i) helping the child to compensate for lack of visual stimulation through use of other sources of information; (ii) helping parents to discover ways to interact with their blind child in a manner which is stimulating for their child and rewarding for them; and (iii) altering those behaviours which 'put people off' and interfere with successful communication.

Parental counselling is often recommended to sensitise parents to the nuances of interaction with their blind child and to suggest strategies for overcoming obstacles to rewarding exchanges. However, the extent and nature of counselling necessary to effect significant changes in parenting style have not been established. Both Fraiberg (1977) and Kekelis and Andersen (1980) reported continued difficulties on the part of both the mothers receiving professional input and the clinicians and researchers in their studies. This suggests that one's responses to non-verbal communication operate on a highly automatic level and are resistant to change.

Hearing impairment
Definitions and important variables
'There are no simple answers. Indeed, there are not even any simple questions in this area' (Savage *et al.* 1981, p. vii). The field of hearing impairment (especially deafness) has been beset by controversy for over 200 years. Parents with deaf children are often amazed and even appalled to find themselves at the vortex of highly emotionally charged professional forces pulling in many different directions, seemingly impervious to the scientific 'evidence' presented by those in opposition.

This is not the place to discuss in detail the historical roots and modern developments of this controversy (Conrad 1979, Freeman *et al.* 1981, Quigley and Kretschmer 1982) but some aspects of it must be appreciated. A consideration of definitions and variables, however, is prerequisite to any further discussion.

Different definitions and terminology may be used in different countries and for different purposes. Audiometric findings under formal test conditions may not be equivalent to functional responses in naturalistic settings (just as visual acuity measures are not a complete picture of functioning with a visual impairment). However, by 'deaf' children we usually mean those whose sensorineural hearing-loss, even with best amplification, cannot be depended upon for the useful discrimination of speech. Amplification may provide awareness of certain loud environmental noises or the general intonation of speech. Usually this is equated with an audiometric loss of 85 or 90 dB or greater. Children with lesser severity of loss may be termed 'partially hearing' or 'hard-of-hearing'. Their losses may be sensorineural, conductive or mixed. Some children have only intermittent hearing-loss (usually due to otitis media) which may be missed entirely on screening examinations, while others have post-lingual onset (either progressive or sudden) after the age of two years. (The dividing line between prelingual and postlingual at age two is somewhat arbitrary.)

Some workers in the field refuse to use the word 'deaf' because they feel all children have some remnant of hearing that is potentially trainable. But as Quigley and Paul (1984) point out, at some point on the audiological continuum there is a functional discontinuity: the person becomes primarily visual in learning, rather than auditory.

The group of deaf children is quite heterogeneous. Among the important variables are: age at onset; hearing status of parents; causation of hearing loss; associated impairments or disorders; language of rearing, adequacy and type of education, and intellectual endowment.

Delay between suspicion and diagnosis
Deafness is most often suspected by parents (not professionals). There may be a long wait for diagnostic confirmation and an intervention program. The more severe the deafness, the shorter the delay (average 10 months for profound deafness, 16 months for severe deafness—see Freeman *et al.* 1975, Freeman 1977). This is a significant delay for parents, who suffer from uncertainty and disagreements about interpretation of the nature, severity, and implications of their child's problem. There are still difficulties in the early identification of hearing loss (Hanson and Ulvestad 1979).

Language disorder in other types of hearing impairment
Much less is known about hard-of-hearing children than about deaf children, though it is known from systematic research that speech intelligibility and reading are likely to be delayed or impaired even with mild losses (Conrad 1979). A common cause of conductive hearing loss in childhood, especially around the time of language acquisition, is secretory otitis media with middle-ear effusion of varying duration and severity. It is reasonable to suppose that the potentially deleterious effects of impaired hearing on decoding of speech will be especially important in children already at risk for delayed language development (with cleft palate or lip, mental retardation, sensorineural hearing loss, brain damage or severe depri-vation). Despite the availability of a relatively simple and non-invasive screening technique (tympanometry), useful prospective studies have yet to be completed

(Rapin 1979). Her review of the literature came to the conclusion that school-age children's verbal skills and scholastic performance (especially reading) are affected by conductive loss. Effects on spontaneous speech are likely to be overlooked, with expressive skills being delayed rather than deviant. No longitudinal studies of effects on preschool children were found, though these would be anticipated. It is not known how long the conductive loss must have been present for a deleterious outcome. An entire monograph has been devoted to the controversial questions posed by this common condition and the research methodology that might lead to answers (Hanson and Ulvestad 1979). In the meantime, early identification and treatment are indicated, especially for high-risk children.

Children with significant continuing hearing loss of early onset (usually sensorineural in type) will have some language and speech deviations. Screening techniques used in schools may be inadequate to identify such problems, due to high levels of ambient noise or other limitations. It is a truism that children with language problems (and those with behaviour disorders in school) should have a competent assessment of their hearing.

Children with postlingual onset of severe or profound levels of hearing loss may experience some gradual deterioration of speech: but their language is likely to be unimpaired if they have no other disability, although there may be some immaturity.

Reasons for language delay and distortion in deaf children
Language is a conventional system of signals for communication which may be spoken/heard, written/read, or may consist of a system of conventionalised movements as in sign languages. These are true languages which have a quite different grammatical structure from those which are spoken; they are adapted to a visual-spatial mode. In the following discussion a number of abbreviations will be used to refer to the different systems of communication. OE will refer to oral/aural English, the usual communication form for the majority of persons. SL will be used to refer to any naturally evolved sign language. At times there will be a need to distinguish between American Sign Language (ASL) and British Sign Language (BSL). Two other terms may be less familiar. Systems have been constructed that purport to transmit English through signs; they are referred to as manually coded English or MCE. When deaf and most hearing people communicate, there tends to be a shift to an intermediate form, with the sign vocabulary strung together in English word order, but without the inflections of English. This is often termed Pidgin Sign English or PSE, though there is now doubt whether it is a true pidgin (Cokely 1983). Fingerspelling is not a sign language; it is merely a visual code for a written language. The systems used in the UK and in North America differ, as do their sign languages. 'Cued speech' is a system of hand signals, used around the mouth, to help distinguish sounds which are not visible on the lips. It is not a sign language and its effectiveness is in doubt (Mohay 1983).

Spoken language and receptive language fail to develop in congenitally or prelingually deaf children after a period of normal babbling. If they have deaf parents who sign, the children (whether deaf, hard-of-hearing, or hearing) will acquire sign language at about the same rate as hearing children acquire receptive and expressive spoken language (Conrad 1979, Chess 1980, Quigley and Paul 1984). Their problems will arise when they encounter the hearing majority who expect them to learn to use and comprehend speech and to read. In the past they would be forbidden to use signs or even gestures and would be limited to amplification, auditory training, and the training of speech and speech reading. If they had not succeeded after many years, they might enter a residential school where signing would be used informally but might still be officially frowned upon.

If the deaf children's parents are hearing (about 90 per cent of cases), they will typically miss much of early incidental learning as well as being linguistically deprived. In the course of daily living, their parents will usually develop (consciously or intuitively) a visual-gestural signalling system with them (though this was discouraged by oralists). Subtleties and complex conversations will be absent.

Prelingually profoundly deaf children usually make many errors in both articulation, voice control, semantics, and syntax. In Conrad's (1979) study of almost all the deaf school-leavers in England and Wales there were very few whose speech was intelligible to strangers (and most not even to their teachers) or could lip-read effectively. He did not find that the few 'successes' with the purely oral/aural method clustered in any one school. The main reasons were attributed to the hearing loss itself, *i.e.* the difficulty of acquiring a language by hearing only fragments of it (if at all) or by seeing a partial representation on the lips.

There has been a major trend in the United States toward combined programs of MCE, OE, amplification, and the teaching of reading. This is known as 'total communication' or TC. The reason for its introduction has been the failure of so many children to acquire facility with *any* language or form of communication. Any language is better than no language at all; but whether it will be more successful with the development of OE is still uncertain (Quigley and Paul 1984).

Intervention and its controversies

There are several levels of controversy. On the first level there is the question of first *modality*: is it better for a deaf child to acquire some form of sign language quickly, for reasons of linguistic and social-emotional development? Or should the longer, more difficult and uncertain route of purely oral/aural education be undertaken? In the past this issue was complicated by the question of whether sign languages are truly languages, albeit in a different mode. (It should be pointed out that they are *not* systems of non-verbal communication. In the sense that 'verbal' refers to specific symbolic meanings, sign languages are verbal languages which are non-vocal or non-speech.)

Important subsidiary questions then have been raised: will the acquisition of signing inhibit the acquisition of speech or speechreading? The answer is no, provided that work in the area of OE is taken seriously (Conrad 1979, Quigley and Paul 1984). What are the risks of not developing any language if the oral/aural route is taken? In other words, what is the success rate and what are the costs of the delay in language development? We have already mentioned Conrad's (1979) results. There is no doubt that the costs are tragically high for many children and their families (Freeman *et al.* 1981, Quigley and Paul 1984).

That there are 'oral successes' cannot be doubted, but they cannot be depended upon, and no one has yet developed a way to predict the winners or losers. Ling (1984 *a, b*) provides detailed descriptions of existing oral/aural and TC programs.

The next question concerns the first *language* to be learned if signing is chosen: will it be a native sign language such as ASL or BSL, or some sign-code (MCE) designed to convey English? This will depend upon the hearing status of the parents, the advice they get, and the availability of different programs.

Teachers are then concerned about the effects of hearing impairment and communication modality upon reading and writing because of academic needs. The question is complicated by a number of factors and issues that can only be touched upon here (but see Conrad 1979, Meadow 1980, Freeman *et al.* 1981, Quigley and Kretschmer 1982, Quigley and Paul 1984, Powell *et al.* 1985). If the usefulness or necessity of manual-gestural communication is accepted, then there are several subgroups of children to consider. Those with signing deaf parents will have SL as their mother tongue, and will have to make a shift to OE if possible, but certainly to some level of instructional MCE and reading/writing. Those with hearing parents may have a delay before their parents learn to sign, and the parents may not both learn, or may not learn beyond a simple level. Which form should the parents learn: that which conforms to English word-order, or a totally foreign language and mode?

In the classroom there has been a tendency to favour MCE, but research seems to indicate that the full structure of English is not transmitted in practice and that something closer to PSE is used (Marmor and Pettito 1979, Maxwell 1983, Quigley and Paul 1984). In the UK the situation is complicated by the use of the Paget-Gorman system, which does not have any significant relationship to BSL (Woll *et al.* 1981).

A new trend in North America has been the concept of bilingual education and English as a second language (ESL). The young child would be exposed to more than one form of language (SL and PSE), or would acquire SL, MCE or PSE first, then add OE at a later point as foreigners do with ESL. The advantages and disadvantages have been discussed fully by Quigley and Paul (1984), and a bilingual program using ASL and PSE within a total communication philosophy has been implemented and evaluated (Freeman *et al.* 1981, Greenberg *et al.* 1984). It can be seen that there are many possibilites, but it is unlikely that any one approach will be best for all subgroups of deaf children. A bilingual approach requires a supportive school and community with equal prestige for both languages. Initiation and evaluation should be carefully planned (Quigley and Paul 1984).

Reading deficits

Language must come before reading, and deaf children's reading, in general, is known to be very poor. In the most complete study (Conrad 1979) the average age-level for those leaving elementary schools was nine (and age eight for those with profound losses). This is a yearly increment of only 0.3 years. Thus the majority could be considered functionally illiterate for such tasks as filling in forms or writing an intelligible letter. Even children with modest losses showed some reading retardation. There are many controversies as to why and what to do about it (Conrad 1979, Quigley and Paul 1984). One of the questions is whether a phonic code (grapheme/phoneme decoding) needs to be internalised in order to read easily. (If so, then signing would not be expected to help directly with reading, and SL syntactical differences might even interfere.) Conrad (1979) asserted that this is not necessary. But since there are some deaf children who do read well, we need to unravel the factors which can account for this. He advocated research into the relationship between signing, speech and reading—preferably involving deaf people who think in signs.

Because MCE more closely parallels what the child is trying to read, it may be more successful than early introduction of SL (Kusché *et al.* 1985). Others advocate the introduction of SL and positive attitudes towards it as the earliest step. Quigley and Paul (1984) even mentioned videotaped ASL as another possibility for learning in place of OE or MCE.

It is clear that much basic research remains to be done. The resolution of one problem (whether signing is bad for OE) results in more questions which will require persistence and skill to answer.

Combined hearing and visual impairment
Definitions and important variables
This group is much more heterogeneous than the phrase 'deaf-blind' would indicate. Many individuals retain some vision or some hearing. The onset of each disability may be at different ages. The factors to be considered are age of onset of each disability and the severity and course (stable or progressive) of each. The presence or absence of additional impairments is also of great importance, though often not easy to determine in young children.

Language acquisition
Literature on the deaf-blind has focused largely on the area of communication, and many other problems (such as behaviour) are typically attributed to communicative deficit (Warren 1977). The disabilities are mutiplicative, not merely additive (Rogow 1980).

It is unclear how to assess cognitive capacity without using language. Observations of the child's behaviour may give hints, but it is most essential to establish a system of signals, however basic. Some of these techniques are described by McInnes and Treffry (1982).

Many, if not all, congenitally deaf-blind children fail to develop language competence which permits normal communication. In particular, they will not initiate conversations and do not ask questions.

Possibilities for intervention
Rogow (1980) emphasised the need to develop consistent responses to the child's

behaviour, followed by a system of signals based on the interests of the child. If these are not evident, they may need to be stimulated. There is stress on enjoyable mutual actions and reciprocal interchanges.

Once a signal has been mastered, differentiation of activities through use of different signals is utilised. Sequential actions are incorporated into play. Progression to understanding of semantic relationships between persons, objects and events may follow before more formal work on syntax is contemplated. Language needs to be linked with action and experience so that the child's language can begin to function as a means of social interaction.

The success of these and other techniques is not well established, which is not surprising since the group is so heterogeneous. Detailed longitudinal descriptions of successful interventions would be helpful.

Conclusions

Disappointingly little has been accomplished, despite many opportunities. Whatever the reasons for this, it should be remedied. The methodology exists. Children and their families are dependent upon clinical judgements which are not soundly based.

Many studies do not specify the representativeness of their samples, do not use control groups, and do not test the assumptions upon which current practices are based. Both types of sensory disability are often associated with other impairments which compound and mask the effect of the primary disability. Subgroups with only one impairment and those with multiple problems must be distinguished and studied: cross-sectionally, longitudinally, and with outcome studies of intervention techniques. This will teach us a great deal about normal children and about developmental resilience to impairment.

REFERENCES

Als, H., Tronick, E., Brazelton, T. B. (1980) 'Affective reciprocity and the development of autonomy: the study of a blind infant.' *Journal of the American Academy of Child Psychiatry,* **19,** 22–40.
Andersen, E. S., Dunlea, A., Kekelis, L. S. (1984) 'Blind children's language: resolving some differences.' *Journal of Child Language,* **11,** 645–664.
Chase, J. B. (1972) *Retrolental Fibroplasia and Autistic Symptomatology.* New York: American Foundation for the Blind.
Chess, S. (1978) 'The plasticity of human development: alternative pathways.' *Journal of the American Academy of Child Psychiatry,* **17,** 80–91.
Cokely, D. (1983) 'When is a pidgin not a pidgin? An alternate analysis of the ASL—English contact situation.' *Sign Language Studies,* **38,** 1–24.
Conrad, R. (1979) *The Deaf Schoolchild: Language and Cognitive Function.* London: Harper & Row.
Dokecki, P. R. (1966) 'Verbalism and the blind: a critical review of the concept and the literature.' *Exceptional Children,* **32,** 525–530.
Elonen, A. S., Cain, A. C. (1964) 'Diagnostic evaluation and treatment of deviant blind children.' *American Journal of Orthopsychiatry,* **34,** 625–633.
Fay, W. H., Schuler, A. L. (1980) *Emerging Language in Autistic Children.* Baltimore: University Park Press.
Fraiberg, S. (1977) *Insights From the Blind: Comparative Studies of Blind and Sighted Infants.* New York: Basic Books.
Freeman, R. D. (1977) 'Psychiatric aspects of sensory disorders and intervention.' *In:* Graham, P. (Ed.) *Epidemiological Approaches in Child Psychiatry.* London: Academic Press. pp. 275–304.

—— Malkin, S. F., Hastings, J. O. (1975) 'Psychosocial problems of deaf children and their families: a comparative study.' *American Annals of the Deaf,* **120,** 391–405.

—— Carbin, C. F., Boese, R. J. (1981) *Can't Your Child Hear? A Guide for Those Who Care About Deaf Children.* Baltimore: University Park Press; London: Croom Helm.

Greenberg, M. T., Calderon, R., Kusché, C. A. (1984) 'Early intervention using simultaneous communication with deaf infants: the effect on communication development.' *Child Development,* **55,** 607–616.

Hanson, D. G., Ulvestad, R. F. (1979) *Otitis Media and Child Development: Speech, Language and Education.* Suppl. 60 to *Annals of Otology, Rhinology and Laryngology,* 88 (5) (Part II).

Jan, J, E., Freeman, R. D., Scott, E. (1977) *Visual Impairment in Children and Adolescents.* New York: Grune & Stratton.

Keeler, W. R. (1958) 'Autistic patterns and defective communication in blind children with retrolental fibroplasia.' *In:* Hoch, P. H., Zubin, J. (Eds.) *Psychopathology of Communication.* New York: Grune & Stratton, pp. 64–83.

Kekelis, L. S., Andersen, E. S. (1984) 'Family communication styles and language development.' *Journal of Visual Impairment & Blindness,* **78,** 54–65.

Landau, B. (1984) 'Blind children's language is not "meaningless".' *In:* Mills, A. E. (Ed.) (1983) *Language Acquisition in the Blind Child: Normal and Deficient.* London: Croom Helm/San Diego: College—Hill Press.

Ling, D. (Ed.) (1984*a*) *Early Intervention for Hearing-Impaired Children: Oral Options.* San Diego: College—Hill Press.

—— (Ed.) (1984*b*) *Early Intervention for Hearing-Impaired Children: Total Communication Options.* San Diego: College—Hill Press.

McInnes, J. M., Treffry, J. A. (1982) *Deaf-Blind Infants and Children: A Developmental Guide.* Toronto: University of Toronto Press.

Marmor, G. S., Petitto, L. (1979) 'Simultaneous communication in the classroom: how well is English grammar represented?' *Sign Language Studies,* **23,** 99–136.

Maxwell, M. M. (1983) 'Simultaneous communication in the classroom: what do deaf children learn?' *Sign Language Studies,* **39,** 95–112.

Meadow, K. P. (1980) *Deafness and Child Development.* Berkeley: University of California Press.

Parke, K., Shallcross, R., Anderson, R. (1980) 'Differences in coverbal behavior between blind and sighted persons during dyadic communication.' *Journal of Visual Impairment & Blindness,* **74,** 142–146.

Peters, A. (1983) *The Units of Language Acquisition.* New York: Cambridge University Press.

Powell, F., Finitzo-Heiber, T., Friel-Patti; S., Henderson, D. (Eds.) (1985) *Education of the Hearing Impaired Child.* San Diego: College—Hill Press.

Prizant, B. M. (1985) 'Toward an understanding of language symptomatology of visually-impaired children.' *In:* Sykanda, A., Jan, J. E., Blockberger, S., Buchanan, B., Groenveld, M. (Eds.) (1985) *Proceedings, Fifth Canadian Interdisciplinary Conference on the Visually Impaired.* Vancouver: The Canadian National Institute for the Blind (B. C.-Yukon Division).

—— Duchan, J. F. (1981) 'The functions of immediate echolalia in autistic children.' *Journal of Speech and Hearing Disorders,* **46,** 241–249.

—— Rydell, P. (1984) 'An analysis of the functions of delayed echolalia in autistic children.' *Journal of Speech and Hearing Research,* **27,** 183–192.

Quigley, S. P., Kretschmer, R. E. (1982) *The Education of Deaf Children: Issues, Theory and Practice.* Baltimore: University Park Press.

—— Paul, P. V. (1984) *Language and Deafness.* San Diego: College—Hill Press.

Rapin, I. (1979) 'Conductive hearing loss; effects on children's language and scolastic skills.' *In:* Hanson, D. G., Ulvestad, R. F. (1979) *Otitis Media and Child Development: Speech, Language and Education.* Suppl. 60 to *Annals of Otology, Rhinology and Laryngology,* 88 (5) (Part II). pp. 3–12.

Rogow, S. (1980) 'Language development in blind multihandicapped children: a model of co-active intervention.' *Child: Care Health and Development,* **6,** 301–308.

Savage, R. D., Evans, L., Savage, J. F. (1981) *Psychology and Communication in Deaf Children.* Sydney: Grune & Stratton.

Thomas, A., Chess, S. (1980) *The Dynamics of Psychological Development.* New York: Brunner/Mazel.

Urwin, C. (1984) 'Communication in infancy and the emergence of language in blind children.' *In:* Schiefelbusch, R., Pickar, J. (Eds.) *The Acquisition of Communicative Competence.* Baltimore: University Park Press. pp. 479–524.

Warren, D. H. (1977) *Blindness and Early Childhood Development.* New York: American Foundation for the Blind.

Wilbur, R. (1978) *American Sign Language and Sign Systems: Research and Applications.* Baltimore: University Park Press.

Wills, D. (1979) 'Early speech development in blind children.' *Psychoanalytic Study of the Child,* **34,** 85–117.

Woll, B., Kyle, J., Deuchar, M. (Eds.) (1981) *Perspectives on British Sign Language and Deafness.* London: Croom Helm.

15
LANGUAGE DEVELOPMENT AND MENTAL RETARDATION

Jean A. Rondal

This chapter reviews and discusses the available data on three major issues: (i) prelinguistic development in retarded babies, (ii) linguistic development in mentally retarded children and adolescents, and (iii) formal and functional aspects of language behaviour in mentally retarded adults.

Particular reference is made throughout the chapter to Down's syndrome subjects, because this syndrome has been studied most intensively during the last 25 years. However, it is recognised that the extent to which findings on Down's syndrome can be generalised to other types of mental retardation is not known.

Prelinguistic development in retarded babies

Following the pioneering work of Bruner (1975), Bates (1976) and Greenfield and Smith (1976), it is now recognised that there are a number of prelinguistic precursors to speech. It is not known whether the behavioural structures to be mentioned are true prerequisites (*i.e.* necessary conditions), or more simply 'facilitators' to further linguistic development (Bretherton and Bates 1979). But most authors in the developmental and remedial literature adopt the working assumption that the behaviours are prerequisites to language.

Among the possible prelinguistic precursors of speech are: (i) the early reciprocal exchanges between mothers and infants (exhibiting so-called preverbal conversation or protodialogue); (ii) joint attention on the mother's and child's part; (iii) smiling, laughing, showing, pointing, giving and receiving activities as early forms of social and communicative sharing; and (iv) babbling and syllable reduplication as protoforms of vocal communication.

Despite large-scale agreement concerning their possible importance for further development, the early signalling and interacting behaviours of retarded infants have received only minimal attention. They should clearly be the subject of more investigations, particularly in the perspective of early intervention, but such data as exist have interesting implications.

For instance, in relation to protodialogue, Jones (1977) has shown that although the quantity of interactions (average rate per minute) between mothers and their normal or Down's syndrome infants is about the same between eight and 18 months, there are important qualitative differences between the two groups of mother-child pairs. Indeed, Down's syndrome infants appear to be less responsive to mothers' verbal as well as non-verbal stimulations. They take the initiative in the interaction much less often than the normally developing infants of similar ages. This in turn determines a more directive style of interaction between mothers and their retarded babies, the mothers trying hard to make the infant respond to their signals and become a more active partner in the interaction. When they do react and take the initiative in the vocal exchange, Down's syndrome infants tend to vocalise in continuous strings or to repeat vocalisations 'on top of each other' with a very short time lapse (less than half a second) left for the partner to take turn in the exchange. Such patterns of vocalisations reveal lapses of interactive turn-taking skills by the Down's syndrome infants. They cause a relatively high frequency of 'vocal clashes' between Down's syndrome infants and their mothers, when compared with non-retarded infants of corresponding ages. Other studies (Buckhalt *et al.* 1978, Berger and Cunningham 1981) confirm the frequent occurrence of vocal clashes between mothers and their Down's syndrome infants. It would appear urgent to establish when the basic turn-taking capacity is operational in Down's syndrome children. There seems to be the possibility of an important developmental delay here that calls for the educator's attention and for the definition and application of a specific remedial procedure.

This developmental lapse in basic communicative skills in Down's syndrome infants must be contrasted with the reported absence of significant delays in various aspects of babbling and phonetic development in Down's syndrome children and other retarded children of various etiologies between the first months and two years (Dodd 1972, Smith 1977, Smith and Oller 1981). The sound characteristics of babbling (vowels, consonants, syllables, reduplicated syllables)—at various stages of babbling—seem to be very similar as to types, tokens (*i.e.* frequencies of appearance) and combinatory patterns in the children whether they are retarded or not at corresponding chronological ages. Along the same line, Smith (1977) has reported that the phoneme (or phonemic) substitutions and approximations leading to the acquisition of co-articulated 'k', 'f', and 'th' correspond rather well for CA-matched Down's syndrome and non-retarded children between two and five years. It may be that certain aspects of prelinguistic development in retarded babies are already deficient in some respect by comparison with normal babies, whereas other aspects of the same development do not exhibit the same problems.

Several studies have reported delayed onset of smiling, laughing, showing, pointing, giving and receiving activities in Down's syndrome babies (Cytryn 1975, Cicchetti and Sroufe 1976, Berger and Cunningham 1981). For example, the onset of smiling comes later for the Down's syndrome babies (between five and nine weeks); and the percentage of time spent smiling at different ages is lower in Down's syndrome infants. It is quite possible that the early forms of social and communicative sharing and reciprocal exchanges are noticeably delayed in retarded babies.

Bruner has emphasised the possible importance of eye-contact and joint attention on the mother and child's part for early communicative development and further language acquisition (*e.g.* lexical development). A small number of studies has been conducted on this topic with mothers and their retarded babies.

Berger and Cunningham (1983) and Gunn *et al.* (1982) have investigated eye-contact between mothers and normal as well as Down's syndrome infants over the first nine months. The Down's syndrome infants show delays in the onset of eye-contact (onset of sustained eye-contact with mother around seven weeks in Down's syndrome infants versus one month in normal babies) and in the establishment of high levels of this behaviour (at six months, Down's syndrome infants exhibit similar levels of eye-contact as observed in normal infants around four months). High levels of eye-contact are attained during the third month. They are maintained in the following months and occur in long episodes (10 seconds and over), whereas the gazing behaviour of the normal infants directed to the mother shows a marked decrease in frequency and duration of episodes after four months.

Frequent and longer episodes of eye-contact with the mother in Down's syndrome babies extending over several months would appear to be beneficial for the formation of the mother-infant bond. Interpersonal looking behaviour may also be regarded as a first step in learning communication skills. But careful attention should be given to the delays and deviations in these children in the relational patterns of mother-child communication, as well as in the timing and referential uses of eye-contact.

These problems imply impairments in both maturational and psychological processes. The age of onset of eye-contact and first increase in normal infants seems to correspond with the reported age of maturation of the macular area of the retina which is considered necessary for sustained focusing on relatively small objects (Browson 1974). The low levels of eye-contact, and the short gaze duration found in Down's syndrome infants during the early months, may be related to some impairments or slower maturation of the macular retina corresponding area in the nervous system. The short gazes might also result from the hypotonia in the muscles of the eyes. There may also be a relationship between Down's syndrome infants' delays in smiling and laughing, and their degree of muscular hypotonia (Cicchetti and Sroufe 1976).

The handicapped infants' greatly prolonged period of frequent and long-lasting eye-contact (while indicating that the visual system has matured sufficiently by three or four months to allow frequent and prolonged eye-contact) suggests new types of difficulties: a possible slower maturation of the peripheral visual field (Salapatek 1975), of the inhibitory mechanisms (Parmelee and Stern 1972), a slow development of competing responses, and a low distractibility (Miranda and Fantz 1974). Alternatively or complementarily, the impairments may be located in the learning processes and information-processing capacity, particularly with respect to the acquisition of the face schema (Miranda 1976). The problem reported by Jones (1977), regarding lapses of interactive turn-taking skills in Down's syndrome infants, may also be cognitive in nature (failure to take the conversational partner into account), or indicate a lack of inhibitory capacity in the auditory-vocal channel, or both. Further research is required to test these hypotheses and suggest ways for remediation.

An explanation of the difference between handicapped and normal infants in looking behaviour does not seem to be related in any gross way to maternal behaviour. In the study by Gunn et al. (1982), looking behaviour by Down's syndrome children was not associated with the amount of mother vocalisation at six months, in contrast to the normal group where a positive correlation was found.

There should be no need to re-emphasise the importance of such research on the early social and communicative behaviours of handicapped infants. If one assumes at least partial sequential dependency between prelinguistic and further linguistic developments, learning more about the early relational problems of the handicapped infant gives the best hope of being able to understand better the impressive delays that follow in the course of ontogenesis and of being able to specify eventually the contents and methods of an efficient early-intervention procedure.

Linguistic development in retarded children and adolescents
One of the important questions in the language development of the retarded subjects is the delay-difference issue. The question is whether language development in retarded children is a delayed but basically similar version of normal development, or whether it follows a different path. It has particular significance for language intervention.

Let us assume that the retarded children acquire language much in the same way as normal children (though it will be slower and less complete). This is the delay position. If this point of view is correct, one intervention strategy is to have the retarded child recapitulate every step in normal language acquisition, although this strategy begs a number of questions. It presupposes that all steps in normal language acquisition are necessary and that they have to be followed in sequence. Studies of other aspects of development indicate that this need not be so. For example, crawling is a normal part of the development sequence of walking, but there are no problems if that stage is missed out. Even so, the main implication for intervention of the delay position is that until demonstrated otherwise, retarded children should be taught language structures in the same order as younger normal children acquire them.

Suppose on the contrary that the language development of the retarded subject proceeds in a different way from the development in normal subjects. In this case, any amount of normative language intervention may not be sufficient.

Current findings differ on this question. At a relatively superficial level and particularly for the phonological, lexical and semantical structural aspects of language, it is possible to compare the retarded to younger normal children. However, when more detailed analyses are made, particularly on the morpho-syntactical aspects of language, the same comparison is far less satisfactory. Additionally, most of the available data are concerned with measurable states of language rather than underlying processes by which the language system is acquired. It is clear that any comprehensive answer to the delay-difference question should take into consideration the processes of language acquisition. In this respect, it must be repeated that we are still in no position to specify whether there is only one or whether there are several alternative ways to the acquisition of the linguistic system in normal as well as in retarded children. Longitudinal studies, supplemented by experimental research, should greatly help to clarify the issue. This work will eventually prompt a more precise tailoring of the language-training and remedial programmes to the specific needs of mentally retarded children.

TABLE I

Evolution of mean length of utterance (MLU) in Down's syndrome children (after Rondal 1978a).

Chronological age (mths.)		MLU (number of morphemes)	Mean upper-bound (i.e. number of morphemes in the longest utterance available for transcription)	
Down's syndrome	Normal		Down's syndrome	Normal
49 (9)*	23 (2)	1.00–1.50	2.86	3.57
78 (25)	27 (2)	1.75–2.25	6.14	6.29
117 (21)	30 (3)	2.50–3.00	11.00	10.57

*Standard deviation

Lexicon

VOCABULARY DEVELOPMENT

This is markedly delayed in moderately and severely retarded children. The onset of meaningful speech (one-word utterance) is delayed at least eight or nine months by comparison with non-retarded children. Around 18 to 20 months, in non-retarded children, about 20 per cent of the utterances are meaningful productions. In retarded children, meaningful speech does not appear before 24 months or so. At this time, the amount of meaningful productions is lower than 5 per cent. This figure increases only slowly with age up to around four years where a good deal more meaningful productions appear. Early stimulation and mental age seem to be two of the key variables in the vocabulary development of the retarded children. At corresponding mental ages, retarded and non-retarded children are able to define, understand and use the same number of words. The word-association tasks also yield similar results for the non-retarded and the retarded subjects at corresponding mental ages (Rondal 1975).

SEMANTICAL STRUCTURAL BASIS OF LANGUAGE

When they begin to combine two or three words in the same utterance (usually not before four years), moderately and severely retarded children seem to make use of the same range of relational meanings as those underlying the two- or three-word utterances of younger non-retarded children. Examples of semantical relations expressed in early language include notice or existence ('that a car'), disappearance ('milk all gone'), recurrence ('more milk'), attribution ('coffee hot'), possession ('my balloon'), and action-agent ('wash cup') (Buium et al. 1974a, Coggins 1976).

It is likely that the semantic relational structure of the language is similar and develops similarly in retarded as well as in non-retarded children. This is true for production as well as for the understanding of the basic semantic relationships of combinatorial language.

MORPHO-SYNTAX

Rondal's study (1978a) indicates that between three years and approximately 11 years the MLU (mean length of utterance) of Down's syndrome children increases from 1.00 to 3.00. Table I summarises these data obtained from 21 Down's

TABLE II

Frequency (in average percentage) of various structural types of sentences and utterances in Down's Syndrome children at three MLU levels (after Rondal 1978a, b).

| | Children | | | | | |
| | Down's syndrome MLU levels* | | | Normal MLU levels | | |
Indices	1	2	3	1	2	3
1. Utterances without verb	0.87	0.76	0.58	0.90	0.74	0.55
2. Modifiers per utterance	0.21	0.29	0.43	0.19	0.35	0.41
3. Sentences	0.10	0.23	0.42	0.07	0.26	0.44
4. Declaratives	0.02	0.14	0.31	0.04	0.18	0.28
5. Imperatives	0.02	0.03	0.05	0.02	0.04	0.07
6. Reversed yes/no questions	0.00	0.00	0.00	0.00	0.00	0.01
7. Yes/no questions based upon intonation	0.00	0.00	0.01	0.01	0.01	0.02
8. Wh—questions	0.05	0.05	0.04	0.00	0.02	0.05
9. Total questions	0.05	0.05	0.05	0.00	0.03	0.08

*MLU level 1: 1.00–1.50; MLU level 2: 1.75–2.25; MLU level 3: 2.50–3.00

syndrome children interacting verbally with their mothers at home (in free-play situations). Table I also supplies information on the children's mean upper-bound (*i.e.* the number of morphemes in the longest utterance available for transcription) at the various MLU levels considered.

Beyond 11 years, MLU values can be obtained that are higher than 3.00. Rondal *et al.* (1980) reported MLU values of about 3.40 for Down's syndrome subjects around 13 years.

Mentally retarded children appear to organise their discourse through use of the same set of utterance and sentence types as non-retarded children. The frequency of use of these different types is not markedly different in retarded and non-retarded subjects at corresponding levels of language development. Table II illustrates this point with data from Rondal (1978a, b) obtained with Down's syndrome and non-retarded children at similar MLU levels (level one: MLU 1.00 to 1.50; level two: MLU 1.75 to 2.25, and level three: MLU 2.50 to 3.00). The speech situation was free-play at home with the mother. The non-retarded children were aged 20 to 32 months. The Down's syndrome children were aged three to approximately 11 years.

Reversed yes/no questions are questions that can be answered by yes or no and that reverse the canonical subject-verb order in the language (for instance, 'Has he arrived yet?' or 'Did you sleep well last night?'). Yes/no questions may also be based upon intonation (*e.g.* 'he has arrived?' or 'you have eaten already?', with a mounting intonation toward the end of the sentence).

As Table II shows, the percentage of utterances without a verb decreases with increasing MLU level for the Down's syndrome as well as for the non-retarded children. In both cases, the dominant discourse modality is declarative (*i.e.* affirmative and negative utterances and sentences). Fewer questions are asked by the children (which probably reflects the difference in conversational status between the mothers and their children partners), and when they are, the wh-questions tend to predominate slightly. The passive category has been withheld from the table. Practically no passive sentences were produced by the Down's syndrome and the non-retarded children at the levels of language development investigated. This is no surprise. Non-retarded adults do not use the passive construction often (actually fewer than 5 per cent of their productions are usually formulated in the passive voice). Furthermore, the use and comprehension of passive sentences are observed in language development only at more advanced levels than those in the studies reported here.

GRAMMATICAL MORPHEMES

The understanding and use of grammatical morphemes is one of the linguistic areas in which mentally retarded children have particular difficulties. Most grammatical morphemes are correctly understood and used in obligatory contexts by non-retarded children around nine or 10 years. A number of researches indicate that retarded children are markedly delayed in this respect. Most often, they do not use the appropriate inflexions on the verb to express the temporal and aspectual relationships or to mark the concordance in number between subject and verb, or when they do use them, they fail to do so properly. They often miss the correct marking of the pronouns for number and gender and they are lost more often than not in the intricacies of the expression of the definite-indefinite contrast through the use of the articles. The deficits reported in the studies seem to go beyond what should be expected on the basis of mental age. That is, the deficiencies in understanding and use of the grammatical morphemes subsist even when the retarded children are matched for mental age with non-retarded children. It is not clear why this should be so. The grammatical morphological marking rests, no doubt, on intricate and momentous discriminative responses within the utterance or the sentence, and such responses are based on existing associative knowledge. It is possible that simply too many operations are involved in grammatical marking for the cognitive capabilities of the moderately and severely retarded subjects, particularly as these operations involve long-term memory knowledge and the retention in short-term memory of several pieces of information (for example, keeping in short-term memory the information on 'plurality' regarding the subject, so that later the verb can be marked appropriately in the sentence). Alternatively, the time available to perform these operations in the real-time processing of the sentence is too short for the retarded children with limited processing capabilities. Such hypotheses can be verified empirically.

Individual differences between retarded subjects have not been systematically studied so far. The 'general' point of view has tended to dominate over the differential one in the last decades. A renewed interest for the study of individual differences among retarded subjects can be found in recent works. Miller *et al.* (1981), for example, have documented significant individual differences in the language acquisition of mentally retarded children.

These authors have gathered and analysed detailed descriptive clinical data on 42 developmentally disabled children evaluated at the Waisman Center on Mental Retardation and Human Development, Madison, Wisconsin. Miller *et al.* report that it is extremely difficult to find a consistent degree of homogeneity in considering the communicative and linguistic abilities of the retarded subjects. With respect to language skills, three major patterns of functioning can be identified relative to cognitive development (assessed by reference to Piagetian theory and measures): a pattern of production delay, a pattern of delay both in production and comprehension, and a pattern of language functioning consistent with cognitive level. These three patterns were identified at every cognitive level, from late sensorimotor to late preoperational stages (the retarded subjects studied were between seven months and seven years cognitively). As Miller *et al.* (1981) pointed out, the existence of three different delayed patterns rules out any simple and unitary conception of language acquisition in the retarded as a slow-motion version of normal development.

There are important individual differences in the speech of mentally retarded adults assessed individually with a non-retarded adult in a dyadic conversational situation (Rondal and Lambert 1983, Rondal 1985). A number of variables must be taken into account in order to explain the differences in the language performance (productive as well as receptive) of the retarded subjects: among them, the relevant subject characteristics of non-verbal cognitive level, type and subtype of mental retardation, time passed in special schools and quality of education received, and quality and stimulating value of home environment. Multivariate studies should be conducted that try to evaluate the main and interactive effects of the relevant variables on the language and communicative developments of retarded subjects.

There has been some concern in recent years regarding the quality and the adaptability of parental (mainly maternal) linguistic environment of the mentally retarded child. Marshall *et al.* (1973) and Buium *et al.* (1974b) found that the language of mothers addressing their mentally retarded children is formally and semantically simpler than the language of mothers addressing their normally developing children. Mothers also tend to be markedly more directive in their verbal (as well as their non-verbal) behaviours when interacting with their retarded children. They also allow their children to take the initiative in the exchange far less often than mothers of normally developing children.

Actually, it can be shown (Rondal 1978a) that once the level of language development of the children (retarded and non-retarded) is carefully controlled (*e.g.* through the use of various psycholinguistic measures, including the MLU index as in Rondal's 1978a study)—a control not usually made in the studies mentioned above—mother's speech to the retarded or the non-retarded children is not significantly different in formal complexity, semantic content, pragmatic intent and in some aspects of language-teaching (like the frequencies of expansions, explicit corrections, approvals and disapprovals of children's linguistic productions). Maternal speech to the retarded children evolves with the increasing linguistic capability of the children in much the same way as for the normal children. At corresponding levels of development in the children, the mothers of the retarded children do not appear to give more directives than the mothers of the non-retarded children (Rondal 1978a). One of the key variables in the reciprocal adaptions between mothers and retarded children seems to be the language level (receptive and productive) reached by the children. This indication is in agreement with the literature on motherese to normally developing children (Rondal 1985).

These results suggest that the maternal linguistic environment of the mentally retarded children is an appropriate one, if by appropriate it is meant the kind of linguistic environment that is generally the one of normal middle-class children at corresponding levels of language development.

But this should not be taken to mean that mothers' speech to the retarded children could not be rendered more efficient for language-teaching, nor that one should dispense with trying to teach the mothers of these children how to maximise the efficiency of their interactions with the children for language development. Numerous interventions carried out since the mid-1970s (MacDonald *et al.* 1974, Rynders and Horrobin 1975, Cheseldine and McConkey 1979) have presented and tested different techniques and procedures involving retarded children and their mothers. Most were able to induce an efficient language-acquisition process in the children.

Formal and functional aspects of language behaviour in mentally retarded adults
Gathering data on the communicative and linguistic functioning of mentally retarded adults is of great significance for professionals in charge of day-care centres, occupational centres, sheltered workshops and institutions, to know exactly what their 'patients' can do in terms of verbal and non-verbal communication both with other retarded and non-retarded people. This knowledge will eventually help the professionals to develop better methods of caring for their subjects.

Several researchers have recently addressed the question of the communicative capability of mentally retarded adults (Sabsay 1975, Veit *et al.* 1976, Bedrosian and Prutting 1978, Berry *et al.* 1978, Bedrosian 1979, Owings and Mc Manus 1980). The available data suggest that mentally retarded adults are able to take part in conversation and to demonstrate similar types of conversational controls and constraints as non-retarded adults. They also use similar communicative functions (questions, statements and commands) with similar frequency as non-retarded subjects. These studies have emphasised the functional and communicative aspects of language behaviour in mentally retarded adults. However, there is also the question of the relationship between formal and functional aspects of language behaviour in the retarded adults. A first study by Rondal and Lambert (1983) supplies specific information on this question. These researchers have recorded the communicative exchanges between a non-retarded adult and 22 monolingual French-speaking mentally retarded adults (Down's syndrome and others) assembled in dyadic natural free conversational situations.

As shown in Table III, there is a constant difference between Down's syndrome and non-Down's syndrome adults, particularly in the morpho-syntactical aspects of the language exchanged with the non-retarded adult. None of these differences proved significant, however, due to the relatively large inter-individual variability in the two groups of subjects. The results were also evaluated in terms of possible differences according to sex, but none of these comparisons proved

TABLE III

Average scores and standard deviations for Down's syndrome (DS) and non-Down's syndrome (NDS) adults. Frequency data on the non-retarded interlocutor's speech (after Rondal and Lambert 1983).

Indices	DS adults		NDS adults	
	Mean	SD	Mean	SD
Retarded adult's speech				
Lexical aspect				
1. TTR (type-token ratio)	0.575	0.075	0.568	0.045
Morpho-syntactical aspect				
2. MLU (mean length of utterance)	5.980	2.620	6.950	2.520
3. Proportion of sentences	0.412	0.311	0.533	0.299
4. Sentence complexity	0.217	0.173	0.327	0.241
5. Number and gender	0.563	0.235	0.690	0.214
6. Proportion of articles	0.381	0.212	0.518	0.154
7. Verbal inflexions	0.547	0.365	0.780	0.379
8. Proportion of pronouns	0.624	0.504	0.876	0.501
Informative aspect				
9. Proportion of informations	0.972	0.046	0.945	0.074
10. Proportion of new informations	0.692	0.121	0.693	0.114
11. Conversational continuity	0.833	0.077	0.824	0.117
Non-retarded interlocutor's speech				
12. Proportion of questions	0.647	0.132	0.661	0.143
13. Proportion of statements	0.112	0.051	0.110	0.080
14. Approval-disapproval	0.095	0.048	0.132	0.105
15. Correction-repetition	0.111	0.093	0.042	0.051

MLU was computed by dividing the number of morphemes in the utterances by the number of utterances. *Sentence complexity* was defined as the ratio of the number of compound verbs (*e.g.* 'is going', 'have made') plus subordinate clauses to the total number of utterances. *Number and gender*: ratio of the number of morphological markers (singular-plural) and for gender (masculine-feminine) to the total number of utterances. *Proportion of informations*: ratio of the number of informations supplied verbally to the total number of utterances. By information is meant a complete relational meaning (*i.e.* a verb with its obligatory arguments in the sense of Chafe 1970), an elliptical statement or a question referring back to an immediately preceding utterance by the interlocutor. The echoic and onomatopoeic productions were not counted as instances of informative utterances. *Proportion of new information*: ratio of the number of informations not previously stated in the conversation to the total number of informations given verbally. *Conversational continuity*: ratio of the number of times the retarded subject correctly followed on the topic introduced or developed by the non-retarded adult. *Approval-disapproval*: ratio of the number of explicit verbal signs of approval or disapproval contingent upon the speech intervention of the retarded subject to the total number of utterances. *Correction-repetition*: ratio of the number of corrections and repetitions of the retarded subject's speech to the total number of utterances.

TABLE IV

Cross-sectional data on mean length of utterance in Down's children and adults

Study	Chronological age (yrs)		MLU	
	Mean	SD	Mean	SD
Rondal (1978a)	4.1	0.9	1.26	0.23
	6.6	2.1	1.94	0.19
	9.9	1.9	2.87	0.14
Rondal *et al.* (1980)	11.6	1.8	3.40	0.95
Rondal and Lambert (1983)	26.0	1.7	5.98	2.62

significant either. Describing the retarded adult's speech, it is necessary to distinguish between formal and informative aspects of the language. As a rule, mentally retarded adults use simple formal means to express meaning. The mean length of utterance averages six or seven (SD = 2.5). Only about half of the utterances are grammatical sentences. Sentence complexity (in terms of compound verbs and subordinate clauses) remains low. Yet despite severe limitations on the formal side, the language of the retarded adults appears to have functional and informative value. It carries organised information and contains a good deal of new information. The topics introduced are dealt with in such a way as to allow for the necessary continuity of the exchange between interlocutors. Severe formal restrictions in the speech of the retarded adults does not mean, therefore, that their discourse is devoid of informative value or grossly deficient in this respect.

A further question is whether there is evidence of linguistic progress between childhood and adulthood in moderately and severely mentally handicapped subjects. According to Lenneberg (1967), no significant progress should be expected in mental retardates beyond puberty. But there is little convincing data to support Lenneberg's hypothesis. Lenneberg *et al.* (1964) studied the language development of 61 Down's syndrome individuals aged from three to 22 and living at home. They indicate that after 14 years any linguistic development practically stopped in their subjects. It should be noted that this conclusion applies only to a relatively small number of subjects who were over age 14 at the end of the study.

Seitz *et al.* (1969) claimed to have found results consistent with Lenneberg's suggestion. They retested high and low MA (mental age) retarded subjects who had been seen 30 months before by Keilman and Moran (1967) on a free word-association task. Seitz *et al.* found that the high MA group (mean CA: 17 years; mean MA: 11.5 years) did not show any significant change in their responses (remaining mostly with syntagmatic word associations as opposed to the paradigmatic associations considered to be developmentally more advanced). By contrast, the low MA group (mean CA: 15.3; mean MA: 7.6) did show changes in their associative responses. It is hard to understand how the authors could have construed their results as supporting Lenneberg's position, as the low MA group in their study that contained a majority of children above 14 years CA did show a significant change in its performance with the time passed since the former examination. Seitz *et al.* (1969) seem to have erroneously interpreted Lenneberg's hypothesis as linked with mental age, when in fact it is concerned with chronological age.

A longitudinal study by Seagoe (1965) supports the view that language development in the retarded may continue after 14 years. This author has reported noticeable linguistic progress in a Down's syndrome person until 30 years. After this age, the person began to exhibit signs of physiological deterioration. The familial environment of this person was exceptional in that it did everything it could to push the child, the adolescent and later the young adult toward always new achievements.

The possibility of substantial linguistic growth in retarded individuals during early adolescence is an important question which needs more systematic investigation.

The figures in Table IV indicate a possible continued language growth in Down's syndrome subjects until the adult age together with a marked increase in the inter-individual variability. However, this indication may be entirely or partially spurious for the following reasons: first, Rondal's study (1978*a*) was conducted with monolingual American-English Down's syndrome subjects whereas the other two studies used monolingual French-speaking subjects; second, these data come from cross-sectional studies (*i.e.* from studies conducted with different individuals at different ages).

It seems reasonable, however, to hypothesise a continuing growth in language performance (particularly as to the morpho-syntactical aspects of language as they are reflected in the MLU index) with chronological age after 12 years in Down's syndrome subjects (at least in some Down's syndrome subjects), and possibly in retarded individuals of other aetiologies.

Overview

This paper has addressed three important questions pertaining to the general issue of language development in mental retardates. As we know, prelinguistic development may be a crucial period for further language acquisition in the child. This period seems to be marked by noticeable delays and failures to acquire basic social and communicative mechanisms in the retarded child. Specific remediation procedures can and should be implemented in order to help establish the behavioural organisation lacking in the retarded babies and to speed up their prelinguistic development.

Regarding the delay-difference issue in the language development of the retarded children, it now appears that neither a delay nor a difference position can account for all the observed facts. The more one penetrates into the details of the linguistic development in the retarded, the more it appears that the course of this development is not comparable to what happens in young normal children: even if, superficially, things appear to be in accordance with a simple concept of delay.

Lastly, the chapter analysed a number of empirical data pertaining to language-functioning in retarded adults, and considered the question of whether significant linguistic progress still occurs after puberty in retarded subjects. No definitive answer can yet be given to this question, but the available data indicate that significant development can occur.

REFERENCES

Bates, E. (1976) *Language and Context. The Acquisition of Pragmatics.* New York: Academic Press.
Bedrosian, J. L. (1979) 'Communicative performance of mentally retarded adults: a topic analysis.' *Paper presented at the Symposium of the American Association on Mental Deficiency. The Linguistic Environment of the Mentally Retarded Child, Miami Beach, Florida.*
—— Prutting, C. A. (1978) 'Communicative performance of mentally retarded adults in four conversational settings.' *Journal of Speech and Hearing Research,* **21**, 79–95.
Berger, J., Cunningham, C. C. (1981) 'The development of eye contact between mothers and normal and Down's syndrome infants.' *Developmental Psychology,* **17**, 678–689.
—— —— (1983) 'The development of early vocal behaviour and interaction in Down's syndrome and non-handicapped infants.' *Developmental Psychology,* **19**, 226–236.
Berry, P., Pountney, C., Powell, I. (1978) 'Meal-time communication in moderately severely retarded

adults: An ethological study.' *Australian Journal of Mental Retardation*, 105–108.

Bretherton, I., Bates, E. (1979) 'The emergence of interactional communication.' *In:* Uzgiris, I. (Ed.) *Social Interaction and Communication during Infancy.* San Francisco: Jossey-Bass.

Browson, G. (1974) 'The postnatal growth of visual capacity.' *Child Development*, **45**, 873–890.

Bruner, J. (1975) 'From communication to language—a psychological perspective.' *Cognition*, **3**, 256–287.

Buckhalt, J. A., Rutherford, R. B., Goldberg, I. (1978) 'Verbal and non-verbal interaction of mothers with their Down's syndrome and non-retarded infants.' *American Journal of Mental Deficiency*, **82**, 337–343.

Buium, N., Rynders, J., Turnure, J. (1974*a*) 'Early maternal linguistic environment of normal and Down's syndrome language learning children.' *American Journal of Mental Deficiency*, **79**, 52–58.

—— —— —— (May 1974*b*) *A Semantic Relational Concepts Based Theory of Language Acquisition as Applied to Down's Syndrome Children: Implication for a Language Enhancement Program. (Research Report no. 62).* Minneapolis, Minnesota: University of Minnesota, Research and Development Center in Education of Handicapped Children.

Chafe, W. (1970) *Meaning of the Structure of Language.* Chicago: University of Chicago Press.

Cheseldine, S., Mc Conkey, R. (1979) 'Parental speech to young Down's syndrome children: an intervention study.' *American Journal of Mental Deficiency*, **83**, 612–620.

Cicchetti, D., Sroufe, L. A. (1976) 'The relationship between affective and cognitive development in Down's syndrome infants.' *Child Development*, **47**, 920–929.

Coggins, T. E. (1976) *The classification of relational meanings expressed in the early two-word utterances of Down's syndrome children.* Unpublished manuscript, University of Wisconsin, Madison (University Microfilms International, Catalogue no. 76-20, 103).

Cytryn, L. (1975) 'Studies of behavior in children with Down's syndrome.' *In:* Anthony, E. J. (Ed.) *Explorations in Child Psychiatry.* New York: Plenum.

Dodd, B. (1972) 'Comparison of babbling patterns in normal and Down syndrome infants.' *Journal of Mental Deficiency Research*, **16**, 35–40.

Greenfield, P., Smith, J. (1976) *The Structure of Communication in Early Language Development.* New York: Academic Press.

Gunn, P. Berry, P. Andrews, R. (1982) 'Looking behavior of Down's syndrome infants.' *American Journal of Mental Deficiency*, **3**, 344–347.

Jones, O. (1977) 'Mother-child communication with pre-linguistic Down's syndrome and normal infants.' *In:* Schaffer, H. (Ed.) *Studies in Mother-infant Interaction.* New York: Academic Press.

Keilman, P., Moran, L. (1967) 'Association structures of mental retardates.' *Multivariate Behavioral Research*, **2**, 35–45.

Lambert, J. L., Rondal, J. A. (1983) 'The language of Down's syndrome adults. Some preliminary data.' *Jornadas Internacionales sobre Sindrome de Down, Instituto Internacional para la Investigacion y asesoramiento sobre la Deficiencia Mental (IAMER)*, Madrid.

Lenneberg, E. H. (1967) *Biological Foundation of Language.* New York: Wiley.

—— Nichols, I. A., Rosenberger, E. F. (1964) 'Primitive stages of language development in mongolism.' *In:* McRioch, D., Weinstein, A. (Eds.) *Disorders of Communication. Research Publications of the Association for Research in Nervous and Mental Diseases Vol. 42* Baltimore: Williams & Wilkins.

MacDonald, J., Blott, J., Gordon, K., Spiegel, B., Hartman, M. (1974) 'An experimental parent-assisted treatment program for preschool language delayed children.' *Journal of Speech and Hearing Disorders*, **39**, 395–415.

Marshall, N. R., Hegrenes, J. R., Goldstein, S. (1973) 'Verbal interactions: mothers and their retarded children *vs.* mothers and their nonretarded children.' *American Journal of Mental Deficiency*, **77**, 415–419.

Miller, J., Chapman, R., Mac Kenzie, H. (June 1981) 'Individual differences in the language acquisttion of mentally retarded children.' *Communication presented at the Biennial Meeting of the Society for Research in Child Development, Boston.*

Miranda, S. B. (1976) 'Visual attention in defective and high-risk infants.' *Merrill-Palmer Quarterly*, **22**, 201–228.

—— Fantz, R. L. (1974) 'Recognition memory in Down's syndrome and normal infants.' *Child Development*, **45**, 651–660.

Owings, N. O., Mc Manus, M. D. (1980) 'An analysis of communication functions in the speech of a deinstitutionalized adult mentally retarded client.' *Mental Retardation*, **18**, 309–314.

Parmelee, A. H., Stern, E. (1972) 'Development of states infants.' *In:* Clements, C., Purpura, P., Mayer, F. (Eds.) *Maturation of Brain Mechanisms Related to Sleep Behaviour.* New York:

Academic Press.

Rondal, J. A. (1975) 'Développement du langage et retard mental: une revue critique de la littérature en langue anglaise.' *L'Année Psychologique*, **75**, 513–547.

—— (1978*a*) 'Maternal speech to normal and Down's syndrome children matched for mean length of utterance.' *In:* Meyers E. (Ed.) *Quality of Life in Severely and Moderately Retarded Children: Research foundations for improvement*. Washington, D. C.: American Association on Mental Deficiency.

—— (1978*b*) 'Patterns of correlations for various language measures in mother-child interactions for normal and Down's syndrome children.' *Language and Speech*, **21**, 242–252.

—— (1985) *Adult-child Interaction and the Process of Language Acquisition*. New York: Praeger Press.

—— Lambert, J. L., Sohier, C. (1980) 'L'imitation verbale et non verbale chez l'enfant retardé mental mongolien et non mongolien.' *Enfance*, **3**, 107–122.

—— —— (1983) 'The speech of mentally retarded adults in a dyadic communication situation: Some formal and informative aspects.' *Psychologica Belgica*, **23**, 49–56.

—— —— (1985) *Langage et communication chez les handicapés mentaux: théorie, évaluation et intervention*. Brussels: Mardaga.

Rynders, J., Horrobin, M. (1975) 'Projet EDGE: The University of Minnesota Communication stimulation program for Down's syndrome infants.' *In:* Friedlander B., Slerritt G., Kirk G. (Eds.) *Exceptional Infant: Assessment and Intervention. Vol. 3*. New York: Brunner/Mazel.

Sabsay, S. (1975) 'Communicative competence among the severely retarded: some evidence from the conversational interaction of Down's syndrome adults.' *Paper presented at the meeting of the Linguistic Society of America, San Francisco*.

Salapatek, P. (1975) 'Pattern perception in early infancy.' *In:* Cohen, L. B., Salapetek, P. (Eds.) *Infant Perception: From Sensation to Cognition*. New York: Academic Press.

Seagoe, M. W. (1965) 'Verbal development in a mongoloid.' *Exceptional Children*, **31**, 269–275.

Seitz, S., Goulding, P., Conrad, R. (1969) 'The effect of maturation on word association of the mentally retarded.' *Multivariate Behavioral Research*, **4**, 79–88.

Smith, B. (1977) 'Phonological development in Down's syndrome children.' *Paper presented at the 85th Annual Convention of the American Psychological Association, San Francisco, August*.

—— Oller, K. (1981) A comparative study of premeaningful vocalizations produced by normally developing and Down's syndrome infants.' *Journal of Speech and Hearing Disorders*, **46**, 46–51.

Veit, S. W., Allen, G. J., Chinsky, J. M. (1976) 'Interpersonal interactions between institutionalized retarded children and their attendants.' *American Journal of Mental Deficiency*, **80**, 535–542.

16
THE SOCIAL CONTEXT: COMMUNICATION IN FAMILIES WITH A HANDICAPPED CHILD

Ann Gath

The complaint that 'we can't get through to him' often heads the list of problems presented by the families of a handicapped child in clinical practice. Siblings as well as parents see difficulty in communication as a major problem in family life.

Infancy

Communication with a baby who is already showing signs of mental retardation may be a problem from the very beginning. Even a small departure from the expected norm may be off-putting to the parents, and inhibit the looking, smiling and talk that mothers and fathers use when getting to know a new child. When the baby is premature, the features are often pointed and sometimes seem more adult, knowing and less appealing than the round-faced innocence of the term newborn. Separation from mother and isolation of the child in a special-care nursery, full of frightening technical equipment, can contribute to a barrier between the newborn child and its mother. The importance of early relationships between parent and child is well known. In recent years, neonatal nurseries have striven to help the parents get to know even the smallest and most frail babies, and deliberately foster mother and child 'bonding' (though see Herbert *et al.* 1982 and Goldberg 1983 for a modern critique of this concept).

The appearance of the child

Many parents have to make an extra effort to relate to a child with an abnormal appearance, especially where there are the facial stigmata commonly associated with mental retardation. In a comparison of parental reaction to children with Down's syndrome and children with cleft lip and palate, it seems that the implication of abnormality is more of a bar to attachment than the severity of facial deformity (Gath 1972). After the initial severe shock, attachment to an infant with even a marked degree of cleft lip proceeded normally—particularly after plastic surgeons had explained what could be done and had shown photographs to illustrate previous successful repairs. Parental grief was much shorter than that experienced by the parents of Down's syndrome children. This finding has been confirmed by work with parents of children with gross facial deformity. In these cases, the parents had been able 'to see beyond the appearance to the baby itself' within a couple of weeks. Despite grotesque and often initially horrifying deformities (but normal intellectual capacities) the children had been able to communicate with their parents and to elicit reciprocal devotion. But in a prospective study of Down's syndrome children (Gath 1978), the baby often remained an enigma for much longer, was rarely addressed by a pet name and—in a few cases—only given a proper first name with much difficulty.

Family background

Certain handicapping conditions may affect vulnerable families. Mental retardation, particularly where no medical cause can be found, is more common in socially disadvantaged families. Other conditions are genetically determined. Where there is a known family history, the parents may feel that they are themselves to blame and that other children may be affected. In some cases the parents themselves may have a related disorder.

Mental state of mother

The early experience of having a handicapped child can seriously damage parents' self-esteem and undermine their capacity to cope with the additional demands made by assessment and treatment. The initial grief is sometimes prolonged, developing into a chronic depressive state. In disorders which are not easily recognised, mothers often feel demeaned by their worries being dismissed repeatedly before being taken seriously.

Depression is common in mothers of young children, particularly where there are other small ones in the home, and additional problems such as poor housing and unsatisfactory relationships (Brown and Harris 1978, Richman *et al.* 1982). The rôle of maternal depression in impeding language development is not clear, but the presence of a silent, over-critical or even abusive mother is not conducive to the development of speech. There is little evidence that mothers of young handicapped children are significantly more depressed than those of normal counterparts, but recent work indicates that mothers of older handicapped children attending school may continue to be anxious and depressed (Gath and Gumley 1985).

Rôle of the child

The first smile of any baby is a delight to the parents, and a strong reinforcer of parental attention. The effect of the first smile of a baby known to be handicapped, such as a child with Down's syndrome, was much more marked than with normal babies in similar families. This sometimes fleeting manifestation of human interpersonal communication was particularly welcome after the initial period of shock and apprehension. Despite the smiles, however, some parents continued to have marked difficulty in their relationship to the baby (often referred to as a problem in 'getting through'), and they described their caring for the child as being mechanical (Gath 1978, Gath and Gumley 1984). In these families, the fathers were able to withdraw unobtrusively: and even the difficulty between mother and handicapped child was not often apparent to an outsider. Only years later, and after experience with other normal children, did the mothers describe the negative feelings they had had in the early months and the lack of joy in the parenting at that time. However, a deep attachment did develop by the end of the first year in the majority of cases, and in only one family of the 22 survivors did the parents regret having persevered.

Mothers' adaptation to the handicapped child

Very little is known about how maternal behaviour is actually affected by the information that the child is handicapped or intellectually impaired. Anecdotal evidence indicates that the mother's behaviour is influenced more by her own feelings about the child than by the information given to her by the clinicians. Much has been written about the way in which parents are told of their child's handicap. The consensus of opinion is that information given in a straightforward but considerate fashion is usually appreciated and leads to better parental adjustment than delay and particularly deception. Even if the parents had not suspected anything was wrong, most interact with the child as they they did before (although there are distressing exceptions).

Stimulating interaction between parent and child may be reduced by the passivity of the child. Mentally retarded children seem less rewarding at first, reacting less frequently and more slowly to parental overtures. The child with Down's syndrome has less intense moods, as well as slower reactions (Sorce and Emde 1982). Experienced mothers do learn to adjust to the differing intensity, but the relative lack of response in the early months can compound the child's innate limitations by reducing environmental stimulation and the opportunity for perception of the surroundings or interaction with adults.

Studies show that mothers of handicapped children are more likely to adopt a teaching rôle and to be more directive of the child's activities than are mothers of normal children. This adaptation takes place spontaneously, but the various infant stimulation programmes do specifically encourage the parent to take a very active teaching rôle, with specific training in modifying and shaping the behaviour of the child. Successful intervention reinforces what happens in all good parenting: the differing needs of children are noted, and the parent intervenes as much or as little as necessary.

There is some evidence, however, that mothers of mentally retarded children resemble mothers of other children with language difficulties in being less able to structure their speech to encourage that of the child (Petersen and Sherrod 1982). Mothers of children with normally developing speech take an active part in leading them towards more complex constructions and ideas: for example, by expanding on what the child has just said (Tizard *et al.* 1983). The mothers of retarded children use less expansion and rely more on imitation, as do, to a lesser extent, the mothers of otherwise normal children with speech delay (Lasky and Klopp 1982).

The rôle of the father

Much less is known of the rôle of the father in most aspects of child development. Most research studies and intervention programmes are scheduled to run in working hours, when the fathers are less often at home. With handicapped children, it appears that mothers are more consistent and more inclined to take the teaching rôle than their husbands. Each spouse is influenced by the presence of the other, but fathers are more inclined to take an active rôle when not with their wives.

Communication in family life

Communication is important in family life for quality of relationships and because of discipline. Parents and siblings need to feel they can understand and be understood by the other members. Failure to communicate on even the most simple terms leads to misunderstanding and strains the relationships, not just between the parent or sibling and the handicapped child, but also between parents and siblings.

As children learn to communicate with their parents and to understand what is expected of them, control moves from physical restraint to verbal reinforcement or discouragement. Families tolerate the constant supervision required of a mobile two-year-old because it is thought to be for a limited time only. When the child understands why she must not touch the cooker or run into the road, then the rest of the family will not have to keep watching. Such supervision remains necessary for a retarded child who cannot communicate or understand instructions, and this is a major cause of strain for a family.

Behaviour and communication

Poor communication skills in early childhood are associated with behavioural problems, which may be persistent (Fundudis *et al.* 1979, Richman *et al.* 1982, Cantwell and Baker 1985). These behaviour disorders may be resistant to treatment, particularly when associated with varying degrees of global retardation; and they cause distress to the child and the rest of the family. The behaviour disorders are clearly associated with a high malaise score in a recent study of handicapped children in Kent (Pahl and Quine 1984).

Severe limitation of language was seen to lead to behaviour problems in several different ways. In the cases where the child is profoundly handicapped and makes neither meaningful utterance nor predictable response, the parents were understandably inclined to think that attempts to control behaviour were doomed to failure, and gave up all attempts to modify it at all. By contrast, parents can greatly overestimate their child's capacity to understand fully what is said. One girl was very talkative, but her comprehension lagged behind her apparent verbal fluency. Her mother used gentle admonishments such as 'I would not do that if I were you' with reasonable success to her other two children, but her Down's syndrome daughter was totally baffled by these complex commands.

Deceptive verbal fluency

Children will sometimes use precocious phrases that they do not really understand. One normal five-year-old offered her aunt a piece of fruit cake about which her mother had been disparaging when she had bought it in a hurry that day. The child asked her aunt if she would like 'some of this alleged fruit-cake'. A similar phenomenon was seen in a nine-year-old boy with the small stature and appealing 'elfin' features of hypercalcaemia. His talk was largely delayed echolalia, and contained many superficially sophisticated phrases. The attention of the surrounding adults strongly reinforced his talking, but there was very little real meaning. He is an example of the so called 'cocktail-party syndrome', originally described in children with arrested hydrocephalus (Hagberg and Sjögren 1966). Other children with infantile hypercalcaemia have also been described as talking excessively to gain adult attention, with both nonsense and mimicry (Arnold *et al.* 1985).

Early intervention
Early intervention has been offered to many families with retarded children for the past 10 years. The best results have often been obtained by home visits, where a teacher trains the mother to be the main therapist of her child. Currently the most popular programme in the UK is the Portage method, usually because it is 'well packaged' and makes use of personnel from a number of different disciplines who do not need an expensive and lengthy training. The efficacy of such programmes has been discussed by Gibson (1983) with regard to Down's syndrome, and by Lazar (1985) in his critical review of the results of 'head-start' programmes. It is arguable how much a cognitive deficit in a condition such as Down's syndrome can be rectified, but there is no doubt that the essential ingredient for success is the change in the mother's attitude towards her child's developmental and educational achievements. One small step forward is recognised by the mother who rewards the child by showing pleasure, and a positive transaction can begin, with small improvements being reinforced by the mother and the child's continuing effort rewarding the mother's interest. The child is not the only reinforcer of the mother's efforts to teach and encourage her child: and the regular visits of the home teacher, and social occasions which give an opportunity to meet other parents, are also very helpful to most parents. The young children with Down's syndrome now starting school at five years of age are apparently brighter and certainly more competent than those who started school 10 years ago. Usually this improvement, noticed in successive cohorts of children, is attributed to the success of early intervention programmes: but the more positive attitude of society as a whole certainly helps to encourage parents who have to put so much work into child-rearing.

Interaction with peers
Language-impaired children have problems in relating to other children of similar age. This has been shown in a study of pairs of children playing together, where the children with language difficulties had particular difficulty engaging another child in play. When equipped with good language skills, a child may take an active rôle in initiating play with a reluctant companion, and carry on the interaction as a leader (Seigel *et al.* 1985). Temperamental factors influence the type of reaction. More outgoing children with language delay react aggressively when they cannot make themselves understood. Tantrums and aggressive outbursts are common reasons why parents of children with poor communication skills seek help from a child psychiatric clinic. The more introverted child with poor speech is inclined to withdraw and become distressed and progressively more shy. The added behaviour problems bring more distress to the mother. An aggressive child often becomes the social outcast of the play-group, and may well be barred from the stimulation and training that is so necessary. The mother also feels ostracised and a depressed woman with low self-esteem may react to the child with yet more aggression,

266

building up a vicious circle. The mother of a shy, withdrawn child is not immune from criticism, which can be deeply hurtful. Her child is labelled 'insecure', and this too is thought to be the fault of the mother.

An understanding of the home and family life is crucial for treatment to be effective. Parents weighed down by frequent or violent tantrums, or exhausted because of sleep disturbance, will be unable to cope with the demands of a home-based treatment to enhance language development. A problem-oriented approach, involving more than one discipline, will enable parents and therapist to work out priorities before a single scheme of treatment is adopted.

Prevention of severe problems in communication
Primary prevention of mental retardation in its different aspects is clearly of major importance, but it is beyond the scope of this chapter.

Early diagnosis is very important in the prevention of the secondary complications of intellectual deficit, which together make up mental handicap, and include behaviour disorders and family disturbance or morbidity. Many parents are demoralised by feeling that their worries about the development of their young children are not taken seriously. Those with an obviously abnormal child may still feel fobbed off with answers like: 'Well what do you expect? He is a mongol, you know'. Mothers whose children look normal are made to feel fussy or inadequate. All doctors are taught how to listen to mothers, but this procedure is sometimes forgotten in the rush to get so much done in ever shorter courses. Deafness must always be looked for. Many children with Down's syndrome suffer from secretory otitis media (Cunningham and McArthur 1981), but this is still often overlooked or neglected. In some children, a large tongue can cause poor breathing, repeated infections and difficulty with speech. There are reports (but no controlled trials) of success following operations to reduce the size of the tongue, helping children to speak more easily and freeing them from upper respiratory-tract infections.

Treatment in early childhood
Early enrolment into an intervention programme that aims to increase parental confidence and skills is the most effective way of diminishing the development of communication and behaviour disorders. The exact programme is of little importance. Some parents, particularly the more verbal, may enjoy and gain much from self-help groups; while others, perhaps less confident to join in a goup, are more comfortable and feel that their children benefit more from the type of programme where a trained home-visitor instructs the parent how to teach the child (as in the Portage schemes, or where local education authorities employ peripatetic preschool teachers). A third group of parents may prefer to keep a strongly medical approach to their child, and are willing to travel some distances to attend developmental clinics—particularly when they have formed a close attachment to a particular doctor or therapist. But many parents feel that attendance at even a local clinic is too expensive and time-consuming.

The vital element is the creation of a mutually reinforcing relationship between parent and child. In earlier studies, it was shown that there were significant language gains in those programmes where the main emphasis was on motor development; and conversely, motor gains were just as common in the language-oriented programmes. The Wessex Revised Portage Language is very clearly laid out for teachers with brief training to use in the home with parents (White and East 1983). However, it can seem over-simplified and patronising to some parents. Other more imaginative approaches include the Early Language Training programme (more often used with a speech therapist) and the book *Let Me Speak* (Jeffree and McConkey 1976).

Rigid adherence to the particular method chosen may be counter-productive, as the greatest gains are made when the parents can grasp the principle behind the method employed, and then improvise to make a programme appropriate for their own child. Intensity of the language treatment does not seem to increase the chances of success (Clements *et al.* 1982).

Whatever form of intervention or treatment programme chosen, it is important not to let the regime put undue stress upon the families. What is stressful will vary from family to family. Programmes based on work done in the home will be the treatment of choice for the majority, but not for all.

Problems with a home-based treatment

Home-based treatment is difficult to carry out where there are many other problems. It has been shown that material deprivation alone is no bar (Gray and Klaus 1976); but where there is no privacy for the mother to receive the visitor, or circumstances make it distressing or embarrassing, it is likely that the visitor will be asked not to call again. It is essential that the parent never feels undermined or at a disadvantage. Extreme parental vulnerability is not confined to those with an obvious social disadvantage. A poor marital relationship is another cause of breakdown of treatment. An insecure young man, whose virility has been seriously damaged by the birth of an abnormal child, can react violently—usually towards the wife, but sometimes to the retarded child or other children. Usually the reaction is much less extreme, but it is hard for the mother to carry out the learning sessions in an atmosphere of criticism.

The presence of other small children can also make it harder for the specific teaching to take place, but here the observant home-visitor can either involve the others in some of the activities, or teach the mother how to plan her day so that at least some time is available for individual attention for the child most in need.

Persistent behaviour problems, or an inability to make the child understand that something is dangerous, will be of high priority to the parents. When it is essential to make a child understand (*e.g.* to stop the child playing with electrical sockets), the child is more likely to understand if more than one modality is used: *i.e.* saying 'No!' in a cross tone of voice, together with gestures such as holding up a finger and shaking the head. Praise is understood best with 'Good boy/girl' said in an exaggeratedly pleased voice with a big smile and a clap of the hands.

The involvement of both parents

Wherever possible, both parents should take part in the teaching sessions with the child. Often the father is not at home when the teacher calls, but his participation can be encouraged. It is sometimes helpful to earmark a particular activity as being 'Daddy's game', or a especially fascinating 'pop-up' book to be kept by him for a special session when he is at home. A very useful idea, put forward by Brinkworth and Collins (1969), is to make bath-time a long leisurely occasion when a lot of learning can take place in a fun atmosphere.

Since it is almost always in the children's best interest to be brought up within their own family, it is essential to maintain the family's external supports. This involves encouraging important relationships (*e.g.* with the maternal grand-mother), and ensuring that the parents have sufficient leisure-time and realise that life has many aspects and should not centre on the handicapped child alone.

The use of sign language

It is not uncommon for teachers to spend many hours teaching sign language, while the parents have no idea that this is happening or what the signs might mean. Some parents feel that the use of a sign language accentuates their child's abnormality, and they will resist it, ignoring or punishing the signs at home. Others see sign language as the last resort, and take it to mean that their child will never learn to speak. Good communication between home and school will prevent these misunderstandings. Parents should be taught the signs and to use speech at the same time.

In the longitudinal study of Down's syndrome, one child was mute with a behaviour disorder at the age of eight. However, Makaton signing had just been introduced at his school. At the next follow-up at the age of 14, he had progressed from signing to quite an extensive spoken vocabulary, and was a happy and well-adjusted boy.

Conclusion

Parents are highly motivated to get their handicapped children to speak, and value this attribute above most others. All language-treatment programmes require the co-operation of parents. Time spent understanding the family and respecting their individuality is time well spent.

REFERENCES

Arnold, R., Yule, W., Martin, N. (1985) 'The psychological characteristics of infantile hypercalcaemia.' *Developmental Medicine and Child Neurology*, **27**, 49–59.

Brinkworth, R., Collins, J. E. (1969) *Improving Mongol Babies and Introducing them to School.* Belfast: National Society for Mentally Handicapped Children.

Brown, G. W., Harris, T. (1978) *Social Origins of Depression. A Study of Psychiatric Disorder in Women.* London: Tavistock.

Cantwell, D., Baker, L. (1985) 'Speech and language: development and disorders.' *In:* Rutter, M., Hersov, L. (Eds.) *Child and Adolescent Psychiatry. Modern Approaches. 2nd edn.* Oxford: Blackwell.

Clements, J., Evans, C., Jones, C., Osborne, K., Upton, G. (1982) 'Evaluation of a home-based language training programme with severely mentally handicapped children.' *Behaviour Research and Therapy*, **20**, 243–249.

Cunningham, C., McArthur, K. (1981) 'Hearing loss and treatment in young Down's syndrome children.' *Child: Care, Health and Development,* **7,** 357–374.

Fundudis, T., Kolvin, I., Garside, R. (1979) *Speech Retarded and Deaf Children: Their ·Psychological Development.* London: Academic Press.

Gath, A. (1972) 'The mental health of siblings of a congenitally abnormal child.' *Journal of Child Psychology and Psychiatry,* **13,** 211–218.

—— (1978) *Down's Syndrome and the Family—the Early Years.* London: Academic Press.

—— Gumley, D. (1984) 'Down's syndrome and the family: follow up of children first seen in infancy.' *Developmental Medicine and child Neurology,* **26,** 500–508.

—— —— (1986) 'Family background of children with Down's syndrome and of children with a similar degree of mental retardation.' *British Journal of Psychiatry (in press).*

Gibson, D. (1983) 'Early stimulation for Down's syndrome: an effectiveness inventory.' *In:* Wolraich, M. L. (Ed.) *Advances in Behavioral Pediatrics Vol, 5.* Greenwich, Conn: JAI Press.

Goldberg, S. (1983) 'Parent–infant bonding: another look.' *Child Development,* **54,** 1355–1382.

Gray, S. W., Klaus, R. A. (1976) 'The early training project–a seventh year report.' *In:* Clarke, A. M., Clarke, A. D. B. (Eds) *Early Experience: Myth and Evidence.* London: Open Books.

Hagberg, B., Sjörgen, I. (1966) 'The chronic brain syndrome of infantile hydrocephalus.' *American Journal of Diseases of Children,* **112,** 189–196.

Herbert, M., Sluckin, W., Sluckin, A. (1982) 'Mother-to-infant "bonding".' *Journal of Child Psychology and Psychiatry,* **23,** 205–221.

Jeffree, D., McConkey, R. (1976) *Let Me Speak. Human Horizon Series.* London: Souvenir Press.

Lazar, I. (1985) 'On bending twigs and planting acorns (Emanuel Miller Lecture, 1984).' *Newsletter of the Association for Child Psychology and Psychiatry,* **7,** (1), 28–32.

Lasky, E. Z., Klopp, K. (1982) 'Parent-child interactions in normal and language-disordered children.' *Journal of Speech and Hearing Disorders,* **47,** 7–18.

Pahl, J., Quine, L. (1984) *Families with Mentally Handicapped Children: A Study of Stress and of Service Response.* University of Kent: Research Report, Health Services Research Unit.

Petersen, G., Sherrod, K. B. (1982) 'Relationship of maternal language to language development and language delay of children.' *American Journal of Mental Deficiency,* **86,** 391–398.

Richman, N., Stevenson, J., Graham, P. (1982) *Pre-school to School. A Behavioural Study.* London: Academic Press.

Seigel, L. E., Cunningham, C. E., Van der Spug, H. I. J. (1985) 'Interaction of language delayed and normal pre-school boys with their peers.' *Journal of Child Psychology and Psychiatry,* **26,** 77–83.

Sorce, J. F., Emde, R. N. (1982) 'The meaning of infant emotional expressions: regularities in caregiving responses in normal and Down's Syndrome Infants.' *Journal of Child Psychology and Psychiatry,* **23,** 145–158.

Tizard, B., Hughes, M., Carmichael, H., Pinkerton, G. (1983) 'Language and social class: is verbal deprivation a myth?' *Journal of Child Psychology and Psychiatry,* **24,** 533–542.

White, M., East, K. (1983) *The Wessex Revised Portage Language Checklist.* Windsor: NFER-Nelson.

17

THE CONSEQUENCES OF LANGUAGE DELAY FOR OTHER ASPECTS OF DEVELOPMENT

Patricia Howlin and Michael Rutter

Although the global term 'language delay' is widely used in the clinical literature it covers a heterogeneous group of problems (Cantwell and Baker 1985). Studies of the psychosocial correlates of language delay vary in their diagnostic criteria. Some are psychometrically precise in the degree of language impairment required for inclusion in the study, but clinically imprecise regarding diagnostic groups; others are the converse. Very few are both psychometrically and clinically adequate. Because most concern children with other handicaps in addition to language delay, often it is not possible to determine the extent to which the associated psychosocial problems stem from the language delay itself *per se*. Only a small proportion of children with a severe language delay have an isolated and specific developmental language disorder (Stark and Tallal 1981).

Nevertheless, despite problems of definition, it is evident that language is a skill that is intrinsically linked with many other cognitive, social and emotional processes; not surprisingly, therefore, abnormalities in language development tend to have far reaching effects on many other areas of children's development.

Language and cognition

Ordinarily, cognitive and linguistic skills tend to develop in close parallel, and it has been argued that language acquisition is dependent on a particular level of cognitive competence (de Zwart 1973, Morehead and Morehead 1976). But just as some children with specific language disorders show language skills well below those expected on the basis of their over-all cognitive level, so also some children exhibit complex syntactic skills in spite of a cognitive level supposedly 'too low' for grammatical competence to be expected. Some aphasic children are capable of understanding conceptual meaning although unable to express it in language (Cromer 1978). Advances in language acquisition may *provoke* as well as derive from, cognitive gains (Karmiloff-Smith 1978). The relationship between language and cognition should be seen as a constructive interaction, rather than as a unidirectional process. The form of the interaction changes according to the experience and maturation of the individual child.

Although it is apparent that thought processes can proceed without the development of spoken language, there is evidence that thinking depends on some sort of symbolic processing. Many theorists have supposed that thinking is entirely verbal, with thoughts always represented by words. Such a view is sustained 'by the incredibility of the alternative notion of thoughts as disembodied images floating in the mind' (Goodman 1982). Although thinking is largely dependent on some sort of symbolic system, be it verbal, notational (as in music) or pictorial, this purely verbal view of thought has many serious flaws. Studies of the cognitive and imaginative development of deaf individuals without any early speech, for example, clearly indicate that thinking does not require words (Furth 1966).

Nevertheless, to some extent words may influence cognitive processes, and even the individual's perception of the world. Whorf (1956) is perhaps the most notable exponent of this hypothesis. He cited many examples of how words supposedly 'shape' our thoughts. For instance, he pointed out that Eskimos have many different words for snow and that they think of snow in terms of subtle distinctions that are essential for their way of life. In contrast we have just one word for snow, and there is evidence that, to a minor extent, the way in which we conceptualize and think about our environment and experiences is influenced by the words we have available. However, as Brown (1976) pointed out: 'It is never the case that something expressed in Zumi or Hopi or Latin cannot be expressed at all in English. Were it the case, Whorf could not have written his articles as he did entirely in English'.

Early studies indicated that individuals from very disparate cultures exhibit similar patterns of recognition—despite very great differences in their lexicon. However, more sophisticated recent research has produced rather ambiguous results. For example, at the moment there is considerable controversy as to whether the lack of subjunctive verb forms (as in Chinese) makes it more or less difficult to deal with hypothetical sentences or 'counterfactuals' (*e.g.* 'if the President were a woman he would think before he spoke'). Results are conflicting (Bloom 1981, Au 1983), but it is probable that in some domains, at least, the Whorfian hypothesis may prove to have a certain amount of validity—if only psychologists could be sufficiently ingenious to devise the appropriate experiments to test it. It may well be that language skills influence the ease with which concepts are formed, but certainly concepts may be achieved in the absence of relevant words. As Hockett (1954) noted, 'Languages differ not so much as to what *can* be said in them, but rather as to what is *relatively easy* to say'.

Inspired by the Soviet psychologists Vygotsky and Luria, there have been many investigations into the rôle of spoken language in the regulation of behaviour. Luria (1957) found that if children used the word 'squeeze' when asked to press a bulb once only, they were more likely to give the correct response than if they did not verbalize. Recent experimental studies indicate that motor control is improved if verbalization occurs *simultaneously* with (rather than prior to) the physical act (Tinsley and Walters 1982, Balamore and Wozniak 1984). But it is the act of speaking, rather than the semantic content of verbalizations, that seems to be important. Even irrelevant verbalizations tend to result in better task performance than no verbalization at all. More naturalistic experiments suggest that the more relevant the language, the greater effects on performance. For example Razran (1961) found that toddlers were better at recognizing particular toys if they were given a variety of attributes associated with them (e.g. rock the doll, dress the doll) rather than the simple semantic label 'doll'. It was hypothesized that the language experience to which these children were exposed enabled them to build up a better representation of what is a doll, rather than having to rely on rote memory for object names.

Although language is only one element in the development of thought processes, it is nevertheless an important one. However, the mechanisms involved remain obscure, and many studies fail to differentiate between language competence and the ability to produce spoken language. In order to make this distinction, it is necessary to consider groups of children with very different degrees of expressive and internal language—deaf children, autistic children and those suffering from developmental language disorders.

Language and thinking in deaf children
Most severely deaf children are greatly handicapped in both the understanding and production of spoken language. Studies of language usage indicate that, compared with hearing children of the same age, they use shorter and much more simplified sentences and utterances tend to be repetitive, stereotyped and characterized by omissions, additions and substitutions. There is an under-use of function words, and an over-reliance on content words. Conversational skills, too, are limited (McKirdy and Blank 1982). Written communication tends to be impaired and associated with simplified syntax. Ivemey and Lachterman (1980) in a study of 11-year-old deaf children found that they were using syntactic structures more appropriate to 2½-year-olds. Their attempts to use these structures to communicate the much more complex interests and intentions of 11 year-old children resulted in syntax that was deviant as well as being delayed. Reading also tends to be impaired; one study of deaf school children found that no child was reading at or above his chronological age (Conrad 1979).

Nevertheless, the potential language capabilities of deaf children (without brain damage) should be normal. Because of the discrepancy between their language competence (which is good) and their spoken language (which is very poor) they provide a useful opportunity to see which faculty is necessary for intellectual growth. In general, deaf children perform as well as normal children on tests of non-verbal ability and when younger there is relatively little evidence of impairment in areas such as pretend play or symbolic reasoning, which might be expected given their limited verbal ability (Furth and Youniss 1976). But as they grow older, there are deficits in representational play and on tests of symbolic logic. Mathematical reasoning also tends to be impaired, in comparison with hearing peers. However, given that deaf children are unable to use subvocalization, which has been postulated as a basis for mathematical calculation (Hitch 1978), they are less handicapped than might have been expected (Wood et al. 1983). Moreover, Suppes (1974) found that, by using computer-assisted programmes, deaf children showed slightly *faster* rates of progress in their mathematical development than hearing children. Some of the conceptual problems reported in older deaf children may be attributable to inappropriate teaching rather than to inherent deficits (Furth 1966).

Cognitive development depends on experience as well as biological potential (Rutter 1985) and it may be that deaf children lack experiences that facilitate cognitive growth. Communication with others is an important source of information as well as a means of exploring ideas. Interestingly, it seems that deaf children reared by deaf parents tend to have somewhat superior communicative skills to deaf children reared by hearing parents (Wilbur and Quigley 1979, Meadow *et al.* 1983). This is particularly striking because deaf parents tend to be less well educated than hearing ones and there may be disadvantages for hearing children in being reared by deaf parents (Schiff and Ventry 1976). However, deaf parents use more gesture and sign in communicating with their deaf children than do hearing parents, and also they may be more understanding of their children's difficulties. It seems that this greater communicative interaction when the parents are deaf is often of benefit to deaf children. It is noteworthy that the environment optimal for the development of normal children may not be optimal for that of handicapped individuals. Therapeutic endeavours need to ensure that children with language delay have experiences that enhance their development but this is not necessarily best achieved by 'normalizing' the environment (see Chapters 7 and 21).

There is little evidence that teaching manual communication systems to deaf children inhibits the development of spoken language. In an extensive review of the literature Caccamise *et al.* (1978) concluded that 'Manual/simultaneous communication not only is not detrimental to the development of oral–aural communication skills . . . but may in fact facilitate the development of these skills.' Whether or not manual training programmes lead to better or worse speech has been questioned in subsequent studies (Geers *et al.* 1984), but certainly children trained in manual systems tend to show more spontaneous communication than those trained in oral systems. However, it is important to be aware of individual differences in response to training, and manual systems may not necessarily be the most effective mode of training for all deaf children. Communication should be encouraged in whatever medium seems most appropriate for the individual child. *Language* is what is needed, and although spoken language is certainly the most efficient form of communication it may well be a disservice to the deaf child to rely on it exclusively.

Language and thinking in children with developmental language disorders
One of the major problems in assessing the cognitive deficits shown by children with severe developmental language disorders is the heterogeneity of this diagnostic category. There is very little adequate description of children described as dysphasic, and many different subgroups have been involved in the various studies undertaken. It is also apparent that although children tend to be classified as suffering from expressive language disorders (which are relatively common, especially in boys), or receptive disorders (which are much rarer and have a more or less equal male to female ratio) the distinction is rarely so clear-cut. Bishop (1979) for example showed that the majority of children with developmental language disorders have both expressive and receptive problems—with girls generally showing greater receptive difficulties than boys. The nature of the

language handicap in this spectrum of disorders remains unclear, with controversy on whether the language is deviant as well as delayed, and on whether the main problem is pragmatic, syntactic or semantic (Cromer 1981, Howlin 1984).

The nature of the associated cognitive deficits is even less well defined. Studies of children with severe language delays, even those within the normal range on standardized IQ tests, have suggested that language impairment may be accompanied by pervasive cognitive deficits. These include problems in representation (Morehead and Ingram 1973, Kahmi *et al.* 1984), associative imagery and short-term memory (Eisenson 1968, Menyuk 1969, Graham 1974).

Sequencing of auditorily presented material tends to be particularly affected (Tallal and Piercy 1973). However, sequencing difficulties have been reported in a whole range of visual and auditory tests (Poppen *et al.* 1969). Cromer (1981) noted that if the sequencing disorder was primarily in the auditory mode one would expect aphasic children to exhibit jumbled words, not disordered syntax; whereas, in fact their errors tend to involve deletion of syntactic forms. One would also expect them to acquire language more easily through visual means (such as lip-reading or writing) but this is clearly not the case, and there are also marked abnormalities in their written language.

Whatever aspects of sequencing deficit are implicated, the evidence suggests that they must be regarded as a corollary to the language difficulty, and not a cause of it. For example, deaf children tend to perform very similarly to language-delayed children on tasks of cognitive peformance, and they also show similar difficulties in sequencing but no one would claim that such deficits are the 'cause' of their deafness. O'Connor and Hermelin (1978) showed that the lack of auditory input does not prevent deaf children from being able to appreciate temporal order, but it makes them unlikely to use that mode of ordering *spontaneously*. Left to themselves they tended to prefer a spatial ordering, but could cope quite adequately with temporal ordering if the experimental conditions required this.

Again, in children with developmental aphasia, a temporal order disability has sometimes been observed but it remains to be shown whether this in any way causes the language impairment. Cromer (1983) suggested that in children suffering from acquired receptive aphasia (as in the Landau-Klefner syndrome) there may be a primary hierarchical ordering deficit that underlies both linguistic and cognitive disabilities. It is important to make a distinction here between executive and receptive language disorders. The latter group is far less common, and very little systematic research has been carried out with these children. However, clinical experience suggests that children with a purely executive language disorder tend to have near-normal intellectual functioning, whereas children with receptive language disorder have greater impairment in conceptual thought. There is also some evidence from the work of Kahmi *et al.* (1984) that problems of symbolic functioning are more pronounced in children with receptive language problems; they argue that a symbolic representational deficit might explain the receptive language handicap better than the expressive one.

Although studies of cognitive development in children with a developmental language disorder remain relatively limited, it would seem that the lack of spoken language as such is of very little *direct* importance for the development of thought and intelligence. Nevertheless, the severity of the language disorder has some implications for the degree of cognitive impairment. Studies of children with a cleft palate but normal IQ, for example, indicate that those with solely executive problems perform significantly better on tests of categorization and associative reasoning than those with additional language handicaps although there are fewer differences on tests involving rote memory. Children with more fundamental language abnormalities display an underlying symbolic mediation deficiency as well as more learning difficulties (Richman 1980).

Although the relationship between language and cognitive development is still poorly understood, it seems clear that the comprehension of spoken language and the availability of 'inner language' are important because they facilitate conceptual development. In addition, language usage in some medium (be it written, gestural or spoken) is of great indirect importance through its rôle in widening experience. In order to promote optimal development it is necessary to combine active learning experiences with a social context that promotes self confidence and an active interest in seeking to learn (Rutter 1985). In order to minimize the effects of their handicap, the social contexts in which language delayed children are raised may well have to be different from the environment in which normal children flourish. It is essential that they are provided with the *special* environmental conditions that are most likely to foster both language and cognitive development. If this is to be achieved, more precise definition of the deficits and needs of different subgroups of children with developmental language disorders is required. Otherwise merely treating language handicapped children as a homogeneous group is likely to be counter-productive both in terms of intervention and research.

Language and thinking in autistic children
In general, the greater the language impairment the more marked are the associated cognitive problems. Autistic children, who show severe deficits in both their expressive and receptive language, are particularly handicapped in their cognitive development (see Chapter 13). Especially when young, they usually show deficits on cognitive tasks that require 'inner language' skills. Compared with non-autistic controls of similar language level and/or mental age they do significantly worse on tests involving sequencing, abstraction, symbolic or conceptual thought, and memory for *meaningful* material (though not on tests of rote memory). Even when autistic children gain spoken language, cognitive deficits usually remain. They are also very much more handicapped when it comes to dealing with stimuli requiring the processing of emotional or social cues. For example, although they are able to complete many object matching tasks just as well as control children, they are noticeably more handicapped when the stimuli relate to people, and particularly when they involve the interpretation of emotions.

When compared with developmental dysphasic controls autistic children also show much greater deficits in internalized language skills (as assessed by the level of their imaginative play and by their use and understanding of gesture). They show more limitations in their use of existing linguistic skills to communicate; and they have more extensive social abnormalities than dysphasic children.

In summary, autistic children perform much worse than mentally retarded controls or children with a specific language handicap in all areas of socialization, symbolization and communication. Thus, these deficits cannot be explained simply on the basis of generalized retardation, nor by a deficit in language *production*. Instead, the deficits seem to be related to a much more fundamental and pervasive language handicap that extends far beyond spoken language and affects many other aspects of cognitive and communicative functions.

Language and educational attainments

Almost all retrospective and prospective studies indicate that language is intrinsically linked with learning in other spheres. Hence, it is hardly surprising that children with some form of language delay are also more likely to show evidence of other learning disorders. Reading, in particular, requires verbal comprehension and internalized language if the child is to make any sense of the written words presented before him. Thus, children who are delayed in talking are also likely to be delayed in reading since both reflect different aspects of language development. Studies of language and speech disordered children have consistently found a high incidence of learning disorders and educational problems. Children suffering from disorders of speech production tend to show milder problems, particularly in reading, although even in this group of children there are higher rates of educational problems (Hall and Tomblin 1978). In children with more extensive language delays, there is an even greater likelihood of educational problems— especially those associated with reading. Ingram (1963) found that the majority of speech retarded youngsters followed up into ordinary primary schools had difficulties in learning to read. Children with more severe language handicaps requiring special education have also been found to have marked reading difficulties (Griffiths 1969, Morley 1973). Garvey and Gordon (1973) found that almost 50 per cent of children with speech disorders showed associated learning difficulties. Hunter and Lewis (1973) found significant differences in all areas of educational achievement between language disordered children and normal controls over a period of two years. Aram and Nation (1980) in a study of 63 pre-school children with language delay found that 40 per cent had reading problems, 24 per cent had spelling difficulties and 28 per cent were below average in maths when they were followed up four to five years later. De Ajuriaguerra *et al.* (1976) also noted that academic delay seemed to increase significantly as children advanced in age, and several other studies have indicated the persistence of early learning difficulties.

Looked at the other way round, Barkley (1981) found that approximately 60 per cent of children with reading disabilities have associated disorders of language; another 10 to 20 per cent have disorders of sequencing, verbal expression and articulation. Older children with severe reading difficulties frequently have a history of speech delay and many still show language impairment and deficiencies in abstract thinking (Rutter *et al.* 1970a). Furthermore, there is some evidence that amongst groups of children with reading disability those with language impairment

277

may have a worse prognosis (Lytton 1968).

Why language impairment should lead to reading difficulties is unclear. Crookes and Green (1963) noted that even children with pure articulation defects frequently had difficulties in learning to read; in this case the difficulties may stem from problems in perception (learning which letter is which) rather than from problems in learning a written language. Bradley and Bryant (1983) found that poor ability to categorize sounds shown by four- and five-year-old children was significantly related to later poor reading performance. Snowling and Stachhausan (1983), in a small scale study of children with verbal dyspraxia and associated reading and spelling problems, also suggested that the difficulty may be caused by problems in the segmentation of words particularly at the speech sound level. Moore *et al.* (1982) found that reading-disabled children had deficits in extracting meaning from linguistic information, and it may be that children with reading problems would benefit from specific exercises in speaking and listening (Scheerer-Neumann 1981, Fox and Routh 1983). On the whole, studies of the association between reading delay and language development suggest that language processes are more powerful determinants of reading than are visuo-perceptual processes. However, as Yule and Rutter (1985) pointed out, few have studied both processes at the same time.

Although differing to some extent in matching and assessment procedures, studies as far apart as Newcastle (Fundudis *et al.* 1979), Waltham Forest (Richman *et al.* 1982) and New Zealand (Silva *et al.* 1983) all reported highly significant differences between language impaired children and normal controls in levels of later educational attainment. Verbal IQ tends to be signficantly lower in the language handicapped group (with over 50 per cent of children having IQs below 85). Moreover, in all three studies the spelling and reading scores of the language delayed children were much lower than in controls. A recent screening study in Dundee (Drillien and Drummond 1983) reported higher rates of school-related problems in the language delayed group. Sheridan and Peckham (1975) in their follow-up of children involved in the National Child Development Study also found that poor performance on scholastic and achievement tests at the ages of 11 and 16 years was associated with language problems at the age of seven.

Unfortunately, these general population longitudinal studies used categories of language delay that did not differentiate specific developmental disorders of language from global mental handicap. As a result it is not possible to tell how far the children's later educational difficulties were a consequence of their earlier language deficit and how far simply a result of low IQ. The recent 10-year follow-up study of preschoolers with language disorders by Aram *et al.* (1984) is one of the very few to provide data on this point. The investigation was systematic, with standardized assessments both initially and at follow-up; however, there is the limitation that only 20 of the original group of 47 were located. 16 of the 20 had an initial non-verbal IQ of 70 or greater; the 16 had a mean IQ of 96 when first seen (mostly at four to five years of age). At follow-up 10 years later, their mean *WISC* Full Scale IQ was 90, five were in special schools or classes for remedial teaching and 10 were in the lowest decile for scholastic achievement in reading, spelling or mathematics (seven, five and eight respectively in each of these subjects). It might be thought that the poor attainments were mainly due to those with IQs on the borderline just above the mental handicap range; however, that was not so. We reanalyzed the data for the 11 children with an initial IQ of at least 90; five of the 11 were in the lowest decile for at least one of three subjects and three were in the lowest decile in at least two of them. It is clear that there is an increased rate of later educational difficulties even when there is a specific developmental language disorder in children of normal IQ. Perhaps surprisingly, these difficulties were as evident in mathematics as in reading or in spelling.

Nevertheless, the authors' findings on the group as a whole showed that both later IQ and scholastic attainment were much better predicted by the children's initial IQ than by their level of language impairment. Thus, for example, the five children in special schools or classes at follow-up had a mean initial IQ of 83, some 14 points below the mean for the group as a whole. It is evident that the worst educational prognosis applies to children who have the combined handicap of both language delay and low IQ.

Because most children who are late in talking ultimately learn to speak reasonably well, there is a tendency to assume that speech delay is of no consequence in most cases. However, early problems do not 'go away', nor do language delayed children rapidly catch up with their peers. Indeed, the younger the child when problems are first evident, the stronger are the associations with later learning difficulties. Silva *et al.* (1983) found that problems of low IQ and later reading difficulties were greatest in children diagnosed as having language delays by the age of three. They found that 60 per cent of these children had subsequent educational difficulties at the age of seven. Thus, although children may catch up in their speaking, many are left with subtle language handicaps that continue to impede their educational progress. The resulting problems may be pervasive and persistent, and the association between language delay and later reading retardation is particularly strong. Progress in schools relies heavily on the ability to read what is written on the blackboard, or in books, or printed out on the computer screen. Even if spoken language skills eventually seem relatively unimpaired, the inability to interpret written material may lead to continuing difficulties in almost all areas of school work.

Language and play
Although there are associations between play and language, it remains uncertain whether one skill underlies the other or whether both are dependent on the development of other skills, such as mental representation (Fein 1981). In a very early study, Luria and Yudovich (1959) described the play and language development over one year of five-year-old identical twin boys. Initially their language comprehension and expression were extremely limited, and their play was primitive and unimaginative. As their language improved, so did their play activities. Furthermore, imaginative play activities improved most in the twin who received language therapy and whose language showed greatest improvement. Although subsequent studies of early language development in both mentally

retarded and normal children have tended to show that particular phases in the development of symbolic play and language tend to occur together (McCune-Nicolich 1981, Casby and Ruder 1983), the relationship is not necessarily a simple one. For example, Hulme and Lunzer (1966) compared the play of normal and retarded children matched for mental age, and found no significant differences even though the retarded children showed deficits in language skills. Kamhi (1981), on the other hand, found that when children were matched for *mental age* the language impaired group were significantly impaired in their symbolic play. They were also deficient in comparison with their same age peers. But when matched for *language level*, the linguistically handicapped group actually showed higher levels of spontaneous play than normal children without language delay—a finding also replicated by Terrel *et al.* (1984). The age of the children concerned also seems to affect the relationship, with the correlation between play and language being apparently higher in younger children. Bates *et al.* (1975) found that between nine and 13 months, symbolic play measures were the best predictors of language development. Rosenblatt (1980) found a significant relationship between advanced language development and representational play in 12 to 24-month-old children. However, by 28 months the correlation between play and language development tends to be less marked (Fein 1981). It is uncertain whether the association becomes attenuated with time, or whether the results found in the younger groups are an artefact of the measures used. After all, the complexity of language skills in 12-month-old infants is much less than in 28-month-old toddlers, and the lack of reported association between play and language at later ages might well be due to the inadequacy of the measures used.

There are further questions about the methods of assessing play that may affect the interpretation of results. Thus, different types of symbolic play may be related to different aspects of language development. Fenson and Ramsay (1980) argued that the use of standard sets of equipment to elicit play and language samples provides better measures of combinatorial ability than do assessments of spontaneous play. However, there are no substantial comparative studies in this area, and Largo and Howard (1979) suggested that structured play settings may restrict both language usage and representational play.

The way in which language development is assessed is also important in the interpretation of comparative studies. Vygotsky (1978) stressed the relationship between cognitive development and internalized (rather than spoken) language. On this basis one would expect to find higher correlations between receptive language and play than between expressive language and play and in fact this tends to be the case (Fein 1981). Deaf children's play tends to be much more closely correlated with their levels of language comprehension than with their expressive language, and children with receptive language disorders often show much greater limitations in their play abilities than do children with executive language delays. Autistic children, who suffer from impairments of both expressive and receptive language, are usually the most severely handicapped of all. Young autistic children, even those with normal non-verbal intelligence, rarely show symbolic play; and their play patterns tend to be even more restricted than their scores on language tests would lead one to predict (Sigman *et al.* 1985). However, even amongst autistic children there is some correlation between the severity of the language handicap and the levels of their play. Howlin (1979) found that autistic children who showed no functional use of objects showed very limited use and understanding of language. Sigman *et al.* (1985) also found that autistic children with higher levels of language ability demonstrated more complex play activities than children with lower levels of language ability. Over-all, compared with normal children of the same mental age (not language age) autistic children engaged far less in symbolic and functional play than controls. Their involvement in doll play was much less and they rarely sought to involve adults in their play activities. They did not show significantly *less* play: it was *how* they played that was so different.

Although play and language are clearly related, both in normal and in handicapped children, there is little convincing evidence that pretend play either develops concurrently with language development, or is a prerequisite for or a consequence of it. Watson and Fischer (1977) noted that precise correspondence is unlikely to be found, since development does not proceed equally across different domains. A number of reports have suggested that treatment designed to increase symbolic play results in improved language development although work in this area is still inconclusive. There are many studies relating imaginative play ability to general adjustment, sociability and popularity with peers (Fein 1981). The child who cannot participate in group and pretend games is at a disadvantage in making social contacts. Make-believe play also serves many other functions; it provides a means of exploring feelings, lessening fears, and increasing excitement. Imaginal processes also seem to be important in helping children to understand and cope with novel events in real life (Sherrod and Singer 1977, Fein 1981). However, although improvements in play patterns may aid cognitive, social and emotional development, the effects on language development remain unclear.

Social, emotional and behavioural development

The high rates of persisting social, emotional and behavioural problems in children attending clinics or special schools for language handicapped has been recognized for some time (Myklebust 1954, Griffiths 1969, Garvey and Gordon 1973, Petrie 1975, Lindholm and Touliatis 1979). Paul *et al.* (1983) found a whole range of psychiatric problems in a longitudinal study of 28 children with severe developmental disorders of language. 61 per cent of children showed disturbances of attention, activity and motor skills, and a similar proportion showed some evidence of EEG abnormalities. They also found that 50 per cent of the group showed some evidence of autistic features. Progress in both language and behaviour was generally poor. Only 2 per cent were described as having near normal language at follow-up, and behaviour problems also tended to persist. One of the best predictors of language progress was the child's initial non-verbal IQ level (Paul and Cohen 1984). Social development did not predict language outcome, although in the group of children with relatively good comprehension skills social behaviour tended to improve with time. On the other hand, when receptive language skills are severely impaired, social abnormalities may sometimes become more prominent as the children grow older (Cantwell *et al.* 1987).

Cantwell and Baker (1977) recorded a 50 per cent rate of psychiatric disorder (as measured by teacher and parent questionnaires) in a sample of 600 children attending a language clinic; and in addition 21 per cent had learning or other developmental disorders (such as enuresis, encopresis or mental retardation). Moreover, a comparison of children who had· no psychiatric disorder with those who did, revealed that speech and language problems were amongst the most significant features to distinguish between the groups.

Children attending schools for the deaf are also known to have higher rates of social and behavioural disturbance than normally hearing children. Amongst the particular problems reported are higher rates of emotional and conduct disorders, personality problems, immaturity and feelings of inadequacy and inferiority (Rutter *et al.* 1970*a*, Schlesinger and Meadow 1972, Hirshoren and Schmittjer 1979). Deaf children transferred to normal schools also tend to have persistently higher rates of problems.

Social and behavioural problems are particularly pronounced in autistic children. Disruptive behaviours such as aggression and temper tantrums are very common; there is a failure to develop normal attachments, and there are gross deficits in empathy and in forming reciprocal relationships.

It could be argued that language handicapped children already attending special schools or clinics would be expected to show higher rates of disturbance than children in the general population. Thus, the reported rates of disturbance in this group might well overestimate the frequency of problems in children with lesser degrees of language impairment. However, screening studies in the general population also indicate much higher rates of disturbance in children with language delay than in normal controls. Follow-up studies of preschool children in Newcastle (Fundudis *et al.* 1979), Dundee (Drillien and Drummon, 1983), London (Richman *et al.* 1982) and New Zealand (Silva *et al.* 1983) have consistently found significantly more behavioural and educational disorders in children identified as having a language delay. These difficulties tend to persist into later childhood and at the age of seven to eight years behavioural disturbance is still considerably higher than in the general population. Moreover even when language delayed children were matched with controls for their behaviour at the age of three, still they showed much higher rates of emotional disturbance at eight (Stevenson *et al.* 1985). In other words, the presence of a language delay at three predisposed to the later development of emotional difficulties. This was most evident for children with poor language structure (perhaps leading to limitations in the ability to formulate ideas and thoughts into words) rather than for those with just a limited vocabulary. The National Child Development Study also found that over 50 per cent of children identified as having language problems at the age of seven years, still demonstrated residual language problems, learning, social and educational difficulties at the age of 16 (Sheridan and Peckham 1975). Stevenson (1984) found that, by the age of six or seven, only 14 per cent of children earlier identified as having language problems did *not* have either low IQ, reading backwardness or disturbed behaviour and he concluded that such children 'are at risk of having one or other of these problems during the later part of their infant schooling'.

The association between speech or language problems and emotional/behavioural disturbance is also evident in general population studies of children with psychiatric disorder (Rutter *et al.* 1970*b*). The association is apparent, too, in groups of children all of whom have some type of neuro-epileptic disorder (Rutter *et al.* 1970*a*).

Although the risk of additional difficulties is considerably raised in children with language problems, the types of behavioural disturbance shown tend to be nonspecific. A whole range of difficulties has been noted, from thumb-sucking to cruelty (Baker *et al.* 1980) and there does not seem to be any specific clinical syndrome. Nevertheless, language delay is often associated with socially withdrawn behaviour (Fundis *et al.* 1979) and observational studies indicate that language retarded children differ from normal children in making fewer social initiations (Siegel *et al.* 1985). Children with global language delays tend to show more hyperactive behaviour and developmental problems than children with executive speech disorders (Baker *et al.* 1980). Somatic complaints are more common in the group with expressive difficulties, but conduct disorders, emotional problems and poor relationships do not distinguish between the groups. Silva *et al.* (1983) found that behavioural and educational problems were frequent in language-disordered children of all levels of intelligence, but the rate was higher in those with an IQ below 90.

On the whole, children with speech impediments show less social and behavioural disturbance than children with more fundamental language deficits. Yet, even children with relatively mild speech defects tend to show higher rates of fears, anxieties, and problems in making friends than do controls (Baker *et al.* 1980). Hall and Tomblin (1978) in a 13- to 20-year follow-up of language impaired and articulation disordered children found that 50 per cent of the language impaired group still showed marked communication problems. Only one out of the 18 articulation impaired children did so. Petrie (1975) found that levels of language ability were closely associated with later social adjustment and progress in communication skills. Cantwell and Baker (1977) in a review of similar studies also concluded that children with global language disorders are more likely to have psychiatric disturbance than children with executive speech difficulties.

There is some evidence that children with *receptive* language difficulties are more prone to psychiatric disturbance than children with expressive delays. Wing (1969) found that most children with developmental receptive language disorders had at some time shown quite severe impairments in social relationships (often of an autistic type). This was true of only a minority of children with expressive problems. Rutter *et al.* (1971) found that by the age of five to seven years few children with receptive disorders were showing autistic features but an appreciable minority showed impaired personal relationships when younger and in some cases the children had shown a syndrome indistinguishable from infantile autism.

The relationship between the extent of the language handicap and the severity of accompanying social and behavioural problems is perhaps best illustrated in the case of autistic children. Although children with receptive language disorders have defects in both the understanding and use of language, they are usually able to communicate in other ways (*i.e.* by gesture, mime and facial expression), and internal language (as demonstrated by imaginative play) is relatively unimpaired. In contrast, autistic children are severely handicapped in all aspects of communication and imaginative skills. The development of autism is associated with a very severe and extensive language disorder. However, it is probably misleading to suggest that the autistic symptoms are 'due to' the impaired language development. Abnormalities in both language and non-verbal skills are probably better explained by an underlying cognitive deficit that particularly affects socialization and communication (Rutter 1983).

In summary, it seems that children with impaired speech or language development show a considerably increased risk of developing other social and emotional problems. This risk is greater when there is a language deficit than when there is only an articulation abnormality, and it is greatest of all when receptive language is severely affected. However, there is considerable individual variation, and some individuals with severe impairments may make a fair social adjustment and hold a steady job (Griffiths 1969). Some studies have found only weak relationships between the severity of language disorder and the frequency of emotional problems (Lewis 1968). Work with deaf children also indicates that personality characteristics are very important, with confident, self-sufficient children being most likely to make a good social and educational adjustment. More detailed knowledge is needed on the characteristics that protect children against the undoubted stresses engendered by severe communication problems.

The type of educational treatment that such children receive and the general environment to which they are exposed may affect outcome. Studies of mainstreaming children with learning or language problems indicate that integration into a normal classroom is not always educationally or socially desirable. On the whole, children with very mild impairments are most easily accepted into normal schools, but those with more pronounced difficulties tend to suffer a degree of isolation, or even rejection. Mainstreaming does not automatically bring about improved academic or social development and studies of the transfer of deaf and language retarded children to normal schools have suggested that some, who were previously making good progress, may suffer many setbacks following the transfer and do far less well than predicted from their earlier progress (Howlin 1985).

Other studies of the environment in which deaf or severely language-delayed children are raised, suggest that a 'normal' environment may not be sufficient to ensure optimal development. We have already mentioned the more sophisticated social and communicative skills of deaf children raised by hearing parents (Meadow *et al.* 1983). Restructuring the verbal environment of autistic children, so that children receive more specific prompting and guidance to encourage speech, also seems to lead to improved communication skills (Howlin and Rutter 1987). Clearly one would not want to deprive deaf or other linguistically handicapped groups of children from the opportunity to lead as normal a life as possible. The arguments for and against segregation are still highly inconclusive (Howlin 1985). However, it is clear that simply placing such children in normal schools, or instructing parents to treat them 'as if they were normal', is not sufficient to overcome their inherent problems. The question perhaps is not *whether* such children should be integrated, but *how* and *when* to offer them the types of education and environments that are best able to overcome their handicaps.

Language delay and later psychosis
The literature includes a variety of rather contradictory claims on possible linkages between language delay in early childhood and the development of psychotic conditions in early adult life. Most systematic follow-up studies of well diagnosed groups of children with infantile autism have not observed the development of schizophrenia (Rutter 1970, Lotter 1978); however, there are isolated reports of schizophrenia arising in a few autistic children (Howells and Guirguis 1984, Petty *et al.* 1984). Also, Wing (1981) has noted that a few adults with Asperger's syndrome (usually thought to be a mild variety of autism) have had psychotic episodes. The interpretation of these reports is complicated by uncertainties on the criteria used to diagnose both autism and schizophrenia. Our own experience indicated that, when the two conditions are diagnosed by generally accepted criteria, it is decidedly unusual for them to be associated. However, it is well recognized that some cases of schizophrenia *are* preceded by developmental problems, although typically not specifically in language alone (Rutter and Garmezy 1983). Moreover, there are undoubted cases of children with developmental disorders of language who show schizophrenic-like psychoses in early adulthood. The diagnostic dilemma arises from doubts as to how to classify both the developmental problems in childhood and the adult psychosis.

A recent report by Lewis and Mezey (1985) provides the first lead regarding the delineation of a possibly distinctive diagnostic subgroup. They described six cases with a cavum septum pellucidum identified in a large series of CAT scans (computerized axial tomography) and noted that they showed an unusual combination of developmental abnormalities (including language delay) in early childhood and the emergence of a paranoid psychosis in late adolescence or early adulthood. The association with a cavum septum pellucidum is puzzling in that it is difficult to imagine why such an apparently innocuous abnormality should have such major consequences for language and behaviour. Nevertheless, the only case with the clinical picture described by Lewis and Mezey that we have encountered since their paper was published showed the identical (rare) CAT scan abnormality. It is clear that further investigation of the association is required.

The relationship between language disorders and educational, psychological and behavioural problems: underlying mechanisms
If the psychological and behavioural difficulties related to language delays are to be minimized, it is necessary to examine some of the possible reasons why language retarded children have a raised rate of associated difficulties. The language disorder may be caused by a psychatric or educational problem; alternatively the language difficulties may lead to psychiatric and educational problems, or all may share an underlying cause.

Despite the strong association between psychiatric disturbance and language delay there is little evidence that mental disorders are a common cause of speech or language retardation. Conditions such as schizophrenia and elective mutism may affect the child's production of speech in certain circumstances, or affect speech content, but there is little evidence that they cause language retardation (Cantwell and Baker 1977). Similarly, there is no good evidence that language difficulties arise as a result of educational problems and indeed, in most cases the language handicap is evident long before other deficits become apparent.

The argument that common antecedents may explain both language and associated problems has been reviewed by Cantwell and Baker (1977). Low IQ is probably the most significant factor associated with psychiatric disturbance, learning difficulties and language delay. Hearing loss and brain damage may also be associated with a combination of linguistic, educational and behaviour problems. The mechanisms that actually cause the disturbances, however, are poorly understood. In the case of brain damaged children there is evidence that brain dysfunction can cause problems of linguistic and cognitive development as well as affecting behaviour. Such abnormalities may also be associated with temperamental differences, making the child less resilient and more susceptible to the usual stresses of growing up. Additional problems, such as hyperactivity and short attention span, may predispose the child to behavioural disorders.

It is possible that the underlying deficits that result in the language and learning delays may also affect the child's ability to form successful peer relationships. In such cases, the language impairment may be important only through its association with a more general defect in brain functioning. But this mechanism probably accounts for only a small minority of the psychological difficulties shown by children with language disorder. The development of behaviour problems is not a necessary result of language delay. Deaf children, for example, frequently show problems of self-adjustment, immaturity and self-confidence, but the extent of these problems can be considerably reduced by appropriate schooling.

Family factors, too, are relevant. Large families and low socio-economic status are associated with low verbal IQ, poor reading skills and conduct disorders. Cantwell and Baker (1977) suggested that the association of large family size with antisocial behaviour is probably mediated through the effects on language, verbal IQ and reading. Thus, the factors that are associated with large family size may well result, at least in some cases, in both a delay in language acquisition and behavioural disturbance. Low social status would seem to be important only in so far as it is associated with other pathogenic factors, such as low IQ, family disorder and family disruption.

Finally, the effects of severe psychosocial deprivation have been noted as a possible cause of social, cognitive and language impairment and certainly there is evidence that in some cases rapid improvements may occur once the previously restrictive or punitive environmental conditions are removed (Skuse 1984). However, in other cases changing the environment does not result in marked improvements. It is possible that those children who did not recover were already suffering from an intrinsic disorder which, although aggravated by severely deleterious conditions of raising, was not primarily caused by them. Cantwell and Baker (1985) concluded that adverse environmental influences may be responsible for some cases of language delay accompanied by behavioural disturbance but that this was not the usual explanation.

The third possibility, that language delay in itself causes psychiatric disturbance and learning difficulties, has recently been the subject of some debate, although (as with the two previous hypotheses) there is still very little in the way of conclusive research evidence. However, there are several ways in which language disturbance may lead directly to psychiatric problems.

First, the failure to develop normal language skills may well have a detrimental effect on parent-child interactions. Evidence from studies of mother–child interaction show that the characteristics of the child may have a marked effect on the nature of family interactions as well as on the child's own response to family stress. It may be that difficulties in communication sometimes evoke disturbed patterns of parent–child interaction and these may contribute in turn to the emotional difficulties shown by the child.

Secondly, it is well established that children with oddities of any kind tend to be particularly prone to rejection by their peers (Corman and Gottlieb 1978), and the child with a language disability is almost certain to be at a disadvantage when it comes to social interaction. Difficulties in early social relationships tend to be one of the most powerful predictors of later emotional disturbance. If speech or language difficulties lead to problems in communication they are also likely to lead to serious problems in developing friendships. It is apparent, too, from studies of successful peer interaction that it is the integration of language and other social skills that is crucial for acceptance by peers. Accordingly, it is possible that although gross language problems may be overcome with time, more subtle aspects of development, particularly the meshing of language with other skills, may remain impaired. It is hardly surprising, therefore, that many children with early language problems show marked behavioural and emotional difficulties, and that these tend to increase rather than decrease as they grow older (Goodman *et al.* 1972).

Thirdly, the problems in symbolic play that are also associated with abnormal language development may reduce the child's ability to join in group games. Since such activities are very important in the development of social relationships any child who is unable to participate fully in make-believe games is likely to be at a great disadvantage when it comes to forming relationships. An impairment in the development of symbolic thinking and make-believe play may also contribute to the development of psychiatric disorder in other ways. It is evident (Rosenblatt 1980) that make-believe play serves several functions—among them exploring feelings, lessening fears, and the rehearsing and developing of social skills. Any child in whom these functions are noticeably impaired may be more prone to the development of emotional problems.

Fourthly, experimental studies of the association between language and behaviour suggest that language is important in inhibiting inappropriate actions and promoting adaptive ones (Luria 1961, Tinsley and Waters 1982, Balamore and

Wozniak 1984). If this ability to control actions by verbal mediation is lacking, then the child may well be at greater risk of behavioural disturbance.

The final way in which language delay may lead to later emotional disturbance has to do with the now well-established relationship between language difficulties and problems in learning to read. Extensive epidemiological studies have demonstrated a strong association between reading retardation and the development of antisocial behaviour in childhood. 30 per cent of children with antisocial behaviour have pre-existing reading problems, and one third of children with serious reading disability have marked antisocial behaviour. Yule and Rutter (1985) concluded that there is no single explanation for the association between reading retardation and psychiatric disorder. For many children, the fact that they are identified as being 'different' from their peers, even if the handicap is relatively mild, means that they are likely to be perceived as less socially acceptable and as academically inferior both by their teachers and their peers (Bradfield *et al.* 1973, Meyers *et al.* 1975). Thus, school failure may lead to rejection by peers, low self-esteem and hence to conduct problems. Moreover, the inability to deal with written material not only leads to the child falling behind in almost all areas of school work, it is also likely to mean that for much of the school day he is under-occupied, and thus more likely to resort to inappropriate and off-task behaviours. But, again it is possible that in many cases temperamental characteristics, such as overactivity, may underlie the children's reading problems and their predisposition to anti-social behaviours. Richman *et al.* (1982) argued strongly for a common antecedent that underlies both the learning and the behavioural problems, and if the hypothesized underlying mechanisms were also responsible for language problems, this might well explain the association between the three conditions.

In summary, there are a number of ways in which the language deficit (or the impairments to which they are related) may lead to emotional or behavioural impairment. The mechanisms involved are poorly understood, but it seems that the more severe the language impairment the greater the risk of associated cognitive problems. This is most obvious in children with autism or severe developmental language disorders, and in such children the underlying cognitive impairment may well be responsible for the related deficits in socio-emotional processing as well as language development. In children with less severe impairments of 'internal' language different mechanisms may be implicated. For all children, the use and understanding of language is important through its role in widening experience. If linguistic input is restricted, as it is in the case of deaf and language delayed children, then this is likely to lead to further deficits in learning and cognitive development. And, as the child grows older, impairments in symbolic development are likely to affect both social and emotional functioning as well as cognitive skills. The inability to cope adequately with written information may restrict cognitive development even further. Since children with pure articulation difficulties are also at risk of developing problems in reading and associated skills it is hardly surprising to find additional cognitive impairments even amongst this relatively mildly handicapped group.

Children with difficulties in communication are likely to suffer disturbances in mother–child relationships and in peer interactions. This in turn may lead to the disruption of normal emotional and social development as well as further limiting the child's experience.

Self-image, too, is likely to be affected by impairments in language. Children's behaviour is much influenced by their self-image and when they see themselves as capable, self-sufficient and popular, they are more likely to behave in ways that fulfil that self-expectation. If parents are unduly distressed, rejecting or over-protective because of the child's handicap, the child's self-confidence will tend to be adversely affected. Rejection by peers is likely to reduce self-confidence even more, and although this may be most marked in children with severe language delays, even children with relatively mild executive disorders may be affected in this way.

Finally, the rôle of associated temperamental difficulties needs to be taken into account. Characteristics such as overactivity, impusiveness and poor concentration tend to cluster together, and may affect the ability to profit from normal social and teaching experiences as well as affecting relationships with parents and other children.

Implications for treatment

The association between language delay and many other impairments of functioning is well demonstrated. It is also clear that these problems do not go away, nor do children 'grow out of them'. Early problems in learning to talk are related not only to later language problems but also to difficulties in emotional and social development and in cognitive and educational attainments. Given that language problems are so closely interwoven with other difficulties, the need seems to be for widely based remedial programmes if associated emotional, behavioural and educational difficulties are to be avoided. Thus, rather than treating delayed speech as if it were a single deficit, it should be considered as one manifestation of a developmental disorder with widespread complex developmental and behavioural implications.

Home intervention programmes that help parents to structure the child's environment in such a way as to encourage communication, and to motivate the child to use inherent language capabilities, may well be more appropriate than highly specific language training programmes. Parents also need to be given appropriate information and advice about the prognosis and possible ways of alleviating the problems associated with language delay.

In schools, lack of knowledge about the sequelae of language delay may result in children receiving inadequate and inappropriate education as they grow older. Teachers need to be more aware of the possible social, emotional and behavioural problems likely to be faced by such children. If teaching can be geared to the 'special' child's particular needs the outcome, both in terms of linguistic, social and educational adjustment, may be much more positive. However, it is apparent that successful integration is most likely to occur only if there are few perceived differences, both behaviourally and intellectually, between learning disabled children and their peers. If children are not to be singled out as being 'different', it is essential that the classroom situation should be structured so as to minimize these disadvantages.

Finally, in order to arrive at a better understanding of potential ways of dealing with language disorder, we need more precise categorization of the different types of language handicap and the different problems they bring in their wake. Instead of becoming embroiled in controversies about the advantages of different therapeutic or educational strategies, we must create an environment that is best suited to reduce early communication difficulties as far as possible.

Avoidance of early communication problems may well reduce the risk of later behavioural and emotional difficulties. Nevertheless, it is important to be aware that the nature of the relationship between language, cognitive, behavioural and emotional development is poorly understood. There may be causal associations between these different areas of functioning but, if there are, the nature of the association clearly varies for different children and at different stages in development. There may also be an underlying deficit that affects performance in all these areas, hence treatment in one domain may have only limited effects on development in others. Our knowledge so far is enough to warn us that problems are very likely to occur in several of these associated domains. Awareness of a child's vulnerability to social, emotional and educational difficulties is not, in itself, enough to ensure that these problems are avoided or overcome. However, it may make teachers, parents and other professionals more sensitive to the needs of these children. Hopefully, too, it may inspire more effective research into the types of strategies required to alleviate language delay and its associated problems.

REFERENCES

Aram, D., Nation, J. (1980) 'Pre-school language disorders and subsequent language and academic difficulties.' *Journal of Communication Disorders,* **13,** 159–198.
—— Ekelman, B., Nation, J. (1984) 'Pre-schoolers with language disorders 10 years later.' *Journal of Speech and Hearing Research,* **27,** 232–244.
Au, T. (1983) 'Chinese and English counterfactuals: the Sapir Whorf hypothesis revisited.' *Cognition,* **15,** 155–187.
Baker, L., Cantwell, D., Mattison, R. (1980) 'Behavior problems in children with pure speech disorders and in children with combined speech and language disorders.' *Journal of Abnormal Child Psychology,* **8,** 245–250.
Balamore, U., Wozniak, R. (1984) 'Speech-action coordination in young children.' *Developmental Psychology,* **20,** 850–858.
Barkley, R. (1981) 'Learning disabilities.' *In:* Mash, E. Terdal, L. (Eds.) *Behavioral Assessment of Childhood Disorders.* New York: Guildford Press. pp. 441–482.
Bates, E., Camaioni, L., Volterra, V. (1975) 'The acquisition of performatives prior to speech.' *Merrill Palmer Quarterly,* **21,** 205–266.
Bishop, D. V. M. (1979) 'Comprehension in developmental language disorders.' *Developmental Medicine and Child Neurology,* **21,** 225–238.
Bloom, A. (1981) *The Linguistic Shaping of Thought: A Study in the Impact of Language on Thinking in China and the West.* Hillsdale: Erlbaum.
Bradfield, H., Brown, J., Kaplan, P., Rickjert, E., Stannard, R. (1973) 'The special child in the regular classroom.' *Exceptional Children,* **39,** 384–390.
Bradley, L., Bryant, P. (1983) 'Categorizing sounds and learning to read—a causal connection.' *Nature,* **301,** 419–421.
Brown, R. (1976) 'Reference—in Memorial Tribute to Eric Lenneberg.' *Cognition,* **4,** 125–153.
Caccamise, F., Hatfield, N., Brewer, L. (1978) 'Manual simultaneous communication research: results and implications.' *American Annals of the Deaf,* **123,** 803–823.

Cantwell, D., Baker, L. (1977) 'Psychiatric disorder in children with speech and language retardation: a critical review.' *Archives of General Psychiatry,* **34,** 583–591.

—— —— (1985) 'Speech and language: development and disorders.' *In:* Rutter, M., Hersov, L. (Eds.) *Child and Adolescent Psychiatry 2nd edn.* Oxford: Blackwell. pp. 526–543.

—— —— Rutter, M., Mawhood, L. (1987) 'A comparative follow-up study of infantile autism and developmental receptive dysphasia.' *(submitted for publication).*

Casby, M., Ruder, K. (1983) 'Symbolic play and early language development in normal and mentally retarded children.' *Journal of Speech and Hearing Research,* **26,** 404–411.

Conrad, R. (1979) *The Deaf School Child.* London: Harper & Row.

Corman, L., Gottlieb, J. (1978) 'Mainstreaming mentally retarded children: a review of research.' *In:* Ellis, N. R. (Ed.) *International Review of Research in Mental Retardation, Vol. 9.* New York: Academic Press.

Cromer, R. (1978) 'Hierarchical disability in the syntax of aphasic children.' *International Journal of Behavioural Development,* **1,** 391–402.

—— (1981) 'Reconceptualizing language acquisition and cognitive development.' *In:* Schiefelbusch, R., Bricker, D. (Eds.) *Early Language Acquisition and Intervention.* Baltimore: University Park Press. pp. 51–138.

—— (1983) 'Hierarchical planning disability in the drawings and constructions of a special group of severely aphasic children.' *Brain and Cognition,* **2,** 144–164.

Crookes, T., Green, M. (1963) 'Some characteristics of children with two types of speech disorder. *British Journal of Educational Psychology,* **33,** 31–37.

De Ajuriaguerra, J., Jaeggi, A., Gulgnard, F., Kocher, F., Maquard, M., Roth, S., Schmid, E. (1976) 'The development and prognosis of dysphasia in children.' *In:* Morehead, D., Morehead, A. (Eds.) *Normal and Deficient Child Language.* Baltimore: University Park Press. pp. 345–385.

de Zwart, S. H. (1973) 'Language acquisition and cognitive development.' *In:* Moore, T. E. (Ed.) *Cognitive Development and the Acquisition of Language.* New York: Academic Press. pp. 9–25.

Drillien, C., Drummond, M. (1983) *Developmental Screening and the Child with Special Needs. Clinics in Developmental Medicine No. 86.* London: S.I.M.P. with Heinemann.

Eisenson, J. (1968) 'Developmental aphasia (dyslogia). A postulation of a unitary concept in the disorder.' *Cortex,* **4,** 184–200.

Fein, G. (1981) 'Pretend play in childhood. An integrative review.' *Child Development,* **52,** 1095–1118.

Fenson, L., Ramsay, (1980) 'Decentration and integration of play in the second year of life.' *Child Development,* **51,** 171–178.

Fox, B., Routh, D. (1983) 'Reading disability, phonemic analysis and dysphonetic spelling: a follow-up study.' *Journal of Clinical Child Psychology,* **12,** 28–32.

Fundudis, T., Kolvin, I., Garside, R. (Eds.) (1979) *Speech Retarded and Deaf Children: Their Psychological Development.* London: Academic Press.

Furth, H. G. (1966) *Thinking Without Language: Psychological Implications of Deafness.* New York: Free Press.

—— Youniss, J. (1976) 'Formal operations: a comparison of deaf and hearing adolescents.' Morehead, M. D., Morehead, A. (Eds.) *Normal and Deficient Child Language.* Baltimore: University Park Press.

Garvey, M., Gordon, N. (1973) 'A follow-up study of children with disorders of speech development.' *British Journal of Disorders of Communication,* **8,** 17–28.

Geers, A., Moog, J., Schick, B. (1984) 'Acquisition of spoken and signed English by profoundly deaf children.' *Journal of Speech and Hearing Disorders,* **49,** 378–388.

Goodman, H. (1982) 'On thoughts without words.' *Cognition,* **12,** 211–217.

—— Gottlieb, J., Harrison, I. (1972) 'Social acceptance of E.M.R's integrated into a non-graded elementary school.' *American Journal of Mental Deficiency,* **76,** 412–417.

Graham, N. (1974) 'Response strategies in the partial comprehension of sentences. *Language and Speech,* **17,** 205–221.

Griffiths, C. (1969) 'A follow-up study of children with disorders of speech.' *British Journal of Disorders of Communication,* **4,** 46–56.

Hall, P., Tomblin, J. (1978) A follow-up study of children with articulation and language disorders. *Journal of Speech and Hearing Disorders,* **43,** 227–241.

Hirshoren, A., Schmittjer, C. (1979) 'Dimensions of problem behavior in deaf children.' *Journal of Abnormal Child Psychology,* **7,** 221–228.

Hitch, G. (1978) 'Developing the concept of working memory.' *In:* Claxton, G. (Ed.) *Cognitive Psychology.* London: Routledge & Kegan-Paul. pp. 154–196.

Hockett, C. (1954) 'Chinese versus English: an exploration of the Whorfian theses'. *In:* Hoijer, H. (Ed.)

Language in Culture. Chicago: University of Chicago Press.

Howells, J. G., Guirguis, W. R. (1984) 'Childhood schizophrenia 20 years later.' *Archives of General Psychiatry,* **41,** 123–128.

Howlin, P. (1979) *Training Parents to Modify the Language of Their Autistic Children: A Home-Based Approach.* Unpublished PhD. Thesis, London University.

—— (1984) 'The acquisition of grammatical morphemes in autistic children: a critique and replication of the findings of Bartolucci, Pierce and Streiner 1980.' *Journal of Autism and Developmental Disorders,* **14,** 127–136.

—— (1985) 'Special educational treatment.' *In:* Rutter, M., Hersov, L. (Eds.) *Child & Adolescent Psychiatry, 2nd edn.* Oxford: Blackwell Scientific. pp. 851–870.

—— Rutter, M. (1987) 'Mothers' speech to autistic children: a preliminary causal analysis.' *Journal of Child Psychology and Psychiatry (in press).*

Hulme, I., Lunzer, E. A. (1966) 'Play, language and reasoning in subnormal children.' *Journal of Child Psychology and Psychiatry,* **7,** 107–124.

Hunter, E., Lewis, H. (1973) 'The dyslexic child—2 years later.' *Journal of Psychology,* **83,** 163–170.

Ingram, T. (1963) 'Delayed development of speech with special reference to dyslexia.' 'The association of speech retardation and educational difficulties.' *Proceedings of the Royal Society of Medicine,* **56,** 199–203.

Ivemey, G., Lachterman, D. (1980) 'The written language of young English deaf children.' *Language and Speech,* **23,** 351–375.

Kahmi, A. (1981) 'Non-linguistic symbolic and conceptual abilities in language impaired and normally developing children.' *Journal of Speech and Hearing Research,* **24,** 446–453.

—— Catts, H., Koenig, L., Lewis, B. (1984) 'Hypothesis testing and non-linguistic symbolic abilities in language impaired children.' *Journal of Speech and Hearing Disorders,* **49,** 169–176.

Karmiloff-Smith, A. (1978) 'The interplay between syntax, semantics and phonology in language acquisition processes.' *In:* Campbell, R. N., Smith, P. T. (Eds.) *Recent Advances in the Psychology of Language: Language Development and Mother-Child Interaction.* New York: Plenum. pp. 1–23.

Largo, R., Howard, J. (1979) 'Developmental progression in play. Behaviour of children between nine and thirty months. I: Spontaneous play and imitation.' *Developmental Medicine and Child Neurology,* **21,** 299–310.

Lewis, M. (1968) *Language and Personality in Deaf Children.* Slough: NFER.

—— Mezey, G. (1985) 'Clinical correlates of septum pellucidum cavities; an unusual association with psychosis.' *Psychological Medicine,* **15,** 43–54.

Lindholm, B., Touliatis, J. (1979) 'Behavior problems of children in regular classes and those diagnosed as requiring speech therapy.' *Perceptual and Motor Skills,* **49,** 459–463.

Lotter, V. (1978) 'Follow-up studies.' *In:* Rutter, M., Schopler, E. (Eds.) *Autism: A Reappraisal of Concepts and Treatment.* New York: Plenum. pp. 475–495.

Luria, A. (1957) 'The role of language in the formation of temporary connections.' *In:* Simon, B. (Ed.) *Psychology in the Soviet Union.* London: Routledge & Kegan-Paul.

—— (1961) *The Role of Speech in the Regulation of Normal and Abnormal Behaviour.* Oxford: Pergamon.

—— Yudovich, F. (1959) *Speech and The Development of Mental Processes in The Child.* London: Staples Press.

Lytton, H. (1968) 'Some psychological and sociological characteristics of "good" and "poor" achievers (boys) in remedial reading groups: clinical case studies.' *Human Development,* **11,** 260–276.

McCune-Nicolich, L. (1981) 'Toward symbolic functioning: structure of early pretend games and potential parallels with language.' *Child Development,* **52,** 785–797.

McKirdy, L., Blank, M. (1982) 'Dialogue in deaf and hearing pre-schoolers.' *Journal of Speech and Hearing Research,* **25,** 487–499.

Meadow, K., Greenberg, M., Erting, C. (1983) 'Attachment behavior of deaf children with deaf parents.' *Journal of the American Academy of Child Psychiatry,* **22,** 23–28.

Menyuk, P. (1969) *Sentences Children Use. Research Monograph, No. 52.* Cambridge Mass: MIT Press.

Meyers, C., MacMillan, D., Yoshida, R. (1975) *Correlates of Success in Transition of M. R. to Regular Class.* US Department of Health Education and Welfare Pomona, California.

Moore, M., Kagan, S., Sahl, M., Grant, S. (1982) 'Cognitive Profiles in Reading Disability.' *Genetic Psychology Monographs,* **105,** 41–93.

Morehead, D. M., Ingram, I. (1973) 'The development of base syntax in normal and linguistically deviant children.' *Journal of Speech and Hearing Research,* **16,** 330–352.

—— Morehead, A. M. (Eds.) (1976) *Normal and Deficient Child Language.* Baltimore: University Park Press.

292

Morley, M. (1973) 'Receptive/expressive developmental aphasia.' *British Journal of Disorders of Communication*, **8**, 47–53.

Mykelbust, H. R. (1954) *Auditory Disorders in Children*. New York: Grune & Stratton.

O'Connor, N., Hermelin, B. (1978) *Seeing and Hearing and Space and Time:* London: Academic Press. pp. 307–318.

Paul, R., Cohen, D. (1984) 'Outcomes of severe disorders of language acquisition.' *Journal of Autism and Developmental Disorders*, **14**, 405–422.

—— —— Caparulo, B. (1983) 'A longitudinal study of patients with severe developmental disorders of language learning.' *Journal of the American Academy of Child Psychiatry*, **22**, 525–534.

Petrie, I. (1975) 'Characteristics and progress of a group of language disorder children with severe receptive difficulties.' *British Journal of Disorders of Communication*, **10**, 123–133.

Petty, L., Ornitz, E. M., Michelman, J. D., Zimmerman, E. G. (1984) 'Autistic children who become schizophrenic.' *Archives of General Psychiatry*, **41**, 129–135.

Poppen, R., Stark, J., Eisenson, J., Forrest, T., Wertheim, G. (1969) 'Visual Sequencing Performance of Aphasic Children.' *Journal of Speech and Hearing Research*, **12**, 288–300.

Razran, G. (1961) 'The observable unconscious and the inferable conscious in current Soviet psycho-physiology: interoceptive conditioning, semantic conditioning and the orienting reflex.' *Psychological Review*, **68**, 81–85.

Richmand, N., Stevenson, J., Graham, P. (1982) *Preschool to School: A Behavioural Study*. London: Academic Press.

Richman, L. (1980) 'Cognitive patterns and learning disabilities in cleft palate children with verbal deficits.' *Journal of Speech and Hearing Research*, **23**, 447–456.

Rosenblatt, D, (1980) 'Play'. *In:* Rutter, M. (Ed.) *Developmental Psychiatry*. Baltimore: University Park Press. pp. 292–305.

Rutter, M. (1970) 'Autistic children: infancy to adulthood.' *Seminars in Psychiatry*, **2**, 435–450.

—— (1983) 'Cognitive deficits in the pathogenesis of autism.' *Journal of Child Psychology and Psychiatry*, **24**, 513–533.

—— (1985) 'Family and school influences on cognitive development.' *Journal of Child Psychology and Psychiatry*, **26**, 349–368.

—— Bartak, L., Newman, S. (1971) 'Autism: a central disorder of cognition and language.' *In:* Rutter, M. (Ed.) *Infantile Autism; Concepts, Characteristics and Treatment*. Edinburgh: Churchill Livingstone. pp. 148–171.

—— Garmezy, N. (1983) 'Developmental psychopathology.' *In:* Hetherington, E. (Ed.) *Handbook of Child Psychology, Vol. 4: Socialization, Personality and Social Development*. 4th edn. New York: John Wiley. pp. 775–911.

—— Graham, P., Yule, W. (1970a) *A Neuropsychiatric Study in Childhood. Clinics in Developmental Medicine No. 35/36*. London: S.I.M.P. with Heinemann.

—— Tizard, J., Whitmore, K. (Eds.) (1970b) *Education, Health and Behaviour*. London: Longman.

Scheerer-Neumann (1981) The utilization of intra-word structure in poor readers experimental evidence and a training programme. *Psychological Research*, **43**, 155–178.

Schiff, N. B., Ventry, I. M. (1976) 'Communication problems in hearing children of deaf parents.' *Journal of Speech and Hearing Disorders*, **41**, 348–358.

Schlesinger, H. S., Meadow, K. P. (1972) *Sound and Sign: Childhood Deafness and Mental Health*. Berkeley: University of California Press.

Sheridan, M., Peckham, C. (1975) 'Follow up at 11 years of children who had marked speech defects at 7 years.' *Child: Care and Health Development*, **1**, 157–166.

Sherrod, L., Singer, J. (1977) 'The development of make believe.' *In:* Goldstein, J. (Ed.) *Sports, Games and Play*. Hillsdale, NJ: Lawrence Erlbaum.

Siegel, L. S., Cunningham, C. E., van der Spuy, H. I. J. (1985) Interactions of language delayed and normal preschool boys with their peers. *Journal of Child Psychology and Psychiatry*, **26**, 77–83.

Sigman, M., Ungerer, J., Mundy, P., Sherman, T. (1985) 'Cognitive functioning in autistic children.' *In:* Cohen, D., Donellan, A., Paul, R. (Eds.) *Handbook of Autism and Atypical Development*. New York: John Wiley.

Silva, P., McGee, R., Williams, S. (1983) 'Developmental language delay from 3 to 7 years and its significance for low intelligence and reading difficulties at age seven.' *Developmental Medicine and Child Neurology*, **28**, 783–793.

Skuse, D. (1984) 'Extreme deprivation in early childhood: theoretical issues and a comparative review.' *Journal of Child Psychology and Psychiatry*, **25**, 543–572.

Snowling, M., Stachhausen, J. (1983) 'Spelling performance of children with developmental verbal dyspraxia.' *Developmental Medicine and Child Neurology*, **25**, 430–437.

Stark, R., Tallal, P. (1981) 'Selection of children with specific language deficits.' *Journal of Speech and Hearing Disorders*, **46**, 114–121.

Stevenson, J. (1984) 'Predictive value of speech and language screening.' *Developmental Medicine and Child Neurology*, **26**, 528–538.

—— Richman, N., Graham, P. (1985) 'Behaviour problems and language abilities at 3 years and behavioural deviance at 8 years.' *Journal of Child Psychology and Psychiatry*, **26**, 215–230.

Suppes, P. (1974) 'Cognition in handicapped children.' *Review of Educational Research*, **44**, 165–176.

Tallal, P., Piercy, M. (1973) 'Defects of non-verbal auditory perception in children with developmental aphasia.' *Nature*, **241**, 468–469.

Terrel, B., Schwartz, R., Prelock, P., Messick, C. (1984) 'Symbolic Play in Normal and Language Impaired Children.' *Journal of Speech and Hearing Research*, **27**, 424–429.

Tinsley, V., Waters, H. (1982) 'The development of verbal control over motor behavior: a replication and extension of Luria's findings.' *Child Development*, **53**, 746–753.

Vygotsky, L. (1978) *Mind in Society: The Development of Higher Mental Processes.* Cambridge Mass: Harvard University Press.

Watson, M., Fischer, K. (1977) 'Development of social roles in elicited and spontaneous behavior during the pre-school years.' *Developmental Psychology*, **16**, 483–494.

Whorf, B. L. (1956) 'Science and linguistics.' *In:* Carroll, J. B. (Ed.) *Language, Thought and Reality: Selected Writings of Benjamin Lee Whorf.* Cambridge, Mass: MIT Press.

Wilbur, R., Quigley, S. (1979) 'Syntactic structures in the written language of deaf children.' *Volta Review*, **77**, 194–203.

Wing, L. (1969) 'The handicaps of autistic children: a comparative study.' *Journal of Child Psychology and Psychiatry*, **10**, 1–40.

—— (1981) 'Asperger's syndrome: a clinical account.' *Psychological Medicine*, **11**, 115–130.

Wood, D., Wood, H., Howarth, P. (1983) 'Mathematical abilities of deaf school leavers.' *British Journal of Developmental Psychology*, **1**, 67–73.

Yule, W., Rutter, M. (1985) 'Reading and other learning difficulties.' *In:* Rutter, M., Hersov, L. (Eds.) *Child and Adolescent Psychiatry. 2nd edn.* Oxford: Blackwell. pp. 444–464.

18
ASSESSMENT: OBJECTIVES AND PRINCIPLES

Michael Rutter

Nature of referral concern

When a child is referred to a clinician with the complaint of language delay, often it is the parent who has expressed concern but sometimes the parents may have been surprised, or even perturbed, that someone else has expressed worry about the development of a child whom they have considered entirely normal. The first goal in assessment is to determine both *who* was concerned and *what* it was that they were concerned about. Not infrequently the referral problem may be expressed in terms of the child being 'slow' to talk, a complaint that carries the hope that the child is basically normal and will 'grow out of it', although the underlying worry is that the child is mentally handicapped, deaf, autistic or emotionally disturbed. Accordingly, it is important to give the parents a chance fully to express their anxieties about the child as well as to explore systematically precisely what it was about the child's functioning that gave rise to concern. Occasionally, too, the overt complaint about the child may be the means of expressing some other concern—such as second thoughts about whether to adopt, or a depressed mother's worry about the ill-effects on the children of her misery and difficulties in playing and talking normally with them. It is never acceptable simply to say 'there's nothing to worry about' if no abnormality is found; the clinician must go on to explain why the parental concern does not indicate pathology and also proceed to deal with any underlying worries when they are present.

Level of language development

When a child has been referred because he is supposedly retarded in speech development, clearly one of the initial tasks is to assess the level of language development. Because normal children vary considerably in the age at which they first use single words, as well as in the age at which they first string words together into phrases (see Chapter 5), there is a tendency among inexperienced clinicians to reassure parents without further assessment if a non-speaking child is within the normal range of first words acquisition. This is not justified because parents may have correctly appreciated that their child is retarded in prelinguistic development (although few will conceptualize their concerns in these terms) or that he is not *using* language appropriately for social communication. Accordingly, before giving reassurance, it is necessary to check that all aspects of the child's development are proceeding apparently normally.

With respect to the milestones of language it is crucial to be quite specific on what is being asked about. Parents are very inclined to interpret all manner of sounds as speech, and especially as 'mama' and 'dada'. Consequently, it may be wise to ask very focused questions such as 'when did he first use simple words with

TABLE I

Scheme for speech and language

1. *Imitation*
2. *Inner language*
3. *Comprehension of spoken language*
    Hearing
    Listening and attention
    Understanding
4. *Vocalization and babble*
    Amount
    Complexity
    Quality
    Social usage
5. *Language production*
    Mode (gesture, speech, *etc.*)
    Complexity; syntactical and semantic
    Qualities (echoing, stereotyped features, *etc.*)
    Amount
    Use for social communication
6. *Word-sound production*
7. *Phonation*
8. *Rhythm*

meaning—that is words other than mama and dada?'; 'what were his first words?'; and 'how did he show that he knew their meaning?'. In addition to the first use of single words it is important to ask about babble, the use of two-or three-word phrases, the use of pointing or gesture or mime, the following of instructions, and immediate or delayed echoing. Again, it is most profitable to concentrate on key age periods that are easily remembered by parents (because they coincide with some event or occasion that is *personally* memorable—such as a birthday or Christmas or when the family moved house or father changed job) rather than to ask for exact dating in calendar or age terms. It is helpful to identify some occasions that the parents obviously remember reasonably clearly and then to focus on what the child was like at that time. In doing so, an attempt should be made to determine what the child was like at about two years, 30 months, and three years. Obviously, parent's memories for the early phases of language development are likely to be more accurate in the case of a young child than when the child is older. This is not so much because memories fade with time (although this occurs), but rather because the recollection of past events or happenings may be distorted and reinterpreted in the light of subsequent course (Yarrow *et al.* 1970), although probably the tendency is less than sometimes thought (Robins *et al.* 1985). Nevertheless, it is always wise to obtain contemporaneous records (such as a baby diary or Health Visitor notes) whenever possible.

Having obtained an outline history of the course of earlier language development, it is necessary to focus in some detail on the child's current level of language functioning. In that connection, it is helpful to have some kind of scheme in mind to ensure that the key aspects of language and language-related functions are systematically covered (see Table I and Rutter 1985). Thus, the questioning should deal in turn with imitation, so-called 'inner language', comprehension of language, vocalization and babble, language production, word-sound qualities, phonation and speech rhythm (Rutter 1974). Imitation in a toddler will be evident by waving goodbye or by baby games such as peek-a-boo or pat-a-cake. It is important to check whether the child does (or did) this spontaneously, rather than just in response to parental request or eliciting. A slightly older child might be expected to copy his parents' vacuuming or mowing the lawn or, indeed, their idiosyncratic social mannerisms. 'Inner language' refers to a child's ability to use a symbolic code in his thought processes—as reflected, for example, in his meaningful use of miniature objects or in pretend play or drawing. Thus, a two-year-old would be expected to 'talk' into a toy telephone, push toy cars instead of just spinning wheels, or to use a baby brush and comb. Similarly, a three- or four-year-old might be expected to create a 'farmyard' with toy animals, to play imaginatively with a tea set or with dolls, or play garages or make races with toy cars. This capacity involves first the ability to recognize the functional use and meaning of objects, secondly an ability to create sequences or stories with the play objects, and thirdly, the imagination to pretend that an imaginary object is used (*e.g.* that there is tea in the pot or cakes on the plate, even though both are empty). The clinician should ask the parent in detail about the way the child plays and the toys that he uses (see Rutter 1974).

There are several different aspects of language comprehension. Thus, 'hearing behavior' includes hearing as such (as shown by the child looking up when an aeroplane flies overhead, or going to the door when the bell rings, or looking up in response to a noise outside); listening and attention (by alerting when called, looking at the person who is speaking to him, and by watching faces); and understanding of spoken language (as shown by the child's ability to follow instructions given without visual, contextual or gestural cues). Especially with a young non-speaking child, most parents naturally (and helpfully) adopt the habit of using pointing, gesture and demonstration when speaking—and, often, are unaware that they do so. Accordingly, once again, questions need to be specific with regard, for example, to whether the child would follow an instruction to fetch something from another room. Would he do so if it was something unfamiliar? Would he follow a two-or three-part instruction (such as go to the hall and fetch my gloves out of the bottom drawer?).

Current vocalization and babble, of course, is relevant only if the child is not yet speaking. But with a non-speaking child it is important to enquire about the amount, range, type and rhythm of the child's sounds. Does the child 'talk' to himself or to you? Are a wide variety of sounds strung together with complex inflections and speech cadences so that sometimes, from the other side of the room, it almost sounds as if the child *is* speaking? Does he babble back when you speak to him (*i.e.* does it have a reciprocal, social quality)?.

When the child is communicating at all, it is important to assess the mode of communication, its complexity, its quality, its amount and its social usage. The clinician will want to know whether the child uses speech or gesture and, if speech, whether this is accompanied by normal gestural accompaniments (pointing, arm movements, *etc.*). The parent should always be asked *how* the child indicates that he wants something. If he takes the parent by the arm, does he grasp the hand or the wrist, does he look at the parent to engage their attention, does he point with a finger or just an outstretched arm, *etc.*? An estimate of the mode of complexity of the speech used may be obtained by enquiring about the average length of utterances (asking for examples and checking that that was exactly how the child put it), whether the small connecting words (such as prepositions and conjunctions) are included, the range of vocabulary, the use of tenses other than the present, and the flexibility of grammatical constructions. The abnormal qualities to be asked about include pronominal reversal (with particular reference to I-you confusion), immediate and delayed echoing, stereotyped phrases, made-up words (neologisms), and odd or idiosyncratic use of words or language. Parents should be asked about the amount that the child talks and the circumstances in which he does so. Particular attention should be paid to the social qualities of the child's communications—whether he 'chats' in a to-and-fro fashion, whether he can sustain a conversation with reciprocal interchange (*i.e.* whether the child's communications show a response to what has been said to him—beyond an answer to a direct question), whether what he says shows an interest in the other person, whether he can give an account of what he did at another time (such as at school or when visiting granny's), and whether his speech is accompanied by appropriate variations in emotional expression and use of eye-to-eye gaze. Lastly, there should be questioning on the child's articulation of speech—that is, his pronunciation (although usually this is best assessed by direct assessment of the child's speech as most parents are not able to identify the particular respects in which articulation departs from the normal); and the phonation and rhythm of speech. The ways in which these various language features can be used in the differential diagnosis of some of the key language disorders are discussed in Chapter 13.

Differential diagnosis
To some extent the next steps in differential diagnosis will depend on what has been determined regarding the child's level and pattern of language functioning. However, almost always it will be necessary to make some appraisal of the child's progress in other aspects of development. These should include social relationships, play, and cognitive functioning.

Social relationships
A scheme for questioning about social interactions is even more necessary than with language because most fond parents tend to perceive some affection in even the most autistic of children, because parents who feel negative towards their child may wrongly describe him as generally unresponsive because he is so with them, and because there is no generally accepted set of constructs about the development of social relationships. A possible scheme of questioning is outlined in Table II; however, the particular structure used in assessment matters less than that there is some structure to ensure systematic coverage. The most basic question is whether the child differentiates between people; whether his response to his parents is reliably different from his response to family friends or to strangers—and how that

TABLE II

Scheme for social interaction

1. *Differentiation between people*
2. *Selective attachment*
   Source of security or comfort
   Greeting
   Separation anxiety
3. *Social overtures*
   Frequency and circumstances
   Quality: visual gaze, facial expression, and emotions
   Reciprocity
4. *Social responses*
   Frequency and circumstances
   Quality: eye-to-eye gaze, facial expression, and emotions
   Reciprocity
5. *Social play*
   Spontaneous imitation
   Cooperation and reciprocity
   Pleasure in the other person
   Humour
   Excitement

TABLE III

Scheme for play

1. *Social aspects*
   Interest in people and in their responses
   Spontaneous sharing of interests and activities
   Playfulness, fun, and entering into the spirit of social games
   Reciprocity, to and fro, and social dialogue
   Emotional expression
2. *Cognitive level*
   Curiosity
   Understanding of how things work
   Complexity; puzzles, drawing, rule-following, inventiveness
   Imagination: pretend-elements, creativity, spontaneity
3. *Content, type and quality*
   Initiation
   Variability or stereotypy
   Unusual preoccupations
   Unusual object attachments
   Rituals and routines
   Resistance to change
   Stereotyped movements
   Interest in unusual aspects of people or objects

differentiation is manifest. The next issue is whether the child shows selective attachments or bonds. It should be appreciated that although in a normal child the phase of clinging, separation anxiety and wariness of strangers usually lasts only to age four or five years, the phenomenon of social bonding is a life-long human characteristic (Rutter 1980*a*). Questions should be asked about the features specific to early childhood but the main focus should be on whether and how specific attachments are used to provide security and reduce anxiety. Does the child stay close to his parents in a strange situation, does he go to them for comfort when upset, does he become clinging when anxious or frightened, does his manner of greeting show pleasure when he sees his parents, does their holding him relieve his distress?

With respect to the child's social overtures, the important question is not whether he approaches other people, but rather *how* social overtures are made and in what circumstances. In the normal child, most social approaches involve a friendly facial expression, some show of positive emotion, the appropriate engagement of mutual gaze and some expression of interest in the other person or his activities. In order to determine whether these characteristics apply, it is necessary, therefore, to obtain a detailed description of just what the child does when he seeks to engage the attention of someone else.

Much the same applies to the style of the child's response to other people's overtures to him. Does he look directly at them, does he smile, and does he show pleasure? The feature of reciprocity is also crucial: does the child show an appropriate response to what the other person says or does; is there a sequence of social dialogue with a to-and-fro; and do the child's emotions and facial expressions vary according to those of the other person? Finally, in what ways, if any, does the child play *with* someone else? Does he *seek* play with other people or does he have to be *brought* into social play? Will he do something together with his parents, sharing, co-operating and taking turns (as in building with bricks, or a board game, or playing ball, or musical games, or chasing games)? If so, does he show pleasure or humour in relation to *other* people's activities in a shared game? Can he follow rules? Does he show social excitement (*i.e.* joining in the 'spirit' of the occasion)? In short, not only will he go through the mechanics of a shared game but is this accompanied by a range of emotions appropriate to the social elements in the interaction? Is there a 'playful' quality to the social interactions in the sense of a shared pleasure and an enjoyment of the 'fun' aspects of the social encounter?

Play
There is a similar need for some kind of structure to questioning about play. Together with social interactions, these tend to constitute the two aspects least well dealt with in history-taking by the inexperienced. The social aspects of play have been considered already in terms of interest, playfulness, reciprocity and emotional expression. Play also constitutes a good guide to the child's cognitive level. Curiosity in the environment is an important quality—does the child explore new toys and show an interest in the world about him; does he seem interested in finding out how things work (toys, tools, household gadgets, *etc.*) and how successful is he in doing so? What is the complexity of the child's play – can he do puzzles on his own (how many pieces?), can he build things with bricks or 'lego' or cope with other constructional toys; what does he draw; how good is he in understanding and following the rules of games; how inventive is he in his play? Questions need to be asked about make-believe play, dressing up, and pretend games (tea parties, schools, cops and robbers, *etc.*, *etc.*) with special reference to the extent to which this is spontaneous, creative and varying.

Thirdly, attention should be paid to the content, type and quality of the child's play. It is helpful to ask what the child does if left to his own devices – will he play in an appropriate fashion or does he tend to engage in repetitive activities or motor stereotypies? What toys or games will he choose if that is left up to him—or does he not use toys or games? In most cases of autism, play tends to be lacking in variability and creativity, so that questions should be asked on these features. Of course, too, attention needs to be paid to the abnormal qualities of play that tend to be characteristic of autism—routines or rituals (are there things that he insists have to be done in a special way or in a special order—what about with mealtimes, or bedtimes, or dressing, or going places?); resistance to change (does he mind if you change the ornaments or rearrange the furniture or vary your household routine?); unusual preoccupations (has he got any special interests that tend to preoccupy him to the exclusion of other activities—such as with numbers, dates, routes or things like that?); unusual object attachments (does he have any things that he likes to carry around with him all the time or that he collects?); and interests in unusual aspects of people or objects (does he tend to smell or feel things inappropriately— either with toys or with people).

Cognitive assessment
Because of its importance in diagnostic evaluation, prognosis and planning of treatment, an accurate assessment of the child's current level of cognitive performance is crucial. Psychological testing is an essential element in such an assessment but the testing should never be considered in isolation (Berger, 1985). In all cases, the history from the parents and from the teachers of the child's behaviour at home and at school should be used to provide an estimate of cognitive level; this should also be made on the basis of what has been observed of the child's behaviour in different settings. Whenever the estimates from history and from observation do not agree with test findings this must be regarded as a matter for further investigation. It is *never* permissible to conclude that the test findings provide the 'true' picture. Some children have specific skills (often in rote memory, visuo-spatial skills, mental arithmetic or music) that are substantially above those evident on routine psychological testing. In such instances, it is necessary to observe the reported skills in the setting in which they occur and, if necessary, to undertake specific testing to assess their validity. Also, sometimes children perform very much better in some settings than others. But, in addition, some parents overestimate their children's skills either because they do not appreciate the cues that are being provided inadvertently, or because they misinterpret the meaning of the child's behaviour in terms of the cognitive skills required. In such circumstances, it is necessary both to provide a valid estimate of the child's level of cognitive functioning at home and to help the parents appreciate the meaning of that level in terms of the child's needs.

Social maturity may be assessed by asking the parents specific questions about the child's performance in the areas of self-help (*e.g.* whether he can dress himself without help, manage buttons and shoe-laces, get his clothes right way round, *etc.*); household activities (in terms of his helping with washing up, clearing the table, *etc.*, and of his ability to run errands or go to the shops); and use of objects

TABLE IV

Cognitive assessment

(i) History of child's behaviour at home and at school
(ii) Observation in different settings
(iii) Psychological testing
1. *Social maturity*
   Self-help: feeding, toileting, dressing, *etc.*
   Household activities: washing up, shopping, errands, *etc.*
   Use of objects: tools, scissors, *etc.*
2. *Play*
   History
   Observation
3. *Intelligence*
   Curiosity in environment
   Finding out how things work
   Style of problem solving
   Social maturity
   Play

(whether he can use scissors, use the radio or record player, *etc*).

As already discussed, the cognitive level of the child's play may be determined from both history and observation.

The child's general intelligence should be assessed from his curiosity in the environment, the extent to which such curiosity is systematically applied to new situations, his ability to find out how things work, his style of problem-solving (does he work things out or try responses at random?), his social maturity and his play. The psychometric assessment of cognitive functioning is discussed in Chapter 19.

Medical assessment
As with any child referred for developmental problems, an adequate screening for medical conditions is essential. This is described in Chapter 20.

Assessment of psychosocial environment
Children learn language in a social context (see Chapter 6) and severe distortions and deficiencies in the social environment can lead to delays in language development (see Chapters 7 and 13). Hence, it is essential to appraise the home environment and to assess parent–child interaction and communication. In that connection it is important to recognize that there are many acceptable ways to bring up young children and many normal sociocultural variations. Stereotypical expectations should be avoided and instead a careful account of key features should be obtained. Ordinarily, quite a good picture will have been provided by the parent's description of the child's play and social relationships. However, in addition, questions should be asked about what sort of things the parents do together with the child, the circumstances of group or family day care (if that is used), and who looks after the child when the parents are out. Perhaps most of all, attention should be paid to the interactions between the parents and the child in the waiting room or consulting room (especially when not obviously the focus of the

clinician's attention). Do they talk or play together? How responsive are they to the child's cues and overtures? Do they show pleasure in interactions with the child? Does the child seem used to enjoyable interactions with them? Is the child physically well cared for?

The assessment of the psychosocial environment is important not only for the detection of possible factors contributing to aetiology, but also for the planning of intervention. Such interventions should include attention to possible family stresses and burdens as well as to the child's handicaps. Accordingly, the initial assessment should involve some appraisal of the parental worries and fears, the degree to which concerns over the child's difficulties have led to parental demoralization or depression, the extent of family burdens and tensions, and particularly the practical and emotional ways in which the family (including siblings) have coped with the 'problem' of having a child with a language disorder.

Diagnostic formulation

As is evident in the style of assessment that has been outlined, one of the main purposes is to move beyond an appraisal of the child's *level* of language to an evaluation of the *pattern* of language skills and deficits. As indicated in Chapters 2, 11 and 13, the delineation of such patterns is crucial for accurate diagnosis. Potentially, too, it should be invaluable for the rational planning of programmes of remediable intervention. Thus, for example, there is a need to decide whether to focus on children's syntax, vocabulary, or articulation, or instead whether to concentrate on social communication, or rather to direct attention to the establishment of some alternative communicative system (see Chapters 24 and 25). Obviously, the therapist must know which aspect is impaired or deviant in order to plan how to intervene successfully. Nevertheless, adequate data are lacking for the choice of whether to teach to strengths or to seek to remedy weaknesses (Rutter 1980*b*, Cromer 1984). An undue focus on weakness may reinforce children's feelings of failure (Cooper and Griffiths 1978); yet an ignoring of weaknesses may result in a lack of the steps needed to remedy the deficits. Probably some mixture is best but much further research is needed on how best to tailor remedial programmes to the specifics of the findings on the pattern of language disabilities.

When is delayed development abnormal?

As indicated in Chapter 5, children vary widely in the age at which they acquire spoken language. A few children who are extremely late in speaking turn out to be entirely normal; once speech develops it progresses rapidly and there are no adverse sequelae of the children's markedly late start. That is exactly what one would expect from a normally distributed characteristic with a wide spread. Conversely, however, there are some children with lesser delays in language development whose delay is due to some disorder and in whom the late start is followed by a variety of associated problems (see Chapter 17). Accordingly, it is necessary to have some means of determining when a language delay is likely to reflect some significant clinical disorder that warrants fuller investigation.

Five main criteria may be employed: severity, course, pattern, associated psychological difficulties, and associated medical conditions. As a general rule, a language delay that is sufficiently severe to fall outside the two standard deviation limits (*i.e.* it falls in the most extreme 2½ per cent) may be regarded as likely to be abnormal. Almost all cases of this severity have significant sequelae. As a rough and ready guide, this means that attention should always be paid to children not using single words by 24 months or not using phrase speech by 33 months (Morley 1965, Reynell 1969). However, many children with lesser degrees of language delay than this have a significant disorder that is likely to be followed by important sequelae; accordingly, other criteria need to be employed in addition.

The level of current severity is of even less use in diagnosis in older children. That is because there is a natural tendency towards progressive improvement. In this situation, the course provides a useful indicator. If the current level of impairment is mild but nevertheless there is a history of a previously severe degree of impairment, the likelihood is that the current functioning represents the sequelae of a significant disorder rather than just normal variation. Conversely, in a young child, if the recent course shows a rapid, wide ranging improvement with apparent 'catch-up', the delay is less likely to represent some clinical disorder.

Thirdly, attention should be paid to the *pattern* of language development. If the child is late in first using simple words, but is progressing normally in all other aspects of language and communication, a variation of normal is more likely than if communication skills are generally delayed. Thus, if babble is developing normally with use of speech-like cadences, if there is good understanding of spoken language, if non-verbal cues are used and responded to appropriately, and if there is normal social interchange, a significant clinical disorder is not likely. Conversely, if the over-all pattern of language is deviant in form (that is, it is not a kind that is appropriate at any age) or if the child's speech or language includes qualitatively abnormal features, a clinical disorder is probable.

Similarly, if a delay in some specific aspect of speech or language is accompanied by abnormalities in any other aspect of development, the delay is unlikely to constitute just a normal variation. Thus, some kind of disorder is probable if there are abnormalities in interpersonal relationships, associated emotional or behavioural disturbances, if there is a global developmental delay (in motor milestones and in adaptive skills), or in older children if there are associated scholastic deficits such as in reading and spelling.

Finally, on the principle of parsimony, if the child has any kind of medical disorder that carries a risk of language problems, it should be assumed that any language delay is pathological until proved otherwise. Thus, for example, a child with hearing impairment, cerebral palsy, or a sex chromosome anomaly who shows any kind of language delay should always have a detailed appraisal of language and communication.

The clear implication is that the initial decision on whether to refer a late speaking child for specialist assessment must be based on a screening of all aspects of language and of development more generally, and not just on the basis of the range of normal variation in acquisition of first words.

Prognosis
Regardless of the diagnosis, parents have the right to expect some guidance about prognosis. Obviously, that is difficult on the basis of a single initial assessment; nevertheless the clinician should give such guidance as he/she can—indicating the range of probabilities and upon what they depend. In that connection, apart from the influence of the underlying medical condition (if there is one), the prognosis is likely to be better if the language delay is *mild* (in terms of degree of departure from normal expectations), if it is *narrow* in the aspects of language affected (that is both comprehension and social usage are near-normal even though expressive language is limited), if it is *specific* and isolated (that is the child is of normal intelligence—see Chapters 1 and 17) and if there is an absence of associated socio-emotional-behavioural problems (see Chapter 17). However, in giving parents a prognosis it is important to be aware that many children with language delay who achieve fully normal language competence nevertheless are left with residual reading/spelling or socio-emotional problems (see Chapter 17). This possibility should be mentioned as a risk to be avoided so far as possible, rather than as an inevitable concomitant, as it applies to only a minority (albeit a substantial minority) of language delayed children.

Preparation for intervention
The last purpose of the initial diagnostic assessment is to provide a basis and preparation for whatever intervention is planned. The parents should be given, not only the diagnosis of their child's disorder, but more importantly an understanding of the nature and pattern of the child's strengths and limitations in the different aspects of language (and of other developmental functions). Parents have the right to expect as full an explanation as is possible on the child's needs with regard to language development. Thus, the clinician should give appropriate guidance on the child's level of understanding and on how the parents should talk and play with the child in order to facilitate language development. Of course, we lack a detailed knowledge of how children learn language from conversational interchanges and we know even less about the special needs of handicapped children (see Chapters 6 and 7). Nevertheless, we know something and certainly our understanding is likely to exceed that of the parents. Hence, while avoiding unwarranted dogmatism, we should give as specific and explicit guidance as we can. General statements such as 'just talk normally with him' are not good enough (*e.g.* does that mean what is normal for a child of his chronological age or his language age?); and broad-based exhortations such as to 'stimulate language' are to be avoided. Instead, the advice should be as precise as can be achieved and should be linked with what has been determined in the assessment. In the same way, the parents should be told whether any professional interventions are required (if not, why not) and, if needed, what are the aims and objectives.

Style of assessment
A further question concerns the *style* of assessment to be employed. In discussing the areas of functioning to be covered in assessment, attention was primarily

focused on the information to be sought during an interview with the parents. However, clearly this is not an adequate data base on its own. So far as possible, all the issues covered in the history taking should be assessed by direct observation of the child. For that purpose, it is highly desirable to see the child in situations that vary greatly in their social context and demands—as each is likely to tap rather different dimensions of the child's functioning. Psychological testing provides the opportunity of observing the child in a structured setting with the context explicitly task-oriented. For older children the school provides another task-oriented environment, but one that differs in the crucial respect of its being a group-setting rather than a one-to-one interaction, and in terms of the less close supervision that that entails. With schoolage children it will always be essential to obtain a detailed report from teachers of the child's behaviour at school. However, in addition, it may be valuable to make a school visit for a direct observation of the child in the classroom and playground, and for a discussion of treatment goals and plans with the teachers in the context of the child's behaviour and attainments at school. At the clinic, the opportunity should be taken of seeing the child with his family—both in order to observe the quality of his interactions with them and in order to assess behaviour in that more familiar social milieu. This may be done in the waiting room but also it may be helpful to have part of the interview time with the family as a whole. As well as providing information on the child's behaviour, it should be informative on the nature of the parent's interactions with the child and on their style of coping with his difficult behaviour. If the parental account of the child's behaviour at home is discrepant from that seen at the clinic a home visit will be essential in order to determine whether there is indeed such situation variability (and, if so, what seems to regulate it), or whether the parents are misinterpreting or misperceiving what the child does.

Finally, the child should be seen by the clinican in a less structured setting than that provided by psychological testing, and with a social rather than a task orientation. The room should be uncluttered with a few well chosen toys appropriate to the child's interests and developmental level on view. These should be selected to provide the opportunity for some form of social interaction and joint play and for the use of imagination and make-believe (a doll's house with family figures may be most suitable for young children). Some additional toys may be kept in reserve on a side table. Initially, after an appropriate social greeting, it may be useful to take a somewhat passive rôle in order to see how the child uses both the toys and the social situation. Then, according to circumstances, the clinician may take a somewhat more active rôle—socially, verbally and with respect to task structure—in order to see how the child responds. However the session is organized and whatever the order followed, it is important to provide a varying social and emotional 'stimulus' to the child so that his reciprocity and responsivity may be evaluated. Although, obviously, it is necessary to tailor the session to the needs, interests, and capabilities of the individual child, also there are great advantages in ensuring that there is broad comparability between the diagnostic interviews with different children. Unless the interview conditions are comparable it will not be possible to know whether variability in the children's behaviour is a function of

TABLE V

Observation of child

(i)	Unstructured with family (clinic and home)
(ii)	Structured and task oriented (psychological testing)
(iii)	Socially oriented, with less structure (psychiatric interview)
(iv)	Group setting with task orientation (school)

1. *Social inhibition/disinhibition*
2. *Social interaction*
3. *Play*
4. *Emotions*
5. *Language*
6. *Abnormal behaviours*

changes in the interview or differences in the children.

Table V summarizes the key elements to be taken note of in observations of the child. Ordinarily, a visit to a clinic and an interview with a doctor whom he has not met before will create a degree of initial social inhibition in a normal child, but with a lessening as the child becomes more at ease and 'gets to know' the doctor. This may not occur with a socially unresponsive autistic child—either in terms of the initial inhibition or the change as the interview proceeds. The quality of the child's social interaction with the clinician and of his play should be assessed in terms of the features discussed above. The range, quality and social appropriateness of the child's emotions should be noted, together with the extent to which emotional expressiveness accompanies social overtures and responses. The child's use and understanding of language should be observed systematically according to the language scheme given in Table I, with whatever systematic attempts to elicit language as are necessary. Ordinarily this is best achieved by talking *with* the child, commenting on the play or responding positively to what the child says or does, rather than by directive questioning. Of course, too, all abnormal behaviours shown should be noted.

A further key issue is when to undertake standardized testing of language, cognition or other developmental functions. Such testing serves several rather different functions. First, it provides a systematic means of quantification that may be related to the child's chronological age. This is of value both in order to determine the extent of the child's retardation or delay in development (expressed in terms of standard deviations from the mean, quotients, or general population percentiles—all of which constitute slightly different ways of quantifying the frequency with which any given level of retardation will occur in the general population of children of a particular age). Secondly, it provides a baseline against which to measure the child's developmental progress during the period of treatment or follow-up.

The simplest means of quantification is provided by the scales based on information given by the parent about the child's skills in particular areas of functioning. Thus, the Vineland Social Maturity Scale (Doll 1953) provides a score representing an over-all social age or social quotient (reflecting global developmental level). A new, extensively revised, version (Sparrow *et al.* 1984) provides a more thorough wide-ranging assessment of social functioning but for a quick sample screening of those aspects that correlate most highly with general intelligence the original has advantages. The Mecham (1958) scale does much the same for language development in terms of providing a rather crude rough and ready estimate of level of language. If direct testing of the child is not to be undertaken, these parental information scales should always constitute part of any specialized assessment of children referred for a possible language delay or disorder.

Direct psychological testing provides a more detailed and generally more accurate means of quantification. It should be undertaken whenever the parental information suggests a clinically significant degree of general or specific retardation. However, direct testing of the child has three additional advantages of particular importance in diagnostic assessment. First, it is designed to assess the child's competence under optimal standard conditions. This may be particularly important when children's social withdrawal or behavioural disturbance leads them to behave in very immature ways in spite of normal intellectual abilities. Skilled psychological testing should allow a differentiation in such circumstances between immaturity in ordinary behaviour as observed and cognitive capacity as elicited. Secondly, testing may demonstrate the level of skills in functions that are difficult to distinguish in ordinary observations. Thus, because children use a variety of non-language cues when following instructions, often it may be difficult clinically to assess the extent of a child's comprehension of spoken language. Tests, such as the Reynell (1969) Developmental Language Scales, that provide measures of both language comprehension and expression are very useful for this purpose. Thirdly, psychological testing should provide a quantified profile of children's cognitive strengths and weaknesses. Thus, the Wechsler Intelligence Scale for Preschool Children (Wechsler 1967) provides measures of both verbal and visuospatial aspects of general intelligence. The topic of psychological testing is discussed more fully in Chapter 19.

Of course, too, all children presenting with a possible language problem should have a medical assessment. The decisions on what can be determined by history and what by physical examination, together with the decisions on when to undertake more specialized medical investigations are considered in Chapter 20.

Scope of assessment
A crucial issue concerns the scope of an initial assessment. Obviously, a family doctor is not going to make as full or as detailed an assessment as the tertiary care expert at a specialized regional centre. Because there is so much individual variation in rates of language development many essentially normal children are going to give rise to transient parental concern that speech seems to be a little slow in development. Clearly it is not necessary that every child who is a little slow should be referred to specialists. On the other hand, clinically important language problems are relatively common (see Chapter 1) and many children with transient language delay are left with adverse sequelae of one type or another (see Chapters 1 and 17). This applies to the *majority* of those with language deficits that persist to age three years and any child of this age with significant language impairment should have a full assessment at a clinic with experience in dealing with

developmental problems. However, clearly it would not be acceptable to wait until three years to decide whether or not to refer.

Screening tests for hearing should be undertaken with *all* children in the general population. However, if there is the slightest doubt about the findings the testing should be repeated whenever there is concern over language development. While it is unlikely these days that cases of total deafness will have been missed, partial hearing losses may be much more difficult to detect. Moreover, children with perfect learning in infancy may develop later auditory impairments as a result of conductive losses following middle ear infections.

The prime question in the initial assessment at primary care level concerns the normality or otherwise of all aspects of development *other* than the use of speech (assuming that the latter is the cause for referral). With respect to language, the parents may be reassured if it is clear that comprehension is normal, that babble is progressing normally, that there is appropriate imitative and symbolic play, that the quality of vocalizations is normal, and that there is appropriate reciprocal social communication using modalities other than speech. However, if any of these aspects of language give rise to concern regarding possible delay or deviance a fuller assessment is indicated. Similarly, specialist referral is called for if there are legitimate worries over other aspects of the child's development—cognition, motor skills, play and socialization. It is *never* acceptable to reassure parents solely on the grounds that the child's level of spoken language is, say, within the 95 per cent population limits. Development must be assessed as a whole.

If a fuller assessment is required the next question is which type of specialist should be consulted. Much will depend on the particular pattern of local services and on the particular skills and interests of the specialists in the area. The important thing is that the assessment be broad-based and well informed. In many cases referral may be most appropriately made to a paediatrician with a special interest in developmental problems, or to a multi-disciplinary district handicap team. However, if the main concern is over hearing, referral to an audiologist; or if over autism to a child psychiatrist may be preferable. In any case, competent specialists of all disciplines should be able to recognize the limits of their expertise and to determine when consultation with colleagues should be sought (such consultation is usually necessary with multi-faced developmental problems). As Chapters 19 and 22 make clear, psychologists and speech therapists have particularly important contributions to make.

Completion of assessment

Finally, there is the question of when assessment stops. Several rather different issues are involved in that apparently simple question. First, there is the matter of making a decision on whether or not there is a language disorder; usually this can be settled on one thorough assessment but sometimes there may need to be further observations or investigations over the next few sessions. Secondly, there is the need to make both a broad-based formulation (including hypotheses on aetiology) and (where possible) a specific medical diagnosis. Sometimes this is a straightforward matter but often specific investigations and/or the appraisal of progress over time are needed. Thirdly, the hypotheses on causation and on the factors in the current situation likely to effect language development need to be translated into testable suggestions on the modes of intervention that are most likely to be effective. Because such treatment plans necessarily involve inferences, they must be evaluated in terms of children's progress in response to the particular interventions employed. As discussed in Chapter 23, this is no easy matter but if treatment is to be rational it must be attempted. Any treatment plan must include monitoring of progress so that it can be decided whether continuing treatment is required and, if it is, whether the original therapeutic hypotheses remain valid or whether some modification is needed. Fourthly, clinicans must always be alert to the possibility that the original diagnostic formulation was wrong. Diagnosis can be a very difficult matter and it is not very uncommon for the initial assessments on, say, hearing or on intellectual level to prove at least partially incorrect. There must be a constant readiness to make reassessments whenever doubt arises. Finally, there is the recognition that children change; an assessment that is valid at 30 months may no longer be appropriate at four years of age. It is clear that there can be no once-and-for-all-time assessment; moreover there can be no sharp demarcation between assessment and intervention. That is *not* to argue for an indecisiveness in diagnosis. Precision and definite decisions are always to be aimed for. Indeed it is only by making definite formulations that clinicians can know when they are wrong. Nevertheless, it *is* to argue that assessment must incorporate not only an evaluation of the child's problems at the time of referral and the problems as they develop over time, but also a systematic monitoring of the intervention procedures in order to cast light on the initial formulation and to determine the efficacy of the interventions used. In that sense assessment must constitute a continuing process that does not stop until clinical contact comes to an end.

REFERENCES

Berger, M. (1985) 'Psychological assessment and testing.' *In:* Rutter, M., Hersov, L. (Eds.) *Child and Adolescent Psychiatry: Modern Approaches (2nd edition).* Oxford: Blackwell Scientific. pp. 264–279.
Cooper, J. M., Griffiths, P. (1978) 'Treatment and prognosis.' *In:* Wyke, M. A. (Ed.) *Developmental Dysphasia.* London: Academic Press. pp. 159–176.
Cromer, R. F. (1984) 'The acquisition of language.' *In:* McGuffin, P., Shanks, M. F., Hodgson, R. J. (Eds.) *The Scientific Principles of Psychopathology.* London: Grune and Stratton. pp. 313–337.
Doll, E. A. (1953) *The Measurement of Social Competence: A Manual for the Vineland Social Maturity Scale.* Minneapolis: American Guidance Service.
Mecham, M. (1958) *Verbal Language Development Scale.* Minneapolis: Educational Test Bureau.
Morley, M. E. (1965) *The Development and Disorders of Speech in Childhood (2nd edition).* Edinburgh: Livingstone.
Reynell, J. (1969) *Reynell Developmental Language Scales.* Slough: NFER.
Robins, L. N., Schoenberg, S. P., Holmes, S. J., Ratcliff, K. S., Benham, A., Works, J. (1985) 'Early home environment and retrospective recall: a test for concordance between siblings with and without psychiatric disorders.' *American Journal of Orthopsychiatry,* **55,** 17–41.
Rutter, M. (1974) 'The child who is slow to talk.' *Update* (March), 777–786.
—— (1980*a*) 'Attachment and the development of social relations.' *In:* Rutter, M. (Ed.) *Scientific Foundations of Developmental Psychiatry.* London: Heinemann Medical. pp. 267–279.
—— (1980*b*) 'Language training with autistic children: how does it work and what does it achieve?' *In:* Hersov, L. A., Berger, M. (Eds.) *Language and Language Disorders in Childhood.* Oxford:

Pergamon Press. p. 1550 ff.
—— (1985) 'Infantile autism.' *In:* Shaffer, D., Erhardt, A., Greenhill, L. (Eds.) *A Clinician's Guide to Child Psychiatry.* New York: Free Press. pp. 48–78.
Sparrow, S., Balla, D., Cicchetti, D. (1984) *Vineland Adaptive Behavior Scales (Survey Form).* Circle Pines, Minnesota: American Guidance Service.
Wechsler, D. (1967) *Wechsler's Preschool and Primary Scale of Intelligence.* New York: Psychological Corporation.
Yarrow, M. R., Campbell, J. D., Burton, R. V. (1970) 'Recollections of childhood: a study of the retrospective method.' *Monographs of the Society for Research in Child Development, Serial No. 138,* **35,** No. 5.

19
PSYCHOLOGICAL ASSESSMENT

William Yule

Psychological assessment, particularly of cognitive abilities, has an important rôle in the assessment and treatment of children with language disorders. As was argued a decade ago, 'Language and cognition are closely interrelated and a careful appraisal of cognitive abilities is necessary for an understanding of possible factors in the genesis and prognosis of language delay, of the nature of the language handicap, and of the child's educational needs' (Berger and Yule 1972). Considering the major advances in developmental psycholinguistics since then, the aim of this chapter is to argue the continuing need for cognitive assessment in the management of the language-retarded child, while discussing what type of psychological assessment is now considered appropriate.

Purposes of psychological assessment

When children fail to begin talking normally, or when their language is developing deviantly, it is important for the problem to be clearly described, a differential diagnosis to be made, appropriate therapy to be started and monitored, and longer-term plans to be made for special education. Formal psychological testing of cognitive ability and language attainment can contribute to each of these areas.

One of the first and most important questions to be considered in the differential diagnosis of language disorder is whether the delay is part of a *general* mental handicap or is a more circumscribed retardation in *specific* skills of language. As discussed in Chapter 15, speech and language disorders are very frequent in mentally handicapped children. Therefore it is necessary to obtain good measures of general intellectual skills and of language attainment, using appropriate psychological tests, to be able to decide whether the child has a specific language disorder or a general developmental retardation (Miller 1981).

Both as an aid in diagnosis and to provide indications for therapy, more detailed descriptions are needed of what the child is able to do and say. There is a need for reliable and objective descriptions of the child's assets and deficits. Any test of general intelligence should cover a wide range of skills. Careful analysis of scores on the test, together with information obtained from parents and teachers and by direct observation of the child may suggest particular skills which need to be assessed in greater detail. Non-verbal skills of perception, motor co-ordination, perceptuo-motor function and attention may all be relevant when designing a treatment programme.

The description of speech and language requires considerable expertise. Ideally, a full assessment of speech and language requires a complete description of phonology, morphology, syntax, semantics and pragmatics (Mittler 1972, Miller 1981, Muller *et al.* 1981, Holland 1984). This is a far cry from listening to the child and estimating that speech is at the two- to 2½-year level, or using formal tests that differentiate comprehension from expression. There are a number of assessment tools and guidelines recently available (Miller 1981), and it is unlikely that many clinical child psychologists or educational (school) psychologists will have the requisite skills to use them without specialist training. It is also unlikely that many speech therapists will have the professional skills to undertake the other aspects of assessment being discussed here. A collaborative effort is needed and we will return to this below. For the present, it is sufficient to note that detailed descriptions of speech and language are required and that recent advances in developmental psycholinguistics have resulted in new assessment techniques.

One of the major advantages of formal testing over clinical judgement is that testing is standardised and the test results can therefore be used as baseline measures against which to judge later progress, be it spontaneous or as a result of deliberate intervention. Test results can also provide a basis for predictions about later language development, social progress and educational achievement, although the data relating to language-disordered children are still very sparse (Lockyer and Rutter 1969, Bartak and Rutter 1971, Miller *et al.* 1984).

General intellectual level enters into most specific skills. Scores on tests of apparently specific skills, like the Frostig test of perceptual motor development (Frostig *et al.* 1964) and the Illinois Test of Psycholinguistic Abilities (Kirk *et al.* 1968), are highly related to scores on tests of general intelligence (Olson 1968, Yule *et al.* 1969). Before one can properly interpret scores on tests of specific skills, one needs to know the child's level of general intelligence.

One final argument can be made for testing the general intelligence of children with language disorders. Such children are relatively uncommon and we do not yet know nearly enough about their cognitive development. To further our knowledge, it is highly desirable that such children are routinely given a full cognitive assessment. We already know that children who are late in speaking are at greater risk of developing reading and spelling problems (Rutter *et al.* 1970). It would be helpful to be able to be more precise and to be able to use test results to make better-informed judgements about the children's progress in language and education.

Some issues of formal assessment

The different questions raised above require different types of assessment to answer them—not merely different tests (verbal IQ, non-verbal IQ, symbolic play, language comprehension, language expression and motor co-ordination), but different *types* of assessment.

Questions concerning diagnosis and especially differential diagnosis will, in part, require *quantitative, normative* assessments. One focus of interest is how the child scores in comparison with other children of the same age. Such assessment allows for broad classification of the presenting disorder. But planning treatment will require much more detailed description of the child's language, using

313

criterion-referenced assessments. The examiner will record the child's language in detail to decide whether particular skills have been mastered or not. Progress can be evaluated using both normative and criterion-referenced assessments. Given that normal language develops so remarkably between the ages of two and four years, it is not uncommon to find that children may make considerable progress by mastering new syntactical structures or morpheme production, but that this forms such a small part of normal language development that the gains are not reflected in normative tests (Howlin 1980). Considerable thought must be given to selecting appropriate indices of progress during treatment.

Appropriate single-case research designs allow therapists to demonstrate whether gains made during treatment can be claimed to result from the treatment as opposed to factors such as maturation. These designs are discussed in detail elsewhere (Hersen and Barlow 1976, Yule and Hemsley 1977) and examples of their application in the treatment of speech and language disorders can be found in Howlin (1980), Hurlbut *et al.* (1982), Schepis *et al.* (1982), and Sisson and Barrett (1984).

Tests of general intelligence

There is no space here to consider all the measures of general intelligence are commonly available, nor to consider the pros and cons of using them with language-handicapped children. Descriptions of most of the tests can be found in Buros (1977) or Levy and Goldstein (1984). Their use in the assessment of mentally handicapped children is discussed in detail in Berger and Yule (1985, 1986). However, for clinicians not familiar with intelligence tests, a brief description of some in common usage is called for.

Below two years of age, most baby tests rely heavily on observing children's motor behaviour—posting objects in matching shaped holes, or building towers of bricks. Such tests may identify children with gross retardation in development: but it is not until later, when verbal language can be tested, that tests of general intelligence have much power to predict later cognitive development (Berger and Yule 1985).

In the preschool period (two to five years), there is a wide range of tests available. Each test usually contains some verbal items and some non-verbal ones. Verbal items take the form of asking children to repeat groups of words, to answer simple questions such as 'what does a dog say?', to define words and later to show awareness of the social rules of living. Non-verbal items range from putting pegs into holes (with the time taken to completion being important), to fitting shapes into a form board, copying drawings of simple line figures and using coloured blocks to copy patterns presented by the examiner. Different tests place different emphases on verbal and non-verbal items (see below).

Despite its age, the Merrill-Palmer Scale (Stutsman 1931) is still a useful test to determine the non-verbal intelligence of language-handicapped children. It presents a variety of tasks which children find interesting, requires a minimum of spoken instructions, and requires little speech from the child. Its scoring system also allows for occasions when the child refuses rather than fails an item—all useful attributes in tests with young language-impaired children.

Some tests are specially devised for hearing-impaired children and others are adapted for them—*e.g.* the Arthur adaptation of the Leiter International Performance Scale (Leiter and Arthur 1955) and the Snijders-Oomen Scale (Snijders and Snijders-Oomen 1959). Others, such as the Columbia Mental Maturity Scale (1959), were designed especially for children with cerebral palsy. However, most psychologists use compendium tests such as the Wechsler Pre-School and Primary Scale of Intelligence (Wechsler 1967), the Wechsler Intelligence Scale for Children—Revised (Wechsler 1974) and the British Ability Scales (Elliot *et al.* 1983). All of these consist of mixtures of verbal and non-verbal tests and each has its strengths and limitations. Here, some of the more important considerations in their use with language-delayed children will be considered.

Firstly, the tester needs to know what each test is supposed to measure so that children are not put at additonal disadvantage. For example, the Binet test has long been known to measure predominantly verbal skills. Therefore it discriminates against children with language disorders, and produces considerable underestimates of their general intelligence. For this reason, and because the most recent versions are not properly standardised (Berger 1970), the Binet should not be used in the assessment of language-disabled children.

Secondly, when testing children with a variety of handicaps, tests may sometimes be administered in non-standard ways. Children with motor handicaps are at a disadvantage on tests requiring fine motor manipulation, particularly under timed conditions. It is tempting to make allowances for them and adjust the timing. It must always be remembered that any departure from the standard way of administering a test may affect the validity of the result.

Thirdly, it is important to consider whether a child failed a particular item because he or she was unable to complete the task, or failed to understand the instructions. This may lead the tester into presenting the items in non-standard ways and seeing what is needed to improve the child's performance. Such information is invaluable in guiding remedial work, but the final result cannot be readily incorporated in a measure of the child's *level* of performance.

Fourthly, care must be taken in making predictions based on the results of intelligence tests completed by handicapped children. As pointed out earlier (Berger and Yule 1972), we still know very little about the structure of abilities of handicapped children. It is inadvisable to generalise the result of studies of normal children to them. Because of the child's handicap, testing may often be less complete. It has already been argued that it is inappropriate to use a verbally biased intelligence test as it will *under*estimate general functioning. However, there are also problems in interpreting the results of non-verbal intelligence tests. Young language-disabled children sometimes do well on visuo-spatial tasks such as puzzles and form-boards, so that on tests such as the Merrill-Palmer they get relatively high scores. However, they still perform badly academically since so much of school instruction is verbally based. As yet, there are insufficient longitudinal studies of language-disabled children to allow one to make accurate predictions of their academic attainment from non-verbal test results.

Fifthly, other technical problems in interpreting test results are considered in detail elsewhere (Berger and Yule 1972, 1985). In brief, one has to be very cautious in using results from partial testing. The fewer test items used, the less reliable will be the result. When a number of short tests are used, one has to be very cautious in interpreting the resulting 'profile'. It is always tempting to believe that one can encapsulate a description of a child's cognitive strengths and weaknesses in a simple profile and that such information will lead directly to better remedial intervention. Unfortunately, all the evidence suggests that we are still a long way from efficient and effective diagnostic-prescriptive interventions.

Finally it is always important to interpret test results along with information obtained by interview from those who know the child well and by direct observation. Indeed, structured interviews and observations of spontaneous play can often give valuable clues about a child's level of receptive and expressive language development—especially useful when trying to assess behaviourally difficult children. Systematic observation of children's symbolic play is an increasingly popular way of assessing their receptive language development (Lowe and Costello 1976, Udwin and Yule 1982a).

From time to time, different assessments will yield apparently different results. Such discrepancies in data should form the basis of hypotheses for further investigation. It could be that the child generally finds some tasks easier than others; it could be that the scores were wrongly added up. Different weight must be placed on positive and negative information. For example, I recently assessed a 3½-year–old boy who did very badly on the British Picture Vocabulary Test, where he has to point to the correct picture (out of four alternatives) when I name it. Usually, this test is a useful ice-breaker with young, shy children, particularly as it does not require them to speak. Later, the boy did far better on the Comprehension part of the Reynell test which involves doing things with miniature toys. As he warmed up, so he spoke some complex sentences and answered sufficient questions to allow his Expressive Language to be rated on the Reynell test. In this case, the *positive* finding that he can use and comprehend language within normal limits (*i.e.* within 2 SD of the scores of boys of his own chronological age) outweigh the *negative* finding on the first test. It may be that he has had insufficient experience in pointing to pictures or that he was initially overwhelmed in a strange setting. Either way, the other findings were sufficient to reassure us that he did not have a global language delay.

When a child is referred because of a suspected language impairment, performing within normal limits at the clinic does not mean that there is no problem at home or nursery school. It demonstrates that in a one-to-one situation, on particular tests, the child has some intact attainments. However, the tests may not be tapping the abnormalities which are worrying the teacher, or the child may only perform well with the undivided attention of an adult. In either case, there should be further discussions with the referring agent and observations of the child in the classroom.

The child with limited language does pose particular problems to the psychologist asked to assess him. As was argued before (Berger and Yule 1972), autistic withdrawal, disruptive behaviour or language delay should never be an excuse for failing to obtain a psychological assessment. It may take several sessions to get to know the child, who may have to be assessed in familiar surroundings. Tests and toy materials must be selected which interest the child, and the psychologist must be able to switch from one task to another very quickly as the child's co-operation dictates. Interviews with parents, teachers and care-staff can provide information sufficient to get estimates of general cognitive and language development, particularly when systematically recorded on developmental and other checklists such as the Mecham (1958), Portage (Bluma *et al.* 1976), Denver (Frankenburg and Dodds 1968) or Gunzburg (1963). These can be supplemented by direct observations of social interactions with peers and adults, of spontaneous play with small toys, and of other social skills. A sound knowledge of child development allows the psychologist to estimate the age-levels of the skills observed, so that it is nearly always possible to provide an assessment of the child's intellectual and language performance.

Assessing language

Having argued that it is important to assess children's level of general ability, let us now turn to the assessment of language itself. Again, different forms of assessment are required for different purposes. For diagnostic and classificatory purposes, it may be sufficient to assess the *level* of language functioning on a normative, standardised test. For the purposes of describing the language problems in detail and using such information to develop intervention strategies, criterion-referenced tests of language processes will be needed.

Normative testing

There now exist a wide variety of assessment tools that claim to measure language age (Muller *et al.* 1981). These vary from tests such as the Edinburgh Articulation Test (Anthony *et al.* 1971) which measure one specific aspect of language to the Reynell Developmental Language Scales (Reynell 1977) and the Illinois Test of Psycholoinguistic Abilities (Kirk *et al.* 1968) which aim to measure both comprehension and production of language. The latter tests have been found to be reasonably reliable indicators of the over-all level of language development, and are therefore of considerable value in confirming the extent of any language delay. However, there are insufficient studies of their use with language-disordered children to warrant their use in making finer-grained assessments of the type of language disorder. For example, the ITPA has been found to have one major component rather than the many proposed by its developers (Mittler and Ward 1970); and in one study of normal and language-disorderd children, the Reynell Expressive Language Scale was found to be a valid measure of syntactical structures whilst the Reynell Comprehension Scale correlated significantly with syntactical structures within groups of normal children but not in the groups of language-disordered children (Udwin and Yule 1982*b*).

The Reynell test (Reynell 1977) was especially designed to measure two very broad areas of language development—comprehension and expression—and to provide normative data on each up to the age of five or six. The examiner uses miniature toys (dolls, animals, toy furniture) to set up small scenes and so structure the interaction with the child. Testing of comprehension moves from simply asking the child to point to a named object ('Show me the doll') to responding to complex requests which require a sophisticated understanding of spatial relationships and prepositions, and a good verbal memory ('Pick up the horse which is eating and put it behind the farmer'). Throughout the testing session, the examiner notes down all spontaneous and provoked language from the child. This is analysed for its complexity of structure. The child is also asked to name objects and pictures, to define simple words and to tell short stories about pictures. The scoring of these parts yields an Expressive Language Age. Tables of data are provided to ascertain the extent to which differences between comprehension and expression are statistically assessed. The test is so constructed that comprehension scores can be obtained from severely physically handicapped children using whatever reliable movement they have to indicate a response. The Reynell test is still useful for measuring *language level*, but it makes no pretence at analysing syntax or semantics in the detailed manner discussed below. It is probably most useful in working with three- to five-year olds.

If there are problems in interpreting scores obtained from specially developed language tests, the situation is much worse when trying to infer language levels from tests devised for other purposes. Unfortunately it is still common to see reports of language ages based solely on the result obtained from parts of intelligence tests. It is true that tests such as the Peabody and British Picture Vocabulary Scales (Dunn *et al.* 1982) yield both standardised (IQ) scores and 'language ages', but the test measures a particular aspect of verbal comprehension, and there are suggestions that they may yield spuriously high scores in handicapped children who are coached in the very skill of pointing to pictures (Wheldall and Jeffree 1974). It is even less justified to infer language level from subtests of conglomerate tests such as the WPPSI or WISC-R (Wechsler 1967, 1974). Individual subtests yield very inexact estimates of ability, and should not normally be used as the sole index of language development. Occasionally they may be the only estimate available if the child refuses to do more tests, but then the results should be treated with extreme caution.

Criterion-referenced testing
Miller (1981) provided a thoughtful, thorough and provocative discussion of experimental procedures useful in the assessment of language production in children. The procedures are 'experimental' in that they derive from studies in developmental psycholinguistics over the past 10 to 15 years, and have not been standardised in the way that normative tests have. Miller used data from such criterion-referenced testing alongside data from standardised tests and interviews with parents and teachers.

Miller argued that a full assessment of the language-disabled child should include assessment of the processes outlined in Table I. He cited a variety of tests, tasks and procedures he had found useful for describing each aspect of language

TABLE I

Processes assessed as the bases for describing language performance (from Miller 1981)

1. *Comprehension*	Understanding of linguistic units
a. Vocabulary	Word meanings
b. Syntax-semantics	Grammatical structure and meaning not separable in assessing comprehension
2. *Production*	Producing linguistic elements
a. Syntax	Sentence structure, grammatical elements
b. Semantics	Sentence meaning, lexical meaning
c. Phonology	Sound elements and rules for ordering in English
3. *Communication*	Use of language
a. Communication functions and intentions	

performance.

The third set of processes would nowadays be called 'pragmatics'. A further set of processes which is increasingly being assessed concerns non-speaking children's abilities to use gestures and to imitate as a prelude to teaching them sign and other augmentative language systems (Kiernan *et al.* 1982, Udwin 1986).

Central to many of these procedures is obtaining a free-speech sample and then analysing the context according to systems developed by psycholinguists. Ever since the early days of Roger Brown and Noam Chomsky, psycholinguists have been writing grammars to describe the productions of individual children. These are time-consuming and tedious procedures, and some short-cuts have been suggested recently.

Miller (1981) recommended obtaining three 15-minute samples of free speech under different conditions. However, below 18 months of age, children give very few utterances in a 30-minute session; from 18 to 24 months they usually produce 30 to 60 utterances, which is not always enough to perform complex analyses on; over 24 months, 100 to 200 utterances are commoner. Cantwell *et al.* (1977) found that the middle 30 minutes of a one-hour audio-tape gave a good approximation to the material contained in the whole hour, but each hour of tape required three to seven hours of transcription and analysis.

These studies illustrate some very important points concerning this type of assessment:

(1) Care must be taken to ensure that the speech sample obtained for analysis is a valid index of the child's normal speech productions. To date, many authors championing the new 'qualitative' analytic methods have largely overlooked the need to obtain representative samples.

(2) It is difficult to obtain large corpuses of utterances from very young and from severely handicapped children. Until the contrary is demonstrated, one must assume that the smaller the number of utterances on which an assessment is based, the less reliable the findings will be.

(3) Obtaining the audiotape is but the first step. Getting from there to a detailed analysis of language production is extremely costly in terms of skilled time. As yet, there are no short cuts and is not clear whether such extra information really does add to cruder assessment techniques, although Bishop's (1984) computer pro-

grammes will assist in using LARSP.

(4) As Miller (1981) made clear, once the speech sample is collected and transcribed, there are no universally agreed ways of analysing the resulting data. One must be concerned about the reliabilty and validity of the methods of analysing the transcripts.

In a revealing study, Klee and Paul (1981) obtained a 30-minute free speech sample from a 41-month-old boy and applied six standard structured analyses procedures to it. The six procedures and their age equivalents were:

(1) Mean Length of Utterance (Miller and Chapman 1979)   35 months
(2) Assigning Structured Stage (Miller 1981)   35 months
(3) Developmental Sentence Score (Lee 1974)   approx. 32 months
(4) Language Assessment, Remediation and Screening
    Procedure (LARSP) (Crystal *et al.* 1976)   approx. 30 months
(5) Language Sampling, Analysis and Training
    (Tyack and Gottsleben 1974)   No norms
(6) Generative Grammar   No norms

The two procedures that yielded data not translatable into normative levels nonetheless reflected similar areas of difficulty noted by the other methods of analysing the data. On the four procedures that allow normed scores, the boy's performance fell (just) within normal limits on MLU and ASS, but way below on the other two. Had either of these been used clinically, the boy could have been given remedial language training. Although the different procedures yielded scores ranging from 30 to 35 months, thereby indicating a measure of agreement, the clinical decision whether or not to provide remedial help would have differed according to the procedure followed.

The moral of this tale is that even with the most carefully developed criterion-referenced procedure, one must still be concerned with the reliability and validity of the procedures used to obtain the speech sample and the procedures used to score it. Clearly the existing procedures—or at least those examined by Klee and Paul (1981)—produce different descriptions of the level and type of a child's problems. Much more work is needed before such procedures can be recommended confidently for general use in clinics assessing children with language disorders.

Conclusion

A comparison of the present chapter with that written by Berger and Yule (1972) gives some idea of the progress in understanding the needs of language-disordered children over the intervening 15 years. There is still a strong case for assessing the general cognitive development of such children, largely for diagnostic and classificatory purposes. There is as great a need as ever to ensure that appropriate psychometric procedures are properly selected, administered and interpreted. In the intervening time, there has been little progress either in developments in intelligence testing in general, or more particularly in assessing cognitive development in language-disordered children. Where there has been a great expansion in basic knowledge—usually in normal developmental

320

psycholinguistics—this is only just beginning to be applied to the assessment of these children.

Miller's (1981) text is an excellent example of how the new knowledge of different aspects of language development can be used in the study and management of language disorders. As yet, such assessment techniques require considerable training and experience to administer and to interpret. There are few standardised assessment tests, and most of them do not meet the accepted standards for good psychometric tests which can be used with individual clients.

Herein lies a current problem—who should be trained to undertake such assessments? There are, at least in Britain, three professional contenders: speech therapists, clinical and educational psychologists, and linguists. The last group, although currently influential, is largely tied to academic pursuits with little clinical training or involvement, so it is unlikely that it will emerge as a new clinical profession. Thus language-disordered children will have to look to speech therapists and psychologists sharing skills and knowledge in this area. District handicap teams should be able to call on both professions to assist in planning and delivery services for such children.

The move towards more detailed, criterion-referenced assessment of psycho-linguistic processes is to be welcomed. However, many practitioners tacitly, and sometimes explicitly, assume that such detailed descriptions will lead directly to prescriptions for remedial intervention (Crystal *et al.* 1976, Crystal 1979). This assumes that we know more about normal language development than is in fact the case, and also that such knowledge can guide remedial intervention with language-disordered children. It assumes that one is dealing more with *delay* (*i.e.* the children pass through the same stages in the same sequence, only more slowly) than *deviance* in language development, and again this premiss is not wholly tenable. It is now clear that autistic children's language is deviant, not merely delayed (Howlin 1980). It is still hotly disputed whether language of other mentally handicapped children should be considered delayed or deviant (Menyuk 1969; see also Chapter 15).

One way of resolving this important issue is to undertake many more well-controlled intervention studies. Surprisingly, there are few reports of studies relating the child's progress during treatment to psychometric measures taken prior to intervention. Beyond the predictable finding that brighter children tend to make better progress—whether on operant language training with autistic children (Howlin 1979), or using sign language more generally (Udwin 1986)—few data exist. One of the exceptions is the study by Kahn (1975), which found that mute children who had reached the stage of object permanence (Stage IV on the Uzgiris-Hunt Scale) made better progress in language training. This finding was independently confirmed by Hillier and Yule (1978). As was argued earlier, good psychological assessment of language-disordered children can help identify features predictive of success in treatment, thereby contributing to more effective service delivery.

Finally, it is increasingly accepted that the modality of communication is far less important than communication itself. While verbal communication remains the ideal goal, written communication, sign language and other augmentative systems are increasingly used at earlier stages. As yet, it is far from clear where alternative systems should be introduced or which children will benefit most from them. Here, again, is an important set of practical and theoretical questions which can be answered, in part at least, by good and appropriate psychological assessment.

REFERENCES

Anthony, A., Bogle, D., Ingram, T. T. S., McIsaac, M.W. (1971) *The Edinburgh Articulation Test.* Edinburgh: Churchill Livingstone.

Bartak, L., Rutter, M. (1971) 'Educational treatment of autism'. *In:* Rutter, M. (Ed.) *Infantile Autism: Concepts, Characteristics and Treatment.* London: Churchill Livingstone.

Berger, M. (1970) 'The third revision of the Stanford-Binet (Form L-M): Some methodological limitations and their practical limitations.' *Bulletin of the British Psychological Society,* **23,** 17–26.

—— Yule, W. (1972) 'Cognitive assessment in young children with language delay.' *In:* Rutter, M., Martin, J. A. M. (Eds.) *The Child with Delayed Speech. Clinics in Developmental Medicine No 43.* London: SIMP with Heinemann Medical.

——— (1985) 'IQ tests and the assessment of mental handicap.' *In:* Clarke, A. M., Clarke, A. D. B., Berg, J. M. (Eds.) *Mental Deficiency: The Changing Outlook (4th edn.)* London: Methuen.

—— —— (1986) 'Psychometric approaches.' *In:* Hogg, J., Raynes, N. V. (Eds.) *Which Assessment? A Guide to Tests, Batteries and Checklists in Mental Handicap.* Beckenham: Croom Helm.

Bishop, D. V. M. (1984) 'Automated LARSP: Computer-assisted grammatical analysis.' *British Journal of Disorders of Communication,* **19,** 78–87.

Bluma, S., Shearer, M., Frohman, A., Hilliard, J. (1976) *Portage Guide to Early Education (Revised Edn.)* Portage, Wisc: Co-operative Educational Service Agency.

Buros, O. (1977) *The Eighth Mental Measurement Yearbook.* New York: Gryphon Press.

Cantwell, D., Howlin, P., Rutter, M. (1977) 'The analysis of language level and language function: a methodological study.' *British Journal of Disorders of Communication,* **12,** 119–135.

Columbia Mental Maturity Scale (1959) New York: Harcourt, Brace & World.

Crystal, D. (1979) *Working with Language Assessment, Remediation and Screening Procedure.* London: Edward Arnold.

—— Fletcher, P., Garman, M. (1976) *The Grammatical Analysis of Language Disability: A Procedure for Assessment and Remediation.* London: Edward Arnold.

Dunn, L. M., Dunn, L. M., Whetton, C. (1982) *British Picture Vocabulary Scales.* Windsor: NFER-Nelson.

Elliot, C., Murray, D. J., Pearson, L. S. (1983) *The British Ability Scales (New edn.).* Windsor: NFER-Nelson.

Frankenburg, W. K., Dodds, J. B. (1968) *Denver Developmental Screening Test Manual.* Denver: University of Colorado Press.

Frostig, M., Lefever, D. W., Whittlesey, J. R. B. (1964) *The Marianne Frostig Developmental Tests of Visual Perception. (3rd edn.)* Palo Alto, CA: Consulting Psychologists Press.

Gunzburg, H. C. (1963) *Progress Assessment Charts.* London: National Association for Mental Health.

Hersen, M., Barlow, D. H. (1976) *Single Case Experimental Designs: Strategies for Studying Behavior Change.* Oxford: Pergamon.

Hillier, J., Yule, W. (1978) 'Object permanence as a prerequisite for language acquisition through operant training in severely mentally handicapped children.' *Unpublished study.*

Holland, A. (Ed.) (1984) *Language Disorders in Children: Recent Advances.* San Diego, CA: College-Hill Press.

Howlin, P. (1979) *Training Parents to Modify the Language of their Autistic Children: A Home Based Approach.* Unpublished Ph.D. Thesis; University of London.

—— (1980) 'The home treatment of autistic children.' *In:* Hersov, L. A., Berger, M., Nicol, A. R. (Eds.) *Language and Language Disorders in Childhood.* Oxford: Pergamon.

Hurlburt, B. I., Iwata, B. A., Green, J. D. (1982) 'Nonvocal language acquisition in adolescents with severe physical disabilities: Blissymbol versus iconic stimulus formats.' *Journal of Applied Behavior Analysis,* **15,** 241–258.

Kahn, J. V. (1975) 'Relationship of Piaget's sensorimotor period to language acquisition of profoundly retarded children.' *American Journal of Mental Deficiency,* **79,** 640–642.

Kiernan, C. C., Reid, B. D., Jones, L. M. (1982) *Signs and Symbols: A Review of Literature and Survey of Use of Non-vocal Communication Systems.* London: Heinemann.

322

Kirk, S. A., McCarthy, J. J., Kirk, W. (1968) *The Illinois Test of Psycholinguistic Abilities (Revised Edn.)* Urbana, Ill.: University of Illinois.

Klee, T. M., Paul, R. (1981) 'A comparison of six structural analysis procedures.' *In:* J. F. Miller (Ed.) *Assessing Language Production in Children.* Baltimore, MD: University Park Press.

Lee, L. (1974) *Developmental Sentence Analysis.* Evanston, Ill.: Northwestern University Press.

Leiter, R. G., Arthur, G. (1955) *Leiter International Performance Scale.* New York: C.H. Stoelting.

Levy, P., Goldstein, H. (1984) *Tests in Education: A Book of Critical Reviews.* London: Academic Press.

Lockyer, L., Rutter, M. (1969) 'A five to fifteen year follow-up study of infantile psychosis. III: Psychological aspects.' *British Journal of Psychiatry,* **115,** 865–882.

Lowe, M., Costello, A. J. (1976) *Manual of the Symbolic Play Test.* Windsor: NFER.

Mecham, M. (1958) *Verbal Language Development Scale.* Minneapolis: Educational Test Bureau.

Menyuk, P. (1969) *Sentences Children Use.* Cambridge, Mass: MIT Press.

Miller, J. F. (1981) *Assessing Language Production in Children: Experimental Procedures.* Baltimore, MD: University Park Press.

—— Chapman, R. S. (1979) 'The relation between age and mean length of utterances in morphemes.' *Unpublished manuscript, University of Wisconsin Madison (cited by Miller, 1981).*

—— Campbell, T. F., Chapman, R. S., Wesmer, S. E. (1984) 'Language behavior in acquired childhood aphasia.' *In:* Holland A. (Ed.) *Language Disorders in Children: Recent Advances.* San Diego, CA: College-Hill Press.

Mittler, P. (1972) 'Psychological assessment of language abilities.' *In:* Rutter, M., Martin, J. A. M. (Eds.) *The Child with Delayed Speech. Clinics in Developmental Medicine, No. 43.* London: SIMP with Heinemann Medical.

—— Ward, J. (1970) 'The use of the Illinois Test of Psycholinguistic Abilities with English four-year-old children: A normative and factorial study.' *British Journal of Educational Psychology,* **40,** 43–49.

Muller, D. J., Munro, S. M., Code, C. (1981) *Language Assessment for Remediation.* London: Croom Helm.

Olson, A. V. (1968) 'Factor analytic studies of the Frostig Developmental Test of Visual Perception.' *Journal of Special Education,* **2,** 429–433.

Reynell, J. (1977) *Manual for the Reynell Developmental Language Scales* (Revised). Windsor: NFER.

Rutter, M., Tizard, J., Whitmore, K. (Eds.) (1970) *Education, Health and Behaviour.* London: Longmans.

Schepis, M. M., Reid, D. H., Fitzgerald, J. R., Faw, G. D., van der Pol, R. A., Welty, P. A. (1982) 'A program for increasing manual signing by autistic and profoundly retarded youth within the daily environment.' *Journal of Applied Behavior Analysis,* **15,** 363–379.

Sisson, L. A., Barrett, R. P. (1984) 'An alternating treatments comparison of oral and total communication training with minimally verbally retarded children.' *Journal of Applied Behavior Analysis,* **17,** 559–566.

Snijders, J. Th., Snijders Oomen, N. (1959) *Non-verbal Intelligence Test.* Groningen: J. B. Walters.

Stutsman, R. (1931) *Mental Measurement of Preschool Children with a Guide for the Administration of the Merrill-Palmer Scale of Mental Tests.* New York: Harcourt, Brace & World.

Tyack, D., Gottsleben, R. (1974) *Language Sampling, Analysis and Training.* Palo Alto, DA: Consulting Psychologists' Press.

Udwin, O. (1986) 'An evaluation of alternative and augmentative systems of communication taught to non-verbal cerebral palsied children.' *Unpublished Ph.D. Thesis, University of London.*

—— Yule, W. (1982*a*) 'Validational data on Lowe and Costello's Symbolic Play Test.' *Child: Care, Health and Development,* **8,** 361–366.

—— —— (1982*b*) 'A comparison of performances on the Reynell Developmental Language Scales with the results of syntactical analysis of speech samples.' *Child: Care, Health and Development,* **8,** 337–343.

Wechsler, D. (1967) *The Wechsler Pre-School Primary Scales of Intelligence.* New York: Psychological Corporation.

—— (1974) *The Wechsler Intelligence Scale for Children (Revised).* New York: Psychological Corporation.

Wheldall, K., Jeffree, D. (1974) 'Criticisms regarding the use of the E.P.V.T. in subnormality research.' *British Journal of Disorders of Communication* **9,** 140–143.

Yule, W., Berger, M., Butler, S., Newham, V., Tizard, J. (1969) 'The WPPSI: an empirical evaluation with a British sample.' *British Journal of Educational Psychology,* **39,** 1–13.

—— Hemsley, D. (1977) Single case methodology in medical psychology. *In:* Rachman, S. (Ed.) *Contributions to Medical Psychology: Vol. 1.* Oxford: Pergamon.

323

20

PAEDIATRIC ASSESSMENT OF THE CHILD WITH A SPEECH AND LANGUAGE DISORDER

Martin Bax

Paediatricians currently are involved in at least three aspects of the assessment of children with communication disorders: (i) the setting up of surveillance systems to identify children with speech disorders, (ii) the examination of children referred from such surveillance schemes, and (iii) the assessment of children referred to them with identified problems. The latter two overlap, so can be considered together.

Surveillance programmes
The first year of life
It is still debatable how far interventions at the prelinguistic level will help the child who has a communication problem. However, there are instances where the earliest possible identification is important: for example, in the case of congenital deafness since this is known to be associated with communication problems. The early identification of children with specific problems such as cerebral palsy or with generalised delayed development is desirable for other reasons besides the higher risks of developing communication disorders. Accordingly, many centres now conduct a surveillance programme during the first year of life, including a neonatal examination at six weeks and a six- to eight-month study. The Neonatal Behavioral Assessment Scale pays particular attention to the neonate's communication system, although follow-up studies have not shown that such elaborate investigations are predictive of later functioning (Lester 1984).

Hearing surveillance
The Linco-Bennet Cradle has been developed to identify the child with a congenital hearing disorder (Bhattacharya *et al.* 1984). The cradle is only a screening device, and a suspect baby must have a full examination—including auditory evoked responses—although many neonatal units are not yet equipped to do this. While the development of such universal neonatal screening is to be encouraged, the child still must be re-evaluated as some forms of sensorineural deafness develop after birth (*e.g.* rubella) and conductive loss is a common problem which can develop throughout early childhood.

At six weeks clinical assessment of hearing is difficult. The baby will locate sound but his responses are not very consistent, and long observation may be necessary to be certain of response. The baby will often 'still' to sound, but reliable observation of this is again difficult (for a review of auditory localisation in the first six months of life, see Muir and Clifton 1985).

At around two or three months the baby localises poorly, but by five months he is localising well again, and accordingly, many centres re-screen hearing between six and eight months. The baby should be observed turning to sounds across the whole human frequency range and high-pitched rattles are available to aid such testing. The clinician gets behind the child and makes noises at ear level with voice and sound-making instruments, observing whether the child turns toward them. Masking of the alternate ear is sometimes difficult in the young child, but becomes easier once s/he is over two years old. Ideally, the tester has an assistant to observe the responses. By eight to 10 months, the child begins to 'look' for the examiner who has to wait till s/he is involved with something else before starting the test. The active child aged between 18 months and two years is the most difficult to test clinically. Distraction testing remains the basis for clinical hearing tests until the child can co-operate with a spoken test (usually around the age of 2½ to three, though some competent two-year-olds can do such a test).

Early vocalisation
By six weeks, the baby and its caretakers should be interacting socially. Nine out of 10 babies will smile at their mother by this age and, less readily, at strangers. The baby will also be making cooing and clucking sounds. By six months, the parents will report (and the clinician will often observe) that the child is making many different sounds. Parents often find it difficult to describe the sort of sounds the baby makes, and it is usually necessary to prompt them to discover that the child has begun to use consonantal sounds, such as 'g' and 'd'.

By 10 months, many children will have begun to use naming words. Although there is great variation in the timing of specific consonantal acquisition (see Chapter 5), the lack of eight to 10 such sounds at this age together with no report of naming words and a lack of 'conversational' activity would necessitate a referral.

During the second year of life, the pace at which speech and language is acquired quickens. Symbolic play may be observed as early as 15 months, and by 18 months new words are appearing daily in many children. By two years up to 200 productive words may be present, and sentence structures of two or more words combined in a selected way are part of the child's daily utterance. Again there is a great range (see Chapter 5), but in a surveillance programme one would consider referral of a child at 18 months who had no words and no evidence of symbolic play. By the age of two a child with fewer than 20 to 25 productive words and no sentence structure should be considered for referral. A delay in using words is a common problem at these ages in children who have apparently good comprehension (indicated by pointing at named objects and obeying simple instructions). An interest in books (from as early as one year old) is reassuring, whereas a failure to look at books and pictures at around 18 months to two years would be cause for concern.

By three, the child should have a wide vocabulary and be able to conduct a simple conversation; a child with no sentence structures and fewer than 50 words should be referred. A clinical assessment at this age, including naming of objects or pictures and the elicitation of simple sentences can be performed quite quickly. We found that such an assessment reliably identified children whose Reynell language scores were 1.5sd below the mean (Bax *et al.* 1980*a,b*). 7 per cent of some 330 three-year-olds had this degree of delay. A further 12 per cent had a lesser degree of delay, but these were children whom a surveillance programme would still wish to observe closely.

As the child approaches five, it is desirable to note systematically what consonantal sounds the child has not acquired (Whitmore and Bax 1986). A child with four or more omissions or substitutions may be difficult to understand (in a school situation) and is at risk of having an associated language problem.

Surveillance programmes also identify children with motor, visual and other problems. Any such child is at higher risk of having a communication problem, and children thus identified will, of course, need full assessment (for a full discussion of the value of surveillance programmes see Drillien and Drummond 1983).

Assessment of a child with speech or language problems

The range of children referred with a speech and language problem can extend from a 2½-year-old who is somewhat behind in speech and language development, to an older severely handicapped child with cerebral palsy who has no apparent communication system. Clearly, the approach to the two children will be different, with emphasis given to different parts of the examination. The difficulty at the moment is that, whereas *associations* between communication problems and various pathologies have been demonstrated, there are few data that allow one to draw clear-cut inferences about particular children. Thus, while the child with a severe hearing loss will almost invariably have a communication problem, the rôle of a fluctuating conductive loss is much less clear-cut. The clinician has to make clinical judgements about the significance of the history and findings and often may feel several factors are acting together to cause the problem.

At all ages, the early history may be relevant in alerting one to the possibility that the child has a speech and language disorder. Many congenital syndromes, including those causing mental subnormality and those associated with hearing problems, are associated also with language disorders. In various conditions such as some chromosome disorders (Mutton and Lea 1980, Evans and Hammerton 1985) and hypothyroidism, language delays are known to occur. Unfortunately many of the studies of individual disorders have used very small groups, and the strength of the association with specific language problems remains uncertain. Some of these syndromes are known to be genetic conditions and here one may elicit a family history of the condition. Clearly, therefore, in taking history from the parents one will ask about language or communication problems, both in the mother's and father's family. Late talking is known sometimes to be a familial condition, but neither parent may know the history of their own early language development. Equally significant is delay in learning to read; if the grandparents of the index child are not alive, it may not be possible to get a good history of this from the parents. However, as something like 5 to 10 per cent of all children suffer speech and language delay to some degree, usually it is not worth extending enquiries beyond a child's close relatives. Nevertheless, it is important to enquire about first cousins in order to detect sex-linked recessive inheritance, as with the fragile x phenomenon.

Clearly, one will also take a careful history from the mother about the pregnancy. Equally, if contemporary records are available, these may provide accurate information. The known association of certain virus infections, such as rubella and cytomegalovirus, with congenital deafness means that it is mandatory to search for evidence of infections or rashes during the pregnancy. Sometimes, if the mother had rubella or rising titres, she will have been investigated at the time, but usually one is faced with trying to assess a rather more vague history. Depending on the levels of health care, one may have more or less good evidence whether or not she had prior immunity, and a more or less convincing account of any infection occurring during the pregnancy. Equally, one will search for information about unusual drugs which the mother may have taken during pregnancy. The administration of potentially dangerous drugs such as streptomycin is now extremely rare in pregnancy, but because of the regular appearance on the market of new products, physicians should be constantly on the alert for unwelcome associations between a child's pathology and drug ingestion by the mother during pregnancy.

No firm relationship has been established between communication disorders and such events as ante-partem haemorrhage or toxaemia. Nor is their link with perinatal events very clear; where proven associations are established (*e.g.* between cerebral palsy and relatively severe brain damage) the children may well suffer communication disorders. However, if we leave aside those children with relatively severe outcomes such as mental subnormality, cerebral palsy, or epilepsy, and review those children who might have sustained some brain damage as a result of a perinatal event, again an association is not clearly apparent.

In a five-year investigation of a group of approximately 350 children born in central London (Stevenson *et al.* 1982), we found no statistically significant association between either the gestational age of the child or the birthweight and the subsequent discovery of speech and language delay at the age of three, although there was a non-significant trend in the expected direction. Neligan *et al.* (1976) suggested that children light for dates or of short gestation might have language difficulties, but most had other problems as well. Numerous other studies discuss the outcome for the small-for-date or short-gestation baby, but the relationship with communication disorders remains unclear. So while one must enquire about these events, often one is uncertain of their significance in individual cases. It is worth recalling that low birthweight is common in most developed countries—up to 7 per cent of the population—and speech and language delay is also common, so chance associations are likely to occur.

As a child gets older, the paediatrician will want to enquire about the way communication developed between the infant and its caretakers. It is important to know what events parents will recall two or three years later. In another study (Hart *et al.* 1978), we investigated the recall of common milestones of parents from whom we had previously collected evidence of their achievement around the age of occurrence. In general, parents tended to improve on nature, reporting the child walking earlier than perhaps s/he did. There was one exception to this: most parents of one- or two-year-olds reported their children as smiling at them later than this milestone had in fact been achieved. Many of them said that the baby was not smiling by three months, although we had records that s/he had smiled by six weeks. The chronological details of this early communication development are not as important, therefore, as parents' recall of the quality. By this time the parents will be anxious about communication, and may overstress minor events in early life that may or may not be significant, but one looks for a history of early eye regard, followed by smiling and chuckling between the child and the caretakers. The quality of the early crying is significant in a few rare disorders and its use has been suggested as an index of brain damage (Michelsson *et al.* 1977). The significance of the amount of crying is hard to assess. Some groups of mentally retarded children have been reported as crying rather little, but this is also reported in many normal children.

Parents in general have difficulty in remembering the way in which sounds developed during the first year, but they can often remember when the first word was spoken (many parents now keep baby books, and it is worth asking the mother to bring this along with her to confirm the age at which her child started using its 'first words'). As the child gets older, and the parents become alarmed about delayed or disorganised vocal communication, the history will become clearer.

Apart from the direct history of the child's speech and language, the paediatrician will want to review other aspects of its development. S/he will often try to make an assessment as to whether the child has a disorder specifically affecting speech and language, or whether there is evidence of global delay. Apart from the specific discussion of spoken language, the doctor will also want to enquire about non-verbal communication and milestones such as the development of gesture (once the child develops the pincer grip and begins using the forefinger to explore manually, s/he will also use it to point and to stress meaning) and facial expression (from smiling to the facial response of the child to those around it). Normally babies are reasonably friendly to all adults at the age of five or six months, and display some wariness of strangers at eight to 10 months; this varies in degree according to temperament. The doctor also should look for a history of affectional behaviour: coming to the parents when distressed by trivial accidents, hugging, cuddling and otherwise displaying affection towards them.

History should be noted also of gross and fine motor development, remembering that both may be slow without generalized delay. Although children who walk earlier do tend to talk earlier, there is not a very strong correlation. More important is fine motor development: a normal history would report a primitive grasp being freely used from five or six months onwards, progressing to the development of forefinger/thumb opposition by about 10 months. Development proceeds apace after this and one would like to hear that between 18 months and two years the child is using objects, such as spoons, crayons or pencils, manipulating them in a meaningful way.

Vision
The child's visual competence should have been displayed from early on. Most normal children have near-adult levels of vision probably by about six months, and one expects a good report of the child being visually alert, noticing small movements and objects from this age. The association of visual impairment with delayed communication is well known.

Hearing
One is obviously going to take a careful history of the child's responses to sound. Parents are probably the best people to diagnose early hearing loss in their child (McCormick 1986), therefore any anxieties that they ever felt about the child's hearing should be carefully documented. In the newborn period, most parents will tell you that they are certain that their child can hear as they have seen it turn to their voices; although the child can use visual cues to do this, the parent is usually correct in this assumption.

Play
When assessing the child's cognitive development, apart from those aspects associated with language, one is dependent on the parents' reports of the child's play activities. It is difficult to do this with children from cultures where toys are not usually provided (sometimes for financial reasons); but in developed societies, one can observe the child's rapid development of exploratory activity with individual objects in the second half of the first year, progressing to activities involving the simultaneous manipulation of more than one object (such as the common 'posting' game—pushing shaped objects into boxes) at around 13 or 14 months. More elaborate play with symbolic objects should begin around 15 months, when a child will also begin to use bricks, possibly stacking two or three on top of each other; simple puzzles may be introduced around this time. A two-year-old will manage a basic form board (circle, square and triangle), or simple commercial puzzles with easy shapes, and will also begin to use paints, crayons and pencils. The earliest activity, commonly, will be to pick up a pencil or piece of chalk and stab it against a piece of paper (or the wallpaper). The grip at this time may be fisted, but in most children some sort of tripod grip develops very soon after the second birthday. The availability of writing equipment and paints is mandatory for the early development of a sophisticated grip. In one unreported study conducted in a poor urban area by myself and Dr Whitmore, we found that 10 per cent of five-year-olds were still using assisted grip; we had the impression, however, that many of these children had had no preschool experience with drawing or painting materials.

History of illness in the child
A small number of children will have had a serious illness during the early years of life which may be of consequence, such as meningitis with resultant neural deafness. These instances will be relatively rare, compared to the very commonly occurring upper respiratory tract infection which may lead to lower respiratory tract infection or, more significantly, to infection of the ear.

Glue ear

Glue ear (secretory otitis media) has been implicated both in language delay and in the later development of hearing disorders, but whereas the association seems to have been clearly demonstrated in some studies, it is often hard to decide how significant the presence or history of glue ear is in relation to any one particular child; many children with glue ear develop normal speech and language. Berko-Gleason (1983) reviewed the studies attempting to document this and concluded:

> Most of them were retrospective and dealt with school age populations, who were tested with a standard instruments such as the Illinois Test of Psycho-linguistic Abilities and the Peabody Picture Vocabulary Test. General conclusions were that children with a history of otitis media with an effusion have normal sounding spontaneous speech, but they have problems with reading, and limited vocabularies and syntax, as compared with the children without a history of otitis media with effusion.

(See Chapter 12 for a fuller discussion of this issue.)

Emotional and social history

Parents provide the best account of their child's developing social responses. Clearly, enquiries at this stage should be directed at assessing the way in which parent/child attachment has developed, as well as relationships between the child, siblings and other members of the family. These issues are discussed further in other chapters. One also makes some sort of assessment of the social circumstances of the child.

Examination of the child

Over the last two decades a lot has been written about the social and emotional development of children, and also about ways other than speech in which human beings signal social concern. Studies of this kind form a scientific basis for the clinician's approach to examining a young child. Clearly, one needs to establish a good, friendly relationship with children in order to obtain any reasonable estimate of their communicative abilities. In examining a child with a communication problem, one is really only interested in the best performance; a child who fails to communicate to the examiner either may not wish to communicate or may have a profound problem, so the first question for the clinician to ask is whether s/he has obtained near maximal performance from the child. The need to achieve a good social relationship is therefore paramount. Up to about six months of age children are not afraid of strangers, and will make a friendly social response to anyone who smiles at them. Soon after this, though, they develop a wariness, so that an immediate approach to an eight-month-old baby may cause tears and distress, depending on a number of variables including the personality of the child, the quality of the parent/child relationship, the frequency of encounters with strangers, the environment in which the encounter takes place and the 'state' of the child (*i.e.* how fatigued s/he is). In examining the communication skills of a toddler aged two to three, the clinician should be aware of a number of features: (i) the child's pace of 'response' is slower than an adult's—it takes time to adjust to new people in a new environment (and one can see the child doing this). If the clinician rushes in on this situation, the child will at once become disturbed; (ii) the child's 'social space' is more restricted than an adult's: s/he can be quite aware of social activity taking place two or three metres away, but may not attend to conversation directed from some distance away; (iii) strange or unusual adult behaviour is alarming: a large man in a white coat, sitting at the other side of a broad desk who suddenly gets up and comes and speaks to a child can be frightening; (iv) the behaviour of known adults (for example the parents) towards the stranger influences a child's own behaviour—s/he will be very aware of how its mother is responding to the doctor.

Furthermore, if the child has easy access to her and can run to her knee readily, then s/he is likely to feel more secure; (v) a child, despite its innate conservatism, is also immensely curious, and this can be used by the clinician to manipulate a situation that will favour a successful interaction with the child. The arrangement of the consulting room is important. I work with my desk against a wall so that the mother and father are sitting in chairs immediately opposite me, and encourage the child either to sit on a parent's knee (if s/he wants to) or to stand by a low table, which provides a barrier between me and the child but does not prevent the child from reaching its mother easily. Apart from greeting the child, the initial remarks are directed to the parents while the child surveys the room. If s/he is obviously at ease, now is the appropriate moment (while still talking to the parents) to introduce an interesting and if possible unusual toy to the child. If s/he displays an interest one can make a remark about it while making frequent friendly smiles towards the child. When one wants to interact with the child it is often sensible to move slowly round behind him/her, 'squat' so that one's face is on the same level as the child's and then touch some of the objects on the table before actually trying to direct the child's responses. If the child shows stress, move rapidly away and encourage the parents (usually the mother) to reassure him/her, then wait for a moment or two before coming back into the situation.

One problem for the clinician is that s/he is usually in a hurry and the easiest way to elicit responses from the child is to ask questions. Wood (1982) has pointed out that this is not a normal form of conversation for a child. While the clinician inevitably will use the interrogatory form it is important to keep it at a conversational level. If the child fails to name an object within five or 10 seconds the examiner should name it for him/her and go on talking in general terms about the pictures and objects that are being displayed, in order to try to make the child feel that s/he is taking part in a conversation rather than a question and answer session. Positive reinforcement is important and whenever the child makes any response at all it should be rewarded; thus, if the clinician sees the child looking at a toy car that s/he has put down, s/he can say: 'yes that's my toy, isn't it a nice red colour?', indicating to the child that s/he is pleased that the child has looked at it. Within two or three minutes, the clinician and the child should be communicating easily. If the child becomes distressed, it is not inevitable that the consultation be aborted; sometimes if the clinician goes away and allows the child to regain its self-possession, a fruitful interaction can still occur. But if this is not the case, a fresh consultation should be arranged. It is very common to meet parents who say, 'Of course s/he wouldn't do anything they told him/her to do, so of course they thought s/he was stupid.' It is very important, therefore, for the parents to feel that their child is at ease. One often wishes to show the parents how their child is functioning in relation to normal children; if they do not think s/he is giving of its best, the demonstration will be fruitless.

It is my practice always to avoid touching the child until a relationship has been firmly established. Often non-verbal activities such as building towers with bricks or pushing cars about are the easiest to start with; the child may then be involved in some speech and language test, use crayons or do puzzles; only finally is a physical examination attempted. It is common to see doctors in busy clinics rush up to a physically ill child and slap a stethoscope on his/her chest. Placing a cold foreign object on anybody's chest without previous intimacies is a form of assault, and the child is aware of this. A child should never be undressed until s/he has been in the clinic for several minutes and it is usually best to lift or pull down clothes rather than strip the child. When using the stethoscope or other instrument, it is best to touch the part to be examined with a warm hand first and say something like 'I'm going to tickle you there', before using an instrument on the child.

The paediatric examination
Every child presenting with a serious communication disorder must have a full physical examination (in whatever order is decided, and taking into account the factors discussed above). This would include the physical dimensions of growth, height, weight and head circumference; the traditional physical examination (particularly of the cardiovascular and respiratory system), together with inspection of the skeletal muscular system, looking out for asymmetries; and also inspecting the skin. Minor congenital abnormalities such as accessory auricles, nipples or minor deviations of the genito-urinary system such as hypospadias are more common in children with a neurodevelopmental disorder. The child should then have a full neurological examination. In children with speech and language disorders, particular attention should be paid to the movements of the tongue, lips and palate. Very young children, at least from the age of co-operation (around 2½), will carry out rapid side-to-side movements of the tongue and protrude the tongue easily, but may find it more difficult to lick the upper and lower lip. The clinician should also feel inside the mouth, test jaw and lip closure and get a good look at the soft palate. Facial expression and vision are both important in terms of communication.

Assessment of hearing is crucial, but with the young and handicapped child who is not co-operative distraction techniques will have to be used clinically as the first approach. The clinician will use a variety of high-pitched rattles (such as the Nuffield or Manchester rattles) and have a variety of sound-making instruments which cover the whole range of human sound. If the child has adequate receptive speech, a spoken word test should be carried out. There are various tests available for the clinician to use, including the Reed, the Kendall Toy Test, and the Stycar equipment. The Reed requires the child to point at one of a set of four pictures; the best sets for assessing the hearing of high-pitched sounds are one containing pictures of a key, a tree, sheep and feet, and another with pictures of a fish, dish, ship and pig. To test the child the clinician stands some six feet from the ear, with the other ear occluded either by the child or parent, and names one of the objects, asking the child to point to the appropriate picture. Some children find it difficult to respond when they cannot see the clinician and in these circumstances one may want to stay in front of the child but cover one's lips with a casually held hand so that the child cannot lip read (which of course a partially hearing child often could do). Sometimes the child initially will not accept occlusion of one ear even by its mother; then a demonstration of normal bi-aural hearing will suggest that deafness is not a major element in the child's problems. With a slightly older child one can proceed to a full audiological test (see Chapter 21). Apart from inspecting the drums, which in serous otitis media can have almost any appearance, and given the great prevalence of glue ear, the clinician nowadays will usually want to carry out impedance testing to check the conduction of the middle ear.

To examine the rest of the central nervous system one will watch the child walk and get him/her to stand on one leg and hop if s/he is an appropriate age to do this and then look at hand movements. For the young child around two, getting them to build a tower gives one a good idea of the smoothness and accuracy of their hand movements. A simple test for older children is to observe them manipulating a pencil, looking particularly for quality of movements as well as accuracy and copying. The child can be asked to make repetitive tapping movements with both hands. This will also assess dominance, although often the significance of this is doubtful. Watching both gait and hand movements should alert one to minor asymmetries, but standard examination of the toe, par and reflexes will also alert one to a minor hemiplegia which may be very important in relationship to a language disorder. When one comes to test the actual speech and language performance, it is usual to start by looking at the child's receptive language before trying to elicit expressive speech.

Some children of school age present psycho-social problems: elective mutism is a classic example which may cause the clinician problems in terms of the examination. Some of these disorders are more fully discussed in Chapter 13. It is worth reminding the paediatrician (and this is of particular importance in relation to elective mutism) that where an examination fails in school, or in the out-patient clinic, a successful outcome may be achieved by going to the child's home. This also enables one to get some idea of the degree to which language is being stimulated in the home, and get a better impression too of some of the emotional and social problems which one sees in school.

Examination of the handicapped child
While speech and language disorders may of course present in the child as isolated phenomena, far more commonly they are associated with the handicaps and quite often the clinician is faced with the need to assess a multiply handicapped child. When it comes to assessing the child's communication system, other aspects of the

handicap may make the examination particularly difficult. The overactive 'psychiatrically disturbed' child may have such attentional difficulties that the clinician finds difficulty establishing social contact. On the other hand the child with severe spastic diplegia may simply lack the motor skills with which to communicate in the ordinary sense of the word. Faced with the apparent absence of any communication system the clinician will ask the family what modes of communication the child normally uses—blinking, nodding or hand movements. Then, having established a social relationship with the child one tries to elicit evidence of these communication systems. In a spastic child with severe dysarthria, perceptive language can often be assessed by eye-pointing techniques, and it is useful to have visual material mounted on cards which can be separated some distance, so that one can be certain that the child is eye-pointing at the relevant picture and not at the one next to it. In assessing the slightly older handicapped child, a rudimentary knowledge of some of the alternative communication systems (see Chapter 24) is clearly necessary if one is going to get some idea of what they can do with, for instance, a sign or some augmented speech system.

Assessment of the handicapped child often is not possible in a single session, and looking at the child's communication systems commonly requires one or two sessions. Again the child's ability to communicate may not be demonstrated well in unusual environments and a visit to the child's classroom or home may be essential. It is worth noting also that many a handicapped child has some useful communication in one situation which does not transfer to another. Hence a report that the child communicates in school may not be reflected in a visit to the home. This may mean simply that efforts have not been made to transfer skills learned in one situation to another.

Investigation
The paediatrician is now faced with an enormous variety of investigations which potentially may be of some interest in the handicapped child; the problem is to decide how many to carry out in specific instances. In the case of a speech- or language-disordered child where the input system is in question, clearly a full audiological assessment will be carried out; where clinical audiological testing has failed, the study of audiological responses may be appropriate. If the child is mentally retarded there is an enormous range of different syndromes, some of which have biochemical features which the clinician may feel it is appropriate to investigate. The common association of communication problems with chromosome disorders implies that cytogenic studies are appropriate for the moderate to severely involved child with language disorders. A report of uneven communication functioning ('S/he seems great one day but says anything the next') may alert the clinician to the possibility of convulsive disorder, and whereas in many language-disordered children an EEG is not very informative, the identification of, for example, minor epileptic status, can give the key to a diagnosis. The newer methods for assessing the electrical functioning of the brain mean that the possibilities for the investigation of language function in the future are expanding, but as yet the potential rôle of such investigations in the ordinary clinical case is

difficult to assess. A CAT scan might demonstrate lesions at particular cortical sites, but most centres would not do it as a routine in a child with language delay.

For a dysarthric child there is now a whole series of investigations available in specialised centres to examine the movements of those parts involved in speech. These include xero-electrolaryngography (XEL) (Berry *et al.* 1982*a,b*) cineradiography (Hardcastle and Morgan 1982) and palatography. Ultrasound has been used to look at tongue movements (Weber *et al.* 1986). While most of these techniques are still on a research basis, in the future they are likely to play an increasing rôle in examinations.

How far should the clinician proceed with the sorts of investigations outlined above in the child of three who presents with speech and language delay? Given the large number of such children (perhaps 10 per cent of the population) a full-scale investigation of every child would be both clinically inappropriate and economically unfeasible. The clinician therefore has to decide which children should have these more detailed investigations. Family history, together with some significant neurological findings, would suggest an investigation was appropriate, as would any untoward event in the child's own life, such as a severe perinatal event or an encephalitic illness in early childhood. Any finding on the rest of the neuro-developmental examination which suggests that the child has another problem should also alert the clinician, *e.g.* if the child has a squint or a minor congenital abnormality. Finally, the assessment of the child's present level of utterance: where this is low but normal, one may guess that the child is in the bottom 3 per cent of a normal developmental curve; but where the child's utterances already display some semantical, syntactical or phonological abnormalities (which the speech pathologists report), one may decide that further investigation is appropriate at this time. For children aged five or older who still have a significant language delay (probably about 1 per cent of the population) full investigations are appropriate in all cases.

It is not the purpose of this chapter to move beyond the paediatric assessment of the speech- and language-disordered child. However, it is important to draw attention to the need in the child with a communication disorder for adequate management of other problems. Vision, for example, must be fully assessed in the child with speech and language disorders—it is distressing how often mentally handicapped and other children turn out at a late age to have a visual defect which was overlooked while attention was being paid to the communicational and physical handicap. This emphasises the importance for all children with communication problems to have full paediatric assessments. Bear in mind, too, that functions which were normal at one age may not be so at the next: the child who hears or sees perfectly normally at three may not be doing so at five, and therapists struggling to alleviate the child's communication problem may not be aware that in the intervening time s/he has developed myopia or is now suffering from a conductive hearing loss which is significant.

It is essential, therefore, to conduct full reviews periodically with the paediatric member of the team caring for a child who has a communication problem.

REFERENCES

Bax, M., Hart, H., Jenkins, S. (1980a) *The Health Needs of the Pre-school Child.* London: Thomas Coram Research Unit.
—————— (1980b) 'Assessment of speech and language development in the young child.' *Pediatrics,* **66,** No. 3, 350–354.
Berko-Gleason, J. (1983) 'Otitis media and language development.' *Pediatrics,* **71,** 636–649. *(Special article.)*
Berry, R. J., Epstein, R., Fourcin, A. J., Freeman, M., MacCurtain, F., Noscoe, N. J. (1982a) 'An objective analysis of voice disorder: part one.' *British Journal of Disorders of Communication,* **17,** No. 1, 67–76.
—————— Freeman, M., MacCurtain, F., Noscoe, N. J. (1982b) 'An objective analysis of voice disorder: part two.' *British Journal of Disorders of Communication,* **17,** No. 1, 77–83.
Bhattacharya, J., Bennett, M. J., Tucker, S. M. (1984) 'Long term follow up of newborn tested with the auditory response cradle.' *Archives of Disease in Childhood,* **59,** 504–511.
Drillien, C., Drummond, M. (1983) *Development Screening and the Child with Special Needs. Clinics in Developmental Medicine No. 86.* London: SIMP with Heinemann Medical; Philadelphia: J. B. Lippincott.
Evans, J. A., Hammerton, J. L. (1985) 'Chromosomal anomalies.' *In:* Clarke, A. M., Clarke, A. D. B., Berg, J. M. (Eds.) *Mental Deficiency: The Changing Outlook.* London: Methuen.
Hardcastle, W. J., Morgan, R. A. (1982) 'An instrumental investigation of articulation disorders in children.' *British Journal of Disorders of Communication.* **17,** No. 1, 47–65.
Hart, H., Bax, M., Jenkins, S. (1978) 'The value of a developmental history.' *Developmental Medicine and Child Neurology,* **20,** 442–452.
Lester, B. M. (1984) 'Data analysis and prediction.' *In:* Brazelton, T. B. (Ed.) *Neonatal Behavioral Assessment Scale. Clinics in Developmental Medicine No. 88.* London: S.I.M.P. with Blackwell Scientific; Philadelphia: J. B. Lippincott.
McCormick, B. (1986) 'Screening for hearing impairment in the first year of life.' *Midwife Health Visitor & Community Nurse,* **22,** 199–202.
Michelsson, K., Sirvio, P., Wasz-Hockert, O. (1977) 'Sound spectrographic cry analysis of infants with bacterial meningitis.' *Developmental Medicine and Child Neurology,* **19,** 309–315.
Muir, D., Clifton, R. K. (1985) 'Infants' orientation to the location of sound sources.' *In:* Gottlieb, G., Krasnegor, N. A. (Eds.) *Measurement of Audition and Vision in the First Year of Postnatal Life: A Methodological Overview.* New York: Ablex Publishing.
Mutton, D. E., Lea, J. (1980) 'Chromosome studies of children with specific speech and language delay.' *Developmental Medicine and Child Neurology,* **22,** 588–594.
Neligan, G. A., Kolvin, I., Scott, D.Mcl., Garside, R. F. (1976) *Born too Soon or Born too Small. Clinics in Developmental Medicine No. 61.* London: SIMP with Heinemann Medical; Philadelphia: J. B. Lippincott.
Stevenson, P., Bax, M., Stevenson, J. (1982) 'The evaluation of a home-based speech therapy for language delayed pre-school children in an inner city area.' *British Journal of Disorders of Communication,* **17,** 141–148.
Weber, F., Wooldridge, M. W., Baum, J. D. (1986) 'An ultrasonographic study of the organisation of sucking and swallowing by newborn infants.' *Developmental Medicine and Child Neurology,* **28,** 19–24.
Whitmore, K., Bax, M. (1986) 'The medical examination of children on entry to school.' *Archives of Disease in Childhood,* **61,** 807–817.
Wood, D. J. (1982) 'Talking to young children.' *Developmental Medicine and Child Neurology,* **24,** 856–858. (Annotation.)

21
ASSESSMENT OF HEARING IN CHILDREN

Denzil Brooks

A healthy baby is wrapped in a blanket of sound from the moment it enters the living world. Indeed it is almost certain that auditory information is being processed long before birth, as the sensory portion of the hearing organ is fully developed by fetal mid-term. During the early period of development the brain is absorbing, classifying, and storing acoustical information. Sound is the antenna that keeps the growing child in close touch with the environment and with human kind. Hence if the normal process of sound acquisition is in any way disturbed or disrupted, the development of the child is likely to be adversely affected. Sound deprivation will occur where a child has a hearing loss, especially if the loss is severe or profound. If this is not discovered and treated, it will interfere dramatically with the normal process of maturation and development. Communication is likely to be disrupted, especially at the linguistic level, with consequent disturbance to parent-child relationships, socialisation and education (viewed in the broadest possible sense). It is therefore vital that hearing loss in children is detected as early as possible, so that appropriate measures can be taken to mitigate the effects of the impairment.

The incidence of severe to profound hearing loss in children in the western hemisphere lies somewhere between one and two per 1000 livebirths (Commission of European Communities 1979). So although it is an extremely severe condition, which poses considerable diagnostic problems and can create substantial social and educational problems, it is also a rare condition: but this rarity means that a high degree of viligance must be maintained, so that a child with this handicap is not overlooked.

Much more common in the developing child is mild to moderate hearing loss affecting the mechanical part of the auditory system—conductive hearing loss. In most cases this arises initially from infection. Approximately 50 per cent of children will have had at least one episode of mild auditory impairment, accompanied by some degree of hearing loss, by the time they reach their first birthday. Usually the condition is transient, with no lasting consequences (Giebink 1984). But for a small percentage of children there may be repeated bouts of infection and auditory dysfunction, and for an unfortunate few the condition can become chronic. The after-effects may continue well into adult life, affecting the potential for achievement and the quality of life.

In the past there has been a tendency to assume that because the degree of hearing impairment in the common forms of conductive hearing loss is small (certainly much smaller than the rarer profound sensorineural hearing loss) there is not the same urgency to detect, diagnose and treat these minor conditions. There is mounting evidence that this view may be too complacent, and that some children with persistent or episodic bouts of middle-ear dysfunction accompanied by mild

337

hearing loss run the risk of falling behind in their educational development, in their acquisition and development of language and in other areas of social maturation (Stewart *et al.* 1984). These consequences may not be directly attributable to the hearing loss itself, but may be due to a combination of factors including the hearing loss, a degree of malaise that can accompany the middle-ear infection or dysfunction, poor socio-economic background (in that middle-ear disorders tend to be more prevalent in the socially disadvantaged), or absence from school due to sickness (Paradise 1980).

Ideally all impairments of auditory function need to be detected at the earliest opportunity, so that accurate diagnosis of the impairment can be made and appropriate treatment—educational, prosthetic or medical—can be instituted. There are two clearly different levels of hearing testing. First there are identification or screening tests, the essential purpose of which is to identify individuals whose hearing falls below a certain well-defined standard. An identification test is a pass/fail test, but as with all such basic screening procedures, it is not feasible to achieve complete accuracy. There will inevitably be some individuals with normal function who fail the simple test, for reasons not associated with hearing: immaturity, disinterest, antipathy to the tester or distraction by extraneous noise. Unfortunately there may also be some individuals with hearing loss who pass the screen, perhaps due to lack of technique or vigilance in the tester or because test equipment is incorrectly calibrated. The aim of the test protocol must be to minimise the number of false negatives (subjects with hearing loss who pass the test) as well as the number of false positives (subjects who fail the test but whose hearing is in fact within normal limits).

Second, there are assessment tests to determine the nature and degree of the hearing impairment. Inevitably such tests are more complex and time-consuming than the identification tests, but are essential as a foundation for diagnosis and treatment.

Identification testing
Nowadays most children are born in hospital maternity wards. This would seem to be the ideal time and place for screening the hearing of neonates to detect the presence of any substantial abnormality of hearing. However, the evaluation of auditory function requires that there is a response to a specific sound stimulus, and that the response can be observed. Infant responses to sound have been observed for well over a hundred years. Charles Darwin said of his newborn son that 'during the first fortnight he often started on hearing sudden sound and blinked his eyes'. Two of the possible responses to acoustic stimulation are noted in those remarks—the startle and the eye-blink. Until quite recently the only responses available to observers have been similar to the one observed by Darwin, physical reactions closely associated in time with the stimulus. These responses tend to be somewhat inconsistent. Depending on the depth of sleep, an infant may or may not stir or waken when a loud sound is made. If a child is awake it may or may not still from motion when a sound is made. Thus there is considerable difficulty in differentiating between responses arising specifically from an acoustical stimulus

and adventitious movement unrelated to the stimulus. Even with highly skilled and self-critical observers such judgements are extremely difficult, especially with the child that is only a few hours or days old (Ling *et al.* 1970). With less skilled observers the likelihood of error increases, and for this reason there has been a search for many years for an objective test—one that does not depend so critically on the experience and skill of the tester.

Respiration is a cyclic phenomenon which in a relaxed adult follows a sinusoidal pattern known as eupnea. Sudden acoustic stimulation may produce a change in the smooth pattern. Observation of changes in recorded respiration pattern in response to acoustic stimulation have been studied for at least 20 years (Bradford 1975). Three major changes in pattern may be seen. There may be a reduction in amplitude (shallow breathing), two cycles compressed together in time (more rapid breathing) or a flattening of the cycle (a temporary cessation of respiration). Interpreting these subtle changes and differentiating them from adventitious changes requires a high degree of skill in the observer, and the method has not yet been validated for use with infants or neonates.

Similar comments and criticisms apply to another technique: cardio-tachometry. As the name implies, this is a procedure for monitoring the heartbeat. In skilled hands the test may provide valid data on hearing in very young children, but such skills are not generally available in maternity departments. (Eisenberg 1975).

Recording the electrical activity of the brain by means of electrodes placed on the surface of the scalp has been practicable for many years. Detection of changes in the brainwave form resulting from acoustic stimulation has been suggested as a possible way of screening hearing. In the USA, large-scale trials are being carried out with relatively unskilled operatives under professional guidance, using specially designed and dedicated equipment (Salamy *et al.* 1982). However, although good reliability has been demonstrated for brainstem recording when carried out by skilled professionals in an intensive-care nursery (Galambos *et al.* 1984), the use of this technique in the wider context of mass infant screening has yet to be validated.

An alternative procedure, instead of looking at the minute voltages developed on the scalp in response to acoustic stimulation, detects the much larger post-auricular myogenic (PAM) response to click stimuli at 60dB.HL. Simple adhesive electrodes are attached to the prepared skin just behind and in front of the pinna. The output from these in response to the acoustical stimuli is averaged (see p. 340). Evaluation of this technique on a sample of 102 subjects produced no false positive results, but a small percentage of normally hearing subjects failed to produce a response (Flood *et al.* 1982). The reasons for these non-responses need to be evaluated and much larger trials performed before PAM testing can be regarded as a possible neonatal hearing screening procedure.

Within the last five or six years, two devices have been developed for the specific purpose of screening babies in the neonatal nursery without the need for specialised techniques and highly skilled personnel. The Crib-o-Gram in the USA (Marcellino 1981), and the Linco-Bennett Auditory Response Cradle in the UK (Bennett and Wade 1980), may have different levels of sophistication but essentially operate on the same principle. They monitor various aspects of a child's physical state (*e.g.* body activity, head turn, startle, respiration), in a specially designed cot before, during and after periods during which there may or may not be an episode of acoustic stimulation. Each episode includes three five-second periods: one prior to test period, one synchronous with the test period (which do not always contain an acoustic stimulus), and one post-stimulus period. During the pre-stimulus period the physical state is monitored and the test proceeds only if the child is in a state of low activity. A microprocessor assesses the activity levels both during the 'stimulus' and post-stimulus periods, and decides whether a response has taken place. The number of trials is not rigid, but depends on the degree of certainty associated with the responses, the microprocessor finally providing an output decision according to a predetermined algorithm—the decision being either 'pass' or 'refer' (NB not 'fail' as there may be reasons for the responses of the infant not coming within the limits defined as normal other than deficiency of hearing). These devices are still undergoing clinical trials, and hence it is not possible to make confident assertions about their value in neonatal hearing screening. Even if the preliminary encouraging results are confirmed (Shepard 1983), other factors such as economic cost of the test equipment and staff involved in the testing may limit the rate at which they can be introduced into the health-care services.

With the current state of the art, therefore, it is probably uneconomic and impracticable to screen every neonate to try and identify the one per 1000 or so with severe/profound hearing loss. More practicable is the testing of specific groups of children who are at high risk for hearing loss. Factors predisposing towards hearing impairment are: (i) a family history of congenital sensorineural hearing loss and especially a sibling with this type of loss; (ii) rubella or other non-bacterial intrauterine fetal infections such as cytomegalovirus; (iii) birthweight less than 1500g; (iv) hyperbilirubinaemia (bilirubin level over 20mg/100ml serum); and (v) craniofacial abnormalities, including cleft palate and lip.

The percentage of children on the high-risk register is only 5 to 10 per cent of the total population of neonates, but screening the hearing of these infants can lead to identification of around 70 per cent of those with severe hearing impairment (Mencher 1977). It has to be borne in mind that having passed a screening test is no guarantee that defects in the hearing may not develop thereafter. Occasionally an infant may have completely normal hearing at birth but then suffer a progressive deterioration in hearing. Hence great attention must be paid to parents who suspect that their child is not responding normally to sound, especially if the child is not their first. Unfortunately parental suspicions are sometimes disregarded and attributed to over-anxiety, with consequent delay in the identification of a genuine hearing deficit.

In normal infants efforts at localisation of a sound source begin at around three months of age, but sound-localising head-turns do not become reliable and efficient until around six to eight months of age. Ewing and Ewing (1944) suggested that this was a suitable age for testing the hearing of infants, combining a high probability of successfully accomplishing a hearing screen with reasonably early identification of hearing loss.

In 1975 the UK Department of Health and Social Security set up the Advisory Committee on Services for Hearing Impaired Persons (ACSHIP 1981). A subcommittee of this parent body was established with the specific task of considering services for hearing-impaired children. This sub-committee recommended that all children should be screened for hearing at around eight months of age. It further suggested that the appropriate person for performing these tests was the health visitor (the visiting nurse). For the hearing screen, however, the ideal situation is that the mother and child attend the local health clinic. Only in such circumstances can the acoustic environment be adequately controlled. The test room should have a low level of ambient noise. Financial constraints may make a fully treated sound-isolated room unattainable, but much can be achieved by relatively simple measures such as fitting double doors with good and effective seals, double-glazing windows and adequate carpeting.

Testing is performed by two health visitors who have received training and whose own hearing has been checked. The baby is seated on mother's knee, slightly forward of the lap, but supported at the waist so that the head can be turned in either direction. One of the testers is situated in front of the child and initially attracts the attention of the child with a suitable toy. The second tester stands behind and to one or other side of the child, and at the correct moment makes the test sound at minimal levels.

Precise timing is essential. The front tester gains the baby's attention, and then removes the toy from the visual field. At that moment, while the child is alert and attentive, the stimulus is presented: and if the child has normal responses, it will most probably turn to try and locate the noise. Since there is a chance that the movement might be purely accidental, two responses are normally required for each specific stimulus, to be certain that they are truly reactions to the sound.

Babies respond best to sounds that have meaning, such as the human voice. To test the hearing for low frequencies, the 'oo' sound as in 'food' may be employed, and for high-frequency hearing, a soft 'ss'. Alternatively a gently tapped chime-bar (middle C) may be used for the low frequencies, and a special high-frequency rattle for the highs. Obviously the tester making the sounds has to be careful not to make any other noise (such as with a squeaky shoe) or to distract the child in any other way (e.g. by allowing a shadow to fall across the child).

As children grow and mature, their reaction to sound also matures. Like adults, they learn to ignore or suppress repeated sounds that have little significance or meaning. Distraction testing becomes less applicable and tests of a greater degree of sophistication are necessary. At around 18 months to two years, children can follow a few simple instructions which form the basis of co-operation testing procedures. Having established that the child can understand a minimum of three simple instructions, and having gained the interest of the child with some simple game, the tester moves out of line of vision and softly asks the child to carry out one of the instructions. Accurate control and knowledge of the tester's voice-level is essential. High-frequency hearing is tested by the distraction technique, which when combined with co-operative testing avoids the problem of inhibition of response to repetitive stimulation.

A further level of sophistication is introduced as the child continues to mature. The test is now made into more of a game. Some action, such as putting a ring on a stick or a ball into a basket, is to be performed but only on the specified signal. That signal may be a soft 'ss' or 'go' for the high and low frequencies.

By the age of three years it will probably be possible to train the child to carry out pure-tone audiometry. Headphones or a bone vibrator have to placed on the head, but with a little persuasion most children will tolerate these, having perhaps seen something similar on TV. Once headphones can be employed, the signals used for testing can be made much more specific both in terms of frequency and intensity.

The ACSHIP report previously referred to with regard to infant screening also recommended that all schoolchildren should have their hearing screened during the first school year, that is between the fifth and sixth birthdays. School hearing screening may be performed by school nurses or by physiological measurement technicians in audiology. Headphones are placed on the child, and tones presented at a fixed level. The actual level is somewhat arbitrary in the UK, although in the USA there are clearly recommended levels for screening (ASHA 1975). The child signifies that he has heard the tone in some well-defined manner (*i.e.* by placing a peg in a board or by tapping on the desk with a stick). No effort is made to find the threshold (softest level) of hearing: only whether tones at the specified level can be heard. Unfortunately, for many reasons, this type of test is prone to substantial error in terms of false positives and false negatives. To overcome the inherent limitations of pure-tone screening it is now suggested that a composite screen be used, with the major rôle being taken by a new form of objective test (see p. 340).

All the tests so far described have the primary purpose of determining if hearing is within normal limits or below some predetermined level. Provided that the tests have been performed according to the rules of procedure, passing the test should imply that at the time of the test hearing was within the range defined as normal. Failure to pass the test does not necessarily imply that a hearing defect exists. There may be many other reasons why, on the day of the test and under the specific conditions of the test, a child does not respond in the acceptable manner (Brooks 1977). It is therefore essential that all those who do not pass the test are rescreened at the earliest possible opportunity. If retesting again indicates the possibility of defective hearing, further and more detailed testing is necessary to determine the true auditory status. If the hearing loss is then confirmed, information is needed of the type and degree of that loss.

Assessment of hearing

Otoscopy—visual examination of the ear canal and tympanic membrane—is the time-honoured method of observing the physical appearance of the ear. In some conditions inferences may be drawn about the degree of hearing loss, but accurate assessment requires other forms of testing. Otoscopy is vital in evaluating the physical condition of the visually observable part of the ear revealing such abnormalities as impacted wax, foreign bodies (stones, peas, paper, insects *etc.*) in the ear-canal, perforations of the tympanic membrane and aural discharge. It is less

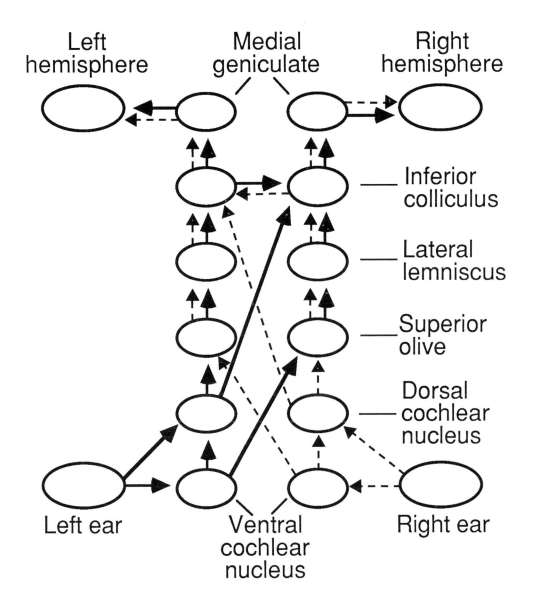

Fig. 1. Diagram of the most important pathways and nuclei from the ear to the auditory cortex. The nuclei illustrated are located in the brainstem. (Reprinted from B. C. J. Moore *An Introduction to the Psychology of Hearing*, by permission of the Academic Press.)

343

reliable in identifying the presence of effusion in the middle ear, which is the commonest aural disorder in children (Haughton and Pardoe 1982). Otoscopy is only partially effective in differentiating conductive from sensorineural hearing loss. In skilled hands the tuning-fork can provide much information. With the co-operation of the subject, the degree of hearing loss can be estimated (in comparison with the hearing of the tester). With minimal co-operation, an experienced user of tuning-forks can determine with reasonable certainty whether a loss is of sensorineural or conductive origin. The differentiation of conductive from sensorineural hearing loss has been greatly enhanced with the introduction of a form of testing known as acoustic impedance or acoustic admittance measurement. The latter term is becoming more acceptable, and probably gives a better indication of the nature of the procedure.

In a normally functioning ear, the rôle of the tympanic membrane (the ear-drum) is to collect (admit) the sound energy that enters the auditory meatus and to efficiently transmit that energy to the inner ear. If the system is disrupted, such as happens when the middle ear is filled with fluid (otitis media), then the response to sound falling on the ear-drum is altered. A higher than normal proportion is reflected from the stiffened ear-drum, and less is 'admitted' and hence transmitted to the inner ear.

The relationship between the energy falling on the tympanic membrane and the amount admitted is examined in acoustic impedance/admittance instruments. A probe that emits an acoustic signal is held lightly to the ear. The instrument does the rest. With such a device it is now possible to tell with a high degree of accuracy and in a matter of seconds whether the middle ear is functioning within normal limits, or whether there is some conductive dysfunction liable to cause loss of hearing. The actual degree of hearing loss cannot be accurately determined in the present state of the art, but inferences can be made that have a direct bearing on the decision processes regarding treatment.

Acoustic impedance testing is practicable at any age. Because it is so quick and non-invasive, and because it requires no co-operation from the subject other than a passive acceptance of the light touch of the probe, it can be used with neonates, with fractious or hyperactive children and with the mentally handicapped. Since mild to moderate hearing loss due to middle-ear effusion (otitis media) is so common, acoustic impedance/admittance testing should be performed on every child failing a screening test. Even where all the indications suggest that the loss is likely to be predominantly sensorineural in type, testing for conductive loss should be carried out as the two types of hearing loss are not mutually exclusive. Indeed there is some evidence to suggest that children with severe/profound sensorineural loss may be more prone to develop significant long-standing conductive hearing losses than are children with otherwise normal hearing (Brooks 1974). The importance of this cannot be overstated. Severe or profound sensorineural hearing loss is a major handicap to learning. The technology of hearing-aids is often stretched to the very limit, especially as regards the ability of earmoulds to cope with the high degree of amplification required. Hence the addition of even a small additional hearing loss, such as can occur with mild middle-ear dysfunction, can produce an effect that seems to be out of all proportion to the actual additional degree of hearing loss, with persistent acoustic feedback from the aid/earmould and greatly increased distortion from the amplifier.

Assessing the degree of hearing impairment is much more age-dependent than determining the type of hearing loss. In very young children one obviously cannot employ test procedures that depend on the co-operation of the subject. With neonates the behavioral tests essentially give only a gross indication about the presence or absence of hearing, and except in the most skilled hands it is not possible to make deductions about the degree of loss. Where there is suspicion of defective hearing, some objective method of testing is necessary to confirm and then to measure the loss. Evoked response audiometry (ERA) is now the method of choice for this purpose.

When a functioning cochlea is acoustically stimulated, electrical impulses are generated which are transmitted by the acoustic nerve through the brainstem to the reception areas of the auditory cortex. The progress of this electrical activity can be detected by means of electrodes placed at suitable locations on the scalp. However, there is a substantial problem in this seemingly simple procedure, in that the stimulus-generated signal is very small and it is by no means the only electrical activity going on within the cranium. There is a high level of 'noise' from other brain activity unrelated to the specific signal of interest to the auditory clinician. If the acoustic signal is large—if the sound is very loud—then the response may be visible over and above the ongoing electrical activity of the brain, but with lesser levels of stimulation the acoustically generated signal merges into the background and is lost. With the ready availability of computers, a technique has become available that enables one to extract certain signals despite their being below the level of the noise. This depends on the reasonably well-founded assumption that the response to a specific type of signal will be consistent in its time-course—i.e. that after an initial latent period, a reproducible voltage change will occur with positive and/or negative peaks at definite periods after the onset of the stimulus. The computer is employed to add up the responses observed at specific intervals after the signal has been initiated. Because the responses of the auditory system is 'time-locked' and reproducible, then the voltage peaks and troughs will gradually grow. The ongoing activity of the brain will, however, tend to average to zero as there is an equal probability at any given time that the random background voltage will be positive or negative. Thus, by using a large number of repetitive stimuli, the response can be extracted from the noise that otherwise obscures it, and responses to signals of much lower intensity can be observed.

It is now possible simply to place electrodes on the head of a neonate and to stimulate the auditory system with a large series of identical tone-bursts or clicks. From the resultant computer-averaged waveform, the expert can deduce much about the degree of hearing present. Brainstem electrical responses (BSER) provide an excellent means of assessing hearing levels in the higher frequencies, although they are less accurate in the lower range. Where doubt remains, or where the findings are equivocal, another type of electrical response test may be employed known as electrocochleography. This tends to be used only as a last resort, since it is an invasive technique. The tympanic membrane is penetrated by an electrode, the tip of which is placed on the bony promontory of the cochlea of the anaesthetised patient. By this means, the very basic electrical activity of the cochlea can be verified.

Although the cost of equipment for performing averaging and processing of acoustically stimulated brain electrical activity has been much reduced over the last decade so that it is now within the budget of many ENT/paediatric departments, the effective use of such equipment requires a high degree of skill and knowledge, as does the even more important interpretation of the findings.

Although electrical response measurement is almost the only definitive method of assessing hearing in neonates, it comes towards the end of a chain of test procedures for measuring hearing in infants and children. Infants who are referred by the health visitor will normally be retested by similar behavioural techniques, but by clinicians who are more specialised. A wider range of stimulus intensities may be employed, together with stimuli of different frequency, so that the hearing loss may be better defined in terms of degree and shape.

Once a child reaches an age when speech is beginning to be understood, then speech (live or recorded) can be used as a test medium. The child may be asked to perform some action (*e.g.* 'put the plate on the table') with a specific toy from a limited range chosen so that there might be a possible confusion if hearing is not normal (*i.e.* picking up the 'plane' instead of the 'plate').

If the child is able and willing to co-operate, multiple-choice picture identification tests may be used. The child is shown a card with a matrix of six pictures. Four are objects that rhyme, the other two being present to reduce the probability of making a correct choice by guesswork. The child is then asked to point to one of the pictures (after first making sure that the names of all the items are known) and the response observed and recorded. Information about the child's hearing is obtained not only from the correct responses, but also from the types of error made. Does the child point to a rhyming picture (suggesting a consonant confusion) or to one of the non-rhyming pictures (possibly suggesting a more severe dysfunction)? For a more detailed review of speech tests of hearing in children, see Martin (1978).

As already noted, children of three years and over can usually be taught to perform pure-tone audiometry: and by this means the degree, shape and type of hearing loss can be determined. However, it is important to recognise that not all children will respond reliably to sounds near their threshold of hearing. Responses will sometimes cease (or change) at some supra-threshold level where the child no longer finds the sound interesting. It is vital that the child is properly instructed in the response required when a sound is perceived, however minimally, and that the observer notes any variation in that response. For example, the child may be asked to make a simple 'yes' response when the tone is heard. As the intensity is progressively reduced, the response may change to 'no', although only being made when the tone is presented. Thus it is apparent that the child can actually hear the tone, but finds it of no interest and so does not give an affirmative response.

Inconsistency between pure-tone thresholds and subjective responses to speech, especially when the pure-tone audiogram shows a predominantly flat loss of around 50 to 70 dB, should alert the tester to the possibility of a functional or non-organic hearing loss (NOHL). Resolving the true nature of the hearing status can be assisted by speech audiometry, impedance testing and a range of other tests of increasing sophistication. NOHL tends to be most common at around 11 to 15 years of age and is probably more prevalent in young girls than boys (McCanna and DeLapa 1981).

Difficulty may arise where there is a marked difference between the two ears, particularly when bone conduction is being tested. A bone vibrator placed on the skull excites both cochleas. The response will then only reflect the hearing of the better of the two ears. To overcome this difficulty and test the poorer ear, a competing signal (usually a filtered white noise sounding rather like escaping steam) is introduced into the non-test ear. Provided the correct level of noise is used, this effectively masks out the uninvolved ear so that the response truly reflects the hearing of the poorer test ear.

Hard-to-test subjects

Apart from the difficulties attributable directly to age (and hence maturity), there may be other reasons why children are difficult to test. Mental retardation, cerebral palsy, blindness, brain damage and combinations of these and other problems can make testing of hearing especially difficult. However the need to know is at least as great and perhaps even greater than in children not so handicapped. The effect of two handicaps greatly compounds learning difficulties.

With the mentally retarded, abnormal or inadequate auditory behaviour is a manifestation of the general intellectual retardation. The response will be at the level of the child's development rather than the chronological age, and this must be a major consideration in the audiological evaluation. It is now well established that children with Down's syndrome have a much higher than normal incidence and prevalence of middle-ear disorders, and hence of mild to moderate hearing loss. The same is generally true of children with cleft palate and craniofacial abnormalities. Acoustic impedance testing is vital in such cases, and should form a part of the evaluation of every child with additional handicaps.

The difficulty in testing the child with cerebral palsy is largely related to the degree of physical disability. Spasticity may prevent the child from making the appropriate responses to indicate hearing, or involuntary movement may make judgement of the response difficult.

Blind children, though initially attempting to localise sound, may (because of the lack of association and reinforcement) cease to turn towards the source, thus appearing not to hear in the behavioural situation.

In testing children with multiple handicaps, or children with handicaps other than hearing loss but where a suspicion of hearing loss exists, correct choice of test procedure is of fundamental importance. The tests used must be appropriate to the child's developmental status. If suitable subjective tests are not practicable, then some form of objective test is required, such as BSER assessment.

Although normal responses may be obtained by ERA, this is not definite proof

347

of normal hearing (in the sense of using sound for the reception and processing of information). It is certainly strongly suggestive of normality, but there may be problems at the receptive and cognitive levels. In children with learning difficulties who appear to have normal hearing, input from other specialists is essential. Psychological assessment and knowledge of the family background may provide information vital to both assessment and remediation.

Purpose of assessment

Accurate assessment must be the precursor of any treatment—medical, surgical, prosthetic or educational. Where the hearing loss is sensorineural in origin, the provision of hearing-aids at the earliest opportunity is desirable. The characteristics of the system—the frequency response, gain and power-output capability and the earmould acoustics—should be tailored to the individual needs of the child. Very few losses are so great as to be beyond the capacity of amplification. For the less severely impaired, radio aids may provide sufficient help to enable the child to function in a normal educational setting. With small hearing losses the advantages of amplification have to be balanced against the acoustical, physical and psychological problems of aid use. Support and encouragement to the family as well as to the child is of great importance if maximum benefit is to be attained and maximum habilitation achieved.

Conductive hearing losses may be remediable, either through medical or surgical treatment or through the natural course of events that characterises middle-ear dysfunction. An expectant 'wait-and-see' approach may still be the wisest policy (Crysdale 1984). Teacher awareness of the presence and effects of hearing loss is also of fundamental importance. Children with small fluctuant hearing loss due to middle-ear effusion are frequently thought to be inattentive, careless or naughty, whereas in reality they may be confused and uncertain. Awareness of the cause of their apparently poor behaviour is the first step towards remediation.

Effective habilitation of the child with hearing loss can only be achieved if the nature of the impairment is known and appreciated. The earlier this can be accomplished the better the prognosis, not only in terms of individual communication skill, but also in terms of quality of life.

REFERENCES

ACSHIP (Advisory Committee on Services for Hearing Impaired People) (1981) *Report of a Sub-committee to consider the rehabilitation of the adult hearing impaired.* (Department of Health and Social Security.) London: H.M.S.O.
ASHA (1975) 'Guidelines for identification audiometry.' *ASHA* , **17** (2), 94–99.
Bennett, M., Wade, K. (1980) 'Automated newborn screening using the auditory response cradle.' *In:* Taylor, I., Markides, A. (Eds.) *Disorders of Auditory Function III.* London: Academic Press. pp. 59–69.
Bradford, L. (1975) 'Respiration audiometry.' *In:* Bradford, L. (Ed.) *Physiological Measures of the Audio-Vestibular System.* New York: Academic Press.
Brooks, D. N. (1974) 'Impedance bridge studies on normal hearing and hearing impaired children.' *Acta Oto-rhino-laryngologica Belgica,* **28,** 140–145.

—— (1977) 'Auditory screening—time for reappraisal.' *Public Health,* **91,** 282–288.
Commission of the European Communities (1979) *Childhood Deafness in the European Community. EUR. Report 6413.* Luxembourg: C.C.E.
Crysdale, W. S. (1984) 'Medical management of serous otitis media.' *Otolaryngologic Clinics of North America,* **17,** 653–657.
Eisenberg, R. B. (1975) 'Cardiotachometry.' *In:* Bradford, L. (Ed.) *Physiological Measures of the Audio-Vestibular System.* New York: Academic Press.
Ewing, I. R., Ewing, A. W. G. (1944) 'The ascertainment of deafness in infancy and early childhood.' *Journal of Laryngology and Otology,* **59,** 309–333.
Flood, L. M., Fraser, J. G., Conway, M. J., Stewart, A. (1982) 'The assessment of hearing in infancy using the post auricular myogenic response. Evaluation of an instrument which simplifies its detection.' *British Journal of Audiology,* **16,** 211–214.
Galambos, R., Hicks, G. E., Wilson, M. J. (1984) 'The auditory brain stem response reliably predicts hearing loss in graduates of a tertiary intensive care nursery.' *Ear and Hearing,* **5,** 254–260.
Giebink, S. (1984) 'Epidemiology and natural history of otitis media.' *In:* Lim, D. J., Bluestone, C. D., Klein, J. O., Nelson, J. D. (Eds.) *Recent Advances in Otitis Media with Effusion.* Philadelphia: B. C. Decker.
Haughton, P. M., Pardoe, K. (1982) 'A comparison of otoscopy and tympanometry in the diagnosis of middle ear effusion.' *Clinical Physical and Physiological Measurement.* **3,** 213–220.
Ling, D., Ling, A. H., Doehring, D. G. (1970) 'Stimulus, response and observer variables in the auditory screening of newborn infants.' *Journal of Speech and Hearing Research* **13,** 9–18.
McCanna, D. L., Delapa, G. (1981) 'A clinical study of twenty-seven children exhibiting function hearing loss.' *Language, Speech and Hearing Services in Schools.* XII, 26–35.
Marcellino, G. R. (1981) 'Neonatal hearing screening utilising microprocessor technology.' *Hearing Instruments,* **32** (6), 12–14, 23.
Martin, F. N. (1978) 'Speech tests of hearing—age one through five years.' *In:* Martin, F. N. (Ed.) *Pediatric Audiology.* New Jersey: Prentice Hall.
Mencher, G. T. (1977) 'Screening the newborn infant for hearing loss; a complete identification program.' *In:* Bess, F. (Ed.) *Childhood Deafness: Causation, Assessment and Management.* New York: Grune & Stratton.
Paradise, J. L. (1980) 'Otitis media in infants and children: a current, critical review.' *Annales Nestlé,* **43,** 7–43.
Salamy, A., Somerville, G., Patterson, D. (1982) 'The infant hearing assessment program.' *Hearing Aid Journal,* **35**(9), 10–12.
Shepard, N. T. (1983) 'Newborn hearing screening using the Linco-Bennett Auditory Response Cradle: a pilot study.' *Ear and Hearing,* **4,** 5–10.
Stewart, I., Kirkland, C., Simpson, A., Silva, P., Williams, S. (1984) 'Some developmental characteristics associated with otitis media with effusion.' *In:* Lim, D. J., Bluestone, C. P., Klein, J. O., Nelson, J. D. (Eds.) *Recent Advances in Otitis Media with Effusion.* Philadelphia: B. C. Decker.

22
SPEECH THERAPY

Kay Coombes

This chapter examines some of the issues facing speech therapists in assessing and treating children with speech and language disabilities. It aims to explain why speech therapists tackle assessment in the ways that they do and outlines some procedures used to evaluate communication. The relationship between assessment and treatment is discussed and the principles underlying current therapeutic practice are described. Particular reference is made to communication disorders that coexist with forms of cerebral palsy and mental handicap (or both), and problems that are likely to arise if such cases are identified.

Preliminary assessment

The speech therapist is unlikely to be the first or only individual concerned in the identification and assessment of speech and language difficulties. The list of colleagues who may also be involved includes health visitors, doctors, physiotherapists, occupational therapists, psychologists, nursery nurses and teachers. The criteria they use in making judgements about delayed or deviant language and speech vary, and the methods used for investigating suspected difficulties range from physical examinations and observation of spontaneous behaviour, through linguistic analyses of the child's expressive language to formal standardised psychometric tests of psycholinguistic behaviour and intelligence.

The first task facing the speech therapist is to decide whether there is a problem; secondly, if there is a problem, she needs to assess it in sufficient detail to describe the presenting difficulties and to formulate a treatment plan. The first task involves the use of standardised norm-referenced procedures by means of which the child's language is compared with that of a sampled normal population. The second task involves a mixture of norm-referenced and criterion-referenced tests as well as non-standardised clinical procedures.

Standardised assessment is relatively new in speech therapy and speech pathology. This may account for the plethora of tests that fail to meet the normal psychometric criteria expected of tests of other psychological functions. For example, McCauley and Swisher (1984) examined 30 language and articulation tests to determine how many met 10 criteria recommended for test construction by the American Psychological Association (1974): criteria such as defining the standardisation sample, descriptive statistics, data on reliability and validity, and clear instructions for examiners.

Only one test met the criterion for test-retest reliability. The authors recommend that the speech-language pathologist notes psychometric flaws in any tests employed, and comment that 'clinical decisions are never properly based on test results alone'. This advice recurs throughout the literature.

Even if a test is psychometrically sound, it will be of little value to speech therapists if it fails to provide the kind of information required for making decisions about clinical intervention. Speech therapists need to compile a picture of the individual child that is as comprehensive as possible. They need to know not only how he compares with other children of the same age but also what he is currently able to do, and how he goes about it. This helps in determining what he has still to learn, and may also give the therapist clues about the learning strategies available to the child. Such information may offer guidelines for selecting appropriate teaching approaches. Hardy (1983) and other clinicians are clearly right in counselling against a reliance on tests that are not related to function. Despite the 'inseparability' of cognition and language (Cruikshank 1976), it is not possible to make inferences about functional communication from intelligence-test data alone. Intelligence test scores may help to determine whether the child has a specific language disorder or a global developmental delay, but they do not, in themselves, provide information which directly guides intervention.

While speech therapists working with mentally and multiply handicapped children may make use of tests and assessment approaches as described in Chapters 20 and 21, there are three reasons why the therapist's assessment is of a particular character. First, its purpose is to assess whether intervention should take place. Secondly, with children who have complex and multiple difficulties, it aims to sort out the place of communication impairment in the child's disorder, and the priorities for intervention in the communication system. This can only be determined by adequate diagnosis. The therapist may have to decide which aspects of treatment should be omitted and which ones stressed. Finally, the therapist's assessment also aims to evaluate treatment, so that the treatment programme, or specific techniques employed, can be changed to obtain the desired result as necessary. In summary, assessment should provide a basis for:

(1) Deciding if and when intervention should take place
(2) Planning treatment
(3) Evaluating on-going therapy.

Description of behaviour must be obtained, in addition to scores (Siegel 1975). Goals or target behaviour(s), and their prerequisites, must be identified. Criteria for success should be clearly stated. Careful record keeping is essential in order to monitor change across a range of behaviours; this is particularly important in the case of multiply handicapped children. Gains in one area may influence performance in another, in unpredictable ways. Performance may be affected by coexisting pathology such as epilepsy, or events such as hospitalisation or changes in medication and in care staff. Monitoring must be wide-ranging and scrupulous, not only to track progress during treatment but also to promote a fuller understanding of those factors that may explain plateau effects, for instance, or regression. Without such records there may be an enormous amount of unnecessary effort expended in teaching skills that are no longer relevant for a particular child.

Assessment and diagnosis

For the speech therapist, diagnosis involves making clinical judgements based on knowledge of a range of normal performance, and on observation of the child's spontaneous and elicited behaviour in various situations. These observations are synthesised with case histories and information collected in parent interviews and from other sources including medical, care staff and teachers, depending on the child's age and situation. It is particularly important that such judgements should be made as objective as possible by being based on explicit criteria. The clinician has to be concerned with qualitative differences as well as with levels of functioning. The neurologist's assessment of co-ordination may be less detailed than the psychologist's in terms of quantification of co-ordination skills, but the qualitative assessment of co-ordination may be superior in the making of observations that generate inferences about the *disordered mechanisms* that may underlie the motor disability. The speech therapist will want to quantify intelligibility of speech using standard procedures when possible, but will also want to provide qualitative assessments that have diagnostic implications.

Developmental checklists can be a useful way of constructing a profile of a child's abilities as well as his difficulties. There are a number of developmental profile charts available, and therapists need to be aware of their reliability, validity and theoretical biases before using them (McCabe and Peterson 1985). To give one example, PIP charts (Martin *et al.* 1984) are widely used in the assessment of children with special needs. Five areas of development are assessed: (i) physical, (ii) social, (iii) eye/hand, (iv) play, and (v) language. Each category is subdivided into sections in which specific activities are identified, together with their (normal) attainment age:

e.g. (9) looks for dropped toys   Yes   No

Skill on each item is directly observed, and it is important that the therapist makes notes on the way activities are attempted so that analysis of task and performance can provide descriptions of all components or subskills. The Portage checklists (Bluma *et al.* 1976) are widely used by health visitors, nursery nurses, nursery teachers and psychologists in the UK to obtain similar information from parents. Audio and videotape recordings increasingly supplement written description and contribute to more analytical observation.

Qualitative analysis and the record keeping previously discussed is crucial. This is clear in cases where children have severe difficulties. Progress is expected to be slow, and a combination of low initial expectations, apparently confirmed by the child's inability to achieve a target behaviour, may result in the child, parents, teacher and therapist all being disheartened. The consequent lowering of morale and expectations is liable to reduce learning further. If qualitative data are omitted, a profile becomes merely another list of attainments. But by focusing parents' attention on small details of skills, slow progress, which would otherwise have gone unnoticed, can be perceived.

Assessment and treatment

Diagnostic procedures themselves may have therapeutic effects. These may stem partly from the evident concern demonstrated by carrying out any investigation, which reassures a family that something is being done: but more particularly they result from discussion between parents and therapists and child-therapist interaction. The clinician is always developing and testing hypotheses as she works with patients and their families. Very often, the most pertinent information about the disorder, its nature and possibly its cause(s), is derived from the patient's responses to intervention. Again, this depends on careful recording and the level of deduction permitted by analyses of tasks and responses.

Perceptions of what might constitute appropriate treatment depend to some extent on views about the nature of communication and language and the development or acquisition of the processes and skills involved. 'Communication' encompasses reception and transmission of signals which might range from spontaneous gestures of facial expression, eye or finger pointing, to sophisticated codes. Any modality may be involved. While communication is one of the functions of language, language itself is more difficult to define. Symbolisation is intrinsic to definitions of language, and conventionally symbols are the acoustic ones of speech or the visual ones of writing (based on spoken language). Alternative systems to speech that have grammars, *e.g.* American Sign Language or British Sign Language, qualify as language systems. Representational gesture such as Amerind does not, although it can provide effective means of communication nonetheless.

The link between assessment and treatment is as controversial in speech therapy as in other disciplines. Detailed descriptions of functional strengths and weaknesses do not, of themselves, tell the therapist whether to plan a treatment programme which builds up weak areas or which ignores them and capitalises on existing strengths. The supposed advantages of a diagnostic-prescriptive approach have long been considered in other fields of special education, and analysis of profiles on tests to date, like the Illinois Test of Psycholinguistic Abilities or the Frostig Test of Developmental Perception have not led to improved treatment procedures (Bateman 1969, Mann 1970, Berger and Yule 1972). Intuitively, however, where developmental checklists and more formal tests indicate areas of delay or deficit, knowledge of normal development reflected in the next few items on the scales can help formulate treatment goals.

Thus, administration of the PIP charts leads to practical suggestions for clearly described activities which parents and teachers can follow (Jeffree and McConkey 1976). Their suggestions on delay with language development accord well with the socio-cognitive perspective of other workers, such as Bricker and Carlson (1981). Similarly, assessment on the Portage material is backed with detailed suggestions for skills training in many areas, including language development (Bluma *et al.* 1976).

The Reynell Developmental Language Scale (Reynell 1969) is probably the assessment tool most commonly used at present by speech therapists in the UK. The test assesses comprehension of language and expressive language separately, and has normative data for children up to age six years. The examiner uses miniature toys to set up as relaxed an atmosphere as possible within which the child is asked to identify various objects, actions or relationships when comprehension is being assessed. Expressive language is quantified from noting the child's spontaneous spoken language as well as responses to pictures. The scales have the advantage that there is a version (Scale B) that can be used with physically handicapped children who cannot manipulate the toys manually. Eye pointing can be used instead. The test is enjoyable for children, is quick to administer and relatively easy to score. Its use in relation to remedial intervention was well described by Cooper *et al.* (1978).

Although widely used and considered very valuable by many speech therapists and psychologists, the test is sometimes criticised for not reflecting some of the more recent developments in psycholinguistics (Muller *et al.* 1981). It assumes that expressive language is preceded by comprehension, and identifies language as a vehicle for thought rather than emphasising the way in which infants use meaning as a clue to language (Macnamara 1972). As with other clinic-based assessment procedures, it may not give a fully accurate picture of the mentally handicapped child's use of language in the natural environment (Beveridge and Buinker 1980). Of course this merely emphasises the need to collect information on language usage from multiple sources.

The RDLS is probably most useful in assessing language at the two- to four-year level. Specific language structures are not well assessed on its expressive scale, and these should be investigated by analysing language samples using LARSP (Crystal *et al.* 1976) or similar procedures described by Miller (1981).

Treatment and theories of language development
Current theories of normal language development stress its generative and functional aspects: children learn rules that enable them to create unique utterances (Brown 1973) and use language because it enables them to communicate more effectively (Bruner 1975). It follows that prime requirements in any remedial programme designed to foster language development must address symbolisation ability and linguistic rules, and employ subject matter and vocabulary that is meaningful and useful for the child concerned. Understandably, it is easier to devise therapy which meets these requirements when children are not severely handicapped physically or mentally.

Cognitive, social and affective processes are intrinsically bound up in children's developing language ability (Bricker and Carlson 1981), and there is increasing emphasis on the communicative and linguistic responsiveness of people in the child's world. Chapman (1981) considered the response of the environment to be more important than the stimulation it provides in the normal development of language. Implications of this hypothesis for speech therapy, at least that designed for multiply handicapped children, are only beginning to be explored. It may be that there is a limited amount of 'environmental surgery' feasible. Nevertheless, in assessing children, therapists seek to identify and describe the opportunities that the child has for acquiring and practising communication, as well as estimating his comprehension of language and describing available communication and the use made of it.

The importance of social interaction in language development is acknowledged by therapy programmes directed at promoting normal mother-baby interaction during daily activities of washing, dressing and feeding. Methods typically involve counselling parents on handling the infant, turn-taking games, and talking with children who may be unable to initiate those preverbal and verbal signals that customarily elicit parental response and maintain interchange.

Additionally, in the case of children with neuromotor impairment therapists assess oral movement in non-speech activities of eating and the adequacy of respiratory adaptation, phonation and oral musculature for speech. In describing speech attempts made by these children, it is necessary to differentiate between linguistic features (such as immature phonology or syntax) and neuromuscular impediment. Both may be present and the therapist uses her clinical judgement to decide whether or not either set of symptoms takes priority in treatment, and also to estimate the interaction between the linguistic and production processes. The impact of dysarthria on developing language is unknown at present.

Speech therapists should be involved in assessing a child's suitability for a system of communication to augment or take the place of speech, and be responsible for selecting and teaching the appropriate system (*e.g.* signing or Bliss symbolics). The choice of system will depend partly on the nature and extent of the child's disabilities, partly on what expertise is available in the schools. Beyond the obvious conclusion that children without control of fine motor movements will be at a disadvantage in learning signing systems that depend on manual dexterity, there is little empirical research to guide the therapist in the choice of a system. Makaton vocabulary within the British Sign Language and Bliss symbolics are currently the most popular systems in Britain (see Chapter 24). However, recent evidence of their use with cerebral-palsied children suggests that the systems are mainly used in artificial teaching sessions rather than as the medium for all communications the child may wish to make. Formal usage amounts to a few minutes per week (Udwin 1986), whereas studies of children with severe communication difficulties find that many hours' tuition per day is often necessary. Increasingly, alternative systems are likely to be electronic devices (see Chapter 25). The speech therapist has a rôle in finding the most suitable interface between the child and the prosthetic device to allow access to the appropriate software.

It may seem paradoxical that despite the current emphasis on interactional models of normal language development, many therapy regimes exploit learning techniques that stress imitation, modelling and reinforcement. Moreover, as Muller *et al.* (1981) pointed out, this behavioural approach has been successful, at least in promoting acquisition of 'lower-order skills' (see Chapter 23). While therapists reared on Chomskyian diets tend to feel wary, there need be no contradiction here. 'Communication' and 'language' are not homogeneous entities; they are umbrella terms, and each covers a complexity of abilities and skills. In the same way, the term 'language disability' merely indicates an impairment of some kind: it does not indicate aetiology, symptoms or prognosis, and it certainly offers no guidance for remediation. It is illogical to eschew learning techniques on the grounds that language is not normally acquired by such means. It is clear that nature needs a nudge from somewhere, and some behavioural regimes anyway appear to extract elements of interactional behaviour commonly considered important in normal development and deliver a stronger dose by removing interference considered inappropriate and confusing for an individual at a particular stage.

A more legitimate objection might concern the way in which clinicians (or teachers or parents) may focus on production above all, possibly eliciting speech from children who do not necessarily comprehend what they are saying or perhaps emphasising an unnatural completeness of structure in the utterance, *e.g.* 'the man is riding on a bicycle', (recently observed). Interestingly, Muller drew attention to an experiment conducted by Pothier *et al.* (1974) that used modelling and reinforcement to influence receptive language. Part of the outcome was an apparent improvement in expressive speech.

Nevertheless, currently there is a continuous stream of new information from all kinds of researchers emphasising the complexities of communication at a multitude of levels. The literature offers a plethora of hypotheses but very little certainty. It would be surprising if therapists were to feel entirely comfortable employing techniques which often appear simplistic and crude to influence any aspect of communicative behaviour.

Bloom and Lahey (1978) advocated a developmental and naturalistic approach in which children are exposed to content/form/use of language interactions commensurate with their level of development. In practice, most speech therapists are likely to adopt a therapy approach that is informed by psycholinguistic theory while employing at least some behavioural techniques.

The impact of motor disability on communication
While all speech therapists possess a detailed knowledge of normal child development, without theoretical and practical understanding of the implications of developmental neuromotor impairment, it is difficult to see how their observations could extend to the interpretative level of differential diagnosis required for treatment planning. If interaction between contributing factors in language development is unclear, it is doubly so in the context of neuromotor handicap.

Essentially, six facts are uncontroversial:

(1) These children are brain-damaged in early life

(2) They have neuromotor impairment

(3) They may also be mentally retarded and have sensory impairments. These may or may not be consequences of the lesion responsible for the motor disorder.

(4) Typically, onset of speech production is delayed

(5) Many have feeding difficulties in infancy, and some continue to have problems in eating and drinking

(6) The most common speech impairments in this group are dysarthrias. Specific disorders of language (developmental dysphasia), and developmental dyspraxia may be present: differential diagnosis is often difficult.

Some of the effects on language development of the neuromotor impairment may be indirect. As Martlew shows (Chapter 4), the reciprocal intervention between caretaker and child in the early years is crucial for establishing turn-taking and other aspects of early communication. Children who cannot respond physically to their caretakers, or who respond in bizarre ways, are likely to elicit reduced or distorted responses from the caretakers, with subsequent effects on their language development.

Interventions and considerations

Effective and well-timed intervention is problematic, partly due to the paucity of assessments that have concurrent and predictive validity. This is hardly surprising given the lack of knowledge about the significance of some features (*e.g.* the impact of dysarthria on language development, already mentioned) and the lack of agreement on others (such as how practice of oral movements for eating might reduce articulatory difficulties). Many of the questions are those inherent in contemporary discussions of language itself, such as what is the relationship between prelinguistic vocalisation and speech?

Some children are identified as being at risk for speech and language problems in infancy due to recognised sensory deficit: blindness or deafness with or without known or suspected brain damage. In children with cerebral palsy the impairment of movement varies in types and extent between individuals, and is likely to coexist with a variety of other problems. Some of these result from the child's responses (automatic and taught) to his condition, and responses elicited from others. Physical, intellectual and psychological features can include one or more of the following: epilepsy, mental retardation, visual impairment, sensory and/or conductive hearing loss, impaired tactile sensation and proprioception, adjustment difficulties, distractibility and hyperactivity. All of these interfere with normal language development.

Communication disorders in such children include problems in acquiring language systems, and in using them due to a range of phonetic, linguistic and paralinguistic production difficulties. These include reduced or distorted gesture, and abnormal facial expression, voice and articulation.

Cerebral palsy may be diagnosed early in infants who are severely handicapped or hemiplegic, but often confirmation is only possible after two years of age. There has been little pertinent and reliable research into the communication difficulties of children with various forms of cerebral palsy, and hardly any evaluation of specific therapy techniques employed by speech therapists working with them. This is not surprising, since few speech therapists work with physically handicapped children; most are concerned with children whose principal handicap is impaired development of one or more components of speech and language associated with various levels of intellectual ability, sensory acuity and perception, and social disadvantage, but not motor disability.

As always, questions facing clinicians fall into four categories:
(1) How to know what to do
(2) What to do (including who to do it to and where)
(3) When to do it

(4) When to stop.

Collaboration between everyone involved in teaching or treating the child is required. Priorities and goals must be determined, together with methods of obtaining them that do not conflict and therefore confound success. It is essential to have a comprehensive appraisal of the factors that influence each individual case. For instance, it could be that in the natural history of spastic quadriplegia, positioning to prevent deformity associated with increased hypertonicity induced by speaking attempts may be justified in the opinion of therapists, while not automatically obvious to the child or his parents. Such issues can be controversial, particularly in the case of older children who may elect not to attend physiotherapy or speech therapy, and may have insufficient information on which to base such a decision. One task of the clinician must be to inform the child, parents and teachers of the reasons for suggesting a particular course of action when these reasons are not self evident. Another task is to prevent secondary handicaps, such as low self-esteem or other maladjustment developing.

Some behaviours of cerebral-palsied children interfere with easy communication. These include:

1. Reduction of an utterance in an effort to produce accurate (phonemic) articulation. This telegrammatic effect can be confused with syntactic or phonological impairment (and, of course, may coexist with either or both). Function words are omitted, and intonation contours flattened or distorted. Children speaking at this level are unlikely to demonstrate an ability to use discourse repair strategies to make their meaning clear when they have not been understood.

2. Individuals with a hearing loss or with fluctuating or basically low tonus sometimes phonate on an ingressive air stream. This may be related to impaired auditory feedback or be a way of maintaining extension against gravity and sufficient muscular tension to produce laryngeal sound.

3. Modification of exaggerated responses, such as facial grimacing, hyperextension of upper or entire body and shrieking may be overlooked or actively encouraged because they indicated pleasure. If they are perceived as the only available means of expression, alternative involuntary movements may be considered inevitable associated reactions, or side-effects, of functional activity, such as using a head pointer, Blissboard, keyboard or other interface with an output device such as a computer.

Differential diagnosis demands that the information gathered is sufficiently comprehensive and accurate. This may entail prolonged assessment at school and at home, instead of (or as well as) in the clinic. It is important to know as much as possible about primary sensory channels of vision and hearing. Even children with no impairment of these senses may be unable to use them effectively because of motor difficulty. For instance, poor head control makes for difficulties in developing a listening attitude, and children who are unable to turn and locate a sound source are likely to respond indiscriminately, possibly with a retained startle reaction. This in turn is likely to distort the auditory visual interaction required in order to develop concepts about auditory and visual perspective and distance.

Assessment and treatment of dysarthria

Children with mental and/or physical handicap may have speech-production difficulties due to varying degrees of neuromuscular inco-ordination. Speech therapists have traditionally analysed dysarthric speech in the following ways:
– a description of oral structures at rest
– assessment of speech and range of non-speech movements
– articulation of isolated speech sounds
– assessment of vocal characteristics, including duration (maximum phonation time), volume and pitch range
– phonetic analyses and, more recently, phonological analysis of connected speech.

There are few data available to guide assessment and treatment. It is not known how closely related oral gymnastics might be to articulatory proficiency, or even how conventional concentration on the physical might be most effectively integrated with the phonological processes approach now used increasingly when tackling unintelligible speech of children who are not physically handicapped (Grunwell 1980, 1981; Crystal 1981).

Phonological simplification processes are observed in both 'delayed' and 'deviant' speech. The resulting reduction of contrasts in a child's sound system reduces intelligibility. Clearly, a careful differential diagnosis is required. The following illustrations might be manifestations of muscular weakness or inco-ordination in articulatory movement and/or due to phonological disorder or immaturity:

dog /gog/ — (velar) assimilation

spade /beI/ — Cluster reduction + labiodental realisation of bilabial /p/ + prevocalic voicing

giraffe /væf/ — weak syllable deletion and /r/ realised as a labiodental frictionless continuant

this /dI/ — stopping for fricatives + final consonant deletion

Some children are unable to make contrasts in production, although aware of the distinction, and it is important to recognise the difference between this physically based speech disorder and a language difficulty involving unawareness of distinction contrast. Hawkins (1985) made this point in commenting on data presented by Harris and Cottam (1985).

There is clearly a need to compare a child's realisation of speech sounds not with an adult model but with systems of other children. Misdiagnosis wastes effort and time and can result in an overemphasis on practising articulatory precision at the expense of work on prosodic features, such as intonation and rhythm and rate. These contribute enormously to intelligibility. Intelligibility must be the prime criterion in any estimate of speech production.

Laboured articulatory movement mitigates against intelligible communication, as do involuntary facial movements, and (conversely) an absence of facial expression. Voice is an important factor in determining potential intelligibility. Even in non-speaking individuals, vocal characteristics (e.g. in laughing) influence listeners' perceptions and contribute to intuitive judgements, however erroneous, of personality and intelligence.

In assessing vocalisation, the speech therapist is concerned to observe respiratory function and the way in which breathing patterns adapt for phonation; to describe characteristics of voice, including pitch, volume and resonance; and to monitor the variety and amount of children's preverbal vocalisation. There are differing views on the relationship between infant vocalisation and later phonation. Interpretations of the development of speech range from those in which infant vocalisation is seen to be at least a natural precursor, and probably a prerequisite of early speech development, to those where prespeech vocalisation, including babbling, is considered unrelated to first words. The latter stance was taken by Jacobsen (1968) while the former is adopted by advocates of the neurodevelopmental approach to the treatment of cerebral palsy (Bobath and Bobath 1964, Mysak 1980, Evans-Morris 1982). Given current theories on the acquisition of complex skills (Bruner 1975) and the phonetic similarity of babbling and first words (Stark 1978), it is probably unhelpful to try to separate non-speech vocalisation from phonation and articulation.

Eating and speech

Traditionally, feeding and prespeech vocalisation have been included among areas for assessment and treatment by speech therapists working with children who are mentally or physically handicapped. Both activities are assumed to be mainfestations of underlying neurological maturation and infants' feeding patterns, and are generally thought to influence early vocalisation and possibly speech. While there are few research data available, circumstantial evidence tends to support this view, although the exact nature and extent of the impact of eating behaviour on other functions remains unclear.

The incidence of feeding difficulties in the general population is unknown. The study by Spence *et al.* (1954) reported that at least 1 per cent of children had attended for hospital treatment of feeding difficulties. Certainly, clinical experience indicates that a number of children referred for speech therapy seem to have had feeding problems even in the absence of structural or neurological impairment.

The rationale for addressing feeding also includes psychosocial considerations. Feeding one's child is an intrinsic part of mothering. Identifying and alleviating difficulties should reduce anxiety and promote bonding in interaction. Prelinguistic behaviours involving reciprocal and mutual gaze and turn taking are well reported in the literature and recognised in infant feeding situations. Typically, mealtimes at any age are social occasions. Eating and postural abnormalities interfere with social interaction, including conversation (Evans-Morris 1982). Oral movements promote oral hygiene; finger feeding provides early eye/hand/mouth activity and a degree of experiential learning.

It is evident from parents' accounts of physically handicapped children that they retain vivid memories of feeding difficulties experienced years earlier. They report feeling unsupported and ill-informed about dietary requirements and methods of feeding (including positioning), and anxious about their child receiving insufficient food or choking fatally. Many had felt angry at the child's non-acceptance of food, failure to 'chew it properly' and vomiting, while usually aware that the child was unable to do better. This was compounded by the fatigue and anxiety incurred in looking after a handicapped child. Guilt and (sometimes bizarre) coping strategies are likely to result and help maintain an unsatisfactory and unsatisfying communicative environment.

The relationship between non-speech movements, such as sucking, swallowing, biting, chewing, burping and babbling and speech is controversial. The fundamentalist view is that reflex-based eating patterns underlie articulatory movement. Other hypotheses discount the significance of some vegetative movement, while holding others, (e.g. lip rounding) to be speech-related. It seems unlikely that an efficient sucking reflex should be a necessary prerequisite for speech, though inability to develop a degree of differentiated jaw and tongue movement as required in chewing may well be a predictor of dysarthria. In a study of 60 children and adults with cerebral palsy, subjects with higher ability in feeding skills appeared to have better speech (Love et al. 1980). Despite the presumed link between acquisition of skills in motor and speech processes, there is still lack of agreement on how best to assess the movements involved.

The first hypothesis is reflected in both the PSAS (Evans-Morris 1982) which includes a section on feeding, and in the Neurophysiological Speech Index (Mysak 1980). Mysak's Index is intended as a means of determining a child's neurophysiological 'speech age', and as a guide for treatment planning and evaluation. Unlike the PSAS it is not standardised, and is less versatile. The PSAS examines feeding, respiration, phonation and sound play. It is appropriate for children who are functioning at, or below, a two-year level including those with developmental disabilities associated with cerebral palsies, mental retardation and verbal dyspraxia. Normal swallowing patterns appear to develop more easily in children who are able to achieve normal head and shoulder alignment, and a certain level of jaw and tongue movement associated with biting and chewing. It should follow that careful appraisal of eating, including posture, would be a first step in planning therapy to develop eating as normally as possible, preventing maladaptive responses and drooling.

It seems that therapy that takes into account positioning, muscle tone and response to oral stimulation, and exploits characteristics of normal experience (such as in self feeding) and food consistency, can at least improve eating function (Treharne 1980). Moreover, the improvements she describes in lip tone and control, and tongue control, might be expected to have implications for articulatory movements. Nevertheless, Jaffe (1984) commented that not all speech-language pathologists in the USA are convinced that their rôle should include remediation of feeding difficulties. As she says, there is undeniably a demand for therapists to do this kind of work, particularly those who are NDT (Bobath) trained. The situation is similar in the UK. Speech therapists expect to be able to provide treatment and advice on eating difficulties to parents of children who are multiply handicapped. Feeding development, assessment and treatment of problems are typically addressed to some extent in speech-therapy courses, even at undergraduate level.

Parents and intervention

Home is obviously where children are likely to learn most, and routinely, parents are expected to play a principal part in therapy. This is only a realistic expectation if they are provided with appropriate guidance and support. It is clear from the enthusiastic response to schemes such as Portage (Bluma *et al.* 1976) that parents will pursue regimes that are clearly laid out and designed, and which involve them (Bluma *et al.* 1976). It is equally clear that parents are no different from the rest of us in being seduced into rigorous, even bizarre, unevaluated regimes, by the promise of dramatic results.

Facilitating interactive play (*e.g.* with mother or with other children) may be helpful in developing pragmatic abilities. Certainly, play provides opportunities for signalling a variety of communicative intentions, such as requests (for a toy or game), protest or rejection (toy removed), or providing comment or information. Modelling and play therapy seem to be effective ways of promoting a child's spontaneous use of language (Martin *et al.* 1984) at least in mentally handicapped children. While there is no published study available for similar approaches with children who are physically handicapped, it would seem likely to hold true for this group, particularly since many of them may be expected to have difficulty in making sense of pictures (a common method of presentation in traditional clinic-based therapy) or transferring their responses to 'what is it' questions to their own communication.

Increasing attention is being paid to interpreting children's communicative intent. It is not surprising that there should be conflict between the child's intention and the recipient of his interpretation of messages. This is particularly likely when children are multiply handicapped and produce ambiguous speech, or non-verbal signals. For example, a physically handicapped girl presented with chocolate, produced head movements that apparently indicated negation. They were interpreted as rejection, but 10 traumatic minutes later it was clear that chocolate was in fact desired. The signal may have resulted from difficulties at several levels, including retained rooting reflex movements and semantic confusion. Even the mothers of handicapped children will not necessarily get the message right, as indeed is the case when they interpret messages from their non-handicapped children. In the past, psycholinguistic research has been directed towards examining rules of language structure and their acquisition. This emphasis has been reflected in clinical practice. Recently there has been greater stress on pragmatics and this has influenced currently developing programmes of therapy for children without mental or motor handicap (*e.g.* Bloom and Lahey 1978). Understanding similar concepts will be increasingly incorporated in therapy for children who are mentally handicapped and multiply handicapped. In assessing the communicative ability of children, clinicians would ideally include an evaluation, or at least a description, of the child's ability to use language appropriately in social interaction, alongside assessment of his language content (semantics), structure, syntax and phonology, and speech production. A number of taxonomies, including those of Halliday, Dore, Greenfield and Smith, are summarised by Chapman (1981).

Whether she works with children and their families at home, or in schools or clinics, the speech therapist's multi-disciplinary training equips her to collect and interpret information, translating it into a practical treatment approach. Two crucial functions of the therapist involve (i) sharing information, especially its implications, and (ii) fostering observational skills and appropriate interaction in front-line workers (parents and teachers). Increasingly, instead of acting as principal interventionist and withdrawing children for short clinical sessions of 'treatment', the speech therapist is adopting a consultative rôle in assessing, treating and monitoring. This would seem to be entirely appropriate, providing communication is maintained between everyone involved. Misunderstandings are bound to occur if information is in jargon, for instance, or if techniques are described without demonstration or supervised practice.

Unambiguous exchange of valid information and informed comment is more difficult than it might appear from textbook ecstasies about the team approach. One of the factors is, of course, that both professional and lay experts (parents, nursery nurses) are likely to have developed communication and linguistic skills without conscious effort. They are also likely to have developed personal prejudices about the way they acquired such skills, and the way others might be taught to acquire them. These include opinions about the contribution of drilled imitation and diligence, for instance.

Another fallacy is the belief that things will necessarily improve on their own. On the contrary, problems in many children with multiple handicap compound over time. There is general agreement that intervention is likely to be indicated as soon as difficulties are suspected. This is not to deny the importance of choosing sequences within the programme carefully in order to foster hierarchies of skills as far as their developmental ordering is known. Increased understanding of memory and learning, for instance, has resulted in recognition that older children and adults can derive benefit from therapy if it is available, while increased understanding of developmental processes has suggested reasons for lack of progress at particular ages. Failure is no longer seen as necessarily indicative of inaccurate assessment and/or inappropriate treatment techniques, but possibly due to mistiming events in the programme. It is often difficult to identify readiness for a particular intervention with any certainty. A notion of 'readiness' is incorporated into current thinking on prerequisites for stages in language development, but it is still a dangerous concept in special education and therapy. It is all too easy to make the judgement that the child is not yet 'ready' for intervention and then to sit back complacently until he is. What is meant here is that a sequence of development or a hierarchy of skills has been recognised and that the child has not yet attained an earlier level or mastered a lower skill which is a prerequisite for learning the current goal. In such circumstances one has effectively reassessed the child's functioning and set different goals. If the child is not 'ready' for one part of a programme, then teach him the skills he needs: do not rely on the passage of time!

In counselling parents, it is clearly necessary to understand their perceptions of the problems. Some intuitive beliefs do not provide a helpful starting point. An illustration would be the debate about permitting gesture rather than insisting on an attempt at speech. There is clear evidence to show that gesture is not inhibitory but actually facilitates speech. Not surprisingly, treatment for complex conditions is the hardest to devise and justify, but the need to pursue its development is clear. Current approaches, on the whole, recognise the central rôle played by parents (not only with very young children but also with those of school age), and multi-disciplinary collaboration. This is compatible with the philosophy embodied in the Warnock Report and 1981 Education Act (see Chapter 28). While it seems appropriate that speech therapists should be specialist consultants, this can result in a remote 'managerial' rôle, and there are likely to be dangers inherent in the trend to reduce contact with individual children and their families. Parents learn most about effective interaction with difficult children, (*i.e.* those who are unable to interact in normal ways at expected ages) from participant observation of a skilled practitioner. The workshop has been demonstrated to be effective in developing appropriate skills and techniques (Yule and Carr 1980). It is also difficult to think how future generations of therapists are going to develop requisite skills, let alone practise, given this kind of regime. More therapists should be going into homes and classrooms, adult training centres and day care centres, to observe functional communication, assess needs and evaluate past and present intervention. This might not only facilitate the development of more effective treatment and education, but also contribute to our understanding of processes involved in normal communication in the way that study of acquired language breakdown has contributed to understanding of language systems and to the development of treatment for adult aphasia.

The need to evaluate

There is a paucity of evaluations of treatment. It is not easy to maintain an objective stance when personally committed to a particular approach by an investment of time, effort and belief. However, if effort is to be expended to real effect by parents or therapists, evaluation must be as objective and comprehensive as possible. This is a formidable demand, especially in the case of complex treatment regimes such as Conductive Education (Peto 1955, Cotton 1976) intended to be holistic. Nevertheless, it is essential if they are to achieve any credibility. It is inevitable that possible benefits are overlooked if criteria for admission, prediction and definitions of measurable achievements are not available. In their absence it is hardly surprising that appraisial attempts that are made (*e.g.* Cottam *et al.* 1985) fail to identify benefits beyond spin-offs, such as the maintenance of morale among staff (in this case teacher, speech therapist and physiotherapist, acting as conductors).

Not that this is an insignificant point in the treatment and management of long term problems. Undoubtedly a sense of purpose and conviction maintains involvement in certain treatment programmes, that critics may consider of little worth. However, in the absence of things proven to be better, such programmes will continue to be attractive to desperate families. It is the duty of all therapists to evaluate the efficacy of their interventions.

Conclusions

Formal and informal assessment provides information on as many aspects of communication as possible. Children's cognition, phonology, phonetics, semantics, syntactics and pragmatics may all be investigated. Remediation programmes aim to promote enhanced performance in any of these areas. Approaches employed might be facilitative, based on developmental or behavioural models, or compensatory (in which symptoms are accommodated, and treatment seeks to minimise their effects) or a combination of both approaches. Effective use of communication and language, and positive responses to the child from others, is testimony to success.

Speech therapists are concerned to intervene directly and indirectly, particularly via parents and teachers, to help those with speech and language problems. If they are to do this effectively, they need both skills and theoretical knowledge. Diagnostic ability is essential, and this presumes proficiency in selecting and using appropriate therapeutic techniques. Neither of these are of much use in securing change however, unless the therapist can also exploit or create a situation and atmosphere in which people can learn. A sensitive appreciation of a family's style of communication is required, and this can only be achieved via developed listening and observation skills. Observation, demonstration and direction are used typically in a way that appears intuitive: a natural application of the therapist's personality and social skills. In fact, apparent spontaneity is exemplified by the most experienced practitioners. They are able to handle an infant with cerebral palsy, for example, in a way that is comfortable and enjoyable for the child which is at the same time informed by a knowledge of neurophysiology to reduce hypertonicity or involuntary movement. They pace a session by timing strategies so that, for example, a parent first observes and then joins in an activity and then can go on to develop an appropriate approach of their own with the child, which will share a similar rationale. Finally, speech therapists are increasingly involved in evaluating the efficacy of their interventions.

REFERENCES

American Psychological Association (1974) *Standards for Educational and Psychological Tests.* Washington, DC.: APA.

Bateman, B. (1969) 'Reading: a controversial view. Research and rationale.' *In:* Tarnopol, L. (Ed.) *Learning Disabilities: Introduction to Educational and Medical Management.* Springfield, Ill.: C. C. Thomas.

Berger, M., Yule, W. (1972) 'Cognitive assessment in young children with language delay.' *In:* Rutter, M., Martin, J. A. M. (Eds.) *The Child with Delayed Speech. Clinics in Developmental Medicine No. 43.* London: SIMP with Heinemann; Philadelphia: Lippincott.

Beveridge, M., Buinker, R. (1980) 'An ecological developmental approach to communication in retarded children.' *In:* Jones, F. M. (Ed.) *Language Disability in Children.* Lancaster: MTP.

Bloom, L., Lahey, M. (1978) *Language Development and Language Disorders.* New York: Wiley.

Bluma, S., Shearer, M., Frohman, A., Hilliard, J. (1976) *Portage Guide to Early Education. Revised Edn.* Portage, Wisc.: Cooperative Education and Service Agency.

Bobath, K., Bobath, B. (1964) 'The facilitation of normal postural reactions and movements in the treatment of cerebral palsy.' *Physiotherapy,* **60,** 246–262.

Bricker, D., Carlson, L. (1981) 'Issues in early language intervention.' *In:* Schiefelbusch, R. L., Bricker, D. (Eds.) *Early Language: Acquisition and Intervention.* Baltimore: University Park Press.

Brown, R. (1973) *A First Language.* Harmondsworth: Penguin Books.

Bruner, J. S. (1975) 'The ontogenesis of speech acts.' *Journal of Child Language,* **2,** 1–21.

Chapman, R. S. (1981) 'Exploring children's communicative intents.' *In:* Miller, J. F. (Ed.) *Assessing Language Production in Children: Experimental Procedures.* Baltimore: University Park Press.

Cooper, J., Moodley, M., Reynell, J. (1978) *Helping Language Development.* London: Edward Arnold.

Cottam, P., McCartney, E., Cullen, C. (1985) 'The effectiveness of conductive education principles with profoundly retarded multiply handicapped children.' *British Journal of Disorders of Communication,* **20,** 45–60.

Cotton, E. (1976) *The Basic Motor Pattern, 2nd Edn.* London: Spastics Society.

Cruikshank, W. (1976) *Cerebral Palsy: A Developmental Disability, 3rd Edn.* Syracuse, NY.: Syracuse University Press.

Crystal, D. (1981) *Clinical Linguistics.* Vienna: Springer.

—— Fletcher, P., Garman, M. (1976) *The Grammatical Analysis of Language Disability.* London: Edward Arnold.

Evans-Morris, S. (1982) *Pre-Speech Assessment Scale.* New Jersey: Preston Corp.

Grunwell, P. (1980) 'Developmental language disorders at the phonological level.' *In:* Jones, M. F. (Ed.) *Language Disability in Children.* Lancaster: MTP Press.

—— (1981) *Clinical Phonology.* London: Croom Helm.

Hardy, J. (1983) *Cerebral Palsy.* Englewood Cliffs, NJ.: Prentice Hall.

Harris, J., Cottam, P. (1985) 'Phonetic features and phonological features in speech assessment.' *British Journal of Disorders of Communication,* **20,** 61–74.

Hawkins, P. (1985) 'A tutorial comment of Harris and Cottam.' *British Journal of Disorders of Communication,* **20,** 75–80.

Jacobsen, R. (1968) *Child Language Aphasia and Phonological Universals.* The Hague: Mouton.

Jaffe, M. B. (1984) 'Neurological impairment of speech production: assessment and treatment.' *In:* Costello, J. (Ed.) *Speech Disorders in Children.* San Diego, CA.: College Hill Press.

Jeffree, D. M., McConkey, R. (1976) *Let me Speak.* London: Souvenir Press.

Love, R. J., Hagelman, E. L., Taimi, E. G. (1980) 'Speech performance, dysphagia and oral reflexes in cerebral palsy.' *Journal of Speech and Hearing Disorders,* **45,** 59–75.

Macnamara, J. (1972) 'The cognitive basis of language learning in infants.' *Psychological Review,* **79,** 1–13.

Mann, L. (1970) 'Perceptual training: mis-directions and re-directions.' *American Journal of Orthopsychiatry,* **40,** 30–38.

Martin, H., McConkey, R., Martin, S. (1984) 'From acquisition theories to intervention strategies: an experiment with mentally handicapped children.' *British Journal of Disorders of Communication,* **19,**

McCabe, A., Peterson, C. (1985) 'A naturalistic study of the production of causal connectives by children.' *Journal of Child Language,* **12,** 145–149.

McCauley, R. J., Swisher, L. (1984) 'Use and misuse of norm-referenced tests in clinical assessment: a hypothetical case.' *Journal of Speech and Hearing Disorders,* **49,** 338–348.

Miller, J. F. (1981) *Assessing Language Production in Children: Experimental Procedures.* Baltimore: University Park Press.

Muller, D., Munro, S., Code, C. (1981) *Language Assessment for Remediation.* Beckenham, Kent: Croom Helm.

Mysak, E. D. (1980) *Neurospeech Therapy for the Cerebral Palsied.* New York: Teachers' College Press, Columbia University.

Petö, A. (1955) 'Konductiv mozgásterápia mint gyógypedagógia.' *Gyógypedagógia,* **1,** 15–21.

Pothier, P., Morrison, D., Gorman, F. R. (1974) 'Effects of receptive language training on receptive language development.' *Journal of Abnormal Child Psychiatry,* **2,** 153.

Reynell, J. (1969) *Reynell Developmental Language Scales.* Windsor: NFER.

Siegel, G. M. (1975) 'The use of language tests.' *Language, Speech and Hearing in Schools,* **6,** 211–217.

Spence, J., Watton, W. S., Miller, F. J. W., Court, S. D. M. (1954) *A Thousand Families in Newcastle upon Tyne.* Oxford: Oxford University Press.

Stark, R. E. (1978) 'Features of infant sounds: the emergence of cooing.' *Journal of Child Language,* **5,** 379–401.

Treharne, D. A. (1980) 'Feeding patterns and speech development.' *In:* Jones, M. F. (Ed.) *Language Disability in Children.* Lancaster: MTP.

Udwin, O. (1986) *An Evaluation of Alternative and Augmentative Systems of Communication Taught to Non-Verbal Cerebral Palsied Children.* Unpublished PhD Thesis, University of London.

Yule, W., Carr, J. (1980) *Behaviour Modification for the Mentally Handicapped.* London: Croom Helm.

23
BEHAVIOURAL APPROACHES TO LANGUAGE TRAINING

Patricia Howlin

Environmental influences on language development

Effects on normal language acquisition

The rôle of environmental influences on normal language development has proved a continuing source of debate (see Chapters 6 and 7). Although early observational studies (Brown 1973, Nelson 1973, Newport *et al.* 1977) suggested that maternal speech styles could influence children's language acquisition, subsequent experimental studies failed to support this thesis. Nevertheless, recent work (Scherer and Olswang 1984, Baker and Nelson 1986, Schwartz *et al.* 1985) has reaffirmed the link between mothers' and children's speech. Certain types of maternal speech style, particularly those involving higher rates of questions, repetitions and extensions of children's utterances, are associated with improved linguistic development at least in some children (Barnes *et al.* 1983, Smolek and Weinraub 1983).

It is unclear whether such styles represent deliberate maternal strategies or are 'natural' responses to the child's developmental level. Individual differences between children must be considered when assessing the apparent rôle of maternal input. Language acquisition is not a one-way process, and the way children respond to and affect their environment is also likely to influence findings. Barnes *et al.* (1983) concluded that the way in which language is learned is ultimately dependent on the child's ability to organise and exploit his or her linguistic environment. But certain features of this environment, particularly in the early stages of development, seem better suited to the acquisition of language than others.

The effects on linguistically handicapped children

Although a number of studies have suggested that inadequate parental input may have a direct *causal* association with language delay (Jones, 1980, Goldfarb *et al.* 1972, Marshall *et al.* 1973; Buium *et al.* 1974) most such claims lack adequate data. Differences between parents of handicapped and normal children exist, but these appear to be a function of the influences of *children's* language level on adult speech, rather than the other way round (Horsborough *et al.* 1985). Much of the apparent 'deviance' in maternal speech tends to disappear if normal and handicapped children are suitably matched for mental and language ages. When this is done, the length and complexity of maternal utterances to normal or language-delayed children tend to be very similar (Rondal 1978, Cunningham *et al.* 1981, Leifer and Lewis 1983). Although most cases of language delay cannot be attributed to inadequate parental communication, the interaction between parents and their handicapped children may be less than optimal for eliciting or encouraging language. Wolchick (1983), for example, in her observations of normal and autistic children, found that parents in the autistic group were likely to use relatively fewer utterances designed to elicit speech from their children. Gardner (1976) also found that mothers of autistic children were less successful than parents of normal children in obtaining co-operative responses.

The most effective language environment for handicapped children may well be very different from the environment in which normal children flourish. Numerous ways of providing such an environment have been explored over recent years. In the course of this research, behavioural techniques have come to be accepted as one of the most effective means of teaching, or re-establishing, language skills.

Behavioural approaches to language training

Behavioural methods involve (i) the use of direct prompting to elicit verbal responses; (ii) the use of reinforcement to increase the frequency of such utterances; (iii) modelling and shaping procedures to increase the complexity of speech, and (iv) fading techniques to bring verbalisations under the subject's own control.

One of the earliest studies to demonstrate the effectiveness of such techniques was that by Isaacs *et al.* (1960). Using cigarettes and chewing-gum as reinforcers, first for lip movements and later for any vocal behaviour, speech was reinstated in two schizophrenic patients who had been mute for 14 and 19 years respectively. Later Sherman (1963, 1965) used similar methods to re-establish speech in institutionalised psychotics. At the same time, studies on the development of speech in non-verbal children began to appear (Hingtgen and Trost 1964, Wolf *et al.* 1964, Hewett 1965, Salzinger *et al.* 1965, Lovaas *et al.* 1966).

Many of these early language-training programmes were designed simply to increase rates of vocalisations, rather than to increase the complexity of utterances. Reinforcement (usually with bites of food) would be given for random vocalisations made by the patient, thereby increasing the frequency of such sounds. Further reinforcements would then be given for closer approximations to the sounds required by the therapist. Lovaas (1966), however, found that although the reinforcement of chance vocalisations could result in children learning a few words, such procedures generally resulted in a very restricted growth in vocabulary. Instead, the direct training of imitative responses resulted in much faster progress. Wolf *et al.* (1964) described the effective use of imitative training with a three-year-old brain-damaged, autistic and mentally retarded boy. Lovaas *et al.* (1966) reported the rapid establishment of a large imitative vocabulary in two initially mute autistic six-year-olds. Kerr *et al.* (1965), Cook and Adams (1966) and Sapon (1969) also used direct imitation training successfully with language-deficient children.

Behavioural intervention programmes with language-handicapped children have continued to proliferate since these early studies. Initially, intervention tended to focus on the use of reinforcers to increase appropriate vocalisations or imitative speech, or on the extinction of inappropriate utterances (Kerr *et al.* 1965). Subsequent programmes have become far more complex and sophisticated with much more detailed assessments of children's language deficits, together with the specific teaching of psycholinguistic rules. A general restructuring of adult-child interaction at home, to facilitate a more effective language-teaching environment, has also played an increasingly important rôle in treatment (Harris *et al.* 1981, Howlin 1981*a*). Recently there have also been successful programmes to teach non-verbal forms of communication to children who do not respond to vocal training (Kiernan 1983).

Methods of treatment used
Although language-modification programmes have tended to follow the procedures initially developed by Lovaas *et al.* (1966) and Sloane *et al.* (1968), the particular stage at which treatment should begin and the ultimate goals of training will depend on the specific problems of the individual child.

Many studies have shown that the effects of language training with children over the age of five years, who totally lack speech, tend to be minimal (Howlin 1981*a, b*; Harris and Wolchick 1982; Koegel *et al.* 1982). Although highly intensive training may be moderately successful in teaching such children to emit specific sounds, there is little evidence that intervention of this kind has any marked influences on general communicative ability. This is particularly true in the case of children who not only lack spontaneous vocalisations, but also show minimal understanding of speech and who have little or no internalised language (as evidenced by imaginative play). For children who are globally handicapped in all areas of language development, it is generally much more useful to focus on the development of simple comprehension skills. This can be done by combining clear verbal instructions with prompts or physical guidance, so that the child learns to associate spoken commands with particular actions. Reinforcement, using praise and possibly tangible rewards, will help to increase co-operation. As the association between the adult's command and the child's action is established, physical prompts and gestures may be withdrawn until the child is able to respond to spoken instructions alone.

Unfortunately, helping to improve the child's understanding in this way does not necessarily lead to significant improvements in spoken language. Improved comprehension should, however, have beneficial effects on the child's interaction with parents and teachers; also it tends to result in decreases in behaviour problems in many children (Howlin 1984*b*).

EXPRESSIVE LANGUAGE TRAINING: THE DEVELOPMENT OF IMITATION
For children who show some spontaneous use of sounds, behavioural techniques can be used to increase the range and complexity of their expressive skills. Again, the outcome of training tends to be highly dependent on the child's initial language level. Koegel *et al.* (1982) showed that it can be very difficult to teach sounds that are not already in the child's repertoire, but shaping, reinforcement and prompting techniques can be used to increase simple vocal imitations. Verbal and kinaesthetic

Syntactical structural acquired in early child language development.
(From Brown 1973, De Villiers and De Villiers 1978)

Morphemes	Example	Transformations	Example
Present progressive	Run*ning*	Imperative	Stop it
Third person singular	Run*s*	Question-inversion	Did he go
Third person regular past	Jump*ed*	Wh-question	Where is mummy
Third person irregular	Went	Negation	Daddy not there
Plural	Dog*s*	Auxiliary	I *can* go
Possessive	Mummy'*s*	Copula	He *is* going
Pronouns and case	My/mine, *etc.*	'Do'-support	I *do* like it
Prepositions	In/on, *etc.*		
Articles	A/the		
Adverbial and adjectival inflections	Quick/quickly		

TABLE Ib
Predominant semantic relationships in early two-word utterances
(From Clark and Clark 1977)

Semantic relationship	Example of utterance
Assertions	
Presence of Object	That car. See sock
Denial of Presence	Allgone shoe. No set
Location of Object	There doggie. Pennyinnere
Possession of Object	Mama dress. Daddy chair
Quality of Object	Pretty boat. Big bus
Ongoing event	Mummy sleep. Hit ball
Requests	
For action	More taxi. Want ball
For information	Where doggie? Sit water?
Refusal	No more

prompts can then be used to extend the range of sounds imitated (Nelson and Evans 1968). Once a variety of sounds can be imitated by the child, these can be chained together to form simple words or word approximations.

Even in the earliest stages of treatment, all the child's 'words' should be associated with familiar objects. Imitation for the sake of imitation is of little practical value. Thus the objects involved in training need to be of direct relevance to the child. Initially any attempts that the child makes at naming should be reinforced, but later, only closer and closer approximations to the stimulus word should be accepted (Howlin 1980*a, b*).

Progress in the early stages of both comprehension and imitation training tends to be slow and arduous, the first few words or commands often taking many weeks to acquire. Thereafter, learning tends to progress more rapidly and it is then possible to teach the child to understand or use many new and different words.

INCREASING SPONTANEOUS LANGUAGE AND THE ACQUISITION OF LINGUISTIC RULES

In the past, language-training programmes tended to be somewhat arbitrary in the selection of the particular linguistic forms taught. The importance of motivational factors was generally ignored, and it is only recently that the need to teach language skills that have a *direct* impact on the child's interaction with his environment has been considered (Guess *et al.* 1976, Carr and Durand 1985). In addition, the language structures taught frequently bore no relationship to the language skills acquired by normal children of a similar linguistic or mental age. Many of the rules taught, for example the differentiation between deictic adjectives (big, small, fat, thin) or pronouns (he/she, I/you) are now known to present difficulties even to normal three- and four-year-olds (De Villiers and De Villiers 1978). There is considerable controversy as to whether the acquisition of syntax or semantics is the same for handicapped children as it is for normal infants. Some authors (Johnston and Schery 1972, Leonard 1972), suggest that morpheme acquisition in language-delayed children follows a normal pattern but that such children reach criterion at higher levels of MLU (mean length of utterance) than normal children. Other studies with deaf, mentally retarded or language-delayed children seem to indicate atypical patterns of rule acquisition (Bartolucci *et al.* 1980, Howlin 1984*a*). Much more information is needed on both normal and abnormal patterns of language acquisition, but clinical findings indicate that those linguistic rules acquired easily by normal children are also the easiest for language-delayed children to acquire.

Table I summarises the types of word-classes and the simple morpheme transformation and semantic rules that are acquired early in the speech of normal children, and which also appear to be relatively easy for handicapped children to master.

DECREASING INAPPROPRIATE SPEECH

Many children with delayed language development also show inappropriate or bizarre speech patterns. Occasional echolalia or repetition of others' speech is common in normal infants around the age of two or three (Fay 1967, Nakashini and Owada 1973). In retarded children, and particularly in autistic children, echolalia is much more prolonged and pervasive (Cantwell *et al.* 1978). Sometimes a child may deliberately use stereotyped and repetitive utterances to gain attention (swear words are a particularly notable example of this). Although echolalia is an indication of immature language development, repetitive and stereotyped speech may persist longer than necessary because of failure to correct the child when he or she uses such utterances. In some cases parents or teachers become so used to the oddities in the child's speech that they cease to notice them; or they may be anxious that, if they begin to correct them, the child may stop speaking altogether. In fact many intervention studies now indicate that echolalic or stereotyped utterances are relatively easy to modify, as long as they are consistently corrected. If the child is prompted and rewarded for using the appropriate (non-stereotyped) form of utterance, rates of echolalia and stereotyped remarks tend to decrease consider-ably. At the same time, spontaneous communicative utterances show a steady improvement. Figure 1 shows how echolalic speech decreased in a group of young autistic children exposed to language training over a six-month period. Over the same time communicative utterances gradually increased. In a matched control

FREQUENCY OF COMPREHENSIBLE UTTERANCES

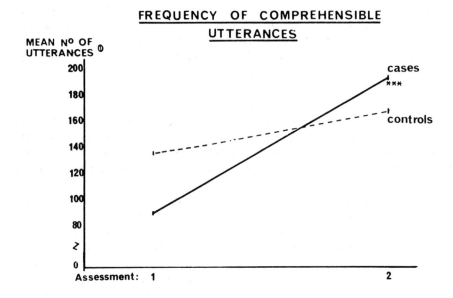

% OF UTTERANCE TYPE

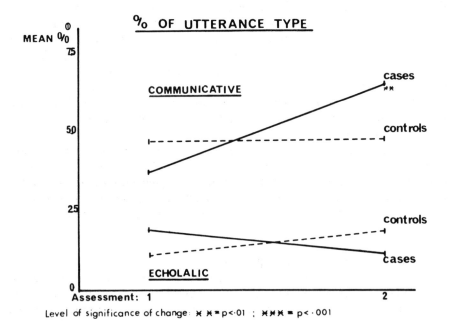

Level of significance of change: ✗✗ = p<·01 ; ✗✗✗ = p< ·001

[0]Figures based on ½ hour recording per. child per. assessment

group few changes were recorded, although echolalic responses rose slightly (Howlin 1980b).

Although the reduction of inappropriate speech is generally desirable, it is important to be aware that echolalic utterances may also serve an important communicative function for some children. Thus in certain cases it may be more appropriate to *modify* echolalic utterances so that they are used to facilitate the child's communicative abilities, rather than to attempt to eliminate them entirely (Prizant and Duchan 1981, Charlop 1983).

ALTERNATIVE FORMS OF COMMUNICATION

For children who fail to respond to spoken-language programmes (either because of the severity of the language impairment or because physical handicaps impair the production of speech sounds), behavioural training in non-verbal communication may prove more effective. A variety of manual sign and symbol systems exist (see Chapters 24 and 25).

Many case studies of non-verbal communication training report on the subsequent acquisition of *spoken* language in children who had not previously responded to treatment (De Villiers and Naughton 1974, Deich and Hodges 1979, Reid 1981). Unfortunately there are no well-controlled group studies of the effectiveness of non-verbal training. Information remains extremely limited on the most successful type of system (signs or symbols, iconic or non-iconic, simplified or syntactical) and on the nature and extent of generalisation from non-verbal to verbal communication. The results of comparative studies are often contradictory (Kiernan 1983) and there is very little information about the types of children who respond best to such training. Nor is there much practical advice to help clinicians select the most appropriate type of alternative system (Shane 1981). Since children with lower IQs are least likely to respond to verbal programmes (Gould 1977, Howlin 1979), it is perhaps advisable to *begin* training with non-vocal systems for the more retarded non-verbal children rather than risk the probable failure of a verbal training programme. If this is successful, vocal imitation training can be implemented at a later stage.

Severely handicapped children may respond to training in the use of symbols and pictures more readily than to signing (Murphy *et al.* 1977). For less retarded children it may be preferable to begin with spoken-language programmes, but it is important to retain a flexible approach to treatment and to be prepared to switch to an alternative, non-vocal system if assessment measures show very few effects of treatment over time.

Children involved in language-training studies

There is now a considerable range of children involved in language programmes. Successful results are reported for children suffering from articulation disorders, apraxia and physical handicaps, hearing problems, Down's syndrome, language delays, elective mutism, aphasia, behavioural disturbances, psycho-social deprivation and mental retardation. Autistic children have also received considerable attention, because of the widespread language difficulties among this group and the importance of language development for prognosis (Howlin 1981a, Harris and Wolchick 1982, Koegel *et al.* 1982).

Range of language skills taught using operant techniques

Although early interventions tended to focus predominantly on the extinction of inappropriate utterances or the increase of simple imitative speech, subsequent studies have tended to be far more sophisticated. Many different linguistic rules have been successfully taught, including pivotal phrases and morpheme and inflectional rules. A variety of simple syntactical and semantic structures have also been taught using behavioural programmes (Mowrer 1984).

Recent studies, however, have tended to emphasise individual needs rather than specific linguistic structures. Thus the level of language taught and the particular treatment goals will depend very much on the child's language level, and may extend from simple receptive skills to highly complex language (Hemsley *et al.* 1978, Cheseldine and McConkey 1979, Harris *et al.* 1981, Jones *et al.* 1983). Studies using sign language with handicapped children also report on the teaching of a fairly wide range of language constructs. Since signing is generally taught as a sort of 'second best' to more severely retarded or autistic children, the programmes tend to be rather more limited in scope than those designed to teach spoken language. Recent reports suggest that abstract concepts and semantic and syntactic rules can be taught using non-verbal communication systems, even to quite severely handicapped children (Layton and Hellmer 1982).

Problems of generalisation and the involvement of parents as co-therapists

Long-term follow-up studies of apparently successful clinic-based programmes indicate that the effects of treatment are not necessarily maintained when intervention ceases (Lovaas *et al.* 1973). Nor do skills acquired in one setting always generalise to other contexts or other therapists (Howlin 1980b, Egel 1981). As Patterson and Reid (1973) showed, even normal children may show problems of generalisation when behaviours have been acquired artificially rather than naturally. Failures of generalisation are particularly common in programmes involving handicapped children. However, generalisation can be planned, and it has been possible to teach basic language rules, which children are then able to generalise to novel utterances (Romanczyk *et al.* 1983). If the child's newly acquired language skills are to be maintained, and if they are to extend to other settings, two factors appear to be crucial. Firstly, the linguistic structures taught should be of functional significance to the child so that they result in more effective and immediate control over his or her environment (Goetz *et al.* 1983). Secondly, all the relevant individuals in the child's environment need to be involved in both the training and the general stimulation of language (Hemsley *et al.* 1978).

Early language-training programmes recommended that treatment should be conducted in a non-distracting clinic setting (Risley and Wolf 1967). However, although the acquisition of novel sounds or utterances may have been made easier under such conditions, the linguistic skills acquired in this way frequently showed little generalisation to more normal environments. For this reason, recent studies have stressed the importance of involving parents in treatment; and with the increasing trend towards community care for the handicapped, much intervention now concentrates almost entirely on home-based treatment and assessment (Howlin 1984*b*).

However, the involvement of parents in therapy needs to be handled with sensitivity (Mittler and Mittler 1983). Therapists must exercise caution in the demands they make on parents, and avoid increasing the burden on families already faced with the multiple practical and emotional problems of caring for a handicapped child.

Effectiveness of language-training programmes

In two detailed reviews of language training programmes, Howlin (1979, 1984*b*) found that although the experimental sophistication of language studies is steadily improving, a substantial proportion of intervention studies are still single-case reports. Fewer than one-third of the studies reviewed employed experimental manipulations, such as reversal techniques or multiple baselines, and only 30 per cent used control groups to assess the effectiveness of treatment.

The need for adequate control groups in evaluating the treatment of developmental problems cannot be overemphasised. In the case of language, as with any other developmental skill, improvements are likely to occur with increasing age, even in handicapped children. Changes attributed to therapy may in fact be due to the passage of time and the child's own maturation. Unfortunately, authors' confidence in the efficacy of their training programmes tends to be negatively correlated with the stringency of their experimental methodology. In general, uncontrolled single case studies tend to be highly optimistic in their reporting of results. For example Welch (1981) concluded that 'the prognosis for the successful development of generative grammar in the majority of mentally retarded children appears to be excellent', in spite of the fact that all the studies he reviewed employed a single-case design, and only two used more than three subjects in all. Many other studies report that treatment resulted in 'important gains' (Goldstein and Lanyon 1971) or even 'normal' speech (Nolan and Pence 1970). It is important to remember, however, that since journals do not readily accept *unsuccessful* single-case studies, the published reports may well be unrepresentative.

It is notable that studies employing control groups have produced disappointingly few significant results. Such studies have compared different types of intervention or have contrasted intervention programmes with no intervention (Tables II and III). Conclusions vary because studies are so mixed in terms of both techniques and samples (see Table II). It would seem from the studies of Lovaas (1977*b*) and Koegel *et al.* (1982), that parent involvement in training is better than no parent involvement. With deaf children, training in non-verbal communication would seem to be significantly more successful than training in verbal communication. And, with autistic children, direct kinaesthetic training would seem to be preferable to indirect training. In the other studies, however, either the numbers

TABLE II
Control studies of language training: comparisons between treatments

Source	Diagnosis	N	Age (yrs)	IQ	Adequacy of data collection etc.	Type of comparison	Outcome
Carrier 1970	Articulation problems	10E 10C	4–7	?	?	Articulation versus imitation training	Articulation therapy = gains in all areas. No statistical analysis
Ney et al. 1971	Autistic	10E 10C	3–15	?	+	Language modification versus play therapy	Both groups improved. No significant differences though some differences in favour of Es after 3m
Jeffree et al. 1973	Down's syndrome	1E 1C	4	MA 2–3y	+	Pivot–open teaching versus non-pivotal training	Pivot–open training more successful (second child also used as own control)
Lovaas et al. 1973	Autistic	20	Mxd	?	+	Parental involvement versus no parental involvement in language therapy	After discharge gains maintained in parental group only
Nelson et al. 1976	ESN(s)	4	3–5	30–50	+	Kinaesthetic versus non-kinaesthetic language therapy	Kinaesthetic group required fewer learning trials—but progress generally limited and considerable individual variation
Brasel and Quigley 1977	Deaf	36E 36C	10–18	?	+	Manual versus verbal communication training	Manual training significantly more effective
Israel and Brown 1977	Disadvantaged	36E 36C	10–18	?	+	Verbal training versus correspondence training	Verbal training no different in outcome to non-verbal strategies
Cheseldine and McConkey 1979	Down's syndrome	7	x̄ 62m	?	+	Parents given language goals, versus parents given direct language training	Goals alone successful in 3/7 families. Direct training more effective in remainder
Oliver and Scott 1981	ESN(s)	8	19–21	SQ 24	?	Group versus individual training in teaching of adjectives	No differences in acquisition. Greater generalisation in group-training condition (counterbalanced design used)

contd. on next page

TABLE II, contd.

Hurlburt *et al.* 1982	ESN(s) PH	3	14–18	MA < 2y	+	Bliss versus iconic symbol training	Bliss symbols took longer to acquire than iconic symbols (multiple baseline used)
Koegel *et al.* 1982	Autistic	?	2–10	$\bar{x}$ = 2.7y	+	Parental involvement versus no parental involvement in language therapy	No significant differences at discharge. At follow-up, significant differences in change scores of parent-training group

+ = adequate information provided
− = no information provided
? = information inadequate or variable

TABLE III

Control studies of language training: treatment versus no treatment

Source	Diagnosis	N	Age	IQ	Adequacy of data collection	Type of comparison	Outcome
Jeffree and Cashdan 1971	ESN(s)	15E 15C	11y.	<50	+	Home language intervention versus no intervention	No significant differences in PPVT, significant improvement in articulation in experiment group
Mash and Terdal 1973	Retarded	45C 5E	4–10y	50–55	+	Training parents in play and verbal interaction with children, versus no training	Increase in mothers' speech. Changes in children not reported
McDonald *et al.* 1974	Down's syndrome	3E 3C	5y	?	+	Language programme at home versus no intervention	MLU increased more in experimental group. No direct statistical comparison
Kaufmann and Kozloff 1977	Autistic	4C 7E	?	?	−	Home intervention versus no intervention (parents given training manual only)	Significant differences in parents' interaction. No differences in children

Study	Population	Ns	Age	Score	Rating	Intervention	Results
Hemsley et al. 1978	Autistic	16E 30C	3–11	60+	+	Language intervention at home, versus no training, versus OP advice	Significant differences in parents' verbal interaction in E group. Significant differences in children's use of speech in E group. Differences in language level generally non-significant
Shelton et al. 1978	Articulation problems	$15E_1$ $15E_2$ 15C	3–4y	93–95	+	Listening training($E1$) versus reading/talking ($E2$) versus no training (C)	No significant differences between groups
Bloch et al. 1980	Autistic	12E 14C	3–4y	50	+	Language intervention in school versus no intervention	More cases than controls improved on the measures used
Cooper et al. 1979	Language delay	$E_1 = 50$ $E_2 = 69$ $C_1 = 39$ $C_2 = 20$	2–10½	?	+	Special language class or clinic (Es 1+2) versus speech therapy group (C_1) versus no treatment (C_3)	All children made progress. 'Accelerated progress' in special class and clinic groups. Low IQ = least progress. Poor statistical comparisons
Harris et al. 1981	Autistic	11E	$\bar{x}$ 47m	$\bar{x}$ 45	+	Intervention with parents versus no intervention	Children served as own controls. No significant differences in pre/post test progress as group, though verbal children did show significant changes
Kahn 1981	Retarded	$4E_1$ $4E_2$ 4C	53m–101m Sens/motor stage 5–6		+	Signing (E_1), versus vocalisation training (E_2), versus no training (C)	No statistical significance between groups (though all Group 1 children learned to use signs and only 50% of Group 2 used words)
Sandow et al. 1981	ESN(s)	$E_1$16 $E_2$16 C15	$\bar{x}$ 2y6	$\bar{x}$ 50	+	Frequent intervention (E_1), versus less frequent (E_2), versus no intervention	Gains faster in E_1 than other groups, but differences not significant
Clements et al. 1982	Preschool retarded) Down's syndrome	14E 17C	5 5	72 45	+	Home intervention versus no intervention	Both groups made progress. No significant differences between groups

+ = adequate information provided
– = no information provided
? = information inadequate or variable

are too small or the statistical analysis too limited to allow any conclusions on the best methods of treatment.

In studies where improvements have been adequately assessed, the effects of treatment often appear disappointingly small. Studies by Ney *et al.* (1971) and Israel and Brown (1977) suggested that programmes involving verbal or non-verbal training strategies had little differential effect on language outcome. Sandow *et al.* (1981) and Shelton *et al.* (1978) reported *no* significant differences between treatment conditions or between treated and untreated groups. Stevenson *et al.* (1982) found that both experimental and control groups showed improvements on all the language tests used and differences in change scores were not significant. Kaufmann and Kozloff (1977) found significant changes in the experimental parents' skills as language therapists, but no significant changes in children's speech. Jeffree and Cashdan (1971) also failed to find differences in most of the group measures they used. The only scores showing a differential improvement in the experimental group were on the Renfrew Articulation test, despite the fact that articulation training played no part in the programme! Similarly, Clements *et al.* (1982) failed to find significant differences between experimental and control groups on any language measures, although the experimental group did show significant improvements on the Personal-Social and Eye Hand Co-ordination Scales of the Griffiths test. Moreover, whilst language changes generally were non-significant, the improvements that occurred were limited to increases in the children's vocabulary; the length and complexity of utterances did not change. Harris *et al.* (1981) also failed to find any significant differences in children following treatment.

Finally, the study by Hemsley *et al.* (1978) employed a short-term and a long-term control group. Following the first six months of treatment, children in the experimental group showed significant gains on several language measures, including frequency of utterances and their use of communicative speech. Echolalic and stereotyped utterances showed a significant decline. However, although the experimental group tended to show greater improvements in their level of language competence, (as measured by the Reynell test and their use of various morpheme and transformational rules), the differences between experimental and control groups were generally non-significant. When compared with the longer-term control group at the end of 18 months of treatment, experimental children again performed better than their matched controls on almost every language measure. Nevertheless, there were few significant group differences in language level, and only a limited number of significant differences in their use of communicative speech. There were, by contrast, large and significant differences between groups on the majority of the behavioural problems assessed in this study (Howlin and Rutter 1987a).

Thus, amongst the few studies employing both control groups *and* adequate data analysis, the results in favour of language training are disappointingly slight. Any gains that are reported tend to be associated with behavioural or social development; changes in language are few and if they do occur, are limited to simple linguistic skills such as improvements in articulation or vocabulary. More fundamental aspects of language such as the semantic, syntactical or transformational complexity of utterances, show little significant change (Howlin 1981a, b; Clements *et al.* 1982). And even if short-term group differences do occur, longer-term follow-ups indicate that many apparently significant treatment effects are short-lived (Hemsley *et al.* 1978).

These results clearly leave us in something of a quandary. If behavioural programmes really are ineffective, why has their use proliferated over the past two decades? Moreover, why should so many well-controlled single-case studies indicate rapid improvements following the implementation of treatment?

One of the major problems in attempting to carry out an evaluation of such studies arises from the very fact that language programmes have expanded so dramatically in range and sophistication over recent years. Behavioural intervention programmes now are far removed from the early attempts to increase simple vocalisations by using food reinforcers. Current behavioural programmes combine techniques borrowed from traditional speech therapy and from developmental psycholinguistic research. Meanwhile, speech therapy programmes almost invariably incorporate behavioural methods, so that there is no longer a real distinction between behaviour therapy and speech therapy. The result is a mixture of techniques that apparently work for some of the children, some of the time, but certainly are not universally effective.

How can we determine the types of children who are most likely to respond to treatment, the particular language problems that are most readily amenable to intervention, and the procedures that are most likely to prove effective?

Individual differences in response to treatment
Although group differences between experimental and control children have been small, the 'swamping' effects of group data may at times obscure changes in individual children. The importance of taking into account individual differences has only rarely been considered in the language-training literature (Howlin 1981a, Clements *et al.* 1982), and perhaps the key question should be not *whether* language training works, but for *whom* it works. More systematic assessment of the children involved in language intervention programmes is badly needed: but despite frequent pleas for better descriptions of subjects who do and who do not respond to treatent (Yule and Berger 1975), relevant details of the children involved are frequently lacking. IQ, age and diagnosis are all factors associated with outcome, but systematic evaluation of these variables is still required.

IQ effects
Epidemiological studies, for example, suggest that language is less likely to be acquired by individuals with IQs below 50, and that almost all children with IQs below 20 will fail to develop language (Spreen 1965, Gould 1977). Nevertheless, although language difficulties are significantly correlated with low IQ, some retarded individuals develop spoken language and respond to language-training programmes. The factors that distinguish those retarded individuals who respond more readily to therapy still have to be identified.

380

Age effects
Although age tends to be related to outcome, in many cases the association is far from perfect. On the whole, language-training studies tend to indicate that young children make faster progress than older ones. Moreover, clinical evidence suggests that many handicapped children, particularly those who are autistic, are unlikely to develop useful speech if spontaneous verbalisations are still lacking by the age of six or seven years (Eisenberg 1956, Rutter 1966, DeMyer *et al.* 1973). There are exceptions, and cases are reported of children developing useful, if simple, language well beyond this age (Rutter 1970).

The underlying condition
The nature of the condition underlying the language delay also has implications for outcome. Although behavioral techniques have been used with a wide range of children, the outcome tends to be less favourable for children with severe mental retardation, profound deafness or infantile autism. Outcome generally tends to be better for children with uncomplicated developmental language disorders, although the differential effects of treatment have not been systematically explored. Many such children will eventually acquire normal speech, but there remains a substantial subgroup who, despite specialist teaching and intensive intervention, fail to gain any useful speech (Paul and Cohen 1984). Again the characteristics of the children who do and do not respond to therapy needs greater investigation.

Severity of language disability
The extent of the language impairment, too, has important implications for treatment. In a controlled study of language training with autistic children Howlin (1981*b*) found that although over-all group differences were not significant, certain children in the experimental group (notably those who were at the single-word stage of development) showed very marked changes in comparison with controls at a similar level. Non-speaking children, on the other hand, particularly those who had low scores on measures of comprehension, social skills and play, made very little progress.

The failure of non-speaking children to respond to treatment has been reported in a number of other studies (Harris and Wolchick 1982). In general the more limited the child's existing language skills the more limited are the effects of treatment. In contrast, many studies have reported that echolalic children tend to respond better to intervention than any other group. Thus Lovaas (1977*a*) claimed that as a consequence of operant training procedures such children 'acquired . . . strikingly complex language behaviours'. Howlin (1981*a, b*) also found that echolalic children seemed to respond best to treatment. However, when the untreated echolalic children in this study were assessed at follow-up, they were found to be doing almost as well as children in the experimental group. These results suggest that children who are using some communicative speech, even if this is predominantly echolalic, are likely to make steady gains in language whether or not they are exposed to special treatment. It has been argued that the very fact of using echolalic speech indicates that children have attained a crucial stage in their cognitive and communicative development, and there is some doubt whether programmes designed to eliminate echolalia are useful or even desirable (Phillips and Dyer 1977, Prizant and Duchan 1981). Certainly, although intervention with echolalic children may have immediate short-term effects and may reduce inappropriate utterances (Howlin 1980*b*), the long-term outcome for such children does not seem to be markedly affected by the implementation of behavioural programmes.

The results of language-training programmes suggest that the children who make most progress are those who already possess at least some of the basic cognitive prerequisites for language learning, and that behavioural techniques are responsible for motivating children to use their *inherent* linguistic abilities more effectively. In other words, intervention programmes may improve linguistic *performance*, but are unlikely to have marked effects on more fundamental aspects of language *competence* (Chomsky 1965).

How does treatment have its effects?

Although reinforcement is accepted as being the crucial element in operant training, this is scarcely ever the only behavioural technique applied. In fact there is evidence that reliance on reinforcers alone has very little effect when it comes to increasing low-frequency responses (Lovaas 1966). Differential reinforcement of appropriate utterances is frequently used in conjunction with modelling, prompting and fading techniques. Operant approaches also involve the breaking down of behaviours into their component parts, so that more complex responses can be systematically shaped. Intervention techniques, derived from psycholinguistic as well as operant methodology, are also frequently incorporated into training programmes.

The relative importance of these various procedures has never been investigated. There is still no evidence that psycholinguistically based procedures are better, or worse, than those derived from learning theory. Experimental studies have tended to concentrate on finding the most effective schedules of reinforcement but the comparative effects of reinforcement with other techniques have not been systematically explored. There is some evidence that reinforcement, combined with modelling and imitation, is more effective than modelling or imitation training alone—although reinforcement procedures on their own have very little effect in severely linguistically handicapped children (Lovaas 1966).

The more general rôle of traditional behavioural techniques is also questionable. Increasing children's opportunities to use their language skills may be a much more crucial element in successful intervention than reinforcement alone (Spradlin and Siegel 1982). 'Functional competence' and motivational factors also need to be considered in any successful programme of language training (Goetz *et al.* 1983). Thus if verbal (or non-verbal) communication strategies can be used more effectively by the child to control the immediate environment, treatment effects are much more likely to endure. Carr and Durand (1985) showed that if self-injurious, retarded children were able to express their needs (and have these rapidly responded to) by simple signs, not only did gestural communication increase but self-injurious responses showed a dramatic fall.

Studies of parents as therapists also indicate that the implementation of operant procedures is not always a necessary part of treatment. Cheseldine and McConkey (1979) found that during a baseline period, in which parents were set specific language goals but given no direct behavioural advice, some families showed marked and rapid changes in their interaction, with a concomitant improvement in children's language skills. Other families needed more direct behavioural programmes in order to effect change.

Short (1984), in a follow-up of the parent training programmes conducted by Schopler and his colleagues, found that improvements in play and language behaviours were associated more with direct physical and verbal guidance from parents than with reinforcement (which actually declined during treatment). Howlin and Rutter (1987b) also found that although parental reinforcements increased, even greater changes occurred in the use of prompts and corrections and in the amount of verbal guidance that they gave to their children. Both these studies suggest that language handicapped children tend to use more appropriate responses as a result of increased parental guidance and structure, rather than through the simple application of reinforcement procedures.

Studies of autistic children in schools have also indicated that structure may be more important than reinforcement alone in increasing positive behaviours (Schopler et al. 1971, Bartak and Rutter 1973, Koegel et al. 1982, Lord 1984). Experimental research, too, indicates that increasing the amount of structure imposed on the child's behaviour is likely to result in increased social and linguistic responsiveness (Clarke and Rutter 1981). These results suggest that successful outcome may not be the result of the reinforcement techniques themselves, but may be due instead to the additional structure imposed on the child's linguistic environment. What this restructuring should consist of will vary from child to child, and very different forms of facilitation may be required according to the child's handicap.

Horsborough et al. (1985) found that mothers' speech to autistic or dysphasic children showed as much evidence of 'fine-tuning' as that in normal dyads. However, maternal speech styles are better at modifying certain aspects of speech than others. The relatively high rate of questions used by mothers of autistic children tends to ensure that autistic children are almost 'forced' to participate in discourse. But this also allows the opportunity for more semantically unrelated responses. Thus in autistic groups, at least, a higher rate of questions may need to be combined with a greater frequency of prompts and corrections if improvements in syntactic, semantic and pragmatic aspects of language are to occur. A recent study by Howlin and Rutter (1987b) concluded that improvements in the language of autistic children were significantly associated with increases in mothers' attempts to elicit and prompt appropriate speech. The ways in which mothers restructured the verbal environment of their children seemed to be important for outcome, although the authors noted that children's language level appeared to influence the amount of change shown by mothers, as well as vice versa.

It is essential that, whatever therapeutic techniques are chosen, these do not rely on pre-determined treatment 'packages'. Instead intervention must be adapted to the individual needs and developmental levels of each child. As Rutter (1980) pointed out, we still know very little about the ways in which language training exerts its effects, nor the most useful types of strategy to use. It is unlikely that a single mechanism accounts for the whole process, or that the same strategies will be equally effective for different groups of children. It is evident that successful treatment will require a detailed assessment of each child's strengths and weaknesses. Careful attention to motivational factors and the functional value of the communication skills taught are also crucial.

Summary

The results of studies using a behavioural approach to the treatment of language disorder suggest that such methods may be effective whether employed by parents or trained therapists. However, the effects of therapy tend to be less dramatic than is often assumed, and even well controlled single-case studies may be misleading if only successful reports appear in print. Long-term follow-ups are lacking, so the permanence of treatment effects is unknown. And even though short-term follow-up periods may indicate significant differences between experimental and control children, some of these differences may be short-lived. In addition, the absence of control groups in many studies means there is no way of knowing how well children might have progressed without treatment.

Studies employing control groups indicate that the effects of treatment vary between children. Mute children tend to show relatively little improvement, whereas those who are echolalic are likely to do reasonably well with or without intervention. On the whole, the children who appear to respond best to training are those who are already on the threshold of developing language and who are at least at the single word stage of language development.

Finally, the aspects of language that show a significant improvement tend to be restricted to the child's language *usage* (*i.e.* increases in vocabulary, a greater use of communicative speech or a decline in echolalic or inappropriate utterances). Language *level*, as measured by syntactical or transformational development, shows fewer improvements. It is unknown whether these often rather limited changes in language usage may affect other areas of the child's functioning, particularly in interactions with other adults and children. The relationships between language measures and measures of other aspects of the child's social behaviour have not been examined in any detail, and the extension of assessments to other areas of functioning may produce more encouraging results. Forehand *et al.* (1979) suggested that it is important to analyse relationships between multiple outcome measures, which may well differ across subjects. The measures of language themselves may also be inadequate (Prutting *et al.* 1975). Standard tests, although necessary for systematic comparisons, may be insensitive to changes in other areas of children's spontaneous language functioning. Increases in communicative intent, for example, may be far more important than whether the child uses past or future tenses, or whether the mean length of utterance is three words or four. A combination of standard tests, together with reliable and objective measures of assessing spontaneous language, is more likely to monitor real changes than formal testing on its own (Cantwell *et al.* 1979, Gerber and Goehl 1980).

Group findings may also overlook important changes in individual children. Despite frequent pleas for better descriptions of subjects who do and do not respond to treatment, individual details of the children involved are frequently inadequate. The use of more homogeneous, well-delineated groups, of adequate size, is required. Finally, we need more information on which aspects of the treatment programme itself are important for success. Almost all the operant studies described employ a variety of different training techniques. As yet, the particular aspects of treatment that are crucial for success remain undetermined. Structuring the child's interaction with parents or caretakers, in order to encourage the use of *inherent* language skills, may well prove to be more important than the use of extrinsic reinforcers. However, the signficance of these variables has rarely been subjected to experimental validation. Indeed, the effectiveness of different components of the language-training programme may well vary according to the type of child in therapy. For normally responsive children, who are already beginning to develop communicative skills, advice that helps parents or other therapists to focus on the general encouragement of language may be all that is required. The child's inherent language competence will then be sufficient to guarantee progress. On the other hand, children with very limited language skills, or less motivation to communicate, may need more structured programmes requiring a high degree of consistency in the use of prompting, modelling and reinforcement, to establish even very simple linguistic rules.

REFERENCES

Baker, N., Nelson, K. (1986) 'Recasting and related conversational techniques for triggering syntactic advances by young children.' *First Language (in press).*
Bartak, L., Rutter, M. (1973) 'Special educational treatment of autistic children: a comparative study. I: Design and study of characteristics of units.' *Journal of Child Psychology and Psychiatry,* **14,** 161–179.
Barnes, S., Gutfreund, M., Satterley, D., Wells, G. (1983) 'Characteristics of adult speech which predict children's language development.' *Journal of Child Language,* **10,** 65–84.
Bartolucci, G., Pierce, S. J., Streiner, D. (1980) 'Cross-sectional studies of grammatical morphemes in autistic and mentally retarded children.' *Journal of Autism and Developmental Disorders,* **10,** 39–50.
Bloch, J., Gersten, E., Korublum, J. (1980) 'Evaluation of a language program for young autistic children.' *Journal of Speech and Hearing Disorders,* **45,** 76–89.
Brasel, K. E., Quigley, S. P. (1977) 'Influences of certain language and communication environments in early childhood on the development of language in deaf individuals.' *Journal of Speech and Hearing Research,* **20,** 93–107.
Brown, R. (1973) *A First Language.* London: George Allen & Unwin.
Buium, N., Rynders, J., Turnure, J. (1974) 'Early maternal linguistic environment of normal and Down's syndrome language learning children.' *American Journal of Mental Deficiency,* **79,** 52–58.
Cantwell, D., Baker, L., Rutter, M. (1978) 'A comparative study of infantile autism and specific developmental receptive language disorder—IV. Analysis of syntax and language function.' *Journal of Child Psychology and Psychiatry,* **19,** 351–362.

—— Howlin, P., Rutter, M. (1979) 'The analysis of language level and language function.' *British Journal of Disorders of Communication,* **12,** 119–135.

Carr, E., Durand, V. (1985) 'The social communication basis of severe behavior problems in children.' *In:* Reiss, S., Bootzin, R. (Eds.) *Theoretical Issues in Behavior Therapy.* New York: Academic Press.

Carrier, J. (1970) 'A program of articulation therapy administered by mothers.' *Journal of Speech and Hearing Disorders,* **35,** 344–348.

Charlop, M. (1983) 'The effects of echolalia on acquisition and generalization of receptive labelling in autistic children.' *Journal of Applied Behavior Analysis,* **16,** 111–126.

Cheseldine, S., McConkey, R. (1979) 'Parental speech to young Down's syndrome children: an intervention study.' *American Journal of Mental Deficiency,* **83,** 612–620.

Chomsky, N. (1965) *Aspects of the Theory of Syntax.* Cambridge, Mass.: MIT Press.

Clark, H., Clark, E. V. (1977) *Psychology and Language: An Introduction to Linguistics.* New York: Harcourt Brace.

Clarke, P., Rutter, M. (1981) 'Autistic children's responses to structure and interpersonal demands.' *Journal of Autism and Developmental Disorders,* **11,** 201–207.

Clements, J., Evans, C., Jones, C., Osborne, K., Upton, G. (1982) 'Evaluation of a home-based language training programme with severely mentally handicapped children.' *Behaviour Research and Therapy,* **20,** 243–269.

Cook, C., Adams, H. E. (1966) 'Modification of verbal behaviour in speech deficient children.' *Behaviour Research and Therapy,* **4,** 265–271.

Cooper, J., Moodley, M., Reynell, J. (1979) The developmental language programme: results from a five-year study.' *British Journal of Disorders of Communication,* **14,** 57–69.

Cunningham, C., Reuler, E., Blackwell, J., Deck, J. (1981) 'Behavioral and linguistic developments in the interactions of normal and retarded children with their mothers.' *Child Development,* **52,** 62–70.

Deich, R., Hodges, P. (1979) *Language without Speech.* London: Souvenir.

DeMyer, M., Barton, S., De Myer, W., Norton, J. A., Allen, J., Steele, R. (1973) 'Prognosis in autism: a follow-up study.' *Journal of Autism and Childhood Schizophrenia,* **3,** 199–246.

De Villiers, J., De Villiers, P. (1978) *Language Acquisition.* Cambridge, Mass.: Harvard University Press.

—— Naughton, J. M. (1974) 'Teaching a symbol language to autistic children.' *Journal of Consulting and Clinical Psychology,* **42,** 111–117.

Egel, A. L. (1981) 'Reinforcer variation: implications for monitoring developmentally disabled children.' *Journal of Applied Behavior Analysis,* **14,** 345–350.

Eisenberg, L. (1956) 'The autistic child in adolescence.' *American Journal of Psychiatry,* **112,** 607–612.

Fay, W. H. (1967) 'Childhood echolalia: a group study of late abatement.' *Folia Phoniatrica,* **19,** 297–306.

Forehand, R., Griest, D., Wells, K. (1979) 'Parent behavioral training: An analysis of the relationship among multiple outcome measures.' *Journal of Abnormal Child Psychology,* **7,** 229–242.

Gardner, J. (1976) *Three Aspects of Childhood Autism.* Unpub. Ph.D.Thesis, University of Leicester.

Gerber, A., Goehl, H. (1980) *The Temple University Short Syntax Test.* Unpublished Manuscript, Temple University, Philadelphia. (Cited by Gerber, A., Bryen, D. N. (Eds.) *Language and Learning Disabilities.* Baltimore: University Park Press.)

Goetz, L., Schuler, A., Sailor, W. (1983) 'Motivational considerations in teaching language to severely handicapped students.' *In:* Hersen, M., Van Hasselt, V., Matson, J. (Eds.) *Behavior Therapy for the Developmentally and Physically Disabled.* New York: Academic Press.

Goldfarb, W., Levy, D. M., Meyers, D. (1972) 'The mother speaks to her schizophrenic child: language in childhood schizophrenia.' *Psychiatry,* **35,** 217–226.

Goldstein, S. B., Lanyon, R. I. (1971) 'Parent-clinicians in the language training of an autistic child.' *Journal of Speech and Hearing Disorders,* **36,** 552–560.

Gould, J. (1977) 'Language development and non-verbal skills in severely mentally retarded children.' *Journal of Mental Deficiency Research,* **20,** 129–143.

Guess, D., Sailor, W., Baer, D. M. (1976) 'To teach language to retarded children.' *In:* Schiefelbusch, R. L., Lloyd, L. L. (Eds.) *Language Perspectives—Acquisition, Retardation and Intervention.* Baltimore: University Park Press.

Harris, S., Wolchik, S., Weiss, S. (1981) 'The acquisition of language skills by autistic children. Can parents do the job?' *Journal of Autism and Developmental Disorders,* **11,** 373–384.

—— —— (1982) 'Teaching speech skills to non-verbal children and their parents.' *In:* Steffen, J., Karoly, P. (Eds.) *Advances in Child Behavioral Analysis and Therapy,* Vol. 2. Lexington: Lexington Books.

Hemsley, R., Howlin, P., Berger, M., Hersov, L., Holbrook, D., Rutter, M., Yule, W. (1978) 'Treating autistic children in a family context.' *In:* Rutter, M., Schopler, E. (Eds.) *Autism: Reappraisal of Concepts and Treatment.* New York: Plenum Press.

Hewitt, F. M. (1965) 'Teaching speech to an autistic child through operant conditioning.' *American Journal of Orthopsychiatry,* **35,** 927–936.

Hintgen, J. N. Trost, F. C. (1964) 'Shaping co-operative responses in early childhood schizophrenics. II. Reinforcement of mutual physical contact and vocal responses.' In: R. Ulrich, T. Stachnik & J. Mabry (Eds.) *Control of Human Behaviour.* Chicago: Scott, Foreman & Co.

Horsborough, K., Cross, T., Ball, J. (1985) 'Conversational interactions between mothers and their autistic dysphasic and normal children.' *In:* Cross, T., Riach, L. (Eds.) Proceedings of the Second Natural Child Development Conference. ACER.

Howlin, P. (1979) *Training Parents to Modify the Language of their Autistic Children: A Home Based Approach.* Unpublished Ph.D. Thesis, University of London.

—— (1980a) 'Language.' *In:* Rutter, M. (Ed.) *Developmental Psychiatry.* London: Heinemann.

—— (1980b) 'Language training with the severely retarded.' *In:* Yule, W., Carr. J. (Eds.) *Behaviour Modification for the Mentally Handicapped.* London: Croom Helm.

—— (1981a) 'The effectiveness of operant language training with autistic children.' *Journal of Autism and Developmental Disorders,* **11,** 89–106.

—— (1981b) 'The results of a home-based language training programme with autistic children.' *British Journal of Disorders of Communication,* **16,** 21–29.

—— (1984a) 'The acquisition of grammatical morphemes in autistic children: a critique and replication of the findings of Bartolucci, Pierce and Streiner (1980).' *Journal of Autism and Developmental Disorders,* **14,** 127–136.

—— (1984b) 'Parents as therapists: a review.' *In:* Miller, D. (Ed.) *Remediating Children's Language.* London: Croom Helm.

Howlin, P., Rutter, M., with Berger, M., Hemsley, R., Hersov, L. and Yule, W. (1987a) *Treatment of Autistic Children.* Chichester: Wiley.

—— —— (1987b) 'Mothers' speech to autistic children: a preliminary causal analysis.' *Journal of Child Psychology and Psychiatry* (in press).

Hurlburt, B., Iwata, B., Green, J. (1982) 'Non-vocal language acquisition in adolescents with severe physical disabilities: Blissymbol versus Iconic stimulus formats.' *Journal of Applied Behavior Analysis,* **15,** 241–258.

Isaacs, W., Thomas, J., Goldiamond, J. (1960) 'Application of operant conditioning to reinstate verbal behavior in psychotics.' *Journal of Speech and Hearing Disorders,* **25,** 8–12.

Israel, A., Brown, M. (1977) 'Correspondence training, prior verbal training and control of non-verbal behavior via control of verbal behavior.' *Journal of Applied Behavior Analysis,* **10,** 333–338.

Jeffree, D. M., Cashdan, A. (1971) 'Severely subnormal children and their parents: an experiment in language improvement.' *British Journal of Educational Psychology,* **41,** 184–194.

—— Wheldell, K., Mittler, P. (1973) 'Facilitating two-word utterances in two Down's syndrome boys.' *American Journal of Mental Deficiency,* **78,** 117–122.

Johnston, J. R., Schery, T. K. (1972) 'The use of grammatical morphemes by children with communication disorders.' *In:* Moorehead, D., Moorehead, A. (Eds.) *Normal and Deficient Child Language.* Baltimore; University Park Press.

Jones, C., Clements, J., Evans, C., Osborne, K., Upton, G. (1983) 'South Wales Early Language Research Project.' *Mental Handicap,* **11,** 30–32.

Jones, O. (1980) 'Prelinguistic communication skills in Down's syndrome and normal infants.' *In:* Field, T., Goldberg, S., Stern, S., Miller-Sostek, A. (Eds.) *High Risk Infants and Children: Adult and Peer Interaction.* New York: Academic Press.

Kahn, J. (1981) 'A comparison of sign and verbal language training with non verbal retarded children.' *Journal of Speech and Hearing Research,* **24,** 113–119.

Kaufman, K., Kozloff, M. (1977) 'New directions in comprehensive programming for parents of autistic children.' Application and Evaluation of "Kozloff-Type" Parent Training Program, Sagmore Children's Center, 1977.

Kerr, N., Myerson, L., Michael, J. (1965) 'A procedure for shaping vocalizations in a mute child.' *In:* Ullman, L. P., Krasner, L. (Eds.) *Case Studies in Behavior Modification.* New York: Holt, Rinehart & Winston.

Kiernan, C. (1983) 'The use of non-vocal communication systems with autistic individuals.' *Journal of Child Psychology and Psychiatry,* **24,** 339–376.

Koegel, R., Rincover, A., Egel, A. (1982) (Eds.) *Educating and Understanding Autistic Children.* San Diego: College-Hill Press.

Layton, T., Hellmer, S. (1982) 'Teaching autistic and developmentally delayed children by sign or speech.' *In:* Berg, J. (Ed.) *Proceedings of the VIth Congress of the International Association for the Scientific Study of Mental Deficiency.* Baltimore: University Park Press.

Leifner, J., Lewis, M. (1983) 'Maternal speech to normal and handicapped children: A look at question asking behavior.' *Infant Behavior and Development,* **6**, 175–182.

Leonard, L. B. (1972) 'What is deviant language?' *Journal of Speech and Hearing Disorders,* **37**, 427–446.

Lord, C. (1984) 'The development of peer relations in children with autism.' *In:* Morrison, F. *Applied Developmental Psychology,* I. pp. 165–229.

Lovaas, O. I. (1966) 'A program for the establishment of speech in psychotic children.' *In:* Wing, J. K. (Ed.) *Early Childhood Autism: Clinical, Educational and Social Aspects.* Oxford: Pergamon Press.

—— (1977*a*) *The Autistic Child: Language Development Through Behavior Modification.* New York: Wiley.

—— (1977*b*) Parents as therapist for autistic children. *In:* Rutter, M., Schopler, E. (Eds.) *Autism: Reappraisal of Concepts and Treatment.* New York: Plenum Press.

—— Berberich, J. P., Perloff, B. F., Schaeffer, B. (1966) 'Acquisition of imitative speech by schizophrenic children.' *Science,* **151**, 705–707.

——Koegel, R., Simmons, J., Stevens, J. (1973) 'Some generalization and follow-up measures on autistic children in behavior therapy.' *Journal of Applied Behavior Analysis,* **6**, 131–166.

McDonald, J. D., Blott, J. P., Gordon, K., Spiegel, B., Hartmann, M. (1974) 'An experimental parent assisted treatment program for preschool language delayed children.' *Journal of Speech and Hearing Disorders,* **39**, 395–415.

Marshall, J., Hegrenes, J., Goldstein, S. (1973) 'Verbal interactions: mothers and their retarded children.' *American Journal of Mental Deficiency,* **77**, 415–419.

Mash, E., Terdal, L. (1973) 'Modification of mother-child interaction: playing with children.' *Mental Retardation,* **10**, 44–49.

Mittler, P., Mittler, H. (1983) Partnership with parents: an overview.' *In:* Mittler, P., McConachie, H. (Eds.) *Parents, Professionals and Mentally Handicapped People: Approaches to Partnership.* London: Croom Helm.

Mowrer, D. (1984) 'Behavioral approaches to treating language disorders.' *In:* Miller, D. (Ed.) *Remediating Children's Language.* London: Croom Helm. pp. 18–55.

Murphy, G. M., Steele, K., Gilligan, T., Yeow, J., Spare, D. (1977) 'Teaching a picture language to a non-speaking retarded boy.' *Behaviour Research and Therapy,* **15**, 198–201.

Nakashini, Y., Owada, (1973) 'Echoic utterances of children between the ages of one and three years.' *Journal of Verbal Learning and Verbal Behaviour,* **12**, 658–665.

Nelson, K. (1973) 'Structure and strategy in learning to talk.' *Monographs of the Society for Research in Child Development,* **38**, 1–2. Serial No. 149.

Nelson, R. O., Evans, I. M. (1968) 'The combination of learning principles and speech therapy techniques in the treatment of non-communicating children.' *Journal of Child Psychology and Psychiatry,* **9**, 111–124.

—— Peoples, A., Hay, L., Johnson, T., Hay, W. (1976) 'The effectiveness of speech training techniques based on operant conditioning: a comparison of two methods.' *Mental Retardation,* **14**, 34–38.

Newport, E., Gleitman, H., Gleitman, O. L. (1977) 'Mother, I'd rather do it myself: some effects and non effects of maternal speech style.' *In:* Snow, C., Ferguson, C. (Eds.) *Talking to Children.* Cambridge: Cambridge University Press.

Ney, P. B., Palvesky, A. E., Markely, J. (1971) 'Relative effectiveness of operant conditioning and play therapy in childhood schizophrenia.' *Journal of Autism and Childhood Schizophrenia,* **1**, 337–349.

Nolan, J. D., Pence, C. (1970) 'Operant conditioning principles in the treatment of a selectively mute child.' *Journal of Consulting and Clinical Psychology,* **35**, 265–268.

Oliver, P., Scott, T. (1981) 'Group versus individual training in establishing generalization of language skills with severely handicapped individuals.' *Mental Retardation,* **19**, 285–289.

Patterson, G., Reid, J. (1973) 'Intervention for families of aggressive boys: a replication study.' *Behaviour Research and Therapy,* **10**, 168–185.

Paul, R., Cohen, D. (1984) 'Outcomes of severe disorders of language acquisition.' *Journal of Autism and Developmental Disorders,* **14**, 405–422.

Phillips, G. M., Dyer, C. (1977) 'Late onset echolalia in autism and allied disorders.' *British Journal of Disorders of Communication,* **12**, 47–59.

Prizant, B., Duchan, J. (1981) 'The functions of immediate echolalia in autistic children.' *Journal of Speech and Hearing Disorders,* **22**, 241–246.

388

Prutting, A., Gallagher, T., Mulac, A. (1975) 'The expressive portion of NSST compared to a spontaneous language sample.' *Journal of Speech and Hearing Disorders*, **40**, 40–48.

Reid, B. (1981) 'An investigation of the relationship between manual sign training and speech development for mentally handicapped children.' Final Report to the DHSS.

Risley, T., Wolf, M. (1967) 'Establishing functional speech in echolalic children.' *Behaviour Research and Therapy*, **5**, 73–88.

Romanczyk, R., Kistner, J., Ponzetti-Dyer, N. (1983) 'Autism.' *In:* Hersen, M., Van Hasselt, V., Matson, J. (Eds.) *Behavior Therapy for the Developmental and Physically Disabled*. New York: Academic Press.

Rondal, J. (1978) 'Maternal speech to normal and Down's syndrome children matched for Mean Length of utterance.' *In:* Meyers, C. G. (Ed.) *Quality of Life in Severely and Profoundly Mentally Retarded People: Research Foundations for Improvement. American Association of Mental Deficiency, Monograph 3.* Washington, DC: AAMD

Rutter, M. (1966) 'Prognosis: psychotic children in adolescence and early adult life.' *In:* Wing, J. K. (Ed.) *Early Childhood Autism: Clinical Educational and Social Aspects*. London: Pergamon.

—— (1970) 'Autistic children. Infancy to adulthood. *Seminars in Psychiatry*, **2**, 435–450.

—— (1980) 'Language training with autistic children. How does it work and what does it achieve?' *In:* L. A. Hersov, M. Berger & R. Nicol (Eds.) *Language and Language Disorders in Children*. Oxford: Pergamon.

Salzinger, K., Feldman, R., Cowan, J., Salzinger, S. (1965) 'Operant conditioning of verbal behavior of two young speech deficient boys.' *In:* Krasner, L., Ullman, L. P. (Eds.) *Research in Behavior Modification*. New York: Holt, Rinehart & Winston.

Sandler, O., Seydon, T., Howe, B., Kaminsky, T. (1976) 'An evaluation of "Groups for Parents". A standardized format encompassing both behavior modification and humanistic methods.' *Journal of Community Psychology*, **4**, 157–163.

Sandow, S., Clarke, A., Cox, M., Stewart, F. (1981) 'Home intervention with parents of severely subnormal pre-school children: a final report'. *Child: Care, Health and Development*, **7**, 135–144.

Sapon, S. M. (1969) 'Contingency management in the modification of verbal behavior in disadvantaged children.' *International Review of Applied Linguistics*, **7**, 37–49.

Scherer, N., Olswang, L., (1984) 'Role of mothers' expansions in stimulating children's language production.' *Journal of Speech and Hearing Research*, **27**, 387–396.

Schopler, E., Brehm, S. S., Kinsbourne, M., Reichler, R. (1971) 'Effects of treatment structure on development in autistic children.' *Archives of General Psychiatry*, **24**, 415–421.

Schwartz, G., Chapman, K., Prelock, P., Terrell, B., Rowan, L. (1985) 'Facilitation of early syntax through discourse structure.' *Journal of Child Language*, **12**, 13–25.

Shane, H. (1981) 'Decision making in early augmentative communication system use.' *In:* Schiefelbusch, R., Bricker, D. (Eds.) *Early Language: Acquisition and Intervention*. Baltimore: University Park Press.

Shelton, R., Johnson, A., Ruscello, D., Arndt, W. (1978) 'Assessment of parent administered listening training for pre-school children with articulation deficits.' *Journal of Speech and Hearing Disorders*, **43**, 242–253.

Sherman, J. A. (1963) 'Reinstatement of verbal behavior in a psychotic by reinforcement methods.' *Journal of Speech and Hearing Disorders*, **28**, 398–401.

—— (1965) 'Use of reinforcement and imitation to reinstate verbal behavior in mute psychotics.' *Journal of Abnormal Psychology*, **70**, 155–164.

Short, A. (1984) 'Short term treatment outcome using parents as co-therapists for their own autistic children.' *Journal of Child Psychology and Psychiatry*, **25**, 443–458.

Sloane, H. N., Johnston, M. K., Harris, F. R. (1968) 'Remedial procedures for teaching verbal behavior to speech deficient or defective young children.' *In:* Sloane, H. N., Macaulay, B. D. (Eds.) *Operant Procedures in Remedial Speech and Language Training*. Boston: Houghton Mifflin.

Smolek, L., Weinraub, M. (1983) 'Maternal speech: strategy or response?' *Journal of Child Language*, **10**, 369–380.

Spradlin, J., Siegel, G. (1982) 'Language training in natural and clinical environments.' *Journal of Speech and Hearing Disorders*, **47**, 2–6.

Spreen, O. (1965) 'Language functions in mental retardation: a review. I. Language development, types of retardation and intelligence level.' *American Journal of Mental Deficiency*, **69**, 482–494.

Stevenson, P., Bax, M., Stevenson, J. (1982) 'The evaluation of home based speech therapy for language delayed pre-school children in an Inner City area.' *British Journal of Disorders of Communication*, **17**, 141–148.

Volkmar, F., Hoder, E., Cohen, D. (1985) 'A naturalistic study of autistic children: I. Effects of treatment structure on behaviour.' *Journal of Child Psychology and Psychiatry,* **26,** 865–878.

Welch, S. (1981) 'Teaching generative grammar to mentally retarded children: a review and analysis of a decade of behavioral research.' *Mental Retardation,* **19,** 277–284.

Wolchick, S. (1983) 'Language patterns of parents of young autistic and normal children.' *Journal of Autism and Developmental Disorders,* **13,** 167–180.

Wolf, M. M., Risley, T. R., Mees, H. I. (1964) 'Applications of operant conditioning procedures to the behaviour problems of an autistic child.' *Behaviuoral Research and Therapy,* **2,** 305–312.

Yule, W., Berger, M. (1975) 'Communication, language, and behaviour modification.' *In:* Kiernan, C., Woodward, F. (Eds.) *Behaviour Modification with the Severely Retarded.* Amsterdam: Associated Scientific Publications.

24
NON-VOCAL COMMUNICATION SYSTEMS: A CRITICAL SURVEY

Chris Kiernan

Introduction

During the last 15 years there has been a rapid increase in the use of non-vocal communication systems with individuals experiencing severe communication difficulties. For people suffering from clear damage to the mechanisms of speech production, these systems are alternatives to speech. For others they augment spoken language, often in the hope that their use will facilitate the development of speech and language.

The systems have been used with individuals with severe physical handicap resulting from surgery for cancer and other causes, cerebral palsy and related problems, and individuals classified as mentally handicapped, autistic and aphasic (Kiernan *et al.* 1982, Kiernan 1983).

Systems are normally grouped as manual sign or graphic symbol systems. Sign systems include derivatives of deaf sign languages and contrived methods of manual communication. Graphic symbol systems range from communication boards, on which three-dimensional objects may be used as 'symbols', through photographs, line drawings, pictographs, ideographs and abstract shapes, to word cards employing modified or traditional orthography.

This chapter will outline the systems employed in the UK, with some mention of those used specifically in the USA. The systems will be compared in terms of a variety of possible strengths in attaining educational and social goals. We will conclude that the situation in the UK is unsatisfactory, not simply because more research needs to be done on the systems but, more critically, because the current pattern of use involves illogicalities which limit the practical value of the systems.

The chapter is written in the context of the central belief that the goal of therapy should be the attainment of normal speech: and that where this goal is unattainable for clear physical reasons, we should try to provide the individual with an alternative system which is maximally acceptable to both user and receiver. In the current state of development of therapy this means that, in addition to sign and symbols systems, we need to consider the use of assistive devices—including microprocessors and equipment which generates synthetic speech (Witten 1982).

Sign languages and systems

A wide variety of sign languages and systems are used or have been used. They are often referred to as unaided systems, since the user does not require apparatus or assistive devices (Lloyd and Karlan 1984).

British Sign Language (BSL)

BSL is the 'natural' language of the deaf population in the UK. The language has evolved in social, educational and work contexts, independent of other sign languages and of spoken English.

For many years BSL has been suppressed as an educational medium, being explicitly rejected by many teachers of the deaf who regard it as a barrier to the development of speech. Probably as a consequence, BSL has until recently been virtually ignored by academics and researchers.

Within the language, individual signs correspond to spoken words. However, just as words in different spoken languages do not necessarily translate precisely into other languages, sign to spoken-word correspondence is not always precise. Kyle and Woll (1981) point out that there are at least three different ways of translating the spoken word 'more'. Different signs are used when the meanings are 'more than' and 'want more', and the word would not be translated directly in the case of 'more people'. Here the sign for people would be modified and 'more' would not appear.

BSL and spoken English differ substantially in their syntax. For example a sentence like 'I ran' or 'I was running' would translate into BSL sign as 'I RUN (PAST)'. Woll (1981), in a study of question structure, gives other examples. 'What's the name of the hospital?' becomes 'HOSPITAL NAME WHAT?'. 'What work does he do?' becomes 'WHAT WORK WHAT?'.

Woll and others have shown that BSL syntax is lawful but, as can be seen in the examples, radically different from spoken English. The rules followed in BSL may well be closer to those revealed in studies of the sign language of the American deaf (American Sign Language or ASL) than to spoken English (Deuchar 1981). This would suggest that the factors that have shaped the languages are related to the visuo-spatial nature of the systems, and that these factors have led to parallel evolution of sign languages. In sign languages it is possible to depict a setting for an event by drawing it in space, with one individual beside a table, and another across the room by a door. Having 'set the scene', the actors can then be signified by position in space, and their movements and actions depicted through movement in the defined area. Since this facility does not exist in spoken English, it gives sign languages particular features which shape some of their syntactic structures.

Use of BSL is limited by lack of documentation. There is no extensive dictionary, although a dictionary containing 2000 signs has long been promised (British Deaf Association, *Sign It*, in preperation). At present the most extensive published lexicon contains 700 to 800 signs (Sutcliffe 1981, 1984). Brennan *et al.* (1980) have produced a mimeographed text (currently under revision) analysing methods through which signs are developed and how they may be described. Two sets of proceedings of conferences and isolated research papers document a number of studies (Deuchar 1979, Woll *et al.* 1981, Kyle and Woll 1983). A text devoted solely to BSL has been published recently (Deuchar 1984).

Use of BSL in education is limited to a few schools and units for the deaf. It is very unlikely that BSL is used at all extensively in any other educational contexts. From several surveys of use of sign languages in schools for mentally and physically handicapped pupils it is clear that, although BSL signs are used very commonly, BSL syntax is not employed. Signs are used in spoken English word-order (Kiernan *et al.* 1982, Reid *et al.* 1983). We will discusss this strategy later.

American Sign Language (ASL)

ASL is the manual language developed by deaf individuals in the United States of America. ASL was introduced in an educational context in the 19th century as a variant of French Sign Language. This origin accounts for its independence from BSL, from which it differs radically in its form of signs. ASL is well documented. A number of dictionaries and manuals have been produced (Stokoe *et al.* 1965), and research on ASL has also been relatively prolific (Wilbur 1979).

In deaf education, ASL has run into as much resistance as BSL (Lane 1980). With non-deaf populations Goodman *et al.* (1978) concluded that, although schools and centres reported use of ASL, in practice they were using ASL signs in spoken English word-order.

Signed English

Deaf sign languages have been rejected by some educators on the grounds that their use would hinder the acquisition of speech. The child who can use sign language may not be motivated to learn to speak, and the syntax of deaf sign languages may interfere with acquisition of spoken English syntax. A compromise is to teach signs in spoken English word-order with accompanying speech. This method is referred to as 'total communication'.

Signed English systems use spoken English word-order and employ additional signs to correspond to 'missing' elements in sign languages. Signs for definite and indefinite articles, affixes or tense endings missing from BSL or ASL, are devised within signed English systems.

Several systems have been derived from ASL, but Signed English (Bornstein and Hamilton 1978) appears to be the most popular in North America. In the United Kingdom a signed English system has been developed and is taught in at least two regular workshops. A published account of UK signed English appeared recently (Sayer 1984). At least one privately produced handbook has been available for several years (Hall 1979).

Signed English is employed in a number of schools for the deaf in the UK, but is used very infrequently by schools for other groups of handicapped pupils. Lack of use has been explained partly by the lack of documentation of UK signed English, and it will be interesting to see how UK signed English is taken up now a readily available manual has been produced.

British Sign Language: Makaton Vocabulary (BSL(M))

In the early 1970s, a group of practitioners developed the use of BSL signs with deaf mentally handicapped adults in four subnormality hospitals (Cornforth *et al.* 1974). Their initial argument was that people who were deaf and mentally handicapped might be helped to communicate by learning to sign in much the way that deaf or deafened people of normal intelligence are helped.

Cornforth and his colleagues suggested that a limited vocabulary of signs be used in spoken English word-order accompanied by spoken words. This approach, and the vocabulary, has been continued and developed by Walker (1976a, 1978).

The Makaton Vocabulary—BSL(M)—is seen by Walker as an implicit language programme, and 'language programmes' have been produced in parallel with the Vocabulary (Walker 1976b). It is important for our purposes to separate the approach to signing and the language-programme aspects of the package, since they require separate evaluation.

As noted, the BSL(M) approach to signing involves the use of grammatical spoken English with accompanying signs. The recommendation is that only key words in spoken sentences are signed. The strategy involves two assumptions. Firstly, it is assumed that acquisitions of understanding of signs (and maybe words) will be facilitated by use of key signs, and that use of signs in grammatical sequences by handicapped people will also be facilitated. Secondly, it is assumed that the system provides all that handicapped users can ever learn. In other words, learners will only be able to acquire a restricted vocabulary and minimal syntax. Neither of these assumptions is backed by evidence.

BSL(M) is disseminated through a set of 'basic' and 'advanced' workshops. The Makaton Vocabulary Development Project has produced record forms and pictures of signs used. The use of the system in schools and other settings is mediated by speech therapists and other professionals who function as 'regional representatives' of the system.

BSL(M) is by far the most commonly used system in the UK. Data from successive surveys between 1978 and 1982 have shown increasing use by schools (Kierman et al. 1982, Reid et al. 1983). In 1982, 84.5 per cent of schools using sign languages or systems employed BSL(M). The system was particularly strong in schools for the severely educationally subnormal where 434 of 457 users (95 per cent) favoured BSL(M). Schools for the physically handicapped (PH) also favoured BSL(M), as did schools and units catering for autistic pupils. Only schools and units for aphasic pupils favoured another system (Kiernan and Reid 1984).

Paget Gorman Sign System (PGSS)
The Paget Gorman Sign System (PGSS) has its own logical structure, and mirrors spoken English in signs. It is based on 21 standard hand postures and 37 basic signs which are formed from these postures. Basic signs represent concepts or classes of objects such as 'ground', 'metals' or 'animals'. The system includes signs for tense endings and for the affixes and suffixes used in spoken English. Crystal and Craig (1978) compared PGSS with various other types of signed English, and concluded that it was the 'most linguistic' system of the available contrived systems.

The system is well documented. An excellent dictionary has been prepared, employing an extremely detailed and precise coding system. Users are expected to attend workshops before using the system, and to obtain diplomas before teaching it to other teachers or therapists. Several discussions of the system have been published (Rowe 1978).

In 1978, 27.91 per cent of ESN(S) schools and 36.36 per cent of PH schools in the

UK used PGSS (Kiernan *et al.* 1982). By 1982 these percentages had fallen to 3.72 per cent of ESN(S) schools (17 of 457 users responding) and 7.55 per cent of PH schools (12 of 159 users responding). Data on the abandonment of systems suggests that the prime reasons were differential adoption of BSL(M) as opposed to PGSS, enforced abandonment of PGSS because of local authority decisions to adopt BSL(M), PGSS users leaving schools and difficulty in using PGSS. Differential adoption often appears to have followed conferences at which BSL(M), PGSS, Blissymbolics and Cued Speech proponents described their systems in fairly brief presentations (see Tebbs 1978).

The different 'images' of the various systems were reflected in data on reasons for adoption (Kiernan *et al.* (1982). PGSS was seen as especially relevant for educational purposes and language-teaching, but in fact the only groups of surveyed schools consistently using PGSS are those catering for aphasic children (Kiernan and Reid 1984). These schools were amongst the first to introduce PGSS, and comments from teachers on the survey forms indicated strong support for the system and conviction that it helps aphasic children to develop speech and language. These feelings are reflected by PGSS users in other types of schools (Rowe 1978).

Informal data suggest that PGSS may also be used in units for language-handicapped pupils in schools for children between the age of five and nine (Kiernan and Reid 1984). These units aim to maintain children in the 'normal' as opposed to the 'special' educational structure. We know of no data that indicate the success of PGSS in helping children to acquire the speech and language skills which would allow them to integrate effectively into normal schools.

It is hard to avoid the conclusion that PGSS has been replaced by BSL(M) partly because of the methods used in presenting the two systems. BSL(M) was offered, and perceived, as easy for staff to learn and easy to teach to pupils. It is taught initially in inexpensive one-day workshops. PGSS, on the other hand, was seen by practitioners as difficult for teachers and children. Learning the system takes time, partly because the commonest method of learning has been a five-day workshop and partly because learners unfamiliar with grammar find it difficult (Kiernan *et al.* 1982). There have been no systematic comparisons of the systems to suggest that one system is 'better' than the other. Practitioners have been forced to make decisions on other grounds and, in the process, PGSS has lost out to BSL(M) in most types of school.

Amer Ind

This system was developed in the USA by a speech pathologist, Madge Skelly, who was working with adults who had lost their ability to speak as a result of strokes, accidents or surgery. It has also been used with other handicapped populations (Skelly 1979). The system, which Skelly calls a 'gestural code based on American Indian Hand Talk' rather than a sign system, has been well documented. Both signs (called gestures) and teaching methods are presented in a text (Skelly 1979). The gestures are seen as representing 'concepts' rather than translating to individual spoken words. So the gestures 'STAND' may be used for the words arise, awake, rise (out of bed), stand up and wake. Skelly's manual includes 236 such concepts and a series of arithmetic concepts. The vocabulary is further extended by a group of suggested 'agglutinations', combined signs which cover terms not accounted for in the initial lists.

Skelly has taught the use of her system in several workshops in the UK. According to our surveys, however, its use in schools is very rare, with only two or three schools reporting use during the period 1978 to 1982. This may well be because it has been in direct competition with BSL(M). There is informal evidence of the employment of Amer Ind by speech therapists and others in stroke clinics and other facilities for adults. It is apparently more commonly used in the USA (Daniloff *et al.* 1983).

Fingerspelling
This 'system' represents the method through which spoken words are spelled out 'on the one hand' through a manual alphabet. In its use with and by deaf people, fingerspelling plays an important educational and communicative function by complementing sign languages. The commonest use of the manual alphabet with other special school groups is in terms of name signs, where the initial letters of proper names are signed. In our surveys, fingerspelling was also mentioned as a means of representing words with aphasic pupils—here, presumably, with more capable individuals.

Two other systems have been used in the UK from time to time: Meldreth Mime (Levett 1970) and Cued Speech (Cornett 1967). We have no evidence of their current use with the non-deaf populations covered in the surveys mentioned.

Graphic symbol systems
There are fewer formal symbol systems in use in the UK than there are manual sign systems. However, as we will see, this situation may be changing.

Communication boards
At its simplest level, communication can be effected by pointing to an object or a pictorial depiction of a desired object or event. Communication boards employ this method at various levels of user sophistication, with three-dimensional representations of objects, colour photographs of objects and line drawings of particular objects, and more abstract pictograms and ideograms.

Communication boards are normally seen as appropriate for physically handicapped pupils, but clearly could be used with pupils with other disabilities. In our surveys we found very little report of the use of boards with any groups. They could be used more frequently as an initial method of allowing handicapped children and young people to indicate needs.

Blissymbolics
This system was developed by Charles Bliss (1965) with the purpose of providing a universal communication system. The system is 'concept-based', in the sense that it is constructed from a limited number of meaningful basic symbols and symbol

elements. The symbols often end up being pictographic (for example the 'male' symbol looks like a stick man) or ideographic (all 'emotion' words are denoted by a heart-shaped symbol). Some symbols are complex. The television symbol is comprised of elements representing the eye, ear, an enclosure or box and electricity: a television set being conceptualised as a box which is seen, heard and which works by electricity.

Blissymbols were first used with handicapped individuals in Canada in 1971. They were introduced on a small scale in the UK in 1974 (Hammond and Bailey 1976). Their use is taught by qualified instructors on courses lasting from three to five days. People attending courses can obtain a handbook (Silverman *et al.* 1978). An excellent dictionary (Hehner 1980) and a variety of back-up materials are also available.

Blissymbols are most commonly used in schools for physically handicapped pupils. By 1982, 124 of 158 PH schools replying to our requests for information used a symbol system and, of these schools, 110 (90.3 per cent) used Blissymbols. Use in other categories of schools was less common. Data from earlier surveys indicated that teachers in ESN(S) schools saw Blissymbols as 'too abstract' for their pupils, although successful use was reported and their use in ESN(S) schools is fairly common (Kiernan *et al.* 1982, Reid *et al.* 1983).

Problems with the relative 'abstractness' of Blissymbols have been recognised by workers involved in the development of Blissymbolics. McNaughton and Warrick (1984) describe a method for 'enhancing' Blissymbols by adding to the form of individual symbols in order to render them more pictorial. So the symbol for 'hurt', in which the dominant forms are the heart and an irregular line, is transformed into a sad face (within the heart) and a figure rubbing a 'hurt' knee. The symbols are normally depicted in black, the additional elements in pink felt-pen.

Rebus systems

The Rebus Reading Series was developed to help mildly mentally handicapped children to learn to read (Woodcock 1969, Clark *et al.* 1974). The symbols used within the system range from pictograms and ideograms to pure rebuses, *i.e.* pictures in which the elements represent syllables of the word referred to. For example, the rebus for 'cannot' constitutes a picture of a can and a picture of a knot. Other symbols within the Peabody scheme compound traditional orthography and pictures. An example is the word 'heat', which is depicted by the symbol for 'eat' (a picture of a child feeding himself with a spoon) prefixed by the letter 'h'. Reid *et al.* (1983) estimated that there were about 880 children using Rebus materials in the UK in 1982, as opposed to Blissymbolics with about 750 users.

The notion of using clear standardised pictures to help children to communicate has attracted teachers of the less able. However, Rebus and phonologically based symbols within the Peabody scheme have not been seen as useful. Until recently no strong alternative has emerged, and consequently many idiosyncratic variants of the system have emerged. Some systematic developments have been documented (Van Oosterum and Devereux 1982). The enhanced Blissymbols represent an interesting alternative.

Sigsymbols

Cregan (1983) has developed a symbol system which employs pictographic and ideographic elements but which also reflects, where possible, the form of BSL signs and symbols. It is designed as a teaching aid for signing children in terms of communication and language development. A very similar scheme is being developed under the auspices of the Makaton Project. It will be interesting to see what advantages justify the addition of the Makaton symbol system.

Premackese

Following the successful attempts by Premack (1970) to teach chimpanzees language-like behavior, the work was extended to handicapped populations. This has led to several developments in the USA and UK where mentally handicapped (Deich and Hodges 1977), aphasic (Hughes 1974/5) or autistic children (Light *et al.* 1981) have been taught to communicate through the use of symbols like those used by Premack. The form of the symbols, which are usually plastic plaques, is deliberately non-representational. Initially Premack used such symbols to ensure the 'arbitrariness' of the language system; but it is questionable whether the continued use of arbitrary symbols is justified.

The Premack approach has been developed in the form of a commercially available teaching scheme by Carrier and Peak (1975). By UK standards the equipment is very expensive and, to our knowledge, has only been used once in the UK (Hand and Carmichael 1979). Our surveys, and the surveys in the USA have shown very little impact of Premackese.

Word cards

Final mention should be made of word cards as a means of communication. Scattered references to their use appear in surveys and in the published literature (De Villiers and Naughton 1974). Less able children are probably responding to words as patterns of elements rather than understanding individual letters in the words. More children may benefit from their use in the future. In fact it is often questioned whether Blissymbols and other abstract symbol systems are really necessary as a teaching device, or whether children could not progress directly to using word cards as a means of communication or for reading.

Relative merits of the systems
CHARACTERISTICS OF STUDENTS

The characteristics of the students to be served must provide the starting point for discussion of the relative merits of the systems. At the broadest level, students may have problems with expressive or receptive aspects of language and communication, or with both aspects. These problems may mean that their expressive skills are well below receptive skills, but that receptive skills are in line with cognitive development. Alternatively, both expressive and receptive skills may lag behind cognitive development; or expressive and receptive skills may be in line with cognitive development, denoting a generalised impairment.

Even at this gross level it is clear that systems need to be deployed differently for different students. One group may need to use an augmentative system purely for expression, relying on speech as a receptive medium. In this case the normal input in teaching may only involve speech. Another student may need to use a system as a receptive *and* an expressive medium. Here the teachers will need to use speech and signs or symbols in some combination. For a student with global impairment the teaching environment may involve speech and sign, but with changes in strategy dictated by hypotheses concerning the most effective ways in which an augmentative system might affect cognitive development. An instance would be the use of graphic symbols to offset sequencing difficulties in the acquisition of syntax (see below).

Expressive problems with speech may result from disorders of muscular control of the speech mechanisms (anarthria or dysarthria) related to cerebral palsy. Alternatively, absent or disordered speech may be caused by disorders of the capacity to programme the positioning of speech muscles or the sequencing of movements in the absence of gross physical problems (apraxia or dyspraxia). Finally, problems may stem from impairment of the capacity to formulate language symbols (expressive aphasia or dysphasia).

Further problems may affect the use of augmentative systems. Poor muscular control of the hands may result in difficulty in producing signs, and, at an extreme, of pointing to graphic symbols. Muscular control of the hands would not necessarily ensure that signs could be learned (sign apraxia) or that sign language could be used meaningfully (sign aphasia).

Similar complexities exist on the receptive side. An individual may be chronically or intermittently deaf, thereby requiring the use of sign or graphic symbols as a receptive medium. In the absence of peripheral deafness, he or she may suffer from some degree of receptive aphasia for speech, but may also suffer receptive aphasia for signs or for graphic symbols.

These considerations lead immediately to the conclusion that assessment needs to be as thorough as possible. Systems need to be considered as aids to teaching, choice being dictated by the needs of the individual student. Finally teaching needs to be seen as a process of cumulative assessment, with the teacher always on the lookout for sign apraxia or receptive aphasia for signs or symbols. More thorough analysis of individual differences is clearly indicated by the wide variation in response to sign-teaching shown in virtually all published studies (Kiernan *et al.* 1982).

TEACHING METHODS

The points also lead to a number of suggestions about teaching, some of which are informed by research findings. One of the commonest findings of research and teaching studies is that vocalisation and speech develops in the context of augmentative communication programmes (Kiernan *et al.* 1982, Kiernan 1983). The mechanisms underlying this phenomenon are unclear. They probably range from generalised effects resulting from increased attention to the student, through helping the imitation of speech sounds as a generalised effect of teaching sign through imitation, to relatively specific sign or symbol linkage to spoken words (Kiernan *et al.* 1987). Investigation leading to the accurate identification of these effects and the development of corresponding teaching strategies represents a high priority.

In the absence of these detailed analyses, several points can be made about teaching. If the aim is to encourage the acquisition and use of speech by students, it would seem sensible to give them experience of relevant speech sounds as they use an augmentative system. One way in which this can be done is for the teacher to translate a student's signs or symbols into speech as he or she produces them. This strategy was used by Schaefer *et al.* (1980) with apparent success. An alternative would be to provide a symbol user with a synthesised speech output from a symbol board. Clearly, as Schaeffer *et al.* point out, effective learning from talk-back will need a component of verbal imitation training in the over-all programme.

Where manual sign is used, and especially where it is seen as both an expressive and a receptive mode for the student, teacher or therapist input represents a model for language development.

There are no data that allow us to compare the relative merits of different systems in potentiating language development. Consequently we do not know whether systems that mirror spoken English (PGSS or Signed English) lead to more rapid learning than true sign languages such as ASL or BSL. However, logic and conventional wisdom would argue that presenting the student with two utterances with widely differing forms, albeit with the same meaning, will not help him to acquire knowledge of corresponding elements in two systems. This argument has lead to the adoption of PGSS or Signed English rather than the natural sign languages.

Several choices remain. Developmental studies would suggest that the ideal strategy for potentiating language development is to present the student with language models that are continuously at the limit of his expressive capacity. Teacher input would, sensibly, match sign and speech through the use of a PGSS or Signed English system, leading the student on to increased vocabulary and more complex syntax. In this context, Walker's notion of the use of normal spoken English with key elements being signed is clearly unsatisfactory (Walker 1978). If the student is learning to use sign as an expressive medium, the strategy precludes the modelling of increasingly complex sign use. Even if the student is 'ready' and able to use normal spoken syntax in sign, the opportunity is never offered. The Makaton approach prevents students from developing, limiting them to a truncated form of expression. Kiernan and Reid (1984) found that teachers reported having to switch students from BSL(M to PGSS) because of the limitations placed by the Makaton approach. The only way in which the approach could be justified is if students are primarily dependent on speech, and signs are acting purely as additional cues for speech production. This is not ostensibly the target group for the system.

This argument leads again to the conclusion that PGSS and Signed English are the two systems which provide enough flexibility for the teacher or therapist to present increasingly sophisticated models in both speech and sign.

To some extent, the problems with the Makaton approach reflect the nature of the Vocabulary. The Vocabulary is said to be based on work on normal language development, but in practice it does not reflect crucial work on early development published in the last decade (Kiernan 1984a, Byler 1985). Because manual sign has to be learned as a second language by most teachers, parents and therapists, there is a clear case for selecting a limited vocabulary which these users can learn. Several vocabularies are now available, based on empirical studies of child development (Gillham 1979, Fristoe and Lloyd 1980). Comparison of these vocabularies with the Makaton Vocabulary confirms the impression that the latter is unsound on developmental grounds (Kiernan 1984a, Byler 1985). It seems clear that the Makaton Vocabulary should be used, if at all, only as a word bank. Additional or alternative vocabulary, including vocabulary necessary to allow more complete syntax to be used, should be added in particular contexts.

Other considerations arise from the different recommended methods of combining speech and sign. Allowing for the suggestion that the syntactic form of speech and sign utterances by teachers should be the same, there is still the question of their temporal arrangement. Most authors argue in favour of simultaneously presentation, but work by Leyton and Helmer (1984) supports Skelly's argument (1979) that successive presentation will lead to more rapid acquisition.

There is a possibility that sign use will lead to direct improvement in basic cognitive skills. One version of this proposal was tested by Bishop (1982, 1983) who found that use of PGSS failed to help children overcome particular problems with syntax. No other direct tests of the hypothesis are available.

There are data that suggest that the use of graphic symbols promotes acquisition of syntactic rules. This is signified by the success of the Non SLIP system (Carrier and Peak 1975; Carrier 1976, 1979). House et al. (1980) have shown how mentally handicapped people may break down the problem of generating descriptive sentences, by first selecting the symbols appropriate for description of a picture in non-standard order, and then sorting them into syntactically correct order. This study suggests that graphic symbols will be valuable only if users can physically rearrange symbols.

The consideration of teaching methods points fairly clearly to the superiority of PGSS and Signed English over BSL or BSL(M). The Makaton Vocabulary and its associated teaching methods are defective in several ways. Graphic symbols may have particular advantages in teaching syntactic rules.

Ease of learning by students represents an obvious dimension of comparison. At the level of attainment of effective communication, the only data available are from the 1978 survey by Kiernan *et al.* (1982). These data have poor grain because of the way in which they were gathered, but suggest that there are no significant differences on a variety of outcome measures amongst various forms of BSL(M), or between BSL, BAL(M) and PGSS. They show a massive unexplained difference *within* the schools using different systems, indicating that pupil and probably teaching-

401

method variables are crucial. The data in the 1978 survey suggest that symbol users may progress faster than sign users. These data reflect the fact that sign use normally requires recall of signs, symbol use requires only recognition. Given that recall is a more complex psychological process than recognition, we would expect pupils to find it easier to use symbols than signs.

Other approaches to comparing ease of learning of the systems involve examining features of the various sign languages and systems. Kiernan (1984b, c) showed that ASL and BSL differ from PGSS in types of sign. The two natural sign languages rely extensively on signs which employ only one hand or signs in which the two hands hold the same posture. By contrast, PGSS contains a large proportion of signs where the hands adopt different postures. Data from a series of studies on the imitation and expressive learning of the different types of sign show that one-hand and two-hand same signs are significantly easier for mentally handicapped children to imitate and learn as names for cartoon figures than are two-hand different signs.

Similar conclusions can be drawn for different kinds of hand postures. ASL and BSL employ significantly more hand postures which are easy to imitate and to learn to use expressively than PGSS (Kiernan 1984c).

These data suggest that BSL or ASL signs will be easier for children to learn than PGSS signs. However, we need to be careful about the conclusion. First of all we are talking about standard PGSS signs. There is no reason why these cannot be simplified initially. Secondly, the conclusion applies to large samples of signs; within a lexicon of 20 signs there may be little difference between systems (Kiernan and Reid 1983). Finally, the conclusion applies only to imitation and expressive learning: it does not hold with receptive learning of sign features (Kiernan 1984c).

It is often suggested that it is easier to learn signs that are depictive or iconic. In practice iconicity is a complex and difficult issue (Mandel 1977), and there are also substantial difficulties in the assessment of iconicity: what is iconic to an adult may not be so to a handicapped child. Kiernan (1984b) concluded that there is little evidence to suggest that iconicity affects acquisition by handicapped children. However, it does reflect 'meaningfulness', and consequently we would expect it to have at least some positive effect on acquisition.

The ease with which mentally handicapped individuals associate meaning with graphic symbols has been assessed in several studies. Hughes (1979) showed that mentally handicapped students learned to recognise Blissymbols more readily than consonant-vowel-consonant nonsense words. Kuntz et al. (1978) found that mentally handicapped children learned to use pictorial Rebus symbols more rapidly than Premack-type abstract symbols. However, in this study, and in a similar one by Worrall and Singh (1983), transfer to traditional orthography was shown to be slower with the more pictographic system than with the more abstract. Worrall and Singh used 'accentuated' words where the form of the word was modified in order to make it depict the meaning (Miller 1968). On the basis of these studies, choice of system must depend on ultimate aim. If it is to provide a communication system, then more pictographic systems are indicated. A more abstract system, or a graded series of systems, needs to be employed if it is transferred to reading.

Surprisingly little discussion has been devoted to the possible effect of the perceptual problems of physically handicapped pupils on symbol use. Blissymbols, especially those which involve combining several elements in verb or adjectival forms, employ relatively inconspicuous cues to modify basic forms. In addition, many symbols involve embedding which might create problems for cerebral-palsied pupils. In one relevant study, five severely mentally handicapped students were shown to have difficulty in responding to Blissymbol modifiers (Kalimikerakis 1983).

Although there are few data on ease of learning signs and symbols, we can draw some tentative conclusions. Form of signs affects the speed with which they are learned, and it would appear that 'natural' sign languages have selected easier sign forms. Pupils also find it easier to learn more concrete graphic symbols: but when it come to transferring to written words, the time saved is likely to be lost by longer transfer time.

Ease of learning by adults probably depends on similar factors to those affecting children in terms of the structural features of systems. However, because of their greater cognitive sophistication, it seems likely that iconic aspects will have a more positive effect for adult learners than for handicapped children. 'Historic iconicity' will clearly affect adults but not handicapped students. Few people are likely to forget that the supposed etymology of the BSL sugar sign, 'scratching' the cheek with a clawed hand, relates to the fact that deaf workers in the Tate and Lyle sugar factory in Liverpool in the 19th century developed sugar dermatitis.

A number of studies have examined the transparency and translucency of signs and related these measures to ease of learning. A transparent sign is one where the meaning can be guessed from the form of the sign: BSL BOOK, for example, where the signer places his flat hands together and then 'opens' them like a book. Translucency refers to the extent to which the form of the sign relates to its referent once the meaning is offered. The BSL sign for BOY, a movement across the chin indicating the lack of a beard, is such a sign.

Several studies have shown Amer Ind to be more transparent than ASL (Kirschner *et al.* 1979, Skelly 1979, Daniloff *et al.* 1983). The only study of transparency and translucency in the UK found no differences between BSL and PGSS (Feinmann 1982).

Luftig and Lloyd (1981) argue that translucency and concreteness of reference may both be crucial in sign-learning. They manipulated the two variables simultaneously: signs with concrete referents (*e.g.* BABY, HAMMER and TRUMPET) with those with low concreteness (IDEA, CHANCE and SCIENCE). Both conditions were indeed shown to influence learning.

Acceptability of systems will clearly be related to ease of learning by pupils and adults, but will also be affected by other variables. In general the study of acceptability has been neglected. Practitioners talk of sign language as being 'more natural' than symbols, although there are reports of parents resisting the use of signing on the grounds that it is non-normalising. In one of the few studies, researchers in Wisconsin found that what was crucial in terms of public acceptance was not so much the form of the system but the rate of transmission of information

(Yoder, personal communication). Systems allowing attainment of normal rates of transmission were preferred regardless of artificiality.

This study investigated transmission through spoken or graphic methods. Clearly there are special problems with sign use. Signing is socially isolating, and systems like PGSS may be excessively isolating if the user does not develop speech. However, it seems reasonable that sign languages or systems which are high on translucency and transparency will be likely to be more acceptable to non-users. This is possibly the strongest argument for the development of Amer Ind. Graphic symbol systems may be difficult to use because they require the student to carry physical representations of the symbols. This may not be a problem for a student in a wheelchair, but it could be for a physically able student. Advances involving use of microprocessors may help here.

Cost of systems relates to initial training costs, costs of equipment and costs of maintaining systems in terms of staff time. It seems likely that PGSS lost out initially to BSL(M), partly because initial workshops took five days, and were often residential, as opposed to the BSL(M) one-day initial course. With severe restrictions on in-service training, PGSS and other courses may soon price themselves out of the market. Equipment costs usually relate to written materials. We have already noted that an otherwise valuable programme, Non SLIP, is probably too high-priced to be taken up by schools.

Time required for staff to maintain systems is difficult to assess. Residential schools find it necessary to have regular in-service training sessions for both teachers and care staff (Kiernan *et al.* 1982). In day schools, where there are only a few users of a system, such sessions may be difficult to justify in terms of a school's priorities. Symbol systems should be easier and cheaper to maintain than sign systems.

Discussion

Blissymbolics is a well-developed and well-established system. The recent addition of enhanced Blissymbols and the emergence of Rebus systems offers a range of teaching aids. There needs to be no conflict amongst systems since elements can readily replace each other from the user's viewpoint. Systems can always be linked to written words or synthetic speech, allowing ready intelligibility.

The potential for teaching syntactic rules through graphic symbols needs further exploration. These developments link up with increased teaching of reading to mentally impaired students.

The position in respect of sign-teaching is equally straightforward but more contentious. It seems clear that Signed English is the system of choice. BSL(M) is a limited and limiting system, both in its structure and in its recommended teaching methods. It can be abandoned as soon as the elements of Signed English are learned by staff. Although PGSS has considerable merits, its greater complexity and lack of continuity with BSL militate against its continued use—except possibly in centres where it reliably leads to development of speech. Even here, effective use of Signed English would render it redundant. Amer Ind may have particular virtues, but it is used very little in schools and its use should probably be discouraged.

Two final points put these considerations in context. The assessment of students in programmes using augmentative systems is typically poor. A greater understanding of the problems of students would allow better use of all types of teaching input. Finally, data from Kahn (1981) show that the use of good structured teaching programmes is more important in producing improved skills than the use of augmentative systems. The quality of language-teaching programmes, especially those for the less able, is generally poor (Kiernan 1984a). We need to improve these programmes, rather than seeing the use of augmentative systems as a panacea.

REFERENCES

Bishop, D. V. M. (1982) 'Comprehension of spoken, written and signed sentences in childhood language disorders.' *Journal of Child Psychology and Psychiatry*, **23**, 1–20.
—— (1983) 'Comprehension of English syntax by profoundly deaf children.' *Journal of Child Psychology and Psychiatry*, **24**, 415–434.
Bliss, C. (1965) *Semantography*. Sydney, Australia: Semantography Publications.
Bornstein, H., Hamilton, L. B. (1978) 'Signed English.' *In:* Tebbs, T. (Ed.) *Ways and Means*. Basingstoke: Globe Education.
Brennan, M., Colville, M. D., Lawson, L. K. (1980) *Words in Hand*. Edinburgh: BSL Project.
Byler, J. K. (1985) 'The Makaton Vocabulary: an analysis based on recent research.' *British Journal of Special Education*, **12**, 109–116.
Carrier, J. K. (1976) 'Application of a nonspeech language system with the severely language handicapped.' *In:* Lloyd, L. L. (Ed.) *Communication Assessment and Intervention Strategies*. Baltimore: University Park Press.
—— (1979) 'Application of functional analysis and a nonspeech response mode to teaching language.' *In:* Schiefelbusch, R. L., Hollis, J. H. (Eds.) *Language Intervention from Ape to Child*. Baltimore: University Park Press.
—— Peak, T. (1975) *Non-speech Language Initiation Program*. Lawrence, Ka.: H & H Enterprises.
Clark, C. R., Davies, C. O., Woodcock, R. W. (1974) *Standard Rebus Glossary*. Circle Pines, Min.: American Guidance Service.
Cornett, O. (1967) 'Cued speech.' *American Annals of the Deaf.*' **112**, 3–13.
Cornforth, A. R. T., Johnson, K., Walker, M. (1974) *The Makaton Vocabulary*. London: RADD.
Cregan, A. (1983) *Sigsymbols*. Cambridge: LDA.
Crystal, D., Craig, E. (1978) 'Contrived sign language.' *In:* Schlesinger, I., Namir, L. (Eds.) *Current Trends in the Study of Sign Language of the Deaf*. New York: Academic Press.
Daniloff, J. K., Lloyd, L. L., Fristoe, M. (1983) 'Amer-Ind transparency.' *Journal of Speech and Hearing Disorders*, **48**, 103–110.
Deich, R. F., Hodges, P. M. (1977) *Language Without Speech*. London: Souvenir Press.
Deuchar, M. (1979) 'The grammar of British Sign Lanuage Supplement of the British Deaf News, June, 1979.
—— (1981) 'Variation in British Sign Language.' *In:* Woll, B., Kyle, J., Deuchar, M. (Eds.) *Perspectives on British Sign Language and Deafness*. London: Croom Helm.
—— (1984) *British Sign Language*. London: Routledge & Kegan Paul.
De Villiers, J. G., Naughton, J. M. (1974) 'Teaching a symbol language to autistic children.' *Journal of Consulting and Clinical Psychology*, **42**, 111–117.
Feinmann, J. L. (1982) 'The visuo-motor complexity, transparency and translucency of the Paget Gorman Sign System and British Sign Language.' Unpublished M.Sc. thesis, University of Manchester Faculty of Education.
Fristoe, M., Lloyd, L. L. (1980) 'Planning an initial expressive sign lexicon for persons with severe communication impairment.' *Journal of Speech and Hearing Disorders*, **45**, 170–180.
Gillham, B. (1979) *The First Words Language Programme*. London: George Allen & Unwin.
Goodman, L., Wilson, P. S., Bornstein, H. (1978) 'Results of a national survey of sign language programmes in special education.' *Mental Retardation*, **16**, 104–106.
Hall, R. (1979) 'Aid to Communication with Signed English.' *Private publication aided by Bedfordshire Education Authority.*

Hammond, J. M., Bailey, P. A. (1976) 'An experiment in Blissymbolics.' *Special Education,* **3**(3), 21–22.

Hand, V., Carmichael, W. T. (1979) 'Teaching a symbol system to non-verbal severely retarded children.' Dissertion for a Diploma in the Education of ESN Children, University of London Institute of Education.

Hehner, B. (1980) *Blissymbols for Use.* Toronto, Canada: Blissymbolics Communication Institute.

House, B. J., Hanley, M. J., Magid, D. F. (1980) 'Logographic reading by TMR adults.' *American Journal of Mental Deficiency,* **85**, 161–170.

Hughes, J. (1974/5) 'Acquisition of a nonverbal "language" by aphasic children.' *Cognition,* **3**, 41–55.

Hughes, M. N. (1979) 'Sequencing of visual and auditory stimuli in teaching words and Blissymbols to the mentally retarded.' *Australian Journal of Mental Retardation,* **5**, 298–302.

Kahn, J. V. (1981) 'A comparison of sign and verbal language training with non-verbal retarded children.' *Journal of Speech and Hearing Research,* **46**, 113–119.

Kalimikerakis, C. (1983) 'Training mentally handicapped children to use Blissymbolics.' Unpublished Master's thesis, University of London Institute of Education.

Kiernan, C. C. (1983) 'The use of non-vocal communication techniques with autistic individuals.' *Journal of Child Psychology and Psychiatry,* **24**, 339–375.

—— (1984*a*) 'Language remediation programmes: a review.' *In:* Muller, D. J. (Ed.) *"Remediating Children's Language" Behavioural and Naturalistic Approaches.* London: Croom Helm.

—— (1984*b*) 'The exploration of sign and symbol effects.' *In:* Hogg, J., Mittler, P. J. (Eds.) *Aspects of Competence in Mental Handicap Research.* Chichester, Sussex: John Wiley.

—— (1984*c*) 'Imitation and learning of hand postures.' *In:* Berg, J. M. (Ed.) *Perspectives and Progress in Mental Retardation: Volume 1—Social, Psychological and Educational Aspects.* Baltimore, Md: University Park Press.

—— Reid, B. D., Jones, L. M. (1982) *Signs and Symbols: A Review of Literature and Survey of Use of Non-Vocal Communication Systems.* University of London Institute of Education Studies in Education, No. 11. London: Heinemann.

—— —— (1984) 'The use of augmentative communication systems in schools and units for autistic and aphasic children in the United Kingdom. *British Journal of Disorders of Communication,* **19**, 47–61.

—— —— Goldbart, J. (1987) *Foundations of Communication and Language.* Manchester: Manchester University Press.

Kirschner, A., Algozzine, B., Abbott, T. B. (1979) 'Manual communication systems: A comparison and its implications.' *Education and Training of the Mentally Retarded,* **14**, 5–10.

Kuntz, J. B., Carrier, J. K., Hollis, J. H. (1978) 'A non-vocal system for teaching retarded children to read and write.' *In:* Meyers, C. (Ed.) *Quality of Life in Severely and Profoundly Mentally Retarded People: Research Foundations for Improvements.* Washington: AAMD.

Kyle, J., Woll, B. (1981) 'British Sign Language.' *Special Education: Forward Trends,* **8**(1), 19–23.

—— (1983) *Language in Sign: An International Perspective on Sign Language.* London: Croom Helm.

Lane, H. (1980) 'A chronology of the oppression of sign language in France and the United States.' *In:* Lane, H., Grosjean, F. (eds.) *Recent Perspectives on American Sign Language.* Hillsdale, New Jersey: Lawrence Erlbaum.

Levett, L. M. (1970) *A Method of Communication for Nonspeaking Severely Subnormal Children.* London: Spastics Society.

Leyton, T. L., Helmer, S. H. (1984) 'Initial language program for autistic and developmentally disordered children.' *Paper to the A.A.M.D. Conference, Chicago.*

Light, P. H., Remington, R. E., Porter, D. (1981) 'Substitutes for speech? Nonvocal approaches to Communication.' *In:* Beveridge, M. (Ed.) *Children Thinking Through Language.* London: Edward Arnold.

Lloyd, L. L., Karlan, G. (1984) 'Non speech communication symbols and systems: where have we been and where are we going?' *Journal of Mental Deficiency Research,* **28**, 3–20.

Luftig, R. L., Lloyd, L. L. (1981) 'Manual sign translucency and referential concreteness in the learning of signs.' *Sign Language Studies,* **No. 30**, 49–60.

Mandel, M. (1977) 'Iconic devices in American Sign Language.' *In:* Friedman, L. A. (Ed.) *On the Other Hand: New Perspectives on American Sign Language.* New York: Academic Press.

McNaughton, S., Warrick, A. (1984) 'Picture your Blissymbols.' *Canadian Journal of Mental Retardation,* **34**, 1–9.

Miller, A. (1968) *Symbol Accentuation—A New Approach to Reading.* New York: Doubleday Multimedia.

Premack, D. (1970) 'A functional analysis of language.' *Journal for the Experimental Analysis of Behaviour,* **14,** 107–125.

Reid, B. D., Jones, L. M., Kiernan, C. C. (1983) 'Signs and symbols: the 1982 survey of use.' *Special Education: Forward Trends,* **10**(1), 27–28.

Rowe, J. (1978) 'Paget-Gorman Sign System: Manual communication as an alternative method.' *In:* Tebbs, T. (Ed.) *Ways and Means.* Basingstoke, Hants: Globe Education.

Sayer, D. J. (Ed.) (1984) *Signed English for Schools. Vol. 1. Structural Language.* Surrey: Working Party on Signed English.

Schaeffer, B., Musil, A., Kollinzas, G. (1980) *Total Communication : A Signed Speech Program for Nonverbal Children.* Champaign, Ill: Research Press.

Silverman, H., McNaughton, S., Kates, B. (1978) *Handbook of Blissymbolics.* Toronto: Blissymbolics Communication Institute.

Skelly, M. (1979) *American Indian Gestural Code Based on Universal American Indian Hand Talk.* New York: Elsevier.

Stokoe, W. C., Casterline, D. D., Croneberg, C. G. (1965) *Dictionary of American Sign Language on Linguistic Principles.* Washington, D.C.: Linston Press.

Sutcliffe, T. H. (1981) *Sign and Say. Book 1.* London: RNID.

—— (1984) *Sign and Say. Book 2.* London: RNID.

Tebbs, T. (Ed.) (1978) *Ways and Means.* Basingstoke: Globe Education.

Van Oosterum, J., Devereux, K. (1982) 'REBUS at Rees Thomas School.' *Special Education—Forward Trends,* **9,** 31–33.

Walker, M. (1976*a*) *Language Programmes for Use with the Revised Makaton Vocabulary.* Chertsey, Surrey, Private publication.

—— (1976*b*) *The Makaton Vocabulary (Revised Edition).* London: RADD.

—— (1978) 'The Makaton Vocabulary.' *In:* Tebbs, T. (Ed.) *Ways and Means.* Basingstoke: Globe Education.

Wilbur, R. B. (1979) *American Sign Language and Sign Systems.* Baltimore, Md: University Park Press.

Witten, I. H. (1982) *Principles of Computer Speech.* London: Academic Press.

Woll, B. (1981) 'Question structure in British sign language.' *In:* Woll, B., Kyle, J., Deuchar, M. (Eds.) *Perspectives on British Sign Language and Deafness.* London: Croom Helm.

—— Kyle, J., Deuchar, M. (Eds.) (1981) *Perspectives on British Sign Language and Deafness.* London: Croom Helm.

Worrall, N., Singh, Y. (1983) 'Teaching TMR children to read using integrated picture cueing.' *American Journal of Mental Deficiency,* **87,** 422–429.

Woodcock, R. (1969) *Rebus.* Circle Pines, Minn: American Guidance Service.

25
TRENDS IN COMMUNICATION AID TECHNOLOGY FOR THE SEVERELY SPEECH-IMPAIRED

Howard Shane

Perspective on non-speaking population

Persons who are non-speaking can be grouped into several etiological categories (Shane 1981). For those who have never developed speech the principal explanations for speechlessness include mental retardation, motor speech impairment (*i.e.* developmental apraxia of speech, dysarthria), and expressive and receptive language disorders. The acquired speechless conditions, on the other hand, generally have a motor speech, emotional (*e.g.* elective mutism) or anatomical/structural etiology. Unlike the childhood cases, however, the acquired neurogenic disorders are typically either degenerative in nature (*e.g.* amyotrophic lateral sclerosis), the result of closed head injury (such as stroke) or head trauma resulting from a physical injury. The anatomically based conditions result from excision (like glossectomy) or non-functioning of mechanism essential for speech production (such as paralysis of vocal cords or inadequate voicing due to tracheotomy).

The individual who is non-speaking is often considered to have a reduced intellectual capacity and/or a language disorder. The inability to speak is not synonymous with mental retardation, incompetence, or ignorance: nor is it synonymous with language impairment, aphasia or any other form of linguistic impairment. Neither of these misconceptions, however, rule out the possibility that the individual who is severely speech impaired may also evidence intellectual impairment or language disorder. Although the condition of speechlessness is sometimes the result of intellectual or linguistic impairment, neither of these impairments necessarily coexist with it. Mental retardation is associated frequently with significant disorders of speech. Despite the relationship between severe speech impairment and mental retardation, the application of augmentative communication with the mentally retarded did not appear until the late 1960s. This work is especially significant because the subjects were mentally retarded and non-speaking, who despite normal hearing were introduced to sign-language instruction, a procedure reserved for the mentally retarded.

A historical review shows that the published literature concentrated on subjects who evidenced little intellectual or language impairment (Goldberg and Fenton, undated; Vicker 1973). Vicker (1974) underscored what seemed to be an early lack of confidence in assistive communication methods with the mentally retarded:

The value of attempting to develop a non-oral method of communication of the type previously described for the very retarded child would seem questionable; it is quite possible that the goals would necessarily be so limited that the system would be no more effective than the child's present mode of communication. Intellectual abilities have a significant effect on the rate and extent of progress which can be expected in the development of a nonoral technique. Consequently, when a limited amount of time is available for developing a technique, intellect may well be the factor which determines whether a nonoral technique will be initiated (p. 64).

Contemporary augmentative communication applications with persons who are retarded and non-speaking demonstrate a more positive belief in these methods. This apparent shift in attitude reflects a greater optimism regarding the capability of the mentally retarded to improve their communication through supplemental or assistive means. It is also the result of greater exposure to these methods by the retarded with a corresponding positive response by the more suitable candidates.

It is critical to successful programming with the retarded that the symbol set that is selected for training be based on an individual's capacity for representation. For the person who is incapable of comprehending the symbolic value of a written word or simple line drawing, for example, one might attempt to introduce a concrete and realistic photograph or a three-dimensional object. No one has yet examined the possible benefits of three-dimensional photography, including the potential application of holography (three-dimensional images in a two-dimensional plane created with laser technology) as a symbol set for the non-speaking mentally retarded.

Some secondary effects of the application of augmentative procedures with the retarded have also been noted. For example, there have been reports of increased attention (Kimble 1975, Balick *et al.* 1976), decreased frustration (Duncan and Silverman 1977), and increased speech production (Schmidt *et al.* 1971, Kimble 1975).

Benefits of communication aids

Because of greater clinical usage and the availability of more written information on the topic, professionals are now in a better position to understand the results of applied augmentative communication system approaches. Several of the functions which assistive communication devices serve are presented below:

(1) As an expressive communication system. The most recognised and commonly assigned task for a communication aid is two fold: to function as an alternative (in the sense of a substitute for a dysfunctional speech system) or as an augmentative (in the sense of an enhancer of existing speech).

(2) As an enhancer of language comprehension. The communication aid as an enhancer of language comprehension is not well understood nor always recognised. In fact, the communication aid is usually viewed exclusively as an expressive communication tool. Undoubtedly, the communication aid does have an influence

on the comprehension of language spoken in context, as well as helping comprehension in general. Clinical recommendations made in the Communication Enhancement Clinic of The Children's Hospital, Boston, frequently include instructions for parents, teachers, and/or therapists themselves to point to symbols (after gaining the user's attention) on the individual's communication aid while simultaneously speaking.

(3) As a facilitator of speech and language development. Perhaps the most troubling prospect to parents, when confronted with the introduction of an augmentative communication system, is the fear that such a system will inhibit or retard speech development. The usual concern of these parents is that their child will no longer need or rehearse speech and consequently will no longer attempt it. Others fear that the communication aid will develop into a 'crutch' which will always be relied upon as the principal form of communication.

Clinical observations suggest that speech is facilitated and not inhibited by the introduction of a supplemental communication system (Silverman 1980). Parnes (1983, personal communication) noted that there may be an initial reduction in speech output when the communication aid is first introduced; but gradually speech returns, at least to its original extent. And there is often an immediate and lasting improvement in the amount of speech output, once a user is proficient with a communication aid.

(4) As an organiser of language. The development of expressive language for some children lags considerably behind their level of language comprehension. A complete explanation for such a comprehension-production gap is not always available. Shane and Bashir (1980) considered a discrepancy between production and comprehension to represent an important factor in the process of determining candidates for an augmentative communication system. They called this the 'election decision' process. The greater the gap, the more readily one would consider the adoption of a supplemental communication method.

The level of comprehension can be used as the standard to which one attempts to train production through the use of the supplemental communication system (Shane 1981). When the communication system is imposed, it apparently helps to organise an aberrant expressive language system. Clinical evidence for this suggested phenomenon stems principally from the observation that when given an organised display, many aid users (with apparently intact motor speech systems) can produce long and frequently complex sentences: whereas without a well-conceived communication aid, their production tends to be telegraphic or agrammatic.

Fitzgerald (1949) introduced an organisational format for teaching grammar to the hearing-impaired. The system she created, now commonly referred to as the Fitzgerald Key, has been adopted widely for use on communication aids for the non-speakiing (Vicker 1974). The success of the Key, as well as other organisational formats, may be related to benefits derived from the visual representation of a sentence which serves to organise the user's expressive language output (Vicker 1974).

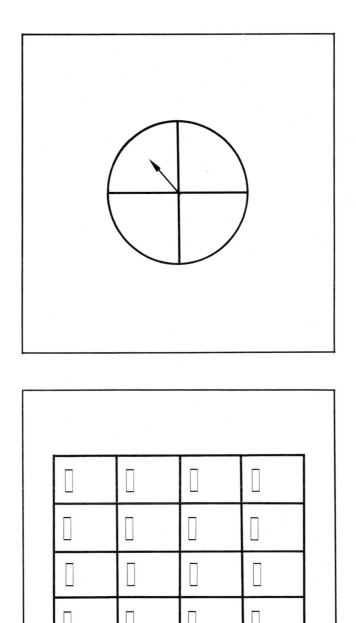

Fig. 1. Diagram of two scanning communication displays. *Top:* information is indicated or selected by the area to which the arrow points, and *(bottom)* by the area in which a cursor or light is highlighted.

411

Technological trends

The first automated communication aids were electric typewriters and simple home-made scanning devices. The former enabled the literate, non-speaking person who could select keys (with an extremity- or head-mounted pointer) to prepare a message in advance or to write independently. The latter helped the more severely physically handicapped patient to select/identify desired vocabulary on a display, or produce a written version if the device interfaced with a typewriter (*e.g.* the Possum Communicator) or contained its own internal printer (*e.g.* Tufts Interactive Communicator). A scanning device enables an individual with the most extreme physical disability to express a thought or make a need known. Any scanning device is composed of three basic elements: the display surface, the indicator and the operating switch. Figure 1 depicts two possible surfaces. Figure 1*a* depicts information arranged in a circular format with a rotating arrow for the indicator. In Figure 1*b*, lighting up various squares is the means of specifying intended information. In either case, the movement (arrow, light or cursor) occurs by operating one of many possible electric switches*.

These first communication aids are designated here as dedicated, for they functioned exclusively as communication devices. The next generation of communication aids, more flexible than the previous, were microprocessor-based, but dedicated in the sense that they too were designed solely to provide assistive communication. Because these devices were computer-based, they allowed features not possible with earlier versions. For example, the microprocessor-based systems allowed for synthetic or digitised voice ouput and rate enhancement (principally through message storage and retrieval). For a more comprehensive treatment of microprocessor-based communication aids, see Kraat and Sitver-Kogut (1985).

The newest or third generation of communication aids are general purpose computers which, with customised software (dedicated for communication purposes) and customised hardware (to enhance access to the computer) or customised output, can perform many of the same functions as dedicated devices, but can also provide a host of additional benefits. In Figure 2, an Apple computer is shown. This general purpose computer has been made wheelchair portable by attachment of the computer to the chair. The system is run by DC (battery) power. In the following sections a description of the benefits accrued from the general purpose computer when it serves as a communication aid is offered.

Benefits of computer technology

Speech is estimated to occur at the rate of 150 to 180 words per minute. Rate estimates for individuals communicating through a variety of assistive devices range between three and 25 words per minute, but typically fall at the lower end of this range. The significant difference between the abled and disabled communicator in the time needed to prepare and transmit a message imposes a profound, negative effect on communicative interaction. In fact, the reduced rate of expression

---

*For a description of commercially available scanning devices see Kraat and Sitver-Kogut (1985).

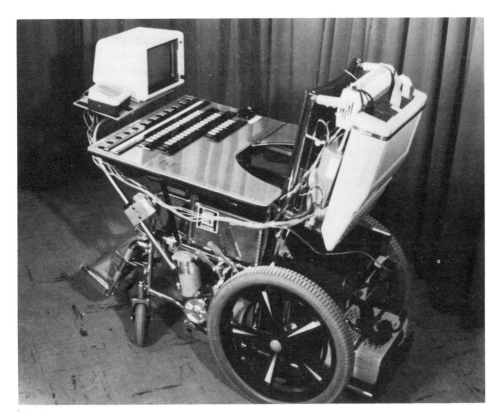

Fig. 2.

represents one of the major deterrents to normal or near-normal communicative interaction between the individual who is non-speaking and the various listeners with whom that person converses. Hagan (1978) offered some insight into these adverse effects:

> Not all present or potential receivers will have the same degree of empathy for the communicatively impaired individual, the same willingness to wait patiently while a message is gradually unfolded. . . as the patient's family and speech pathologist have.

In order to normalise the conversational opportunities of the severely speech-impaired, procedures for enhancing over-all rate of message preparation, retrieval and transmission become critical. A host of procedures, both technical and non-technical, can be employed in order to enhance the over-all rate of communication. The computer, however, presents a flexible and powerful tool for equalising the rate discrepancy. Ways in which the computer enhances expressive communication rate include: (i) letter and linguistic prediction; (ii) multiple-level accessing; (iii) abbreviated expansion; and (iv) semantic coding.

413

The redundant nature of language makes it possible to predict the occurrence of future letters, words, and even whole thoughts based on previous information. It has been suggested that speakers of a language process implicitly have an enormous understanding of the statistical properties of their language. This inherent knowledge or familiarity enables one to anticipate letters (*e.g.* the strong tendency for the letter h to follow t, or for u to follow q), to predict grammatical or word classes (*e.g.* the auxiliary 'has been' can only be followed by a verb conjugated in the present progresssive aspect, and nouns are typically preceded by articles), or to complete unfinished phrases in conversation. Observation of familiar listeners conversing with non-speaking communicators provides ample evidence of this latter ability. For example, a familiar listener is often adept at predicting an incomplete thought or phrase of a non-speaking conversational partner. When prediction is an acceptable strategy by both partners, a great deal of time can be saved.

The predictive quality of language can be computer or machine-based and used to increase rate of message generation by the person who is non-speaking. Crochetière *et al.* (1977), for example, envisaged a communicative device for the non-speaker, based on the statistical properties of the next letter of occurrence. He suggested that such an anticipatory device would predict the next letter from the occurrence of previous ones and subsequently display the most probable choice for the user to either accept or reject. Rombola and Childress (1977) applied this logic with a non-speaking woman, and noted a 50 per cent increase in communication rate when a dynamic anticipatory display was used. Wilson (1981) developed a computer-based linguistic predicting device which anticipated both grammar and word selection. Their predictive program was based on the statistical properties of language, as well as the recurring word and grammar schemes of specific users.

Abel (1984) is a dedicated communication software program containing letter-prediction capability. Letters are selected through a scanning procedure controlled by a single switch. As letters are selected by the user, the next most likely letters appear on the computer monitor. The user has the option of selecting one of these letters (if a correct prediction is offered), rather than having to return to the original display. The program uses English letter-combination frequency as well as the user's previous selections as the basis for the letters offered for selection.

Two factors underlying the slow rate of expression by communication-aid users are (i) the small and limited vocabulary generally available on the surface of a communication aid, and (ii) the slowness with which additional vocabulary can be retrieved. Typically, the smaller the surface vocabulary, the slower the rate of expression. Frequently multiple displays or pages are employed as a means of accessing additional vocabulary; they are used most effectively with a computer-based communication system. The computer allows generically coded or arranged vocabulary to be rapidly accessed. It also allows for the retrieval or access of situational displays containing vocabulary relevant to a specific conversational topic (such as conversing in a restaurant) or relevant to a particular educational or vocational topic (like a science or maths lesson). 'Touch and speak' (Shane *et al.* 1984) is an Apple computer-based communication software program that uses a flat membrane keyboard programmed to offer a maximum of 128 targets, measuring approximately one inch square. For each of its five layers, up to 128 distinct areas can be programmed to contain individualised letters, words or phrases. By touching a specific area, the message contained within the target can be spoken (via an electronic voice), printed, and/or displayed on a monitor.

Access to stored and logically arranged information can speed up the rate of expression, because it reduces the number of keystrokes or movements the user must make in order to gain access to the stored information. 'Message Maker' (Shane *et al.* 1983) is a conversational and writing software program designed to enhance rate of conversation by way of a word and phrase accessing system. By selecting the initial letter of a desired word and continuing to hold the key representing that initial letter, several coloumns of words beginning with that letter, will appear on the monitor screen. A user can spell the word letter-by-letter, or select the intended word with a cursor (the specific words contained in the program memory and subsequently listed on the monitor screen can be customised for a given user). The program also allows access to stored, customised phrases which are accessed with minimal keystrokes.

Many commercially available, dedicated microprocessor-based communication aids also process multiple-level accessing capability. For example, the Express 3 (Prentke-Romich Company) contains 128 targets on 99 levels. Plastic overlays, giving representations of the information contained with a given level, can be affixed to the device. The numerous levels enable a considerable vocabulary to be stored, and this can be organised to accommodate specific situations (*e.g.* vocabulary relevant to a trip to the museum can be entered on level 35, an oral book report on level 50, and general conversational words on level 3).

One of the major problems surrounding multiple-level accessing is the difficulty of cataloguing information stored within levels. Generally some visual form is needed for a user to recall the level where information is stored, as well as the actual layout of that information. This problem can be solved partially by the use of a monitor screen which can display information retrieved from storage. At present, portable monitors are too small for easy reading, while large screens are not easily portable. The next generation of flat-screen monitors should solve this problem. Flat screens can be interfaced with touch screens (allowing retrieval of new levels of stored information), thereby becoming the 'lap trays' of the future.

ABBREVIATED EXPANSION

The fewer the number of keystrokes or movements needed to access a stored message or generate a new one, the faster that message can be expressed. This rather obvious conclusion is the basis for the abbreviated expansion technique. Essentially, the technique attempts to provide access to an extensive stored listing of words, phrases, or sentences. Recall or retrieval of a word or phrase can be enhanced when a coded or mnemonic representation is used. For example, one might code all information pertaining to food under the general heading 'F'. Specific 'F' or food-related items would also have an abbreviated (yet relational) listing. Thus, one could designate an apple as 'FA'—'F' (for food) and 'A' (to specify apple within the food grouping). By the same token, an orange could be represented by 'F-O', or a peach by 'F-P'. In each of these cases the coded representation for the fruit requires fewer actual keystrokes than if the entire word was spelled letter by letter. The task of recalling a coded representation for a word or lists of words is a task easily handled by a microprocessor-based communication system.

Generally the abbreviated expansion technique is not the only method used by a particular user. It is usually used in conjunction with other methods, to supplement a word-processing approach.

Speech Pak (available from Adaptive Communication Systems Inc., Pittsberg, Pennsylvania) is a communication program which uses the Epson HX-20 computer and an attached Echo speech synthesiser. The dedicated software has the capability of storing words, sentences or phrases. Stored information can be retrieved by making a user designate a combination of one, two or three letters. For example, the letters 'NJ' can be used instead of the sentence 'I live in New Jersey'.

Opportunity for spoken output
Three types of voice output are available for use on electronic assistive communication devices: pre-recorded, digitised and synthesised. The benefit of using pre-recorded speech is its ability to produce a gender- and age-appropriate voice. Its principal disadvantages are the length of time needed to access or retrieve selected vocabulary, and the fixed and non-generative nature of the vocabulary itself. Both digitised and synthesised speech are created by a computer. Vocabulary represented in digitised voice, like pre-recorded voice, must be created in advance. This approach does not allow smaller elements of speech (*i.e.* phonemes or speech sounds) to be combined in order to form whole words, thereby causing the stored vocabulary to be fixed or permanent. Synthesised speech, on the other hand, allows infinite message-creation through a finite set of symbols.

The voice-quality offered through digitised speech is currently superior to the quality of voice available through synthesis. However, the technology of voice synthesis is increasing at a remarkable pace. While it is technically possible even now for speech synthesis to produce appropriate age and gender output (*e.g.* DEC talk by Digital Equipment Corporation), the cost remains too high for widespread use.

At present voice output is available on dedicated communication devices (*e.g.* Form-a-phrase), dedicated microprocessor-based communication aids (*e.g.* Vois 130, 135 or Express 3), and general purpose computers which run both dedicated communication software and standard word-processor software which can serve as a communication system for the non-speaking individual.

There is little doubt about the communicative value of voice output for the individual whose own speech is difficult or impossible to understand. Nevertheless, the actual value remains unstudied. One can speculate with reasonable assurity, however, that voice output does offer considerable benefits to the speechless. Several of these benefits are listed below:

(1) Opportunity to interject
(2) Ability to communicate in a group
(3) Ability to communicate in the dark
(4) Ability to communicate with non-literate listeners (includes non-symbol readers). Implicit in this is an increase in audience size.
(5) Increased opportunity for employment
(6) Increased over-all social opportunities.

The motivational and learning value of voice output represents another unstudied issue. Clinical observations indicate clearly that a voice output substantially increases the non-speaking person's motivation to use an assistive device. Many people who are reluctant to use non-electronic systems become willing users when voice is the output result. Speech feedback given after the selection of targets on one's communication aid seems to facilitate the learning of a symbol-set, as well as the placement of such information on or within the communication aid itself. Reading and spelling may be improved, as letters and words are spoken aloud as a user makes selections.

Assistance to the visually impaired, non-speaking person
Typically, the visually impaired use tactile perception or enhanced visual material (*e.g.* enlarged graphics) as a means to receive and send alphanumeric information. When physical disability accompanies a visual impairment, however, the use of braille becomes less likely. A visual impairment, therefore, presents a significant obstacle to the acquisition of a suitable symbol set for use with an alternative or augmentative communication system.

One recent and major computer-based innovation to assist the visually impaired is the Kurzweil Reader. This assistive device reads aloud (with a synthetic voice), thus diminishing the problem for the visually impaired of receiving written information.

Computer-assisted expressive communication is also possible for the visually impaired, non-speaking individual. This can be accomplished in several ways: (i) morse code input, which in turn is 'translated' into written or spoken form; (ii) enlarged graphics on a computer monitor; and (iii) user selection of desired letter, word, or sentence choices which are presented in spoken form (synthetic speech) to the user, who activates a switch when the desired choice is offered. 'Say It' (Geiger 1983), for example, is a software program designed to present choices in spoken form, from which the user can select desired information. The specific categories and sub-categories of information and vocabulary are custom-designed for each user. 'Audscan' (Bequaert 1987) represents another auditory scanning program which, like 'Say It', allows the user to select from vocabulary presented through a speech synthesiser. Unlike 'Say It', however, 'Audscan' allows a user to select letter elements of a sentence or word (when the letter-spelling mode is used) to form or create a desired message. Message Making (scanning version) (Shane *et al.* 1984) offers a third auditory scan format in which selections are spoken to the user.

When the initial letter of a word is chosen, a series of words beginning with that letter are presented, for the user to make a whole word selection.

Technology offers the non-speaking visually impaired a number of options to enhance communication heretofore unavailable to this population. The abilities and needs of the user dictates the specific hardware and software requirements which will bring about improved communication.

Enhanced education opportunity

Enhanced educational possibilities and opportunities are a natural outcome of the improved writing and reading potential offered through computer access. Some other potential benefits are listed below:

(1) Analysing and/or creating spread sheets

(2) Writing computer programs to aid in school-related work (*e.g.* a program to calculate mathematical problems) or to modify existing school-related software programs

(3) Creating graphs and charts

(4) Supplementing specific academic subject areas with relevant software

(5) Making notes, with the help of a 'Scratch Pad' (Assistive Communication Center, Sacramento, California), or doing mathematical calculations (Smith 1980)

(6) Creating computer graphics for art projects and entertainment

(7) Developing logical thinking, precision, order, creativity, and the scientific method.

In summary, computers in the educational setting can potentially offer a level of independence previously unavailable to the physically handicapped, non-speaking child. Typically, the educational opportunities for such an individual have been restricted, because of limited access to educational materials and poor tools for competing with children who could use paper and pencil for calculating, notetaking, graph-making and writing. It is fortuitous, in this age of educating handicapped children in the least restrictive setting, that the computer is available as an educational tool. In this sense, one might view the computer as an educational equaliser—a facilitator of mainstreaming.

Potential for improved reading

The ability to read and write is a certain predictor of educational success. Unfortunately, reading problems ranging from subtle, yet identifiable difficulties, to profound disturbances occur concomitantly with severe speech impairments. For the person with persistent difficulties in adequate speech production, a most suitable communication alternative would be the employment of an alphabetic symbol system. However, because of specific developmental reading problems, one must investigate substitute symbol sets for traditional orthography or to explore other methods to enhance reading skills. Knowledge of the difficulties experienced by cerebral-palsied children who attempt to break the reading code, led Kates and McNaughton (1974) to experiment with a set of symbols which Charles Bliss had created as an international multilingual communication system. After a period of symbol instruction, Kates and McNaughton concluded that severely speech-impaired children could use these symbols (which are now popularly known as Blissymbols) for purposes of communication. They suggested that Blissymbols could bridge the gap between the use of line drawings and the use of an alphabet system for communication. Shane and Melrose (1974) introduced the Initial Teaching Alphabet (ita) to two non-speaking adolescents who were having difficulty learning to read and write using traditional orthography. These researchers found that both subjects learned the sound-symbol associative value of 16 of the 44 "ita" letters, and were able to generalise this symbolic learning to create words which had not been introduced during the training sessions.

Neither the exact nature nor the etiology of the reading problems of the non-speaking is well understood. Nevertheless, efforts to improve reading-skill levels must continue. The use of language arts computer-based software to promote reading-skill acquisition represents one such method.

At present there is a mass of software developed expressly to aid in the acquisition of reading readiness skills, site word learning, sound-symbol associations, *etc.* Reading software can help the child with potential reading problems, for several reasons: (i) the computer is highly motivating, and particularly when the software is colorful, appealing, and reinforcing; (ii) the computer is non-threatening and non-critical; (iii) the computer allows the child to work independently; and (iv) the computer, with the right peripherals, can say any word which the child has difficulty decoding. For example, 'Message Maker' (Shane *et al.* 1983) allows the computer to speak words listed in a vocabulary which can be customised for a particular child. So if a child is unable to read a word, he or she can 'toggle on' a speaking mode which speaks (reads) each listed word to the child.

Enhanced writing (hard copy) opportunities
Through his typewriter Christy gained release from his tongue-tied world
(Bernadette Nolan—*Dam Burst of Dreams*)

The manual and electronic typewriter were probably the first mechanical and electronic communication aids. They both offered the individual who could access a keyboard (typically with a single finger or headstick/wand selection method), and who could spell, the capacity to produce a written (hard copy) record: thereby increasing the opportunities to work independently on homework, correspondence, poetry, *etc.* Although the typewriter offers numerous benefits, it does not eliminate all problems. There is still the problem of inserting and removing paper; output is generally slow because of the frequent single-letter selection technique; corrections are difficult on some machines and impossible on others.

With the availability of computer-based word processing, the writing opportunities for the severely handicapped are considerably improved. One might speculate that the technology leap from the typewriter to the computer (word processor) is even more important than the leap from the manual communication aid to the typewriter. Word processing, for example, allows for easy and independent correction of words, sentences and order of paragraphs—all of which are inordinately difficult for the person with physical disability. A computer can also store and retrieve files, advance paper, control the environment and perform other office tasks.

The following case report is from the record of an 18-year-old male seen for the purpose of selecting a writing aid.

The etiology of N.'s current communication problems stems from a severe head trauma suffered 18 months prior to this evaluation. Although N. continues to make slow but steady progress in all developmental areas he continues to experience problems with fine and gross motor difficulties and short term memory deficits. N. is repeating his fourth year or senior year in high school. He acknowledged that his greatest difficulty in school currently is his inability to write. At the present time he employs scribes to record relevant class notes. In addition, he complained of difficulties in math particularly related to the inability to use a 'scratch pad' for calculating. N. recently had to drop an accounting course because he was unable to place entries in a ledger. He reportedly spends two hours per day doing homework. His future plans include obtaining a college (business degree) education. N.'s speech was judged to be highly intelligible even to naive listeners.

In summary, N. is an 18-year-old male who wishes to continue his education. These plans are greatly hampered by an inability to write. Although he experiences some fine motor control difficulties, he does have sufficient control to select keys on a regular typewriter keyboard. The use of a keyguard may be of some assistance in preventing the activation of unwanted letters, particularly when tired which tends to exaggerate a slight intention tremor.

RECOMMENDATIONS
(1) Regarding notetaking—N. should utilize several approaches which include; (a) use of a portable hand held typewriter; (b) a voice activated tape recorder by which N. can review recordings of class lectures and subsequently transcribe relevant information; (c) a home (stationary) computer which can serve as a word processor, a scratch pad, and a spread sheet.

Conclusion
This chapter has attempted to describe the computer in service of individuals needing supplemental communication. As a communication aid, the computer is a powerful tool. In fact, serving that function alone would be sufficient to justify an entire chapter being devoted to its applications. But the computer is, for the non-speaking individual, more than just a communication device. It can serve as a motivator and enhancer of learning, open up previously unimagined vocation opportunities, as well as provide recreation and environmental control. Given the relative youth of the computer, it must be viewed here as a tool whose full potential in all of these domains has not been fully realised.

REFERENCES

Abel, S. T. (1984) *Aaron* (Software) Aesir Software Engineer. Pinedale, California.

Balick, S., Spiegel, D., Greene, G. (1976) Mime in language therapy and clinician training. *Archives of Physical Medicine and Rehabilitation,* **57,** 35–38.

Bequaert, F. (1987) *Audscan* (Software). *In preparation.*

Crochetière, W. J. *et al.* (1977) Society for Information Display Digest. pp. 150–151.

Duncan, J. L., Silverman, F. H. (1977) 'Impacts of learning American Indian Sign Language on mentally retarded children: a preliminary report.' *Perceptual and Motor Skills,* **44,** 1138.

Fitzgerald, E. (1949) *Straight Language for the Deaf.* Washington, D.C.: The Volta Bureau.

Geiger, C. (1983) *Say It* (Software), Schneier Communications Unit, Syracuse, New York.

Goldberg, H. R., Fenton, J. Aphonic Communications for those with Cerebral Palsy: *Guide for the Development and Use of a Conversation Board.* New York: United Cerebral Palsy Associations of New York State, *(n.d.)*

Hagan, C. (1978) 'Assistive communication systems for the anarthric and severe dysarthria patient: a rationale for their use and criteria for their selection.' *Scandinavian Journal of Rehabilitative Medicine,* **10,** 163–168.

Kates, B., McNaughton, S. (1974) 'The first application of Blissymbolics as a communication medium for nonspeaking children: history and development, 1971–1974.' Toronto: Blissymbolics Communication Foundation.

Kimble, S. L. (1975) 'A language teaching technique with totally nonverbal, severely mentally retarded adolescents.' *Paper Presented at the 50th Annual Meeting of the American Speech and Hearing Association, Washington, D. C.*

Kraat, A., Sitver-Kogut, (1985) *Features of Commercially Available Communication Devices.* Chart available from Prentke Romich Company, 1022 Heyl, Wooster, Ohio.

Rombola, G. E., Childress, D. S. (1977) 'Computer-based control and communication systems for severely disabled persons.' *Proceedings of the National Electronics Conference,* **21,** 362–366.

Schmidt, M. J., Carrier, J. K., Jr., Parsons, S. D. (1971) 'Use of a nonspeech mode in teaching language.' *Paper presented at the 46th Annual Meeting of the American Speech and Hearing Association, Chicago.*

Shane, H. C. (1981) 'Early decision-making in augmentative communication.' *In:* Schiefelbusch, R., Bricker, D. (Eds.). *Early Language Intervention.* Baltimore: University Park Press.

—— Bashir, A. S. (1980) 'Election criteria for the adoption of an augmentative communication system: preliminary considerations.' *Journal of Speech and Hearing Disorders,* **45,** 408–414.

—— Dawson, K. E., Bonfiglio, A., Field, A., Geier, M. J. (1983) *Message Maker* (Software), Communication Enhancement Clinic, Boston, Children's Hospital, Boston, Massachusetts.

—— Field, A. F., Geier, M. (1984) *Touch and Speak* (Software). Communication Enhancement Clinic, Boston, Children's Hospital, Boston, Massachusetts, 1984.

—— Melrose, J. (1974) An electronic conversation board and an accompanying training program for aphonic expressive communication. *Paper presented at the meeting of the American Speech and Hearing Association, Washington, D.C., November.*

Silverman, F. (1980) *Communication for the Speechless.* Englewood Cliffs, New Jersey: Prentice-Hall.

Smith, B. (1980) *Handicapped Typewriter* (Software). Rocky Mountain Software, Vancouver, B.C.

Vicker, B. (1974) *Nonoral Communication Systems Project: 1964/1972.* Iowa City: Campus Stores.

Wilson, W. (1981) *Nonoral Communication Systems Project.* Seattle: University of Washington.

26

THE USE OF ALTERNATIVE SYSTEMS AND MICROELECTRONICS AS AIDS TO COMMUNICATION AND LANGUAGE DEVELOPMENT

P. Fuller and T. Southgate

Introduction

Establishing effective channels of communication must be a major objective for those concerned with the education of children with special needs. To enable linguistic development to take place, it is often necessary to provide multiply handicapped children with one or more alternative systems in order to augment their existing means of communication. For children who have physical and perhaps sensory impairments, and who are also without speech, it is very unlikely that any one channel will be sufficient to meet all expressive and receptive communication needs. In recent years, microtechnology has begun to provide an additional augmentative channel and has been increasingly used in therapy and special education (Goldenberg 1979, 1984; Fuller *et al.* 1983*a*; Adams 1984; Rostron and Sewell 1984).

Sensitively used, the power and flexibility of this new technology can enable multiply handicapped children to improve both the quality and quantity of their communication. Appropriate interfaces in the form of switches or specialised keyboards make it possible to utilise any small, reliable movement to operate the computer. Given software which is sophisticated enough to respond to the child's input, and flexible enough to be modified as communication needs develop, the computer can greatly enhance the child's output and opportunities for learning. As a result, the child is often able to demonstrate a greater potential for language interaction than had previously seemed possible.

This chapter will illustrate how microtechnology can complement other approaches to the education of two children with communication and learning disabilities. Neither child is able to communicate through speech: so both need to develop a language system through which they can communicate meaningfully and reciprocally, make sense of their environment, and develop and handle their thoughts. The term 'non-communicating' is sometimes applied to non-speaking children. However, Lloyd and Karlan (1984) suggested that 'non-speech' is a more appropriate description. According to Krauss (1979): 'We communicate—speak, but also gesture, grimace, *etc.* — in order to affect the behaviour of others'. Even as infants, without access to language, these two children did communicate with those around them in that their signals, facial expressions, vocalisations and gestures, were able to influence others' behaviour. They needed to develop the linguistic skills necessary not only for cognitive growth ('As a cognitive instrument . . . . to represent and systematically transform the regularities of experience with greater power and regularity than before'—Bruner 1964), but also for affective and social skills. Fouts *et al.* (1979) stated that 'The inability to speak creates a tremendous loss of control over one's environment, producing a situation analogous to that of learned helplessness.' Such children, he maintains, demonstrate generalised passivity, over-all lower motivation and greater emotionality than those who speak. 'By teaching these children communicative behaviours that can be transmitted to, and interpreted by, others (thus providing the children with more control over their environment) their expectations about the use of communication can be changed. These communicative behaviours could be produced either by helping them to establish and develop vocal speech or by introducing a means of communication not requiring the use of the possibly impaired vocal apparatus. Pointing to symbols or using manual communication are excellent ways of establishing a non-vocal communication system' (Fouts *et al.* 1979).

Michael

Michael, who is nine, has a severe sensorineural hearing loss (audiometric testing in 1982 showed 70dB in the left ear, 80dB in the right ear at 200Hz, and 110dB at 1000Hz in both ears.) He also has athetoid cerebral palsy and was extremely floppy as an infant. He was unable to lift his head until six months or sit until 20 months. At 3:9 years he took a few unsteady steps, but even at this stage his preferred method of locomotion was crawling. He now walks and runs unaided but, although his fine motor control is steadily improving, his efforts at writing are laborious and unsatisfactory for a boy of his age and intellectual ability.

Assessment of a multiply handicapped child is invariably difficult. Michael's parents were convinced of his intelligence, although others thought he must be mentally retarded because of his floppiness and lack of response (he often appeared to avoid eye-contact, although he made good use of his eyes for information which was meaningful to him in other ways). For over two years, specialists ignored his parents' protestations that he was deaf: and it was not until he was 2½, when electric response tests were carried out, that the extent of his communication difficulties was appreciated. Such a misdiagnosis of mental retardation in cases of multiple handicap is not uncommon, and a similar case is described in Fuller *et al.* (1983*b*).

Michael's mother describes how, before he was two years old, he would indicate in picture books where all the familiar objects in the pictures were in his house, thus matching picture symbols with real objects. She was convinced of his ability, and asked to be shown a few signs to see if Michael could learn to use them. At this time he was attending a playgroup for mentally handicapped children. He quickly grasped five signs associated with meal-times (*e.g.* bowl, food and biscuit) and began using them to make requests. At this stage it was felt that Michael had somehow 'proved himself'. He was no longer considered to be mentally retarded and was admitted to a school for physically handicapped children where he began receiving formal tuition in the Paget Gorman Signed Speech (AEDE 1971). (See Chapter 24 for a further description.)

Since PGSS is a translation of English, it allows for an easy transference from the signs to the grammar and correct word-order of written English. The disadvantage is that it is an artificial sign language and is not used or approved of by the deaf population. This means that a child learning PGSS is likely to develop good English-language skills, but will remain isolated from the deaf community. However, since Michael has an additional physical handicap, he needs a communication aid which requires literacy skills, and Paget seemed the most appropriate system. It might be that Signed English, developed in recent years and based upon British Sign Language, offers a useful alternative for children with Michael's difficulties.

By the time Michael was 3½ years old he had a signed vocabulary of over a hundred words, including adjectives, nouns, verbs, adverbs and prepositions. He used these signs to make requests and comments and to identify objects, pictures and words. He was able to use language creatively and to generalise. He readily generalised the 'animal' sign, for example, which he learnt originally for 'dog', even spontaneously calling a bird an animal. He was also beginning to use language to control his environment. He signed 'chair' one day when he wanted his teacher to leave him alone and go and sit down—a more complex request than asking for food or drink. Michael's potential for developing good language skills was becoming apparent. When he was four, he began signing words from flash-cards and matching words to pictures. It was decided not to wait for 'reading readiness' but to combine signs with both spoken and written words where possible. 'For the severely deaf, reading does not stand on the shoulders of speech but is rather their first acquaintance with English language' (Chapman and Wilby 1982). He soon demonstrated his ability to learn to read. However, because of his physical handicap he was unable to produce the written symbols for himself. Michael's athetosis resulted in such poor motor control that he had no reliable way of drawing or forming clear letters. He could hold a pencil but could not copy letters accurately. His hand jerked away from the line he was drawing, making his efforts unrecognisable. Therefore he was unable to reinforce his learning by creating for himself the sequences of written symbols which make up words and meaningful sentences.

In an attempt to overcome the problem presented by his poor hand control, Michael was provided with magnetic letters to form words. Although this was better than nothing (he learnt to spell his name and 'mummy' and 'daddy'), it was a poor substitute for his own writing, and there was no permanent record for him or his teacher. By the time he was five years old, however, his hand control had improved sufficiently for him to use an electric typewriter with a keyguard. This is a piece of sheet metal or perspex through which finger-holes have been punched corresponding to the layout of the keyboard. When mounted a short distance above the keyboard, a more deliberate effort is needed to press a key; consequently children with poor co-ordination, or those who cannot lift their hands easily, are less likely to make mistakes and typing becomes a possibility. The main advantage of an electric typewriter for those with motor impairments is that the paper is held firmly and the letters are formed correctly by the machine. A number of control systems for electric typewriters have been developed, which range from the simple keyguard, through mini- and expanded-keyboards with variable delays, to the single- and double-switch operation of a matrix display. However, typewriters also have a number of serious disadvantages. Often it is difficult for a physically disabled person, particularly a small child, to see what has been typed because the ribbon or typewriter-case gets in the way. Even if the letters are visible, they may be in an unsuitable typeface. Another problem is that once letters and words have been committed to paper, they cannot be edited, deleted or corrected without great difficulty.

Although Michael was soon able to copy-type short sentences and to match the upper-and lower-case letters on the keyboard with finger-spelling, the many errors he produced frustrated and discouraged him. Although at the age of 6:6 his reading age for accuracy on the Neale Analysis was 6:9, and 6:6 on the Picture Aided Reading Test, he was very reluctant even to copy-type without the support of a teacher sitting beside him, and he rejected free writing altogether. The 'leap' into free writing, even for children with good spelling abilities and normal manual dexterity, can be difficult to make. For Michael, who had severe spelling problems without phonic clues, this leap seemed insurmountable. He was very unsure of himself and quite unmotivated to type on his own. His typed output of a few short copy-typed sentences each week was not sufficiently rewarding for him to make real progress and to reinforce his language development. A more satisfactory means of handling the written word was required if his use of language was to make the progress of which he was capable.

The MAC (Microprocessor Assisted Communicator) was designed to improve the communication rate of severely physically impaired individuals (Head and Poon 1982). It consists of a small microcomputer, to which can be connected a standard keyboard and a number of other switches and interfaces, a monitor and a printer. The most important features of the system, however, are in the computer programme. The MAC is a sophisticated word-processor programme that enables the disabled user to 'type' directly on to the monitor screen as if it were the paper in a typewriter. The problem of visibility is therefore eliminated. The characters produced are relatively large and clear, and the text is not permanent so it can be corrected and deleted easily. It is not necessary to commit anything to paper until the user is quite satisfied with what is on the screen. Pressing a sequence of keys then results in a hard-copy printout.

The clear text on the screen, the ability to correct and the neat printout have proved very satisfying and motivating for Michael and the other children who use the MAC. One boy, Christopher, had a severe speech impairment in addition to his physical handicap, and his verbal and written output were both unsatisfactory. He used the MAC as a writing aid when working with his teacher, and after some months his articulation improved considerably. For the first time he was able to produce words that were both clear and clearly distinguishable. James (aged 10) was not physically impaired, but was referred because of severe reading problems which had resisted the efforts of a number of teachers. His experience had left him cautious of committing himself to paper. But the computer screen was different, since his mistakes—instead of remaining to remind him of his failure—could be quickly eradicated. His enthusiasm was revived and his reading and writing skills began to improve.

Because the original MAC overcame the problems of visibility and correctability, most children became more motivated and their written output increased in quantity. However, as words had still to be entered letter by letter, the rate of this output may remain very slow. Since Michael cannot use speech to practise his use of language or 'think aloud', he needed a quick way of handling words which he could read but not write easily. To meet such a need, Patrick Poon incorporated word-lists into the MAC programme. Words from these lists could be entered whole into the text by the user. Unfortunately, the original MAC programme was written on an Eprom, a Read Only Memory chip, and consequently any word-lists would have had to be entered by the programmer and could not be altered later by a child or teacher. Therefore the programme was rewritten to run on an Apple computer which uses programmes that are stored on discs. In the MAC-Apple programme, word-lists may be customised continually to suit the changing needs of the individual user, and can include the names of friends and relatives and those words the child most commonly uses. In the keyboard version of MAC-Apple, the child can call up a shortlist of general words by pressing a switch and choose from these by entering a reference letter. The whole word is then added to the text. If the first letter of the desired word is known, the child types this and again presses the switch. This time only words beginning with that letter will appear, and selection is again made by typing a reference letter. If the first two letters are known and are typed before the switch is pressed, then only words beginning with these two letters will appear, thus limiting the number of words that have to be scanned and making selection quicker. Children using MAC-Apple should have their own discs on which they store each piece of work. Work is saved under different file names and can be printed out at any stage. Michael has files for 'News', 'Story', 'English Workcard', 'Spelling', 'Topic', and a special file for 'Talking' which he uses if he wants to converse with a non-signer.

Michael has taken to the MAC-Apple system very readily. The computer is performing an 'emancipatory rôle' (Odor 1984) in removing the obstacles to writing. Not only does it reduce his problems of poor manual control so that, with the editing facilities, he can produce as clear and neat a piece of work as any other child (or indeed adult): it also removes the problem of spelling out each word letter by letter and allows him to handle whole words, using his reading skills to convey his thoughts through meaningful sentences. The easy editing means that he can play with the position of words in his sentences until he is satisfied with what he is trying to say. For this particular child's difficulties, the system is very satisfactory. He quickly grasped the idea of speeding up communication by using the word-lists and, even if he can spell a word or it is there for him to copy, he will often choose instead to select it from the lists. Occasionally he plays with this facility just for fun. Recently he wanted the word 'tight' but it was not on the list. So he selected 'tiger' instead, deleted the 'er' and added 'ht'. This rather laborious procedure in fact took eight key presses as opposed to the five he would have needed to type 'tight'. He was delighted with his idea, however, and signed with great pride how clever it was.

It is difficult to say as yet how much Michael's reading ability is being helped by MAC-Apple. This seems likely as he is constantly searching for the word he needs to convey his meaning. There is no doubt that the system has improved his confidence. He will now type on his own for 15 minutes at a time and his output has slowly expanded to four or more lines of type instead of a single sentence. The following is an example from his 'News' file at age 9:10.

> October the 12th
> Granny's electricity is broken. She came to my house for 1 night. When I was in bed My Daddy took Granny home in Daddy's car. Granny waited for the workmen to come. She had no light and no TV and no electric sockets working.

Michael's increased output has also made it possible to see some of the confusions that have developed in his use of language. Many Paget signs are small and precise and are therefore difficult for him to sign accurately. His approximations are accepted but the intended word is sometimes unclear. 'Have' and 'has' or 'is' and 'am' are little signs with only small movement or directional differences to distinguish them. Michael fails to make these differences when he is signing, so although he receives the correct form, his own output is indistinct and he frequently confuses such words in his writing. To overcome this problem, a large flat overlay keyboard was used. The surface of this keyboard is divided into 32 50mm × 50mm squares, which can be programmed individually or in groups; and when they are pressed, the screen registers whole words from which sentences can be formed. The teacher can produce a paper overlay and a related computer file to match the child's reading and physical abilities. Using this keyboard, Michael is able to practise forming sentences which include his 'problem' words, without having to spell out every word.

There is little doubt that the use of these computer systems has enabled Michael to increase and improve his use of language, and that this in turn has helped him to communicate more widely. One application which demonstrates this is his inclusion in a small 'Story Writing' group. Using the MAC-Apple system on the computer, the children create, print and illustrate a story between them and Michael takes a full part in this co-operative activity. Since he is no longer confined to communicating with those who can use his sign system, Michael's isolation has been greatly reduced.

Mark

Mark's communication problem is equally severe but very different. He has no speech, but his hearing is unimpaired and he understands speech. On the other hand, at the age of 11 his expressive communication is still extremely limited. Various computer programmes have been developed in an effort to meet his needs, and these will be described in some detail.

The communication needs of children who understand speech but cannot talk often seem less pressing than those of children who cannot understand speech, and who therefore demand an effort on the part of the others to penetrate their isolation. The child who does understand speech runs the risk of having his needs and thoughts interpreted for him. All too often such children will agree with this interpretation of their intentions, because such agreement seems expected of them and seems to elicit some kind of effect. It is hoped that by enabling Mark to use speech synthesis (even if only in a limited way), the ambiguity which has surrounded his attempts at communication will be reduced and his expressive language will improve.

Most schools for children with physical impairments have children like Mark, so severely disabled that they are dependent on others for every activity of daily living. Mark has no independent mobility, is unable to feed or to toilet himself and has so little effective communication that, even at the age of 11, no one can be sure just what his intellectual potential might be. Mark's traumatic birth left him with severe athetoid and spastic cerebral palsy. By the age of four, his only form of mobility was rolling on the floor—and even this was poorly directed and not very functional. He had not acquired distinct 'yes' and 'no' responses, and his athetosis and spasticity was so severe that he could neither grip or release objects intentionally. An educational psychologist noted that in addition to his lack of mobility and virtual absence of any effective means of communication, Mark's poor attention-span would prove a major obstacle to assessment and teaching.

Mark was admitted to a special-school nursery class, and after some months during which he was only a spectator in his class, he began to receive some individual teaching. The primary aim was to try to establish correct and reliable 'yes' and 'no' responses. His teacher worked with him on an electronic scanning device, which Mark operated by hitting a single switch with his hand. While his concentration with this apparatus was quite impressive, Mark was inclined to get excited and trigger the device by involuntary movements, reducing his success rate to little better than chance.

Although he might be able to make use of two or three simple signs and gestures, the severity of Mark's cerebral palsy meant that sign language could not provide him with a comprehensive system of communication. After an unsuccessful attempt to use words on cards, he was introduced to Blissymbolics at the age of five. His concentration was improving and he was able to sustain his efforts with his teacher for up to half an hour. Within four months, he had learnt about 20 symbols and was beginning to combine one or two symbols to describe a picture or convey an idea. For the first time he was using communication to influence events around him. However, the severity of his physical handicap meant that his pointing was often ambiguous, and this also limited the number of symbols he could use.

As well as developing his use of Blissymbolics, attempts continued to try to give Mark some form of writing-based communication aid. He would not be able to use an electric typewriter, and a writing aid such as the Possum scanning system would only be of value once he had developed language skills. His history has consisted of short bursts of progress, interspersed with lengthy periods of frustrating stagnation. This slow and erratic progress has almost certainly undermined Mark's morale and motivation. His teachers have all felt frustrated and guilty because of the amount of time that he has had to sit just watching and waiting. The main problem has always been to find the most effective combination of apparatus and switch: the former to meet Mark's needs and to motivate him, and the latter to harness whatever reliable movements he may have.

Michael and some other children have benefited from using the text-editing facilities of the MAC-Apple system. However, for younger and less able children who are still non-readers, operating this system presents too many difficulties. The letters on the screen are too small and they appear too quickly. A child who is concentrating hard on pressing the right letter on the keyboard may well look up to find that it has already appeared on the screen. The essential connection between cause and effect may be lost. In order to overcome these difficulties, a new computer programme called 'Write' was produced. A word is 'written' across the screen in very large letters, and when this is completed the child presses the space bar on the keyboard. The word is moved down to the bottom of the screen where a sentence is built up. The programme allows for the flexible use of speech synthesis, so that letters may be spoken as they are added to the sentence. When the child is satisfied with the sentence, pressing a full stop causes it to be read out and printed. The first part of the Write programme, in which a word is constructed in large letters across the screen, is conceptually similar to the Word Maker in the 'Breakthrough to Literacy' reading scheme (McKay et al. 1970), with which the physically able child builds up a word by placing cardboard letters in a plastic rack. The second part, when whole words are combined to make a sentence, is an electronic analogy to the 'Breakthrough' Sentence Maker. A further feature of the Write programme is the 'teacher's line' at the top of the screen, on which the teacher can enter a word for the child to copy.

As Mark could not use a normal-sized keyboard, a large 'expanded' keyboard was constructed and the Write programme modified to run in conjunction with it. The keys are large and well spaced (approximately 35mm between centres) and a variable delay can be set by the teacher, so that a key must be held down for a certain time before a letter appears on the screen. Thus keys inadvertently pressed for a short period are not registered by the computer.

Mark was used to pointing at the symbols and pictures on his wheelchair-mounted communication board with a spread hand. This made understanding his intentions difficult, and much patient negotiation was needed before he could be understood. A spread hand is completely inappropriate for operating the expanded keyboard, since any of the fingers might make contact with a key. It proved impossible for Mark to control his fingers sufficiently; but with much effort, and helped by his very strong desire to work in the same way as the other children, he eventually learned to press some of the keys with the thumb of his clenched hand. Unfortunately, while his athetosis made wide spacing essential, the resulting keyboard had to be very large to accommodate the keys and his spasticity then prevented him from reaching them all (a similar problem to the one he faced with his Bliss Board). More important, the Write programme itself proved inappropriate for him at that stage. Although he was quick to learn the sequence necessary to effect a printout, this was motivated not by a desire to produce written work but by the noise and excitement of the printer. While he could identify some individual letters and words, he was not yet ready for the task of constructing words from letters and he found even copying a word which was written on the teacher's line very difficult. It was not helpful that Mark was required to deal with two different letter styles—those on the keys and the large letters on the screen.

In order to give Mark practice in letter-matching without requiring him either to relate dissimilar letter styles or to press individual keys, a different programme was used (Head and Poon 1982). The screen displays a test-item letter, in a clear character set and of a size chosen by the teacher. A number of other selected letters are also displayed either vertically or horizontally. The child scans the row of letters using one switch, and when the one which he thinks matches the test-item letter is reached, he makes his selection with another switch. Again Mark was hampered by the problem of finding switches he could operate reliably. He could not bring his hand down quickly or accurately enough, so he had to keep his hand on a large switch and release it only when the cursor reached the letter he thought matched the test item. He then selected that letter with a foot-switch which had been constructed to make use of the relatively good control he had over his left foot. When he made his selection, the whole screen was printed—showing the test-item letter the other letters and the position of the cursor.

Many computer programmes for use in education react with equal enthusiasm whether the user is right or wrong, and so fail to reinforce correct responses. A modification was made to this programme, so that Mark was rewarded with the printout only when he chose the correct letter. In order to make this reward even more effective, the programme was further modified to incorporate speech synthesis. When Mark made his choice, using the two switches, the screen showing his selection was printed out and the speech synthesiser would say the correct letter and announce that Mark made his choice, using the two switches, the screen showing his selection was printed out and the speech synthesiser would say the correct letter and announce that Mark was 'very clever'. This enthusiastic response from the computer made Mark very excited, and sometimes he triggered the switches accidentally. However, it also helped to motivate him and he made good progress with letter-matching. From this he progressed to a variant of the same programme, in which he was required to match whole words.

With simple matching exercises such as these, the computer can be made to respond only when the child is correct. However, if the words are to be used for sentence construction, then a free choice must be allowed or of course only one sentence is possible. A new programme called Sentence Scan was written, to enable Mark to build up sentences by selecting from a list of words on the screen (Fuller *et al.* 1983*a*). The programme can be operated using one or two switches. Work with the previous two programmes had shown that Mark had appreciably better control over his foot than his hand, and for this reason the programme was set up with the cursor scanning automatically at a speed determined by the teacher. Mark makes a selection by pressing his toes when the cursor reaches the word he wants. The teacher negotiates the content of the sentence with Mark and then puts the words on the screen, initially in the correct order. As he builds up his sentence at the bottom of the screen by selecting the words in order, each word is spoken by the computer. At the conclusion of the sentence, a full stop is selected and the whole sentence is read aloud and printed out.

Mark was eventually able to use the Sentence Scan programme. He became steadily more reliable with his foot-switch, and particularly enjoyed using the system to write letters and notes to others. It was apparent from his enthusiasm for this kind of interaction that the development of literacy skills needed to be complemented by some form of direct, unambiguous communication. The emphasis on literacy was perhaps premature. His real need was to be able to communicate more directly. Although further work on the Sentence Scan programme might have improved his word recognition, it could not provide him with an independent means of communication since the words and their order are chosen by the teacher. Even if the words displayed constituted a sentence that Mark wished to say, the selection would take some time and so the immediacy of communication is lost. For this reason a new programme, Speak, was developed. This programme uses the Concept overlay keyboard and a speech synthesiser. The teacher produces an overlay for the Concept keyboard, showing words that the child might want to use (*e.g.* food, drink, please, yes, no and hello). An acrylic sheet with large holes cut through it was fixed over the Concept keyboard, and Mark chose the word he wanted to say by pressing his fingers through the holes. The word was then spoken immediately. In spite of his very poor hand control, Mark found using this system so motivating that he became surprisingly quick and accurate. He often started by saying 'hello' and was soon joining words together (*e.g.* 'food please').

The Concept keyboard has 128 touch-sensitive squares. These squares are too small for those with poor hand control to press individually, so the Speak programme groups them into fours, giving 32 larger squares. However, since spaces must usually be left between words to 'insulate' them from their neighbours, it was possible in practice to have only 12 or 16 words available for Mark to use. In order to increase the available vocabulary, the programme was developed into 'Speak Plus,' in which up to six 'layers' of words may be provided. When pressed, each of the 32 squares can be made to speak any one of the six words or phrases. Changing layers is achieved by pressing one square allocated for that purpose. It was not long before Mark was using two layers and with practice he may eventually use more. It is now planned to attach a large Concept keyboard and portable computer to Mark's powered wheelchair so that he can talk to people as he moves around the school. For Mark, therefore, microtechnology is beginning to give him the opportunity to escape his isolation and establish communication with the world around him.

Conclusions

The computer can be employed in a number of different educational rôles. Odor (1984) distinguished between the instructional, revelatory, conjectural and eman-

431

cipatory rôles. Many teachers have found that children working at a computer are highly motivated. As a result, computers are often used to instruct children in specific skills such as arithmetic computation which may not intrinsically be very motivating. Unfortunately, most of the programmes which employ this approach are not sufficiently flexible to enable the teacher to adapt them closely to individual needs. In the revelatory rôle, children interact with the computer through a game or simulation, and so discover what the teacher intends them to learn. A number of computer programmes using this approach have been produced, and some of them are designed to encourage children of very limited ability to interact with their environment. For example, a picture may appear on the computer screen and the child is able to colour the scene by pressing a switch. Learning that the picture can be modified by performing an action can be the first stage of communication for some profoundly handicapped children. Rostron and Lovett (1981) described a microelectronically controlled electric car which a child could drive by making a simple movement. By enabling children to manipulate their environment it is hoped that communication can be developed.

In the conjectural rôle, the computer is used to give the child some control over the learning process. Papert (1980) helped to develop the computer language 'logo' for this purpose. Logo is a 'high-level' computer language which is similar to English. Among other things, it can be used to draw shapes either on the screen or on the floor using a Turtle. This involves the child in decision-making and problem-solving processes which can boost the child's understanding and confidence.

In the emancipatory rôle, the computer is used to remove or reduce unproductive workload and blocks to performance. For example, given a word-processor such as MAC-Apple which can be accessed with a single switch, a severely motor impaired child may have the opportunity to develop written language skills without the need to hold a pencil or form letters. If this child is also without speech, written language may provide the channel of communication which is essential for linguistic and cognitive development.

Any movement a child can make voluntarily and consistently may be harnessed to activate a switch and thus control a computer. The movement might be of the head, hand, foot, eye or tongue. Even a sound can be a means of control. In deciding which switch a child should use, it is important to explore all possible voluntary movements and also to ensure that the child is seated in such a way that effective and continuous use of the switch is possible. Depending upon the degree of disability, the child may use one or more switches, a special keyboard or a guard over the computer keyboard itself. However, while it is clearly important to find the most appropriate switch and optimum position, effective use of a switch or keyboard depends very much upon how motivating the child finds the activity presented. For example, Mark did not find the efforts to develop his literacy particularly rewarding. While his teachers were concerned with language development, he was concerned with communication; and when he was given the means to communicate more directly, the physical skill he demonstrated surprised those working with him.

Computer software can only meet the needs of a disabled child such as Mark if it is sufficiently flexible to be adapted to each individual. Such sophisticated and powerful software can only result from close co-operation between skilled and sensitive programmers and those working with the children.

The computer is only one of many tools available for helping children overcome difficulties of communication and learning. The computer is enabling Michael to increase and improve his written output in a way that previously had not been possible. It has also revealed particular language problems and provided possible means of remediation. Mark has at last been given access to the curriculum and has discovered a new motivation. Perhaps more importantly for both children, the power and flexibility of the microcomputer is such that it offers them the promise of eventually overcoming their isolation.

Postscript
Michael: an integrated future
In September 1985 Michael moved from his special school to a nearby middle school. This move formed part of the special school's integration scheme which meant that Michael was not on his own but shared the experience with five other children from his year. These children are not in a unit or special class but are fully integrated into the host school. A teacher from the special school has moved with them to ensure that their educational, physical and social needs are met and to augment the teaching strength of the middle school. This teacher signs to Michael. He also has a signing welfare assistant who is able to interpret lessons for him as well as several sessions each week with a specialist signing language teacher.

Michael's integration appears to be extremely successful. Enormous effort has been made to ensure that he communicates as fully as possible with the children and teachers in his new school environment. He is equipped with his own work station for written work. His MAC-Apple programme is now run on an Apple IIc with a small monitor and portable printer. The equipment needed to be as compact and unobtrusive as possible. Michael's written output since joining his middle school peers has at least doubled. At the same time he is receiving a curriculum appropriate to a child of his age and intelligence.

MAC-Apple still offers Michael the most suitable writing aid. Although he is the only signing child in his school, the children in his class voluntarily attend signing lessons during the lunch break so that they can talk to him. It is now felt that he also needs a portable letter-based social communication aid, and so he is being given a Toby Churchill Lightwriter. This device works off rechargeable batteries and has a very clear LED two-sided display as well as a memory for stored words and phrases.

The resource implications of integrating Michael in terms of hardware and teaching/welfare time are not negligible but to have succumbed to his communication handicaps and so ignored his potential would have isolated him even more from the society in which he belongs. There is no doubt that the alternative and augmentative communication systems which he uses are helping to penetrate that wall of isolation which would otherwise have surrounded him.

A portable communication system for Mark

In order to provide Mark with greater opportunities for communication, and hopefully to cultivate his language and communication skills, it was decided to devise a portable system. Around school he tried to make his wants known by pointing to symbols, words and pictures on a large board attached to his wheelchair. The use of this board requires that the other person can both see and read it and consequently Mark is unable to communicate with many children who have physical or sensory disabilities. Even when an adult or child can see what Mark is pointing at, it is difficult for communication to take place 'face-to-face' and so many non-vocal aspects of expression may be missed.

Mark's board is approximately A2 in size, that is mm × mm. As an A2 Concept Keyboard had become available, one of these was obtained and mounted on his wheelchair. An Apple IIc computer which is very compact was mounted in a box on the back of the chair. Computers are very sensitive to variations in electric current, and it was not possible to power the system from the wheelchair battery as these are periodically heavily drained to provide propulsion. Instead, a separate battery is built into the computer box along with a speech synthesiser. The speakers are mounted under the wheelchair seat.

When using the Speak Plus programme, Mark did not use the monitor to read the words he selected. Instead he listened to them being spoken out by the computer. He would not require a monitor, or indeed a printer, with his portable system as the intention was to provide a means of immediate, face-to-face communication. However, a monitor is required in order to enter the vocabulary, and if this programme were to be used with a portable system it would inhibit the teacher from making changes to the vocabulary. Because of this, the programme was entirely rewritten so that the system could be used without reference to a monitor screen. Instead of a menu of instructions being displayed, the teacher received spoken instructions and responses from the computer. In this way, appropriate vocabulary can be entered very quickly and in any situation.

Custom-building microcomputer-based systems requires considerable technical expertise and the task of developing Mark's system took much more time than had been anticipated. Many of these technical problems have been overcome and Mark is now able to 'speak' to others, albeit in a rather rudimentary way. However, many other problems have yet to be addressed. The quality of electronically produced speech is still not good, although there are promising signs that improvements in this area will soon be available. The rate at which utterances may be made is still extremely slow, and the listener's attention may wander. Sudden interjections into conversation are impossible. If Mark does eventually make much fuller use of the system, then a means will have to be devised to provide him with a larger and more flexible vocabulary.

Mark's system is enhancing his ability to communicate with others. As it offers solutions to some problems, however, this new technology is presenting new problems which make it necessary for us to appreciate more fully the complexities of the communication process.

REFERENCES

Adams, J. (1984) *Learning to Cope.* London: Educational Computing.

AEDE (1971) *The Paget Gorman Sign System.* London: Association for Experiment in Deaf Education.

Bruner, J. (1964) 'The course of cognitive growth.' *American Psychologist,* **19.**

Chapman, B. L. M., Wilby, J. F. (1982) 'Language and silence.' *Computers in Schools,* **4,** 3.

Fouts, R. S., Couch, J. B., O'Neil, C. R. (1979) 'Strategies for primate language training.' *In:* Schiefelbusch, R. L., Hollis, J. H. (Eds.) *Language Intervention from Ape to Child.* Baltimore: University Park Press.

Fuller, P., Poon, P., Southgate, T. (1983*a*) 'Microcomputers at Ormerod School.' *Special Education—Forward Trends,* **10**(3), 30–33.

—— Newcombe, F., Ounsted, C. (1983*b*) 'Late language development in a child unable to recognize or produce speech sounds.' *Archives of Neurology,* **40,** 165–168.

Goldenberg, E. P. (1979) *Special Technology for Special Children.* Baltimore: University Park Press.

—— (1984) *Computers, Education and Special Needs.* Reading, Massachusetts: Addison-Wesley.

Head, P., Poon, P. (1982) 'The enabling micro.' *Learning to Cope,* **1,** 39.

Krauss, R. M. (1979) 'Communication models and communicative behaviour.' *In:* Schiefelbusch, R. L., Hollins, J. H. (Ed.) *Language Intervention from Ape to Child.* Baltimore: University Park Press.

Lloyd, L. L., Karlan, G. R. (1984) 'Non-speech communication symbols and systems: where have we been and where are we going?' *Journal of Mental Deficiency Research,* **28,** 3–20.

MacKay, D., Thompson, B., Schaub, P. (1970) *Breakthrough to Literacy—Teachers' Manual.* London: Longman for the Schools Council.

Odor, P. (1984) 'Hard and soft technology for education and communication.' *CALL Centre Occasional Paper No. 9.* CALL Centre: Edinburgh.

Papert, S. (1980) *Mindstorms.* Brighton: Harvester Press.

Rostron, A. B., Lovett, S. (1981) 'A new outlook with the computer.' *Special Education-Forward Trends,* **8**(4), 29–31.

—— Sewell, D. (1984) *Microtechnology in Special Education.* London: Croom Helm.

435

27
SPECIAL EDUCATION

Harry Purser

Help for children with speech and language difficulties has grown steadily over the past 20 years, but the identification and description of these difficulties is often complex. Parents and professionals are confronted with a daunting array of theory and research in their pursuit of a focus for intervention. Much of this research is the product of a multidisciplinary effort to understand the development of normal human language: only a portion focuses directly on the development of children with pronounced communication difficulties. Both research perspectives have contributed to our current knowledge of language remediation, and together with the growth of the speech-therapy services in recent years, have considerably increased the availability of individual and group-based programmes for childhood language disorders. But it is at school where these problems are most acutely obvious, and where the main opportunities for intervention exist.

Language difficulties exist both as a feature of many broader handicapping conditions, and, more frequently today, as relatively specific forms of handicap in their own right. Language disorders can be conceived as distributed along a continuum of severity, but in most cases they are to be found in combination with other types of developmental difficulties. The challenge for educationalists and clinicians is to develop comprehensive curricula and specific programmes of intervention which are capable of addressing language difficulty, regardless of the context in which they occur.

Before considering the range of educational provision that is currently available to language-handicapped children, and the form that provision takes, it is worth looking at the aims of special education, and the means of access to these services. Given the complexity of language problems, and the frequent co-occurrence of other forms of developmental difficulties, it is often useful to be aware of the issues which influence the provision of special education.

USA PL 94–142

In the USA the 'Education for All Handicapped Children Act' (Public Law 1975) came into force in the late 1970s, and forms a powerful bill of rights for all handicapped children. Welcomed by educationalists as 'the end of a quiet revolution' (Abeson and Zettel 1977), this legislation entitles handicapped children to a free appropriate public education (and any other related services such as transportation, physiotherapy and speech therapy) and encourages the active involvement of the child's parents throughout the process. The new legislation is estimated to have drawn into public education some four million handicapped children who had previously been excluded by virtue of their particular profile of handicap, which suggested they were uneducable.

Handicapped children are defined in the Act as children who are 'mentally retarded, hard of hearing, deaf, orthopedically impaired, other health impaired, speech impaired, visually handicapped, seriously emotionally disturbed or having specific learning disabilities'. It is the responsibility of States and schools to provide an adequate evaluation of the needs of each child. Each state is required under the Act to submit detailed plans of the special educational opportunities it intends to provide for handicapped children; indeed, federal funding for special education is contingent upon the approval of these plans by the US Bureau of Education for the Handicapped.

The Law also emphasises the rôle and rights of the child's parents in special education. Parents are consulted at each stage in the process of assessment and placement, and have considerable powers of appeal in the event of dissatisfaction with particular arrangements. Special education must be provided in the 'least restrictive environment'. As far as possible, handicapped children should be educated alongside non-handicapped children within mainstream schools; only where the handicap is particularly severe are more restrictive alternatives contemplated (*e.g.* resource rooms within ordinary schools, special classrooms, special day or residential schools).

Perhaps the most significant feature of PL 94–142 is its emphasis on developing an Individual Education Programme (IEP) for each handicapped child. This is a formal definition of the particular special educational needs of each child, and is followed by clear statements of the goals provision is designed to achieve. The IEP is the product of a multidisciplinary evaluation process, and must contain information about the child's present level of performance, the annual and short-term learning objectives set for each child, the form of education and related services which will be available to meet these objectives, and the extent to which it will be possible for the child to participate in the ordinary school programme with non-handicapped children. The IEP must also specify when special services will begin, and for how long each service or special programme will be offered. It must also indicate clearly both the form and timing of future reassessments to gauge progress, and thus evaluate the effectiveness of the special educational provision detailed in the IEP. A comprehensive re-evaluation of the child's needs (and a new IEP) must be made every three years, or more frequently at parental request.

UK Education Act 1981

Within the last decade, three major government enquiries have highlighted the need for fundamental revisions of the public services provided to handicapped children. The Bullock Committee (1975) was commissioned to consider the issue of identifying and helping children with reading and language difficulties in school; the Court Committee (1976) reviewed the national provision of child health services and made recommendations which were only partially adopted as Government policy. But it was the Warnock Committee (1978) which undertook a fundamental review of the issues in special education. The subsequent Education Act (Special Educational Needs) of 1981 incorporated some (but by no means all) of the Warnock committee's recommendations.

Like their American counterparts, each local education authority (LEA) has a duty under the Education Act of 1944 to provide a free public education for all children. LEAS must also ensure that 'special educational provision is made for pupils who have special educational needs' (EA 1981), and such provision must be available for all children between the ages of two and 19 years. Children are entitled to receive these services with or without full parental consent. Appeal opportunities are available to parents, not only to challenge particular educational placements, but also to compel LEAS to review any decision *not* to make special provision available for a particular child. LEAS also have a duty to make detailed assessments and provide educational services for children under two years of age, but only where informed parental consent is obtained.

With the advent of EA 1981, the traditional categorical model of developmental handicap was abandoned. In its place came a new emphasis upon defining the specific learning needs of individual children. This multi-axial emphasis in assessment has effectively broadened the scope of special education: a change in approach which was the central recommendation of the Warnock Committee. Children are now deemed to require special education if they can be shown to have 'special educational needs', *i.e.* if they exhibit a 'learning difficulty', which is defined in three ways: if a child (i) has 'significantly greater difficulty in learning than the majority of children of his age'; (ii) has 'a disability which either prevents or hinders him from making use of educational facilities of a kind generally provided in schools for children of this age'; or (iii) is under five years old and is considered likely to fall into one of the above categories if special educational provision is not made.

Where it appears a child may warrant special educational provision, each LEA must arrange for a comprehensive multidisciplinary assessment of that child's needs. Four sources of advice are required for the assessment: educational, medical (including psychiatric), psychological and parental. The written advice from the assessment team covers the identification of current needs, as well as the child's likely future needs. This advice, and the education authority's response to it, may eventually form part of a legal undertaking known as the Statement of Special Educational Needs. In cases where adequate educational provision can be made within the ordinary school, there is no need to make such a formal statement. But whenever a child has moderate to severe difficulties, and is placed in a special school or special unit within an ordinary school, there will be a need for a statement under the Act.

Statements must be reviewed annually, but this does not usually entail a further multidisciplinary reassessment. Rather these reviews constitute a process of continuous assessment of the child's needs. A formal reassessment must be undertaken where there has been 'a significant change in the child's circumstances', or at parental request. A full reassessment is required by law only between the ages of 13 and 15 years, and then only where the last assessment was undertaken under the age of 12½ years.

Comparing the legislation in the UK and the USA, it is clear that there is a shared commitment to provide individualised education for exceptional children and to involve parents fully in the process of determining special needs. There is also agreement on the need to review educational arrangements as development proceeds. In the USA these aims are legally binding through the power of PL 94–142, and many educationalists feel that the law has stimulated a period of unprecedented development in special education. The main source of difference between the approaches lies in the extent to which they promote the issue of integration of handicapped children within the regular school system.

Under PL 94–142 it is the duty of education agencies to provide special curricula in the 'least restrictive environment', and to indicate in the IEP the amount of contact with ordinary schoolchildren that will be available. This emphasis has been derived from arguments about the artificiality of operating a 'dual system' educational programme. Stainback and Stainback (1984) make the telling point that the very existence of a dual educational system (ordinary and special) reinforces the idea that children fall into a similar dichotomy. They argue that all children should be considered special; every child has individual educational needs as a consequence of his unique physical, intellectual and psychological make up. All children would benefit from individualised instructional programmes, not just those with a significant learning difficulty (Blankenship and Lilly 1981). EA 1981 promotes integration only where it is compatible with the efficient use of resources.

The arguments for integrating children with handicaps into the ordinary school system on social grounds appear compelling to many parents and professionals; but on educational grounds, the balance of evidence is far from clear (Howlin 1985). In recent years a wider public approval of 'normalisation' policies towards handicapped people has considerably improved the prospect of further educational integration (Wolfensberger 1972). A new awareness of the possibilites for integration has emerged from professional rejection of the idea of special education as implying the existence, and the need for, special instructional methods (Gardner 1977). Many involved in special education would accept that there are no unique methods for use with exceptional children, only new aims for the curriculum. This type of reasoning has led to the promotion of 'mainstreaming' for even the most severely handicapped children in the USA (Brinker and Thorpe 1984).

Special education for language-handicapped children

Language difficulties are seldom easy to disentangle from a complex picture of learning difficulties. In some cases speech and language difficulties are seen as the fundamental cause of other social, emotional, behavioural and intellectual handicaps; in others it may appear that impaired communicative ability is the consequence of more tangible forms of handicap. The most obvious examples of the latter proposition would be communication difficulties found in children with significant hearing loss, as well as in non-communicative children with known neurological pathology. There is evidence that language problems also arise as a consequence of physical handicap (Anderson and Spain 1977).

There are a number of distinct approaches to the treatment of child language disorders. The study of normal language acquisition has suggested a sequence in which communicative abilities are acquired, as well as a range of 'cognitive prerequisites' for language learning. These theoretical perspectives have a clear implication for the non-communicating child. For the child whose language is not comparable with other children of his age, it is the first task of intervention to determine how that child's communicative abilities deviate from the expected developmental course. This type of assessment can lead to direct individual intervention in the child's communicative system; many aspects of speech and language development may be addressed. The child's fundamental phonological system may be examined if the child's speech is unintelligible to an adult (Ingram 1976, Grunwell 1979). The structure of the child's linguistic skills can be evaluated in order to prescribe individualised remedial action, and to promote further syntactical development (Crystal *et al.* 1976). The child's use of language to influence and regulate social encounters will be studied. This functional analysis may lead to structured programmes of intervention aimed at eliciting and maintaining communication within a variety of contexts, including the home (McConkey 1981, McLean and Snyder-McLean 1984, Mowrer 1984).

Before reaching an over-all plan of management for the child, it is necessary to assess all the relevant information about the child's medical and cognitive status, behavioural difficulties and particular emotional or social factors. In an individual case it may be considered necessary for the child to attend a preschool day nursery in order to provide a suitable language learning environment, and to receive individual treatment from a speech therapist. There may also be a social worker allocated to the family in order to help with concurrent difficulties. If the child's general level of cognitive development was impaired, and the communication difficulty was severe, then a more suitable placement might be in a nursery class within a special school. The activities offered in this setting would differ significantly from what would be practical within a preschool day nursery. If the child was also suspected of having some degree of hearing impairment, then a further form of specialised educational placement might be considered.

Comprehensive assessment leads to a comprehensive formulation of the child's needs; having established the aims of special education for an individual child, it then becomes a matter of selecting the most appropriate setting for that education. Much will depend on the availability of particular programmes for children with specific types of handicap. For children with a number of areas of handicap, the type of provision selected needs to have resources which can address multiple learning difficulties. Where there is a fundamental medical or psychological handicap the provision must be able to address these problems in detail, as well as providing for the child's development in more general ways.

Early recognition of childhood language difficulties has generated the need for early intervention and preventative services for preschool children. For children of school age, the development of special language units, and partially hearing units within ordinary schools, is an important step towards providing more individualised educational opportunities while fulfilling some of the principles of educational integration. The aims of some common forms of language intervention programmes in these two settings will be outlined.

Preschool provision
The majority of language-handicapped children under five years who are brought
to the attention of LEAs will have been identified and assessed by the health
services. The primary care network provides access to such specialised services as
paediatric assessment units, child development centres, speech therapy services as
well as child psychology and psychiatry departments. Following these specialist
assessments (and communication of the findings to parents) early intensive
intervention is provided either through the specialist services, or through district
and community handicap teams. The child's LEA will be informed of the need for
special educational provision, and further arrangements for preschool placement
will be made after a Statement of Special Educational Needs has been formulated.
Several educational options may be available for preschool children with varying
degrees of language handicap and associated behavioural difficulties.

Social Services departments maintain preschool day nurseries for children and
families with special social needs. Many of the children who attend these nurseries
also have special educational needs, and additional specialist help can be made
available within the nursery from visiting speech therapists, psychologists and
peripatetic teachers. Most children attending day nurseries will be aged between
two and five years. The types of language problems that are likely to be seen in
these settings can range from pure expressive language disorders to much more
diffuse forms of communicative handicap. Research undertaken for the Warnock
Committee in a number of Scottish regions (Clark and Cheyne 1979, Clark *et al.*
1982) suggests that many nursery teachers see speech and language difficulties as
one of the most prevalent handicaps amongst young children. This research also
highlighted the willingness of teachers to address these problems, given adequate
resources (Clark and Cheyne 1979, Chazan *et al.* 1980).

Often, however, children with moderate to severe language handicap require a
placement with a more favourable child-teacher ratio. Nursery classes are available
in some special-school settings, but access to this type of provision is invariably
limited to children with a predominantly severe sensory, intellectual or physical
handicap. Such settings are usually better equipped to address multiple severe
handicap, and have access to the full range of specialist services as needs arise.
Children with a significant degree of hearing impairment, mental retardation or
physical handicap would be likely to be found in these settings.

Where profound deafness is identified in a preschool child, there is the
possibility of placement in one of the special day/residential schools for the deaf.
But much depends on the geographical location of these facilities; for the child
under four years, residential placement at some distance from home would only be
considered when severe behaviour problems are present. Day attendance, on the
other hand, may be feasible in some locations.

Special educational provision for preschool language-handicapped children
need not necessarily imply institutional provision. The Warnock Committee
recommended the development of a comprehensive peripatetic teaching service to
train parents as educators of their young handicapped children within the home.
This type of service has been successfully established for both deaf and partially

hearing preschool children, and extensive use has been made of this model in early-intervention programmes for mentally handicapped children (Shearer *et al.* 1972, Cameron 1982). Much has been written about the importance of parents in early special education, and there is ample evidence that parents can be trained to become their child's 'language therapist' (Mahoney and Geller 1980, Lombardino and Mangan 1983, Howlin 1984). Initial intensive input from professional teachers can gradually be reduced as parents gain confidence in their ability to stimulate language development through structured play. These home-based teaching schemes have made a considerable impact on the provision for preschool language-handicapped children (Cooper *et al.* 1978, White and East 1983). When this type of programme is supplemented with attendance at playgroups or access to toy libraries, it offers new possibilities for individual instruction.

Within the context of the nursery class there are a number of approaches to intervention with language handicap. Bloom and Lahey (1978) offer an intervention model which focuses on the individual child's communicative abilities, and describe them in terms of impairments in the form, content and use of language. Particular attention is given to the goals for early language learning. Three main precursors of language use have been identified: reciprocal gaze patterns, regulating the behaviours of others, and calling attention to objects and events. The first stage of an intervention programme for young children lacking functional language would be to address use through systematic modelling of these behaviours and reinforcement of the child for their consistent performance. Attention is also given to the precursory goals of language form. Production of a linguistic signal is encouraged via the imitation of specific motor/gestural movements and patterns of vocalisation. In the first instance this may be approached by copying a behaviour instigated by the child, and gradually increasing the time-delay between that behaviour and its imitation. New sequences of responses are then built up from these already familiar individual actions. Further non-verbal behaviours are seen to precede linguistic development, and are believed to reflect the development of the prerequisite cognitive skills for representational thinking. These behaviours suggest teaching goals for a prelinguistic intervention programme which focus on the child's play with objects. General goals, such as teaching the child to search for objects that disappear, are broken down into a number of sequential subgoals. First the child will be encouraged to gaze in the direction of a moving object and track its progress, then the object is made to disappear behind a screen. The child is then taught to anticipate its reappearance, and ultimately to search actively for an object concealed amongst a number of other objects. It is hypothesised that in order to perform these actions a child must develop some prelinguistic representation of both objects and object relations, which leads on to the development of linguistic representation.

The Wolfson language development programme (Cooper *et al.* 1978) also offers practical suggestions for early intervention. Here the learning of language is broken down into specific developmental stages, with 'attention control' being seen as the primary prerequisite for initial language development. Six distinct stages in the normal development of attention control are considered, with language-delayed children typically clustering in the most basic stages. By careful structuring of the teaching environment to exclude sources of distraction, and by capitalising on the child's interests, the programme encourages the development of sustained attention. A range of non-verbal cognitive skills are also targeted for intervention in this approach. Concept formation is stimulated via simple concrete one-to-one matching tasks to establish concepts like colour and shape. Classification tasks are then introduced, where size and quantity as well as positional concepts are taught. The programme subsequently moves on to the development of symbolic understanding through representational play opportunities; here the child begins with large doll play, where there is high saliency, and progresses towards two-dimensional pictorial play materials.

There is a great deal of agreement between these two approaches to early intervention in language handicap. Both begin with the need for detailed assessment of the child's cognitive skills, and emphasise the need to teach fundamental object relations. Where progress is slow, it may emerge that there are more specific types of cognitive difficulties present than initial assessment suggested.

The Portage Guide to Early Education (Bluma *et al.* 1976) was developed both to encourage parents to take an active rôle in their handicapped child's education and to provide a continuous educational environment for children between birth and six years. The guides are based on developmentally sequenced checklists of behavioural skills and encompass socialisation, language, self-help skills, cognitive abilities and motor development. The Portage teaching model begins by identifying the child's skill level in each of the above areas, and then offers parents clear guidelines on how to carry out specific activities with the child which form the next step in development. Parents are encouraged to record the child's progress as particular skills are acquired, and any specific difficulties are discussed with a visiting Portage professional.

The Portage scheme has been further developed for use with young language-handicapped children between birth and four years (White and East 1983). The Language checklist has been expanded to include a range of infant communication items, and the more complex language goals have been broken down into smaller component steps in order to make learning easier. Parents whose child does not vocalise in response to their speech may be offered the following guidelines for intervention:

(1) Talk to the child as you carry out daily activities—name objects, food, clothing *etc.* Name the activities carried out by yourself and the child.

(2) Look at objects and picture books. Ask the child to show you objects and pictures. Read to the child.

(3) Ask the child to tell what has happened.

(4) Say 'hi' and 'bye' to the child when going in and out of sight.

(5) While playing with the child reinforce the sounds he makes by making more sounds and vocalising back to him.

The revised Portage Language Checklist may be used to amplify language development within the general Portage scheme, or as a specific programme in its own right.

Early intervention for language disorders within the nursery environment typically involves individual and class activities based upon the principles outlined above. With additional specialist help aimed at particular individual difficulties a comprehensive programme for language development is built up, but the importance of parental involvement in language-development programmes for preschool children cannot be underestimated. Even so, the pioneering projects described here fall short of demonstrating the effectiveness of early intervention for all language delays. As is argued elsewhere (see Chapter 23), intensive training can sometimes increase the use of existing language without improving the general level of language development. It is essential that all language-intervention programmes are subjected to critical evaluation.

Special language units
The growth of special language classes or units within ordinary schools is a relatively recent innovation and parallels the development of partially hearing units in ordinary schools for hearing-impaired children. Language units vary in the severity and complexity of communication handicaps that they address. In some units, teaching is aimed at children between the ages of four and 11 years who fit criteria for language delay; in others, more complex language disorders are addressed with support from special-school resource centres. Language units within special schools generally cater for children with severe communication difficulties (and often multiple handicap) who are likely to require instruction in a non-vocal system of communication.

The curriculum of the language unit within the ordinary school setting varies according to the needs of the children enrolled and the resources available. In some areas the work of the unit is centred around structured remediation programmes which have been developed from behavioural principles. The Distar Language Program (Engelman and Osborn 1976) has been a useful vehicle for teaching linguistic concepts in special education for many years. Originally developed as part of the USA 'Follow-through' project (and among the most successful programmes included in that project) the Distar scheme aims to teach children the 'language of instruction'; it was reasoned that children were likely to fail at school unless they understood their teachers. The programme is therefore based on an analysis of the skills and concepts required to understand and follow basic instructions presented by a teacher. Although many modern educationalists would now question the central aims of this scheme, and its relevance to language-handicapped children, there is some evidence that it can lead to significant gains for children within special language units (Gregory *et al.* 1982).

Psycholinguistic training approaches (Kirk and Kirk 1971, Bush and Giles 1977) have also proved popular. Here a broad spectrum of the child's communicative abilities is examined in order to identify specific areas where the child needs remedial help. Although this type of approach often seems to be based on a very abstract conception of functional communication, there have been several detailed studies where encouraging results have been obtained (Kavale 1981).

444

In many language units the approach to intervention may be based on the principles of the Wolfson programme, or Bloom and Lahey's approach to language teaching outlined earlier. The Derbyshire Language Scheme (Knowles and Madislover 1982) is becoming increasingly popular as a framework for intervention within such units. Following a detailed assessment of the child's language comprehension he is assigned to one of three stages in the scheme: the Early Vocabulary or Single Word Level, the Simple Sentence Stage, or the Grammar and Complex Sentence Stage. Teaching is based around game-like situations and many activities are suggested which are geared to improving the child's comprehension skills. Expressive language-teaching features a 'rôle-reversal' procedure where the child, having learned how to 'play the game', takes over as 'the teacher'. This latter aspect of the scheme reflects a conscious effort by the authors to broaden the basis of language teaching. Rather than have the child become a rather passive respondent in the classroom, this approach emphasises the need to provide genuine functional communication situations where the child has to learn to control other people, obtain objects, and obtain information.

In units catering for children with more complex language disorders greater emphasis is placed upon the development of basic functional communication abilities. In these settings teachers may employ more behavioural methods of instruction in order to reinforce emergent communicative abilities (Guess *et al.* 1976, Rose 1982). Where severe language disorders exist there are invariably complex behavioural, emotional and social difficulties. Here a more comprehensive approach to educational programming is desirable, rather than a narrow focus upon language skills (Harris 1975, Gardner *et al.* 1983). Children who do not develop oral communication skills may be taught a particular form of sign language, such as the Makaton vocabulary (Walker 1976, 1978). This is perhaps the most widely used alternative communication system in British special school settings (Reid *et al.* 1983), and similar programmes are employed in the USA (Fristoe and Lloyd 1980, Siverman 1980, Musselwhite and St. Louis 1982). The Makaton programme consists of some 350 words which are taught in a series of nine stages to form a progressive sequence of communication. To date however there has been surprisingly little research addressing the longer term outcomes of these alternative communication systems with severely handicapped children (Kiernan 1977, 1984).

Children whose language handicap is primarily a consequence of inadequate hearing may be placed within specialist units for the partially hearing or in language units within ordinary schools. A moderate to severe conductive hearing loss is usually involved which results in an impoverishment of linguistic processes, and in many cases, unintelligible speech. With modern hearing aids the majority of such children can benefit from the normal school curriculum, but the methods of instruction need to be tailored to the child's specific handicap. Education is geared to developing and extending the child's residual communicative abilities through employing the aural/oral method. In this approach careful amplification of the speech frequencies is achieved in order that oral speech, supplemented by lipreading, can be employed in the classroom. Teachers exaggerate their lip movements in order to supplement the aural signal.

Those children with a severe to profound sensorineural hearing loss, where amplification is of little help and the quality of speech is insufficient for oral communication, are usually trained in a manual communication system such as American or British Sign Language. Although there has been some debate regarding the status of signing as a true language there is little doubt that such manual communication systems, particularly when supplemented by fingerspelling, are capable of generating the same range of semantic forms that oral language can achieve.

It is rather artificial to make such a sharp distinction between groups of children with hearing loss; and it is often difficult to be prescriptive about hearing impairment. In many schools and units for deaf and partially hearing children, a happy mixture of oral and manual communication systems is employed under the title of Total Communication.

Conclusion

Special education for children with speech and language disorders clearly makes a major contribution to their development. In recent years our ideas about the nature of language, and its relation to general cognitive development, have grown considerably. The study of semantic development (Macnamara 1972) has highlighted the need to consider pragmatic aspects of language development (Bates 1976, Hart 1981). Here the natural function of communication is emphasised, rather than the teaching of isolated language structures within artificial contexts. It is fair to say that pragmatics has now become the dominant force in contemporary language remediation (Aldred 1983, Gallagher and Prutting 1983, McLean and Snyder-McLean 1984) and this will undoubtedly have a further significant impact on the education of language handicapped children in the future.

REFERENCES

Abeson, A., Zettel, J. (1977) 'The end of a quiet revolution: the United States Education for All Handicapped Children Act, 1975.' *Exceptional Children,* **44,** 115–128.
Aldred, C. (1983) 'Language in use.' *Bulletin of the College of Speech Therapists,* August, 1–4.
Anderson, E. M., Spain, B. (1977) *The Child with Spina Bifida.* London: Methuen.
Bates, E. (1976) *Language and Context.* New York: Academic Press.
Blankenship, C., Lilly, S. (1981) *Mainstreaming Students with Learning and Behavior Problems.* New York: Holt, Rinehart & Winston.
Bloom, L., Lahey, M. (1978) *Language Development and Language Disorders.* New York: Wiley.
Bluma, S., Shearer, M., Frohman, A., Hilliard, J. (1976) *Manual of the Portage Guide to Early Education.* Windsor: NFER.
Brinker, R. P., Thorpe, M. E. (1984) 'Integration of severely handicapped students and the proportion of IEP objectives achieved.' *Exceptional Children,* **51,** 168–175.
Bullock, Sir A. (1975) *A Language for Life. Report of the Committee of Enquiry into Reading and the Use of English.* London: HMSO.
Bush, W. J., Giles, M. T. (1977) *Aids to Psycholinguistic Teaching, 2nd Edn.* Columbus, Ohio: C. E. Merrill.
Cameron, R. J. (Ed.) (1982) *Working Together—Portage in the UK.* Windsor: NFER-Nelson.
Chazan, M., Laing, A. F., Shackleton Bailey, M., Jones, G. (1980) *Some of our Children.* London:

Open Books.

Clark, M. M., Robson, B., Browning, M. (1982) *Pre-school Education and Children with Special Needs.* Birmingham: Faculty of Education, University of Birmingham.

—— Cheyne, W. M. (1979) *Studies in Pre-school Education* London: Hodder & Stoughton.

Cooper, J., Moodley, M., Reynell, J. (1978) *Helping Language Development.* London: Edward Arnold.

Court, S. D. M. (Chairman) (1976) *Fit for the Future. Report of the Committee on Child Health Services.* London: HMSO.

Crystal, D., Fletcher, P., Garman, M. (1976) *The Grammatical Analysis of Language Disability: a Procedure for Assessment and Remediation.* London: Edward Arnold.

Education Act (1981) *An act to make provision with respect to children with special educational needs.* London: HMSO.

Engelman, S., Osborn, J. (1976) *Distar Instructional System: Distar Language 1.* Chicago: Science Research Associates.

Fristoe, M., Lloyd, L. L. (1980) 'Planning an initial expressive sign lexicon for persons with severe communication impairment.' *Journal of Speech and Hearing Disorders,* **45,** 170–180.

Gallagher, T. M., Prutting, C. A. (1983) *Pragmatic Assessment and Intervention Issues in Language.* San Diego: College Hill Press.

Gardner, J., Murphy, J., Crawford, N. (1983) *The Skills Analysis Model.* Kidderminster: British Institute of Mental Handicap.

Gardner, W. (1977) *Learning and Behavior Characteristics of Exceptional Children and Youth.* Boston: Allyn & Bacon.

Gregory, P., Richards, C., Hadley, M. (1982) 'Using DISTAR language in a unit for children with language disorders.' *Mental Handicap,* **10,** 102–104.

Grunwell, P. (1979) 'Developmental language disorders at the phonological level.' *In:* Jones, F. M. (Ed) *Language Disability in Children.* Lancaster: MTP.

Guess, D., Sailor, W., Keogh, W., Baer, D. (1976) 'Language development programs for severely handicapped children.' *In:* Haring, N., Brown, L. (Eds.) *Teaching the Severely Handicapped—a Yearly Publication. Vol II.* New York: Grune Stratton.

Harris, S. L. (1975) 'Teaching language to non-verbal children with emphasis on problems of generalisation.' *Psychological Bulletin,* **82,** 565–580.

Hart, B. (1981) 'Pragmatics: how language is used.' *Analysis and Intervention in Developmental Disabilities,* **1,** 299–313.

Howlin, P. (1984) 'Parents as therapists: a critical review.' *In:* Muller, D. J. (Ed.) *Remediating Children's Language.* London: Croom Helm.

—— (1985) 'Special educational treatment.' *In:* Rutter, M., Hersov, L. (Eds.) *Child and Adolescent Psychiatry: Modern Approaches. 2nd Edn.* Oxford: Blackwell.

Ingram, D. (1976) *Phonological Disability in Children.* London: Edward Arnold.

Kavale, K. (1981) 'Functions of the Illinois Test of Psycholinguistic Abilities (ITPA): are they trainable?.' *Exceptional Children,* **47,** 496–510.

Kiernan, C. (1977) 'Alternatives to speech: a review of research on manual and other forms of communication with the mentally handicapped.' *British Journal of Mental Subnormality,* **23,** 6–28.

—— (1984) 'Language remediation programmes.' *In:* Muller, D. J. (Ed.) *Remediating Children's Language.* London: Croom Helm.

Kirk, S. A., Kirk, W. D. (1971) *Psycholinguistic Learning Disabilities: Diagnosis and Remediation.* Urbana, Ill.: UIP.

Knowles, W., Madislover, M. (1982) *The Derbyshire Language Scheme.* Ripley, Derbyshire: private publication.

Lombardino, L. & Mangan, N. (1983) 'Parents as language trainers: language programming with developmentally delayed children.' *Exceptional Children,* **49,** 358–361.

Mahoney, G., Geller, E. (1980) 'An ecological approach to language intervention.' *In:* Bricker, D. (Ed.) *Language Intervention with Children.* San Francisco: Jossey Bass.

McConkey, R. (1981) 'Sharing knowledge of language with children and parents.' *British Journal of Disorders of Communication,* **16,** 3–10.

McLean, J & Snyder-McLean, L. K. (1984) 'Recent developments in pragmatics: remedial implications.' *In:* Muller, D. J. (Ed.) *Remediating Children's Language.* London: Croom Helm.

Macnamara, J. (1972) 'Cognitive basis of language learning in infants.' *Psychological Review,* **79,** 1–13.

Mowrer, D. E. (1984) 'Behavioural approaches to treating language disorders.' *In:* Muller, D. J. (Ed.) *Remediating Children's Language.* London: Croom Helm.

Musselwhite, K., St. Louis, K. W. (1982) *Communication Programming for the Severely Handicapped: Vocal and Non-vocal Strategies.* San Diego: College Hill Press.

447

Reid, B. D., Jones, L. M., Kiernan, C. C. (1983) 'Signs and symbols: the 1982 survey of use.' *Special Education: Forward Trends,* **10,** 27–28.

Rose, R. (1982) 'Constructing language comprehension programmes: an approach for use with mentally handicapped children.' *Mental Handicap,* **10,** 117–120.

Shearer, D. E., Billingsley, J., Froham, S., Hilliard, J., Johnson, F., Shearer, M. S. (1972) *The Portage Guide to Early Education.* Wisconsin: CESA.

Silverman, F. H. (1980) *Communication for the Speechless.* Engelwood Cliffs, NJ: Prentice-Hall.

Stainback, W., Stainback, S. (1984) 'A rationale for the merger of special and regular education.' *Exceptional Children,* **51,** 102–111.

United States of America: Public Law 94–142 (1975) 'Education for All Handicapped Children Act, November 29, 1975.' 42 Federal Register 42474, Aug 23, 1977. Washington, DC: US Government.

Walker, M. (1976) *The Makaton vocabulary (Revised Edition.)* London: Royal Association in aid of Deaf and Dumb.

—— (1978) 'The Makaton vocabulary.' *In:* Tebbs, T. (Ed.) *Ways and Means.* Basingstoke: Globe Educational.

Warnock, H. M. (Chairman) (1978) *Special Educational Needs. Report of the Committee of Enquiry into the Education of Handicapped Children and Young People.* London: HMSO.

White, M., East, K. (1983) *The Wessex Revised Portage Language Check List.* Windsor: NFER-Nelson.

Wolfensberger, W. (1972) *The Principle of Normalisation in Human Service.* Toronto: National Institute of Mental Retardation.

28
FAMILY ISSUES

Sheila Hollins

Language disorder has been called a 'hidden handicap' by the Association For All Speech Impaired Children.* That the child looks normal and has no obvious external sign of disability is both a blessing to him and his family, and an additional handicap. More than one parent has said she couldn't bring herself to claim attendance allowance for her child because he looked normal. But an impairment of the ability to communicate with one's family, and later with the outside world, may have as many ramifications as a more obvious physical disability. Lansdown (1980) said of hearing-impaired children: 'They sound different. . . . and do not respond to words as they are expected to. This leads some people to assume they are stupid. It is no accident the word "dummy" is in common use.'

This chapter will explore how the professional can gain an understanding of the rôle played by the family in the life of the individual who has a language impairment.

The rôle of the family

A full paediatric and psychological assessment of the child will have included details of the medical and social history. Since accurate diagnosis of language disorders is characteristically difficult, the specialist will be looking to the child's parents to offer some extra clues about ability and willingness to communicate. He will need to assess the parents' views alongside more empirical evidence, and he will have to make his own assessment of the parents' contribution to understanding. In unravelling all the evidence he must attempt to understand the emotional impact of the diagnostic assessment on the family, and the parents' desperate need to know what is wrong and why. However, the successful and precise labelling of the disability and the definition of what the child cannot do, may strike the parents as being fairly pointless. The recognition of the child's potential achievements and strengths will offer genuine comfort and hope. The disability can then be seen in terms of specific needs, for which detailed plans can be drawn up with the family.

For example, Neil is seven years old and has two sisters, one older and one younger. His strengths include the fact that he is attractive and friendly, can dress himself and can hoover the carpet. He enjoys swimming and watching cartoons on television, he can ride a bicycle and sleeps well at night.

Needs identified include the fact that his communication skills are limited to gesture and two-word phrases. He is frustrated by difficulties in saying what he wants. He is nervous of traffic and may have a visual perceptual problem which puts him at special risk on the roads. The cause of his disability is not known and his

*AFASIC, 347 Central Markets, Smithfield, London EC1.

parents are worried about the risk of another child being affected. An individual chart for this child would include columns for strengths, needs and for action.

If the assessment is to be meaningful, it must address itself to identifying strengths and needs in both the child and family. Some of the needs will be emotional ones, and attention must be given to the reality of the person's disability as he and his family see it. The difficulties and disadvantages he and his family experience in adjusting to the disability will make up his social handicap (Pless and Pinkerton 1975, World Health Organization 1980, Baird and Hall 1985). The extent to which a child's disability will be a handicap depends partly on the 'socially desirable rôles and behaviour' he achieves with the help of his family. In this chapter it is taken for granted that the essential attempt to understand the basic impairment and to find appropriate remediation is one of the primary goals of assessment. The brief here is to examine the impact on the family of the realisation of delayed or disordered language development. The emotional work to be done by families before they can be engaged as partners in remediation programmes will also be considered.

Diagnosis

For whom is the assessment of child and family being done? Although the child may be an interesting 'case' for diagnosis, this must never be the primary objective of the enquiry. It must be directed to identifying the special supports needed by the child and family, and providing an introduction to services such as education, therapy, and aids. The assessment may concentrate on one particular area of need; for example it may be required as part of a statement of special educational need.

Diagnosis of the child's impairment is only the beginning, and should be defined in terms of success rather than failure. Parents, teachers and therapists are interested in the child's achievements as well as in areas of difficulty, and any report must direct their skills to further the child's language development, and to prevent secondary emotional, behavioural and educational handicaps (Rutter 1977). Parents will certainly want to know if the primary impairment is likely to become a handicap, and what action they can take to minimise the handicapping effects.

Validity of parental suspicion in relation to diagnosis

The diagnosis of language delay and disorder occurs late, and often in many stages, in sharp contrast to the diagnosis of a visible handicap such as Down's syndrome. Since parents will have information and insights to add to the assessment of their child, the professional will wish to make the best use of their contribution. Sadly, where the diagnosis is not readily apparent, parental suspicions that something is amiss are often met with bland reassurance and considerable delay before a diagnosis is made. In Freeman's Canadian study (1977) he found that parents of deaf children were not shocked when the diagnosis was confirmed. From the parents' first suspecting something was wrong, to the diagnosis being made, the delay varied from 9.4 months (profoundly deaf) to 16.4 months (severely deaf).

Young parents with a first child and no other recent experience of childcare, separated through social mobility from grandparents and the wider family circle, may lack confidence in their own suspicion that something is wrong. Comparison with the children of friends, or information from books on child development, are likely to be discounted by the general practitioner or health visitor as one of the worries of motherhood, or the well-known 'fact' that boys talk later than girls. This reassurance feeds the parents' own wish to deny the possibility that anything is wrong. Where the parental suspicion is about a second or subsequent child, such anxieties are not so readily brushed aside.

The clinician will find it helpful to interview both parents to ascertain the extent of their agreement. The greater the differences, the less likely the suspicion of handicap will be validated. Parental reports of the grandparents' views will also be useful. Detailed notes of parents' observations should be made. If asked the right questions, parents may provide the specific details of language and communication difficulties. The subtleties of word-finding difficulties, for example, may be missed on crude assessment measures. Sadly, discrepancies between home accounts and school or clinic reports are often discounted as parental exaggeration. However, language skills may not be generalised from the security of the home environment, or may be situation-dependent. Perhaps it is safer to err on the side of believing the parents.

Breaking the news
The decision about when to share the professional viewpoint varies, but a delay between parental suspicion and professional confirmation can destroy trust. Any delay in sharing the diagnosis may be due to a reluctance to break the news to the family, but parents express a preference for the doctor's lack of certainty to be shared with them (Cunningham and Davis 1985). The shared knowledge of uncertainty about the extent of an impairment might lighten the burden for the parents. Indeed, the prolonged assessment itself demands the professional's exposure to the reality of the parents' response. But such sharing confers burdens on the specialist who may be reluctant to act as a container for the parents' feelings.

Parental reaction to the diagnosis
The discrepancy between the parental expectations for their presumed normal child and the adjustments now demanded of them may be so great that the loss they have experienced must be mourned (Solnit and Stark 1977). This experience of loss will be coloured by both personal and environmental factors. We all bring to relationships past experiences of coping with loss. We also place differing values on certain developmental skills. Literacy and spoken communication may be more important in an academic or an artistic family, just as impaired hearing will have special significance in a musical family. This 'bereavement' work must be done in order to release some emotional energy for coping and making the most use of the available professional skills (Hollins 1985).

Final diagnosis and labelling, although seemingly harsh and even inaccurate, can enable families to experience the full force of the shock and panic they have been avoiding. Feelings of inadequacy, and a wish to deny the reality of the diagnosis, turn into grief. Sadness may be expressed as anger towards the conveyor

451

of the bad news—perhaps towards the very person who has demonstrated the capacity to understand—or grief may be internalised as guilt about possible contributory causes of the impairment. Ultimately a sense of duty and resignation may lead to adjustment and acceptance of the individual child as he has turned out to be (Bicknell 1981). But continued uncertainty, misdiagnosis, inadequate remedial help for special educational needs will all serve to prolong or rekindle the pain of the loss.

Parents may find themselves in a world in which diagnoses are made, programmes and futures planned, and yet with no concrete knowledge of what is *wrong*. It may be as though important decisions are being taken on what seem like totally inadequate grounds. This fear may lead to hostility and despair. The common complaint 'nobody told me anything' could be expanded to 'nobody told me anything which *meant* anything to me'. This meaning must take into account the emotional content and context of the communication. The communication of the diagnosis of disability requires lots of time, and there must be several separate opportunities for questions to be answered and implications explored. The busy clinician may choose to delegate some of this task to a social worker.

The rôle of the social worker

As more emphasis is placed on the social and emotional problems associated with disability, experienced social workers must be available to discuss and accept referrals and 'help to place the patient and his complaint more fully in the framework of family patterns of stress and reaction to illness' (Court 1978). Social workers have special responsibilities for people with handicaps, and—because their work will include rather more than the provision of allowances, home helps and respite care—they must have knowledge of normal and abnormal child development, and family psychopathology. They will also be concerned with how social resources can be utilised to help families, bearing in mind that children's problems often occur in the setting of family difficulties or social disadvantage—or may contribute to the development of these. For example, Watson and Midlarsky (1979) found that mothers of children with mental handicap were less likely to be in full employment than other mothers, and to have more difficulty in arranging childcare.

Enabling a family to use the resources designed to help them will require sensitivity. 'The first time the social worker spoke of taking Arthur into care. . . . my stomach turned over. Of course it is the professional jargon, but it has such connotations in our society, implying inadequacy in the mother' (Young 1985). The social worker in regular contact with the health-care team is in a position to anticipate events which may lead to a crisis in the family's ability to cope and to co-operate: for example, a sibling starting school and forcing comparison with the child who has a handicap.

Referral to a psychiatrist

At the end of the diagnostic interview, the paediatrician will be in a position to decide if referral to a child psychiatry department is necessary. Graham (1984) said that referral should be made only if symptoms are disabling in everyday life, have lasted several weeks or more, and if the family needs more resources in time or skill than the paediatrician is able to provide. An emotional cause for the disturbance in communication must be excluded (for example a traumatic separation or serious marital disharmony). Referral to a child psychiatrist is essential if such factors predominate. However, the psychiatrist's involvement may have less to do with elucidating the diagnostic aspects of the primary impairment, and more to do with facilitating acceptance of the diagnosis and all its implications. If Graham's statement is considered in the context of a child with a handicap, then even though cure of the handicap is not the aim, the psychiatrist may be able to make a contribution to treating coincidental psychiatric or emotional distress in the child or another family member. Along the path to remediation, preventive measures may also be required. For example maladaptive responses on the part of the child, or the family, may turn the impairment into a handicap (overprotectiveness is common). In practice there is considerable overlap between the rôle of the psychiatrist, social worker and clinical psychologist.

Parent/professional partnership
Professional preparedness
How does the professional enlist the help of the people who have full-time responsibility for the child in question? How does he know when he has engaged in a working relationship with the parents? Is he in touch with the feelings aroused in himself by his inability to cure the child? The skills required are those of counselling.

Certainly he will not be able to bring standard answers, nor will he be able to retain his professional isolation as 'the expert'. It is probable that he will make more progress if he is prepared to admit ignorance, does not use jargon, and takes time to establish some understanding and goals in common with the parents. Parental compliance with his recommendations has been shown to be related to the quality of the client/consultant interaction, and to the client's attitudes and beliefs about the recommendation (Cadman *et al.* 1984). Written material to supplement the areas covered in discussion with the parents may simply be a copy of the case summary, or a strengths/needs/action chart drawn up during the interview. Written details of relevant voluntary organisations should also be provided. At the end of the interview the parents should be given the name, address and telephone number of the key worker who will be co-ordinating the assessment and any interventions with their child, and whom they should contact with any questions arising from this last meeting.

Parental preparedness
Who is the ideal parent? Unlike professionals, parents are not prepared for their rôle. They may adopt a passive rôle, assuming that the professional is the expert. But parents are people with widely differing experiences of life, and with skills and insights from other parts of their lives which will be brought to bear on their child rearing. What did the school doctor have in mind when she told the medical mother

of a child with a language disorder to 'take off her white coat' because she could not possibly have an opinion about her son's needs? Some other parents needed help to bring different parts of their lives closer together when they sought help for their son's behaviour problems, and at the same time were seeing a marriage guidance counsellor for their marriage, a psychoanalyst for the wife's neurosis, a physiotherapist for their child's clumsiness, a speech therapist for his language delay, and an ophthalmic surgeon for his visual perceptual problem—all of whom were unaware of anyone else's involvement, though all the problems originated from the son's delayed development.

Parents generally wish to conform, and want to know how other parents behave. However, they are not reassured either by simplistic or by sophisticated explanations which do not match their own understanding. Different parents will arrive at each stage of assessment with different expectations, and different limitations, and for every child this must be taken into account.

Is a parent/professional partnership a realistic goal in the exercise of continuous assessment and decision making about the child's management? If the parents are seen to be on the same side as the professional team, then their need for full information and training will be readily understood. Since the 1981 Education Act in the UK, parents have had a right to submit their own statement of their child's special educational needs, and to see the professional reports which make up the remainder of the statement. Education authorities and individual professional bodies differ in their response to this provision, some welcoming it and willingly involving parents according to the spirit of the act, others resisting and resenting what they see as the unwelcome involvement of 'the opposition' in assessment. But there is no turning back, and without help and information from professionals, parents will support each other and become powerful advocates of their own rights.*

People change in response to experience, and it is unwise to judge a parent once and for all as having any characteristic, whether positive or negative. Parents who are distressed may be described as over-anxious and difficult; such comments recorded in the clinical notes may reappear time and again, photocopied for newly involved professionals in years to come. Such comments may discourage the therapist from endeavouring to engage with a particular family, or he may use these comments as an excuse for failing to make a lasting contact. Other judgemental comments include descriptions such as 'over-protective', 'denying' or 'shopping around'. While opinions about the current status of parental adjustment may be made, to form the basis of immediate management, the institutionalisation of such opinions must be avoided.

Parents who cannot cope
The question to ask here is 'what can't they cope with?' and 'who thinks they cannot cope?'. For example, is it that they cannot cope with the sheer physical work of looking after a larger dependent child? Is it because of the responsibility, which

*For example the Parents' Campaign for Integrated Education in London, 25 Woodnook Road, London SW16.

454

never seems to diminish, or is it the guilt they feel and of which they are reminded daily by the presence of their child? Does their failure to cope simply reflect their ignorance of essential information, or do they fail to cope with other aspects of their lives as well?

Ballard (1982) argued that if family members cared for each other in an 'adequately caring and loving manner', then they would cope better with the handicapped child, who would in turn pose fewer problems. In other words, the stress associated with chronic problems may affect family members in different ways: but in a cohesive and caring family, individual members will find successful coping strategies.

Crnic *et al.* (1983) described a model of family adaptation to having a retarded child in which 'the response to stress is moderated by the interaction of available coping resources and ecological contexts'. Other studies have demonstrated the increased stresses experienced by these families (Friedrich and Friedrich 1981, Beckman 1983), and research into life events is increasing as it becomes apparent that many changes in lifestyle are related to having a disabled child. For example, parents may move to a neighbourhood where there is better provision for speech therapy or a recognition of their child's particular disability by the local education authority. For similar reasons, parents may suffer financially because they turn down job promotion in order to stay close to trusted services.

How to assess the family
Family history
This is required to elucidate not only important medical facts, but also significant previous and current experiences of disability, and the attitudes of different family members to disability. Ideas about the possible cause of a child's delay, whether reasonable or extremely unlikely, are all important clues to the family's level of understanding. It may be important to establish whether the family's ideas are based on an objective view and the external reality, whether they arise from the individual's own past experiences of success and failure, or from current and past relationships. Genetic counselling must be made available, and if necessary the implications of no known aetiology explored. It is worth considering the possibility of continuing litigation proceedings for personal injury damages where medical negligence is suspected, and consequent delays in adjustment expected.

Psychosocial and cultural factors may be relevant; and observation of the parental interaction with their child in play and in verbal and non-verbal communication will be important. Home visits can be illuminating, providing information about the richness or poverty of a child's environment: for example, the presence of suitable toys, or someone to play with the child. In assessing the family, one might hope to predict their later adjustment and adaptation to the disability, but in fact prospective studies of parents' adaptation have not been done. Niaira *et al.* (1981) have shown that familial coping at home influences the retarded child's adaptation in different environments. Their study delineated specific factors of the home environment that were significantly related to the personal and social adjustment of children with severe mental handicap in school. Those considered most important were the harmony and quality of parenting, the degree of available educational and cognitive stimulation, and emotional support and parental approval for learning. The traditional indices of family background, such as socio-economic status or number of children, were less important. It is common sense that part of the task must be to identify parents' existing resources, and then help families find additional coping strategies.

What help should be offered?

Appropriate supports might include practical help, information, counselling, and an introduction to voluntary associations and special education services. Techniques of skills development can be taught, which for the parent as teacher might include sessions on communicating with your handicapped child (Newson and Hipgrave 1982), or involvement in an early-intervention programme such as Portage (Revill and Blunden 1979). Intensive speech therapy is as essential as providing a wheelchair for a child with a physical handicap, or hearing aids for a hearing-impaired child. Some parents may want to try any intervention, appropriate or otherwise; and the round of hypnotherapists and faith healers or the search for a 'second opinion' from a third or fourth specialist is often exhausting.

Attitudes and beliefs

The intensity of a family's religious beliefs may appreciably affect their adjustment to caring for a child with an impairment. Zuk *et al.* (1961) explored maternal acceptance of a child who was retarded, using structured interviews and an attitude questionnaire. They found that Catholic mothers were more accepting of a handicapped child than non-Catholic mothers. They suggested that this difference might have its origins in the different churches' understanding of the rôle handicap plays in our society and the church. Young (1985) quotes a hired minibus driver, collecting some children with handicaps, as saying 'What on earth have the parents done to have children like these?' Since guilt feelings slow down the acceptance of a disability, it might be helpful if there was an injunction discouraging guilt and emphasising the special nature of a handicapped child as a gift from God.

The philosophy of normalisation increasingly attracts interest (Wolfensberger 1972). Ferrara (1979) showed that the parents of children with mental handicap were in favour of normalisation, and of increasing independence for people with mental handicap, but not for their own children! The principle of normalisation provides a framework for thinking about services for handicapped people which has been widely adopted by service providers. It is an ideal which favours the use of ordinary experiences and social integration as the means of reducing social difference and handicap.

The particular impact of impaired language

Diagnoses that are delayed, uncertain or contradictory may lead to the parents 'shopping around' for the most favourable prognosis. The search for a label, which will relieve some of the pain of 'not knowing what is wrong', may mean that labels such as autistic or aphasic become more attractive, if not completely accurate. This parental activity will be reinforced by the diagnostic interest shown in a difficult-to-diagnose 'case'. Continued uncertainty about the degree of associated cognitive impairment, for example, may mean that parents' feelings of anxiety will predominate over grief.

Communication is so fundamental that its lack can put a strain on relationships; and the pattern of relating to the child with the language problem may affect conversational styles in the family as a whole. One sibling complained that the other children at school used much longer words than she was hearing at home. Spoken language may be unwittingly replaced by physical or gestural prompts. For example, the normal child in a pushchair who drags his feet on the pavement quickly learns to respond to a spoken request to lift his feet; but when no response is forthcoming from the receptive dysphasic or deaf child, the carer will learn instead to lift the feet on the child's behalf, thus taking away an element of self control.

In the work on preverbal communication, reviewed by Grove and Walker (1985), the importance of the relationship with the first communicator is stressed. Communicative behaviour includes gaze and gesture as well as vocal signals, and requires the development of awareness of people and objects. From early infancy the normal child turn-takes with his mother as the mother-infant interactions develop. For each language-disordered child, different aspects of communicative behaviour will be disturbed. For the child whose disorder mainly affects spoken language, turn-taking may not be distorted and mother and child will achieve empathy in their relationship. On the other hand, the child whose awareness of other people is disturbed will fail to develop this rapport, with obvious consequences for the carer.

Behavioural problems are commonly associated with difficulties in communicating, perhaps due to frustration, loss of self esteem and lack of motivation. The development of social and emotional relationships is impeded by severe language impairment (Rutter 1977). However, where the child is able to establish a normal emotional rapport and to make close relationships with his parents and siblings, motivation to communicate will persist.

For the parents of a young deaf child, the true long-term implications of deafness may remain unrecognised while effort is concentrated on encouraging speech as opposed to life experience, learning and language. Carbin (1976) has designed a programme for the deaf child and family which uses a deaf person as the teacher of sign-language within the home. It seems that many parents favour the purely oral approach rather than 'total communication' (which includes sign-language for all the family), perhaps because it demands less adjustment on their part. Society's attitude towards people who cannot hear is often one of annoyance (Freeman 1977). For the child who has a profound hearing impairment and who masters sign-language, there is the prospect of him becoming part of a deaf community in adulthood. Although such a community will be a segregated subculture, full human rôles and relationships may be possible. For the partially hearing-impaired person, the conflict between the desire for integration and the isolation imposed by an intolerant world will resemble the struggle of the language-disordered individual.

Family assessment—the essentials

The child's strengths and needs can only be seen within his current life context. Attempts to devise a comprehensive assessment tool or multiaxial classification have been made (Rutter *et al.* 1975, Disability Assessment Schedule 1980), taking into account associated psychosocial stresses. In preparing to meet the family for the first time, the professional must consider his different rôles as interviewer (eliciting as much factual information as possible), and counsellor (allowing the expression of emotion, and fostering understanding and adjustment). Rutter and Cox (1981) examined different psychiatric interview styles used in the initial diagnostic interview with parents attending a child psychiatry clinic, and concluded that a combination of techniques to obtain high factual information and high expression of emotion was both possible and useful.

A structured approach to information-gathering can be used in such a way that diversions to take account of both verbal and non-verbal expressions of emotion are still possible. In other words, the clinician should concern himself as much with process as content.

Counselling begins before the diagnosis is given to the parents, and continues in all subsequent communication. All professionals working with families where there is a child with a handicap will need basic counselling skills. Cunningham and Davis (1985) pointed out that this should not be seen as the treatment of abnormal pathology, but that the reactions of the majority of parents should be seen as normal and healthy. Only a minority of parents, who develop severe depression or disruption on learning that their child has a handicap, should be referred for more specialised counselling. In their chapter on 'early parent counselling', Cunningham and Davis discussed some approaches to counselling which have proved successful—increasing parental satisfaction with services provided. They described the professional's rôle as 'to provide parents with the necessary information and guidance to develop coping strategies without undermining their feelings of self esteem and confidence'.

Eliciting information

No preconceptions about the family's knowledge or expectations are possible. The assessment must begin by developing a picture of the family and seeing where the referred child fits in. However, before seeking any answers to his own questions, the clinician must note the questions that the parents have come with. What do they want to know? What are they worried about? Unless these are acknowledged and dealt with as fully as possible, the consultation will be seen as unsatisfactory.

> To the professional this is just one case among hundreds. To the person on the receiving end, it is the moment for which they have made a special and sometimes difficult journey, the moment for which they have been waiting for a long time, the moment of anxiety, perhaps of hope that something useful will be done (Young 1985).

458

Drawing a family tree is one way of compiling a family history, and provides an easy reference point for later discussion. The present carers (even if not the family of origin) should be clearly marked. The home environment and parents' occupations should be described. Key informants such as grandmother or a child-minder must also be noted, as their co-operation with any intervention may be relevant. Judgements will be made about the quality of parenting and the appropriateness of the care currently provided, to decide how much change can be introduced into the family system. Recent stresses within the family, such as the birth of a new baby, a bereavement, or a serious illness in the child or family member, will all impair the family's ability to engage in a working alliance. Realistic goals must be negotiated with all the key carers, bearing in mind the other stresses they have to face.

Practical advice
(1) Allow enough time for the interview so that the family do not feel rushed
(2) Leave some pauses to give the family time to think and to ask questions
(3) Avoid jargon and check constantly for understanding
(4) Listen carefully
(5) Respect the information and opinion parents express. Try to see things from their position
(6) Be honest if you do not know all the answers
(7) Be objective in the information you give, emphasising neither positive nor negative aspects
(8) Offer another appointment as soon as possible
(9) Offer an introduction to a parent who has faced the same problem, or suggest reading about another person's experience (*e.g.* Browning 1972)
(10) Suggest reading material about the handicap to supplement verbal information given
(11) Provide a written summary of the assessment
(12) Introduce to appropriate voluntary organisations (*e.g.* AFASIC)
(13) Avoid dependency by sharing own competence with family and continually reinforcing and building on their successes
(14) Consult the community-based service for children with handicaps, to identify the most appropriate person to co-ordinate the child's continuing care in partnership with the family.

Conclusion
I have tried to heighten awareness about some of the issues that will be important with respect to some families. One cannot make generalisations from individual cases, although the clinician's experience may encourage some lines of enquiry and intervention more than others. Many of the points made in this chapter apply to the families of any child with a handicap. Findings which relate to the special areas of language and communication disability must be seen in this broader context.

The parents' rôle is clearly very important in enabling the child to adjust to his impairment and to make the most of his communicative abilities—in other words to reduce his social handicap. One cannot overemphasise the importance of professional workers recognising the fundamental part played by a child's family in enabling his best possible adjustment.

REFERENCES

Baird, G., Hall, D. M. B. (1985) 'Developmental paediatrics in primary care: what should we teach?' *British Medical Journal,* **291,** 583–586.

Ballard, R. (1982) 'Taking the family into account.' *Mental Handicap,* **10,** 75–76.

Beckman, P. J. (1983) 'The influence of selected child characteristics on stress in families of handicapped infants.' *American Journal of Mental Deficiency,* **88,** 150–156.

Bicknell, D. J. (1981) 'The psychopathology of handicap.' *British Journal of Medical Psychology,* **56,** 167–178.

Browning, E. (1972) *I Can't See What You're Saying.* London: Elek Press.

Cadman, D., Shurvell, B., Davies, P., Bradfield, S. (1984) 'Compliance in the community with consultant's recommendations for developmentally handicapped children.' *Developmental Medicine Child Neurology,* **26,** 40–46.

Carbin, C. F. (1976) 'A total communication approach: a new programme for deaf infants and children and their families.' *British Columbia Medical Journal,* **18,** 141–142.

Court, S. D. M. (1978) *Fit for the Future.* London: HMSO.

Crnic, K. A., Friedrich, W. N., Greenberg, M. T. (1983) 'Adaptation of families with mentally retarded children: a model of stress, coping and family ecology.' *American Journal of Mental Deficiency,* **88,** 125–138.

Cunningham, C. C., Davis, H. (1985) 'Early parent counselling.' *In:* Craft, M., Bicknell, D. J., Hollins, S. (Eds.) *Mental Handicap—A Multidisciplinary Approach.* Eastbourne: Bailliere Tindall.

Disability Assessment Schedule (1980) MRC Social Psychiatry Unit, Institute of Psychiatry, De Crespigny Park, London SE5 8AF.

Ferrara, D. M. (1979) 'Attitudes of parents of mentally retarded children toward normalization activities.' *American Journal of Mental Deficiency,* **84,** 145–151.

Freeman, R. (1977) 'Psychiatric aspects of sensory disorders and intervention.' *In:* Graham, P. J. (Ed.) *Epidemiological Approaches in Child Psychiatry.* London: Academic Press.

Friedrich, W. N., Friedrich, W. L. (1981) 'Comparison of psychosocial assets of parents with a handicapped child and their normal controls.' *American Journal of Mental Deficiency,* **85,** 551–553.

Graham, P. (1984) 'Paediatric referral to a child psychiatrist.' *Archives of Disease in Childhood,* **59,** 1103–1105.

Grove, N., Walker, M. (1985) *Communication Before Language. Research Information Service. Vol 2 Issue 2.* Makaton Vocabulary Development Project, 31 Firwood Drive, Camberley, Surrey.

Hollins, S. (1985) 'Families and handicap.' *In:* Craft, M., Bicknell, D. J., Hollins, S. (Eds.) *Mental Handicap—A Multidisciplinary Approach.* Eastbourne: Bailliere Tindall.

Lansdown, R. (1980) *More than Sympathy. The Everyday Needs of Sick and Handicapped Children and their Families.* London: Tavistock Publications.

Newson, E., Hipgrave, T. (1982) *Getting Through to Your Handicapped Child.* Cambridge: Cambridge University Press.

Nihara, K., Mink, I. T., Meyers, C. E. (1981) 'Relationship between home environment and school adjustment of trainable mentally retarded children.' *American Journal of Mental Deficiency,* **86,** 8–15.

Pless, I. B., Pinkerton, P. (1975) *Chronic Childhood Disorder: Promoting Patterns of Adjustment.* London: Henry Kimpton.

Revill, S., Blunden, R. (1979) 'A home training service for preschool developmentally handicapped children.' *Behaviour Research and Therapy,* **17,** 207–214.

Rutter, M. (1977) 'Speech delay.' *In:* Rutter, M., Hersov, L. (Eds.) *Child Psychiatry: Modern Approaches.* Oxford: Blackwell Scientific.

—— Shaffer, D., Sturge, C. (1975) *A Guide to a Multiaxial Classification Scheme for Psychiatric Disorders in Childhood and Adolescence.* Dept. of Child & Adolescent Psychiatry, Institute of Psychiatry, London, England.

—— Cox, A. (1981) 'Psychiatric interview techniques. 1. Methods and measures.' *British Journal of Psychiatry,* **138,** 273–282.

Solnit, A. J., Stark, M. H. (1977) 'Mourning and the birth of a defective child.' *In:* Eissler, R. S. (Ed.) *Physical Illness and Handicap in Childhood.* Newhaven, Connecticut: Yale University Press.

Watson, R. L., Midlarsky, E. (1979) 'Reactions of mothers with mentally retarded children: a social perspective.' *Psychological Reports,* **45,** 309–310.

World Health Organization (1980) *International Classification of Impairments, Disabilities and Handicaps. A Manual of Classification Relating to the Consequences of Disease.* Geneva: W.H.O.

Wolfensberger, W. (1972) *The Principle of Normalisation in Human Services.* Toronto: National Institute on Mental Retardation.

Young, F. (1985) *Face to Face.* London: Epworth Press.

Zuk, G. H., Miller, R. L., Bartram, J. B., Kling, F. (1961) 'Maternal acceptance of retarded children: a questionnaire study of attitudes and religious background.' *Child Development,* **32,** 525–540.

29
SERVICES

Martin Bax and William Yule

There are two distinct, but closely related, aspects to distinguish when considering comprehensive services for children with delayed or deviant speech and language development. The first is to determine the needs of the children and their families, and how these needs can best be met. This raises issues of service policy and priorities, and different communities and different countries have addressed the problem in varying ways. The second aspect concerns how an individual family, worried about their child's language development, can access whatever services are available.

Any child who has, or is suspected of having, a speech or language problem needs first to be identified. Thereafter, thorough assessment should lead to clear diagnosis and appropriate intervention as necessary. Intervention may include direct therapy with the child, although increasingly it is recognised that parents, teachers, care-workers and other aides are better placed to assist in intervention when adequately advised. Such intervention can vary in its intensity, and parents often need counselling and advice on general management as well as help with specific treatment programmes. Given the nature of the problems considered earlier in this text, there is a clear need for periodic reassessment and follow-up. How are these goals best attained?

Identification

McCormick (1986) has shown that parents are often the best people to identify the child who is deaf. Indeed, Freeman (1977) demonstrated that parents were well aware that something was badly wrong, long before they convinced professionals of the existence of the problem. One lesson for professionals of all disciplines is to listen carefully to parental concerns and to respect the views of parents.

However, one has to be cautious about using the identification of hearing loss as a model for all services identifying other language problems. As more sophisticated technology becomes more widely available (see Chapter 25), it becomes possible to assess hearing in young babies in special cradles, as well as in frightened, unco-operative infants. The problem is no longer that of audiological investigation, but one of alerting parents, nurses and others to the tell-tale signs that something may be wrong.

Even so, it still seems likely to us that parents are among the most appropriate people to identify a child with speech and language problems, although we know of no data suggesting how effectively they can do this. Clinically, one has seen parents who are concerned about development when it is well within normal limits, and equally, one has seen children with quite profound delay where the parents have seemed to deny that the child's language was behind. But most parents are very acute at observing the levels of their child's development and give good and accurate information about speech and language development. They are in an ideal position to identify that their child has a problem, but they must be able to see somebody who can confirm whether or not the child has a problem, and, if so, what further steps need to be taken.

In the first two years of life (at least in the United Kingdom) the worried mother is most likely to turn to staff at the child health clinic or to the family's general practitioner. Thus general practitioners, health visitors and community nurses need to know the course of normal language development, and to observe that babble, non-verbal communication and the like are normal. As Simpson (1972) pointed out, there is quite good attendance of infants at child health clinics up until about two years of age, when it tails off sharply. Of course, this is precisely the age at which delays in language can begin to be identified more readily – a mismatch between the needs of the child and the services, as presently organised. The problem is not so acute in communities where child health clinics are held in group general practices and where, in the first five years of life, most children are taken to see their general practitioner for other reasons three or four times per year.

From two or three years of age until five years, when formal schooling begins, many children attend play-groups, nursery schools run by the local education authority or day nurseries run by the departments of social services. Each of these facilities is staffed by differently trained personnel and has different formal links with specialist support services. Given that these are the years when language delays and deviations become noticeable, it is important that someone on the staff is trained not only in general aspects of child development but in spotting abnormalities of language and other cognitive development (see below).

Once at school, there is a heavy onus on the reception class teacher to differentiate shy, unforthcoming behaviour from language delay. At least in school there are clearer links with school doctors, educational psychologists and, increasingly, speech therapists, all of whom can then advise on what further steps need to be taken.

Screening

Given the size of the problem at different ages (see Chapter 1), it is difficult to say who should be the first to assess the child, and how thoroughly. Simpson (1972) argued that many children will be diagnosed too late if it is left to the parents to initiate contact with specialist services. Some form of population screening is needed. As commented earlier, this is comparatively easy to contemplate in relation to the screening of hearing defects. Of course one has to ensure that the tests are repeated, especially with children with mental and multiple handicaps; and doctors must be alert to transient as well as permanent hearing loss associated with recurrent otitis media. We are now all sufficiently sophisticated to know that pure-tone audiometry is only the beginning of a screening for hearing loss. Even with hearing loss, the efficiency of mass screening is in doubt (Bellman 1986). Should population screening be replaced by surveillance of 'high-risk' groups? In the late 1960s and early 1970s, the 'at-risk' registers did not prove to be efficient ways of picking out handicapped children in general (Alberman and Goldstein 1970), largely because they were geared to perinatal factors and many handicaps do not have that origin. Things have probably improved with the development of community handicap teams, usually centred on district general hospitals, and with an increase in the provision of trained professional staff (to say nothing of the fall in birthrate leaving fewer children to survey). However, that still leaves us with the question of which children would be identified as at high risk of developing a language disorder, how they should be screened, and by whom.

Apart from screening for hearing loss, which can nowadays be done at the general practitioner's surgery or at school entry (which is too late), mass screening for other language problems is difficult to achieve. Better education of parents about language development and better training of clinic and community nurses, health visitors, general practitioners, social workers and so on seems more promising. Fortunately, this advice is not as grandiose as it seems at first. There are increasingly available developmental check lists which such professionals can use when seeing infants and young children to alert them to the possibility of serious delays. Many of these rely on systematic interviews with parents and here is where our optimistic view of the parental rôle fits in. These checklists (Meecham 1958, Frankenburg and Dodds 1968, Shearer and Shearer 1976) are invaluable to primary care workers, and their judicious use should improve referrals for more detailed investigations. A recent community study found that children who prove to be below 1.5sd on the Reynell can be identified by a quick screening test (Hart et al. 1978).

Assessment and diagnosis

So far we have made it clear that a full assessment of the child and the family involves professionals from many disciplines, depending on the nature and extent of the presenting problem (cf. Chapters 18 to 22). Simpson (1972) recommended that: 'As a minimum, assessment should include an evaluation of neurological and general medical function, response to sounds, intellectual level, and overall psychological development, as well as speech and language competence' (p.255). The needs of the children have not altered in the meantime, but fortunately the availability of child psychologists (both clinical and educational) and of speech therapists has noticeably improved.

Recent British government reports on child health and special education services agree that there is a strong case for having speech therapists and psychologists as full members of multi-disciplinary teams charged with the identification and management of children with language disorders (Court Committee 1976, Warnock Committee 1978). We stress 'identification and management' since assessment should ideally not be divorced from treatment. Of course there will always be a need to refer some children to specialist centres for some investigations, but the over-all management should remain as local as possible. This implies that most assessment should take place at local facilities: in clinics, schools and local hospitals. This facilitates forward planning across health, education and social service departments, particularly in relation to recognising and meeting children's special educational needs (see Chapter 27).

At present in most parts of the world, there are too few trained speech pathologists (or speech therapists in the UK) for them to be actively involved in the routine assessment of all children with suspected language problems. However, their expertise must be available to the district handicap team and they must be involved in determining criteria locally which will help the primary contact decide when to involve the speech therapist directly.

As the Warnock Committee (1978) discovered, teachers in special classes and units in mainstream schools had less regular contact with speech therapists than did teachers in special schools, although even there the contact can be very variable. A survey of teachers undertaken for the Committee established that teachers want more contact with speech therapists. Clearly, these observations are very important when it is realised that most children with language handicap will receive education at least partly integrated within ordinary schools. The ways in which health and education services in general (and speech-therapy services in particular) need to be co-ordinated to meet these children's needs will be returned to below.

Management and therapy

'The care of children with speech delay requires a multi-faceted approach, including: a) the specific treatment of medical disorders (such as deafness); b) the prevention of secondary handicaps; c) advice and counselling of parents; d) speech and language therapy; e) nursery school provision; and f) remedial education. In some cases, other facilities, such as social assistance or genetic counselling will be needed' (Simpson 1972). A comparison of the contents (and length) of the 1972 volume with the present one illustrates the expansion in our knowledge and understanding of language disorders, but Simpson's list of management needs remains essentially the same. There is now less emphasis on 'remedial education' in the sense of separate schooling, and much more on integrated education (see Chapter 27), although it is still far from clear that the social advantages of fully integrated education outweigh the disadvantages for children with speech, language and hearing difficulties. Specific treatments have been discussed in previous chapters. Here we will consider the rôles of some of the professionals involved in providing the services. We are very conscious that we are writing about what we know of services in Britain. We make no claim that these are 'better' than those provided elsewhere, and indeed we would welcome some cross-national comparison of service delivery for these children.

In the United Kingdom, responsibility for children's services is divided among the district health authority, the local education authority and the local social services department. Where these have co-terminous geographical boundaries, collaboration is easier than in inner cities, where they do not. Health services are organised between primary health care (centred on the family doctor and other community-based services) and secondary referral services, usually based in district general hospitals. Children with language delay are likely to be referred to departments of paediatrics, child psychiatry or the district handicap team.

Primary services
Doctors
In most countries now, a child will be assigned to a family physician, or in some circumstances (in the USA), will be seen by a paediatrician as a first physician. In the UK, the family doctor or general practitioner increasingly works in a group practice. In general, the amount of training that this doctor has had in child development will vary, but the GP is usually the first person who is likely to see the preschool child and should be capable of identifying whether there is a problem or not. Increasingly, in group practices, one partner will specialise in working with children.

Health visitors
Most mothers take their very young babies to the clinics run by health visitors to check on both physical and psychological development. Increasingly, health visitors are asked for advice on the management of children's behaviour problems, and their training has expanded to deal as much with child development as with problems of feeding, growth and so on. In many parts of the UK, health visitors are actively involved in Portage-based schemes, giving advice to parents of developmentally delayed children.

Secondary services
In the United Kingdom, most health districts have set up district handicap teams, usually working out of a child assessment centre situated in the district general hospital. As a rule, these teams include paediatrician, psychologist, teacher, social worker, physiotherapist, occupational therapist and speech therapist. This is the usual remedial referral centre for children with communication problems. The different children's services departments are represented within the team, facilitating the collaboration needed across services and settings.

Other European countries have very similar systems. Some of the child centres will provide preschool facilities which help with the assessment of the young child, but many young children with language problems will, of course, be attending nursery or other preschool provision. It is vital that the personnel in these settings have access to members of the handicap team for advice and help on the management of preschool children with language and behaviour problems, as the Chazan et al. (1983) study demonstrated.

Education provision
Local education authorities in the UK are empowered to meet the special educational needs of children from two years onwards (earlier in some circumstances). There is a long tradition of providing peripatetic teachers of deaf children who work both directly with the child and through the parents. All LEAS have some provision for preschool children (although the UK lags behind the rest of Europe in this respect), and within that there may be special classes or units for children with severe language impairment. These will be staffed by specially trained teachers and usually have sessions from speech therapists.

For school-age children, integrated education within ordinary schools is the goal officially espoused by legislators and welcomed by most parents and professionals on humanitarian grounds. To what extent fully integrated education is in the best interests of *all* children with language disorders remains to be seen. Already, it is clear that merely placing partially hearing or other language-impaired children in mainstream schooling does not automatically result in integration at a social level with their peers (Levy-Schiff and Hoffman 1985). Both handicapped and non-handicapped children need active help from adults if the ideals of integration are to be achieved (Odom *et al.* 1985, Tin and Teasdale 1985).

Social services provision
Social services departments provide a wide range of day care and residential services for children and families. Although day care is provided primarily for social reasons, infants and toddlers attending are at high risk of having behavioural disorders and language delay (McGuire and Richman 1986). It is vital that staff in such day-care facilities are trained to develop children's language skill and are able to get advice from other professionals when doubts are raised about development. Often they are in a good position to provide practical help to parents—advice on how to involve children in language games, or how to play with everyday materials.

It is also important that field social workers get an adequate training in child development (CCETSW 1978). As society expects more statutory duties to be undertaken on its behalf by social workers, so must they be trained to recognise deviations in children's development, be they social, emotional or cognitive.

Children with complex problems
There are relatively few children with autism or dysphasic syndromes, so any individual health district is likely to have only limited experience with any particular problem. Special experience should exist at regional handicap children's centres and in certain special schools. Some centres have been designated in the UK as having special skills in certain areas, such as communication. One problem with the planned integration of language-handicapped children into normal school is to see that such expertise is maintained while the child is helped in a more normal environment.

The adolescent and young adult with a communication problem
The services for preschool and school children are becoming more adequate, but in many parts of the developed world there are few, if any, services for adolescents and young adults. There is no question that there are many handicapped young people who still have communication problems at the end of their formal secondary school years, and it can be assumed that without regular help thereafter their communication skills are likely to deteriorate. In any case, the young person's needs change and there may be physical changes accompanying early ageing processes in some conditions. Regular reviews of handicapped people who have communication problems are essential into adult life (Thomas *et al.* 1985).

It is worth emphasising the gap between services for schoolchildren and those for adults, and also worth stressing that leaving school should not be treated as an unforeseen crisis. It is one of the very few highly predictable 'life events'. Fortunately, in Britain, the new legislation on children's special educational needs mandates that handicapped children's needs should be reviewed a year before leaving school, so that the transition to adult life can be better managed.

One of the additional needs of young adults is for their new social and work environments to be able to understand them. Sign languages depend on mutual signing skills if they are to be effective. Unless positive steps are taken to ensure that work colleagues and friends can learn the sign system or learn to interpret other augmentative systems, the language-disabled young adult will be further handicapped. More sophisticated microtechnology requires frequent servicing of the hardware and updating of the software. Periodic reassessment of interface needs is also essential. Whereas all of these needs can be considered within a school system, it is not clear whose responsibility it is —health, social services or voluntary agencies—to co-ordinate surveillance after school-leaving age. There are various people who may work between primary and secondary care, or have rôles in either, and these we now briefly discuss.

Paediatricians

The paediatrician will be involved in the assessment and diagnosis of children with speech and language disorders, and should be particularly concerned when there are physical problems, such as serous otitis media, in management. He or she may also have a major rôle to play in training primary health-care staff in the identification in the preliminary assessment of children with speech and language problems.

In most cases, the paediatrician is best placed to provide genetic counselling to the parents and to the affected young adults. As noted earlier, careful family histories are an essential part of all diagnostic work-ups. As modern behavioural genetics, coupled with findings from cytogenetic studies, clarify the mode of inheritance of many language disorders, so those assessing and caring for children with language disorders need to discuss the implications of these findings for having other children. Where parents feel unduly guilty at contributing to their child's disability, it may be necessary to call on the counselling skills of other professionals.

The community paediatrician in the district handicap team will often be the person involved in seeing that all aspects of the child's care are satisfactorily integrated.

Parents

Parents are undoubtedly the most influential people in developing children's early language. The importance of early exchanges for the development of communication is now well documented (see Chapter 4). The need to ensure that such mutually reinforcing exchanges continue with handicapped children is gradually becoming recognised (see Chapters 4 and 15). As noted earlier, parents need more help—partly through general education, television programmes, baby books and the like, and partly through easier access to primary health-care staff – in

468

recognising language delays.

Thereafter, they need advice on how to encourage language development through activities such as playing reciprocal games, encouraging young children to ask questions, reading to their child, telling rhymes and singing songs. Such general advice can be translated for some into practical activities merely by suggestion or modelling. This can be done individually or informally at parent group meetings at clinics, and this sort of advice may be sufficient for children with minor delays in language.

A major problem in the expansion of any therapeutic service is our lack of evidence from suitably controlled trials about the effectiveness of various treatments and other forms of intervention in helping these children. It is obviously important that further research should go forward to identify effective means of therapy, but we would not see it as appropriate to delay the development of some service to help families with language-delayed children while that research is under way.

Children with major delays, or deviant language development consequent on some other handicapping condition, will require more intensive help (see Chapters 22, 24 and 25). Although the professional advisors will play a key rôle, they must involve the parents as co-therapists from the start. There is no point in teaching a sign system to the child if the parent does not also know it! Apart from the need to remember that we are always talking about two-way communication, parents and siblings are in the best position early on to reinforce the work done sporadically at the clinic. The advent of systematic training packages such as the Portage System (Scrutton 1984) has been a boon for many parents, but requires that supervising professionals must know when to reassess and refer children for further help as necessary.

Of course, parents of language-impaired children will also need the opportunity to discuss the nature of the disorder, its likely prognosis and their fears and worries about all of this. Some of this needs to come from medical personnel, much from social workers—it all depends on who is the key worker.

Speech therapists

In the UK these professionals are referred to as 'speech therapists', and in the USA they are called 'speech pathologists'. There is still a severe shortage of qualified speech therapists, which limits the number of children with whom they can work directly. Increasingly, their work will be as members of teams advising parents, teachers and child-care staff, and so they must have training in skills of supervision.

We noted earlier that teachers want more contact with speech therapists. In discussing this, the Warnock Committee (1978) drew attention to another potential gap in services. Where nursery classes are seen as the main base for service delivery, the arrangements must be made to continue treatment and its supervision throughout the long school holidays. Quite how health authorities can do this remains to be seen.

Psychologists

Local education authorities employ educational psychologists who will have degrees in psychology, followed by teacher training and experience, followed by one or two years of professional training. Health authorities employ clinical psychologists who also have first degrees in psychology followed by a two- or three-year professional training, a mandatory part of which involves working with the mentally handicapped. During basic training, neither profession is sufficiently well trained in working with preschool children and children with language problems. This is obtained by experience and post-qualification training.

Psychologists of both professions who are members of handicap teams and who work in assessment centres will usually be of fairly senior status and have complementary skills in helping children with language impairment.

Psychiatrists

While all psychiatrists will have had some training in child development during their early medical training and their basic psychiatry training, this is not at a detailed level except in those who specialise in child psychiatry or the psychiatry of mental handicap. Since children with severe developmental delay, infantile autism, selective mutism and other complex problems are likely to present to child psychiatric clinics, it is important that training in language development and disorders remains a part of child psychiatric training.

Teachers

From five to 16 years, children spend much of their waking time in school during term-time. Teachers are in an excellent position to identify language disorder and to assist in its treatment. However, teachers and others involved in preschool provision must be the main targets for helping these children. Children cannot wait until five or six years before their problems are identified. Given the previously noted division of responsibility for preschool provision, considerable thought must be given as to how best to harness the goodwill of adults involved with preschool children. What sort of training do they need, and how can services be co-ordinated?

Social workers

Field social workers working with families must be able to make screening assessments of many aspects of children's development, including their language. They must be able to explain to parents the reasons for particular courses of action and intervention. They must be able to demonstrate what is meant by 'providing a linguistically stimulating environment'. All this is asking a great deal from generically trained social workers, and underlines the great need for continuing education and post-qualification training in working with young children. Day-care and residential social workers need advice in recognising language impairment and in participating in treatment.

Integration of services

Given the range of services that may be needed by a child with language problems involving many different disciplines, the integration of such services with clear communication between professionals and with the child and his family can prove difficult. The case conference with the family is the time-honoured method of achieving such integration, but it is expensive and can prove cumbersome. The appointment of a key-worker who funnels information to the family is another suggested approach (Court Committee 1976), but the family may elect to by-pass that person on occasion or prefer different workers at different ages and in relation to different problems. Those who spend most time with the child, parents or teachers, need most information about the child, and if other professionals visit the child on his or her ground (*i.e.* at home or at school) effective exchange with those closest to the child often takes place automatically.

Conclusions

A cursory comparison of the current text with its predecessor (Rutter and Martin 1972) indicates how much our understanding of children's language development and disorders has grown in the past 15 years. It is not that some authors have become more verbose! There has been a genuine growth of knowledge. As always, there is a delay between research findings appearing in specialist publications and clinical practice being influenced. In part, it is a matter of resource allocation. If children with language disorders are to receive the best service possible, this implies that they are identified early, given comprehensive assessment by multi-disciplinary teams, and provided with skilled therapy. The preceding chapters in this book have indicated what is currently considered to be good practice. Many questions are raised, and most are answerable by careful research. We need not wait for further research evidence, however, before implementing what is already known, thereby improving the services for children and their families.

REFERENCES

Alberman, E., Goldstein, H. (1970) 'The "at-risk" register: a statistical evaluation.' *British Journal of Preventative and Social Medicine*, **24**, 129.

Bellman, S. (1986) 'Hearing screening in infancy.' *Archives of Disease in Childhood*, **61**, 637–638. *(Annotation.)*

CCETSW (1978) *Good Enough Parenting: Report of a Group on Work with Children and Young People and the Implications for Social Work Education*. London: Central Council for Education and Training in Social Work.

Chazan, M., Laing, A. F., Jones, J., Harper, G. C., Bolton, J. (1983) *Helping Young Children with Behaviour Difficulties*. Beckenham: Croom Helm.

Court, S. D. M. (Chairman) (1976) *Fit for the Future. Report of the Committee on Child Health Services*. London: HMSO.

Frankenburg, W. K., Dodds, J. B. (1968) *Denver Developmental Screening Test Manual*. Denver: University of Colorado Press.

Freeman, R. (1977) 'Psychiatric aspects of sensory disorders and intervention.' *In:* Graham, P. J. (Ed.) *Epidemiological Approaches in Child Psychiatry*. London: Academic Press.

Hart, H., Bax, M., Jenkins, S. (1978) 'The value of a developmental history.' *Developmental Medicine and Child Neurology*, **20**, 442–452.

Levy-Schiff, R., Hoffmann, M. A. (1985) 'Social behaviour of hearing impaired and normally hearing pre-schoolers.' *British Journal of Educational Psychology*, **55**, 111–118.

McCormick, B. (1986) 'Screening for hearing impairment in the first year of life.' *Midwife, Health Visitor and Community Nurse*, **22**, 199–202.

McGuire, J., Richman, N. (1986) 'Screening for behaviour problems in nurseries: the reliability and validity of the preschool behaviour checklist.' *Journal of Child Psychology and Psychiatry,* **27,** 7–32.

Meecham, M. (1958) *Verbal Language Development Scale.* Minneapolis: Educational Test Bureau.

Odom, S. L., Hoyson, M., Jamieson, B., Strain, P. S. (1985) 'Increasing handicapped preschoolers peer social interactions: cross-setting and component analysis.' *Journal of Applied Behavioural Analysis,* **18,** 3–16.

Rutter, M., Martin, J. A. M. (1972) *The Child with Delayed Speech. Clinics in Developmental Medicine, No. 43.* London: SIMP with Heinemann Medical; Philadelpia: J. B. Lippincott.

Scrutton, D. (1984) *Management of the Motor Disorders of Children with Cerebral Palsy. Clinics in Developmental Medicine, No. 90.* London: SIMP with Blackwell Scientific; Philadelphia: J. B. Lippincott.

Shearer, D. E., Shearer, M. S. (1976) 'The Portage Project: a model for early childhood intervention.' *In: Intervention Strategies for High Risk Infants and Young Children.* Baltimore: University Park Press.

Simpson, E. (1972) 'Services for children with delayed speech.' *In:* Rutter, M., Martin, J. A. M. (Eds.) *The Child with Delayed Speech. Clinics in Developmental Medicine, No. 43.* London: SIMP with Heinemann Medical; Philadelphia: J. B. Lippincott.

Thomas, A., Bax, M., Coombes, K., Goldson, E., Smyth, D., Whitmore, K. (1985) 'The health and social needs of physically handicapped young adults: are they being met by statutory services?' *Developmental Medicine and Child Neurology,* Supplement No. 50.

Tin, L. G., Teasdale, G. R. (1985) 'An observational study of the social adjustment of spina bifida children in integrated settings.' *British Journal of Educational Psychology,* **55,** 81–83.

Warnock, H. M. (Chairman) (1978) *Special Educational Needs. Report of the Committee of Enquiry into the Education of Handicapped Children and Young People.* London: HMSO.

INDEX

474

Tympanic membrane 344
Typanometry 240

U

Ultrasound scanning 142

V

Variable responses to sound associated with
    expressive/receptive language problems 36
Verbal auditory agnosia 147
Verbal deprivation 28
Verbal dyspraxia (apraxia of speech) 29, 278
Verbal fluency, deceptive 265–6
Verbal labelling 62
Verbally unrestrained language disorder 34
Vineland Social Maturity Scale 307–8
Visual impairment 64, 65, 234–9
    aids to non-speaking person 417–18
    autistic-like blind children 237
    definitions 234
    echolalia associated 236–7
    flat facial expression 238
    hearing impairment combined 244
    imitation 236
    language development 234–6
    non-verbal communication 238–9
    parental counselling 239
    parent-child interaction difference 237–8
    possibilities for intervention 239
    restriction in early life 135

sensitive period 135
social routines 236–7
variables 234
Visuospatial defects in very young children 155
Vocabulary increase 165
Vocalisation, early 325–6

W

Wada test (intracarotid sodium amytal test) 131,
    132
    stutterers 137–8
Waltham Forest study 9–10
Warnock Committee (UK, 1978) 437, 438, 441,
    464, 465
Wechsler Intelligence Scale for Children—
    Revised 315
Wechsler Pre-School and Primary Scale of
    Intelligence 308
Wernicke's area 199
Wernicke's dysphasia 151
Whorfian hypothesis 272
Wilson's disease 224
Wolf children 200
Wolfson language development programme
    442–3
Word blindness (developmental dyslexia) 155
Word cards 398
Working-class children 28, 107–8
Writing (written language) 44